psychology
of education
new looks

psychology
of education
new looks

edited by

GARY A. DAVIS
University of Wisconsin

THOMAS F. WARREN
Beloit College

D. C. Heath and Company

Lexington, Massachusetts   Toronto   London

To   Rachel
Kirsten
Ingrid
Sonja

preface

rev·o·lu·tion (rĕv′ə -lōō′ shən), n. **1.** A complete overthrow of an established system. **2.** A radical and pervasive change in society and the social structure, especially one made suddenly. **3.** A complete or marked change in something.

There is indeed an accelerating revolution in the psychology of education. Each year brings new ideas for classroom organization, new curriculum packages and media, and new insights into the abilities and needs of children. Sometimes, the changes only modify in piece-meal fashion the existing policies, such as when we add a zesty creative writing unit to the English curriculum or install rock-polishing tools in the school shops. Other changes, such as ungraded schools, open classrooms, and Project Head Start, mark a more radical shift in educational traditions. We are departing from the old paths and ignoring the risks of getting lost.

Educational innovation will continue, as certainly it must, either bit by bit or in sudden shake-ups. Once in a while, however, we must snap the shutter, stop the action, and see what we have. The purpose of this book is to place under one cover some of today's most significant ideas in the psychology of education. Some developments clearly show their roots in such traditional academic topics as human learning, development, motivation, and educational measurement. Other innovations reported in these pages were not born in psychology, in education, or, in some cases, even in the U.S.A.

It is interesting that some of the most exciting educational ideas were hatched in other disciplines, in other professions, and in other countries. The high-impact concepts of *schools without failure* and *classroom meetings,* for example, were engineered by Dr. William Glasser, a sensitive innovator trained in medicine. The fields of drama and psychotherapy have inspired classroom exercises in creative dramatics that are designed to sharpen the senses and free the spirit, rather than stuff the student with information. Linguists are forcing us to take more informed second looks at supposedly "culturally deprived" and "linguistically disabled" minority-group children. New developments in computer capabilities individualize instruction either by direct student-computer teaching sessions, or by the latest technique of computer-managed classrooms, in which the progress of every student in every subject undergoes separate diagnosis and prescription. Great Britain is providing a number of exciting imports: The Summerhill idea and other freedom-based "integrated day" schools. Finally, a group of teachers-turned-novelists have artfully spelled out the touching problems of urban classrooms, problems that still face the next generation of teachers.

The organization of this book is quite simple. We wanted to present recent (and some time-tested) insights into classroom-related principles of learning, development, motivation, and testing. These academic-looking topics comprise four parts. We wanted also to include some of the newest looks in revolutionizing education, material which one reviewer of this book referred to as our "pop stuff." Finally, we wanted to present the strongest parts we could create on two critical but overlooked topics—training creative thinking and educating the culturally different learner (a section with more pop stuff). Throughout, we tried to select interesting and readable articles (some, in fact, are downright entertaining), yet articles which are academically worthwhile and meaningful for today's teachers. Almost half of the selections are abridged, condensing the authors' main points into fewer words and pages.

At the end of each article, two or more memory-stimulating and thought-stimulating questions provide a brief review, a test of understanding, an exercise in integration and application, or all of these functions. The form of the review exercises varies among articles, appearing sometimes as a true-false quiz, sometimes as multiple-choice questions, and other times in a more strenuous form.

Finally, we gratefully acknowledge the suggestions and comments of Terry Belcher, Bill Looft, Frank Farley, Jim Peterson, Jim Buchholz, and Norma Sadler.

Gary A. Davis
Thomas F. Warren

contents

psychology
of education
new looks

part i

PSYCHOLOGY AND EDUCATION: ISSUES AND PRACTICES

We begin with a spoof by Harold Benjamin (under the pseudonym of J. Abner Peddiwell) of some timeless educational issues. Problems of behind-the-times and irrelevant curricula, resistance to change, and "how many college credits of what" make a good teacher seem to have changed little from Paleolithic times to the present.

We often legitimately ask, "What has psychology to offer teaching?" In article 2 Goodwin Watson outlines some answers—fifty of them, to be exact. Categorized under the headings *learning process, motivation, teaching methods, subject matter, evaluation, growth, group relations,* and *social stratification,* the author's conclusions do not exhaust all of psychology's contributions to education. His list is, however, fairly safe in view of academic disagreements that characterize psychology.

In the next group of articles we look specifically at the area of psychology dealing with the process of learning. As noted by Gary Davis in article 3, psychologists have *not* studied learning and conditioning in order to improve our educational practices. Rather, under the assumption that 99 per cent of our thoughts, emotions, habits, and skills are learned, psychologists have sought to understand the human psyche by studing basic principles of learning. While his review is necessarily short and selective, Davis covers a good portion of the ABCs of traditional stimulus-response psychology.

B. F. Skinner is no doubt the most influential living psychologist. Beginning with the most basic principle of learning theory—that rewards control learning and behavior—Skinner outlines how most of human life is in fact controlled by reinforcement-dispensing agencies and social norms. He further prescribes how the more systematic management of behavior may solve some pressing problems of war, pollution, and overpopulation. Part of his prescription includes the controversial scrapping of individual *freedom* and *dignity*—troublesome concepts that give the individual credit (or blame) for actions and accomplishments not under his own control.

It is debatable whether or not Skinner's new book is properly understood. Perhaps he is understood, but disagreed with. Walter Arnold, in article 5, itemizes his points of agreement and dispute with Skinner. For example, while he lauds Skinner's real concern for the survival of society, he proposes that it may be possible to have social control without forfeiting all individual freedom. Most of all, Arnold rejects Skinner's too objective view of man-devoid-of-personality.

The clearest application of learning theory to education is found in teaching machines and in programmed learning. In article 6, a condensation and combination of two separate articles, Skinner sketches the need for and rationale behind programming. Primarily, he sees individualization of instruction, prompt reinforcing feedback, and careful sequencing of information as essential conditions for effective classroom learning. According to Skinner, the fact that programming meets these conditions accounts for the highly favorable results with programming as compared with more traditional classroom procedures.

A standard criticism of stimulus-response psychology is that it presents an incomplete picture of the total human being. In article 7, from *Compulsory Mis-Education,* Paul Goodman paints a fiery picture of programming and "behavior controllers" which includes more than charges of incompleteness. For one thing, he questions whether or not programmers have the constitutional right to control the content of learning and the behavior of children as free citizens. He further argues that programming encourages thoughtless conformity at the expense of individual initiative and "inward meaning." Comparing programming with learning by discovery, Goodman observes that the latter not only resembles meaningful learning in the real world, but stimulates interest in further learning. Programming, on the other hand, *prevents* learning—according to Goodman.

If we were to speculate on the state of education 100 or 1,000 years into the future, we would likely put the student in front of a computer terminal for a session on . . . well, on whatever will comprise future educational curricula. In describing the computer-assisted instruction (CAI) capabilities of the IBM 1500, Ezra Bowen, in article 8, proves the future is closer than we think. By talking to the pupil, drawing pictures, and playing games on the cathode-ray tube screen, reinforcing the learning with smiles and verbal encouragement—along with keeping attendance and administering and marking tests—the computer functions as a patient private tutor ". . . as well informed and responsible as Aristotle." Aware of critics of automated learning, Bowen points out that *things* should be taught by machines, *values* and *meaning* by a teacher.

While CAI was designed to teach, computer-based instructional management systems (CBIMS) are being created to handle the busywork that accompanies individualized education. According to Frank Baker in article 9, the major functions of CBIM systems are test-scoring, diagnosing, prescribing, and reporting. Baker describes several CBIM systems and spells out some difficulties with this newest of computer applications to classroom learning. For example, data processing is too slow, varying from overnight to even a few days. On the positive side, the cost of CBIMS is a fraction of the cost of CAI, and in fact it may be technologically and financially within the reach of the individual classroom instructor. We might mention that the system of individually guided education outlined by Klausmeier in article 30 functions considerably smoother when a CBIM system performs the testing, record-keeping, and other management services.

Using the language of the learning theorist, Arthur Staats, in article 10, says that an overwhelming amount of learning takes by imitating or "matching" the behavior of others. This explains how imitative acts from sitting properly to learning speech skills are reinforced by parents, and hence are acquired. The degree to which imitative behavior itself becomes reinforcing determines how much the child will continue to learn by imitation. Staats further explains that attention, as a type of behavior, is necessary for imitation and for learning in general, and that punishing undesirable matching leads to negative imitation. Finally, the author notes that basic repertoires of imitation behaviors are significant constituents of intelligence which, in fact, contribute to higher scores on standard IQ tests.

Many school psychologists use token reinforcement systems to motivate remedial learning. In article 11 Roger Severson summarizes how his reward-based methods go even further than activating reading and arithmetic. Indeed the author's procedures are engineered to remove *underground school phobia,* the highly negative attitudes that are born in continual failure and frustration.

Education is not complete even with test-confirmed evidence that skills and information have been mastered. The individual also must be able to remember and use his school experiences in the real world. In article 12, Blair, Jones, and Simpson describe the importance of *transfer* and its related concepts of generalization and the learning of principles. One dilemma facing educators, they note, is the difficulty in predicting what skills will be useful decades from now. They also emphasize that not only specific information transfers, but also *attitudes,* toward mathematics for example, will influence later encounters with mathematics. The authors point out fallacies regarding transfer that are still common. Specifically, both the position that "formal discipline" with difficult topics will sharpen mental facilities, and the opposite view that nothing transfers but facts, facts, facts, were judged inaccurate, to say the least. The authors conclude with a number of reasonable recommendations for teaching for transfer.

one

From *The Saber-Tooth Curriculum*

J. ABNER PEDDIWELL

The first great educational theorist and practitioner of whom my imagination has any record . . . was a man of Chellean times whose full name was *New-Fist-Hammer-Maker* but whom, for convenience, I shall hereafter call *New-Fist*.

New-Fist was a doer, in spite of the fact that there was little in his environment with which to do anything very complex. You have undoubtedly heard of the pear-shaped, chipped-stone tool which archeologists call the *coup-de-poing* or fist hammer. New-Fist gained his name and a considerable local prestige by producing one of these artifacts in a less rough and more useful form than any previously known to his tribe. His hunting clubs were generally superior weapons, moreover, and his fire-using techniques were patterns of simplicity and precision. He knew how to do things his community needed to have done, and he had the energy and will to go ahead and do them. By virtue of these characteristics he was an educated man.

New-Fist was also a thinker. Then, as now, there were few lengths to which men would not go to avoid the labor and pain of thought. More readily than his fellows, New-Fist pushed himself beyond those lengths to the point where cerebration was inevitable. The same quality of intelligence which led him into the socially approved activity of producing a superior artifact also led him to engage in the socially disapproved practice of thinking. When other men gorged themselves on the proceeds of a successful hunt and vegetated in dull stupor for many hours thereafter, New-Fist ate a little less heartily, slept a little less stupidly, and arose a little earlier than his comrades to sit by the fire and think. He would stare moodily at the flickering flames and wonder about various parts of his environment until he finally got to the point where he became strongly dissatisfied with the accustomed ways of his tribe. He began to catch glimpses of ways in which life might be made better for himself, his family, and his group. By virtue of this development he became a dangerous man.

This was the background that made this doer and thinker hit upon the concept of a conscious, systematic education. The immediate stimulus which put him directly into the practice of education came from watching his children at play. He saw these children at the cave entrance before the fire engaged in activity with bones and sticks and brightly colored pebbles. He noted that they seemed to have no purpose in their play beyond immediate pleasure in the activity itself. He compared their activity with that of the grown-up members of the tribe. The children played for fun; the adults worked for security and enrichment of their lives. The children dealt with bones, sticks, and pebbles; the adults dealt with food, shelter, and clothing. The children protected themselves from boredom; the adults protected themselves from danger.

"If I could only get these children to do the things that will give more and better food, shelter, clothing, and security," thought New-Fist, "I would be helping this tribe to have a better life. When the children became grown, they would have more meat to eat, more skins to keep them warm, better caves in which to sleep, and less danger from the striped death with the curving teeth that walks these trails by night."

Having set up an educational goal, New-Fist proceeded to construct a curriculum for reaching that goal. "What things must we tribesmen know how to do in order to live with full bellies, warm backs, and minds free from fear?" he asked himself.

To answer this question, he ran various activities over in his mind. "We have to catch fish with our bare hands in the pool far up the creek beyond that big bend," he said to himself. "We have to catch fish with our bare hands in the pool right at the bend. We have to catch them in the same way in the pool just this side of the bend. And so we catch them in the next pool and the next and the next. Always we catch them with our bare hands."

Thus New-Fist discovered the first subject of the first curriculum—fish-grabbing-with-the-bare-hands.

"Also we club the little woolly horses," he continued with his analysis. "We club them along the bank of the creek where they come down to drink. We club them in the thickets where they lie down to sleep. We club them in the upland meadow where they graze. Wherever we find them we club them."

So woolly-horse-clubbing was seen to be the second main subject in the curriculum.

"And finally, we drive away the saber-tooth tigers with fire," New-Fist went on in his thinking. "We drive them from the mouth of our caves with fire. We drive them from our trail with burning branches. We wave firebrands to drive them from our drinking hole. Always we have to drive them away, and always we drive them with fire."

Thus was discovered the third subject—saber-tooth-tiger-scaring-with-fire.

Having developed a curriculum, New-Fist took his children with him as he went about his activities. He gave them an opportunity to practice these three subjects. The children liked to learn. It was more fun for them to engage in these purposeful activities than to play with colored stones just for the fun of it.

They learned the new activities well, and so the educational system was a success.

As New-Fist's children grew older, it was plain to see that they had an advantage in good and safe living over other children who had never been educated systematically. Some of the more intelligent members of the tribe began to do as New-Fist had done, and the teaching of fish-grabbing, horse-clubbing, and tiger-scaring came more and more to be accepted as the heart of real education. . . .

In due time everybody who was anybody in the community knew that the heart of good education lay in the three subjects of fish-grabbing, horse-clubbing, and tiger-scaring. New-Fist and his contemporaries grew old and were gathered by the Great Mystery to the Land of the Sunset far down the creek. Other men followed their educational ways more and more, until at last all the children of the tribe were practiced systematically in the three fundamentals. Thus the tribe prospered and was happy in the possession of adequate meat, skins, and security.

It is to be supposed that all would have gone well forever with this good educational system if conditions of life in that community had remained forever the same. But conditions changed, and life which had once been so safe and happy in the cave-realm valley became insecure and disturbing.

A new ice age was approaching in that part of the world. A great glacier came down from the neighboring mountain range to the north. Year after year it crept closer and closer to the headwaters of the creek which ran through the tribe's valley, until at length it reached the stream and began to melt into the water. Dirt and gravel which the glacier had collected on its long journey were dropped into the creek. The water grew muddy. What had once been a crystal-clear stream in which one could see easily to the bottom was now a milky stream into which one could not see at all.

At once the life of the community was changed in one very important respect. It was no longer possible to catch fish with the bare hands. The fish could not be seen in the muddy water. For some years, moreover, the fish in this creek had been getting more timid, agile, and intelligent. The stupid, clumsy, brave fish, of which originally there had been a great many, had been caught with the bare hands for fish generation after fish generation, until only fish of superior intelligence and agility were left. These smart fish, hiding in the muddy water under the newly deposited glacial boulders, eluded the hands of the most expertly trained fish-grabbers. Those tribesmen who had studied advanced fish-grabbing in the secondary school could do no better than their less well-educated fellows who had taken only an elementary course in the subject, and even the university graduates with majors in ichthyology were baffled by the problem. No matter how good a man's fish-grabbing education had been, he could not grab fish when he could not find fish to grab.

The melting waters of the approaching ice sheet also made the country wetter. The ground became marshy far back from the banks of the creek. The stupid woolly horses, standing only five or six hands high and running on four-toed front feet and three-toed hind feet, although admirable objects for clubbing, had one dangerous characteristic. They were ambitious. They all wanted to learn to run on their middle toes. They all had visions of becoming powerful and aggressive animals instead of little and timid ones. They dreamed of a far-distant day when some of their descendants would be sixteen hands high, weigh more than half a ton, and be able to pitch their would-be-riders into the dirt. They knew they could never attain these goals in a wet, marshy country, so they all went east to the dry, open plains, far from the paleolithic hunting grounds. Their places were taken by little antelopes who came down with the ice sheet and were so shy and speedy and had so keen a scent for danger that no one could approach them closely enough to club them.

The best trained horse-clubbers of the tribe went out day after day and employed the most efficient techniques taught in the schools, but day after day they returned empty-handed. A horse-clubbing education of the highest type could get no results when there were no horses to club.

Finally, to complete the disruption of paleolithic life and education, the new dampness in the air gave the saber-tooth tigers pneumonia, a disease to which these animals were peculiarly susceptible and to which most of them succumbed. A few moth-eaten specimens crept south to the desert, it is true, but they were pitifully few and weak representatives of a once numerous and powerful race.

So there were no more tigers to scare in the paleolithic community, and the best tiger-scaring techniques became only academic exercises, good in themselves, perhaps, but not necessary for tribal security. Yet this danger to the people was lost only to be replaced by another and even greater danger, for with the advancing ice sheet came ferocious glacial bears which were not afraid of fire, which walked the trails by day as well as by night, and which could not be driven away by the most advanced methods developed in the tiger-scaring courses of the schools.

The community was now in a very difficult situation. There was no fish or meat for food, no hides for clothing, and no security from the hairy death that walked the trails day and night. Adjustment to this difficulty had to be made at once if the tribe was not to become extinct.

Fortunately for the tribe, however, there were men in it of the old New-Fist breed, men who had the ability to do and the daring to think. One of them stood by the muddy stream, his stomach contracting with hunger pains, longing for some way to get a fish to eat. Again and again he had tried the old fish-grabbing technique that day, hoping desperately that at last it might work, but now in black despair he finally rejected all that he had learned in the schools and looked about him for some new way to get fish from that stream. There were stout but slender vines hanging from trees along the bank. He pulled them down and began to fasten them together more or less aimlessly. As he worked, the vision of what he might do to satisfy his hunger and that of his crying children back in the cave grew clearer. His black despair lightened a little. He worked more rapidly and intelligently: At last he had it—a net, a crude seine. He called a companion and explained the device. The two men took the net into the water, into pool after pool, and in one hour they caught more fish—intelligent fish in muddy water—than the whole tribe could have caught in a day under the best fish-grabbing conditions.

Another intelligent member of the tribe wandered hungrily through the woods where once the stupid little horses had abounded but where now only the elusive antelope could be seen. He had tried the horse-clubbing technique on the antelope until he was fully convinced of its futility. He knew that one would starve who relied on school learning to get him meat in those woods. Thus it was that he too, like the fish-net inventor, was finally impelled by hunger to new ways. He bent a strong, springy young tree over an antelope trail, hung a noosed vine therefrom, and fastened the whole device in so ingenious a fashion that the passing animal would release a trigger and be snared neatly when the tree jerked upright. By setting a line of these snares, he was able in one night to secure more meat and skins than a dozen horse-clubbers in the old days had secured in a week.

A third tribesman, determined to meet the problem of the ferocious bears, also forgot what he had been taught in school and began to think in direct and radical fashion. Finally, as a result of this thinking, he dug a deep pit in a bear trail, covered it with branches in such a way that a bear would walk out on it unsuspectingly, fall through to the bottom, and remain trapped until the tribesmen could come up and despatch him with sticks and stones at their leisure. The inventor showed his friends how to dig and camouflage other pits until all the trails around the community were furnished with them. Thus the tribe had even more security than before and in addition had the great additional store of meat and skins which they secured from the captured bears.

"Fishnet-making and using, antelope-snare construction and operation, and bear-catching and killing," the radicals pointed out, "require intelligence and skills—things we claim to develop in schools. They are also activities we need to know. Why can't the schools teach them?"

But most of the tribe, and particularly the wise old men who controlled the school, smiled indulgently at this suggestion. "That wouldn't be *education*," they said gently.

"But why wouldn't it be?" asked the radicals.

"Because it would be mere training," explained the old men patiently. "With all the intricate details of fish-grabbing, horse-clubbing, and tiger-scaring—the standard cultural subjects—the school curriculum is too crowded now. We can't add these fads and frills of net-making, antelope-snaring, and—of all things—bear-killing. Why, at the very thought, the body of the great New-Fist, founder of our paleolithic educational system would turn over in its burial cairn. What we need to do is to give our young people a more thorough grounding in the fundamentals. Even the graduates of the secondary schools don't know the art of fish-grabbing in any complex sense nowadays, they swing their horse clubs awkwardly too, and as for the old science of tiger-scaring—well, even the teachers seem to lack the real flair for the subject which we oldsters got in our teens and never forgot."

"But, damn it," exploded one of the radicals, "how can any person with good sense be interested in such useless activities? What is the point of trying to catch fish with the bare hands when it just can't be done any more. How can a boy learn to club horses when there are no horses left to club? And why in hell should children try to scare tigers with fire when the tigers are dead and gone?"

"Don't be foolish," said the wise old men, smiling most kindly smiles. "We

don't teach fish-grabbing to grab fish; we teach it to develop a generalized agility which can never come from so base an activity as bear-killing."
to club horses; we teach it to develop a generalized strength in the learner which he can never get from so prosaic and specialized a thing as antelope-snare-setting. We don't teach tiger-scaring to scare tigers; we teach it for the purpose of giving that noble courage which carries over into all the affairs of life and which can never come from so base an activity as bear-killing."

All the radicals were silenced by this statement, all except the one who was most radical of all. He felt abashed, it is true, but he was so radical that he made one last protest.

"But—but anyway," he suggested, "you will have to admit that times have changed. Couldn't you please *try* these other more up-to-date activities? Maybe they have *some* educational value after all?"

Even the man's fellow radicals felt that this was going a little too far.

The wise old men were indignant. Their kindly smiles faded. "If you had any education yourself," they said severely, "you would know that the essence of true education is timelessness. It is something that endures through changing conditions like a a solid rock standing squarely and firmly in the middle of a raging torrent. You must know that there are some eternal verities, and the saber-tooth curriculum is one of them!"

After the new fishnet era was well under way . . . there was marked dissatisfaction with the traditional school. This dissatisfaction was really directed towards the teachers, for in those days the patrons of the school had the notion that a particular curriculum was really a certain kind of teacher, that a particular system of methods was a certain kind of teacher, and that the whole philosophy of the school was also just a certain kind of teacher. It was a peculiar notion, I admit—unbelievably simple, and all that—but the people had it. Of course they were courteous enough not to *say*, in most cases, that it was the teacher who was at fault. They talked about a better educational philosophy, an improved organization, and all that sort of thing very much as we do today.

By the beginning of the fishnet era, the profession of teaching was pretty well developed, and after the era was well under way, the status and preparation of teachers were rather adequately standardized. In the earlier days of the real-tiger era, teachers had been largely recruited from the ranks of those tribesmen who were too clumsy to grab fish, too weak to club horses, or too timid to face a saber-tooth. By the middle of the fishnet era, this situation had been vastly improved. Teachers were still selected to some extent from the more stupid and less aggressive elements of the population, but any slight disadvantage arising from that condition was more than offset by the new requirements for possession of the teacher's bone.

The chiefs of the tribe were the ones who made the rules in this regard as they did in any other matters affecting the peace, prosperity, security, and happiness of the people. According to these rules, every teacher had to carry with him at all times an official bone, usually the thigh bone of an antelope, upon which was scratched the amount of fish-eats' credit he possessed in pedagogy and in one or more of the standard cultural subjects. Since the paleolithic day was divided into periods between the six meals which the tribe liked to have when food was plentiful, and since fish had formed an important part of the diet from time immemorial, the distance from one fish-eat to another came naturally to be regarded as the proper unit for measuring education.

The elementary teacher's bone had to carry at least fifteen fish-eats' credit in special methods of beginning fish-grabbing, the same amount of credit in the methods of teaching elementary horse-clubbing, but only twelve fish-eats for the corresponding methods course in tiger-scaring. Tiger-scaring was a subject which was not offered until the second year of the elementary school, and it was, therefore, recognized as not demanding quite so much preparatory training as the other two subjects. In addition to special methods, the elementary teacher also needed a certificate on his bone that he had earned thirty fish-eats in the theory and practice of paleolithic education.

The secondary teacher's bone requirements were quite different. He had to have only five fish-eats of special methods in each of the cultural fields in which he taught. If he taught only the various branches of horse-clubbing, he needed only a notation on his bone of special methods in that one field. In general theory and practice of paleolithic education on the secondary level, moreover, he needed only twenty-two and one-half fish-eats. The greater surface of his bone had to be covered by notations concerning strictly subject-matter training in his major and minors. The exact number of fish-eats required varied according to the subject. A major in fish-grabbing required forty-five fish-eats, whereas one in horse-clubbing was only thirty-three. This difference arose from the insistence of the professors of ichthyology that secondary-school graduates entered college ignorant of many of the elements of fish-grabbing. It was therefore necessary, claimed the professors, to devote the first fifteen fish-eats of college work in the subject to teaching what should have been learned in the secondary schools. The professors of equinology, moreover, as soon as they became fully aware of the ichthyologists' success in getting an increase in fish-eats, also protested loudly that they too needed more time for teaching the simplest elements of horse-clubbing to ignorant secondary-school graduates. It was generally conceded by the big chiefs of the tribe, however, that since the ichthyologists had been the first professors to think of making this claim they should be the ones to secure the advantage of extra fish-eats. The equinologists were allotted merely an additional sop of three fish-eats over the standard thirty for college work to quiet their clamor. When the professors of defense engineering, for whose instruction tiger-scaring was a prerequisite, finally awoke to what was going on and made their demand for more fish-eats on the same grounds as their colleagues had cited in the two other fields, the big chiefs rejected the application completely and kept the defense-engineering major at thirty fish-eats.

One group of observers concluded that the chief mistakes in the current educational methods came simply from the circumstance of having too much direction of the learning. "Let the child grow naturally into his learning activities," they advised the teachers. "Let all his purposes and procedures be self-impelled.

Without teacher interference or domination, let him always decide what he wants to do, plan what he has proposed, carry out what he has planned, and judge the worth of what he has done."

The teachers were disturbed. "But where, then, do we come in?" they inquired. "If the children are going to do it all, they don't need any teachers."

"Oh, no!" assured the experts. "The teacher is a very necessary guide. He will lead the child in the direction of wise choices of right activities and show him how to engage more intelligently and effectively in those activities in which he would have engaged anyway."

"And suppose," said one teacher guardedly, "that a child wants to engage in cutting up fishnets. Shall I show him how to do it better than he could without my guidance?"

"You are being facetious," smiled the experts. "Get the real progressive spirit and such questions will not occur to you."

Whereupon the teachers withdrew and consulted among themselves. "It is very clear," suggested one, "that we are still supposed to teach fish-grabbing."

"Yes," agreed another, "but we must not tell the children they *have* to learn fish-grabbing. We must just arrange everything so they themselves will think of learning to grab fish and ask us if they can't do it."

"Ah, I see," said a third, "and then we give them permission and guide— guide—"

The teachers then went back to their classes and proceeded enthusiastically upon this new basis.

"Now, children, what would you like to learn today?" one of them began to a class of twelve-year-olds.

The children stared in astonishment. "We're supposed to learn fish-grabbing, aren't we?" they asked.

"Well—er—not unless you *want* to. What do you really *want* to do?"

"I want to leave school and go to work," announced one of the duller boys.

"Ah, but you *have* to go to school," explained the teacher. "Our compulsory education laws, you know—"

"Who is going to decide whether we pass into the next grade in June?" asked a thin, freckled, myopic girl.

"Why—I am, of course," admitted the teacher.

The members of the class looked at one another a little dubiously, drew a deep collective breath, and then chanted in polite unison, "We want to learn fish-grabbing!"

REVIEW QUESTIONS

1.   Do many college courses resemble fish-grabbing, horse-clubbing, and tiger-scaring in their relevance to contemporary problems? Or are these courses worth-

while as purely academic matters—as valuable as Egyptian history or Renaissance art?

2.   What is *not* taught in today's schools of education which, like fishnet-making and antelope-snaring, would better prepare students for the real world?

3.   What forces in today's schools resist change?

two

From *What Psychology Can We Trust?*

GOODWIN WATSON

Educators and others who wish to apply psychology in their professional work have long been troubled by controversies among psychologists themselves. Behaviorism arose to challenge the introspective method; Thorndike's connectionism was controverted by Gestalt concepts; psychoanalysts talked an almost completely different language. It was natural for teachers to say, "Let's wait until the psychologists themselves straighten out their various systems!" It looked for a while as if one could support almost any educational practice by citing the appropriate psychologist.

Gradually, however, a body of fairly firm facts has accumulated. While it remains true that research findings will be somewhat differently expressed and explained within different theoretical frameworks, the findings themselves are fairly solid.

A workshop of educators recently asked me to formulate for them some statements of what we really know today about children and learning. I set out to list some propositions, important for education, with which I thought few knowledgeable psychologists of any "school" would disagree. To my own surprise, the list grew to fifty.

In no science are truths established beyond the possibility of revision. Einstein modified thinking about gravity, even though Newton's observations were essentially correct. Psychology is much younger and more malleable than physics. New facts are constantly accumulating in psychological research, and these will doubtless introduce some qualifications and modifications—conceivably even a basic contradiction. The educator who bases his program on the propositions presented here, however, is entitled to feel that he is on solid psychological ground and not on shifting sands. Most psychologists, I think, would agree with them.

The fifty propositions follow, somewhat revised and with brief comments, under nine (sic) major headings.

Source: Reprinted by permission of the publisher from Goodwin Watson, *What Psychology Can We Trust?* (New York: Teachers College Press, copyright 1961 by Bureau of Publications, Teachers College, Columbia University).

I. LEARNING PROCESS

1. Behaviors which are rewarded (reinforced) are more likely to recur.
This most fundamental law of learning has been demonstrated in literally
thousands of experiments. It seems to hold for every sort of animal from
earthworms to highly intelligent adults. The behavior most likely to emerge
in any situation is that which the subject found successful or satisfying previously in a similar situation. No other variable affects learning so powerfully. The best-planned learning provides for a steady, cumulative sequence
of successful behaviors.

*2. Reward (reinforcement), to be most effective in learning, must follow
almost immediately after the desired behavior and be clearly connected
with that behavior in the mind of the learner.* The simple word, "Right,"
coming directly after a given response, will have more influence on learning
than any big reward which comes much later or which is dimly connected
with many responses so that it can't really reinforce any of them. Much of
the effectiveness of programmed self-instruction (teaching machines) is that
success is fed back immediately for each learner response. A total mark on a
test, the day after it is administered, has little or no reinforcement value for
the specific answers.

*3. Sheer repetition without indications of improvement or any kind of
reinforcement (reward) is a poor way to attempt to learn.* Practice is not
enough. The learner cannot improve by repeated efforts unless he is informed about how well each one has succeeded.

*4. Threat and punishment have variable and uncertain effects upon learn-
ing; they may make the punished response more likely or less likely to recur;
they may set up avoidance tendencies which prevent further learning.* Punishment is not, psychologically, the reverse of reward. It disturbs the relationship of the learner to the situation and teacher. It does not assist the
learner in finding and fixing the correct response.

II. MOTIVATION

*5. Readiness for any new learning is a complex product of interaction
among such factors as (a) sufficient physiological and psychological maturity, (b) sense of the importance of the new learning for the learner in his
world, (c) mastery of prerequisites providing a fair chance of success, and
(d) freedom from discouragement (expectation of failure) or threat (sense
of danger).* Conversely, the learner will not be ready to try new responses
which are beyond his powers or which are seen as valueless or too dangerous.

*6. Opportunity for fresh, novel, stimulating experience is a kind of reward
which is quite effective in conditioning and learning.* Experiments indicate

that even lower animals (rats, dogs, monkeys) will learn as effectively when they receive rewards of new experience or satisfied curiosity, as they will when the rewards gratify desires for food, water, sex, or rest. One trouble with the typical school day is that it is too dull; pupils find too few stimulating new insights to reward their efforts.

7. *The type of reward (reinforcement) which has the greatest transfer value to other life-situations is the kind one gives oneself—the sense of satisfaction in achieving purposes.* Any extrinsic reward—candy, or stars on a chart, or commendation—depends on its dispenser. There is no need to strive if the reward-giver is out of the picture. Also, cheating (detour behavior) can sometimes win the extrinsic reward. The internal reward system is always present for the learner, and he sees little gain in fooling himself.

8. *Learners progress in any area of learning only as far as they need to in order to achieve their purposes. Often they do only well enough to "get by"; with increased motivation they improve.* One of the earliest psychological studies showed that telegraph operators with years of practice seldom rose in speed beyond the acceptable "main line" rate; they could, however, learn to send and receive much faster if special incentives were provided. Studies of reading speed show that practice alone will not bring improvement; a person may have read books for years at his customary rate, but with new demands and opportunities he may be able to double that rate.

9. *The most effective effort is put forth by children when they attempt tasks which fall in the "range of challenge"—not too easy and not too hard—where success seems quite possible but not certain.* A good illustration is the dart game. Where is it most fun to stand? So close that you can't miss? So far away that you can't make a decent score? The maximum fun is at the level of maximum challenge. If it proves too easy, one steps further back; if it proves too hard one steps a little closer. It is not reasonable to expect a teacher to set an appropriate level of challenge for each pupil in a class; pupils can, however, learn to set their own goals to bring maximum satisfaction and learning.

III. TEACHING METHODS

10. *Children are more apt to throw themselves wholeheartedly into any project if they themselves have participated in the selection and planning of the enterprise.* Genuine participation (not pretended sharing) has been found to increase motivation, adaptability, and speed of learning.

11. *Reaction to excessive direction by the teacher is likely to be (a) apathetic conformity, (b) defiance, (c) scape-goating, or (d) escape from the whole affair.* Autocratic leadership has been found to increase dependence of members on the leader and to generate resentment (conscious or uncon-

scious) which finds expression in attacks on weaker figures or even in sabotage of the work.

12.   Over-strict discipline is associated with more conformity, anxiety, shyness, and acquiescence in children; greater permissiveness is associated with more initiative and creativity in children. Comparison of children whose parents were at the most permissive extreme of home discipline with those who were most strict (both groups of parents loving and concerned) has shown more enterprise, self-confidence, curiosity, and originality in the youngsters from permissive homes. These children were also more friendly and less hostile than the strictly disciplined children. The demand for more restrictive discipline runs counter to the call for more individuality.

13.   Many pupils experience so much criticism, failure, and discouragement in school that their self-confidence, level of aspiration, and sense of worth are damaged The pupil who sees himself at his worst in school is likely to place little value on study and to seek his role of importance outside the classroom. He may carry through life a sense of being not good for much. He is likely also to feel resentment at schools, teachers, and books.

14.   When children (or adults) experience too much frustration, their behavior ceases to be integrated, purposeful, and rational. Blindly they act out their rage or discouragement or withdrawal. The threshold of what is "too much" varies; it is lowered by previous failures. Pupils who have had little success and almost continuous failure at school tasks are in no condition to think, to learn, or even to pay attention. They may turn their anger outward against respectable society or inward against themselves.

15.   Pupils think when they encounter an obstacle, difficulty, puzzle, or challenge in a course of action which interests them. The process of thinking involves designing and testing plausible solutions for the problem as understood by the thinker. It is useless to command people to think; they must feel concerned to get somewhere and eager to remove an obstruction on the way. A situation in which the customary responses work smoothly does not call for thought; when they no longer serve, then one needs to think.

16.   The best way to help pupils form a general concept is to present the concept in numerous and varied specific situations, contrasting experiences with and without the desired concept, then to encourage precise formulations of the general idea and its application in situations different from those in which the concept was learned. For example, the concept of democracy might be illustrated not only in national government but also in familiar situations of home, school, church, jobs, clubs, and local affairs. It is best understood when it is contrasted with the power structures such as autocracy, oligarchy, or laissez faire.

17.   The experience of learning by sudden insight into a previously confused or puzzling situation arises when (a) there has been a sufficient background and preparation, (b) attention is given to the relationships operative in the whole situation, (c) the perceptual structure "frees" the key elements to be shifted into new patterns, (d) the task is meaningful and within the range of ability of the subject. The term "cognitive reorganization" is sometimes applied to this experience. Suddenly the scene changes into one that seems familiar and can be coped with.

18.   *Learning from reading is facilitated more by time spent recalling what has been read than by rereading.* In one experiment (typical of many), students who spent eighty per cent of their learning periods trying to remember what they had read surpassed those who spent only sixty per cent of the time on recollection; sixty per cent was better than forty per cent; forty per cent was better than twenty per cent; and the poorest plan was to spend all the time reading and rereading the assignment. Trying to interpret and apply the ideas noted in reading is another good procedure.

19.   *Forgetting proceeds rapidly at first—then more and more slowly; recall shortly after learning reduces the amount forgotten.* Within twenty-four hours after learning something, a large part is forgotten unless efforts are made to prevent forgetting. A thing can be relearned more quickly than it was learned originally, however; and if it is reviewed several times at gradually increasing intervals it can be retained for some time. Some people apply this idea in remembering names of several persons to whom they have just been introduced. The first recall must come immediately; a second recall should follow about five minutes later, a third after half an hour, a fourth some hours later, and perhaps a fifth the next day. Then names will stick.

20.   *People remember new information which confirms their previous attitudes better than they remember new information which runs counter to their previous attitudes.* Studies consistently show that individuals who feel strongly on a controversial issue, and who are asked to read presentations of both sides, remember the facts and arguments which support their feelings better than they recall those on the opposite side.

IV. SUBJECT MATTER

21.   *No school subjects are markedly superior to others for "strengthening mental powers." General improvement as a result of study of any subject depends on instruction designed to build up generalizations about principles, concept formation, and improvements of techniques of study, thinking, and communication.* In Thorndike's classic investigation, high school pupils whose programs included "hard" subjects like mathematics and ancient languages did not consistently improve in "selective and relational thinking" during a school year any more than did students whose programs had substituted allegedly easier activities like dramatics or typewriting. Whether any subject develops general abilities or not depends very much on how it is taught. Memorizing won't strengthen memory, but students can learn how

to use better techniques of remembering. Pupils who study science may or may not master the processes of scientific thought.

22.   *Children (and adults even more) tend to select groups, reading matter, TV shows, and other influences which agree with their own opinions; they break off contact with contradictory views.* Parents want children taught what they themselves value and believe. One of the basic educational problems is to preserve minds from being closed in—surrounded by like-minded associates, like-minded commentators, and like-minded publications.

23.   *What is learned is most likely to be available for use if it is learned in a situation much like that in which it is to be used and immediately preceding the time when it is needed. Learning in childhood, then forgetting, and then relearning when need arises is not an efficient procedure.* It was once thought that childhood was the golden age for learning. We now know (see Proposition 33) that adults of forty can learn better than youths of fourteen and much better than seven-year-olds. The best time to learn is when the learning can be useful. Motivation is then strongest and forgetting less of a problem. Much that is now taught children might be more effective if taught to responsible adults.

24.   *The superiority of man over calculating machines is more evident in the formulation of questions than in the working out of answers.* Is education too much concerned with answers, not enough with the generation of better questions? "Always the beautiful answer who asks a more beautiful question" (E. E. Cummings).

25.   *Television is the most frequently reported activity of elementary school pupils, occupying about the same number of hours per week as are given to school—far more than would voluntarily be given to school attendance.* Television is qualitatively as well as quantitatively influential. The pictures and sound have a lifelike impact, far more impressive than print. The proportion of their total knowledge which children today acquire in school has dropped to a small fraction. Communities deeply concerned about finding better textbooks have given very little effective attention to the more potent educational medium.

V. EVALUATION

26.   *If there is a discrepancy between the real objectives and the tests used to measure achievement, the latter become the main influence upon choice of subject matter and method.* The biggest difficulty with our present standard tests, and with the machines proposed for offering programmed instruction, is that they don't cover what we believe to be our most important educational aims and values. Curriculum and teaching geared to such tests and machines are likely, then, to ignore these great goals, and to concentrate only on learnings which can be easily checked and scored.

VI. GROWTH

27. *Every trait in human behavior is a product of the interaction of hered-*
ity (as determined at conception by genes) and environmental influences.
The classic argument on the relative importance of heredity and environment is futile; both influence every human act and trait. Some traits (preferences in food or clothing, for example) are easily influenced by nurture,
others (height, rate of skeletal ossification) only when extreme environmental differences are involved.

28. *There are specific stages in individual development during which cer-*
tain capacities for behavior appear. The manner in which these capacities
are then utilized sets a pattern for later behavior which is highly resistant
to change. If unutilized then, they are likely not to develop later. The object
which a baby duck regards as its mother and follows about is that which
appears at a certain brief stage shortly after the egg has hatched. Children
born blind who later recover their sight have lifelong difficulty recognizing
objects which seem simple and obvious to youngsters with normal visual
development. A child who does not experience affectionate care from one
person (not necessarily the biological mother) during the period from six
months to eighteen months of age may be emotionally handicapped for life.
It is very difficult in later years to learn to speak a second language without
a foreign accent. Adolescents who do not develop independence from parents and a normal interest in the opposite sex during the 'teen years may
never do either very well.

29. *The most rapid mental growth occurs during infancy and early child-*
hood; the average child achieves about half of his mental growth by the
age of five. In the first two years a normal child transforms the "big, buzzing,
blooming confusion" of his first conscious experience to organized perception of familiar faces, spoken words, surroundings, toys, bed, clothing, and
foods. He differentiates himself from others, high from low, many from
few, approval from disapproval. He lays a foundation for lifelong tendencies
toward trust or mistrust, self-acceptance or shame, initiative or passivity;
and these vitally condition further mental growth.

30. *During the elementary school years (ages six to twelve) most children*
enjoy energetic activity—running, chasing, jumping, shouting, and rough-
house. For most staid adults this is uncomfortable. Boys are generally more
vigorous, active, rough, noisy, and non-conforming than are girls. Only in
relatively recent periods of human history have children been cooped up in
classrooms, confined to desks, and marched in silent order. There is reason
to doubt the biological appropriateness of the traditional school.

31. *Not until adolescence do most children develop the sense of time*
which is required for historical perspective. The so-called facts of history—
1492, 1776, and all that—can be learned by children but without any real
grasp of what life was like in another period or in a different country. Most

instruction in Biblical, ancient, medieval, and even modern history is no more real to children than are fairy tales.

32. *The significance of the important biological transformations of pubescence (growth of primary sex organs, development of secondary sex characteristics, skeletal and muscular growth, glandular interaction) lies mainly in the meaning which cultural norms and personal history have given to these changes.* Adolescence is not necessarily a "stormy" period. It is vital in our culture because it is then that we expect boys and girls to achieve their *identity*. They must work out their vocational plans, their social life, their marriage, their politics, their religion, and, above all, their concept of who and what they really are. They have one role at home, another with friends of their own sex, another with friends of the opposite sex, another at work, and still another in a school class. What is the true self behind all these masks?

33. *Ability to learn increases with age up to adult years.* The apparent decline is more a matter of motivation (see Proposition 8) than of inability. Most adults don't need to take the trouble to change and to learn new skills. We can coerce children into school activities; adult education is mostly voluntary. Men and women *can*, if they wish, master new languages, new ideas, and new ways of acting or problem-solving even at sixty and seventy years of age.

34. *No two people make the same response to any school situation. Differences of heredity, physical maturity, intelligence, motor skills, health, experiences with parents, siblings, playmates; consequent attitudes, motives, drives, tastes, fears—all these and more enter into production of each individual's unique reaction. People vary in their minds and personalities as much as in their appearance.* Because conformity can be coerced, the ever-present differences are often ignored. Almost everyone around us stops at the red light, comes to work on time, sees the favorite TV programs. Children assemble in classes and take out their arithmetic books when told to do so. These similarities are misleading; the inner reactions are always varied.

35. *Pupils vary not only in their present performance but in their rate of growth and the "ceiling" which represents their potential level of achievement. Some "late bloomers" may eventually surpass pupils who seem far ahead of them in grade school.* Rates of growth are, moreover, irregular; mental growth is even more so than physical growth because it varies with encouragement and opportunity.

36. *Children's gains in intelligence test scores and IQ's are positively related to aggressiveness, competitiveness, initiative, and strength of felt need to achieve.* Some apparent dullness is due to lack of encouragement in the development of verbal and arithmetic skills. When these are not valued at home or by friends, it is hard to take them very seriously. Studies have shown gradual decline in IQ's in culturally deprived groups.

37. *Pupils grouped by ability on any one kind of test (age, size, IQ, read-*

ing, arithmetic, science, art, music, physical fitness, and so forth) will vary over a range of several grades in other abilities and traits. Homogeneous grouping is literally impossible except for a given limited task. On another task, a little later, these same children will not perform alike. No teacher is justified in teaching children, however they may be grouped, as if they were all alike—little mechanical robots. A challenging assignment (see Proposition 9) for one pupil may be too hard or too easy for another despite similarity in grade, age, IQ, sex, size, and school marks.

VIII. GROUP RELATIONS

38.   The right size of group for any activity depends on both the maturity of the individual and the nature of the activity. Hundreds or thousands may be spectators at a film, a TV presentation, or a spectacle. Working, inter-acting groups seem to do best when composed of five to eight members. If the group is larger, some become performers and other spectators. At age six, spontaneous groups seldom exceed three or four children. Sizes now accepted for school classes are much too large for good cooperative work.

39.   When groups act for a common goal there is better cooperation and more friendliness than when individuals in the group are engaged in competitive rivalry with one another. Some studies indicate that the more cooperative groups also produce results of better quality. The competitive emphasis directs attention toward winning rather than toward excellence of performance.

40.   Children learn at an early age that peer consensus is an important criterion; they are uncomfortable when they disagree with their peers, and especially when they find themselves in a minority of one against all the others. Children naturally conform; they do not want to be seen as "different" from all the others. This is an important aid in socializing the human animal. "Independence" emerges in some adolescents as conformity to a specially selected reference group—often one not present at the moment.

41.   Pupils learn much from one another; those who have been together for years learn new material more easily from one of their own group than they do from strangers. Traditioned groups develop their own customary norms. They have signals which recall shared experiences. Peers can communicate economically and without barriers of status.

42.   Children who differ in race, nationality, religion, or social class background, but who play together on a footing of equal status and acceptance, usually come to like one another. This is a particular instance of an important law in social psychology: frequency of interaction brings increased liking for one another. Generally, best friends are those who are most frequently seen—classmates, neighbors, work associates, companions in recreation. The relationship is circular. Those best liked are most often chosen as companions; those with whom we more frequently associate become better liked.

43. *In most school classes, one to three pupils remain unchosen by their classmates for friendship, for parties, or for working committees. These "isolates" are usually also unpopular with teachers.* A vicious circle operates. The rejection by peers and teachers intensifies the disagreeable characteristics and behavior of the isolates and makes it even more difficult to accept them. The task of the teacher is to break through the vicious circle—to try to bring out traits which will enable the isolate eventually to make friends. The relationship to an accepting and understanding teacher is the bridge to all other human beings.

44. *Leadership qualities vary with the demands of the particular situation. A good leader for a football team may or may not be a good leader for a discussion group, a research project, or an overnight hike; leadership is not a general trait.* In some groups, leadership is distributed among members. One person may propose an idea; someone else may lead in its development; a third person may remind the group of its goals or time limits; still another may help to raise morale. No one leader is required. Agenda may be adopted by consensus and followed by cooperative reminders as needed.

IX. SOCIAL STRATIFICATION

45. *The socioeconomic class into which a child happens to be born strongly influences his life chances.* Studies show differential infant-mortality rates, health services, mental growth, school performance, housing, recreation, vocational opportunities, type of church, and extent of community influence—all favoring the upper-class neighborhoods. Schools have a peculiar problem with social class: the school boards represent largely the upper strata; the teachers are drawn mainly from the middle layers; most pupils come from the lower classes.

46. *Two thirds of the elementary school children of America come from lower-class homes; the one third who come from the lower-lower class usually find school very uncongenial.* This is education's biggest unsolved problem. Even in the elementary schools, most teachers are reluctant to work in the culturally deprived areas of cities or of rural regions. As we try to keep all American adolescents in school until sixteen or eighteen years of age, we increase the problem. The "Blackboard Jungle" of the city slums and the "Tobacco Road" schools of the rural slums are tough for teachers and are unrewarding for the resistant pupils. Few successful experiments have yet been reported in devising publicly approved educational programs with strong appeal for these students and for teachers.

47. *Children who are looked down upon (or looked up to) because of their family, school marks, social class, race, nationality, religion, or sex*

tend to adopt and to internalize this evaluation of themselves. Studies have shown that Negro children in a white-dominated society are more likely to pick the black-skinned doll than the white-skinned doll as "looking bad"; they unconsciously accept the prevailing norms of white superiority. Race and class and sex discrimination lead to self-concepts of over-valuation in the dominant group and under-valuation in the subordinate group.

48.   Attitudes toward members of out-groups are usually acquired from members of one's in-group. White children get their attitudes toward Negroes not primarily from direct contact with Negroes but from their white parents and playmates. Similarly, attitudes toward other classes, other faiths, and other nationalities are acquired (like speech dialects or food preferences) from the nurturing group.

49.   Children choose most of their "best friends" from homes of the same socioeconomic class as their own. An effort in one junior high school over a three-year period to increase interaction across the lines of socioeconomic class led to a drop in same-class choices from seventy-five to sixty-six per cent. The norms of the larger community were more powerful than those generated within the school.

50.   More girls than boys wish, from time to time, that they could change their sex. Sex discrimination in our culture has received much less attention than has race discrimination. While there has been some progress toward equality of opportunity in education, our culture still sees boys as primarily concerned with vocational achievement and only secondarily with love, marriage, and parenthood. For girls, the order is reversed; it is thought that their vocational achievement should properly be secondary. Thus it comes about that the top positions in government, industry, commerce, science, education, and religion are reserved for males. The conflict may be particularly acute in girls gifted with high intelligence and outstanding capacity for executive leadership.

REVIEW QUESTIONS

1.   True or false:
   a. A novel experience is a kind of reward.
   b. Tasks that are not too easy and not too hard—the range of challenge—elicit the most effort.
   c. Strict discipline is associated with initiative and creativity in children.
   d. Concepts are best learned by demonstrating numerous examples and by encouraging formulation and application.
   e. It is better to practice recalling, rather than to reread written material.

f. Adults of forty learn better than youths of fourteen.

g. Children spend more time in school than watching TV.

h. There are specific age periods during which certain behaviors must be developed, or they may never develop normally.

i. Adolescence is a storm-and-stress period, regardless of cultural norms and meanings associated with puberty.

j. Because of the influences of encouragement and opportunity, mental growth is more irregular than physical growth.

k. Optimal group size depends upon the activity.

l. Nonconformity may be unpleasant for children.

m. Social isolates are usually liked by teachers.

n. Prejudices are acquired from one's in-group.

2. Reread item 50. Have times changed since Watson wrote this?

Answers to question 1: a. true, b. true, c. false, d. true, e. true, f. true, g. false, h. true, i. false, j. true, k. true, l. true, m. false, n. true.

three

Dogs, Rats, and People:
Basic Conditioning Concepts

GARY A. DAVIS

Almost all human behavior is learned. We learn a language, the meaning of words and how to pronounce them. We learn motor skills, such as walking, writing, and hitting a golf ball. We learn attitudes too—our likes and dislikes of rock music, school, spinach, and foreign policy. Skills, knowledge, habits, even most of our thoughts are the result of learning.

Since psychology is the study of human behavior, and most of this behavior is learned, it logically follows that the study of learning lies at the core of twentieth-century psychology. To understand human behavior, we study principles of human learning. In fact, the terms *behavior theory* and *learning theory* are synonymous and completely interchangeable. One of the main thrusts of psychology has been to identify the simplest, most elementary types of learning and to study the processes, variables, and characteristics of these learning types.

PSYCHOLOGY OF LEARNING
AND EDUCATION

It may seem strange to say that *learning* has almost nothing to do with teaching. Yet this has generally been the case—at least in that area called the psychology of learning. The large body of research and theory in learning has sought mainly to describe and explain principles of learning as a means of understanding the human psyche. There has been pitifully little attention given to principles of teaching and instruction. Over the past half century, major textbooks devoted to learning and conditioning or to experimental psychology in general may not even contain the words *teaching, education, classroom learning,* or *instruction.* The primary exception has been the interest in programmed instruction which, as we will see later, does constitute a clear application of learning theory to practical problems.

If learning has little to do with teaching, why should an education-oriented person invest his precious time studying in this area? There are two reasons, both of which are quite good. First of all, as a matter of general education a student in any social science field should acquaint himself with a topic that has played so central a role in modern psychology. Indeed, a knowledge of learning theory and learning principles constitutes a fair knowledge of the science of psychology. Secondly, a teacher versed in learning theory will possess a powerful explanatory tool. For example, she will be more sensitive to the role of reinforcements and punishments in motivation and learning and will more quickly detect instances of positive and negative transfer. She will understand the theory behind programmed texts, computer-assisted instruction, and the conditioning-based remediation strategies of the school psychologist and the speech therapist.

In our precious few pages, which cannot begin to summarize so vast a literature as human learning, we shall sketch two basic forms of learning—classical and instrumental conditioning. Within these two sections, selected principles and concepts will be inserted wherever they fit most conveniently. Throughout, examples from both the laboratory and the real world will serve to clarify the particular ideas.

CLASSICAL CONDITIONING

Most readers are acquainted with Ivan Pavlov's famous demonstrations. Using a dog as an experimental subject, he paired an arbitrary stimulus, such as the ringing of a bell, with food. After a few trials, the dog apparently had learned the association between the bell and the food and would salivate just to the ringing of the bell. Pavlov called this a *conditioned reflex.*

Now some shop talk. Before training, the dog's physiological machinery was such that he would automatically salivate to the food—meat powder—in his mouth. The meat powder was therefore called the *unconditioned stimulus;* the salivating, the *unconditioned response.* Also before training, the bell was considered "neutral" as a stimulus. That is, the dog would not salivate to the bell. He might have cocked his head and looked at Pavlov, wondering why such a fine scientist was ringing that silly bell; or if the bell were very loud the dog might have jumped a bit, just as you or I would. But before training, he did not respond to this neutral stimulus, and that is the important point. After the pairing of the bell with the meat powder, the bell alone would elicit the salivating, and so the bell became a *conditioned stimulus.*

SIGNIFICANCE OF THE CONDITIONED REFLEX: ASSOCIATIONISM

What is so important about Pavlov's obvious demonstration? After all, any hungry person will begin to salivate if he approaches a hot dog stand or sees a steamed lobster through a restaurant window. Did Pavlov succeed only in teaching the dog to drool on cue?

Pavlov demonstrated experimentally the scientific conditions for the formation of a mental *association*. The main condition was just the stimulus-stimulus *contiguity* of the bell and the food. For at least 2400 years, philosophers had speculated about the nature of the human mind. By introspection it was apparent that "thinking about" one thing led to thoughts about related things; and the related thoughts led to further related thoughts, and so on. To these philosophers, *thinking* appeared to be a matter of remembering associated ideas and events, including many of the mental images, tastes, smells, loves, and fears initially experienced with these ideas and events. *Learning* was forming associations, and *thinking* was recalling those associations.

Beginning with Aristotle, and continuing with such men as Hume, Locke, Descartes, Hobbes, Berkeley, John Stuart Mill and James Mill, and William James, *laws of thought* became *laws of association*. Always, *contiguity* was the primary law—things which occur together tend to become associated. Aristotle's own list contained the laws of *contiguity, similarity,* and *contrast.* For example, think about the word *sea.* You might visualize a sunny beach, which you have experienced in *contiguity* with the word *sea;* or you might think of the word *ocean,* which is *similar* in meaning to *sea.* Now consider the word *up.* You cannot prevent yourself from thinking of its *contrast—down.* More recent seventeenth- to nineteenth-century philosophers added to Aristotle's basic list. For example, the *law of repetition* states that the more frequent the contiguous occurrence of two stimuli, the stronger the mental association between them. The *law of intensity* says that if a stimulus situation is brighter, louder, more startling or fear-provoking, it is more likely to enter into associative relationships and, therefore, be remembered.

With his dog, bell, and saliva-drop counter Pavlov demonstrated the scientific conditioned-reflex basis for many of these time-tested laws of association.

GENERALIZATION, TRANSFER, AND DIFFERENTIATION

When trained to salivate to a certain tone, the dog would also salivate to similar tones. The greater the similarity, the stronger the salivation. We could say that the dog *generalized* from the initial tone to similar tones. We could also say that the dog *transferred* his learned response to a new situation. If a low tone is paired with food while a higher tone is not, the dog will learn to *differentiate* the two stimuli, salivating only to the lower tone. In the classroom, a student solving an algebra problem will be aided if he recalls a similar problem with a transferable solution strategy. The more similar the problems, the greater the amount of *positive transfer*. On the other hand, *transfer* may be *negative*: An inappropriate solution will interfere with his problem solving, and the student must learn to *differentiate* situations requiring different responses.

Positive and negative transfer, generalization, and differentiation are common classroom-learning phenomena. For example, a social studies student who understands prejudice in America will quickly grasp the plight of blacks in South Africa or Rhodesia. A student who has learned about the Industrial Revolution in Great Britain and America will better understand the economical and technological struggles of today's underdeveloped countries. Some information, however, may transfer negatively from one situation to another. Technological development today does not depend upon *inventing* the gas engine, railroad, cotton gin, or light bulb, but upon the speedier process of adopting existing processes and inventions. The student must differentiate some details of technological development today versus 200 years ago.

LANGUAGE LEARNING:
THE SECOND SIGNALLING SYSTEM

Pavlov's explanation of language learning is virtually identical to more current conditioning-based explanations. He coined the term *second signalling system* to describe this *higher-order conditioning*. For example, through basic classical conditioning, or first signalling system, the child learns to associate the taste of a marshmallow with the sight of the marshmallow as a stimulus object. After some eating experience, the sight of the marshmallow stimulus will elicit conditioned taste and touch associations. According to the higher-order conditioning model, if the word "marshmallow" is often paired with the object marshmallow, eventually the word "marshmallow" alone will elicit some of the same conditioned marshmallow responses as did the physical marshmallow object. This is a silly example, but it illustrates with no serious distortion Pavlov's notion that in the second signalling system (or speech), through the contiguous occurrence of the *word* with the *object*, the child comes to respond to the word as a symbol for the object. In Pavlov's [1970] words, ". . . speech constitutes . . . the signal of the first signals."

OTHER EXAMPLES OF CONDITIONED REFLEXES

There are other examples of complex human behavior that are more understandable if we look at them as instances of classical conditioning. Emotional reactions, such as fear, phobias, dislikes, love, sadness, and even racial prejudice appear to fit the model. If you were ever frightened by a snarling Doberman pinscher, the next Doberman—friendly or not—is guaranteed to elicit your conditioned fear reaction, although it will be weaker than in the first frightening case. A child who continually "fails" or is otherwise frustrated or unhappy in school will acquire a conditioned aversion to school. Severson calls this conditioned aversion an *underground school phobia*.[1] A teacher, mother, friend, or sweetheart who has been associated with warmth, love, satisfaction, and happiness will elicit these wonderfully happy yet conditioned responses.

About prejudice, consider the child of bigoted parents who categorically dislike all Jewish and Catholic people. The words "Jews" and "Catholics" are initially "neutral stimuli" which elicit no particular emotional reaction by the child. However, if parents and friends systematically pair the "neutral stimuli" with words such as *bad, rotten, greedy, no good,* and so on, the neutral stimuli will become conditioned stimuli which will elicit conditioned bigot responses.

Of course, the situation may be reversed. Imagine a liberal all-men-are-created-equal person who sincerely wishes to help the plight of American blacks. Then, on *CBS News* he sees black men burning and looting their own brothers' businesses, shooting at firemen, and overturning and burning the cars of whites who happened to drive by at a bad time. The liberal may become negatively conditioned by this contiguous association of distasteful events with black people.

OVERVIEW OF PAVLOVIAN CONDITIONING

We have covered the fundamentals of basic classical, or Pavlovian, conditioning. We indicated its relationship to the earlier philosophical concepts of learning as forming associations and of thinking as associating. We further demonstrated how such complex behaviors as language learning and the conditioning of emotional reactions, including school fears and racial prejudice, may be simplified by viewing them as instances of classical conditioning. Finally, it must be mentioned that Pavlov's ideas and concepts influenced the thinking of virtually all later experimental psychologists in all parts of the world.

INSTRUMENTAL CONDITIONING

With classical conditioning, the basic learning condition was simply the contiguous occurrence of the two stimuli, leading to the formation of a mental association between them. With *instrumental conditioning,* or *operant conditioning* as B. F. Skinner prefers, the basic learning condition is the *selective reinforcement of correct responses.* Skinner's demonstration, which is just as famous as Pavlov's, lies in his Skinner box. In its ultimate simplicity, a rat presses a bar which dispenses a food pellet. The food pellet, or reinforcement, strengthens the conditioned bar-pressing response.

---

[1] See article 11.

SHAPING

The rat initially acquires the bar-pressing response by the experimenter care-fully *shaping* the rat's behavior. The untrained naive rat, running about and sniffing at the Skinner box corners, is awarded a pellet for behaviors that come closer and closer to the desired pressing of the bar—for coming near the bar, for sniffing it, touching it with his little hand, and eventually he is rewarded only for pressing the bar with sufficient force to activate the automatic dispenser.

Animal trainers have used the shaping strategy for centuries, for example, re-warding the hungry elephant only for coming closer and closer to the actual de-sired behavior of standing on his head or bowing to the king. Further, every mother "shapes" the behavior of her children with rewards and punishments; and she does this without reading any of Skinner's books. The selective reinforce-ment of correct responses is a basic, face-valid principle of learning.

SELECTIVE REINFORCEMENT IN EVOLUTION

Some psychologists have noted the similarity of instrumental conditioning to natural selection in evolution. Here, favorable characteristics of species are selectively rewarded by members surviving to propagate, and unfavorable characteristics are "extinguished" through punishment. For example, only the fastest rabbits with the best camouflage and the warmest coats survive the foxes, hawks, and cold weather. Even today, insects continually become im-mune to the newest insecticides because the immunity of the strongest members is reinforced (by survival), leading to new generations of hardy bugs.

SUPERSTITIOUS BEHAVIOR

Returning to our hungry rat learning to press the bar, occasionally he loses track of the exact response required to produce the reinforcement. The result is a chain of irrelevant and sometimes bizarre behavior which the rat apparently "thinks" will lead to rewards. For example, the only rat which this author ever trained learned to place his right paw on the lever, turn his head upside down, then simultaneously bite and press the bar. Sure enough, he was rewarded. And since rewarded behavior persists—the most basic law of all psychology—*Rattus rattus* continued to place his right paw on the lever, invert his head, bite and press—and receive his reward.

Such extraneous, adventitiously rewarded responses as this rat's head action were reported early by Skinner and were appropriately labeled *superstitious be-havior*. It is easy to note human instances of superstitious behavior. For example, we all can look at the religious beliefs and rituals of others and call them supersti-tious. To the believer, of course, these chants, dances, prayers, sacrifices, contributions, and unusual garments are necessary for future reinforcements—"blessings," good crops, victory over the enemy, salvation, reincarnation, or admission to Valhalla or the happy hunting ground. Do you know students who will not take an exam without their lucky charm? Lucky shirt? Or lucky pen?

There are many, many examples of superstitious behavior, responses which we think are reinforced, but in fact are not.

PARTIAL REINFORCEMENT EFFECT

Another interesting Skinnerian concept is the *partial reinforcement effect* (PRE). According to Skinner's tongue-in-cheek story, in his early rat-training days he manufactured his own food pellets using a pharmacist's pill-making machine. Since pill rolling was tedious work, Skinner felt he could get more rat-miles to the pellet if he rewarded not every bar press, but every second, third, fifth, or tenth press. That is, he put his rats on a *partial reinforcement schedule*. Intriguingly, the rats seemed to work harder and longer for the more meager rewards. When Skinner disconnected the pellet dispenser entirely, the rats continued pressing the bar for a long time before finally *extinguishing* (stopping their nonreinforced bar-pressing). Rats on a 100 per cent schedule, one pellet for each response, responded less vigorously and stopped pressing (extinguished) more rapidly when Skinner disconnected the dispenser.

Human examples of the PRE—the highly motivated responding with great resistance to extinction—are common. Have you ever visited the casinos of Las Vegas? On your way to dinner you might notice a lady patiently pumping nickels or dollars into a slot machine. Returning from your midnight show you could pass her again, still standing in front of the same one-armed bandit, hypnotically watching the wheels spin, and occasionally collecting her unpredictable rewards. You could see the same thing at the roulette, black-jack, and crap tables. Closer to home, how many compulsive bridge players do you know? Perhaps you are one. Many college students daily spend hours and hours counting their points and overbidding, all for the unpredictable rewards—a thirty-point hand, a game contract made, and, once in a great while, a grand slam contract bid and made. The partial reinforcement effect in any game or sport, such as bridge, bowling, golf, or poker, is guaranteed to maintain highly motivated responding and strong resistance to extinction.

BEHAVIOR MODIFICATION AND BEHAVIOR THERAPY

The Skinnerian concept of operant conditioning has found application in several practical areas. The terms *behavior modification* and *behavior therapy* are used to describe conditioning methods used in the treatment of mental illness and by school psychologists in the remediation of academic difficulties.

In conditioning-based clinical psychology, a disturbed patient is defined as having acquired a set of maladaptive behavior patterns through past reinforcements and punishments. For example, he may have acquired an aversion to school, an addiction to heroin, an attraction to members of the same sex, or an inability to cope with business or personal pressures. The role of the therapist is to extinguish the disruptive responses and condition more socially acceptable patterns of behavior. One psychiatrist might administer an electric shock when the addict sticks a needle in his arm, hoping to condition an aversion to needles. Another therapist might administer punishment when the homophile views pictures of members of the same sex. Patients with fears and phobias might be *desensitized* by the application of positive reinforcers in fear-provoking situations. For example, the school psychologist might use money, smiles, verbal encouragement, candy, or other valued items to simultaneously reward learning to read and liking school.

PROGRAMMED LEARNING

The entire field of programmed learning, including teaching machines, programmed texts, and computer-assisted instruction, is based upon the instrumental conditioning model of selectively rewarding correct responses. In fact, Skinner himself is directly responsible for the strong current interest in programming.[2] In case the reader has never seen programmed materials, the format is a series of questions. The learner actively responds to each question and immediately receives reinforcing feedback about the correctness of his response. The sequence of questions is carefully engineered so that the learner can be correct on at least eighty-five or ninety per cent of the questions. According to Skinner, programming provides several critical learning conditions that the traditional classroom cannot always provide: Active responding, including *echoic behavior,* is elicited; rewards are frequent and immediate; and the material is carefully sequenced, with built-in graduated difficulty and repetition. According to Skinner, the result is motivated, efficient learning.[3]

A TRUE SKINNERIAN

There are some academic peculiarities of Skinner and "Skinnerians" that set them apart from other learning theorists. First of all, Skinner considers himself *atheoretical*—he does not have a *theory,* but a *system* of behavior. He feels that the true purpose of psychology as a science is to establish *low-order laws,* direct relationships between environmental stimuli, behavioral responses, and reinforcing events. We should not formulate higher-level theories in terms borrowed, say, from philosophy or physiology.

Skinner also emphasizes *behavior control.* We should not use large groups of subjects in our research, nor should we compute means, standard deviations, or other statistics. Rather, we should seek to control the behavior of the individual

---

[2] Sidney Pressey, however, is credited with inventing the first teaching machine in the early 1920's.
[3] See article 6.

organism better, thus making statistics unnecessary. The prototype Skinnerian researcher then, uses few subjects, describes the behavior of each subject in response to reinforcement contingencies, and his research is rarely published in psychological journals that require large subject samples and elaborate statistics.

SUMMARY

In this short report we have summarized the essentials of classical (Pavlovian) and instrumental (operant or Skinnerian) conditioning, along with some concepts associated with these basic learning types. Pavlov's contiguity-based conditioned reflex—a laboratory demonstration of the formation of a mental association—led to his concepts of generalization, differentiation, transfer, and his second-signalling system theory of speech. We also saw how fears, prejudices, and other attitudes and emotions may fit a classical conditioning model.

B. F. Skinner, whose shadow covers almost as much psychological ground as Pavlov's, emphasized the powerful learning principle of immediate and selective reinforcement of correct responses. Superstitious behavior, the partial-reinforcement effect, behavior modification in therapy, and programming were concepts and applications that grew from his research in the Skinner box.

I would repeat that the psychology of learning has not contributed greatly to the psychology of teaching because it never intended to. While a study of the literature on human learning, therefore, will not guarantee improvement in the effectiveness of the average teacher, such a study will increase her professional understanding of psychological principles of human learning—learning which takes place in the crib, on the street, in front of the TV, and in the classroom.

REFERENCE

Pavlov, I. P. Classical conditioning. In W. S. Sahakian (Ed.), *Psychology of Learning*. Chicago: Markham, 1970, pp. 3–18.

REVIEW QUESTIONS

1. A super-strict "conditioning" theorist, otherwise known as a behaviorist, sees man as a switchboard. Through either Pavlovian or instrumental conditioning, input signals become connected to proper output responses. What is missing from this view of man?

2. Can you think of instances of conditioned fears? Partial reinforcement effects? Superstitious behavior?

four

"A Technology of Behavior"
from *Beyond Freedom and Dignity*

B. F. SKINNER

In trying to solve today's terrifying problems of war, overpopulation and pollution, we naturally play from strength, and our strength is science and technology. But while we have made many advances, things grow steadily worse, and it is disheartening to find that technology itself is increasingly at fault. War has acquired a new horror with the invention of nuclear weapons; sanitation and medicine have made the problems of population more acute, and the affluent pursuit of happiness is largely responsible for pollution.

Man must repair the damage or all is lost. And he can do so if he will recognize the nature of the difficulty. The application of the physical and biological sciences alone will not solve our problems because the solutions lie in another field.

What we need is a technology of behavior. We could solve our problems quickly enough if we could adjust the growth of the world's population as precisely as we adjust the course of a spaceship, or move toward a peaceful world with something like the steady progress with which physics has approached absolute zero (even though both presumably remain out of reach). But we do not have a behavioral technology comparable in power and precision to physical and biological technology, and those who do not find the very possibility ridiculous are more likely to be frightened by it than reassured.

Twenty-five hundred years ago man probably understood himself as well as he understood any other part of his world. Today he is the thing he understands least. Physics and biology have come a long way, but there has been no comparable development of anything like a science of human behavior. Greek physics and biology are now of historical interest only, but the dialogues of Plato are still assigned to students and cited as if they threw light on human behavior.

One can always argue that human behavior is a particularly difficult field. It is, and we are especially likely to think so just because we are so inept in dealing with it.

But modern physics and biology successfully treat subjects that are certainly no simpler than many aspects of human behavior. The difference is that the instruments and methods they use are of commensurate complexity. That equally powerful instruments and methods are not available in the field of human behavior is not an explanation; it is only part of the puzzle.

It is easy to conclude that there must be something about human behavior that makes a scientific analysis, and hence an effective technology, impossible. But we have by no means exhausted the possibilities. In a sense, we have scarcely applied the methods of science to human behavior. We have used the instruments of science: we have counted and measured and compared, but something essential to scientific practice is missing in practically all current discussions of human behavior. It has to do with our treatment of the causes of behavior.

Man's first experience with causes probably came from his own behavior: things moved because he moved them. If other things moved, it was because someone else was moving them; if the mover could not be seen, it was because he was invisible. Gods and demons served in this way as the causes of physical phenomena.

Physics and biology soon abandoned such explanations and turned to more useful kinds of causes, but the step has not been taken decisively in the field of human behavior. Intelligent people no longer believe that men are possessed by demons (although the daimonic has reappeared in the writings of psychotherapists), but they still commonly attribute human behavior to indwelling agents. They say, for example, that a juvenile delinquent suffers from a disturbed personality. There would be no point in saying it if the personality were not somehow distinct from the body that got itself into trouble. The distinction is clear when people say that one body contains several personalities that control it in different ways at different times. Psychoanalysts have identified three of these personalities—the ego, superego and id—and say that interactions among them are responsible for the behavior of the man in whom they dwell. And almost everyone still attributes human behavior to intentions, purposes, aims and goals.

Most persons concerned with human affairs—as political scientist, philosopher, man of letters, economist, psychologist, linguist, sociologist, theologian, anthropologist, educator, or psychotherapist—continue to talk about human behavior in this prescientific way. They tell us that to control the number of people in the world we need to change *attitudes* toward children, overcome *pride* in size of family or in sexual potency, and build some *sense of responsibility* toward offspring. To work for peace we must deal with the *will to power* or the *paranoid delusions* of leaders; we must remember that wars begin in the *minds* of men, that there is something suicidal in man—a *death instinct,* perhaps—that leads to war, and that man is aggressive by *nature.* This is staple fare. Almost no one questions it. Yet there is nothing like it in physics or most of biology, and that fact may well explain why a science and a technology of behavior have been so long delayed.

The important objection to mentalism is that the world of the mind steals the show. Behavior is not recognized as a subject in its own right. Psychotherapists, for example, almost always regard the disturbing things a person does or says as merely symptoms, and compared with the fascinating dramas staged in the depths of the mind, behavior itself seems superficial indeed. Linguists and literary critics almost always treat what a man says as the expression of ideas of feelings. Political scientists, theologians and economists usually regard behavior as the material from which one infers attitudes, intentions, needs and so on. For more than 2,500 years close attention has been paid to mental life, but only recently have we made any effort to study human behavior as something more than a mere by-product.

We also neglect the conditions of which behavior is a function. The mental explanation brings curiosity to an end. We see the effect in casual discourse. If we ask someone, "Why did you go to the theater?" and he says, "Because I felt like going," we are apt to take his reply as a kind of explanation. It would be much more to the point to know what happened when he went to the theater in the past, what he heard or read about the play he went to see, and what other things in his past or present environments might have induced him to go or to do something else.

The professional psychologist often stops at the same point. A long time ago William James corrected a prevailing view of the relation between feelings and action by asserting that we do not run away because we are afraid but are afraid because we run away. In other words, what we feel when we feel afraid is our behavior—the very behavior that in the traditional view expresses the feeling and is explained by it. But how many of those who have considered James's argument have noted that no antecedent event has in fact been pointed out? Neither "because" should be taken seriously. No explanation has been given as to why we run away *and* feel afraid.

Unable to understand how or why the person we see behaves as he does, we attribute his behavior to a person we cannot see, whose behavior we cannot explain either, but about whom we are not inclined to ask questions. We probably adopt this strategy not so much because of any lack of interest or power but because of a long-standing conviction that for much of human behavior there *are* no relevant antecedents. The function of the inner man is to provide an explanation that will not be explained in turn. Explanation stops with him. He is not a mediator between past history and current behavior; he is a *center* from which behavior emanates. He initiates, originates and creates, and in doing so, he remains, as he was for the Greeks, divine. We say that he is autonomous—and so far as a science of behavior is concerned, that means miraculous.

The position is, of course, vulnerable. Autonomous man serves to explain only the things we are not yet able to explain in other ways. Autonomous man's existence depends upon our ignorance and he naturally loses status as we come to know more about behavior.

The task of a scientific analysis is to explain how the behavior of a person as a physical system relates to the conditions under which the human species evolved and the conditions under which the individual lives. Unless there is indeed some capricious or creative intervention, these events must be related, and no intervention is in fact needed. The contingencies of survival responsible for man's genetic endowment would produce tendencies to *act* aggressively, not feelings of aggression. The punishment of sexual behavior changes sexual *behavior,* and any feelings that may arise are at best by-products. Our age is not suffering from anxiety but from the accidents, crimes, wars and other dangerous and painful things to which people are so often exposed. The fact that young people drop out of school, refuse to get jobs and associate only with others of their own age is not due to feelings of alienation but to defective social environments in homes, schools, factories and elsewhere.

We can follow the path taken by physics and biology by turning directly to the relation between behavior and the environment and neglecting states of mind. We do not need to try to discover what personalities, states of mind, feelings, traits of character, plans, purposes, intentions or other perquisites of autonomous man really are in order to get on with a scientific analysis of behavior.

There are reasons why it has taken us so long to reach this point. The outer man whose behavior is to be explained could be very much like the inner man whose behavior is said to explain it. We have created the inner man in the image of the outer.

A more important reason is that we seem at times to observe the inner man directly. Indeed, we do feel things inside our own skin, but we do not feel the things we have invented to explain behavior. We feel certain states of our bodies associated with behavior, particularly with strong behavior, but as Freud pointed out, we behave in the same way when we do not feel them; they are by-products and not to be mistaken for causes.

A yet more important reason why we have been so slow in discarding mentalistic explanations: it has been hard to find alternatives. Presumably we must look for them in the external environment, but the role of the environment is by no means clear. The history of the theory of evolution illustrates the problem. Before the nineteenth century, people thought of the environment as simply a passive setting in which many different kinds of organisms were born, reproduced themselves and died. No one saw that the environment was responsible for the fact that there *were* many different kinds (and that fact, significantly enough, was attributed to a creative mind). The trouble was that the environment acts in an inconspicuous way: it does not push or pull, it *selects.* For thousands of years in the history of human thought the process of natural selection went unseen in spite of its extraordinary importance. When it was eventually discovered, it became, of course, the key to evolutionary theory.

The effect of the environment on behavior remained obscure for an even longer time. We can see what organisms do to the world around them, as they take from it what they need and ward off its dangers, but it is much harder to see what the world does to *them.*

The triggering action of the environment came to be called a "stimulus"—the Latin for goad—and the effect on an organism a "response," and together they were said to compose a "reflex." Reflexes were first demonstrated in small decapitated animals, and it is significant that people challenged the principle throughout the nineteenth century because it seemed to deny the existence of an autonomous agent to which they had attributed the movement of a decapitated body.

When Ivan Pavlov showed how to build up new reflexes through conditioning, he created a full-fledged stimulus-response psychology that regarded all behavior as reaction to stimuli. The stimulus-response model was never very convincing, however, and it did not solve the basic problem because something like an inner man had to be invented to convert a stimulus into a response.

It is now clear that we must take into account what the environment does to an organism not only before but *after* it responds. Behavior is shaped and maintained by its *consequences*. Once we recognize this fact we can formulate the interaction between organism and environment in a much more comprehensive way.

There are two important results. One concerns the basic analysis. We can study behavior that operates upon the environment to produce consequences ("operant behavior") by arranging environments in which specific consequences are contingent upon behavior. The contingencies have become steadily more complex, and one by one they are taking over the explanatory functions previously assigned to personalities, states of mind, feelings, traits of character, purposes and intentions.

The second result is practical: we can manipulate the environment. Though man's genetic endowment can be changed only very slowly, changes in the environment of the individual have quick and dramatic effects. A technology of operant behavior is already well advanced and it may prove to be commensurate with our problems. However, that possibility raises another problem that we must solve if we are to take advantage of our gains.

We have dispossessed autonomous man, but he has not departed gracefully. He is conducting a sort of rear-guard action in which, unfortunately, he can marshal formidable support. He is still an important figure in political science, law, religion, economics, anthropology, sociology, psychotherapy, philosophy, ethics, history, education, child care, linguistics, architecture, city planning and family life. These fields have their specialists, every specialist has a theory, and almost every theory accepts the autonomy of the individual unquestioningly. Data obtained through casual observation or from studies of the structure of behavior do not seriously threaten the inner man, and many of these fields deal only with groups of people, where statistical or actuarial data impose few restraints upon the individual. The result is a tremendous weight of traditional "knowledge" that a scientific analysis must correct or displace.

Two features of autonomous man—his freedom and dignity—are particularly troublesome. In the traditional view, a person is free. He is autonomous in the sense that his behavior is uncaused. We therefore can hold him responsible for what he does and justly punish him if he offends. We must reexamine that view, together with its associated practices, when a scientific analysis reveals unsuspected controlling relations between behavior and the environment.

Of course, people can tolerate a certain amount of external control. Theologians have accepted the idea that man must be predestined to do what an omniscient God knows he will do, and the Greek dramatist took inexorable fate ·as his favorite theme. Folk wisdom and the insights of essayists like Michel de Montaigne and Francis Bacon imply some kind of predictability in human conduct, and the statistical and actuarial evidences of the social sciences point in the same direction.

Autonomous man survives in the face of all this because he is the happy exception. Theologians have reconciled predestination with free will, and the Greek audience, moved by the portrayal of an inescapable destiny, walked out of the theater free men. Very little behavioral science raises "the specter of predictable man." On the contrary, many anthropologists, sociologists and psychologists have used their expert knowledge to prove that man is free, purposeful and responsible. Freud was a determinist—on faith, if not on the evidence—but many Freudians have no hesitation in assuring their patients that they are free to choose among different courses of action and are in the long run the architects of their own destinies.

This escape route slowly closes as we discover new evidences of the predictability of human behavior. Personal exemption from a complete determinism is revoked as a scientific analysis progresses, particularly in accounting for the behavior of the individual.

By questioning the control exercised by autonomous man and demonstrating the control exercised by the environment, a science of behavior also seems to question dignity or worth. A person is responsible for his behavior, not only in the sense that he may be justly blamed or punished when he behaves badly, but also in the sense that he is to be given credit and admired for his achievements. A scientific analysis shifts the credit as well as the blame to the environment, and traditional practices can then no longer be justified. These are sweeping changes and persons committed to traditional theories and practices naturally resist them.

There is a third source of trouble. As the emphasis shifts to the environment, the individual seems to face a new kind of danger. Who is to construct the controlling environment, and to what end? Autonomous man presumably controls himself in accordance with a built-in set of values; he works for what he finds good. But what will the putative controller find good and will it be good for those he controls? Answers to questions of this sort are said, of course, to call for value judgment.

Freedom, dignity and value are major issues and unfortunately become more crucial as the power of a technology of behavior becomes more nearly commensurate with the problems we must solve. The very change that has brought some hope of a solution is responsible for a growing opposition to the kind of solution proposed. This conflict is itself a problem in human behavior and we may approach it as such. A science of behavior is by no means as far advanced as physics or biology, but it has an advantage in that it may throw some light on its own difficulties. Science *is* human behavior, and so is the opposition to science. What has happened in man's struggle for freedom and dignity, and what problems arise when scientific knowledge begins to be relevant in that struggle? Answers to these questions may help to clear the way for the technology we so badly need.

REVIEW QUESTIONS

1.   Can you paraphrase the gist of Skinner's complaints about "mentalism"? His use of the term "autonomous man"?

2.   Do you really understand Skinner's problems with *freedom* and *dignity?* Before reading article 5, formulate your own support for or rebuttal of Skinner's freedom-and-dignity position.

five

Beyond Freedom and Dignity: A Review

WALTER ARNOLD

Many would say we are already beyond freedom and dignity. But B. F. Skinner does not think so. One measure of the oddity of his new book is that he deplores this laggardness and urges us to move steadily ahead. We may just be ready for the prompting. It is said that desperate straits call for desperate remedies, and this book seems to be one. In fact, it is one of the strangest amalgams of compassion and misanthropy that has ever been my puzzlement to read.

Actually, there is nothing surprising to old Skinner-watchers about the lines he follows in *Beyond Freedom and Dignity* [Skinner, 1971]. Although addressed to the acuteness of contemporary crises, and more explicit about designing a future society than his earlier works, it is really a nonfiction statement of the principles behind *Walden Two* [Skinner, 1960], his widely read novel of a "behavioral utopia" published in 1948. *Science and Human Behavior* [Skinner, 1953] elaborated further upon Skinner's deterministic convictions about men and society. So the stir that has already begun over the present book seems a delayed reaction to those acquainted with the author's general approach to human problems. The flap must indeed, and possibly ominously, have to do with the revolt against individualism and permissiveness which is beginning to accompany the present cultural expression of those tendencies.

Some men are fired by a vision of freedom; some, like Skinner, by one of control. In a sense, his new book is about survival, and he sees hope for the survival of the species and of the culture of the West only in a designed society, one that is based upon "the science of behavior" and its attendant technology. This means the directed control of individuals by an environment so designed. For Skinner holds that behavior is shaped and ultimately completely determined by the contingencies of the environment. Change the environment and you change the behavior responding to it. For the most part, that is now done haphazardly—or maliciously—by powerful men and institutions. It can be done for "mutual aid" by, Skinner must trust, benevolent leaders.

Source: Reprinted from *Saturday Review*, October 9, 1971, pp. 47–48, 52. Copyright 1971 Saturday Review, Inc. Reprinted by permission of the author and the publisher.

The author obviously believes in progress (he may be one of the last of the believers), and "operant conditioning," which is his technical term for environmental control of behavior, is the simple basis upon which social progress can be made, according to his present catechism. The trouble is, freedom as commonly understood, particularly in what Skinner almost obsessively calls "the literatures of freedom and dignity," is now in his view the chief antagonist of such progress. "Life, liberty, and the pursuit of happiness are basic rights," he says, in some contradiction to what follows. "But they are the rights of the individual and were listed as such at a time when the literatures of freedom and dignity were concerned with the aggrandizement of the individual. They have only a minor bearing on the survival of a culture." What culture? is a question the critic will want to keep in mind.

Adopting Skinner's view, then, means abandoning the old notions of choice, "free will," individual initiative, and especially "autonomy." These to him are "prescientific" ideas, along with such other moral fictions as "the inner man," the thinking, feeling "self," and of course the "mind." Following Pavlov, J. B. Watson and other behaviorists, materialists, and nominalists before him, Skinner sees these inner realities as constructs of "mentalism" which must be demythologized according to the true science. "It is in the nature of scientific progress that the functions of autonomous man be taken over one by one as the role of the environment is better understood." Indeed "a self is a repertoire of behavior appropriate to a given set of contingencies," a nexus of conditioning, very far from the existentialists' "abyss of longing." For Skinner, the alternative is to admit behavior without a cause—in other words, truly original action. The choice, as it were, is between science and miracle-mongering. Some choice.

If people do not really decide, if they are not able to originate judgments or actions, they are also not responsible for what they do or bring about. "A scientific analysis shifts the credit as well as the blame to the environment, and traditional practices can then no longer be justified." I am reminded of Chesterton's remark that one of the consequences of accepting a complete determinism in human actions is that it becomes pointless to thank someone for passing the salt at the table. In fact, in the community of Walden Two nobody thanks anybody for services or commends anyone for achievements. There are no heroes in Walden Two. But no tragedy either, and not much deep laughter.

Plainly, this view of human actions militates against the vaunted "dignity of man," and against moral values generally as they are understood by most people. Skinner does not exactly throw such values out. Doing what one does when one wants to keep the name of a quality without its old substance, he redefines "good" and "bad" in keeping with his "behavioral technology." Accordingly, "the only good things are positive reinforcers, and the only bad things are negative reinforcers." These "values" are strictly utilitarian; they are solely means and in no sense ends. It does not seem to bother Skinner that what he means is not all that we mean when defining such values as "good" and "bad," or "evil." It is perfectly meaningful, and critical, to ask about a given "positive reinforcer": Does it operate to a person's good? Is it really good?

Skinner does indeed have a quarrel with "the literatures of freedom and dignity" which have so dominated the modern period in the West. In this tradition he includes both nonfiction and fiction, Tom Paine's *Common Sense* and Dostoevsky's *Notes from the Underground*. He admits that such works have been effective both as "good" counter-controls against tyranny and, unfortunately from his point of view, as "conditioners" against achieving a more successfully designed society. For this last reason such literatures would gradually diminish in a Skinnerian world. "We shall not only have no reason to admire people who endure suffering, face danger, or struggle to be good, it is possible that we shall have little interest in pictures or books about them."

What is to be thought of all this? Is *Beyond Freedom and Dignity* perhaps a Swiftian "modest proposal," a deliberate deadpan put-on contrived as a stimulus to evoke a highly aversive response? I am afraid not. Certainly there is unconscious irony and self-satire in the book: "Almost everyone who is concerned with human affairs—as political scientist, philosopher, man of letters, economist, psychologist, linguist, sociologist, theologian, anthropologist, educator, or psychotherapist—continues to talk about human behavior in this prescientific way." And for good reason.

Dr. Skinner is too tightly hinged to premises and principles that are highly arguable and, in any case, not necessary to the mitigation of the very real social problems that concern him and ought to concern his readers. For example, to work for effective social controls it is not necessary to accept either determinism, environmentalism, or the denial of human "inwardness." Control is not coercion, and we can accept the need for control in many circumstances without giving up *relative* individual autonomy. In fact, without freedom, there is no control.

But since *Beyond Freedom and Dignity* will receive its fair share of attacks, including, I am sure, a share that will be unfair—name-calling, *ad hominem* arguments, and the rest—let me briefly state what I think is in favor of the book. First of all, Dr. Skinner pays admirable attention to social problems at a time when psychology, as well as so many other aspects of our society, seems ever more turned in upon itself. In particular he helps to focus attention on the crucial issue of control, both of the individual and society. Skinner's sharp critique of punishment as largely ineffectual control is pertinent to the pressing question of prisons. Surely, too, individualism is not enough, and Skinner is right in warning against the potentially disastrous consequences of a prolific and arrogant individualism. He does a service to concentrate our attention on these concerns, and, contrary to his own convictions, should be thanked for that.

Having said this much for the book, I must add that its most important service is the negative one of providing an example of the absurdity to which the superstition of scientism leads. In the end nothing is left in Skinner's world but a concatenation of environments with no real persons to experience or control them. For in what I can only call his lust to objectivize everything, Skinner has effectively abolished personality and hence man. As the great Russian philosopher Nikolai Berdyaev pointed out, "Personality cannot be recognized as an object, as one of the objects in a line with other objects in the world. . . . In that way man is looked at partially: but there is in that case no mystery of man, as personality, as an existential center of the world. Personality is recognized only as a subject, in infinite subjectivity, in which is hidden the secret of existence." Skinner cannot have it both ways. Since he wants a manipulable creature he must assert, as he does, "To man *qua* man we readily say good riddance."

Another dream of reason has ended as a nightmare of an eminent psychologist, in this case perhaps the most influential of living American psychologists. But was it a good dream to begin with? Was it even an especially rational one? We all know some of the devastating results of following the old imperative to control and subdue nature outside man, of adopting the dictum of Skinner's spiritual forebear, Francis Bacon, that "knowledge is power." Are we about to try the same experiment with "manipulable man"? Skinner wants to see the survival of our culture. I am not certain survival is the highest human value, but to accept his principles and means would, I am sure, guarantee the extinction of everything that presently energizes our inmost beings and hence our culture. For man, nothing exists "beyond freedom and dignity" but atoms and the void. Thus only if the views of this book are for the most part rejected will it really have a good effect on the social environment.

REFERENCES

Skinner, B. F. *Beyond Freedom and Dignity*. New York: Alfred A. Knopf, Inc., 1971.

Skinner, B. F. *Walden Two*. New York: The Macmillan Company, 1960.

Skinner, B. F. *Science and Human Behavior*. New York: The Macmillan Company, 1953.

REVIEW QUESTIONS

1.   Reread the author's last sentence. Can you think of at least one line of reasoning supporting Skinner? Another argument in support of Arnold's last sentence?

2.   Imagine a low SES high-school dropout who is repeatedly arrested for petty theft. Imagine also a high-school valedictorian from the "other side of the tracks." Can environment control behavior?

six

Excerpts from "Teaching Machines" and "Why We Need Teaching Machines"

B. F. SKINNER

I. From *Why We Need Teaching Machines*

It is true that the psychology of learning has so far not been very helpful in education. Its learning curves and its theories of learning have not yielded greatly improved classroom practices. But it is too early to conclude that nothing useful is to be learned about the behavior of teacher and student. No enterprise can improve itself very effectively without examining its basic processes. Fortunately, recent advances in the experimental analysis of behavior suggest that a true technology of education is feasible. Improved techniques are available to carry out the two basic assignments of education: constructing extensive repertoires of verbal and nonverbal behavior and generating that high probability of action which is said to show interest, enthusiasm, or a strong "desire to learn."

The processes clarified by an experimental analysis of behavior have, of course, always played a part in education, but they have been used with little understanding of their effects, wanted or unwanted. Whether by intention or necessity, teachers have been less given to teaching than to holding students responsible for learning. Methods are still basically aversive. The student looks, listens, and answers questions (and, incidentally, sometimes learns) as a gesture of avoidance or escape. A good teacher can cite exceptions, but it is a mistake to call them typical. The birch rod and cane are gone, but their place has been taken by equally effective punishments (criticism, possibly ridicule, failure) used in the same way: the student must learn, or else!

By-products of aversive control in education range from truancy, early dropouts, and school-vandalism to inattention, "mental fatigue," forgetting, and apathy. It does not take a scientific analysis to trace these to their sources in edu-

Source: Sections I and III are abridged from *Cumulative Record: A Selection of Papers,* Third Edition, by B. F. Skinner. Copyright © 1972 by Appleton-Century-Crofts, Educational Division, Meredith Corporation. Reprinted by permission of the author and the publisher. Section II is abridged from *Science,* Vol. 128, October 24, 1958, pp. 969–77. Reprinted by permission of the author and the American Association for the Advancement of Science.

cational practice. But more acceptable techniques have been hard to find. Erasmus tells of an English gentleman who tried to teach his son Greek and Latin without punishment. He taught the boy to use a bow and arrow and set up targets in the shape of Greek and Latin letters, rewarding each hit with a cherry. He also fed the boy letters cut from delicious biscuits. As a result, we may assume that the boy salivated slightly upon seeing a Greek or Latin text and that he was probably a better archer; but any effect on his knowledge of Greek and Latin is doubtful.

Current efforts to use rewards in education show the same indirection. Texts garnished with pictures in four colors, exciting episodes in a scientific film, interesting classroom activities—these will make a school interesting and even attractive (just as the boy probably liked his study of Greek and Latin), but to generate specific forms of behavior these things must be related to the student's behavior in special ways. Only then will they be truly rewarding or, technically speaking, "reinforcing."

We make a reinforcing event contingent on behavior when, for example, we design a piece of equipment in which a hungry rat or monkey or chimpanzee may press a lever and immediately obtain a bit of food. Such a piece of equipment gives us a powerful control over behavior. By scheduling reinforcements, we may maintain the behavior of pressing the lever in any given strength for long periods of time. By reinforcing special kinds of responses to the lever—for example, very light or very heavy presses or those made with one hand or the other—we "shape" different forms or topographies of behavior. By reinforcing only when particular stimuli or classes of stimuli are present, we bring the behavior under the control of the environment. All these processes have been thoroughly investigated, and they have already yielded standard laboratory practices in manipulating complex forms of behavior for experimental purposes. They are obviously appropriate to educational design.

In approaching the problem of the educator we may begin by surveying available reinforcers. What positive reasons can we give the student for studying? We can point to the ultimate advantages of an education—to the ways of life which are open only to educated men—and the student himself may cite these to explain why he wants an education, but ultimate advantages are not contingent on behavior in ways which generate action. Many a student can testify to the result. No matter how much he may *want* to become a doctor or an engineer, say, he cannot force himself to read and remember the page of text in front of him at the moment. All notions of ultimate utility (as, for example, in economics) suffer from the same shortcoming: they do not specify effective contingencies of reinforcement.

The gap between behavior and a distant consequence is sometimes bridged by a series of "conditioned reinforcers." In the laboratory experiment just described a delay of even a fraction of a second between the response to the lever and the appearance of food may reduce the effectiveness of the food by a measurable amount. It is standard practice to let the movement of a lever produce some visual stimulus, such as a change in the illumination in the apparatus, which is then followed by food. In this way the change in illumination becomes a conditioned reinforcer which can be made immediately contingent on the response. The marks, grades, and diplomas of education are conditioned reinforcers designed to bring ultimate consequences closer to the behavior reinforced. Like prizes and medals, they represent the approval of teachers, parents, and others, and they show competitive superiority, but they are mainly effective because they signalize progress through the system—toward some ultimate advantage of, or at least freedom from, education. To this extent they bridge the gap between behavior and its remote consequences; but they are still not contingent on behavior in a very effective way.

Fortunately, we can solve the problem of education without discovering or inventing additional reinforcers. We merely need to make better use of those we have. Human behavior is distinguished by the fact that it is affected by small consequences. Describing something with the right word is often reinforcing. So is the clarification of a temporary puzzlement, or the solution of a complex problem, or simply the opportunity to move forward after completing one stage of an activity. We need not stop to explain *why* these things are reinforcing. It is enough that, when properly contingent upon behavior, they provide the control we need for successful educational design.

II. From *Teaching Machines*

If our current knowledge of the acquisition and maintenance of verbal behavior is to be applied to education, some sort of teaching machine is needed. Contingencies of reinforcement which change the behavior of lower organisms often cannot be arranged by hand; rather elaborate apparatus is needed. The human organism requires even more subtle instrumentation. An appropriate teaching machine will have several important features. The student must *compose* his response rather than select it from a set of alternatives, as in a multiple-choice self-rater. One reason for this is that we want him to recall rather than recognize—to make a response as well as see that it is right. Another reason is that effective multiple-choice material must contain plausible wrong responses, which are out of place in the delicate process of "shaping" behavior because they strengthen unwanted forms. Although it is much easier to build a machine to score multiple-choice answers than to evaluate a composed response, the technical advantage is outweighed by these and other considerations.

A second requirement of a minimal teaching machine also distinguishes it from earlier versions. In acquiring complex behavior the student must pass through a carefully designed sequence of steps, often of considerable length. Each step must be so small that it can always be taken, yet in taking it the student moves somewhat closer to fully competent behavior. The machine must make sure that these steps are taken in a carefully prescribed order.

The success of such a machine depends on the material used in it. The task of programming a given subject is at first sight rather formidable. Many helpful techniques can be derived from a general analysis of the relevant behavioral processes, verbal and nonverbal. Specific forms of behavior are to be evoked and, through differential reinforcement, brought under the control of specific stimuli.

This is not the place for a systematic review of available techniques, or of the kind of research which may be expected to discover others. However, the machines themselves cannot be adequately described without giving a few examples of programs. We may begin with a set of frames (see Table 1) designed to teach a third- or fourth-grade pupil to spell the word *manufacture*. The six frames are presented in the order shown and the pupil moves sliders to expose letters in the open squares.

TABLE 1.   A Set of Frames Designed to Teach a Third- or Fourth-Grade Pupil to Spell the Word *manufacture*

---

1.   Manufacture means to make or build. *Chair factories manufacture chairs.* Copy the word here:

$$\square\,\square\,\square\,\square\,\square\,\square\,\square\,\square\,\square\,\square\,\square$$

2.   Part of the word is like part of the word factory. Both parts come from an old word meaning *make* or *build.*

m a n u $\square\,\square\,\square\,\square$ u r e

3.   Part of the word is like part of the word manual. Both parts come from an old word for *hand.* Many things used to be made by hand.

$\square\,\square\,\square\,\square$ f a c t u r e

4.   The same letter goes in both spaces:

m $\square$ n u f $\square$ c t u r e

5.   The same letter goes in both spaces:

m a n $\square$ f a c t $\square$ r e

6.   Chair factories $\square\,\square\,\square\,\square\,\square\,\square\,\square\,\square\,\square\,\square$ chairs.

The word to be learned appears in bold face in frame 1, with an example and a simple definition. The pupil's first task is simply to copy it. When he does so correctly, frame 2 appears. He must now copy selectively: he must identify *fact* as the common part of *manufacture* and *factory*. This helps him to spell the word and also to acquire a separable "atomic" verbal operant. In frame 3 another root must be copied selectively from *manual*. In frame 4 the pupil must for the first time insert letters without copying. Since he is asked to insert the same letter in two places, a wrong response will be doubly conspicuous, and the chance of failure is thereby minimized. The same principle governs frame 5. In frame 6 the pupil spells the word to complete the sentence used as an example in frame 1. Even a poor student is likely to do this correctly because he has just composed or completed the word five times, has made two important root-responses, and has learned that two letters occur in the word twice. He has probably learned to spell the word without having made a mistake.

A simple technique used in programming material at the high-school or college level . . . is exemplified in teaching a student to recite a poem. The first line is presented with several unimportant letters omitted. The student must read the line "meaningfully" and supply the missing letters. The second, third, and fourth frames present succeeding lines in the same way. In the fifth frame the first line reappears with other letters also missing. Since the student has recently read the line, he can complete it correctly. He does the same for the second, third, and fourth lines. Subsequent frames are increasingly incomplete, and eventually—say, after twenty or twenty-four frames—the student reproduces all four lines without external help, and quite possibly without having made a wrong response. The technique is similar to that used in teaching spelling: responses are first controlled by a text, but this is slowly reduced (colloquially, "vanished") until the responses can be emitted without a text, each member in a series of responses being now under the "intraverbal" control of other members.

"Vanishing" can be used in teaching other types of verbal behavior. When a student describes the geography of part of the world or the anatomy of part of the body, or names plants and animals from specimens or pictures, verbal responses are controlled by nonverbal stimuli. In setting up such behavior the student is first asked to report features of a fully labeled map, picture, or object, and the labels are then vanished. In teaching a map, for example, the machine asks the student to describe spatial relations among cities, countries, rivers, and so on, as shown on a fully labeled map. He is then asked to do the same with a map in which the names are incomplete or, possibly, lacking. Eventually he is asked to report the same relations with no map at all. If the material has been well programmed, he can do so correctly. Instruction is sometimes concerned not so much with imparting a new repertoire of verbal responses as with getting the student to describe something accurately in any available terms. The machine can "make sure the student understands" a graph, diagram, chart, or picture by asking him to identify and explain its features—correcting him, of course, whenever he is wrong.

Difficult as programming is, it has its compensations. It is a salutary thing to try to guarantee a right response at every step in the presentation of a subject matter. The programmer will usually find that he has been accustomed to leave much to the student—that he has frequently omitted essential steps and neglected to invoke relevant points. The responses made to his material may reveal surprising ambiguities. Unless he is lucky, he may find that he still has something to learn about his subject. He will almost certainly find that he needs to learn a great deal more about the behavioral changes he is trying to induce in the student. This effect of the machine in confronting the programmer with the full scope of his task may in itself produce a considerable improvement in education.

The machine itself, of course, does not teach. It simply brings the student into contact with the person who composed the material it presents. It is a labor-saving device because it can bring one programmer into contact with an indefinite number of students. This may suggest mass production, but the effect upon each student is surprisingly like that of a private tutor. The comparison holds in several respects.

i.   There is a constant interchange between program and student. Unlike lectures, textbooks, and the usual audio-visual aids, the machine induces sustained activity. The student is always alert and busy.

ii.   Like a good tutor, the machine insists that a given point be thoroughly understood, either frame by frame or set by set, before the student moves on. Lectures, textbooks, and their mechanized equivalents, on the other hand, proceed without making sure that the student understands and easily leave him behind.

iii.   Like a good tutor, the machine presents just that material for which the student is ready. It asks him to take only that step which he is at the moment best equipped and most likely to take.

iv.   Like a skillful tutor, the machine helps the student to come up with the right answers. It does this in part through the orderly construction of the program and in part with techniques of hinting, prompting, suggesting, and so on, derived from an analysis of verbal behavior.

v.   Lastly, of course, the machine, like the private tutor, reinforces the student for every correct response using this immediate feedback not only to shape his behavior most efficiently but to maintain it in strength in a manner which the layman would describe as "holding the student's interest."

III. From *Why We Need Teaching Machines*

Exploratory research in schools and colleges indicates that what is now taught by teacher, textbook, lecture, or film can be taught in half the time with half the effort by a machine of this general type. One has only to see students at work to understand why this is a conservative estimate. The student remains active. If he stops, the program stops (in marked contrast with classroom practice and educational television); but there is no compulsion for he is not inclined to stop. Immediate and frequent reinforcement sustains a lively interest. (The interest, incidentally, outlasts any effect of novelty. Novelty may be relevant to interest, but the material in the machine is always novel.) Where current instructional procedures are highly efficient, the gain may not be so great. In one experiment involving industrial education there was approximately a 25 per cent saving in the time required for instruction, something of the order of a 10 per cent increase in retention, and about 90 per cent of the students preferred to study by machine. In general, the student generally likes what he is doing; he makes no effort to escape—for example, by letting his attention wander. He need not force himself to work and is usually free of the feeling of effort generated by aversive control. He has no reason to be anxious about impending examinations, for none are required. Both he and his instructor know where he stands at all times.

No less important in explaining the success of teaching machines is the fact that each student is free to proceed at his own rate. Holding students together for instructional purposes in a class is probably the greatest source of inefficiency in education. Some efforts to mechanize instruction have missed this point. A language laboratory controlled from a central console presupposes a group of students advancing at about the same rate, even though some choice of material is permitted. Television in education has made the same mistake on a colossal scale. A class of twenty or thirty students moving at the same pace is inefficient enough, but what must we say of all the students in half a dozen states marching in a similar lock step?

In trying to teach more than one student at once we harm both fast and slow learners. The plight of the good student has been recognized, but the slow learner suffers more disastrous consequences. The effect of pressure to move beyond one's natural speed is cumulative. The student who has not fully mastered a first lesson is less able to master a second. His ultimate failure may greatly exaggerate his shortcomings; a small difference in speed has grown to an immense difference in comprehension. Some of those most active in improving education have been tempted to dismiss slow students impatiently as a waste of time, but it is quite possible that many of them are capable of substantial, even extraordinary, achievements if permitted to move at their own pace. Many distinguished scientists, for example, have appeared to think slowly.

One advantage of individual instruction is that the student is able to follow a program without breaks or omissions. A member of a class moving at approximately the same rate cannot always make up for absences, and limitations of contact time between student and teacher make it necessary to abbreviate material to the point at which substantial gaps are inevitable. Working on a machine, the student can always take up where he left off or, if he wishes, review earlier work after a longer absence. The coherence of the program helps to maximize the student's success, for by thoroughly mastering one step he is optimally prepared for the next. Many years ago, in their *Elementary Principles of Education,* Thorndike and Gates considered the possibility of a book "so arranged that only to him who had done what was directed on page one would page two become visible, and so on." With such a book, they felt, "much that now requires personal instruction could be managed by print." The teaching machine is, of course, such a book.

In summary, then, machine teaching is unusually efficient because

1. The student is frequently and immediately reinforced,
2. He is free to move at his natural rate, and
3. He follows a coherent sequence.

These are the more obvious advantages, and they may well explain current successes. But there are more promising possibilities: the conditions arranged by a good teaching machine make it possible to apply to education what we have learned from laboratory research and to extend our knowledge through rigorous experiments in schools and colleges.

REVIEW QUESTIONS

1.   Review the claimed advantages of teaching machines. Do you think these claims are justified?

2.   Do you see a role for programming in today's schools?

seven

"Programmed" from
Compulsory Mis-Education

PAUL GOODMAN

I

Programmed teaching adapted for machine use goes a further step than conforming students to the consensus which is a principal effect of schooling interlocked with the mass media. In this pedagogic method it is *only* the programmer—the administrative decision-maker—who is to do any "thinking" at all; the students are systematically conditioned to follow the train of the *other's* thoughts. "Learning" means to give some final response that the programmer considers advantageous (to the students). There is no criterion of *knowing* it, of having learned it, of Gestalt-forming or simplification. That is, the student has no active self at all; his self, at least as student, is a construct of the programmer.

What does this imply? Let me analyze a very high-level argument for such teaching by Lauren Resnick, "Programmed Instruction of Complex Skills," in *The Harvard Educational Review* of Fall 1963.

In the conclusion of this perspicuous article, Dr. Resnick tells us:

By explicit instruction I mean the deliberate modification of the behavior of other human beings. Programmed instruction is not interested in the teacher as stimulator of interest, role model, or evaluator of progress. It is interested in him as instructor, or controller of behavior. This means that programmed instruction is applicable only where we do in fact want to change behavior in a given direction. There are cases where for political or ethical reasons we do not want to. We do not, for example, want to train all students to be active partisans of a given political or religious viewpoint, or make everyone like the same kind of literature or music. In such cases . . . "exposure" is the most we should attempt. (p. 467)

Source: From *Compulsory Mis-Education* by Paul Goodman. Copyright 1964, reprinted by permission of the publisher, Horizon Press, New York.

Let me put this dramatic statement in juxtaposition with an earlier statement in her essay:

> In the context of behavioral analysis, knowledge, skill, and ability can be dealt with only insofar as they can be described in terms of performance. This description is not a matter of listing "correlates" of ability or knowledge, but of deciding what observable behaviors will be accepted as evidence of their existence. The behaviorist simply eschews the question of whether knowledge, for instance, exists apart from observable behaviors. While, in so doing, he may fail to answer to the philosopher's satisfaction the question, "What is knowledge?", he very effectively provides himself with a set of usable goals for instruction. (p. 448)

I do not much want to discuss the pedagogic relevance of these ideas. The only evidence of "performance" that school people ever draw on for their experiments is scoring on academic tests, and it seems to be impossible to disabuse school people of the notion that test-passers have necessarily learned anything relevant to their further progress or careers; or of advantage to the body politic; or indeed anything whatever that will not vanish in a short time, when the *real* life-incentive, of passing the test, has passed away. But I want to ask if this kind of *formulation* of teaching does not involve serious legal difficulties, in terms of civil liberties, especially where schooling is compulsory, when the child *must* go to school and submit to having his behavior shaped.

It may seem odd that I keep referring to the constitutional question; but it is a way of asking what kind of democracy we envisage in our curriculum and methods of schooling. Besides, since the young have become so clearly both an exploited and an outcast class, we must begin to think of legal rights.

II

Our Bill of Rights guarantees were grounded in a very different epistemological theory from operant-conditioning, the method that Dr. Resnick has learned from B. F. Skinner. Roughly, the Enlightenment conception was that intellect, like conscience, was something "inward," and the aim of teaching was to nurture its "growth" by "knowledge." Even more important, behavior was the "external" effect of an initiating or self-moving of the "soul"; therefore the student was or became "responsible." In my opinion, the inner-outer metaphor of this conception is quite useless; there is not much use in a psychological theory for entities that are not observable as behavior. But the Aristotelian emphasis on the self-moving organism is solid gold.

Now compulsory schooling, as I have pointed out, was justified in this theory, e.g. by Jefferson, as necessary to bring children to the point of self-government, of exercising citizenly initiative, as well as the animal and social initiative that they had by "nature" and the moral initiative that they had by "conscience." Democracy required an educated electorate. To this was later added the justification that only by compulsory education could the poor get an equal democratic opportunity with the rich; poor parents were likely to put their children to work too early, and not give them a chance to develop to their full powers.

In turn, any course of the curriculum or detail of method was justified by showing that it nurtured the growth of the inward intellect, encouraged initiative, and fitted the young to take a free part in political society. On this view, school teaching was precisely not "training," though parents were allowed to train minor children and the masters of apprentices were allowed to train their bonded apprentices. School subjects either had to contain values ideal in themselves, as good, true, or beautiful, which were "liberal" by definition; or they strengthened the "logical faculty," which the young citizen would then apply to all kinds of matters (this was the traditional notion of "transfer"); or they gave him orientation in space and time—as I have mentioned, especially History was prized, because its horrible and noble examples inspired youth to preserve freedom.

Of course, the late nineteenth century compulsory education in the mechanical arts, to the degree that they were merely utilitarian, could not so easily be justified in these "inward" ways—it tended to seem like apprentice-training at the public expense. But in an expanding economy with high social mobility, and where there was considerable self-employment and much new enterprise, there was no occasion to cavil; a free soul would want such advantageous skills of its own volition. Few adolescents went to school anyway, and children never did have many rights, though plenty of privileges.

III

Dr. Resnick's system explicitly excludes all notions of "inward" meaning. And she is also unhappy about the sneaking in of any factor of initiative. For example, in discussing Shaping—the approximation of the responses to the final response —she sharply disagrees with those experimenters who wait for the organism to make a small move in the right direction, to reinforce it. "Programmed instruction," she says, "cannot afford to proceed in this way." (But she never does make clear, at least to me, how she gets the beast to move *ab extra*, in order to have something to shape.)

Also, unlike the liberal or "faculty-developing" curriculum of the Enlightenment theory, no particular subject of learning is chosen because of its characteristic appeal to or stimulation of the powers, liberation, or needs of the learner. Operant-conditioning theory, she says, is essentially "contentless"; it is a pure technique that can teach anything to almost anybody. This might be Dr. Conant's "national needs"; it might be the "improved attitudes" of the Continuation branch of Milwaukee Vocational; it might be the vagaries of Big Brother.

In sum, on this view, if compulsory schooling, so far as it is programmed, is identical with compulsory training to the goals of the controllers of behavior, and such goals are set by the "we want" of the first paragraph I have cited, then I am curious to hear from Dr. Resnick the constitutional justification for compulsory schooling in terms of the "we want" and "we do not want" of that paragraph. Who, we? and what limitation is there to "want" or happen to want? The title of her essay, let us remember, is "Instruction of Complex Skills"; she is not restricting behavior-control to rote and drill subjects, but extending it to the higher branches, to criticism, problem-solving, appreciation, except where "we do not want to."

Needless to say, curriculum, methods, and the school-system itself have *always* been determined by social goals and National Goals, parental ambitions, and the need to baby-sit and police the young. But it is one thing to believe—or pretend—that these educate the children, and quite another thing to *say* that they are behavior-controllers.

IV

Our author's indifference to this kind of consideration appears strongly in an otherwise excellent analysis of the "Discovery Method" as contrasted with step-by-step programmed instruction. One advantage claimed for the Discovery Method—for which, we saw, Dr. Zacharias and the National Science Foundation have manifested enthusiasm—is that the leap over the gap is itself exciting and reinforcing, providing stronger motivation. Dr. Resnick agrees that this might be true for bright students; but she wisely points out that culturally-deprived, poorly achieving youngsters get more satisfaction from steady success, without risk of new failure. A second advantage claimed is that the trial and error in the Discovery process fits the student for the kind of learning that he will have to do outside the classroom; but here Dr. Resnick doubts that the student learns from his errors unless he is trained in what to ask about them, that is, to notice them. (She is right. For example, a good piano teacher will have the student deliberately play the wrong note that he repeats inadvertently.) Finally, it is claimed, the quality of what is learned by Discovery—the synoptic, the law, the solution of the problem—is superior. This, says Dr. Resnick, is because programmed instruction has so far concentrated almost exclusively on teaching mere concepts and information, rather than complex wholes of learning.

What is astonishing in this thoughtful analysis, however, is that she entirely omits the *salient* virtue that most teachers, classical or progressive, have always hoped for in letting the student discover for himself, namely the development of his confidence that he *can,* that he is adequate to the nature of things, can proceed on his own initiative, and ultimately strike out on an unknown path, where there is no program, and assign his own tasks to himself. The classical maxim of teaching is: to bring the student to where he casts off the teacher. Dewey's model for curriculum and method was: any study so pursued that it ends up with the student wanting to find out something further.

Apparently Dr. Resnick cannot even conceive of this virtue, because it is contradictory to the essence of controlled behavior toward a predetermined goal. It is open. From her point of view, it is not instruction at all. In terms of social theory, it posits an open society of independent citizens—but she and Dr. Skinner think there is a special "we" who "want." Also, scientifically, it posits a more open intellectual future than the complex-skill which programming seems to envisage. Is it indeed the case that so much *is* known—so definitely —that we can tightly program methods and fundamental ideas? Much of the program is bound to be out-of-date before the class graduates.

V

This is a fundamental issue. Intellectually, humanly, and politically, our present universal high-schooling and vastly increasing college-going are a disaster. I will go over the *crude* facts still again! A youngster is compelled for twelve *continuous* years—if middle class, for sixteen years—to work on assigned lessons, during a lively period of life when one hopes he might invent enterprises of his own. Because of the school work, he cannot follow his nose in reading and browsing in the library, or concentrate on a hobby that fires him, or get a job, or carry on a responsible love-affair, or travel, or become involved in political action. The school system as a whole, with its increasingly set curriculum, stricter grading, incredible amounts of testing, is already a vast machine to shape acceptable responses. Programmed instruction closes the windows a little tighter and it rigidifies the present departmentalization and dogma. But worst of all, it tends to nullify the one lively virtue that any school does have, that it is a community of youth and of youth and adults.

Dr. Resnick can assert that there are areas where "we do not want" to control behavior—political, religious, esthetic, perhaps social. But the case is that for sixteen years it is precisely docility to training and boredom that is heavily rewarded with approval, legitimacy, and money; whereas spontaneous initiation is punished by interruption, by being considered irrelevant, by anxiety of failing in the "important" work, and even by humiliation and jail. Yet somehow, after this hectic course of conditioning, young men and women are supposed, on commencement, suddenly to exercise initiative in the most extreme matters: to find jobs for themselves in a competitive market, to make long career plans, to undertake original artistic and scientific projects, to marry and become parents, to vote for public officers. But their behavior has been shaped only too well. Inevitably most of them will go on with the pattern of assigned lessons, as Organization Men or on the assembly-line; they will vote Democratic-Republican and buy right brands.

I am rather miffed at the vulgarity of the implication that, in teaching the humanities, we should at most attempt "exposure"—as if appreciation were entirely a private matter, or a matter of unstructured "emotion." (There is no such thing, by the way, as unstructured emotion.) When Dr. Resnick speaks of the unshaped response to the kind of literature or music "they like," she condemns their esthetic life to bring a frill, without meaning for character, valuation, recreation, or how one is in the world. Frankly, as a man of letters I would even prefer literature to be programmed, as in Russia.

That is, *even if behavioral analysis and programmed instruction were the adequate analysis of learning and method of teaching, it would still be questionable, for overriding political reasons, whether they are generally appropriate for the education of free citizens.*

VI

To be candid, I think operant-conditioning is vastly overrated. It teaches us the not newsy proposition that if an animal is deprived of its natural environment and society, sensorily deprived, made mildly anxious, and restricted to the narrowest possible spontaneous motion, it will emotionally identify with its oppressor and respond—with low-grade grace, energy, and intelligence—in the only way allowed to it. The poor beast must do something, just to live on a little. There is no doubt that a beagle can be trained to walk on its hind legs and balance a ball on the tip of its nose. But the dog will show much more intelligence, force, and speedy feed-back when chasing a rabbit in the field. It is an odd thought that we can increase the efficiency of learning by nullifying *a priori* most of an animal's powers to learn and taking it out of its best field.

It has been a persistent error of behaviorist psychologies to overlook that there are overt criteria that are organically part of *meaningful* acts of an organism in its environment; we can observe grace, ease, force, style, sudden simplification— and some such characteristics are at least roughly measurable. It is not necessary, in describing insight, knowledge, the kind of assimilated learning that Aristotle called "second nature," to have recourse to mental entities. It is not difficult to *see* when a child *knows* how to ride a bicycle; and he never forgets it, which would not be the case if the learning were by conditioning with reinforcement, because that can easily be wiped away by a negative reinforcement. . . .

On the other hand, it is extremely dubious that by controlled conditioning one *can* teach organically meaningful behavior. Rather, the attempt to control *prevents* learning. This is obvious to anyone who has ever tried to teach a child to ride a bicycle; the more you try, the more he falls. The best one can do is to provide him a bicycle, allay his anxiety, tell him to keep going, and *not* to try to balance. I am convinced that the same is true in teaching reading.

VII

As is common in many (sometimes excellent) modern scientific papers— whether in linguistics or studies of citizen participation or the theory of delinquency—Dr. Resnick asks for more money; and of course, for purposes of pure research, the higher investigations that she asks for should be pursued as long as her enthusiasm lasts and should be supported. Any definite hypothesis that is believed in by a brilliant worker is likely to yield useful by-products that can then be reinterpreted; nor is there any other guide for the advancement of science except the conviction and competence of the researchers.

But I am puzzled at what widespread social benefits she has in mind that warrant a *lot* of expense in brains and machinery. She seems to agree that bright children do not learn most efficiently by these extrinsic methods; and for the average the picture is as I have described it: average employment in a highly automated technology requires a few weeks' training on the job and no schooling at all, and for the kind of humane employment and humane leisure that we hopefully look toward, we require a kind of education and habit entirely different from programmed instruction.

But I am more impressed by what is perhaps Dr. Resnick's deepest concern, the possible *psychotherapeutic* use of more complex programming for the remedial instruction of kids who have developed severe blocks to learning and are far behind. For youngsters who have lost all confidence in themselves, there is a security in being able to take small steps entirely at their own pace and entirely by their own control of the machine. Also, though the chief use of schools is their functioning as a community, under present competitive and stratified conditions it is often less wounding for a kid who has fallen behind to be allowed to withdraw from the group and recover. And this time can usefully and curatively be spent in learning the standard "answers" that can put him in the game again.

There is a pathos in our technological advancement, well exemplified by programmed instruction. A large part of it consists in erroneously reducing the concept of animals and human beings in order to make them machine-operable. The social background in which this occurs, meanwhile, makes many people out-caste and in fact tends to reduce them as persons and make them irresponsible. The refined technique has little valid use for the dominant social group for which it has been devised, e.g. in teaching science; but it does prove to have a use for the reduced out-castes, in teaching remedial arithmetic.

REVIEW QUESTIONS

1. Does Paul Goodman *really* need to worry about whether or not programmers, or "controllers of behavior," violate the civil rights of children?

2. Based upon article 6 and this one, can you imagine a conversation between Skinner and Goodman about programmed learning?

eight

The Computer as a Tutor

EZRA BOWEN

Inside the low, windowless building, eighteen computer terminals—each with a teletypewriter keyboard, cathode-ray tube, earphones and projection screen—were lined up in back-to-back rows. One wall of the room looked like a dark mirror but actually was one-way glass. Near it, a half-dozen men and women holding clipboards waited anxiously; the results of four years of planning and preparation in the complex world of electronic education were finally about to be put into regular, classroom use.

A side door burst open and in trooped a dozen scrabbling little first-grade children, some wide-eyed, some smiling, some a little scared. The children were seated at the terminals and the computer quickly took them in hand. "Well, hello, Jimmy," the machine said into an astounded 6-year-old's earphones. "I've been waiting for you." Thus began the most eerie—and perhaps the most promising—dialogue ever carried on in a United States grade school.

The windowless chamber was a new first-grade room of the Brentwood Elementary School at East Palo Alto, Calif., and the exotic computer system was Brentwood's new math and reading teacher. Since that first day, Nov. 1, 1966, half the kids in the first grade at Brentwood have been taking all their arithmetic and the other half most of their reading from the IBM 1500 computer, and they will continue doing so until the end of the current school year. Other elementary school children have occasionally faced off with a computer for short-term experiments, but this is the first time a machine has ever been handed the responsibility for a full chunk of the regular first-grade curriculum. Furthermore, the 1500 is taking up the challenge in a neighborhood where teaching has not always flourished. The Brentwood area is a mélange of gas stations, drive-ins and tiny ranch houses, where eighty-five per cent of the population is Negro, and too many of the school children are a year or two behind the national norm in elementary reading. But, in these first few months at least, the 1500 has thrived in this environment.

"We really wanted something like this," says Brentwood's principal, William Rybensky. "We're committed here to innovation." Indeed, Brentwood has offered up 100 of its children to the computer, and the machine's proctors, programmers and assorted spear carriers outnumber the rest of the Brentwood faculty. So far, everyone involved in the experiment seems absolutely delighted with it.

The IBM Corporation is especially happy since it has invested some $30 million in the research and development of computer-based instruction. "There may be a lot of profit in this one day," says Leonard Muller, Director of Instructional Systems Development for IBM. Executives of other heavyweight electronics corporations agree. They have begun to hear the rustle of the new money that is falling like autumn leaves onto educational ground.

Most important, the kids love the experiment, although that first day, when they confronted the eighteen terminals hooked into the computer, some of them shied away. "If I touch it, it'll hurt me," said one small girl, stepping back. One of the proctors assigned to teach the children and tend the program touched the face of the cathode tube and slipped on a set of earphones. Reassured, the girl and her classmates allowed themselves to be seated and the earphones drawn over their heads.

Soon the terminals in front of them began to dance with images—white-dot and white-line drawings of a dog, a bone, a cat—all flickering from the brain of the computer onto a gray screen. Through the earphones, a voice said, "Bow-wow, woof-woof. . . . Touch the dog with your light-pen and see what he does." Each child, at his own terminal, touched the dog with the light-projecting pen he held, and the dog went for the bone. An electronic snail crawled onto the tube, veered away from a turtle and went to visit his friend, a butterfly. The voice at each terminal murmured new instructions—"Touch the snail" or "Touch the turtle." As the lessons progressed, a child who touched the correct image heard the voice ooze a gentle "Good." When an incorrect image was touched, the voice softly said "Nooooo," then repeated the original command. Sometimes a tiny arrow popped onto the screen above the correct picture. If there was a hesitation of more than five or ten seconds, the voice said, with a slight rigidity, "Do it now." And if a child made two or three mistakes, or did nothing at all, the computer tapped out a distress signal on a monitor, and the teacher came—even as she once did for you and me—to find out what the trouble was and correct it.

The kids were fascinated. One boy, when he finished his lesson, twined his legs around the base of the swivel chair and refused to move. His proctor gently pulled him away. As he dug his heels into the rug, she pushed him out the door.

"He didn't want to leave because he was so absorbed," said Pat Suppes, the Stanford philosopher and mathematician who, along with Stanford psychologist Dick Atkinson, developed the mechanized reading and math programs for Brentwood. "Usually he gets so bored in regular class, he starts trouble."

By the end of the first week, the computer had subtly moved half the class into its first exercises in New Math. (The other half of the class was on reading.)

Brackets popped up around the dogs and the voice in the earphones explained to the kids, in its best New Math jargon, that they were now looking at the set with dog as its member. Guided by the computer, every child moved along at his own pace.

In the course of a day each of the terminals had several pupils assigned to it. At the start of his session the pupil would see his name on the cathode tube and would confirm his identity to the computer by touching his name with his light-projecting pen. Then the computer would start the pupil off with audio-taped instructions exactly where he had ended the last lesson. The brighter children quickly jumped ahead, skipping over the practice drills, taking on more complex problems. Whenever the slower ones faltered, the computer automatically branched them onto a sequence of corrective drills.

Meanwhile, the other half of the class was using computerized exercises and word games to learn how to read. When the child faced the terminal, a baseball diamond and a list of words flashed onto the tube and the voice said, "Touch a four-legged hairy animal that goes meow." If the child touched the cat, a tiny runner zipped to first base. Four hits and the student won that part of the game. In more formal drills, if the student made a mistake, the computer would branch him through as many as five corrective exercises. Within three months the computer's audio-tape deck was reading aloud *"Peter, Peter, Pumpkin Eater"* as the written words appeared on the tube and each child was reading along with good old IBM 1500.

Simultaneously the computer was also taking attendance, giving tests and marking them, recording every child's responses and measuring the reaction times down to the last millisecond.

"We're on the edge of some very new stuff, very deep," says Suppes. "With this technology we may be able to give each kid the personal services of a tutor as well-informed and as responsible as Aristotle. Right now teachers teach to the middle fifty per cent of each class. The machines offer the chance to do much better teaching on an individual basis for the top twenty-five per cent and the bottom twenty-five per cent."

Every human being has a different learning style: some people gather knowledge quickly, others slowly or not at all. Everybody comes into a learning situation with a different background, different vocabulary, different attitude and a different supply of what is called intelligence. In a typical sixth-grade classroom, for example, the mental age level of the pupils, according to a widely accepted study, ranges from nine years to sixteen. But measured intelligence is no true indication of the capacity to learn. There is, however, some agreement among psychologists that a student, whatever his supply of intelligence may be, seems to learn best when his lessons are tailored to his own pace of learning. The Brentwood computer system does adjust to each pupil's personal speed.

"I think this thing of individualizing instruction is the most important single principle of learning," says Suppes. "We're trying to go deeper and deeper into it, to find out whether we can write curricula so they reflect the personality, the learning characteristics of each child. Computers can collect for us the data to do a real, microscopic analysis of the curricula. There will be no guessing here. Data! Data! And that's what I think is really exciting."

Suppes's partner, Atkinson, agrees. "We're really interested in the psychology of learning," Atkinson says. "How does a kid master a concept like math or reading? What *should* be the exact sequencing of the materials?" Unlike many of their colleagues who carry out their experiments in the canned atmosphere of a laboratory, Pat Suppes and Dick Atkinson believe that the answers can best be found in the daily struggle and confusion of a classroom.

It is natural for Suppes and Atkinson to feel a strong paternal pride in their computer system. Nevertheless, there are critics who think that the IBM 1500 has a face that only its father could love. The critics of computer education complain, first, about the cost. Computer technology today is too expensive for any ordinary school system without heavy underwriting by the federal or state government, a major foundation or a corporation. Most of the men involved in computer-based learning are convinced the cost will come down, and it is possible that within ten to fifteen years every school—or at least every school district—can pay for its own computer system. But right now, although the price of computers themselves is already dropping, the costs of sophisticated terminals and programming remain quite high. . . .

Furthermore, to a lot of people the Pat and Dick Show, with its humming computers, one-way mirrors and the automated sincerity in the electronic voice, comes too close to 1984. But the critics, it appears, will have to learn to live with it. The Brentwood spectacular is only one of perhaps a thousand projects in computerized learning which have been installed at all educational levels across the U.S. in the past half-dozen years. In fact, about the same time the 1500 met the Brentwood first-graders:

> Fifty graduate students at Carnegie Tech's Graduate School of Industrial Administration were deep in a scrimmage with a computer that simulates the activities of nine make-believe corporations. As part of the exercise, the students formed management teams, bought stock, began to run the companies, grappled with accounting, taxes, labor, production quotas, sales figures and inflation and generally tried to drive each other out of business.

> At Illinois a computer nick-named PLATO gave a short audio-taped lecture and quiz to a junior studying electrical engineering. The student flunked the quiz and pressed a button literally marked "Help!" Patiently, PLATO gave a simpler, fuller explanation; the boy got the message, punched a button marked "Aha!" and PLATO went on with the lecture.

> Using a talking typewriter he developed, social psychologist Omar Khayyam Moore of the University of Pittsburgh was teaching three- and four-year-olds to read and write up to a fifth-grade level. The talking typewriter generated careful enunciations and cheery pictures of a B-A-R-N. The child sitting at it ran his fingers over the keyboard. All the letters were locked except for a "B". The child hit the "B" and the letter appeared in the

paper in the roller. With the keyboard continuing to lock in proper sequence, the child spelled out the word "barn."

At M.I.T. a graduate engineer took a light-pen and made a sketch of a bridge on the face of a cathode tube; a computer then whipped the rough lines into the symmetry of a functional bridge and rotated the image to give a three-dimensional view of the work, while a high-speed print out device disgorged stresses and force vectors for such a bridge.

In Santa Barbara, Calif., a high school physics student used teletypewriter computer terminals to whip through algebraic equations that would have taken hours of tedious hand-calculating.

At the computerized National Library of Medicine in Bethesda, Md., a medical student asked a machine for research sources on Occupational Dermatitis. Among the recommended readings hammered out by the machine was: "A Study on Dermatitis in Rice Farmers, Yang KL, et al. *Chinese Medical Journal* (Peking) 84: 143–59, March 1965."

Basically the computer is used as a tool, to speed up the clerical routines of calculation or of combing through archives. In the more sophisticated programs it also takes over the role of a tutor—sometimes a rather fatuous tutor at that. A machine at a California school greets its fourth-to-eighth grade pupils with "Hello, I'm your friendly computer." Another computer has presented German to college students by dropping German words, one by one, into English sentences, until it arrives at a dialogue straight out of the old Cinderella Hassenpfeffer satires: *"Der sky war klar, die Winde hatten sich* died, *und der* moon went brightly *im Westen* down."

"People are so fascinated by the miracle of the computer," Suppes says, "that no matter how awful the stuff programmed into it is, they think it's wonderful."

Over the past fifteen years people have been unduly fascinated by many kinds of educational hardware. Classroom television was supposed to change the world of learning by bringing the cosmic events and the voices of great men into the schools. But it has mostly brought the same old professors droning along on the little gray screen. Multiple-station recording machines called "Language Laboratories" were supposed to improve the study of foreign languages, by handling pronunciation and grammar drills with taped lessons, thereby freeing the teacher to conduct stimulating classroom sessions. But all too often the recording machines have been fed uninspired, rote drills by teachers whose old-fashioned training has not prepared them to utilize fully either the hardware or the extra time the machines could give them. Mechanical teaching machines—most of them metal boxes with a viewing window—were supposed to speed and individualize learning by serving up simple, step-by-step lessons. But most of the teaching machines have been no more than vastly expensive page-turners, with programs so dull that neither teachers nor pupils could stand the tedium of clicking through them.

Classroom television, language laboratories and teaching machines appeared in schools in the 1950's as part of the postwar technological upheaval. At the same time there was an intellectual upheaval, and a wave of curriculum reform aimed at shooting new life into course content swept classrooms. It included the broad concepts and ordered jargon of the New Math, and new courses in physics and biology built on the sensible notion that science students should spend their time like real scientists, experimenting and discovering, instead of memorizing outdated charts of elements. Some of the new courses were better, but they still had shortcomings. The main problem, according to one junior high teacher, was that "It's fine to talk about getting high school kids to think like scientists and the inductive method of reasoning and all that, but how are you going to get some dunce in the back of the room to induce when he's asleep? You've got to wake him up first. We've got to get these kids involved." With the computer, says Suppes, "the kid *can't* just sit there. He's got to do something. And the computer checks him out at every step."

Last year, at Grant Elementary School near Brentwood, Suppes had thirty children a day working on computerized math drills at a simple teletypewriter terminal—a machine with a keyboard, but no cathode tube or projection screen. Most of the children were able to learn two years' worth of math in one year, but simply to keep the thirty pupils busy only five minutes a day over the 160 days of the school year, the programmers had to develop 96,000 exercises, a chore that took some 1,600 man-hours.

Besides putting heavy pressure on the programmers, the new machines force the classroom teacher into a unique new role. There is no way a single human teacher can present 96,000 drill and practice problems to a class, let alone mark the results and give review exercises. Nor, in a computerized class, is there any reason why the teacher should. "A teacher who only dispenses information can be dispensed with," says Harold Gores, president of the Ford Foundation's Educational Facilities Laboratory. "From now on, *things* should be taught by machines. And the teacher is raised to the level of *meaning*. *Things* from machines, *values* from people." That is, in the simplest terms, D-O-G is dog, whether it comes from Miss Jones or an IBM 1500, but whether or not all dogs are created equal is a matter for the pupil and Miss Jones alone.

More broadly, the teacher becomes a trouble shooter, both intellectual and mechanical. And there is plenty of both kinds of trouble in any computer classroom. An electronic teaching system is a fallible instrument, subject to the vagaries of overheated circuits and faulty wiring. In the first two months of the Grant School's teletypewriter math program last year, the computer broke down an average of 100 minutes a day. And when the machine falters, the children drift off into what psychologists solemnly call "random behavior"; in an emergency phone call, one of Suppes's teachers described it more colorfully as "hanging from the rafters." On one particularly troublesome day at Grant, a nine-year-old marched to the principal's office and said, "That machine has caused more trouble than anybody else today. If it acts up again, I think my teacher will start crying."

The breakdown average was eventually honed to seven minutes, but even on its good days the computer, at this stage of its development, has severe limitations as a tutor. In most instances it can act as little more than a lightning-fast memory device, able to respond only to those words, numbers, instructions and questions which have been painstakingly programmed in. And while a clever programmer can make a computer that couples a teletypewriter with audio-tape response behave as if it is carrying on a conversation with a human, actually the machine is just picking out one or two key words and giving back canned replies. As of today, it has very little flexibility. For example, if a computer has been programmed with the question and answer for "Who assassinated Abraham Lincoln?" it does not know who *shot* Abraham Lincoln, or who assassinated *Honest Abe.*

In time, as more and more material is programmed into it, the computer will be able to answer more questions, but it may never be able to handle a free dialogue, particularly a teaching dialogue. Many of the most advanced computer researchers—among them, Robert Callan, a G.E. computer expert, and Dr. Robert Fano, head of M.I.T.'s Multiple Access Computer System—feel it never should. They regard the computer as an intellectual power tool, capable of extending the power of a man's memory or his computational skills in the same way that a chain saw extends the power of his hands or an automobile the power of his legs. "Computers should compute," says Callan, "teachers should teach, and kids should turn their own pages." At most, a computer should be a training device to encourage logical thinking.

Pat Suppes, on the other hand, is continually trying to push his machines into the outer limits of research and beyond. "You know, with technology you always have a gleam in your eye about what you're going to do next," he says. Particularly, he hopes for the day when a student can have a free dialogue with a computer that can recognize the student's voice, understand his words and talk back with flexible replies.

Already, in select experiments, computer programmers are moving their machines closer and closer to human consciousness. At Stanford one computer, by matching the sound waves in a human voice to wave forms already programmed in, can recognize some 200 words spoken directly to it through a microphone. At General Electric's laboratory in Santa Barbara and at M.I.T., other computers are inching toward the ability to understand and reply to questions they have never before received.

And, finally, there is the ultimate concept. At Syracuse Univerity, Dr. S. Seshu is working on the total teaching machine, an electronic input system which will transfer factual information on punch cards or magnetic tape directly into the human brain and memory. Dr. Seshu has not yet mastered the details, but he says, "All that we need to do is find the input terminals in the human brain, and the necessary code."

Such talk, while alarming to most adults, does not disturb the students—from first grade to graduate school—who meet the computer every day in their classrooms. They are growing up with the machine, and to them it is no more alarming than any other common piece of hardware, like a pop-up toaster or an automatic phonograph. At Brentwood the veterans of last year's computerized math drills at the Grant School are completely blasé about the machine. They show no sign of having been dehumanized or damaged in any way. If anything, they have become rather fond of the machine, which they seem to regard as a simple-minded and fragile friend. On one occcasion last year the computer, whose code name was THOR, suffered a particularly severe breakdown. The next day the teacher was handed an envelope containing something signed by the whole class. It was a get-well card for THOR.

REVIEW QUESTIONS

1.   Imagine that IBM is trying to sell their IBM 1500 system to your school board for use in teaching mathematics, English, and some science. What would be your carefully considered recommendation to the board? What questions would you ask the IBM representative?

2.   How would CAI change the role of the teacher?

3.   In article 7 Paul Goodman argued that programming, among other things, violates civil rights, fails to teach "inward meaning," and fails to stimulate either learning by discovery or individual initiative. Do these arguments apply also to CAI?

nine

Computer-Based Instructional Management Systems: A First Look

FRANK B. BAKER

A recurring theme in American educational thought has been the individualization of instruction. The durability of this theme is attested to by two yearbooks of the National Society for the Study of Education devoted to this topic that were published nearly four decades apart [Whipple, 1925; Henry, 1962]. These two yearbooks reported a wide range of approaches to the individualization of instruction as well as research on individual differences. New approaches to the individualization of instruction often result from technological developments such as tape recorders, teaching machines, etc. Thus, when digital computers became available, it was inevitable that this powerful technology would be employed in attempts to solve the persistent problem of individualization of instruction.

The first application of the digital computer to the task of instruction was reported by Rath, Anderson, and Brainerd [1959]. Since that time, numerous other computer-assisted instruction (CAI) systems have been constructed. Initially it was considered a simple task to write computer programs that would present instructional materials to the student, collect his responses, analyze them, and select the next step to be performed by the student. The computer was viewed as the means by which the in vogue concepts of programmed instruction could be implemented [Coulsen, 1962]. Unfortunately, this early conceptualization of CAI grossly underestimated both the complexity of the learning process and the level of computer-related equipment necessary for wide scale implementation of CAI. As a result, many CAI systems were developed, but most demonstrated only the feasibility of CAI, not its practicality. Currently, the initial flush of enthusiam for CAI has subsided and a relatively small number of research groups are engaged in the laborious task of transferring CAI from the laboratory to the classroom.

Source: Abridged from *Review of Educational Research*, 1971, 41:51–70. Copyright by American Educational Research Association, Washington, D.C. Reprinted by permission of the author and the publisher.

The best known of these CAI systems is the one at Stanford [Suppes, 1966]; it is representative of what can be done in this area with present technology.

In recent years, a number of researchers have been developing curricular approaches and instructional materials that would enable implementation of individualized instruction without involving CAI. Through these efforts it became quite clear that one of the most difficult aspects of a program of individualized instruction is that of management. A situation develops rather quickly in which each pupil is employing a different set of instructional materials, progressing at his own rate, and experiencing a unique set of successes and learning difficulties. In the center of this milieu is the classroom teacher who somehow must regulate this activity, diagnose each child's difficulties, and prescribe his activities for some future period of time. If instruction were individualized in several subjects at the elementary-school level, the cognitive load would be too great for a single teacher or even a small group of teachers. It quickly becomes apparent that in order to operate in such a context a teacher must be provided with assistance in the management aspects of individualized instruction.

The successful use of computers as an aid to management in the commercial world was not unnoticed by educators, and a number of groups turned to the computer to perform tasks associated with managing an individualized instructional environment. A major facet of this managerial task is composed of the mechanical tasks of scoring seat work and test papers, recording the scores, creating descriptions of pupils based on their scores, and keeping track of what instructional materials a student has used. The larger goal, however, is to provide the teacher with the tools of management via a computer-based instructional management system (CBIMS). Such systems would be the means by which a teacher manages an educational enterprise that provides each child with an optimum set of educational experiences.

The present review describes a number of existing computer-based instructional management systems and ascertains their level of development. Because of the interests of the reviewer, the emphasis is on the basic structure of these systems and on the manner in which digital computers are employed. By and large, only systems designed expressly for the purpose of instructional management are considered and the management aspects of CAI generally are ignored. The learning theory basis and the curriculum philosophies facilitated by such systems are deferred to reviewers interested in such aspects.

Before describing specific examples of CBIMS, a general overview based on a composite of existing systems is presented below to acquaint the reader with the basic features of such systems. The curriculum with which one uses a CBIMS is usually built around units of instruction. Typically, these are specified in terms of educational objectives: desired student behavior, levels of competence, concepts to be learned, or a given program of instruction. The term *objective* is used rather loosely in this paper to include all of these. The objectives can be fractioned to any desired level, and means of achieving subobjectives can be embedded within the educational tasks and materials related to the larger objectives. The definition of curricular objectives and the development of the related instructional materials, measuring instruments, teaching techniques, etc., are major endeavors which despite their enormity are prerequisites to instructional management systems. Once an appropriate curriculum exists, a computer-based system can be developed to assist the teacher in the management of instruction.

The four major functions performed by computers in existing instructional management systems are test scoring, diagnosing, prescribing, and reporting. These are incorporated into the curriculum in the following way:

At the beginning of each unit of instruction, a pretest is taken by each pupil to determine his status relative to instructional objectives. The pupil's answer sheet is read by an optical scanner and scored via a computer program. The test may be simultaneously scored for achievement in several main objectives and sub-objectives. On the basis of the pretest results, the pupil is assigned to specific learning tasks. Such assignments can be made by computer programs which implement decision rules relating test scores to learning tasks or, if full automation is not desired, the computer can generate the test results in a printed report. The report then becomes one of several information sources used by the teacher to prescribe learning tasks for the pupil. These prescribed tasks can be any of a number of educational experiences, e.g., seat work, group activities, reading books, tutoring, even CAI.

At various points within a unit the pupil may take diagnostic or progress tests; these assess his progress toward specific objectives contained within the unit. These tests are also computer processed and the reports generated can be used by the teacher to ascertain whether the pupil is progressing satisfactorily.

When the pupil has completed the assigned tasks, he takes a protest covering the unit of instruction. This test is criterion-referenced and the pupil is scored on one or more objectives. If he achieves a score of eighty-five per cent or greater on a given objective, he is considered to have mastered it. If a pupil fails to reach criterion performance, two alternatives are available. He can be subjected to remedial procedures, or the failure can be ignored and he can proceed to the next unit of instruction.

After the administration of each test, the teacher receives several printed reports. One report lists each pupil, the unit of instruction he is working on, the objectives of that unit, and the percentiles he achieved for each objective covered by the test. Using this report, the teacher can study the pattern of accomplishment of each pupil and identify those who warrant additional attention. A second report shows the proportion of pupils working on a specific unit who achieved criterion performance on each of the objectives covered by the test. On the basis of this report the teacher can determine common strengths and weaknesses of the group and adjust the instruction to fit the situation.

The basic pattern of pretest, diagnosis, prescription, and posttest is repeated for each unit of instruction. A very desirable feature of this cycle is that it can be used without modification in the usual classroom. Thus, once established in a school, it facilitates the transition from the group-oriented classroom to individualized instruction.

Most of the existing CBIM systems follow the model given above in their general plans, but they differ considerably in their origins and in actual implementations. In the next section, several CBIM systems are presented to acquaint the reader with the specific approaches.

DESCRIPTION OF SPECIFIC SYSTEMS

One of the interesting aspects of computer-based instructional management systems is that a number of research groups across the country conceptualized their systems nearly simultaneously. As a result it is difficult to credit any one group with the basic idea. However, the first such system to become operational was developed by the Systems Development Corporation for the Southwest Regional Educational Laboratory at Los Angeles [Silberman, 1968; Bratten, 1968].

SYSTEMS DEVELOPMENT CORPORATION—IMS

The computer-based instructional management system developed by the staff of the Systems Development Corporation (SDC) was given the mnemonic IMS (Instructional Management System) [Silberman, 1968]. The system was implemented initially in several first-grade classrooms with reading as the subject of interest. Each class was divided by its teacher into several reading groups. The groups received first-grade level instruction based on a state-adopted reading series. A file of self-administered tests based on the reading series, a file of self-administered pencil and paper exercises used for followup work, and a "listening post" where pupils could listen to audio tapes were placed in the classroom. Upon completion of a typical lesson, a reading group would be seated at the listening post and they would take the self-administered tests, following instructions received via their headsets. After class, the answer sheets were taken by courier to the SDC computer facility where they were optically scanned and the item response choices punched into cards. The cards served as input to a large computer that scored the tests and generated the appropriate reports. These reports were available to the teacher before class the next morning for use in planning.

The data resulting from a test taken by a reading group was presented to the teacher in several different reports. The basic report was for the particular test taken and contained information concerning the specific objectives covered in the test. When the group score was below the criterion level of eighty-five per cent, the report prescribed a number of remedial activities for the teacher to consider. These activities were specified by a number indicating a folder in the followup materials file. In addition to the group information, the report also listed each pupil, his score on the test, the number of tests he had taken, and his cumulative average score. At the end of each week, a summary report was produced listing the score made by each pupil on all tests taken to date and his ranking within his reading group. The teacher could also obtain a special report for a given pupil which listed the pupil's performance on general objectives embedded within a sequence of lesson-related tests. In addition, a teletype terminal was available in the school for the teacher to use as an inquiry device. By means of this teletype, the teacher could instruct the computer to search the data base and report specific information. The flexibility of the underlying data management computer program allowed the researchers at SDC to easily redesign the reports, or delete or add information as new needs arose [Bratten, 1968].

The IMS development is a very pragmatic approach to implementing a computer-based instructional management system within a conventional classroom setting.

PITTSBURGH RESEARCH AND DEVELOPMENT CENTER IPI/MIS

The computer-based instructional management system at the Pittsburgh Learning Research and Development Center grew out of the individually prescribed instruction (IPI) project [Glaser 1968]. It is called the IPI management and information system (IPI/MIS). The instructional model underlying the IPI project was Glaser's six part model [Glaser 1969] that corresponds roughly to the paradigm described above for computer-based instructional management systems.

The Pittsburgh center has been engaged in developing and operating an elementary-school curriculum allowing individualization of progress for the past four years. During the first three years, instructional materials were developed, teachers trained, and a particular elementary school was reorganized. Manual procedures were developed for test scoring, diagnosis of test results, prescription of instructional tasks, and record keeping. Experience with this system led rather naturally to thoughts of using digital computers to automate many, if not all, of the manual tasks. Thus, the introduction of digital computers into the program was the next logical step. It is important to note that the staff was not faced with the monumental task of trying to develop the instructional scheme and the computer-based capabilities simultaneously.

When the data processing is completed, the results are transmitted to the remote input/output terminal in the school which prints three basic types of report. First, a unit summary for each student reporting his scores on the pretest and curriculum embedded tests is printed, along with a task prescription suggested by the computer. The teacher uses this report to trace the activities of the pupil within a unit and to ascertain how well he performed on the unit. Second, there is a homeroom report listing each pupil, the unit of instruction, the skill, and the number of days he spent on the unit. Pupils who are perseverating on a unit can be identified by means of this report. Third, an instructional report lists the names of the pupils working on a given unit and the specific objectives each pupil is attempting to master. Again, this report is useful for informing the teacher of the status of the pupils, each of whom may be engaged in a different task.

AMERICAN INSTITUTE FOR RESEARCH: PROJECT PLAN

The Program for Learning in Accordance with Needs (PLAN) was developed by the American Institute for Research as a means for correcting the deficiencies in our educational system revealed by project TALENT [Flanagan, Dailey, Davis, Goldberg, Heyman, Orr, and Shaycraft, 1964]. Although the actual implementation of PLAN resembles that of other CBIM systems, there is an emphasis on long-term educational goals as they relate to career planning and educationally relevant decision-making.

The computer is relegated to a rather minor role within the framework of PLAN. For example, Flanagan [1967, p. 31] stated: "The computer will be an inconspicuous and incidental part of the program as far as the teacher and student are concerned. Neither of them may ever see the input/output terminal in the school building or the computer itself." In a later article [Flanagan, 1969], the functions of the computer were described as scoring tests, maintaining files on the experiences and progress of each student, and keeping records of the results achieved by the pupils on the teaching-learning units and on the guidance and planning procedures. It was also indicated that the pupil characteristics files are updated at two or three month intervals.

At the time of Flanagan's report, project PLAN involved classrooms in grades 1, 2, 5, 6, 9, and 10 in 14 school districts. The teaching-learning units were developed by a staff of specialists but the actual execution of these units appears to have been controlled at the local school district level. The mechanisms and extent of the diagnosis and prescription aspects of PLAN were not described by Flanagan [1967, 1968, 1969]. However, Sponberg [1968] reported that the computer used test scores and stored pupil characteristics to recommend three alternative teaching-learning units. The teacher and the pupil then jointly determined the specific unit to study.

Since Flanagan's reports, the computer-based aspects of project PLAN have been assumed by the Westinghouse Learning Corporation. They offer project PLAN as a commercial service.

ALLEN KELLEY'S TIPS

The concepts underlying computer-based instructional management systems were independently developed by Kelley [1968a, 1968b] in the context of an introductory economics course at the University of Wisconsin. Although the Teaching Information Processing System (TIPS) was developed in isolation, it follows the general CBIMS model very closely and contains all of the basic features of other systems. The TIPS program was employed within a conventional university-level economics curriculum in which a professor presented the lectures and teaching assistants conducted small group sessions.

Approximately six to ten times per semester a ten- to fifteen-item questionnaire was administered to 200 students in the course. These questionnaires were structured according to the objectives of the course and the economic concepts to be attained by the students. The students were assured that the instruments were surveys, not quizzes, intended only to help them with the course. The multiple choice answer sheets were optically scanned and the punch cards produced were used as input to the TIPS computer programs. These programs scored the surveys, performed the diagnosis and prescription functions, and generated reports. Three different reports were generated: the student report, the teaching assistant report, and the professor report. Kelly [1968a] indicatd that these reports were available within a few hours after the students responded to the questionnaire, a response time much better than that typically achieved.

The student's report contained a listing of the item choices made by the student and the correct response, his score on the survey, a statement about his level of achievement, and a series of prescribed activities. In sharp contrast to other systems, the prescriptions generated were in the form of paragraphs rather than the usual cryptic lesson numbers. The paragraphs described what the student should do, whether it was optional or required, and the date the assignment was due. The prescriptions ranged from the usual homework assignment to attendance at lectures given by instructors in other economics courses. In some cases, the student was referred to the teaching assistant for help in a small group setting.

The teaching assistant's report listed the section leader, the survey taken, each student's name, and a short description of the assignments. Special messages to the section leader named pupils recommended for special help or alerted him to lectures of interest on campus. In addition, an analysis of each item in the survey was given and subscores on the embedded concepts were reported.

The professor's report summarized the materials in the student and teaching assistant reports. The project also involved feedback from the student to the professor so that communication could proceed in both directions. Questionnaires were administered to measure students' reactions to the degree of individualization afforded by TIPS and to identify areas needing improvement. Kelley [1968b] reported that 86 per cent of the students thought that TIPS had helped them to learn economics better and only 12 per cent did not care for the system.

TIPS, as developed and implemented by Kelley, shows what can be accomplished by an individual instructor who is concerned about the quality of instruction. Despite his being unaware of the other CBIM systems, Kelley's TIPS is based on the same basic model as those systems developed by educational researchers. The mechanisms of the TIPS approach are such that they could be applied easily to other college-level courses.

INSTRUCTIONAL MANAGEMENT ASPECTS OF THE STANFORD CAI PROJECT

Because the early CAI systems were designed to be a means of instruction, the major concern was the pupil-computer dialogue; the teacher was essentially an interested bystander. The recent shift in emphasis of the Stanford CAI project to computer-based drill and practice in elementary arithmetic has resulted in the teacher having regained a role within the total system. The CAI procedures for diagnosis and prescription have been supplemented with report generation capabilities aimed at providing the teacher with instructional management information. These instructional management capabilities are used with both the "block" and "strand" approaches to drill and practice in elementary arithmetic. Under the block approach, the arithmetic content of a particular grade level is divided into twenty-four blocks, each block containing a pretest, five days work, and a posttest. Under the strand approach, a given topic in arithmetic is followed across grade levels to whatever level the pupil is capable of handling. Each day's lesson is divided into thirds, according to difficulty: material at, above, and below the student's current average performance level is included in the lesson.

The instructional management aspects are quite similar under both these approaches to CAI implemented drill and practice in arithmetic. For the block system, the computer generates a daily report and an end of block report [Jerman, 1969]. The daily report identifies pupils who are performing within twenty per cent, at least twenty per cent below, or 20 per cent above their average score, and lists the blocks that are currently being studied. The end of block report identifies the concept embodied in the block and lists each pupil's performance on the seven days of the block. The daily report [Jerman, 1970] for the strand approach lists each pupil, his grade equivalent on the eleven strands, his average grade placement, and the standardized change in his average grade placement. The minimum, maximum, and average grade placement of the class is also reported for each strand. A weekly report contains nearly the same information for the longer time period.

The instructional management procedures and the generated reports of the Stanford CAI project are similar to those of the CBIM systems. An interesting aspect of the diagnosis and prescription procedures is the use of a standardized average grade placement score, maintained by the computer for each pupil. This standardized average is used in the prescription of drill and practice units. The algorithms underlying the prescriptive procedures were reported by Jerman [1969]. Although there is an excellent instructional management component to the Stanford CAI system it has not been reported as such. The description of these features is scattered in newsletters and teachers' handbooks [Jerman, 1970]. As a result, one tends to overlook the instructional management aspects of this CAI system.

FEATURES COMMON TO EXISTING SYSTEMS

It can be seen from the descriptions of the specific CBIM systems that they all follow the same basic model. They differ in the original impetus for developing the system and somewhat in the level of implementation, but the underlying pattern of test scoring, diagnosis, prescription, and reporting is embodied in all of the existing systems. In addition, they are all based on a curricular approach in which educational objectives are defined in detail. These objectives then serve as the basis for the design of instructional procedures, materials, and other aspects of the curriculum. In several of the CBIM systems these objectives are specific to a given subject at a given grade level [see Kelley, 1968; Silberman,

1968]. In others, they go across grade levels within a subject matter area (see Cooley and Glaser, 1968). . . . Achieving these objectives requires that instructional materials related to objectives be available to each pupil. The majority of the CBIM systems employ conventional instructional materials such as textbooks, workbooks, etc. Only the Pittsburgh group [Cooley and Glaser, 1968] reported using instructional materials developed expressly for the project. The extensive use of conventional materials reflects the extremely high cost of design, development, and projection of materials associated with specific instructional objectives.

Given the instructional objectives and the correspondent procedures and materials, a means must be available for determining whether or not a pupil using them has achieved a particular objective. Universally, the approach has been to use criterion-referenced tests [see Popham and Husek, 1969]. Such tests are typically administered as pretests to determine a pupil's present level of achievement and as posttests to determine if specific objectives have been achieved. In several cases [Kelley, 1968; Cooley and Glaser, 1968], tests were administered during the course of instruction to ascertain the progress of a student rather than waiting until the posttest to discover nonachieving pupils. Typically, these test scores were then used as the basis for the procedures of diagnosis and prescription.

The end product in all CBIM systems is a series of computer-generated reports containing pupils' names, test scores, and the related prescriptions. These reports are generally structured by objectives and by groups of pupils (e.g., reading groups). In several systems the computer-stored data allows one to trace a given pupil over a period of time greater than that of a single unit of instruction [see Cooley and Glaser, 1969]. . . . It is interesting that the reports produced by the CBIM systems contain nearly the same kinds of detailed and summary information yielded by the Standard CAI system [Jerman, 1969, 1970].

SUMMARY

The published papers describing the existing CBIM systems dealt primarily with the reasons for developing such systems and with their data processing mechanics. These papers described the computer-generated reports in some detail but were vague when it came to describing the procedures for diagnosis and prescription. Completely lacking has been a description of how the teachers employ these reports to manage the classroom and any evidence that the CBIM systems result in a more effective role for the teacher. These omissions seem to be associated with an emphasis on "getting something to work"; hopefully, this phase will pass quickly. A similar phenomenon occurred in the early days of CAI when most of the systems were constructed to demonstrate that CAI systems could be implemented and many larger questions were ignored.

In the process of demonstrating the feasibility of computer-based instructional management systems, it became apparent that a wide range of problems exist which are intrinsic to individualization of instruction. These problems exist both in CBIM systems that were designed to assist the teacher and in CAI systems that were designed to be a means of instruction.

The most fundamental need is a definition of individualized instruction. All of the CBIM systems were used to facilitate a curriculum based on a common content that was to be learned by all the pupils. Individualization occurred only in regard to the rate at which a pupil moved through this common curriculum and in the assignment of a limited range of remedial tasks to pupils not achieving mastery. Wilhelms [1962] indicated that the individualization provided by such rate of progress schemes is largely illusory and such schemes have been given more credence than they deserve.

Significant problems arise in the areas of diagnosis and prescription since individualization essentially depends on how well one can diagnose and the effectiveness of the resulting prescriptions. In the existing CBIM systems, diagnosis consists of determining if a test score obtained from a criterion-referenced test meets the level set for mastery of the objective or subobjective. In some cases patterns of item responses are reported [Kelley, 1968a, 1968b], but they do not seem to be used diagnostically. Current diagnostic procedures report their findings in a very sterile fashion, and interpretation of the data is left to the teacher. A much more viable reporting of diagnoses could be accomplished via the computer-generated descriptive paragraphs such as proposed by Baker [1970] and by Finney [1967]. In these paragraphs, the test score at hand would be used in conjunction with past performance data to create a verbal description and interpretation of a pupil's performance on a unit of instruction.

Rudimentary prescriptive procedures are a part of most existing CBIM systems. These procedures generally consist of table look-up schemes in which the test score distribution is divided into several score intervals, and remedial actions such as seat work, review sessions, etc. are assigned a priori to each score interval. The obtained test score is compared to the distributions; the interval in which it falls determines what tasks are prescribed for the pupil. The computer merely produces an identification number indicating a folder in a materials file or a particular chapter in a text book.

Although he employs the same table look-up mechanisms, Kelley's [1968a] prescriptions are the most interesting. His computer programs yield paragraphs describing what the student is to do and when the assignment is due. The prescriptions are also a bit more lively in that they consist of homework, attendance at other courses, attending lectures, and writing reports, rather than the usual file folder number.

A final instructionally related problem shared by CBIM and CAI is that of criterion-referenced tests. The present practice is to use existing multiple choice items or locally developed items and assemble them into achievement tests covering an objective. Because of the manner in which such instruments are employed, it will take a considerable period of time to identify and correct their deficiencies. In the meantime, many educational decisions will have been based on pupils' scores on these tests. The testing problem is greatest in completely individualized systems where only a few pupils may take a given instrument within a period of time. It is less of a problem in conventional group-oriented systems such as IMS and TIPS where all testing is done on a group basis.

One must tread rather cautiously in this area since criterion-referenced tests are naught but a new label for the mastery tests used in an earlier era [see Rice, 1893]. A considerable literature relating to the evils of mastery tests exists, and much of the work of early educational psychologists was in reaction to the unreal requirement that all pupils achieve criterion performance. There is real danger that CBIM systems might inadvertently be the vehicle for reestablishing mastery tests under the guise of progress.

Because CBIM and CAI share many instructionally related problems, it is very easy to regard the former as a poor man's or slow-speed CAI. To do so would be a major error. CBIM systems should exist as a distinct mode of computer involvement implementing a carefully orchestrated interaction among pupils, instructional procedures, and instructional materials, managed by the teacher. The teacher should use the computer as a vehicle for obtaining the timely, accurate, and relevant information needed to fulfill the role of an educational manager. Because CBIM systems are management systems rather than means of instruction, this reviewer foresees their development along lines distinctly different from those of CAI. There will be considerable interaction between the two, but eventually CAI will be one of several instructional procedures managed by computer-based instructional management systems. The success of future CBIM systems depends on a definition of individualization, on improved curriculum, on better diagnostic and prescriptive techniques, and on an adequate conceptualization of the teacher as the manager of an educational enterprise. Progress in these areas is not readily achieved, and even small gains require a great investment in time, talent, and funds.

As is the case with CAI, the promise of CBIM systems far exceeds the present accomplishments. The present systems are rudimentary, provide the teacher precious little management assistance, and are available on a very limited basis. Primary attention has been given to getting such systems up and running, and their role as a management tool for the teacher has been nearly ignored. Hopefully, now that the feasibility of CBIMS has been demonstrated, attention can turn to the reason for their existence.

REFERENCES

Baker, F. B. Automation of test scoring, reporting and analysis. In R. L. Thorndike, *Educational Measurement*. American Council on Education, 1970.

Bratten, J. E. Educational applications of information management systems. SP 3077/000/01, Systems Development Corporation, Santa Monica, Calif., 1968.

Cooley, W. W., and Glaser, R. An information and management system for individually prescribed instruction. Working Paper No. 44, Learning Research and Development Center, University of Pittsburgh, 1968. (A revised version appears in R. C. Atkinson and H. A. Wilson (Eds.), *Computer-assisted instruction: A book of readings.* New York: Academic Press, 1969).

Coulsen, J. E. (Ed.) *Programmed learning and computer based instruction.* New York: John Wiley, 1962.

Finney, J. C. Methodological problems in programmed composition of psychological test reports. *Behavioral Science,* 1967, 12: 142–52.

Flanagan, J. C. Functional education for the seventies. *Phi Delta Kappan,* 1967, 48: 27–32.

Flanagan, J. C. Individualizing education. Address presented to Division 15, American Psychological Association, San Francisco, California, 1968.

Flanagan, J. C. Program for learning in accordance with needs. *Psychology in the Schools,* 1969, 6: 133–36.

Flanagan, J. C., Dailey, J. T., Davis, F. B., Goldberg, I., Heyman, C. A., Jr., Orr, D. B., and Shaycraft M. F. The American high school student. Cooperative Research Project No. 635, 1964, University of Pittsburgh, United States Office of Education.

Glaser, R. Adapting the elementary school, curriculum to individual performance. *Proceedings of the 1967 Invitational Conference on Testing Problems,* Educational Testing Service, 1968.

Glaser, R. Evaluation of instruction and changing educational models. In M. C. Wittrock and D. Wiley (Eds.), *Evaluation of instruction.* New York: Holt, Rinehart and Winston, 1969.

Henry, N. B. (Ed.) *National Society for the Study of Education 61st yearbook.* Part I. *Individualizing instruction.* Chicago: University of Chicago Press, 1962.

Jerman, M. *Teacher handbook.* Stanford, Calif.: Stanford University, Institute for Mathematical Studies in the Social Sciences, 1969.

Jerman, M. *Supplement to the Teacher Handbook.* Stanford, Calif.: Stanford University, Institute for Mathematical Studies in the Social Sciences, 1970.

Kelley, A. C. The economics of teaching: The role of TIPS. Paper presented at conference on new developments in the teaching of economics, Stanford University, 1968.(a)

Kelley, A. C. An experiment with TIPS: A computer aided instructional system for undergraduate education. *The American Economic Review,* 1968, 58: 446–57.(b)

Popham, J. W., and Husek, T. R. Implications of criterion-referenced measurement. *Journal of Educational Measurement,* 1969, 6: 1–10.

Rath, G. J., Anderson, N. S., and Brainerd, R. C. The IBM Research Center teaching machine project. In E. H. Galanter (Ed.), *Automatic teaching: The state of the art.* New York: Wiley, 1959.

Rice, J. M. *The public school system of the United States.* New York: Century, 1893.

Silberman, H. G. Design objectives of the instructional management system. SP

3038/001/00, Systems Development Corporation, Santa Monica, Calif., 1968.

Sponberg, R. A. Teacher written TLU. *The Instructor,* 1968, 77: 101.

Suppes, P. The uses of computers in education. In *Information.* San Francisco: Freeman Press, 1966.

Whipple, G. M. (Ed.) *National Society for the Study of Education 24th yearbook.* Part II. *Adapting the schools to individual differences.* Chicago: University of Chicago Press, 1925.

Wilhelms, F. T. The curriculum and individual differences. In N. B. Henry (Ed.), *National Society for the Study of Education 61st yearbook.* Part I. *Individualizing instruction.* Chicago: University of Chicago Press, 1962.

REVIEW QUESTIONS

1.   What do CAI and CBIMS have in common, and how do they differ?

2.   Do computer-based instructional management systems pose a dehumanizing threat of robot schools? Or would they improve the efficiency of individualizing instruction?

ten

Imitation Learning and Learning Through Imitation

ARTHUR W. STAATS

. . . The child acquires much of his speech skill as well as other social and sensory-motor skills on the basis of imitational learning. Imitation consists of several types of learning. And imitation skills play various roles in the child's general behavior development. For example, the child's imitation is selective; that is, through learning children come to imitate certain things and not others. Moreover, they will learn imitation to varying degrees of skill. The manner in which imitation is learned and some of the ways imitation functions in further learning are thus important topics for understanding the behavioral development of children. This chapter will describe several aspects of the imitational skill acquisition . . .

REWARD VALUE OF IMITATION

Basic to the action of imitation of the adult by the child is the acquisition of reward value of the adult for the child. Simply stated, if the adult as a complex stimulus acquires reward value for the child, then it will be reinforcing if the child does something like the adult—if he imitates the adult. Thus, the learning of imitational skills first depends upon the stimuli of the adult becoming rewarding.

It has been stated that because of the fact that the parent's voice becomes rewarding to the child, he gradually learns to make sounds like that of the parent. These are imitative behaviors. In addition to the speech sounds of the parent, it would be expected that his other stimuli would also become rewarding. Thus, at

Source: Abridgment of pp. 97–101, 123–28 from *Child Learning, Intelligence, and Personality* by A. W. Staats. Copyright © 1971 by Arthur W. Staats. Reprinted by permission of the author and Harper & Row Publishers, Inc.

a later age we see that the child finds it rewarding to dress like the parent. There is no special reason that clothes the parent wears should be rewarding for the child except through the process described. We will also see that the child will find it rewarding to mimic the parent's mannerisms in various ways and to do various things like the parent.

It would be expected that the child would learn many imitational behaviors in this manner. However, the present section is concerned with the motivational (reward) properties of imitation, and it is important to indicate that there are additional ways that imitational stimuli become reinforcing. That is, the child ordinarily receives specific (if informal) training experiences that also contribute to making imitation of the parent rewarding. In describing this it is relevant to indicate that the imitation response in any case results in the production of a stimulus circumstance by the child that is like the stimulus produced by the parent. This may be taken as a definition of an imitation or matching response. It is when the child's stimulus matches that of the parent (or other child or adult) that we say the child has imitated.

The child will have many experiences when he is reinforced after producing such matching, or imitational, behavior. To illustrate, the child will be told by the parent, "Do it like I do," and so on, and be rewarded to the extent that he produces a good match of the parent's behavior. The child will be told, "Sit up at the table like so and so does," and he will be rewarded if his behavior is like that of an older brother or sister. The child will be told to comb his hair like . . . , brush his teeth like . . . , not cry like . . . , and to perform many other imitative acts. Each time the child is reinforced when his behavior or other attributes match those of another person, this will have the effect of making such matching or imitational events (stimuli) into rewards. [See Baer and Sherman, 1967; Staats, 1963, pp. 123–26; 1968, pp. 425–27, 441–51.]

It would be expected that the extent to which the child is rewarded when he has produced such imitational stimuli will determine in part the extent to which the child will find imitation reinforcing. The parent may in his interactions with the child arrange (usually informally) many such training experiences, or, conversely, relatively few. The extent to which the child will learn through imitation will in part be determined by how much reward value imitational stimuli have for the child. Other things being equal, the more reward value imitational events have for the child, the more he will learn through imitation.

The foregoing thus suggests the manner in which it becomes rewarding for the child to learn to imitate. A child who has a deficit in this type of training, and thus a deficit in imitation motivation, will not learn as developed an imitation repertoire as the child who has had more such experience.

Actually, the child may in certain cases even learn to do the *opposite* of what someone else does. Then, in many situations that call for imitation, rather than learning appropriate behaviors he may learn the opposite. A moment may be spent in describing a learning situation that could produce such a "negativistic" child. Let us take the case where the child has sparse experience in which he is rewarded for doing something like the parent. Rather, it is when the child *refuses* to do something like the parent that he receives much social reward in the form of the parent coaxing and wheedling the child to perform the action. Such training conditions, inadvertently conducted, can lead in many circumstances to a deficit in imitation reward for the child as well as the learning of obstinate, or negative imitation repertoires.

One other general problem of imitation motivation may be mentioned here. Ordinarily, although at first imitation of both parents will be equally rewarding (depending of course upon the child's experience), after a certain age it is our custom to discourage the child from imitating to the same degree the parent of the opposite sex—at least in certain areas of behavior. The child will continue to be rewarded for imitating the same-sex parent in a wider number of behaviors than in the opposite-sex parent, and conversely punishment in the form of social disproval will follow "incorrect" imitation of the opposite-sex parent. This can be expected to ordinarily affect the imitational motivation of the child along sex lines. Where such differential training does not occur in some form, the child may not demonstrate the desirable differentiation in motivation.

ATTENTION AND IMITATION

An important aspect of the imitation repertoire is that the child look at the actions of other people and the stimulus events that are controlling those actions. Some children when in a situation where their own behavior is not controlled by the situation—for example, problem situations where the child has no learned responses that produce a satisfactory result—will look at the ways that others behave. These attentional responses are basic to learning through imitation, for in such a situation if there is someone else who has learned a response the child will then observe (see, hear, touch, or what have you) the response.

Thus, basic to the imitational repertoire are the attentional behaviors that allow the child to sense the actions of another individual, as well as the relevant stimuli that are controlling the individual's behavior. Two children can be in the same situation where someone else performs a desirable response. Yet the two may profit differently, because one has closely observed the action and the controlling stimuli for the action while the other child has not.

The fact is that we learn to observe other people's behaviors when we have had the training to do so. This may occur in many, many parent-child interactions, as well as in interactions the child has with others. A child may be instructed, for example, to "watch how I do it." This can be done in great detail, with the trainer drawing the attention of the child to the relevant stimuli, as well as to the stimulus events of his own behavior. A child who has had a rich experience of this kind—where he observes and imitates and is then reinforced when he behaves in kind—will acquire a rich attentional repertoire for observing other people's behavior, as well as a rich imitational repertoire.

For example the child in class who watches the teacher closely as she performs actions which the children in class are later to perform, and also pays attention to the stimulus objects she manipulates, and so on, will learn rapidly. The child who does not have this repertoire of attentional behaviors will not even observe what has occurred, let alone be able to imitate the action. Other things being equal, the second child will not learn as rapidly. In addition, of course, as will be discussed, the child must have learned the actual imitational repertoire that is involved. That is, in this example the child must to some extent be able to repeat what the teacher has written, said, or done, for the learning to be complete.

It should be noted that in many cases the first step in imitating a behavior that is different from one that we have in our own repertoire may be to first discriminate the difference. As one example, before we can imitate a spoken dialect that is slightly different from our own, we must be able to discriminate the dialect— be able to respond to it differentially. . . . The extent to which the child can discriminate stimuli that are similar will depend upon the extent to which he has been presented with the different stimuli and has learned to respond differently to them. Once an individual has discriminated two types of dialects, for example, or other sets of like responses, he can practice the speech that is different from his own and learn to make imitational responses that match the new dialect. The reinforcement for this learning is provided when a sound is produced that matches or imitates the new dialect.

NEGATIVE IMITATION

In general, through this and various other experiences, the attitude or reward value of social stimuli come to control the imitative and following behavior of the child. The stronger the reward value, the stronger the positive control over such behavior. It would also appear that the child learns, conversely, *not* to imitate some people and some types of actions, and so on. It may be suggested that one of the important mechanisms involved here is analogous to that just described, except rather than learning to imitate people with positive reward value, the mechanism involved is learning not to imitate when the person has negative attitude value. Nonimitating behavior may also involve negative imitation—that is, doing the opposite of what someone else has done. Thus, it is suggested that the child ordinarily receives training in which in the presence of nonrewarding models he is reinforced for nonimitating or negative imitating behavior.

For example, a young boy who as is customary has been admonished or teased (both punishing) for imitating girls will have less reward value for girls. In this process the boy will also have learned not to imitate girls, and more generally not to imitate people who elicit in him negative attitudes. The learning processes involved in this may be considered to be the same as those in the positive rewarding case—except the opposite in reward valued is involved, and the opposite type of imitation behavior is learned.

Thus, the negative reward value of a person ordinarily comes to strongly control negative imitation, or nonimitation, in the child. This type of basic behavioral repertoire is also important in what the individual will learn. For example, we depend upon this mechanism when we attempt to lower the reward value of a political candidate or movement by invective. By lowering the reward value we decrease the extent to which the candidate will be followed (imitated).

MANIPULATING IMITATION BY MANIPULATING SOCIAL ATTITUDES

This analysis indicates that the reward value of other people (that is, the type and intensity of attitudes we have toward them) is an important variable that helps determine the extent to which the child will imitate people, and thus the extent and content of what the child will learn in many situations. For example, in the schoolroom if the teacher has a good deal of positive reward value for the child, the teacher's behavior will control imitational behavior in the child. The same is true for other children in the class. If for a particular child other able, hardworking, children have high reward value, then their behavior will be more highly imitated by the child. Anything that lessens the reward value of these able children will lessen the controlling effect they have in producing like behaviors in the child. On the other hand, if a group of rebellious, negligent students have a good deal of reward value for the child, he will imitate their behavior instead.

Once the mechanism has been learned by the child so that people who have positive reward value tend more to control his imitation, and those having negative reward value control negative imitation, then the extent of the child's imitation behavior is affected by the manipulation of the reward value of people. It is then not necessary that the imitator previously have had any direct experience with the particular model. The analysis thus indicates why celebrities, leaders, and so on are imitated even though the imitator has had no direct contact with the model. It may also be noted here that these effects of reward value on imitation can be manipulated by increasing or decreasing the reward value of the model—and this can be done in various ways. Reward value may be increased or decreased by words, for example, through communication procedures that will be described more fully later on.

An illustration is pertinent at this point, however, in the context of imitation. Let us say that the parent associates negative emotional words with able, hardworking students. He does this, let us say, because the child is having a difficult time in school and the parent, who has little value for education himself, attempts to provide solace for the child by saying such things as, "Those bookworms spend all their time studying, and they don't know how to do anything worthwhile." This experience would have the effect of lessening for the child the reward value of other children in the class who were diligent, college-bound students. Moreover, lowering the reward value of these successful students would lessen the extent to which the child would imitate them in school. By the same token, the parent who gives relatively high verbal praise to baseball players, football players, fighters, and so on will be ensuring that these types of individuals are rewarding for his child and consequently that his child will emulate the behaviors of these types of individuals.

IMITATION AND INTELLIGENCE

In a gross way it has been realized for a long time that imitation is important to human adjustment and to human learning. The traditional conception, as has been indicated, has been that imitation skills are an innate given of the individual. The conception presented herein is that imitation consists of types of skill that are acquired directly through learning, beginning in the child's early experience. It is suggested also that these imitation skills constitute a basic behavioral repertoire which, also according to the same learning principles, enable the child to adjust positively in many situations and to learn profitably in many situations. . . . A central purpose of the present section, specifically, is to illustrate that the types of imitation that have been shown to be learned constitute important constituents of what we call intelligence, as measured by intelligence tests.

In indicating the importance of imitation to the common conception of intelligence, it is edifying to consult . . . the items of intelligence tests for young children. It becomes clear when this is done that many items measure the extent of the child's learning of the two aspects of imitation that have been discussed. Take, for example, an item . . . on the revised Stanford-Binet Intelligence Test . . . The child is instructed to watch the test administrator construct a tower of blocks and, with the blocks left standing as a model, to build one just like it. The child must have learned the attentional responses involved in watching the administrator and scrutinizing the block model, under the control of the verbal stimuli. And he must have the sensory-motor skills in imitating the tower.

This item is at the two-year level of the test. At the three-year level the child has to imitate a more complex block design. As other examples will also suggest, the same task of imitation, as well as other basic behavioral repertoires, appears in somewhat more complex form as the level of the test items advances. Thus, as in the present case, the level of skill in the particular basic behavioral repertoire is tested a number of times. In the present case, this demonstrates that imitation is not only important for the very young child but continues to be an item of his measured intelligence as he grows older and meets more complex learning tasks.

On another item at the 2½-year-level the child is told, "Watch what I do," a classic instruction that will establish control of an imitation act in the child who has had the necessary training. The examiner then takes three geometric forms out of the corresponding holes in a board and says, "Now put them back into their holes" [Terman and Merrill, 1937, p. 75]. This may be considered to call for a type of imitation behavior that is the model's behavior run backwards. Ordinarily, the child receives training in this backward imitation skill when the parent plays various kinds of "replacement" games with the child—as well as in the child's own experience in doing and undoing things. Another imitation item of this type occurs at the three-year level.

At the three-year-level the child is told again to watch while the examiner strings wooden beads on a shoestring. The child is then instructed to string beads himself like the examiner. By the six-year level the imitation behavior required by this type of item is consideraby more difficult. The child is told, "Watch what I do." The examiner then makes a chain of seven beads using alternately square and round beads. Then the examiner says, "When I'm through, I'm going to take this one away and see if you can make one just like it. . . ." At the nine-year level the child has a similar item where he has to imitate the examiner in folding and cutting paper. The instructions must control very assiduous attending behavior.

There are also a number of items that involve the child imitating what the test administrator has said, upon command. For example, at the three-year level there is an item in which the child is instructed to repeat two numbers pronounced by the examiner. The examiner says, "Listen! Say two." "Now four . . . seven, . . ." and so on. These are straightforward speech imitation terms. At the five-year level, also, one item consists of the examiner asking the child to imitate a sentence ten words in length, which is another type of speech imitation item.

As with the other items illustrated in this and the other chapters, these are but examples. Many more of the skills of the basic behavioral repertoire of imitation could be illustrated by the use of intelligence test items.

. . . If the child has learned negative attitudes toward adults, the examiner may elicit negative imitation behaviors, or general nonresponding. Furthermore, the stimuli presented by the examiner must control the sensory-motor responses of the actual imitation acts. If the child has had the necessary learning history, and thus has the necessary behaviors, he will respond appropriately to these items and receive points toward his intelligence rating. Thus, the basic behavioral repertoires of imitation that have been described also contribute toward the child's measured intelligence; in fact, the repertoires are constitutents of intelligence, one part of personality.

REFERENCES

Baer, D., and Sherman, J. Reinforcement of generalized imitation by reinforcing behavioral similarity to a model. *Journal of Experimental Analysis of Behavior,* 1967, 10: 405–416.

Staats, A. W. *Learning, Language, and Cognition.* New York: Holt, 1968.

Staats, A. W., and Staats, C. K. *Complex Human Behavior.* New York: Holt, 1963.

Terman, L. M., and Merrill, M. A. *Measuring Intelligence.* Boston: Houghton Mifflin, 1937.

REVIEW QUESTIONS

1. What types of behavior, information, skills, and so on are acquired in the classroom by imitating the teacher or other models?

2. What kind of imitation behavior, positive or negative, will an unpleasant teacher stimulate?

3. Do you agree that imitation tendencies may be a basic part of innate intelligence?

eleven

Teaching Academic Skills, Assertiveness, and Improved Self-Concept to Learning Disabled Children

ROGER A. SEVERSON

Several years ago I began to explore the possibilities of applying behavior modification techniques to children with severe learning disabilities. At the time, the only published work was that of Staats [1964; Staats, Minke, Finley, Wolf, and Brooks, 1964], which indicated that reading behaviors could be successfully modified by appropriate reinforcement. We began to teach children with severe reading disabilities to acquire a sight vocabulary. We also improved oral reading skills, comprehension, and mastery of phonic rules. The initial success was encouraging, but we failed to see visible changes in the attitudes of the children toward school and learning. About that time, another article by Staats was published [Staats and Butterfield, 1965], indicating apparent success in teaching reading to a delinquent adolescent. The boy, however, ended his treatment by being returned to an institution because of further delinquent behaviors. Somehow, the reported success with reading behaviors did not make much sense when the more impairing anti-social behaviors were not successfully changed. Thus, we experienced a sense of dissatisfaction with the narrow approach to improving reading behavior alone.

Two problems were seen in trying to develop a more adequate approach with these children. First was the problem of deciding what behaviors represented deficiencies. While appearing on the surface to be very agreeable and cooperative children, these appearances were very deceptive. When we looked at their patterns of performing and reacting more carefully, the compliance was seen as a kind of behavior that masked underlying patterns which were frequently quite maladaptive. Borrowing a term from DeCharms [1968], the children were "pawns," extremely unassertive in situations where withdrawal and overcompliance worked to their disadvantage. In fact, some of the children were depressed in varying degrees, failing to believe in their own talents or to have hope that they could overcome the obstacles preventing them from becoming high achievers. These problems showed up in elusive ways and it took many children to reveal the picture clearly. Dudek and Lester [1968], noting a similar pattern in severe learning disabilities, referred to these behaviors as the "good child facade." We concluded that the picture of apparent adjustment was deceptive, and that these children needed to be taught to be more assertive as well as to have a stronger sense of self-esteem.

The second problem was to devise an approach based on behavior modification principles which would allow effective change of these patterns into more personally adaptive patterns. Implicit in our approach is the assumption that helping a child to become a person who can choose his own goals, has confidence in achieving them, and does so without sacrificing a sense of personal enjoyment, is a better, if more complex, treatment goal than simply trying to teach the child reading behaviors. We had already satisfied ourselves that with these children such improvements do not come about spontaneously when reading skills improve. We began our efforts to modify the overcompliant behaviors by giving the child a chance to choose what he wanted to do in the treatment session. We offered them alternatives in the form of games.

The children varied considerably in the way they reacted to the offer to either work on reading skills or play games. Some chose immediately to play games and showed no interest in the academic tasks, even when they knew they would be rewarded for spending time learning. Others chose the reading task, but seemed conflicted by the choice. With continuing reminders that they could truly choose to do whatever they wished, they soon chose to play and seemed relieved to be away from the reading task. A small number of children, however, stuck determinedly to the job of learning to read, and verbalized a belief that it would not be proper to play games instead of practicing reading skills. A few children were completely unable to make a choice and merely asked the clinician which they should do.

THE BEHAVIOR HIERARCHY MODEL

Many of the children obviously wished to avoid reading activities, and in fact would have chosen to play games most of the time if we had let them. Many felt uncertain or uncomfortable about having to choose. We needed procedures which would preserve their right to choose, yet help in their ability to make personal choices and increasingly encourage them to engage in reading activities. Behavior modification seemed to offer some suggestions for this goal. Systematic desensitization is a format developed by behavior modifiers to allow a person to overcome fear of an object (for example, snakes) by gradually helping the person to come closer to the object, either physically or imaginally, while at the same time engaging him in something incompatible with fear reactions, such as relaxing or eating. Frequently, a hierarchy of situations is employed, ranging from some only mildly related to the feared object to some which arouse maximal fear reactions.

Borrowing from this basic approach, we employ a hierarchy of activities with academic tasks at the top. Each subsequent step involves a task with decreasing emphasis on academic skills and increasing emphasis on having fun. We use academic games to fill the intermediate levels. Further down the hierarchy we include nonacademic games which are clearly enjoyed by the child. Lastly, we put the item "Leave the room," allowing the child to completely terminate the session whenever he desires. We break up the treatment sessions into five-minute periods, asking the child at the beginning of each five-minute period what he wishes to do next. With sessions averaging forty-five minutes each, this forces the child to make nine choices in each session.

It is necessary to develop schedules of reinforcement which strengthen the appropriate behaviors. The kinds of reinforcers we use are social reinforcement and secondary reinforcers in the form of various kinds of tokens which can be exchanged for a wide variety of back-up reinforcements. Various contingencies are involved for dispensing reinforcers. Social reinforcement is employed systematically for effort and learning, with more intense reinforcement being offered initially, according to known principles of operant reinforcement [Sulzer and Mayer, 1972]. The effort to make such reactions more effective by obeying certain principles of operant reinforcement are always secondary to communicating a sense of genuine interest in the growth of the child.

Dispensing of tokens is done more precisely. On a variable interval schedule (random time intervals between each reinforcement), tokens are given to the child with a statement similar to the following: "Here's a token just for being here, Jimmy. It's nice to have you here." These reactions are meant to let the child know the clinician is pleased to spend time with the child and to strengthen the child's positive feelings about being at the clinic. Other tokens are given at the end of each five minutes for being involved in a particular activity. For the academic tasks only, tokens are given in various amounts for different levels of successful accomplishment.

The differences in the amount of tokens earned for each level of the hierarchy provides one of the more powerful incentives during the early stages of behavior therapy for the child to engage in the top academic task a portion of the time. Tokens for each five minutes of task involvement range from zero (for tasks with high intrinsic enjoyment) to fifteen or more for the top task when the child is extremely reluctant to choose an academic task. The selection of effective back-up reinforcers is a matter of diagnostic art, whereas the determination of effective exchange rates is a matter of careful mastery of principles of behavior modification. Both the content of the behavior hierarchy and the exchange value of tokens are adjusted between sessions to maximize the reinforcing power of the various contingencies. The details of the kinds of tokens, reinforcers, and exchange patterns which have proven to be maximally effective with this population of children have been reported in greater detail in an earlier account [Severson, 1972]. In general, as a group they are much more responsive to social praise than children in general, and tend to value sweets very highly. Often a fairly dramatic change in behavior can be observed by the opportunity to work for a Coke. The development of complete reinforcement schedules for individual children, however, generally involves not only a within-session back-up reinforcer such as a soft drink or candy bar, but opportunities to earn money ranging up to a dollar a session. Further tokens are put in a "bank" and generally add up to long-term reinforcers requiring between 500 and 3,000 tokens.

Many persons have strong ideas against the appropriateness of employing tangible reinforcers to enhance learning in children [O'Leary, Poulos, and Devine, 1972]. Such reactions are usually based on ignorance of the techniques involved, or represent value systems which reject the idea of rewarding children for doing things they should do as ends in themselves. Tangible reinforcers are effective aids in changing behaviors, but can easily be abused if misunderstood. In our work they represent "pump primers," ways of getting the children to make appropriate efforts when the task itself lacks adequate reinforcing properties. We know, however, that getting the child to learn with the use of unusual patterns of reinforcement is not the whole objective. We will have succeeded only when we have restored the child to willingness to learn with the kinds of available and acceptable reinforcers he will have after discharge. This is the distinction between *acquisition* and *maintenance*, and people who criticize behavior modification approaches often do not understand that establishing maintenance of behavior patterns is just as important as getting the initial behaviors in the repertoire of the person.

THE TYPICAL STAGES OF BEHAVIOR THERAPY

Once we have set up the session according to the freedom and structure described above, together with the various conditions for dispensing social and tangible reinforcement, we watch the child carefully to see what patterns he will show in making task selections. The choices provide important diagnostic clues as to the child's reaction to achievement-related tasks. Although the patterns vary considerably, we consider the first phase to be completed when the child is choosing the top task at least once during the session and shows no persistently deviant patterns of avoiding academic material or enjoyable activities. Also, no unusual reactions to reinforcers are noted, and the schedules of reinforcement are clearly effective in improving the degree of effort shown and amount of learning achieved.

Evidence of improvement is shown both in the amount of time the child spends engaged in the academic tasks and in changes in the rate of learning and retention, together with the increases in effort shown by the child while engaged in learning. The careful clinical observer gets a great deal of useful information by watching the physical posture of the child during learning activities. A pure behavior modifier would probably reject this kind of diagnostic information, but it is definitely more behavioral than inferential. During the initial assessment period a baseline is obtained to see how rapidly the child shows postural tension and increases in frequency of errors as the difficulty of the material increases and the clinician's reaction changes. This approach is known as diagnostic teaching and provides much more precise information about the learning process than extensive batteries of IQ tests or static assessments of curriculum knowledge. During subsequent remedial sessions the clinician makes careful notes as to apparent changes in effort and rate of learning, and from time to time he returns to the precision of the diagnostic teaching format in order to be more certain of his observations. The rather precise approach to documenting the behavior patterns, which is one of the basic distinctions between diagnosis and remediation, continues through this early phase of therapy.

Once the child begins to choose the top task more frequently, several things seem to be occurring. The child is building up confidence in his ability to master new learning, and his attitude toward learning and himself is more amenable to influence. In order to further the development of these attitudes and feelings, and help the child to anticipate the future in a more positive way, we introduce at this point the long-term bonus arrangement and increase the options within the session which will allow the child to earn tokens. For example, if the top task involves learning new words, we build in a *success* contingency such that the larger the number of new words learned in a five-minute session, the greater the number of tokens that can be earned. Additional tokens can also be earned by demonstrating retention of the new words at the end of the session and at the beginning of the following session. This second phase involves two major ingredients, the effort to involve the child as much as possible in academic tasks during the session, and a more systematic effort to change the child's attitudes toward himself. By this time we have usually worked through the problems associated with self-punitive behaviors which lead the child to reject activities involving enjoyment. Thus, when the child chooses the top task time after time, he usually has learned his own limits and will drop down to a game temporarily if he gets too fatigued.

Now the child is usually showing the kind of effort that provides us with ample opportunity to systematically help him to improve his feelings about himself. This area, however, provides a clear challenge to a behavioristic approach. The existence of a self-concept has been strongly challenged by some, but we only assume that persons have attitudes toward their own behaviors which influence their behavior in achievement-related situations. If we can not only influence the probability of success in such situations, as well as help to modify the way in which the child views himself, the two lead to more enduring changes. We attempt this in the following manner. First we get a baseline on self-attitudes either through the administration of an inventory during the diagnostic period, or by asking the child how he feels about what he has done in the early stages of behavior therapy. Then, as the child achieves success, the clinician offers praise clearly reflecting how he feels about the child's performance. After a period of initial success, the comments by the clinician take on a different quality. He may say, "You're really trying harder, George. You seem to have a new sense of confidence in yourself." Later he begins to make statements such as, "My, how proud you must be of yourself for doing so well!" Later, in the presence of the parent, the clinician asks the child to relate how he feels about his achievement. This is a real clinical art, since efforts to force this too soon may get an embarrassed silence from the child, or some self-belittling comment. The intent is not only to strengthen the child's willingness to think positively about himself, but to begin the process of weaning the child from dependence upon tokens and tangible reinforcers.

When the child is clearly making the most effective use of the sessions and showing some capacity to work on materials between sessions, we enter the third phase. This involves a much more systematic extension of the program outside of the clinic. A key ingredient is the extent to which we can create effective conditions of learning in the home. The parents are a critical part of this extension of the program. As part of our initial diagnostic evaluation we usually have asked the child to interact with one or both of the parents with material of similar difficulty to that used in the initial academic evaluation. We start with the parent who is most likely to be able to continue in the home. Despite the kind of interaction observed during the initial evaluation, we now put the parent on the hierarchy. This means the child can elect to have the parent as clinician during one or more of the five-minute sessions. It is an interesting operational measure of the child's feelings about the parent selected to see if he willingly chooses to introduce the parent into the session. The parent is put at the top of the hierarchy, so there is a maximum tangible reinforcement to elect this alternative. It is necessary to alert the parent that often the child does not choose to do this task with the parent the first time offered. If he does not, we continue the opportunity in a second session, with a bonus attached for electing this.

If the child still does not choose the task involving the parent, it is clear there is considerable resistance for one reason or another. We know this may be for a variety of reasons, including shyness, a feeling that the child may somehow lose this cherished opportunity with the permissive and supportive clinician, or a strong aversion to interacting with the parent. It is an important diagnostic task to evaluate which of these is uppermost in the thinking of the child. Thus, at the end of the second session the clinician discusses this with the child in a nonjudgmental way. At that time it is tentatively mentioned that the clinician does not intend for the parent to take over the sessions at the clinic, but he would like to know if both the parent and the child are interested in doing something similar to the clinic interaction within the home. The advantages of this are discussed with the child, including the continuing opportunity for the child to decide each week whether to do it or not, the opportunity to introduce games into the interaction, and the opportunity to earn additional bonus tokens by the activity. If this helps the child to reverse the avoidance of the task, with the child's permission the parent is introduced into this session at the end. If both parent and child handle the interaction reasonably well, after two or three successful sessions some discussion is given to setting up a weekly elective session in the home. Simple hierarchies are constructed for use by the parent and they are taught how to introduce the opportunity for having a session and wait for a definite indication of interest on the part of the child. It is often necessary to spend time each week dealing with the parent's reaction to the session.

If, as is reasonably frequent, the child is ready for learning tasks at home but wishes to avoid introducing the parent into the situation at this point, we look for other possible home tutors, such as a sibling, or we engineer learning activities which the child can do by himself. We know that academic tasks in the home are likely to generate negative reactions that we cannot observe and correct, so we escalate slowly until it is clear the child can effectively cope with the special conditions. We need to carefully introduce cues in the home which do not lead to negative experiences. Sometimes we can do this by sending home a tape recorder, or just a book with high-interest content. At the beginning of the next session we reward the child for effort and accomplishment, once again shaping the behavior slowly in order to insure high probability of success. If the activity is reading, we may initially reward self-report of number of pages read. In subsequent sessions we tighten up by asking the child to tell us about the theme of the story, read words from the story on request, or spell some of the new words. We always set up these situations in advance and give the child the option of working for these bonus tokens at the start of the next session.

CHILDREN WITH MALADAPTIVE VARIATIONS

The foregoing description refers to the normative sequence which all children eventually go through. At all stages of this sequence there are children with unusual response patterns who require modified treatment programs. When we find a child who shows a marked unwillingness to select academic tasks if given a choice, we call this child a "hedonistic nonlearner." Usually they are much more immature than the average child with a learning disability. Family patterns often reflect a nagging parent who continuously pushes the child to accept responsibility or a parent who shows permissive toleration of regressive behaviors. The child often has younger playmates, is a clown in the classroom, and in general shows a strong dislike of changes associated with growing up. We need to rearrange the tasks in such a way that the top tasks are only slightly academic in nature, and see that the child has a great deal of fun and success in the early stages. When he chooses games, the clinician offers little in the way of social praise but carefully avoids any critical reaction even if the child chooses games throughout the session. Between sessions the reinforcement contingencies are adjusted to pair highly-valued reinforcers, such as candy, with the tasks that the clinician desires the child to choose. The disparity between token values is made greater to increase the temptation for the child to choose the top task at least once. Gradually the child finds it less rewarding to choose games and more rewarding to try something academic. When he finds that he gets a great deal of positive reinforcement for choosing an academic task, it is usually only a matter of time before he changes his pattern. Social praise and candy are usually very powerful reinforcers for this kind of child.

In contrast to this is the child who cannot let down and enjoy himself. Dubbed the "obsessed learner," he gets tense easily, may reject the use of tangible reinforcement in the early stages, and must be encouraged to choose a game activity. In the background there is almost always a punitive parent with a profound orientation toward the work ethic. The child has picked up the idea that his worth is determined solely by how well he achieves in school. In the early sessions his motor tension is clearly high and he may even bite his nails or the insides of his mouth. The intense concentration almost always takes a high toll in quality of performance. With this kind of child behavior modification procedures are useful, but the child often ignores or rejects tangibles, and techniques borrowed from insight therapies are necessary. We point out to the child the effects of his tension, such as impaired performance, the self-inflicted pain, and his loss of enjoyable experiences. Often we need to get the family together to try to break up the child's frequently exaggerated acceptance of the family attitudes, or to help the parents see the maladaptive course of their message. Insight, however, is seldom enough, and we need to engineer the learning environment to elicit behaviors incompatible with the child's usual pattern. One effective technique is to get the child to engage in an activity requiring him to move about physically. One very constricted child was brought completely out of his withdrawn pattern by using a treasure hunt game requiring him to hop on squares on the floor and engage in active bodily turning.

Some children show selective inability to tolerate positive reinforcement. An example of this is a girl who responded to the verbal reinforcer "Good!" by saying, "No, it's not good." With any effort on the part of the clinician to positively reinforce her, the praise would cause her to chain into a critical comment about herself. The pattern is reflected in the home interaction where she has acquired the role of scapegoat. We concluded that any form of praise would elicit a self-critical comment so we replaced social praise with an almost totally nonevaluative reinforcer. The clinician rigged a white card in such a way that it could be spun. When the girl made a correct response the clinician hit the card and made it spin. Soon the clinician instructed the girl to spin the card (a form of self-administered praise of low intensity), and next introduced a bell which the clinician rang at the same time that the child spun the card. Then we faded out the card, had the child ring the bell for right responses, and the clinician spoke the word *correct*. The clinician gradually progressed from *correct* to *OK* to *yes,* and dropped out the bell completely. Whenever the clinician moved too fast, the girl came up with the predictable negative comment and we backed up temporarily. Eventually the girl was restored to accepting high levels of social praise. Although an extreme example, this girl illustrates the kind of child who shows such a deviant pattern of reaction to reinforcers that modifications in the choice of reinforcers are necessary, together with retraining regarding this acceptability of positive reinforcement.

Yet another kind of deficiency is occasionally seen with a child who cannot learn to make a choice of task on the hierarchy. In this case we give tokens and praise for the child making a choice within a given number of seconds. Other modifications may involve the opposite strategy of lengthening the task intervals to ten or fifteen minutes for a child who is overly hyperactive and cannot sustain involvement at a task for very long. The format is sufficiently flexible to allow accommodation to most unique behavior problems, but each must be carefully engineered with regard to both cuing and reinforcement aspects of the session.

EXTENSION OF THE PROGRAM INTO THE SCHOOL AND HOME

If comprehensive and enduring improvement is to be obtained in the learning patterns of learning-disabled children, not only must the child show clear progress in the clinic, but these behaviors must carry over into the schools. One of the more challenging findings of research in the area of behavior modification is that improved behaviors do not generalize unless this generalization is brought about by systematic extension of the appropriate cues into the new settings, and the new behaviors are also appropriately reinforced in that setting. Thus, it is entirely possible to see new kinds of behavior in the child at the clinic, with him learning effectively and enthusiastically, but then see the child continue as an under-achiever in the schools where everyone expects and reinforces such behaviors. Therefore, when it becomes feasible to do so, we generally visit the school in order to observe the specific behaviors shown by the child in the classroom, and to review his performance patterns with the teacher. After getting an anecdotal listing of the kinds of deficient or excessive behaviors shown by the child in school, we pinpoint the more important behaviors and work with the teacher in order to get baseline information on the frequency and intensity of these. Then we set up appropriate contracts with the child for getting rewarded at the clinic when he demonstrates classroom improvement. By now the relationship with the clinician is quite important for the child, and unless serious behavior problems are found, improvement within the school progresses rather quickly, assuming the teacher is cooperative.

Extension of attention to nonacademic behaviors in the home is also necessary to complete the clinical program. The approach is similar, moving from anecdotal listing of the important behavior problems to a more precise retrieval of baseline information through parent charting. If the parents are cooperative in making a careful record of problem behaviors, and are willing to read about and subscribe to concepts of behavior management, this part usually goes very easily. When the behaviors are more severe, however, the parents may disguise their records because of defensiveness, or else reject the basic behavioral approach. We then begin looking at family patterns within the clinical setting and only gradually extend into the home setting, gathering more accurate information either through tape recordings or actual visits.

IMPLICATIONS OF THIS MODEL FOR THE LEARNING PROCESS

What has been described is obviously a very complex and extensive clinical model when all aspects are considered. Several implications seem to emerge from our work. First is the fact that persons who truly wish to help restore learning-disabled children to effective functioning *can do so,* but it is a much more demanding task than is generally realized. A second implication is the general superiority of behavior modification in approaching this population. Although most of these children would have accrued fancy diagnostic labels if seen in a medical setting, seldom do these diagnostic efforts significantly advance the child's learning skills beyond a superficial level. Third, the traditional behavior modification approaches are generally insufficient to deal with the complex affective and cognitive pictures seen in these children. Since these children manifest what has been called an *underground school phobia* [Severson, 1972], a willingness to deal with affective reactions through labeling and interpretation are important clinical measures.

Our work would also seem to have implications for the kinds of environments that can optimize learning for these children in school settings. Precisely because these children tend to cope with school stress through withdrawal, an environment that emphasizes success and failure in group settings is definitely a handicap. On the other hand, these children, as a group, lack the qualities for completely independent functioning and would probably always need guidance in choosing learning sequences. We found some of the children surprisingly assertive, once persons began to tolerate and reward these behaviors, but the general pattern of compliance seems to suggest they could adjust rather easily to any academic setting once they had overcome the initial handicaps. As support for this, after five years of working in an early intervention program we believe our easiest successes have been with the kind of child described here. Although the general passivity has resulted in many of them being overlooked until the picture crystallizes into a severe learning disorder, if they receive special help in the early grades they respond quickly. What seems to be significant is that they can be helped to become the kind of independent learner which many persons prize, but that early structure in the teaching environment is necessary in order to bring it about.

Whether philosophies similar to those of the open classroom take root widely, or settle down to special populations where the children come equipped with the necessary adaptive behaviors, will probably depend, in part, on the recognition that many children will need specific preparation to function in such environments. We have started out with a technique identified in the minds of many people as being heavily structured, worked with a population of children in which overcompliance is a prominent feature, and successfully moved them toward becoming the kind of independent learner who can control his own learning sequence.

REFERENCES

DeCharms, R. *Personal Causation.* New York: Academic Press, 1968.

Dudek, S. Z., and Lester, E. P. The good child facade in chronic underachievers. *American Journal of Orthopsychiatry*, 1968, 38: 153–60.

O'Leary, K. D., Poulos, R. W., and Devine, V. T. Tangible reinforcers: bonuses or bribes? *Journal of Clinical and Consulting Psychology*, 1972, 38: 1–8.

Severson, R. A. Behavior therapy with learning disabled children. In M. Rosenberg and R. Schneider (Eds.), *Educational Therapy*, Vol. III. Seattle: Special Child Publications, 1972.

Staats, A. W. Conditioned stimuli, conditioned reinforcers, and word meaning. In A. W. Staats (Ed.), *Human Learning.* New York: Holt, Rinehart and Winston, Inc., 1964.

Staats, A. W., and Butterfield, W. H. Treatment of nonreading in a culturally deprived juvenile delinquent: An application of reinforcement principles. *Child Development,* 1965, 4: 925–42.

Staats, A. W., Minke, K. A., Finley, J. R., Wolf M. M., and Brooks, L. O. A reinforcer system and experimental procedure for the laboratory study of reading acquisition. *Child Development,* 1964, 35: 209–31.

Sulzer, B., and Mayer, G. R. *Behavior Modification Procedures for School Personnel.* Hinsdale, Ill: Dryden Press, 1972.

REVIEW QUESTIONS

1. Severson's concept of *underground school phobia* calls attention to problems that *accompany* learning disabilities. What are the bases and symptoms of these problems?

2. Can you think of methods for removing *underground school phobia*, other than hiring Professor Severson?

twelve

The Transfer and Application of Learning

GLENN MYERS BLAIR, R. STEWART JONES,

AND RAY H. SIMPSON

TRANSFER—THE ULTIMATE GOAL OF TEACHING

The ultimate goal of teaching is to produce desirable changes in behavior which will carry over into new situations. Teachers intend training in English composition to produce better writing, mathematics to make pupils better able to solve problems, and civics to lead to better citizenship. At first glance, the attainment of these aims appears simply a matter of providing sufficient training so that what is learned is remembered. But achievement of goals such as these entails much more. Each new situation which confronts the child contains elements of uniqueness, and requires him to use previous learnings in a new way. The child must not only be able to remember, but also must be able to select from his experience those responses which are appropriate in the learning of new and different ideas and skills. When learning thus carries over into new situations, the resulting improvement, or in some cases the interference which is developed, is known as transfer of learning.

There can be little defense of schooling if it does not transfer. Learning for the sake of learning alone is hardly defensible in a system of universal education. All of learning should, of course, not be judged in terms of its "transfer value." Many skills are learned for their own intrinsic worth, their immediate value in the child's life, or for recreational purposes. In such cases proficiency in relatively unchanging situations may be a legitimate goal of teaching. However, it is impossible to predict for the pupil in exactly what situations he will use the things he has learned. People who learned to drive automobiles fifteen years ago now have to make adjustments to a changed gear shift location, automatic drives, power steering, and the like. The farmer who once acquired skill in the use of horses has been forced to change to machinery, and the pilot who learned to fly by the feel of the plane has had to learn to use instruments.

Source: Abridged with permission of The Macmillan Company from *Educational Psychology* by Blair, Jones, and Simpson. Copyright © 1968 by The Macmillan Company.

THE MEANING OF TRANSFER IN TEACHING

Transfer of learning exists whenever a previous learning has influence upon the learning or performance of new responses. Thus anything which can be learned may be transferred. A simple case of transfer would be the following:

A pupil learns	$4 \times 9 =$	36
This should help him learn	$9 \times 4 =$	36
and	$40 \times 90 =$	3600

Note that in this simple example there are not only associations and discriminations that children may have been presumed to have learned (the numbers themselves and the meaning of $\times$) but rules, viz., the commutative principle[1] and the rule that the same number of zeros must be added to the product as to the multiplier and multiplicand. Evidence in recent years suggests that the way in which these rules are learned and practiced is important in determining whether or not transfer will take place. In short, having learned these simple operations, there is a question of how well a student will be able to use them in long division or in algebraic manipulations.

These apparently simple feats of transfer are not always easy for the beginner. It has been found, for example, that many students who learn to do algebra problems involving x and y as unknowns may not be able to solve the same problems when a and b are used for unknowns. A specific check of the effect of changed symbols showed that twenty-eight per cent of a group of college students were unable to square $b_1 + b_2$, but of the same group only six per cent failed to square $x + y$ correctly [Thorndike, 1922].

The above examples of transfer are of a highly specific nature. Suppose a student comes to enjoy arithmetic greatly. Will such attitudes transfer to algebra and geometry? Or suppose the student learns to solve problems in geometry. Will he, as a consequence, be more likely to use the methods learned in solving other kinds of problems? Immediately one sees that transfer of learning is inextricably bound up with the broader objectives of education. How well the schools are achieving these broader goals is considered in the next section.

APPRAISAL OF PRESENT SCHOOL PRACTICES

Most teaching is done with the implicit assumption that what is taught will be available for future use. But research has shown that this assumption is not always warranted. For one thing, the content of school subjects is all too often outmoded and unrelated to students' interests and needs or social usage. For instance, an analysis of spellers from Grades 2 through 8 has shown that many

---

[1] A principle stating that the order in which the elements of certain operations are given is immaterial, as in arithmetic, 4 X 9 is the same as 9 X 4.

are filled with spelling words typical of our grandparents' day—words that are rare and difficult and must be studied some years ahead of the infrequent times they will ever be used [Hildreth, 1951]. Surely analyses of this kind should convince teachers and educators that closer attention be paid to the relation between subject matter and the later use of learned materials.

At all levels of schooling the question of relevance of both materials and methods is an important one. Countless examples could be cited of educational programs that are so far divorced from the present levels of ability of learners and from their interests that there is little possibility of transfer.

COMMON MISCONCEPTIONS ABOUT TRANSFER

There are a number of erroneous notions about how children's learning carries over to subsequent tasks, a common failure to clarify teaching objectives as they relate to transfer, and inadequate understanding of issues due to poorly defined terms. For example, mathematicians on the one hand defend geometry as a most excellent means of teaching reasoning—on the other hand they admit that there may be little carry-over of this ability to nonmathematical fields. Some experiments have shown considerable transfer between foreign language study and English vocabulary, others have found little or no effect, and still others have found an actual decrease in understanding of English vocabulary after foreign language study [Mead, 1946]. As positive transfer is the main objective of teaching, it is essential that teachers avoid misconceptions and lay their teaching plans on a groundwork of good understanding of the ultimate purposes of instruction. Some common erroneous views about transfer of training will now be discussed.

The first and most common error in thinking about transfer is that it takes place through a process of "formal discipline." This outmoded idea of education was based on faculty psychology, a theory that separate elements or powers of the mind such as will, memory, and cognition were trained or sharpened by practice. In this view was the assumption that what was practiced was less important than the difficulty or disciplinary value of what was practiced. Also, there was the notion that learning should be somewhat "painful" if it were to achieve the best results. Thus the hard memory work in classical languages and difficult problems in mathematics and science were viewed as the most promising media for sharpening the mind. Instead of defending these subjects for their own intrinsic worth, teachers of classics, mathematics, and sciences frequently defended them on the basis of their ability (better than other subjects) to improve the mind. Two comprehensive experimental studies which sought to test this hypothesis (that certain subjects or courses are best able to improve the mind) have found no evidence to support it. The first conducted by Thorndike [1924] compared the gains in "thinking ability" made by students studying various combinations of subjects. His conclusion was that the subjects studied were of little apparent importance, especially when the influence of the subject was compared with the initial ability of the students. He believed that the apparent superiority of mathematics and science in producing good thinkers was an artifact caused by the fact that better students *take* these courses. If better students were to study vocational arts and social sciences, these subjects would *appear* to produce the best thinkers.

A more recent study [Wesman, 1945] similar to Thorndike's, but in some ways a better-designed experiment, found almost identical results. There was no clear-cut superiority for any particular school subject. Students who took the most courses made the greatest gains, and (as shown in Thorndike's work) the bright students made greater gains than the slow ones. Even though the idea of mental discipline has long since been discredited by dozens of experimental studies [Mead, 1946], it is still a part of the thinking of some present-day educators and is still used as an argument to justify the inclusion of various subjects in the school curriculum. It is unfortunate that certain subjects such as geometry, Latin, and English grammar have most frequently been targets of attacks. There is little question that such subjects can be a rich source of learning for some pupils, and may be taught so that much that is learned transfers. On the other hand their defense on the basis of the discredited idea of disciplinary value may lead to unrealistic objectives and methods of teaching which are sterile. (The aforementioned subjects are not singled out as representative of this kind of non-functional teaching, for there is probably not a single subject in our schools which would escape this censure to some degree.) When courses are conceived in terms of the values of transfer and on the basis of their own intrinsic worth, there is a greater likelihood that they will be taught in a manner which will make them useful.

The second misconception is just the opposite of the first, and probably grew up as a reaction against it. This is the notion that nothing transfers from one situation to another except specific facts or definite identities. In the extreme, this point of view leads to a curriculum composed only of materials which are believed immediately useful. Transfer is minimized and subjects are all learned only for immediate values. What are the results of such a program? One author [Spaulding, 1939] notes that special trade courses (as in the vocational-industrial curricula) may *not* prepare students to shift from one vocation to another or one job to another because students have never learned to see relationships or look for similarities among jobs. These students are unable to adjust to the rapidly changing industrial scene brought about by technological advances.

If this idea of transfer (that is, thinking of transfer in its narrowest sense) were followed, education would become largely rote memorization and skill training—a process almost devoid of understanding, generalization, and problem solving.

A third error which emasculates the effect of teaching nearly as much as the first two, is the notion that transfer of learning is automatic. This view puts the main burden of achieving transfer upon the curriculum builder and neglects the important contribution of teaching method. The arrangement of subject matter into related sequences, plans for common learnings or core curricula, and other curricular plans do not guarantee that children will see relationships apparent to the adults who plan the program. (It is certainly true, of course, that such curricular plans may make more likely the teaching for transfer which is so important a function of school.)

The acquisition of information does not guarantee its utility. Most teachers have experienced the disappointment of seeing pupils learn in school but later fail to apply information in situations which call for its use. A well-worn story in educational circles tells of three college professors who were building a cabin in the north woods, and were unable to start with a square corner because they did not have a square. While they were trying to solve this problem, a farmer riding by, stopped, and when told the difficulty suggested that they measure three feet along one side, four feet along the other, and if the distance diagonally across the points measured on the sides was five feet, they would have a square corner. All the professors of course were familiar with the Pythagorean theorem, yet were unable to apply it in a practical way. The reader might pause at this point and consider ways in which this theorem could have been taught in the first place so that it would have been more likely to have been recalled under these circumstances.

Finally, the emphasis which books about learning and psychology have given to the topic of transfer has tended to create the impression that somehow transfer and learning are different. Actually transfer is a part of the learning process. There is indeed such a thing as learning to learn, learning how to secure transfer, and learning how to work. There is no learning which does not involve a part of a person's past experience, and in a sense all retention or remembering is a kind of transfer, because original circumstances of learning are rarely, if ever, duplicated in a new situation. Children should learn to expect change—to have the experience of applying even the simplest learnings in a number of different situations. As it is, many times drill precedes understanding and then teachers attempt to teach transfer as a separate step—something different from the initial learning. Actually learning and transfer are best produced when the learning situation offers a variety of experiences so as to better equip the student with the varieties of applications and changed conditions he will find in other school subjects and in out-of-school life.

HOW AND IN WHAT WAYS DOES TRANSFER OCCUR?

The most obvious form of transfer is that in which an identity carries over from one situation to another. The following are examples:

Transfer of an identity when a single response is appropriate to two stimuli:

Stimulus$_1$ "Casa" (in Spanish) ⟶
                                      Response—House
Stimulus$_2$ "Casa" (in Portuguese) ⟶

Negative transfer or interference when one stimulus requires two different responses:

Stimulus "Mas" (spoken)———————→Response 1 (Portuguese) But

—————————————————————→Response 2 (Spanish) More

This kind of transfer which is a result of stimulus similarity (or identities between two stimuli) was first treated systematically by Thorndike [1906], whose theory held that a function is changed by another only insofar as the two functions have identical or common elements of substance or procedure. Thorndike and . . . Woodworth [1901] began a series of investigations of the problem of transfer at the beginning of the century. They tested persons in one function, such as estimating the size of geometric figures, then gave practice in another function, such as estimating areas of a quite different magnitude. Finally, they retested them in the first function to see how much improvement was brought about by the intervening practice. They found that the amount of improvement in estimating size was inversely proportional to the degree of change in size and/or shape between the function initially tested and that which was practiced. They concluded that practice did not lead to a general change in such things as discrimination, attention, quickness, and the like, but that it improved these functions with respect to particular sorts of data.

STIMULUS GENERALIZATION

One may see quite clearly in the Portuguese-Spanish example how an identity transfers (with negative or positive effect) from one situation to another. In this case the only change is in the situation. But how about the case when the actual stimuli themselves are markedly changed?

One term applied to this kind of transfer is *stimulus generalization*. The young child who learns "dada," at first calls all men "dada." He says "ball" for his own particular ball and later applies this term to numerous other elastic objects regardless of changes in color, shape, and size. Stimulus generalization is not limited to the development of young children. Numerous studies have shown the same phenomenon in older children and adults.

A child who has become conditioned to fear one reading book, or one text, may show similar reactions when confronted with other books or texts. Likewise the dislike of one teacher may transfer to another teacher in a different classroom. In such cases youngsters overgeneralize from specific cases. They have not learned to make necessary discriminations.

TRANSFER AND THE LEARNING OF PRINCIPLES

Closely akin to stimulus generalization is the transfer of a general principle from one situation to another. Even before children are aware of it, they begin to generalize or make rules which they apply in several situations. Without ever being told a rule, they learn the generalization that most words form plurals by adding "s," hence "mouses" and "feets" are not uncommon in the speech of young children. Also the fact that "ed" makes the past tense of verbs, leads to such verb as "runned" and "doed."

One of the earliest experiments which showed how principles could influence subsequent behavior was that of Judd [1908], who used the principle of refraction of light when it travels from one medium into another. One group of boys was taught this principle, while a second group received no such instruction. Both groups were then given a trial in shooting bows and arrows at underwater targets. Although both groups did equally well when the targets were at a fixed depth, the instructed group excelled the other when the targets were moved to a new depth. The learning of the principle had made them more adaptable under changed conditions. More recently a similar experiment (using air-rifles instead of bows and arrows) obtained like results [Hendrickson and Schroeder, 1941].

What are the implications of this kind of transfer for teachers? Clearly a general principle has much broader possibilities for use than detailed facts. Also, . . . these kinds of learning are more enduring. It would seem then that a major emphasis of schooling should be upon principles and their use in a number of situations, rather than upon memorization of such details as may be quickly forgotten.

METHODS OF WORK AND TRANSFER

Students who have received practice and guidance in methods of work and study report that such training in one course helps them in other courses. Research dealing with both elementary and high school pupils showed that time spent in training children how to outline was rewarded with gains in achievement not only in the specific subject in which training was given but also in other subjects as well [Salisbury, 1935]. Any kind of "how to study" course is predicated on the belief that such training will generalize or transfer to other course material.

The pupil who learns a skill in one context should be able to apply it in many contexts. Thus a pupil who has learned in his English class the skills of outlining, note taking, reading, and participation in class discussion should be able to use these proficiencies in all of his courses. These skills are more apt to become generalized when:

1. The teacher uses examples from various subjects and materials as vehicles for the illustration and practice of methods and skills. (The English teacher might ask a student to use his history notes as material to be outlined.)

2. Students are asked (or ask each other) to explain why one method or skill is better than another. In other words, students are led to understand the rationale for various methods of work and study.

3.   The class as a whole, with the teacher's guidance, develops criteria for appraising various methods and skills.

4.   "Situational tests," which call for application of methods, give direction to students' work and bring more attention to method than tests which deal with facts. A part of the testing program might well involve exercises in which students were asked to point out relationships between solving a problem in geometry and one in social science or physics.

5.   Teachers work together toward this important common goal. The English teacher should work with others to determine whether writing skills show improvement in classes other than English.

ATTITUDES AND TRANSFER

A complex form of carry-over from previous experiences is the effect of previously formed attitudes upon new learning. The child who has had unpleasant emotional experiences in an English class will not approach the next class in English with the same attitudes as one whose experiences have been gratifying.

Since a person's attitude about himself (his self-concept) is quite likely to become overgeneralized, it is extremely important that youngsters obtain ideas of positive self-reference; that they see difficulties as problems to be solved rather than troubles which call for retreat. Such attitudes are products of successful and gratifying learning experiences. Insofar as such experiences are within the control of the teacher, pupils should receive due praise for their achievement especially when they solve problems under their own initiative.

TEACHING FOR TRANSFER

Good teaching always involves teaching for transfer. It is another way of saying that good teachers have a definite objective of making learned material a functioning part of the youngster's response system. It is thus essential that teachers think through their own subject matter and study the generalizations, relationships, and methods which may transfer. The extent to which students learn *how* to transfer will depend on how well teachers can lead students to see the similarities between the subject matter and its applications.

Following is a list of suggestions which should form the basis of teaching for transfer:

1.   Have clear-cut objectives. Decide what students should be able to *do* as a result of their work.

2.   Study the course content to find what it contains that is applicable to other school subjects and to out-of-school life.

3.   Select instructional materials which are best suited to the job of making relationships apparent.

4.   Let students know when to expect transfer, what kinds to expect, and the benefits which it can bring them.

5.   Use methods of teaching (e.g., problem-solving, discussion, leading questions) which will facilitate transfer.

6.   Provide practice in transfer. It is not enough to point out relationships. Pupils should be given practice in finding relationships on their own. Tests of application, guided discussion, and actual class projects ought to provide this kind of experience.

7.   Concentrate on the process of learning as well as upon products. Do not be satisfied with a right answer or solution, but probe to find out why a certain answer was given, and discuss with the class the steps which led to their answers.

EMPHASIZING RELATIONSHIPS AND UNDERSTANDING

Teachers who stress understanding tend to stimulate learning of a useful and an enduring nature. On the other hand, emphasis upon facts and memorization of rules and procedures which are not fully understood by pupils, may result in a superficial lip service which has neither permanence nor utility. A study of the learning of mathematics of three thousand pupils reveals that youngsters learn what teachers stress as important in the classroom. The school which glorifies abstract computation in mathematics is likely to produce pupils who excel in this respect, but who may or may not understand what they are doing or be able to use the computations in changing situations.

DIRECTING DISCOVERY

Experiments have indicated that the way in which a child learns a generalization will affect the probability of his recognizing a chance to use it. As Hendrix [1947] has shown, "persons who know that six times eight is forty-eight, will often count to forty-eight to find the number of chairs in a room containing six rows of eight chairs each." The question of how best to teach a generalization is of utmost importance to the teacher. Evidence shows that one important element may be discovery. One investigator compared methods in which the teacher gave the class a mathematical generalization and then gave several examples of application with methods in which the generalization was a product of the student's own discovery. The latter method proved much more effective in producing transfer [Hendrix, 1947].

Students actually resent too much supervision. It is only natural that teachers should want to help children, but in the very act of helping they may actually be robbing them of the chance to learn how to solve problems and use information.

Exactly what function, psychologically, is served by students' discovery is not at this time clear. Undoubtedly one of the major gains is an increased enthusiasm for the work. Teachers of the University of Illinois Committee on School Mathematics who have used the discovery method in much of their work have all noted the heightened motivation when students work things out for themselves, in fact a major aim of the project is that the study of mathematics be an adventure. Pupils should be encouraged to make their own mathematical discoveries. Some teachers believe the discovery process itself is so exhilarating that it becomes its own motive for academic work. It is likely that zest for work, self-confidence and ego-involvement may all be increased by the discovery process.

Aside from a greater zest for school work, the act of discovering something seems to assure a better understanding. This is not to say that students understand something only when they can manipulate objects as in a science laboratory, or do experimental work on their own. Many insights come from reading and listening. It is probable that the brighter students can make discoveries through verbal media better than can their less bright peers.

Finally, it seems likely that having once discovered something for himself the person achieves a "set" to discover other things. In short, he is applying the scientific method to his own thought processes. If the latter achievement is realized, there are indeed broad values to be attained by courses that allow students to find out things for themselves.

SUMMARY

Tranfer of learning is not a new idea to most persons who read this book. It must have occurred to everyone who has given serious thought to teaching, that ultimately class work is designed to equip pupils to solve effectively the problems of living and to make them happier and more effective citizens. These goals are apparent.

Too often, however, teachers and pupils alike neglect to think through the significance of present activities in terms of future usefulness or applicability. One reason for this is that, although everyone shares the above stated desires about transfer, attempts to reach it are blocked by common, erroneous notions about it. Some of these erroneous notions are:

1. That training *per se* strengthens an ability,
2. That only that which is immediately useful should be taught,
3. That transfer is automatic, in other words, that once a child learns, the learning will lead to transfer, and
4. That transfer and learning are separable elements.

Transfer may occur when there is a similarity between two activities either in substance or procedure. Anything which can be learned can be transferred including such things as attitudes, a feeling of self-confidence, sets, and interests, as well as skills, facts, and other items generally thought of as constituting school work. Transfer may be quite specific, as when elements of one learning situation occur in identical or similar form in another. In such cases the effects may be either positive or negative, that is, a previous learning may either facilitate a new learning, or may cause interference. Also transfer may be general, in that a given learning such as a principle, a set, or method has influence upon any number of later learning situations.

Teaching for transfer requires that the objectives of schooling be clearly defined, that teachers study content and method to find interrelationships among materials and the applicability to other situations or learned skills, and that the teaching method be such that students are given practice in transfer. Children should learn to expect to see a relationship between present learning and future situations. They should also learn not only to search for such relationships, but also to probe into problems to find reasons for the facts and principles which they are asked to believe. Out of the habit of critical appraisal youngsters will develop the ability to bring past experiences to bear upon the new problems and new learning situations.

REFERENCES

Hendrickson, G., and Schroeder, W. H. Transfer of training in learning to hit a submerged target. *Journal of Educational Psychology,* 1941, 32: 205–13.

Hendrix, G. A new clue to transfer of training. *Elementary School Journal,* 1947, 48: 197–208.

Hildreth, G. An evaluation of spelling word lists and vocabulary studies. *Elementary School Journal,* 1951, 51: 254–65.

Judd, C. H. The relation of special training to general intelligence. *Educational Review,* 1908, 36: 28–42.

Mead, A. R. Transfer of training again. *Journal of Educational Psychology,* 1946, 37: 391–97.

Salisbury, R. Some effects of training in outlining. *English Journal* (College Edition), 1935, 24: 111–16.

Spaulding, F. T. *High school and Life: Report of the Regents' Inquiry into the Character and Cost of Public Education in the State of New York.* New York: McGraw-Hill, 1939.

Thorndike, E. L. *The Principles of Teaching.* New York: A. G. Seiler, 1906.

Thorndike, E. L. The effect of changed data upon reasoning. *Journal of Experimental Psychology,* 1922, 5: 33–38.

Thorndike, E. L. Mental discipline in high school studies. *Journal of Educational Psychology,* 1924, 15: 1–22, 83–98.

Thorndike, E. L., and Woodworth, R. S. The influence of improvement in one mental function upon the efficiency of other functions. *Psychological Review,* 1901, 8: 247–61, 384–95, 553–64.

Wesman, A. G. A study of transfer of training from high school subjects to intelligence. *Journal of Educational Research,* 1945, 39: 254–64.

REVIEW QUESTIONS

1.   How much of your own elementary and secondary school learning "transferred" to later situations? Were the nontransferable skills and information wasted?

2.   Do many aspects of the educational psychology course you are now taking contribute to your understanding of classroom learning and teaching? Which do and which do not?

3.   Do you "read constructively"? That is, do you ask yourself how this material *will* transfer to real-world situations?

part ii

PERSPECTIVES IN
HUMAN DEVELOPMENT

The impact of Jean Piaget at least rivals that of B. F. Skinner. The reason is simple—both men are fantastically brilliant and perceptive, and both are dedicated to understanding the world's most complicated animal. Currently, the average college course on human development almost amounts to a course on Jean Piaget. In article 13, Read Tuddenham sketches a brief biography of Piaget, along with some main Piagetian ideas. The reader should look especially for the concepts of *schema, assimilation* and *accommodation, equilibrium,* and most important, for his four stages of cognitive growth—*sensory motor, preoperational, concrete operations,* and *formal operations.*

Another outstanding psychologist-educator is Jerome Bruner. In article 14 Bruner summarizes the results of two years of studying and speculating upon interrelationships between education and human development. Did we say *human*? Bruner creatively stood back—way back—and compared the "education" of young East African baboons to that of Kung Bushmen children and children in more complex societies. Baboon juveniles seemed to learn adult protective behaviors by play-practice with their peers. Kung children, however, learn directly from adults in playing, story telling, and hunting and from playing imitatively with tools and weapons. In literate societies, we find the strange concept of "school," with its abstract "practice," "drill," and "rote learning." Bruner also summarizes how a culture provides *amplifiers* of action, senses, and thought, and explains conditions necessary for successful cultural transmission. In order to stimulate thinking and sensitize fifth-grade children to the human condition, Bruner outlines the content and problems of *A Course in Man,* created by a group of anthropologists, zoologists, linguists, engineers, and many others.

The moral development of a child is a topic of interest not only to the scholar, but also to the teacher faced with moral sensitivities related to, for example, a trivial fib, a drug transaction, political assassinations, the Vietnam War, and sermons on the good life. In article 15 developmental psychologist Lawrence Kohlberg describes three levels of moral thinking, each with two substages, which he identified during a twelve-year study of seventy-five boys. In an oversimplification, his six stages begin with the *preconventional* child, responsive to potentially punishing superior power (stage 1) and then to need satisfaction (stage 2). Stage 3 of the *conventional* level is based upon approval seeking, while in stage 4 the child responds more to fixed rules and legitimate authority. At the *postconventional* level, moral beliefs in stage 5 stem from society's critically examined rights and standards. The highest level of moral development, stage 6, centers upon abstract self-chosen ethical principles such as the golden rule. According to Kohlberg, the speed of progressing through the stages may vary with culture, religion, or socioeconomic level, but the order in which one passes through the six stages is absolutely invariant.

Piaget's writings during 1929 included the concept of animistic thinking—the imputation of life and lifelike qualities to inanimate objects. In article 16 William Looft summarizes four developmental stages of animistic thinking proposed by Piaget: attributing life to *usefulness* or *activity in general* (age 4–6 years), to *things that move* (6–7 years), to *things that move spontaneously* (8–10 years), and finally to the adult-level *plants and animals* (11 and older). In the remainder of this article, Looft reviews psychological research on animistic thinking in normal and retarded children, and even in adults. The author also pinpoints problems of semantics and response bias that contaminate research and then discusses the theoretical alternative that in fact, animistic thinking does not exist.

Psychologists have uncovered a surprising number of traits and behavior patterns that differentiate first-born from later-born children. For example, no less than ninety-four per cent of our American Astronauts are first born. Looking specifically at educational matters, Richard Bradley, in article 17, points to the high numbers of first-born children who win scholarships and attend college. While first-borns may or may not be innately more intelligent than second- and later-borns, they tend to be more dependent, which leads them to be achievement oriented. First-borns also tend to be less interested in athletics and in popularity and are less aggressive.

thirteen

Jean Piaget and the World of the Child

READ D. TUDDENHAM

It is difficult to characterize Piaget's work, for it is both deep and broad in scope. He has been in turn a biologist, psychologist, philosopher, and logician, and in all four fields he has made major contributions. He is currently Professor of Psychology at the University of Geneva and at the Sorbonne. He is coeditor of the *Archives de Psychologie* and of the *Revue Suisse de Psychologie*. He is Director of the Institut des Sciences de l'Éducation (successor to the Institut Jean Jacques Rousseau), founder of the Centre d'Epistemologie Génétique, and Director of the Bureau International de l'Éducation, an affiliate of the United Nations Educational, Scientific, and Cultural Organization, which entitles him to the black passport of diplomatic status. Widely traveled, he has been honored by many foreign universities and governments. He is a member of the French Légion d'Honneur and holds honorary doctorates from the Sorbonne, from Brussels, Brandeis, Harvard, and other universities.

Since his book, *Language and Thought of the Child* appeared in 1923, Piaget and his collaborators have published more than twenty full-length books and largely filled thirty bulky annual volumes of the *Archives de Psychologie;* in all, over 180 major studies covering thousands of pages, of which the barest fraction has been translated into English. I am acquainted with only a small part of this fantastic productivity, and considering the brief time at my disposal, it may be just as well that my knowledge of it is not encyclopedic. In any case you will understand why this talk is scarcely a preface to an introduction to Piaget.

Now in spite of his stature in the field, there is nothing remotely pretentious about Piaget. As many of you know, he paid a brief visit to Berkeley in March 1964. If you were fortunate enough to attend his evening lecture, I need not tell you of his personal charm and wit which withstood the rigors of translation from one language to another. For those who did not attend, a word of description may not be amiss.

Source: Abridged from *American Psychologist*, 1966, 21:207–17. Copyright 1966 by the American Psychological Association. Reprinted by permission of the author and the publisher.

Imagine a man approaching seventy, a man of average build, of clear and ruddy complexion, and with snow-white hair worn long over his collar. He moves deliberately, but his blue eyes sparkle with youth, good humor, and zest. Benevolent enough, but not heavy enough, to look like Santa Claus, he reminds one faintly of the pictures of Franz Liszt that have come down to us. A man of great vigor, he still bicycles the several miles from his home to his office in the Palais Wilson and back again each day; and despite a man-killing schedule of conferences and meetings here in Berkeley, he wore out relays of us who tried to entertain him, and had energy left to spare for private hikes in Strawberry Canyon.

It was my privilege to introduce him to San Francisco on a Sunday of perfect temperature and brilliant sunshine. He found San Francisco "formidable," but astonished me by saying that what he particularly wanted to do, was drive the Lombard Street hill, "the one that curves back and forth like a snake." I had never driven it and did not much want to, so I took him up to Coit Tower in the hope he would settle for seeing the street in the distance. He enjoyed the view from Telegraph Hill and appreciated not only the tower itself but also its name. (Parenthetically, there has been some question about the influence of Freud upon Piaget. There is not much evidence of influence, but I assure anyone who doubts it, that he is familiar with psychoanalytic symbolism and loves a pun.) — But then he said, "Now let's go drive down the twisting street." — So there was no help for it. We went, and a child on a roller coaster could not have enjoyed the steep climb and abrupt descent any more than he did.

Later he admired Sausalito and Muir Woods, but although a passionate botanist by avocation, his real affection is reserved not for redwoods, but for succulents—especially sedums. If there are present today any residents of Mill Valley, you may have seen us stopping before several gardens containing sedums, while Piaget got out and took a promising cutting to carry back to Geneva. If a policeman had stopped us, I would probably have just kept still and left it to Piaget's warm smile and eloquent French to keep us out of jail.

Now Piaget's botanical interests represent, to a degree, a change from his earliest interest, which was in zoology. Born in Neuchâtel in 1896, he published his first paper when he was ten years old on an albino sparrow he found hopping in the public garden. His interest soon turned to molluscs. Before he was twenty-one, he had published twenty papers on molluscs and related topics, and had been offered sight unseen the curatorship of molluscs at Geneva while still in secondary school. He took his baccalaureate at Neuchâtel in 1915 followed by his doctorate in 1918.

Throughout these early years he read widely in other fields—religion, philosophy, and psychology. He came thus to the view that biology should contribute to the solution of classical problems in epistemology, but realized that something was needed to bridge the two. In later years, his developmental psychology came to provide the link, culminating in his three-volume work of 1950 on genetic epistemology, unfortunately still untranslated.

After receiving his doctorate, his interests shifted more explicitly to psychology, and he left Neuchâtel to visit and study at various other centers, including

Bleuler's psychiatric clinic and the Sorbonne. Binet had died in 1911, but in Paris, Piaget was given the opportunity by Simon, Binet's collaborator in the Simon-Binet tests, to work in Binet's old laboratory at a Paris grade school. The problem suggested was a standardization of Burt's reasoning tests on Paris school children. Although Piaget was not much interested in the psychometric aspects of the problem, he found himself fascinated by the processes whereby the child achieved his answers—and wrong answers were often more enlightening than right ones.

The psychiatric examining procedures learned at Bleuler's clinic were pressed into service to elucidate the child's reasoning, and came ultimately to constitute the *méthode clinique* by which much of Piaget's data have been collected. This method of intensive interrogation is common enough among psychiatrists, but it is likely to scandalize the American psychologist trained in the canons of objectivity and standardization of procedure, because it risks leading the child and putting words in his mouth. Yet in skillful hands, it yields subtle insights which our "measurement" approach precludes.

In view of his work in Binet's laboratory, it is interesting to trace Piaget's relation to the great French psychologist who had died when Piaget was in adolescence. Certainly Piaget has relatively little in common with the Binet of the famous intelligence tests, because Piaget has never been much interested in mental testing or in individual differences. But he has much in common with the Binet of earlier years, whose interests, like Piaget's, ranged over much of science. More specifically, he seems the direct heir of the Binet who wrote the famous volume *The Psychology of Reasoning*, a book which anticipates Piaget in its concern with the subtle qualitative aspects of thought, and further anticipates him in the employment of the psychologist's own children as experimental subjects—a procedure which might be impractical in this country where statistically adequate samples of forty or fifty are a desideratum for the simplest investigation!

In 1921 Piaget published four papers describing the results of his work with Burt's tests and other such problems. On the strength of them, Claparède, who was then the Professor of Psychology at Geneva, invited Piaget to the post of Director of Studies at the Institut Jean Jacques Rousseau, and Piaget accepted. Although at first he divided his time between Geneva and Neuchâtel, and until fairly recently spent part of each week at the Sorbonne, his work for the last forty years has been largely identified with the University of Geneva.

In all the vast corpus of Piaget's work are there unifying trends or concerns which can serve to orient us in this brief survey? Apart from his zoological studies and a few mathematical papers on logic as such, the central preoccupation has been with epistemology—the fundamental problem of how we come to know our world. But this problem is approached, not via traditional philosophical speculation, but rather via scientific observation and experimentation, although sometimes of an unconventional kind. The subjects are infants, children, and adolescents, and the emphasis is always developmental.

Some of this work is on perception, and is concerned with discovering the laws of perceptual development and the differences between perceptual and cognitive functions. To this end, the Geneva workers have shown a persistent interest in optical illusions. For example, they have systematically altered various aspects of the stimulus configuration and measured the magnitude and direction of the observer's errors as a function of his age. These perception studies, over forty in number, are more rigorous and quantitative than the studies on cognitive development, and substitute for the *méthode clinique* the traditional experimental approach.

In summary, Piaget finds a general tendency, though by no means a linear one, nor one found in all instances, whereby perceptual judgments grow more accurate with age. However, he regards perceptual development as essentially continuous, and he does not consider that the developmental stages, which are so important in his cognitive theory, exist in the perceptual domain. Indeed, he has repeatedly contrasted the perceptual versus the conceptual or inferential process even in the young child, and emphasized that the two functions follow very different paths in development. Wohlwill [1962] has suggested that Piaget's denial of stages in perception while affirming them for cognition stems not from the finding that ontogenetic change in perception is necessarily more gradual, but rather because the differences between successive perceptual achievements are only quantitative, whereas one can find structural criteria—that is to say the presence or absence of particular logical operations—to differentiate the stages of conceptual development.

Let us turn first to Piaget's theory of cognitive development. Here a confusing situation arises for the English-speaking student. Piaget's four important books of the early 1920's were translated fairly promptly into English in the first flurry of interest in his work. These volumes—*Language and Thought of the Child, Judgment and Reasoning in the Child, The Child's Conception of Physical Causality,* and *The Moral Judgment of the Child*—are widely available. It is their contents—the famous inquiries about what makes clouds move, the origins of dreams, the basis of rules for games, and a host of other such topics—which come to mind for many people when Piaget is mentioned.

Now these works were gradually superseded in Piaget's theoretical formulations, but the point has not been sufficiently appreciated. In this country, there was a decline of interest in Piaget during what Koch [1959] has called the "Age of Theory" in American psychology—roughly from the early '30's to the end of the war—a tough-minded period dominated by the rules of "hypothetico-deduction" and "operational definition" and animated by belief in the imminence of a precisely quantitative behavior theory. Piaget's work was not easily reconciled with the fashions of the period, and little was translated. Now the tide has turned, and at least a portion of Piaget's recent work is available in English, not to mention several excellent "explanations" of him by Wolff [1960], Wohlwill [1960], Hunt [1961], and especially Flavell's comprehensive volume of 1963. However, the essential continuity of development of Piaget's ideas is obscured by the discontinuity of translation. So different are the recent works from the old ones, that to read them one must master a new vocabulary and a new theoretical formulation, and this time the task is made more difficult by the heavy emphasis upon propositions of symbolic logic to explicate the developmental stages of reasoning.

To the early Piaget belonged the painstaking compilation of the forms of verbal expression according to age level from three years to ten years: the demonstration that children's "explanations" of phenomena pass through *stages,* from early animistic, through magical and artificialist forms, to rational thought, and that at each level, the child constructs a systematic "cosmology" according to the modes of reasoning available to him at this stage. The empirical bases for these finding were the children's verbalizations as elicited by the *méthode clinique,* with its inherent risks of misinterpretation of what the child is trying to express. Piaget was severely and perhaps unjustly criticized on this account, for he was sharply aware of the problem. As he put it [1929],

> It is so hard not to talk too much when questioning a child, especially for a pedagogue! It is so hard not suggest! And above all, it is so hard to find the middle course between systematization due to preconceived ideas, and incoherence due to the absence of any directing hypothesis! . . . In short, it is no simple task, and the material it yields needs to be subjected to the strictest criticism [p. 8].

In retrospect, Piaget [1952a] recognizes that his method in those years was much too exclusively verbal.

> I well knew that thought proceeds from action, but believed then that language directly reflects the act, and that to understand the logic of the child one has to look for it in the domain of verbal interactions. It was only by studying the patterns of intelligent behavior of *the first two years* that I learned that for a complete understanding of the genesis of intellectual operations, manipulation and experience with objects had first to be considered [p. 247].

As Piaget notes, the shift from reliance on verbalization to observation and experiment is most important for genetic epistemology because it permits one to study infants as well as the later stages of growth, and by more or less comparable methods.

The cognitive theory starts from the central postulate that motor action is the source from which mental operations emerge. The *action* of the organism is central to the acquisitions of the operations (i.e., ideas, or strategies), which we acquire for coping with the world. In the Hegelian dialectical form which his lectures often assume, Piaget contrasts his emphasis upon the active interplay of organism and environment, both with the environmentalist view in which experience or conditioning is impressed upon a passive organism, and with the nativist view that intellectual capabilities exist preformed and merely unfold in the course of development.

Motor action is *adaptive,* and so are the cognitive activities which more and more replace motor behavior. Piaget's biological orientation is seen in his assertion that intelligence is an adaptation, and only one aspect of biological adaptation. Intelligence is an organizing activity which extends the biological organization. With respect to intelligence, a subject to which Piaget has given much attention, it should be noted that his interest is in the typical, not in the range of variation. For him, the word "intelligence" lacks the mental-testing connotations with which it is usually invested in English, and corresponds rather to "intellect" or to intellectual activity or adaptation.

Life is a continuous creation of increasingly complex forms, and a progressive balancing of these forms with the environment [Piaget, 1952b, p. 3].

Intellectual adaptation is the progressive differentiation and integration of inborn reflex mechanisms under the impact of experience. The differentiation of inborn reflex structures and their functions give rise to the mental operations by which man conceives of objects, space, time, and causality, and of the logical relationships which constitute the basis of scientific thought. [Wolff, 1960, p. 9].

Another central postulate is that intellectual operations acquired by interaction between organism and environment are acquired in a *lawful sequence*. It should be emphasized again that Piaget's concern is with elucidating the sequence, *not* with establishing exact age norms for its stages. It should also be noted that Piaget has set out to write the ontogenetic history of cognition—*not* a complete account of personality development. What lies outside the cognitive domain is rigorously excluded.

The innate equipment consists of reflexes present at birth. A few reflexes, e.g., yawning or sneezing, are relatively fixed and unmodifiable by experience, though some, like the Babinski, change with maturation. The majority of reflexes, for example, grasping, *require* stimulation for their stabilization, are modified as a result of experience, and constitute the basic behavioral units from which more complex forms of behavior emerge. Most important, the feedback from the activation of a reflex alters all subsequent performance of that reflex. Thus, behavior is simultaneously determined by: first, the inborn structure; second, past activations, i.e., experience; and third, the particular present situation.

Now corresponding to each innate reflex there is assumed to exist in the mind a reflex *schema,* which will not become a stable structure unless repeatedly activated by external stimulation. The concept of schema is difficult. It is described as a flexible mental structure, the primary unit of mental organization. It is too invested with motor connotations to translate as "idea"; and being initially innate, it can hardly be a memory trace. Yet it covers both, and when fully developed bears some resemblance to Tolman's sign Gestalt.

When a reflex responds to a suitable external stimulus, the total sensory perception *and* motor activity are incorporated into the schema of that reflex, and change it; so that when the reflex is again stimulated, the schema has been modified. The stimulus is never again experienced in quite the same way, nor is the response quite the same. Thus the schema is invoked to account for the modification of response, *and* for the alteration of perception in the course of learning. In other words, the organism experiences and reacts to the environment always in terms of an existing organization. All experiences of a particular kind are molded into the already present schema, and in turn alter it according to the reality conditions. Hence, experiences are not recorded as isolated stimulus-response connections, or engrams impressed on a passive brain field, but are integrated into a constantly changing structure.

For the dual aspects of learning, Piaget has used the terms *assimilation* and *accommodation*. He points out first that there exists a fundamental coordination or tuning of the organism to its environment. We have eyes and skin receptors preadapted for the photic and thermal radiation found on earth, ears for sensing rapid waves of pressure in earth's atmosphere, and so forth. There exists, moreover, a fundamental tendency of organisms to take in substances and stimulations for which there already exist the appropriate internal structures and organization. This taking in is called *assimilation*. At a biological level, it refers to the physical incorporation of suitable nutrients into organic structure. At a primitive psychological level, it refers to the incorporation of the sensory and motor components of a behavioral act into the reflex schema they have activated. At more complex levels, assimilation refers to the tendency of the mental apparatus to incorporate ideas into a complex system of thought schemata.

Parallel to assimilation is the function of *accommodation*, i.e., the process by which a schema *changes* so as to adapt better to the assimilated reality. At the biological level, accommodation refers to modification of the organism in response to stimulation, e.g., skin tanning in response to sunlight, or muscle growth in response to exercise. At the lowest psychological level, it refers to the gradual adaptation of the reflexes to new stimulus conditions—what others have called conditioning or stimulus generalization. At higher levels it refers to the coordination of thought patterns to one another and to external reality.

While assimilation and accommodation seem not too far from conventional learning theory, the concept of *aliment* is more unfamiliar. Whatever can be assimilated to a schema is aliment for that schema. Now the aliment is not the *object* which seems from the point of view of the observer to activate behavior, but rather those properties of the object which are assimilated and accommodated to. For example, a nursing bottle filled with milk may be organic aliment for the metabolism, sucking aliment for the reflex sucking schema, and visual aliment for the visual schema. And if the idea strikes you as bizarre that a reflex requires to be fed, as it were, by appropriate stimulation, consider Riesen's [1947] report on the degeneration of the visual apparatus in chimpanzees reared in the dark—or the more familiar degeneration of unstimulated muscles when polio destroys the motor pathways.

Why the careful distinction between an object and its properties? Because for the infant the object does not exist! The idea of an object grows gradually out of the coordination of several schemata—that which is perceived by several sensorial avenues *becomes* the object. At first, the infant has not even awareness of the boundaries of his own body. Objects in the perceptual field—including his own hands and feet—are responded to according to the infant's limited reflexive repertoire. He sucks in response to oral stimulation, grasps in response to palmar stimulation, but makes no attempt to grasp the nursing bottle which he competently sucks, or to follow visually the bottle he can clutch if placed in his hand. Only gradually, by a process called generalizing assimilation, do stimuli which were initially specific aliment for one schema become aliment for other schemata. In parallel accommodation, a schema becomes attuned to more complex inputs, and tends to become coordinated with other schemata which are simultaneously activated. When this happens, things previously known tactilely by being grasped can be recognized by sight alone. Similarly, grasping attempts of increasing accuracy can be directed toward sources of visual stimulation. In such a fashion does the baby come to populate the world with objects, one of which is his own body, which supplies him at once with visual, tactile and kinesthetic stimuli—and when he cries, with auditory ones.

However, the infant still does not attach the concept of permanence to objects. "Out of sight" is quite literally "out of mind." One of Piaget's most interesting experiments—and one which can be repeated by any parent of an infant —concerns the growth of the idea of permanent objects. If you catch a young baby's attention with a small toy, and then hide it, he will make little response. When somewhat older, he will show diffuse motor behavior. If now he once happens to touch it, he will gradually learn to search more efficiently where the object is hidden. However, if the object is hidden in a different place, in full sight of the baby, he will search not where he saw it hidden, but where previously he had touched it. It is an intellectual achievement of some magnitude when the very young child learns to coordinate the space of things seen with the space of things touched, and seeks to touch an object where hitherto he has only seen it.

We can conclude our rapid survey of Piaget's basic concepts with a brief reference to *equilibrium*. Bruner [1959], otherwise most sympathetic, regards the notion of equilibrium as excess baggage, contributing to Piaget a comforting sense of continuity with biology, but offering little else. Perhaps the idea of disequilibrium is more easily described. A schema is in disequilibrium if adaptation (i.e., assimilation and accommodation) to the stimulus is incomplete.

It seems to me that the ideas of equilibrium and disequilibrium constitute most of Piaget's theory of motivation, which is a rather underelaborated part of his psychological system. The organism has a basic need to continue contact with an object as long as adaptation to it is incomplete—or, as Piaget would say, as long as the corresponding schema is in disequilibrium. The need for commerce with an object persists until the child's behavior has been wholly adapted to whatever novelty it presents, that is to say, it persists until the child has acquired mastery. Once accommodation is complete and assimilation is total, the schema is said to be "in equilibrium," and there is no further adaptation. There is, in short, no learning without a problem.

Further, two *schemata* are in disequilibrium until they have mutually accommodated and assimilated, and thereby been integrated into a new superordinate mental structure. This tendency to integrate schemata into more and more complex wholes is assumed by Piaget to be a native propensity of the mind, and as fundamental as the tendency toward equilibrium in physical systems. To put the matter in less cosmic terms, the person strives continually for more and more comprehensive mastery of his world. At each *stage*, however, he is concerned with those things which lie just beyond his intellectual grasp—far enough away to present a novelty to be assimilated, but not so far but what accommodation is possible. Phenomena too simple—i.e., already in equilibrium—and phenomena too complex for present adaptation are ignored in favor of those in the critical range. Anyone who has ever watched the persistence, and resistance to satiation, of a baby intent on mastering a developmental task—for example, learning to walk—will agree with Piaget as to the strength of the motivation, whether or not he accepts Piaget's thermodynamic metaphor.

What then are the general *stages* of intellectual development, and how may they be characterized? Piaget's stages are one of the best known aspects of his work, but he has not been altogether consistent either in the number of them or in the names assigned. Moreover, the stages are linked to particular chronological ages only rather loosely, and Piaget has himself offered data to show that the age at which a particular stage is reached differs for different content domains. For example, conservation (i.e., invariance under transformation) of a plastic object, such as a lump of clay, is acquired first with respect to mass, a year or so later with respect to weight, and a couple of years after that with respect to volume. Moreover, the Geneva group are concerned to demonstrate the invariance of the *sequence* of stages, not the age at which a given stage is achieved. In Martinique the children are four years retarded compared to those in Montreal [Laurendeau and Pinard, 1963], and certain Brazilian Indians appear never to achieve the last stage—but the sequence is everywhere the same.

When Piaget visited Berkeley, he deplored the preoccupation of American psychologists with accelerating a child's progress through the successive stages, and commented on recent work of Gruber, who found that kittens achieve awareness of the permanence of objects in three months, the human baby only in nine months; but the important fact is that the cat never acquires the power to think in terms of formal logic, and the human being may!

The more recent books from Geneva usually divide development into four stages: the sensorimotor, from birth to two or three years; the preoperational stage, from around two to around seven years; the stage of concrete operations, from roughly seven years to eleven or twelve; and finally the stage of formal operations. Each stage in turn has substages—no less than six for the sensorimotor period alone. . . .

The sensorimotor period as a whole (i.e., from birth up to age two) carries the child from inborn reflexes to acquired behavior patterns. It leads the child from a body-centered (i.e., self-centered) world to an object-centered one. During this period the various sensory spaces, of vision, touch, and the rest, are coordinated into a single space and objects evolve from their separate sensory properties into *things* with multiple properties, permanence, and spatial relationships to other objects. Altogether this stage comprises a most important set of intellectual achievements.

The preoperational stage (two years to around seven years) covers the impor-

tant period when language is acquired. This permits the child to deal symboli-
cally with the world instead of directly through motor activity, though his
problem solving tends to be "action ridden." The child is himself still the focus
of his own world, and space and time are centered on him. Time is only "before
now," "now," and "not yet"; and space moves as the child moves. When he is
taken for an evening walk, the moon follows *him*. Traces of this attitude are
present even in adults, who often locate places and things in terms of distance
and direction from themselves, rather than in terms of objective spatial relationships. By a process of "decentering," the child during this stage learns gradually
to conceive of a time scale and of a spatial world which exist independent of
himself. In dealing with physical objects and quantities, the child pays attention
to one aspect to the neglect of other aspects. He concludes, for example, that
there is more water in a glass graduate than in a beaker—though he has just
seen it poured from the one vessel into the other—because in the graduate the
column of water is taller, and the child neglects the reduction in diameter.

The stage of concrete operations has its beginnings as early as age six or seven.
Now the child grows less dependent upon his own perceptions and motor actions
and shows a capacity for reasoning, though still at a very concrete level. Among
his "logical" acquisitions are classifying, ordering in series, and numbering.
Asked to put a handful of sticks in order by length, he need no longer make all
the pair comparisons but can pick out the longest, then the longest one left, and
so forth, until the series is complete. When shown that Stick A is longer than
Stick B, and Stick B is longer than Stick C, he can infer without actual demonstration that A is longer than C.

Here at Berkeley, my students and I have been developing test materials
based on Piaget experiments, and intended to measure the abilities of children in
the primary grades, i.e., at the transition point from the perceptual attitude of
the preoperational stage to the reasoning attitude of the stage of concrete operations. Thus far, fifteen tests have been developed and administered to more
than 300 school children. Although we abandoned the *méthode clinique* for a
strictly standardized psychometric approach, we have observed precisely the
same types of behavior which Piaget had previously reported.

The last of Piaget's major stages of intellectual development begins usually
somewhere around eleven or twelve years and matures a couple of years later. He
calls it the stage of formal operations. Now the child can deal with abstract relationships instead of with things, with the form of an argument while ignoring
its content. For the first time he can intellectually manipulate the merely hypothetical, and systematically evaluate a lengthy set of alternatives. He learns to
handle the logical relationships of Identity (I), Negation (N), Reciprocity (R),
and Correlation (C), which permit him to deal with problems of proportion-
ality, probability, permutations, and combinations.

I have just referred to the INRC logical group whose acquisition marks the
last stage of intellectual growth. In Piaget's writings over the years, the char-

acteristics of each stage and the differences between them have increasingly been formulated in the notation of symbolic logic—a circumstance which does not increase the comprehensibility of his latest books for nonmathematicians.

What finally are the implications of Piaget's work? . . . Certainly they have a major bearing upon education.

If Piaget is correct—and much work now substantiates his empirical findings at least in broad outline—methods of education will be most effective when they are attuned to the patterns of thought which are natural to a child of the age concerned. It may not be true that you can teach a child *anything* if your approach is correct, but it does look as if you can teach him a great deal more than anyone might have guessed. Of course, teachers long before Piaget recognized intuitively that a child learned better when problems were approached at a concrete rather than at an abstract level. But there is more to it than that. Bruner, at Harvard, and others in this country are attempting to find ways to introduce children to some of the abstract ideas of mathematics—for example, the algebraic concept of squaring a number—by concrete, geometric models. They hope thus possibly to accelerate a child's progress—a goal which Piaget has his reservations about. Perhaps the most dramatic evidence of a revolution which owes a great deal of its impetus to Piaget is the new elementary school mathematics, in which children even in the lower grades are being taught, and learning, and actually enjoying learning basic arithmetical and geometrical ideas introduced via set theory, which most of their parents have never heard of.

I could not better conclude this appreciation of Piaget than by quoting from William James [1890] who wrote seventy-five years ago in his famous *Principles of Psychology* as follows: "To the infant, sounds, sights, touches and pains form probably one unanalyzed bloom of confusion [p. 496]." We can now go beyond the philosopher's speculations and describe in some detail how the unanalyzed "bloom of confusion" of the infant becomes the world of the child—in which not only objects, but time, space, causality and the rest acquire a coherent organization. And we owe this achievement in large measure to the analyses of Jean Piaget.

REFERENCES

Bruner, J. S. Inhelder and Piaget's *The Growth of Logical Thinking*. I. A psychologist's viewpoint. *British Journal of Psychology*, 1959, 50: 363–70.

Flavell, J. H. *The Developmental Psychology of Jean Piaget*. Princeton, N.J.: Van Nostrand, 1963.

Hunt, J. McV. *Intelligence and Experience*. New York: Ronald Press, 1961.

James, W. *The Principles of Psychology*. New York: Holt, 1890.

Koch, S. (Ed.) *Psychology: A Study of a Science*. Vol. 3. *Formulations of the Person and the Social Context*. New York: McGraw-Hill, 1959.

Laurendeau, Monique, and Pinard, A. *Causal Thinking in the Child, a Genetic and Experimental Approach*. New York: International Universities Press, 1963.

Piaget, J. *The Child's Conception of the World*. New York: Harcourt, Brace, 1929.

Piaget, J. Autobiography. In E. G. Boring (Ed.), *A History of Psychology in Autobiography*. Vol. 4. Worcester, Mass.: Clark Univer. Press, 1952. (a)

Piaget, J. *The Origins of Intelligence in Children*. (2nd ed.) New York: International Universities Press, 1952. (b)

Riesen, A. H. The development of visual perception in man and chimpanzee. *Science*, 1947, 106, 107–108.

Wohlwill, J. F. Developmental studies of perception. *Psychological Bulletin*, 1960, 57: 249–88.

Wohlwill, J. F. From perception to inference: A dimension of cognitive development. In W. Kessen and Clementina Kuhlman (Eds.), Thought in the young child. *Monographs of the Society for Research in Child Development*, 1962, 27(2, Whole No. 83).

Wolff, P. H. The developmental psychologies of Jean Piaget and psychoanalysis. *Psychological Issues*, 1960, 2(1, Whole No. 5).

REVIEW QUESTIONS

1. What do Piaget's stages tell you about adjusting the learning experiences to the child?

2. Were your schemas related to child development put in a state of disequilibrium as a result of assimilating and accommodating Piaget's ideas?

fourteen

The Growth of Mind

JEROME S. BRUNER

These past several years, I have had the painful pleasure—and it has been both—of exploring two aspects of the cognitive processes that were new to me. One was cognitive development, the other pedagogy. I knew, as we all know, that the two were closely related, and it was my naive hope that, betimes, the relation would come clear to me. Indeed, two years ago when I first knew that in early September 1965 I would be standing here, delivering this lecture, I said to myself that I would use the occasion to set forth to my colleagues what I had been able to find out about this vexed subject, the relation of pedagogy and development. It seemed obvious then that in two years one could get to the heart of the matter.

The two years have gone by. I have had the privilege of addressing this distinguished audience [Bruner, 1964] on some of our findings concerning the development of cognitive processes in children, and I have similarly set forth what I hope are not entirely unreasonable ideas about pedagogy [Bruner, 1966]. I am still in a very deep quandary concerning the relation of these two enterprises. The heart of the matter still eludes me, but I shall stand by my resolve. I begin on this autobiographical note so that you may know in advance why this evening is more an exercise in conjecture than a cataloguing of solid conclusions.

UNIQUENESS OF MAN

What is most unique about man is that his growth as an individual depends upon the history of his species—not upon a history reflected in genes and chromosomes but, rather, reflected in a culture external to man's tissue and wider in scope than is embodied in any one man's competency. Perforce, then, the growth of mind is always growth assisted from the outside. And since a culture,

Source: From *American Psychologist*, 1965, 20:1007–17. Copyright 1965 by the American Psychological Association. Reprinted by permission of the author and the publisher.

particularly an advanced one, transcends the bounds of individual competence, the limits for individual growth are by definition greater than what any single person has previously attained. For the limits of growth depend on how a culture assists the individual to use such intellectual potential as he may possess. It seems highly unlikely—either empirically or canonically—that we have any realistic sense of the furthest reach of such assistance to growth.

The evidence today is that the full evolution of intelligence came as a result of bipedalism and tool using. The large human brain gradually evolved as a sequel to the first use of pebble tools by early near-man. To condense the story, a near-man, or hominid, with a slightly superior brain, using a pebble tool, could make out better in the niche provided by nature than a near-man who depended not on tools but on sheer strength and formidable jaws. Natural selection favored the primitive tool user. In time, thanks to his better chance of surviving and breathing, he became more so: The ones who survived had larger brains, smaller jaws, less ferocious teeth. In place of belligerent anatomy, they developed tools and a brain that made it possible to use them. Human evolution thereafter became less a matter of having appropriate fangs or claws and more one of using and later fashioning tools to express the powers of the larger brain that was also emerging. Without tools the brain was of little use, no matter how many hundred cubic centimeters of it there might be. Let it also be said that without the original programmatic capacity for fitting tools into a sequence of acts, early hominids would never have started the epigenetic progress that brought them to their present state. And as human groups stabilized, tools became more complex and "shaped to pattern," so that it was no longer a matter of reinventing tools in order to survive, but rather of mastering the skills necessary for using them. In short, after a certain point in human evolution, the only means whereby man could fill his evolutionary niche was through the cultural transmission of the skills necessary for the use of priorly invented techniques, implements, and devices.

Two crucial parallel developments seem also to have occurred. As hominids became increasingly bipedal, with the freed hands necessary for using spontaneous pebble tools, selection also favored those with a heavier pelvic bony structure that could sustain the impacting strain of bipedal locomotion. The added strength came, of course, from a gradual closing down of the birth canal. There is an obstetrical paradox here: a creature with an increasingly larger brain but with a smaller and smaller birth canal to get through. The resolution seems to have been achieved through the immaturity of the human neonate, particularly cerebral immaturity that assures not only a smaller head, but also a longer period of transmitting the necessary skills required by human culture. During this same period, human language must have emerged, giving man not only a new and powerful way of representing reality but also increasing his power to assist the mental growth of the young to a degree beyond anything before seen in nature.

It is impossible, of course, to reconstruct the evolution in techniques of instruction in the shadow zone between hominids and man. I have tried to compensate by observing contemporary analogues of earlier forms, knowing full well that the pursuit of analogy can be dangerously misleading. I have spent many hours observing uncut films of the behavior of free-ranging baboons, films shot in East Africa by my colleague Irven DeVore with a very generous footage devoted to infants and juveniles. I have also had access to the unedited film archives of a hunting-gathering people living under roughly analogous ecological conditions, the !Kung Bushman of the Kalahari, recorded by Laurance and Lorna Marshall, brilliantly aided by their son John and daughter Elizabeth. I have also worked directly but informally with the Wolof of Senegal, observing children in the bush and in French-style schools. Even more valuable than my own informal observations in Senegal were the systematic experiments carried out later by my colleague, Patricia Marks Greenfield [1966].

Let me describe very briefly some salient differences in the free learning patterns of immature baboons and among !Kung children. Baboons have a highly developed social life in their troops, with well-organized and stable dominance patterns. They live within a territory, protecting themselves from predators by joint action of the strongly built, adult males. It is striking that the behavior of baboon juveniles is shaped principally by play with their peer group, play that provides opportunity for the spontaneous expression and practice of the component acts that, in maturity, will be orchestrated into either the behavior of the dominant male or of the infant-protective female. All this seems to be accomplished with little participation by any mature animals in the play of the juveniles. We know from the important experiments of Harlow and his colleagues [Harlow and Harlow, 1962] how devastating a disruption in development can be produced in subhuman primates by interfering with their opportunity for peer-group play and social interaction.

Among hunting-gathering humans, on the other hand, there is *constant* interaction between adult and child, or adult and adolescent, or adolescent and child. !Kung adults and children play and dance together, sit together, participate in minor hunting together, join in song and story telling together. At very frequent intervals, moreover, children are party to rituals presided over by adults—minor, as in the first haircutting, or major, as when a boy kills his first Kudu buck and goes through the proud but painful process of sacrification. Children, besides, are constantly playing imitatively with the rituals, implements, tools, and weapons of the adult world. Young juvenile baboons, on the other hand, virtually never play with things or imitate directly large and significant sequences of adult behavior.

Note, though, that in tens of thousands of feet of !Kung film, one virtually never sees an instance of "teaching" taking place outside the situation where the behavior to be learned is relevant. Nobody "teaches" in our prepared sense of the word. There is nothing like school, nothing like lessons. Indeed, among the !Kung children there is very little "telling." Most of what we would call instruction is through showing. And there is no "practice" or "drill" as such save in the form of play modeled directly on adult models—play hunting, play bossing, play exchanging, play baby tending, play house making. In the end, every man in the culture knows nearly all there is to know about how to get on with life as a man, and every woman as a woman—the skills, the rituals and myths, the obligations and rights.

The change in the instruction of children in more complex societies is twofold. First of all, there is knowledge and skill in the culture far in excess of what any one individual knows. And so, increasingly, there develops an economical technique of instructing the young based heavily on *telling* out of context rather than *showing* in context. In literate societies, the practice becomes institutionalized in the school or the "teacher." Both promote this necessarily abstract way of instructing the young. The result of "teaching the culture" can, at its worst, lead to the ritual, rote nonsense that has led a generation of critics from Max Wertheimer [1945] to Mary Alice White [undated] of Teachers' College to despair. For in the detached school, what is imparted often has little to do with life as lived in the society except insofar as the demands of school are of a kind that reflect *indirectly* the demands of life in a technical society. But these indirectly imposed demands may be the most important feature of the detached school. For school is a sharp departure from indigenous practice. It takes learning, as we have noted, out of the context of immediate action just by dint of putting it into a school. This very extirpation makes learning become an act in itself, freed from the immediate ends of action, preparing the learner for the chain of reckoning remote from payoff that is needed for the formulation of complex ideas. At the same time, the school (if successful) frees the child from the pace setting of the round of daily activity. If the school succeeds in avoiding a pace-setting round of its own, it may be one of the great agents for promoting reflectiveness. Moreover, in school, one must "follow the lesson" which means one must learn to follow either the abstraction of written speech—abstract in the sense that it is divorced from the concrete situation to which the speech might originally have been related—or the abstraction of language delivered orally but out of the context of an ongoing action. Both of these are highly abstract uses of language.

It is no wonder, then, that many recent studies report large differences between "primitive" children who are in schools and their brothers who are not: differences in perception, abstraction, time perspective, and so on. I need only cite the work of Biesheuvel [1949] in South Africa, Gay and Cole [undated] in Liberia, Greenfield [1966] in Senegal, Maccoby and Modiano [1966] in rural Mexico, Reich [1966] among Alaskan Eskimos.

AMPLIFIERS OF ACTION, SENSES, AND THOUGHT

What a culture does to assist the development of the powers of mind of its members is, in effect, to provide amplification systems to which human beings, equipped with appropriate skills, can link themselves. There are, first, the amplifiers of action—hammers, levers, digging sticks, wheels—but more important, the programs of action into which such implements can be substituted. Second, there are amplifiers of the senses, ways of looking and noticing that can take advantage of devices ranging from smoke signals and hailers to diagrams and pictures that stop the action or microscopes that enlarge it. Finally and most powerfully, there are amplifiers of the thought processes, ways of thinking that employ language and formation of explanation, and later use such languages as mathematics and logic and even find automatic servants to crank out the consequences. A culture is, then, a deviser, a repository, and a transmitter of amplification systems and of the devices that fit into such systems. We know very little in a deep sense about the transmission function, how people are trained to get the most from their potential by use of a culture's resources.

But it is reasonably clear that there is a major difference between the mode of transmission in a technical society, with its schools, and an indigenous one, where cultural transmission is in the context of action. It is not just that an indigenous society, when its action pattern becomes disrupted falls apart—at a most terrifying rate—as in uncontrolled urbanization in some parts of Africa. Rather, it is that the institution of a school serves to convert knowledge and skill into more symbolical, more abstract, more verbal form. It is this process of transmission—admittedly very new in human history—that is so poorly understood and to which, finally, we shall return.

CONVERSION OF KNOWLEDGE

There are certain obvious specifications that can be stated about how a society must proceed in order to equip its young. It must convert what is to be known—whether a skill or a belief system or a connected body of knowledge—into a form capable of being mastered by a beginner. The more we know of the process of growth, the better we shall be at such conversion. The failure of modern man to understand mathematics and science may be less a matter of stunted abilities than our failure to understand how to teach such subjects. Second, given the limited amount of time available for learning, there must be a due regard, for saving the learner from needless learning. There must be some emphasis placed on economy and transfer and the learning of general rules. All societies must (and virtually all do) distinguish those who are clever from those who are stupid —though few of them generalize this trait across all activities. Cleverness in a particular activity almost universally connotes strategy, economy, heuristics, highly generalized skills. A society must also place emphasis upon how one derives a course of action from what one has learned. Indeed, in an indigenous society, it is almost impossible to separate what one does from what one knows. More advanced societies often have not found a way of dealing with the separation of knowledge and action—probably a result of the emphasis they place upon "telling" in their instruction. All societies must maintain interest among the young in the learning process, a minor problem when learning is in the context of life and action, but harder when it becomes more abstracted. And finally, and perhaps most obviously, a society must assure that its necessary skills and procedures remain intact from one generation to the next—which does not always happen, as witnessed by Easter Islanders, Incas, Aztecs, and Mayas.

FAILURE OF PSYCHOLOGY

Unfortunately, psychology has not concerned itself much with any of these five requisites of cultural transmission—or at least not much with four of them. We have too easily assumed that learning is learning is learning—that the early version of what was taught did not matter much, one thing being much like another and reducible to a pattern of association, to stimulus-response connections, or to our favorite molecular componentry. We denied there was a problem of development beyond the quantitative one of providing more experience, and with the denial, closed our eyes to the pedagogical problem of how to represent knowledge, how to sequence it, how to embody it in a form appropriate to young learners. We expended more passion on the part-whole controversy than on what whole or what part of it was to be presented first. I should except Piaget [1954], Köhler [1940], and Vygotsky [1962] from these complaints—all until recently unheeded voices.

Our neglect of the economy of learning stems, ironically, from the heritage of Ebbinghaus [1913], who was vastly interested in savings. Our nonsense syllables, our random mazes failed to take into account how we reduce complexity and strangeness to simplicity and the familiar, how we convert what we have learned into rules and procedures, how, to use Bartlett's [1932] term of over 30 years ago, we turn around on our own schemata to reorganize what we have mastered into more manageable form.

Nor have we taken naturally to the issue of knowledge and action. Its apparent mentalism has repelled us. Tolman [1951], who bravely made the distinction, was accused of leaving his organisms wrapt in thought. But he recognized the problem and if he insisted on the idea that knowledge might be organized in cognitive maps, it was in recognition (as a great functionalist) that organisms go somewhere on the basis of what they have learned. I believe we are getting closer to the problem of how knowledge affects action and vice versa, and offer in testimony of my conviction the provocative book by Miller, Galanter, and Pribram [1960], *Plans and the Structure of Behavior.*

Where the maintenance of the learner's interest is concerned, I remind you of what my colleague Gordon Allport [1946] has long warned. We have been so concerned with the model of driven behavior, with drive reduction and the *vis a tergo* that, again, until recently, we have tended to overlook the question of what keeps learners interested in the activity of learning, in the achievment of competence beyond bare necessity and first payoff. The work of R. W. White [1959] on effectance motivation, of Harlow and his colleagues [Butler, 1954; Harlow, 1953] on curiosity, and of Heider [1958] and Festinger [1962] on consistency begins to redress the balance. But it is only a beginning.

The invention of antidegradation devices, guarantors that skill and knowledge will be maintained intact, is an exception to our oversight. We psychologists have been up to our ears in it. Our special contribution is the achievement test. But the achievement test has, in the main, reflected the timidity of the educational enterprise as a whole. I believe we know how to determine, though we have not yet devised tests to determine, how pupils use what they learn to think with later in life—for there is the real issue.

I have tried to examine briefly what a culture must do in passing on its amplifying skills and knowledge to a new generation and, even more briefly, how we as psychologists have dealt or failed to deal with the problems. I think the situation is fast changing—with a sharp increase in interest in the conversion problem, the problems of economy of learning, the nature of interest, the relation of knowledge and action. We are, I believe, at a major turning point where psychology will once again concern itself with the design of methods of assisting cognitive growth, be it through the invention of a rational technology of toys, of ways of enriching the environment of the crib and nursery, of organizing the activity of a school, or of devising a curriculum whereby we transmit an organized body of knowledge and skill to a new generation to amplify their powers of mind.

A COURSE IN MAN

I commented earlier that there was strikingly little knowledge available about the "third way" of training the skills of the young: the first being the play practice of component skills in prehuman primates, the second the teaching-in-context of indigenous societies, and the third being the abstracted, detached method of the school.

Let me now become highly specific. Let me consider a particular course of study, one given in a school, one we are ourselves constructing, trying out, and in a highly qualitative way, evaluating. It is for schools of the kind that exist in Western culture. The experience we have had with this effort, now in its third year, may serve to highlight the kinds of problems and conjectures one encounters in studying how to assist the growth of intellect in this "third way."

There is a dilemma in describing a course of study. One begins by setting forth the intellectual substance of what is to be taught. Yet if such a recounting tempts one to "get across" the subject, the ingredient of pedagogy is in jeopardy. For only in a trivial sense is a course designed to "get something across," merely to impart information. There are better means to that end than teaching. Unless the learner develops his skills, disciplines his taste, deepens his view of the world, the "something" that is got across is hardly worth the effort of transmission.

The more "elementary" a course and the younger its students, the more serious must be its pedagogical aim of forming the intellectual powers of those whom it serves. It is as important to justify a good mathematics course by the intellectual discipline it provides or the honesty it promotes as by the mathematics it transmits. Indeed, neither can be accomplished without the other. The content of this particular course is man: his nature as a species, the forces that shaped and continue to shape his humanity. Three questions recur throughout:

What is human about human beings?

How did they get that way?

How can they be made more so?

In pursuit of our questions we explore five matters, each closely associated with the evolution of man as a species, each defining at once the distinctiveness of man and his potentiality for further evolution. The five great humanizing forces are, of course, tool making, language, social organization, the management of man's prolonged childhood, and man's urge to explain. It has been our first lesson in teaching that no pupil, however eager, can appreciate the relevance of, say, tool making or language in human evolution without first grasping the fundamental concept of a tool or what a language is. These are not self-evident matters, even to the expert. So we are involved in teaching not only the role of tools or language in the emergence of man, but, as a necessary precondition for doing so, setting forth the fundamentals of linguistics or the theory of tools. And it is as often the case as not that (as in the case of the "theory of tools") we must solve a formidable intellectual problem ourselves in order to be able to help our pupils do the same. I should have said at the outset that the "we" I employ in this context is no editorial fiction, but rather a group of anthropologists, zoologists, linguists, theoretical engineers, artists, designers, camera crews, teachers, children, and psychologists. The project is being carried out under my direction at Educational Services, Incorporated, with grants from the National Science Foundation and the Ford Foundation.

While one readily singles out five sources of man's humanization, under no circumstances can they be put into airtight compartments. Human kinship is distinctively different from primate mating patterns precisely because it is classificatory and rests on man's ability to use language. Or, if you will, tool use enhances the division of labor in a society which in turn affects kinship. So while each domain can be treated as a separate set of ideas, their teaching must make it possible for the children to have a sense of their interaction. We have leaned heavily on the use of contrast, highly controlled contrast, to help children achieve detachment from the all too familiar matrix of social life: the contrasts of man versus higher primates, man versus prehistoric man, contemporary technological man versus "primitive" man, and man versus child. The primates are principally baboons, the prehistoric materials mostly from the Olduvai Gorge and Les Eyzies, the "primitive" peoples mostly the Netsilik Eskimos of Pelly Bay and the !Kung Bushmen. The materials, collected for our purposes, are on film, in story, in ethnography, in pictures and drawings, and principally in ideas embodied in exercises.

We have high aspirations. We hope to achieve five goals:

1. To give our pupils respect for and confidence in the powers of their own minds.

2.   To give them respect, moreover, for the powers of thought concerning the human condition, man's plight, and his social life.

3.   To provide them with a set of workable models that make it simpler to analyze the nature of the social world in which they live and the condition in which man finds himself.

4.   To impart a sense of respect for the capacities and plight of man as a species, for his origins, for his potential for his humanity.

5.   To leave the student with a sense of the unfinished business of man's evolution.

One last word about the course of study that has to do with the quality of the ideas, materials, and artistry—a matter that is at once technological and intellectual. We have felt that the making of such a curriculum deserved the best talent and technique available in the world. Whether artist, ethnographer, film maker, poet, teacher—nobody we have asked has refused us. We are obviously going to suffer in testing a Hawthorne effect of some magnitude. But then, perhaps, it is as well to live in a permanent state of revolution.

FOUR PROBLEMS

Let me now try to describe some of the major problems one encounters in trying to construct a course of study. I shall not try to translate the problems into refined theoretical form, for they do not as yet merit such translation. They are more difficulties than problems. I choose them, because they are vividly typical of what one encounters in such enterprises. The course is designed for 10-year-olds in the fifth grade of elementary school, but we have been trying it out as well on the fourth and sixth grades better to bracket our difficulties.

One special point about these difficulties. They are born of trying to achieve an objective and are as much policy bound as theory bound. It is like the difference between building an economic theory about monopolistic practices and constructing policies for controlling monopoly. Let me remind you that modern economic theory has been reformulated, refined, and revived by having a season in policy. I am convinced that the psychology of assisted growth, i.e., pedagogy, will have to be forged in the policy crucible of curriculum making before it can reach its full descriptive power as theory. Economics was first through the cycle from theory to policy to theory to policy; it is happening now to psychology, anthropology, and sociology.

1. WHICH WAY OF THINKING? A PROBLEM OF CONVERSION

Now on to the difficulties. The first is what might be called *the psychology of a subject matter*. A learned discipline can be conceived as a way of thinking about certain phenomena. Mathematics is one way of thinking about order without reference to what is being ordered. The behavioral sciences provide one or perhaps several ways of thinking about man and his society—about regularities, origins, causes, effects. They are probably special (and suspect) because they permit man to look at himself from a perspective that is outside his own skin and beyond his own preferences—at least for awhile.

Underlying a discipline's "way of thought," there is a set of connected, varyingly implicit, generative propositions. In physics and mathematics, most of the underlying generative propositions like the conservation theorems, or the axioms of geometry, or the associative, distributive, and commutative rules of analysis are by now very explicit indeed. In the behavioral sciences we must be content with more implicitness. We traffic in inductive propositions: e.g., the different activities of a society are interconnected such that if you know something about the technological response of a society to an environment, you will be able to make some shrewd guesses about its myths or about the things it values, etc. We use the device of a significant contrast as in linguistics as when we describe the territoriality of a baboon troop in order to help us recognize the system of reciprocal exchange of a human group, the former somehow provoking awareness of the latter.

There is nothing more central to a discipline than its way of thinking. There is nothing more important in its teaching than to provide the child the earliest opportunity to learn that way of thinking—the forms of connection, the attitudes, hopes, jokes, and frustrations that go with it. In a word, the best introduction to a subject is the subject itself. At the very first breath, the young learner should, we think, be given the chance to solve problems, to conjecture, to quarrel as these are done at the heart of the discipline. But, you will ask, how can this be arranged?

Here again the problem of conversion. There exist ways of thinking characteristic of different stages of development. We are acquainted with Inhelder and Piaget's [1958] account of the transition from preoperational, through concrete operational, to propositional thought in the years from preschool through, say, high school. If you have an eventual pedagogical objective in mind, you can translate the way of thought of a discipline into its Piagetian (or other) equivalent appropriate to a given level of development and take the child onward from there. The Cambridge Mathematics Project of Educational Services, Incorporated, argues that if the child is to master the calculus early in his high school years, he should start work early with the idea of limits, the earliest work being manipulative, later going on to images and diagrams, and finally moving on to the more abstract notation needed for delineating the more precise idea of limits.

In "Man: A Course of Study" [Bruner, 1965], there are also versions of the subject appropriate to a particular age that can at a later age be given a more powerful rendering. We have tried to choose topics with this in mind: The analysis of kinship that begins with children using sticks and blocks and colors and whatnot to represent their own families, goes on to the conventional kinship diagrams by a meandering but, as you can imagine, interesting path, and then can move on to more formal and powerful componential analysis. So, too, with myth. We begin with the excitement of a powerful myth (like the Netsilik Nuliajik myth), then have the children construct some myths of their own, then examine what a set of Netsilik myths have in common, which takes us finally to Lévi-Strauss's [1963] analysis of contrastive features in myth construction. A variorum text of a myth or corpus of myths put together by sixth graders can be quite an extraordinary document.

This approach to the psychology of a learned discipline turns out to illuminate another problem raised earlier: the maintenance of interest. There is, in this approach, a reward in understanding that grows from the subject matter itself. It is easier to engineer this satisfaction in mathematics, for understanding is so utter in a formal discipline—a balance beam balances or it does not; therefore there is an equality or there is not. In the behavioral sciences the payoff in understanding cannot be so obviously and startlingly self-revealing. Yet, one can design exercises in the understanding of man, too—as when children figure out the ways in which, given limits of ecology, skills, and materials, Bushmen hunt different animals, and then compare their predictions with the real thing on film.

2. STIMULATING THOUGHT

Consider now a second problem: *how to stimulate thought in the setting of a school*. We know from experimental studies like those of Bloom and Broder [1950], and of Goodnow and Pettigrew [1955], that there is a striking difference in the acts of a person who thinks that the task before him represents a problem to be solved rather than being controlled by random forces. School is a particular subculture where these matters are concerned. By school age, children have come to expect quite arbitrary and, from their point of view, meaningless demands to be made upon them by adults—the result, most likely, of the fact that adults often fail to recognize the task of conversion necessary to make their questions have some intrinsic significance for the child. Children, of course, will try to solve problems if they recognize them as such. But they are not often either predisposed to or skillful in problem finding, in recognizing the hidden conjectural feature in tasks set them. But we know now that children in school can quite quickly be led to such problem finding by encouragement and instruction.

The need for this instruction and encouragement and its relatively swift success relates, I suspect, to what psychoanalysts refer to as the guilt-ridden oversuppression of primary process and its public replacement by secondary process. Children, like adults, need reassurance that it is all right to entertain and express highly subjective ideas, to treat a task as a problem where you *invent* an answer rather than *finding* one out there in the book or on the blackboard. With children in elementary school, there is often a need to devise emotionally vivid special games, story-making episodes, or construction projects to reestablish in the child's mind his right not only to have his own private ideas but to express them in the public setting of a classroom.

But there is another, perhaps more serious difficulty: the interference of intrinsic problem solving by extrinsic. Young children in school expend extraordinary time and effort figuring out what it is that the teacher wants—and usually coming to the conclusion that she or he wants tidiness or remembering or to do things at a certain time in a certain way. This I refer to as extrinsic problem solving. There is a great deal of it in school.

There are several quite straightforward ways of stimulating problem solving. One is to train teachers to want it and that will come in time. But teachers can be encouraged to like it, interestingly enough, by providing them and their children with materials and lessons that *permit* legitimate problem solving and permit the teacher to recognize it. For exercises with such materials create an atmosphere by treating things as instances of what *might* have occurred rather than simply as what did occur. Let me illustrate by a concrete instance. A fifth-grade class was working on the organization of a baboon troop—on this particular day, specifically on how they might protect against predators. They saw a brief sequence of film in which six or seven adult males go forward to intimidate and hold off three cheetahs. The teacher asked what the baboons had done to keep the cheetahs off, and there ensued a lively discussion of how the dominant adult males, by showing their formidable mouthful of teeth and making threatening gestures had turned the trick. A boy raised a tentative hand and asked whether cheetahs always attacked together. Yes, though a single cheetah sometimes followed behind a moving troop and picked off an older, weakened straggler or an unwary, straying juvenile. "Well, what if there were four cheetahs and two of them attacked from behind and two from in front. What would the baboons do then?" The question could have been answered empirically—and the inquiry ended. Cheetahs *do not* attack that way, and so we do not know what baboons *might* do. Fortunately, it was not. For the question opens up the deep issues of what might be and why it is not. Is there a necessary relation between predators and prey that share a common ecological niche? Must their encounters have a "sporting chance" outcome? It is such conjecture, in this case quite unanswerable, that produces rational, self-consciously problem-finding behavior so crucial to the growth of intellectual power. Given the materials, given some background and encouragement, teachers like it as much as the students.

3. PERSONALIZATION OF KNOWLEDGE

I should like to turn now to the *personalization of knowledge*. A generation ago, the progressive movement urged that knowledge be related to the child's own experience and brought out of the realm of empty abstractions. A good idea was translated into banalities about the home, then the friendly postman and trashman, then the community, and so on. It is a poor way to compete with the child's own dramas and mysteries. A decade ago, my colleague Clyde Kluckhohn [1949] wrote a prize-winning popular book on anthropology with the entrancing title *Mirror for Man*. In some deep way, there is extraordinary power in "that mirror which other civilizations still hold up to us to recognize and study . . . [the] image of ourselves" [Lévi-Strauss, 1965]. The psychological bases of the power are not obvious. Is it as in discrimination learning, where increasing the degree of contrast helps in the learning of a discrimination, or as in studies of concept attainment where a negative instance demonstrably defines the domain of a conceptual rule? Or is it some primitive identification? All these miss one thing that seems to come up frequently in our interviews with the children. It is the experience of discovering kinship and likeness in what at first seemed bizarre, exotic, and even a little repellent.

Consider two examples, both involving film of the Netsilik. In the films, a single nuclear family, Zachary, Marta, and their 4-year-old Alexi, is followed through the year—spring sealing, summer fishing at the stone weir, fall caribou hunting, early winter fishing through the ice, winter at the big ceremonial igloo. Children report that at first the three members of the family look weird and uncouth. In time, they look normal, and eventually, as when Marta finds sticks around which to wrap her braids, the girls speak of how pretty she is. That much is superficial—or so it seems. But consider a second episode.

It has to do with Alexi who, with his father's help, devises a snare and catches a gull. There is a scene in which he stones the gull to death. Our children watched, horror struck. One girl, Kathy, blurted out, "He's not even human, doing that to the seagull.'" The class was silent. Then another girl, Jennine, said quietly: "He's got to grow up to be a hunter. His mother was smiling when he was doing that." And then an extended discussion about how people have to do things to learn and even do things to learn how to feel appropriately. "What would you do if you had to live there? Would you be as smart about getting along as they are with what they've got?" said one boy, going back to the accusation that Alexi was inhuman to stone the bird.

I am sorry it is so difficult to say it clearly. What I am trying to say is that to personalize knowledge one does not simply link it to the familiar. Rather one makes the familiar an instance of a more general case and thereby produces awareness of it. What the children were learning about was not seagulls and Eskimos, but about their own feelings and preconceptions that, up to then, were too implicit to be recognizable to them.

4. SELF-CONSCIOUS REFLECTIVENESS

Consider finally the problem of *self-conscious reflectiveness*. It is an epistemological mystery why traditional education has so often emphasized extensiveness and coverage over intensiveness and depth. We have already commented on the fact that memorizing was usually perceived by children as one of the high-priority tasks but rarely did children sense an emphasis upon ratiocination with a view toward redefining what had been encountered, reshaping it, reordering it. The cultivation of reflectiveness, or whatever you choose to call it, is one of the great problems one faces in devising curriculum. How to lead children to discover the powers and pleasures that await the exercise of retrospection?

Let me suggest one answer that has grown from what we have done. It is the use of the "organizing conjecture." We have used three such conjectures—what is human about human beings, how they got that way, how they could become more so. They serve two functions, one of them the very obvious though important one of putting perspective back into the particulars. The second is less obvious and considerably more surprising. The questions often seemed to serve as criteria for determining where they were getting, how well they were understanding, whether anything new was emerging. Recall Kathy's cry: "He's not human doing that to the seagull." She was hard at work in her rage on the conjecture what makes human beings human.

There, in brief, are four problems that provide some sense of what a psychologist encounters when he takes a hand in assisting the growth of mind in children in the special setting of a school. The problems look quite different from those we encounter in formulating classical developmental theory with the aid of typical laboratory research. They also look very different from those that one would find in an indigenous society, describing how children picked up skills and knowledge and values in the context of action and daily life. We clearly do not have a theory of the school that is sufficient to the task of running schools—just as we have no adequate theory of toys or of readiness building or whatever the jargon is for preparing children to do a better job the next round. It only obscures the issue to urge that some day our classical theories of learning will fill the gap. They show no sign of doing so.

THE TASK AHEAD

I hope that we shall not allow ourselves to be embarrassed by our present ignorance. It has been a long time since we have looked at what is involved in imparting knowledge through the vehicle of the school—if ever we did look at it squarely. I urge that we delay no longer.

But I am deeply convinced that the psychologist cannot alone construct a theory of how to assist cognitive development and cannot alone learn how to enrich and amplify the powers of a growing human mind. The task belongs to the whole intellectual community: the behavioral scientists and the artists, scientists, and scholars who are the custodians of skill, taste, and knowledge in our culture. Our special task as psychologists is to convert skills and knowledge to forms and exercises that fit growing minds—and it is a task ranging from how to keep children free from anxiety and how to translate physics for the very young child into a set of playground maneuvers that, later, the child can turn around upon and convert into a sense of inertial regularities.

And this in turn leads me to a final conjecture, one that has to do with the organization of our profession, a matter that has concerned me greatly during this past year during which I have had the privilege of serving as your President. Psychology is peculiarly prey to parochialism. Left to our own devices, we tend to construct models of a man who is neither a victim of history, a target of economic forces, or even a working member of a society. I am still struck by Roger Barker's [1963] ironic truism that the best way to predict the behavior of a human being is to know where he is: In a post office he behaves post office, at church he behaves church.

Psychology, and you will forgive me if the image seems a trifle frivolous, thrives on polygamy with her neighbors. Our marriage with the biological sciences has produced a cumulation of ever more powerful knowledge. So, too, our joint undertakings with anthropology and sociology. Joined together with a variety of disciplines, we have made lasting contributions to the health sciences and, I judge, will make even greater contributions now that the emphasis is shifting to the problems of alleviating stress and arranging for a community's mental health. What I find lacking is an alignment that might properly be called the growth sciences. The field of pedagogy is one participant in the growth sciences. Any field of inquiry devoted to assisting the growth of effective human beings, fully empowered with zest, with skill, with knowledge, with taste is surely a candidate for this sodality. My friend Philip Morrison once suggested to his colleagues at Cornell that his department of physics grant a doctorate not only for work in theoretical, experimental, or applied physics, but also for work in pedagogical physics. The limits of the growth sciences remain to be drawn. They surely transcend the behavioral sciences cum pediatrics. It is plain that, if we are to achieve the effectiveness of which we as human beings are capable, there will one day have to be such a field. I hope that we psychologists can earn our way as charter members.

REFERENCES

Allport, G. Effect: a secondary principle of learning. *Psychological Review,* 1946, 53: 335–47.

Barker, R. On the nature of the environment. *Journal of Social Issues,* 1963, 19: 17–38.

Bartlett, F. *Remembering.* Cambridge, England: Cambridge Univer. Press, 1932.

Biesheuvel, S. Psychological tests and their application to non-European peoples. *Yearbook of Education.* London: Evans, 1949, pp. 87–126.

Bloom, B., and Broder, L. Problem solving processes of college students. *Supplementary Educational Monograph, No. 73.* Chicago: Univer. Chicago Press, 1950.

Bruner, J. The course of cognitive growth. *American Psychologist,* 1964, 19: 1–15.

Bruner, J. Man: a course of study. *Educational Services Inc. Quarterly Report,* 1965, Spring-Summer, 3–13.

Bruner, J. *Toward a Theory of Instruction.* Cambridge: Harvard Univer. Press, 1966.

Butler, R. A. Incentive conditions which influence visual exploration. *Journal of Experimental Psychology,* 1954, 48: 19–23.

Ebbinghaus, H. *Memory: A Contribution to Experimental Psychology.* New York: Teachers College, Columbia University, 1913.

Festinger, L. A theory of cognitive dissonance. Stanford: Stanford Univer. Press, 1962.

Gay, J., and Cole, M. Outline of general report on Kpelle mathematics project. Stanford: Stanford University, Institute for Mathematical Social Studies, undated. (Mimeo)

Goodnow, Jacqueline, and Pettigrew, T. Effect of prior patterns of experience on strategies and learning sets. *Journal of Experimental Psychology,* 1955, 49: 381–89.

Greenfield, Patricia M. Culture and conservation. In J. Bruner, Rose Olver, and Patricia M. Greenfield (Eds.), *Studies in Cognitive Growth.* New York: Wiley, 1966, Ch. 10.

Harlow, H., and Harlow, Margaret. Social deprivation in monkeys. *Scientific American,* 1962, November.

Harlow, H. F. Mice, monkeys, men, and motives. *Psychological Review,* 1953, 60: 23–32.

Heider, F. *The Psychology of Interpersonal Relations.* New York: Wiley, 1958.

Inhelder, Bärbel, and Piaget, J. *The Growth of Logical Thinking.* New York: Basic Books, 1958.

Kluckhohn, C. *Mirror for Man.* New York: Whittlesey House, 1949.

Köhler, W. *Dynamics in Psychology.* New York: Liveright, 1940.

Lévi-Strauss, C. The structural study of myth. *Structural Anthropology.* (Trans. by Claire Jacobson and B. Grundfest Scharpf) New York: Basic Books, 1963, pp. 206–31.

Lévi-Strauss, C. Anthropology: Its achievements and future. Lecture presented at Bicentennial Celebration, Smithsonian Institution, Washington, D.C., September 1965.

Maccoby, M., and Modiano, Nancy. On culture and equivalence. In J. Bruner, Rose Olver, and Patricia M. Greenfield (Eds.), *Studies in Cognitive Growth.* New York: Wiley, 1966, Ch. 12.

Miller, G., Galanter, E., and Pribram, K. *Plans and the Structure of Behavior.* New York: Holt, 1960.

Piaget, J. *The Construction of Reality in the Child.* New York: Basic Books, 1954.

Reich, Lee. On culture and grouping. In J. Bruner, Rose Olver, and Patricia M. Greenfield (Eds.), *Studies in Cognitive Growth.* New York: Wiley, 1966, Ch. 13.

Tolman, E. Cognitive maps in rats and men. *Collected Papers in Psychology.* Berkeley and Los Angeles: Univer. California Press, 1951, pp. 241–64.

Vygotsky, L. *Thought and Language.* (Ed. and trans. by Eugenia Hanfmann and Gertude Vakar) New York: Wiley, 1962.

Wertheimer, M. *Productive Thinking.* New York and London: Harper, 1945.

White, Mary A. The child's world of learning. Teachers College, Columbia University, undated. (Mimeo)

White, R. W. Motivation reconsidered: The concept of competence. *Psychological Review,* 1959, 66: 297–333.

REVIEW QUESTIONS

1. What are the differences in "education" among baboon troops, primitive African societies, and Western cultures?

2. What does Bruner mean by *amplification systems* and *knowledge conversion?*

3. What do you think about his fifth-grade study-of-man course?

fifteen

The Child as a Moral Philosopher

LAWRENCE KOHLBERG

How can one study morality? Current trends in the fields of ethics, linguistics, anthropology, and cognitive psychology have suggested a new approach that seems to avoid the morass of semantical confusions, value bias and cultural relativity in which the psychoanalytic and semantic approaches to morality have foundered. New scholarship in all these fields is now focusing upon structures, forms, and relationships that seem to be common to all societies and all languages rather than upon the features that make particular languages or cultures different.

For twelve years, my colleagues and I studied the same group of seventy-five boys, following their development at three-year intervals from early adolescence through young manhood. At the start of the study, the boys were aged ten to sixteen. We have now followed them through to ages twenty-two to twenty-eight. In addition, I have explored moral development in other cultures—Great Britain, Canada, Taiwan, Mexico, and Turkey.

Inspired by Jean Piaget's pioneering effort to apply a structural approach to moral development, I have gradually elaborated over the years of my study a typological scheme describing general structures and forms of moral thought that can be defined independently of the specific content of particular moral decisions or actions.

The typology contains three distinct levels of moral thinking, and within each of these levels distinguishes two related stages. These levels and stages may be considered separate moral philosophies, distinct views of the sociomoral world.

We can speak of the child as having his own morality or series of moralities. Adults seldom listen to children's moralizing. If a child throws back a few adult clichés and behaves himself, most parents—and many anthropologists and psychologists as well—think that the child has adopted or internalized the appropriate parental standards.

Actually, as soon as we talk with children about morality, we find that they

Source: Reprinted from *Psychology Today* Magazine, September 1968. Copyright © Communications/Research/Machines, Inc. Reprinted by permission of the author and the publisher.

have many ways of making judgments that are not "internalized" from the out-side, and that do not come in any direct and obvious way from parents, teachers, or even peers.

MORAL LEVELS

The *preconventional* level is the first of three levels of moral thinking; the second level is *conventional,* and the third *postconventional,* or autonomous. While the preconventional child is often "well behaved" and is responsive to cultural labels of good and bad, he interprets these labels in terms of their physi-cal consequences (punishment, reward, exchange of favors) or in terms of the physical power of those who enunciate the rules and labels of good and bad.

This level is usually occupied by children aged four to ten, a fact long known to sensitive observers of children. The capacity of "properly behaved" children of this age to engage in cruel behavior when there are holes in the power structure is sometimes noted as tragic (*Lord of the Flies, High Wind in Jamaica*), sometimes as comic (Lucy in *Peanuts*).

The second, or conventional, level also can be described as conformist, but that is perhaps too smug a term. Maintaining the expectations and rules of the individual's family, group, or nation is perceived as valuable in its own right. There is a concern not only with *conforming* to the individual's social order but in *maintaining,* supporting, and justifying this order.

The postconventional level is characterized by a major thrust toward autono-mous moral principles that have validity and application apart from authority of the groups or persons who hold them and apart from the individual's identi-fication with those persons or groups.

MORAL STAGES

Within each of these three levels there are two discernible stages. At the pre-conventional level we have:

Stage 1: Orientation toward punishment and questioning deference to superior power. The physical consequences of action, regardless of their human meaning or value, determine its goodness or badness.

Stage 2: Right action consists of that which instrumentally satisfies one's own needs and occasionally the needs of others. Human relations are viewed in terms like those of the marketplace. Elements of fairness, of reci-procity, and equal sharing are present, but they are always interpreted in a physical, pragmatic way. Reciprocity is a matter of "you scratch my back and I'll scratch yours," not of loyalty, gratitude, or justice.

And at the conventional level we have:

Stage 3: Good-boy—good-girl orientation. Good behavior is that which pleases or helps others and is approved by them. There is much conformity to stereotypical images of what is majority or "natural" behavior. Behavior is often judged by intention; "he means well" becomes important for the first time, and is overused, as by Charlie Brown in *Peanuts*. One seeks approval by being "nice."

Stage 4: Orientation toward authority, fixed rules, and the maintenance of the social order. Right behavior consists of doing one's duty, showing respect for authority, and maintaining the given social order for its own sake. One earns respect performing dutifully.

At the postconventional level, we have:

Stage 5: A social-contract orientation, generally with legalistic and utilitarian overtones. Right action tends to be defined in terms of general rights and in terms of standards that have been critically examined and agreed upon by the whole society. There is a clear awareness of the relativism of personal values and opinions and a corresponding emphasis upon procedural rules for reaching consensus. Aside from what is constitutionally and democratically agreed upon, right or wrong is a matter of personal "values" and "opinion." The result is an emphasis upon the "legal point of view," but with an emphasis upon the possibility of *changing* law in terms of rational considerations of social utility, rather than freezing it in the terms of Stage 4 "law and order." Outside the legal realm, free agreement and contract are the binding elements of obligation. This is the "official" morality of American government and finds its ground in the thought of the writers of the Constitution.

Stage 6: Orientation toward the decisions of conscience and toward self-chosen *ethical principles* appealing to logical comprehensiveness, universality, and consistency. These principles are abstract and ethical (the Golden Rule, the categorical imperative); they are not concrete moral rules like the Ten Commandments. Instead, they are universal principles of justice, of the reciprocity and equality of human rights, and of respect for the dignity of human beings as individual persons.

UP TO NOW

In the past, when psychologists tried to answer the question asked of Socrates by Meno, "Is virtue something that can be taught (by rational discussion), or does it come by practice, or is it a natural inborn attitude?" their answers usually have been dictated not by research findings on children's moral character but by their general theoretical convictions.

Behavior theorists have said that virtue is behavior acquired according to their favorite general principles of learning. Freudians have claimed that virtue is superego identification with parents, generated by a proper balance of love and authority in family relations.

The American psychologists who have actually studied children's morality have tried to start with a set of labels—the "virtues" and "vices," the "traits" of good and bad character found in ordinary language. The earliest major psychological study of moral character, that of Hugh Hartshorne and Mark May in 1928–1930, focused on a bag of virtues including honesty, service (altruism or generosity), and self-control. To their dismay, they found that there were *no* character traits, psychological dispositions, or entities that corresponded to words like honesty, service, or self-control.

Regarding honesty, for instance, they found that almost everyone cheats some of the time, and that if a person cheats in one situation, it does not mean that he *will* or *won't* in another. In other words, it is not an identifiable character trait, *dis*honesty, that makes a child cheat in a given situation. These early researchers also found that people who cheat express as much or even more moral disapproval of cheating as those who do not cheat.

What Hartshorne and May found out about their bag of virtues is equally upsetting to the somewhat more psychological-sounding names introduced by psychoanalytic psychology: "superego strength," "resistance to temptation," "strength of conscience," and the like. When contemporary researchers have attempted to measure such traits in individuals, they have been forced to use Hartshorne and May's old tests of honesty and self-control, and they get exactly the same results—"superego strength" in one situation predicts little about "superego strength" in another. That is, virtue words like honesty (or superego strength) point to certain behaviors with approval but gives us no guide to understanding them.

So far as one can extract some generalized personality factor from children's performance on tests of honesty or resistance to temptation, it is a factor of ego strength or ego control, which always involves nonmoral capacities like the capacity to maintain attention, intelligent task performance, and the ability to delay response. "Ego strength" (called "will" in earlier days) has something to do with moral action, but it does not take us to the core of morality or to the definition of virtue. Obviously enough, many of the greatest evil-doers in history have been men of strong wills, men strongly pursuing immoral goals.

MORAL REASONS

In our research, we have found definite and universal levels of development in moral thought. In our study of seventy-five American boys from early adolescence on, these youths were presented with hypothetical moral dilemmas, all deliberately philosophical, some of them found in medieval works of casuistry.

On the basis of their reasoning about these dilemmas at a given age, each boy's stage of thought could be determined for each of twenty-five basic moral concepts or aspects. One such aspect, for instance, is "motive given for rule obedience or moral action." In this instance, the six stages look like this:

1. Obey rules to avoid punishment.
2. Conform to obtain rewards, have favors returned, and so on.

3.   Conform to avoid disapproval, dislike by others.

4.   Conform to avoid censure by legitimate authorities and resultant guilt.

5.   Conform to maintain the respect of the impartial spectator judging in terms of community welfare.

6.   Conform to avoid self-condemnation.

In another of these twenty-five moral aspects, "the value of human life," the six stages can be defined thus:

1.   The value of a human life is confused with the value of physical objects and is based on the social status or physical attributes of its possessor.

2.   The value of a human life is seen as instrumental to the satisfaction of the needs of its possessor or of other persons.

3.   The value of a human life is based on the empathy and affection of family members and others toward its possessor.

4.   Life is conceived as sacred in terms of its place in a categorical moral or religious order of rights and duties.

5.   Life is valued both in terms of its relation to community welfare and in terms of life being a universal human right.

6.   Belief in the sacredness of human life as representing a universal human value of respect for the individual.

I have called this scheme a typology. This is because about fifty per cent of most people's thinking will be at a single stage, regardless of the moral dilemma involved. We call our types stages because they seem to represent an *invariant developmental sequence.* "True" stages come one at a time and always in the same order.

All movement is forward in sequence, and does not skip steps. Children may move through these stages at varying speeds, of course, and may be found half in and half out of a particular stage. An individual may stop at any given stage and at any age, but if he continues to move, he must move in accord with these steps. Moral reasoning of the conventional, or Stage 3–4, kind never occurs before the preconventional Stage 1 and Stage 2 thought has taken place. No adult in Stage 4 has gone through Stage 6, but all Stage 6 adults have gone at least through 4.

While the evidence is not complete, my study strongly suggests that moral change fits the stage pattern just described. (The major uncertainty is whether there are two alternate mature orientations.)

HOW VALUES CHANGE

As a single example of our findings of stage sequence, take the progress of two boys on the aspect "the value of human life." The first boy, Tommy, is asked "Is it better to save the life of one important person or a lot of unimportant people?" At age ten, he answers "all the people that aren't important because one man just has one house, maybe a lot of furniture, but a whole bunch of people have an awful lot of furniture and some of these poor people might have a lot of money and it doesn't look it."

Clearly Tommy is Stage 1: he confuses the value of a human being with the value of the property he possesses. Three years later (age thirteen) Tommy's conceptions of life's value are most clearly elicited by the question, "Should the doctor 'mercy kill' a fatally ill woman requesting death because of her pain?" He answers, "Maybe it would be good to put her out of her pain, she'd be better off that way. But the husband wouldn't want it, it's not like an animal. If a pet dies you can get along without it—it isn't something you really need. Well, you can get a new wife, but it's not really the same."

Here his answer is Stage 2: the value of the woman's life is partly contingent on its hedonistic value to the wife herself but even more contingent on its instrumental value to her husband, who can't replace her as easily as he can a pet.

Three years later (age sixteen) Tommy's conception of life's value is elicited by the same question, to which he replies: "It might be best for her, but her husband—it's a human life—not like an animal; it just doesn't have the same relationship that a human being does to a family. You can become attached to a dog, but nothing like a human you know."

Now Tommy has moved from a Stage 2 instrumental view of the woman's value to a Stage 3 view based on the husband's distinctively human empathy and love for someone in his family. Equally clearly, it lacks any basis for a universal human value of the woman's life, which would hold if she had no husband or if her husband didn't love her. Tommy, then, has moved step by step through three stages during the ages ten through sixteen. Tommy, though bright (IQ 120), is a slow developer in moral judgment. Let us take another boy, Richard, to show us sequential movement through the remaining three steps.

At age thirteen, Richard said about the mercy killing, "If she requests it, it's really up to her. She is in such terrible pain, just the same as people are always putting animals out of their pain," and in general showed a mixture of Stage 2 and Stage 3 responses concerning the value of life. At sixteen, he said:

> I don't know. In one way, it's murder, it's not a right or privilege of man to decide who shall live and who should die. God put life into everybody on earth and you're taking away something from that person that came directly from God, and you're destroying something that is very sacred, it's in a way part of God and it's almost destroying a part of God when you kill a person. There's something of God in everyone.

Here Richard clearly displays a Stage 4 concept of life as sacred in terms of its place in a categorical moral or religious order. The value of human life is universal, it is true for all humans. It is still, however, dependent on something else, upon respect for God and God's authority; it is not an autonomous human value. Presumably if God told Richard to murder, as God commanded Abraham to murder Isaac, he would do so.

At age twenty, Richard said to the same question:

There are more and more people in the medical profession who think it is a hardship on everyone, the person, the family, when you know they are going to die. When a person is kept alive by an artificial lung or kidney it's more like being a vegetable than being a human. If it's her own choice, I think there are certain rights and privileges that go along with being a human being. I am a human being and have certain desires for life and I think everybody else does too. You have a world of which you are the center, and everybody else does too and in that sense we're all equal.

Richard's response is clearly Stage 5, in that the value of life is defined in terms of equal and universal human rights in a context of relativity ("You have a world of which you are the center and in that sense we're all equal"), and of concern for utility or welfare consequences.

THE FINAL STEP

At twenty-four, Richard says:

A human life takes precedence over any other moral or legal value, whoever it is. A human life has inherent value whether or not it is valued by a particular individual. The worth of the individual human being is central where the principles of justice and love are normative for all human relationships.

This young man is at Stage 6 in seeing the value of human life as absolute in representing a universal and equal respect for the human as an individual. He has moved step by step through a sequence culminating in a definition of human life as centrally valuable rather than derived from or dependent on social or divine authority.

In a genuine and culturally universal sense, these steps lead toward an increased *morality* of value judgment, where morality is considered as a form of judging, as it has been in a philosophic tradition running from the analyses of Kant to those of the modern analytic or "ordinary language" philosophers. The person at Stage 6 has disentangled his judgments of—or language about—human life from status and property values (Stage 1), from its uses to others (Stage 2), from interpersonal affection (Stage 3), and so on; he has a means of moral judgment that is universal and impersonal. The Stage 6 person's answers use moral words like "duty" or "morally right," and he uses them in a way implying universality, ideals, impersonality: He thinks and speaks in phrases like "regardless of who it was," or "I would do it in spite of punishment."

ACROSS CULTURES

When I first decided to explore moral development in other cultures, I was told by anthropologist friends that I would have to throw away my culture-bound moral concepts and stories and start from scratch learning a whole new set of values for each new culture. My first try consisted of a brace of villages, one Atayal (Malaysian aboriginal) and the other Taiwanese.

My guide was a young Chinese ethnographer who had written an account of the moral and religious patterns of the Atayal and Taiwanese villages. Taiwanese boys in the ten to thirteen age group were asked about a story involving theft of food. A man's wife is starving to death, but the store owner won't give the man any food unless he can pay, which he can't. Should he break in and steal some food? Why? Many of the boys said, "He should steal the food for his wife because if she dies he'll have to pay for her funeral and that costs a lot."

My guide was amused by these responses, but I was relieved: they were, of course, "classic" Stage 2 responses. In the Atayal village, funerals weren't such a big thing, so the Stage 2 boys would say, "He should steal the food because he needs his wife to cook for him."

This means that we need to consult our anthropologists to know what content a Stage 2 child will include in his instrumental exchange calculations, or what a Stage 4 adult will identify as the proper social order. But one certainly does not have to start from scratch. What made my guide laugh was the difference in form between the children's Stage 2 thought and his own, a difference definable independently of particular cultures.

Figure 1 indicates the cultural universality of the sequence of stages that we have found. Figure 1a presents the age trends for middle-class urban boys in the United States, Taiwan, and Mexico. At age ten in each country the order of use of each stage is the same as the order of its difficulty or maturity.

In the United States, by age sixteen the order is the reverse, from the highest to the lowest, except that Stage 6 is still little-used. At age thirteen, the good-boy, middle stage (Stage 3) is not used.

The results in Mexico and Taiwan are the same, except that development is a little slower. The most conspicuous feature is that at the age of sixteen, Stage 5 thinking is much more salient in the United States than in Mexico or Taiwan. Nevertheless, it *is* present in the other countries, so we know that this is not purely an American democratic construct.

Figure 1b shows strikingly similar results from two isolated villages, one in Yucatan, one in Turkey. While conventional moral thought increases steadily from ages ten to sixteen, it still has not achieved a clear ascendency over preconventional thought.

Trends for lower-class urban groups are intermediate in the rate of development between those for the middle-class and those for the village boys. In the three divergent cultures that I studied, middle-class children were found to be more advanced in moral judgment than matched lower-class children. This was not due to the fact that the middle-class children heavily favored some one type of thought that could be seen as corresponding to the prevailing middle-class pattern. Instead, middle-class and working children move through the same sequences, but the middle-class children move faster and further.

This sequence is not dependent upon a particular religion, or any religion at

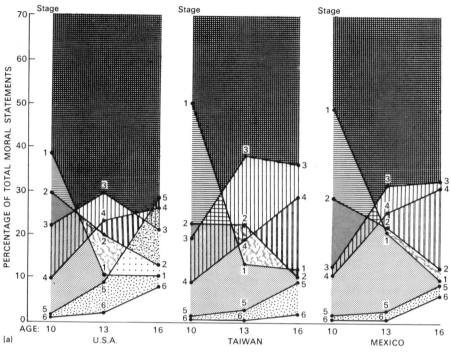

(a)

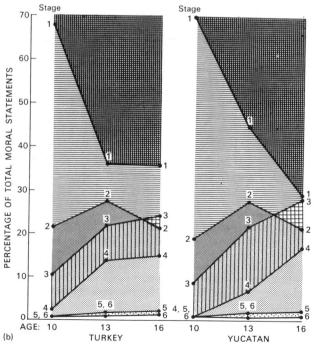

Figure 1. Cultural universality of the sequence of stages in moral development. a. Stages for middle-class urban boys in the United States, Taiwan, and Mexico. b. Stages for boys from isolated villages in Turkey and Yucatan.

(b)

all in the usual sense. I found no important differences in the development of moral thinking among Catholics, Protestants, Jews, Buddhists, Moslems, or atheists. Religious values seem to go through the same stages as all other values.

TRADING UP

In summary, the nature of our sequence is not significantly affected by widely varying social, cultural, or religious conditions. The only thing that is affected is the *rate* at which individuals progress through this sequence.

Why should there be such a universal invariant sequence of development? In answering this question, we need first to analyze these developing social concepts in terms of their internal logical structure. At each stage, the same basic moral concept or aspect is defined, but at each higher stage this definition is more differentiated, more integrated, and more general or universal. When one's concept of human life moves from Stage 1 to Stage 2, the value of life becomes more differentiated from the value of property, more integrated (the value of life enters an organizational hierarchy where it is "higher" than property so that one steals property in order to save life), and more universalized (the life of any sentient being is valuable regardless of status or property). The same advance is true at each stage in the hierarchy. Each step of development, then, is a better cognitive organization than the one before it, one that takes account of everything present in the previous stage but makes new distinctions and organizes them into a more comprehensive or more equilibrated structure. The fact that this is the case has been demonstrated by a series of studies indicating that children and adolescents comprehend all stages up to their own, but not more than one stage beyond their own. And importantly, *they prefer this next stage.*

We have conducted experimental moral discussion classes that show that the child at an earlier stage of development tends to move forward when confronted by the views of a child one stage further along. In an argument between a Stage 3 and a Stage 4 child, the child in the third stage tends to move toward or into Stage 4, while the Stage 4 child understands but does not accept the arguments of the Stage 3 child.

Moral thought, then, seems to behave like all other kinds of thought. Progress through the moral levels and stages is characterized by increasing differentiation and increasing integration, and hence is the same kind of progress that scientific theory represents. Like acceptable scientific theory—or like *any* theory or structure of knowledge—moral thought may be considered to partially generate its own data as it goes along, or at least to expand so as to contain in a balanced, self-consistent way a wider and wider experiential field. The raw data in the case of our ethical philosophies may be considered as conflicts between roles, or values, or as the social order in which men live.

THE ROLE OF SOCIETY

The social worlds of all men seem to contain the same basic structures. All the societies we have studied have the same basic institutions—family, economy, law, government. In addition, however, all societies are alike because they *are* societies—systems of defined complementary roles. In order to play a social role in the family, school, or society, the child must implicitly take the role of others toward himself and toward others in the group. These role-taking tendencies form the basis of all social institutions. They represent various patternings of shared or complementary expectations.

In the preconventional and conventional levels (Stages 1–4), moral content or value is largely accidental or culture bound. Anything from "honesty" to "courage in battle" can be the central value. But in the higher postconventional levels, Socrates, Lincoln, Thoreau, and Martin Luther King tend to speak without confusion of tongues, as it were. This is because the ideal principles of any social structure are basically alike, if only because there simply are not that many principles that are articulate, comprehensive, and integrated enough to be satisfying to the human intellect. And most of these principles have gone by the name of justice.

Behavioristic psychology and psychoanalysis have always upheld the Philistine view that fine moral words are one thing and moral deeds another. Morally mature reasoning is quite a different matter, and does not really depend on "fine words." The man who understands justice is more likely to practice it.

In our studies, we have found that youths who understand justice act more justly, and the man who understands justice helps create a moral climate that goes far beyond his immediate and personal acts. The universal society is the beneficiary.

REVIEW QUESTIONS

1. What do Kohlberg's stages mean for the elementary school teacher? For the ghetto teacher? For the high school teacher?

2. Do school systems and political systems sometimes seem "stuck" at stage 4 (law and order) instead of moving to stage 5 (agreed-upon-but-modifiable rights)? In what ways?

3. Does a school system or government reach stage 6 (self-chosen ethical principles)? Why or why not?

sixteen

Animism Revived

WILLIAM R. LOOFT

WAYNE H. BARTZ

Abstract: The literature on animistic thought is reviewed, beginning with the initial work by Piaget. In addition to the coverage of the empirical work methodological and theoretical issues are discussed extensively, including ... semantic problems and response bias, the stage concept, and the influence of specific experiences. Animism in adults is also discussed and concluded to be not of the same character as that found in children.

In the *Zeitgeist* of current psychological research, considerable attention is conferred to questions initially investigated by Jean Piaget in his developmental studies of cognition in children. Among the more popular Piaget-inspired topics are conservation of mass and number, formation of the object concept, and moral development, to name a few. However, animism, a concept accorded much consideration in Piaget's early work, is an issue which has received meager attention in the recent literature. In the two decades following the first published reports on his studies of animistic thinking in children [Piaget, 1929, 1933], a flurry of investigations by other workers appeared. Since that time, with few exceptions, very little research has been concerned with this question. Indeed, Bronfenbrenner [1963] noted that the content of a recent handbook of child psychology [Stevenson, 1963], in comparison with a similar handbook 30 years back [Murchison, 1931], excludes "the familiar trinity of 'realism, animism, and artificialism' " [p. 528]. A perusal of the earlier studies, however, rather clearly indicates that the issues involved were far from settled. In view of the findings of a recent large-scale investigation [Laurendau and Pinard, 1962], which revealed that animistic thinking is still very much prevalent among children and youth, the question appears to be of sufficient importance to merit revival.

Source: Abridged From *Psychology Bulletin*, 1969, 71:1–19. Copyright 1969 by the American Psychology Association. Reprinted by permission of the first author and the publisher.

THE CLINICAL STUDIES OF JEAN PIAGET

Though the existence of animistic thinking has long been acknowledged [Dennis, 1938], it is Jean Piaget who is credited with the first systematic investigations [Piaget, 1929, 1933]. Piaget referred to animism as "the tendency among children to consider things as living and conscious [1933, p. 537]." Actually, his primary concern was with what might be called the development of the concept of life. As a child grows older, Piaget noted that he tends to attribute life to inanimate objects with decreasing frequency, until eventually he reaches a mature cognitive state in which life is attributed only to what educated adults consider alive, that is, animals and plants.

Piaget conducted what he called the "clinical method" of studying the content of child thought, which consisted of the investigator informally questioning the child and attempting to pursue his reasoning. The following is a typical question and answer session:

> Vel (8:6): "Is the sun alive?—*Yes.*—Why?—*It gives light. It is alive when it is giving light, but it isn't alive when it is not giving light.*—Is a gun alive?—*Yes, it shoots.*" Vel even goes so far as to say that poison is alive—"*. . . because it can kill us*" [1929, p. 196].

At this stage of development, Piaget observed that a child attributes life to *usefulness* or *activity in general*. In the next stage life is attributed solely to *things which move*.

> Zimm (8:1) "Is a stone alive?—*Yes.*—Why?—*It moves.*—How does it move?— By rolling.*—Is the table alive?—*No, it can't move . . .*" [1929, p. 199].

According to Piaget, a third stage in this development is characterized by the restriction of life to those *things which move spontaneously.*

> Sart (12:6): "Is a fly alive?—*Yes.*—Why?—*Because if it wasn't alive it couldn't fly.*—Is a bicycle alive? *No.*—Why not?—*Because it is we who make it go . . .*— Are streams alive?—*Yes, because the water is flowing all the time . . .*" [1929, p. 202].

Piaget indicated that the fourth and final stage is that in which the concept of life is confined to *plants and animals*. In general, the responses given by a child at this level are consistent and approximate to those concepts acceptable to educated adults. Piaget found that Stage One corresponded roughly to ages 4–6 years; Stage Two: 6–7; Stage Three: 8–10; Stage Four: 11 and over.

VARIATIONS AND EXTENSIONS OF
PIAGET'S ANIMISM RESEARCH

As indicated previously, Piaget's studies on this and other concepts gave the impetus to substantial further research, some of which was highly critical in nature, but most of which was seen as improvements upon Piaget's method. One of the most salient criticisms pertained to the lack of a standardized procedure and a consequent lack of quantitative analysis of his data. An allied criticism suggested that Piaget, by the very nature of his questioning, may have often suggested answers to the children. For example, instead of asking "Who put the snow there?", which suggests some personal agency, he should have asked, "How did the snow get there?" [Munn, 1965]. A further criticism was that the stages of animistic thought advanced by Piaget may have been imposed upon the data by Piaget himself. The pertinent question was whether other observers would discern the same stages, given the same data. The remainder of the present paper concerns primarily the subsequent research efforts which attempted to deal with these questions; in addition, attention is paid to the peculiar methodological and theoretical issues intrinsic in them.

EARLY ATTEMPTS AT REPLICATION OR REFUTATION

The Russell-Dennis Studies. The criticisms leveled at Piaget's investigations made apparent the need for carefully standardizing his procedures with respect to (a) the statement of the questions, (b) the specific objects upon which the questions are to be focused, and (c) the interpretation of responses with regard to classification into developmental stages. In response to these needs, a rigorous standardization was developed by Russell and Dennis [1939] and was employed in several subsequent studies.

The questions in the Russell and Dennis procedure were focused upon twenty objects (examples: stone, watch, broken dish, comb). Some objects, such as those just enumerated, were present in the interview room; others were merely referred to verbally (e.g., tree, clouds). The child was told the following: "We are going to play a game. I am going to ask you some questions and we will see how many you can answer. You know what living means? A cat is living but if an automobile runs over it, it is dead." A comparison was made of the responses from two comparable groups of children, one group with and the other without this orientation. This statement was not found to be suggestive to the subjects; on the contrary, it appeared to serve the desired function of acquainting the subjects with the nature of the questions to follow [Russell and Dennis, 1941].

The subsequent procedure was as follows: The child was shown an item (e.g., a chair) and was asked, "Is the chair living or dead?" If he said the object was dead and then added that this was so because it did not move, the investigator moved the object and asked, "Is the chair living or dead when it is moving?" If the child attributed life to the item under these conditions, a further question was asked in order to determine whether the child meant imparted or spontaneous movement: "Can the chair move by itself or does something move it?" The same procedure was followed for each item in turn. The answers were classified according to standardized directions. Upon application of this procedure to the responses of 385 American school children (ages 3–15½ years), Russell and Dennis obtained results in general agreement with those of

Piaget. At the lowest level no concept was in evidence at all; next, life was attributed to anything of utility or in good condition; then to anything that moved; then to anything exhibiting spontaneous movement; and at the highest level only to animals and plants. Three other independent judges showed 87 per cent agreement with Russell and Dennis' assignment of responses to the specific levels of animistic thought, and test-retest reliability was .81 for the test itself. One point of disagreement with Piaget was that any one of the stages of maturity was found to contain at least a few cases from the entire age range. Generally, however, maturity in thought increased with age level.

In further research utilizing this standardized procedure, Russell [1940a] found that 98.5 per cent of American school children ($N = 774$) were readily classifiable into the stages of animism suggested by Piaget. The development of this concept was found to be constant over geographic locations and socioeconomic status (urban, suburban, rural). No differences were evident between sexes, and the same stages and sequential development were found in children at every level of intelligence. Generally, however, curves for the percentage of cases in each stage revealed increasing maturity with increasing mental age. This study also gave further evidence of the impossibility of limiting the age range of the stages as Piaget attempted to do. In another investigation [Russell, 1942], 611 older children between the ages of 8 and 20 years were also found to be readily classifiable into one of the stages of animistic thought (98 per cent). A definite increase in the percentage of individuals at the adult level (Stage Four) accompanied progressive increases in mental and chronological age.

ANIMISTIC THOUGHT IN THE MENTALLY RETARDED

In addition to these investigations with normal children, the early literature reveals three studies with mentally retarded subjects [Granich, 1940; Russell, Dennis, and Ash, 1940; Werner and Carrison, 1944]. The three investigations concur in their conclusions that a high incidence of animism exists in the deficient population. Granich [1940] and Russell et al. [1940] specifically investigated the effects of experience on the development of the life concept. In general, the degree of animism exhibited in any response was negatively related to the retardate's amount of experience with the phenomenon in question. Russell et al. additionally found that a comparison between retarded adults and normal children of corresponding mental age showed the retarded to be more advanced with regard to their conception of life, but the subnormal adults were nearer to the children in this respect than to normal adults.

RECENT EMPIRICAL EFFORTS

The major recent undertaking, under the direction of Laurendeau and Pinard [1962] of the University of Montreal, had as its primary objective the systematic replication of Piaget's early experiments under stricter methodological requirements. After constructing and administering their own standardized question-naires to 500 school children, these researchers identified several inadequacies in Piaget's classification scheme. A major criticism had to do with the question of anthropomorphic responses, which are not taken into account by Piaget. An allied criticism dealt with the limited number of stages contained in Piaget's model. They found that most children, at any age, gave a combination of re-sponses, including generated and spontaneous movement, activity, and anthro-pomorphism. Consequently classification was problematic. Other problems concerned children who could not explain their responses or made several con-tradictions, which also led to classification difficulties. Laurendau and Pinard proposed a new scheme to remove these inadequacies. Stage 0 is labeled "Incom-prehension or Refusal," in which the meaning of the questions is not understood; Stage 1 is "Animistic Thinking based on Usefulness, Anthropomorphism, Move-ment"—these subjects possess imperfect criteria; Stage 2 is "Autonomous Move-ment with some Residual Animistic Thinking"—this is essentially a transition stage; Stage 3 is "Total Disappearance of Animistic Thinking"—this corresponds to Piaget's Stage Four. This scheme was found by its creators to better classify the responses obtained in their testing.

METHODOLOGICAL ISSUES

THE SEMANTIC PROBLEM

When a child says that something is "living," just what does he mean? To an educated adult, the use of this term most likely implies a number of concepts, including birth, growth, metabolism, reproduction, a progression toward death, and in human beings, perhaps also moral conscience and reasoning. As Huang [1943] aptly observed, "Obviously the child does not mean all that . . . [p. 101]."

Russell [1940b] attacked the semantic problem by posing this question: Is the development of animism by characteristic stages merely a function of a child's usage of the terms "living" and "dead," or is this development actually due to more inclusive ideas concerning the nature of "life" in general? The standardized Russell-Dennis questionnaire was employed with respect to "knowing" and "feel-ing" rather than "living" or "dead." All but 3 out of 335 subjects followed the general stage progression. The correlations between the stages of animism and the stages of these allied concepts were much higher than the correlations of either series with mental age or chronological age. Since most subjects attributed "knowing" and "feeling" to the "living" objects, and since the development of the two series of concepts followed the same progression, Russell felt justified in the use of the term "animism" as descriptive of the subjects' ideas of life. How-ever, on a conceptual level, it appears that Russell's approach to the problem does not get at the real issue. "Living" and "dead" as two polar categories are considerably different than those of "living" and "not living." "Dead" implies that an object at one time had life, but this is not necessarily the case with a "not alive" category. There is evidence that unless specific instructions are given, some children are uncertain as to which of these two non-"alive" categories they are to use [Looft and Charles, 1969]. Russell and Dennis [1939] themselves found that some children would classify a chipped button or a chipped dish as "dead" because they were broken and therefore of no use.

Contrary to Russell's [1940b] findings, Klingensmith [1953] found that a majority of his subjects who stated that an inanimate object was alive did not attribute "knowing" and "feeling" to that object. Also, his group much more frequently stated that inanimate objects were alive than they attributed sensory and functional attributes to these objects. He suggested one possible reason for this discrepancy is that Russell used the term "Why?" to elicit explanations for the classification of an object as animate or inanimate, which may be suggestive to a child. This may in fact be the case, for it has been shown that subjects asked *why* an object is alive produce more animistic responses than do subjects asked *how* they know an object is alive [Nass, 1956]. A possible explanation for this finding might be that "Why?" and "How?" pose two quite different problems for the child. "Why?" may be interpreted by the child that he is to *justify* the categorization he just made (cf. the Russell-Dennis procedure: "Why do you say it is alive?"). This request for immediate justification may very likely have a higher probability of eliciting a superficial, immature (i.e., animistic) reply from the child. On the other hand, "How?" may indicate to the child that he is to support his categorization by more analytical means; therefore he may tend to take more time before giving his reply, and consequently he may produce a more mature explanation.

It appears that a semantic difference may even exist between the words "living" and "life." Klingberg [1957] obtained more animistic responses to the question "Is it living?" than to "Has it life?" He suggested that "living" may have other concepts associated with it (e.g., moving, sounding) than the word "life," which may be more abstract. The difference found here, however, might be better accounted for by an examination of the linguistic properties of these two words. "Living" and "life" represent two different syntactic categories and therefore may contain somewhat different meanings for the child. The -*ing* ending may indicate an equivalence of the object with this particular condition, whereas "life" may represent a property that the object can possess.

Response Bias. It may well be that response bias in younger children is the major methodological problem in this questioning type of research. In this situation, the possibility exists, at least, that a child can be induced to say almost anything. Deutsche's [1937] position was much stronger, for she felt that the individual method of questioning forces a young child to answer at any cost. In such a situation, the child takes recourse to imagination and pure chance, and therefore, Deutsche concluded, nothing proves that the child is thinking of natural phenomena in precausal terms.

Piaget has warned of several pitfalls inherent in any study of children's ideas and beliefs, including the necessity to tread a narrow line between missing or ignoring what is actually there (due to excessive interpretative timidity, methodological inflexibility, etc.) and overinterpreting what the child may have said out of experimenter suggestion or momentary fancy.

> It is, as always, open to question exactly how far the children believe what they are saying and at what point they start romancing. But the important thing is to realize that they have nothing with which to replace this artificialism. Whether they make up the details or not they can only explain things by having recourse to human activity and not to things themselves [Piaget, 1929, p. 313].

The child is seen to make associations and connections rather than causal relations between successive elements in a chain of reasoning. As Piaget calls it, he tends to *juxtapose* elements rather than associate them because of logical necessity; the two terms just "go together." Similarly, the child's reasoning is *syncretic* in that diverse terms are imperfectly but intimately correlated within an all-encompassing schema. Because of this juxtapositional and syncretic reasoning, the child tends to find a reason for anything when pressed to do so [Flavell, 1963].

As a guideline for interpreting the data, Piaget [1929] suggested that the specific beliefs which the child expresses, whether elicited spontaneously or through skillful questioning, should be taken as only symptomatic of his turn of mind, a general intellectual orientation toward the world. They should not be accepted as evidence for highly organized and coherent systems of thought.

Admittedly, children have seldom, if ever, reflected on these phenomena about which they are questioned. The ultimate concern, however, is not an examination of ideas which children have already thought out, but rather in determining *how* their ideas are formed and what direction their thinking leads them. What the answer reports is subjective in some proper sense, to be sure, but the fact that *that particular* answer is given is as objective a datum as any which scientific inquiry can yield. It is only necessary to corroborate these kinds of data with other kinds of data.

THEORETICAL ISSUES

The literature on animism displays two features which are particularly salient: One is the presence of animistic thought among populations of all age ranges and of great cultural differences. The percentages reported and the interpretations offered for these figures vary widely, but the research clearly indicates, almost without exception, that in each group at least *some* people give *some* responses which appear to be animistic. The other prominent feature is the controversy revolving around the explanation of this phenomenon. There can be little question that animistic-like responses exist; the question which remains unanswered is, what do they mean?

In response to this question, Piaget, once again, is a reasonable starting point, for it was he who provoked the initial empirical interest in the topic. It should be noted that the development of infantile concepts of reality and causality does not occupy a very large place in Piaget's total writings. The two books [1929, 1930] and one article [1933] which deal most extensively with this question date back to the very first part of his psychological work, and Piaget considered these early publications as preliminary endeavors to his total program of research. Commenting upon these works, he recently described them as "un peu adolescents [Piaget, 1959, p. 10]." Nevertheless, these early investigations on the various forms of representation of the world still remain of interest and are still stimulating research. This continued interest is probably due to the fact that these writings were translated early, are readily accessible, and are not filled with the complex logical schemata which characterize his later publications.

For purposes of this discussion, it should be sufficient to provide a most cursory outline of this portion of Piaget's theory; a definitive account is provided by Flavell [1963]. In his study of a child's representation of reality, Piaget [1930] sees the child at first as having no image of itself or of the external world; these are two universes compounded into a single reality. These two worlds separate and take shape very gradually through a process of differentiation. Indeed, this period of total egocentrism is a difficult concept for observers to grasp, for it is characteristic of an age at which it is virtually impossible to question a child in any ordered manner. Not until about age four can the child be verbally questioned systematically, and by this time the process of dissociation or differentiation is already well underway. In acknowledging the child's inability to communicate verbally his conception of reality at this stage, Piaget [1951] later emphasized the fact that he formed his notion about the existence of this phenomenon from an accumulation of all types of evidence. At any rate, the child is seen to cling to fewer and fewer subjective notions. "Precausality," the term used by Piaget to describe these adherences to egocentric notions about the world, is an expression which was introduced to represent the explanations intervening between those based on pure psychological and those relating to pure physical causality. Gradually these precausal beliefs are replaced by more objective conceptions of the world.

THE REALITY OF THE ANIMISTIC MODE OF THOUGHT

Among the first criticisms leveled at Piaget's theory were those which disputed the very existence of animism. Upon reviewing the early investigations, Huang [1943] concluded that Piaget and other child investigators were trying to establish the existence of elaborate mental systems in a child's head which are not actually there. Huang proposed that the supposed animism phenomenon could be better explained by a differentiation process quite unlike that proposed by Piaget. His analysis went like this: At first a child is in a neutral or undetermined state, which is not animistic. Gradually the animate-inanimate dichotomy develops, due to repeated definitions and contrasts. It is granted that the child will certainly make errors before reaching perfect differentiation. The more an object shares the typical properties of living things, the greater the tendency for the child to confuse it with these.

Huang made much of the experimenter's inability to investigate adequately very young children. He pointed out that when a young child is closely questioned, he is bewildered, answers at random, and seems entirely at the mercy of suggestion. He felt that it is impossible to pin down the child to a definite statement which could be accepted as representing his belief. "The picture presented is not one of mystic precausality, but the *absence of any definite idea* [Huang, 1943, p. 112]." Even under the apparent animistic forms, Huang went on, precausal thinking is neither typical nor universal among children. He referred to his own investigations in which the instances of precausal thinking were rare and often ambiguous [cf. Huang and Lee, 1945]. He suggested that animism is readily noted because it is so infrequent and striking that it could not escape attention; physical and naturalistic explanations are so commonplace that they tend not to be noticed. Thus, Huang concluded, the observer is left with an illusion of animism.

Safier [1964] suggested that Huang's notions might be called a "computer theory." She noted that Huang denied any special type of childish logic that would result in different types of animism, and that he considered the child to be different from an adult only to the extent that he lacks information about the "real" world. The child is thus like a computer in that he can give correct answers only to the extent that he has the correct amount of information fed into him.

Klingberg [1957] also challenged the existence of a global animistic trend in very young children. He proposed that pananimism can never be verified empirically because of its presence at such an early age that children cannot be successfully questioned. His position is similar to that of Huang in that he stated that although children may appear to be animistic, nothing proves it as Piaget understood it. Instead of progressing from universal animism toward greater objectivity, mental development is better seen as a transition from a state of total ignorance to a more accurate knowledge of reality.

An examination of the theses of Huang and Klingberg, therefore, seems to reveal the following line of thought: In lieu of predominantly precausal (animistic) thinking in a child, it is preferable to assume the existence of a progression of concept differentiations stemming from a continual accumulation of knowledge. Thus the differences between children and adults, according to this view, are purely quantitative. However, as Jahoda [1958] has observed, this thesis offers no sound alternative to that of Piaget, for in their postulation of the existence of an undetermined or neutral state (or initial state of ignorance), they have avoided giving any explicit definitions. Just what a "neutral" or "undetermined" state might represent is not at all clear. One quite valid interpretation would be that a child in such a state would respond in the same way whether confronted by either an animate *or* an inanimate object. But, as very aptly pointed out by Laurendeau and Pinard [1962], this is precisely one of the salient features of animistic thought!

Perhaps a return to Piaget's [1929] original work can lend some amount of clarity to the issue. Until the ages of four to five, Piaget postulates a state of *diffuse* animism, in which a child's thought begins with a lack of differentiation between living and inert bodies since it possesses no criteria by which to make the distinction. As long as this egocentric indissociation holds sway, the child fails to distinguish between action and purpose, fusing them into a primitive continuum. Animism is held to be a special form of this indissociation, "which consists in attributing to things, characteristics similar to those which the mind attributes to itself—such as consciousness, will, etc. [Piaget, 1929, p. 237]." After age five animism is seen to be more transitional and no longer all pervasive. It thereafter appears spontaneously when the child encounters phenomena which are unexpected and incomprehensible. Obviously, this is quite different from Huang's "neutral" state.

THE NOTION OF STAGES OF THOUGHT

Numerous objections have been raised to Piaget's proposition that the animistic mode of thought progresses steadily and invariably through clearly delineated levels or stages. Deutsche [1937], Bruce [1941], and Huang [1943] all have observed that at no age is it possible to classify all the responses of those subjects into the same category; each age level always includes children whose responses belong to stages of thought more descriptive of other age levels. Indeed, Russell and Dennis [1939] and Russell [1940a] demonstrated quite conclusively that the age ranges assigned to the stages of animism by Piaget were not precise. It is important to note, however, that they also demonstrated quite conclusively that virtually every child could be classified readily into one of Piaget's stages, disregarding age. Using a somewhat different classification scheme, Laurendeau and Pinard [1962] also found that each child could be categorized readily, according to his response pattern.

Nevertheless, a number of persons have still found reason to criticize the hypothesis of stages of animism as opposed to the notion of a gradual transition in precausal thought. One critic recently made the following observation: "There is reason to question any breaking up of the data into rigid stages . . . one who was not biased by Piaget's original analysis into stages might discern a gradual transition [Munn, 1965, p. 361]." Regardless of whether the actual progression is saltatory or gradual, however, it does appear that such statements, of which the preceding is typical, reflect a superficial reading or a misunderstanding of Piaget's intentions. It is therefore important to know how Piaget arrived at the notion of the stage concept.

His thesis is that thought passes through distinctive stages before adult ideas are attained. It is not that a child grasps adult ideas with varying degrees of adequacy, but rather that a child forms ideas which differ *qualitatively* from those of the educated adult. Furthermore, this transition from precausal toward natural explanations occurs by a succession of substitutions; that is, the final belief is not derived from an initial belief, but is *substituted* for it. Therefore these cognitive stages are essentially discontinuous and qualitatively distinct; each one represents an equilibrium state derived from an equilibration process which is continuous throughout ontogenesis [Flavell, 1963]. Piaget agrees that much overlapping among stages is involved, but he emphasizes that the total *pattern* of a child's responses must be considered. Two stages are defined largely by their differences. Thus the positing of stages is basically a process of abstracting high-lights, within some frame of reference, from a panorama of gradual change.

ANIMISM BEYOND CHILDHOOD?

One perplexing problem which remains is the nature and meaning of the animism that has been reported in adult populations. Although this discussion has considered animism as basically a characteristic of child thought, percentages as high as fifty per cent—sometimes up to seventy-five per cent—have been reported for adults. This finding appears to deny the supposition of a progression toward consecutively more sophisticated modes of thought, and therefore to deny the Piaget theory. It should be noted, however, that Piaget never questioned any adults.

Dennis and Mallinger [1949] administered a concept-of-life questionnaire to a group of people seventy years and older. Surprisingly, seventy-five percent of this group gave animistic responses, many of which were similar to those given by children. The investigators suggested that a *regression* to infantile modes of thinking may have occurred in this group due to neurological deterioration, senility, and the like. This reasoning may be valid in this instance, but it does not reasonably apply to adults in general. The incidences of animistic responses from adults in subsequent research are much too high to be attributable to mental deterioration or other pathological conditions. Other factors need to be called upon to explain adult animism.

Following the Dennis and Mallinger study, several investigations have revealed the presence of a persistent cast of animism among adults. These data raised considerable doubt as to the veracity of the notion of the infantile and primitive character of this mode of thought. Dennis [1953] found that about one-third of the students sampled in various American colleges and universities attributed life to one or more inanimate objects. A perusal of detailed responses convinced Dennis that the students were not being poetic, philosophic, or whimsical. Typical examples were these: lighted match—"*Living because it has flames which indicate life*"; sun—"*Living because it gives off heat* [pp. 248–249]." Dennis [1957] found a much higher percentage (seventy-nine per cent) of a sample of college students in Beirut, Lebanon, gave one or more animistic answers. Further evidence came from Crannell [1954], who found results verifying those of Dennis. Bell [1954], Lowrie [1954], Voeks [1954], Crowell and Dole [1957], and Simmons and Goss [1957] all conducted investigations with college populations and obtained analogous results: Considerable percentages of subjects gave at least a few animistic responses.

Dennis [1953] found that college students with courses in biology gave fewer animistic responses than those without this background. He similarly concluded that the high incidence of animism among college students in the Near East could be accounted for in terms of weak scientific instruction [Dennis, 1957]. A number of other studies failed to confirm these results, however [Bell, 1954; Crannell, 1954; Crowell and Dole, 1957; Simmons and Goss, 1957]. All of these investigators reported relatively high frequencies of students with courses in biology giving animistic answers.

An analysis of these experiments leaves the impression that adult animism does not have the same meaning as that in children. It appears that in many cases the animism observed was artificially induced by the experimental setup. Some of the factors may have been these: The questions posed were greatly different from those given to children; some items appear to be excessively difficult and perhaps even give rise to philosophical issues (e.g., atom, seed) ; some questions were posed in a suggestive manner (e.g., "When an automobile tire blows out, does the tire feel it?") ; subjects were usually not informed that they were to make a distinction between scientific and metaphoric language. Questionnaires in multiple-choice form obtained smaller numbers of animistic answers than those offering a simple alternative [Bell, 1954]. The frequency of precausal answers could also be modified according to the instructions given [Simmons and Goss, 1957]. Again, the semantic problem is undoubtedly influential. Voeks [1954] reported that many of her subjects admitted that "living" simply meant to them "real" or "existing."

Obviously, "living" and similar words are used abundantly in metaphorical expressions: a living language, a live battery, a live wire, etc. The prevalence of such lay descriptions led Simmons and Goss [1957] to conclude that animistic responses could be attributed to response-mediated generalization. The use of these characteristics as reasons for animistic response, according to them, indicates that the same or similar responses were also aroused by the test words. As a consequence, to the degree that verbalization of these reasons elicits responses such as "living" and "alive," generalization of these responses to the test items would be anticipated.

Ignorance as to what constitute the criteria of life is widespread. Apparently, even college science courses do not present this information in such a way that it can be transferred to the world outside textbooks and the classroom (or at least to the questionnaires devised by psychologists). As Simmons and Goss [1957] have remarked, the emphasis in biology is more likely to be upon characteristics of living things rather than upon the absence of such characteristics in nonliving things. Therefore, the amount of background in science may be largely irrelevant to the extent of experience in distinguishing between living and nonliving things. Furthermore, possibly, and quite probably, many people have just never thought about the matter.

REFERENCES

Bell, C. R. Additional data on animistic thinking. *Scientific Monthly,* 1954, 79: 67–69.

Bronfenbrenner, U. Developmental theory in transition. In H. W. Stevenson (Ed.), *Child Psychology, the 62nd yearbook of the National Society for the Study of Education.* Chicago: National Society for the Study of Education, 1963.

Bruce, M. Animism vs. evolution of the concept "alive." *Journal of Psychology,* 1941, 12: 81–90.

Crannell, C. N. Responses of college students to a questionnaire on animistic thinking. *Scientific Monthly,* 1954, 78: 54–56.

Crowell, D. H., and Dole, A. A. Animism and college students. *Journal of Educational Research,* 1957, 50: 391–95.

Dennis, W. Historical notes on child animism. *Psychological Review,* 1938, 45: 257–66.

Dennis, W. Animistic thinking among college and university students. *Scientific Monthly,* 1953, 76: 247–49.

Dennis, W. Animistic thinking among college and high school students in the Near East. *Journal of Educational Psychology,* 1957, 48: 193–98.

Dennis, W. and Mallinger, B. Animism and related tendencies in senescence. *Journal of Gerontology,* 1949, 4: 218–21.

Deutsche, J. M. *The Development of Children's Concepts of Causal Relations.* Minneapolis: University of Minnesota Press, 1937.

Flavell, J. H. *The Developmental Psychology of Jean Piaget,* Princeton, N.J.: Van Nostrand, 1963.

Granich, L. A qualitative analysis of concepts in mentally deficient boys. *Archives of Psychology,* 1940, 35: No. 251.

Huang, I. Children's conception of physical causality: a critical summary. *Journal of Genetic Psychology,* 1943: 63, 71–121.

Huang, I., and Lee, W. H. Experimental analysis of child animism. *Journal of Genetic Psychology,* 1945, 66: 69–74.

Jahoda, G. Child animism: I. a critical survey of cross-cultural research. *Journal of Social Psychology,* 1958, 47: 197–212.

Klingberg, G. The distinction between living and non-living among 7–10-year-old children, with some remarks concerning the animism controversy. *Journal of Genetic Psychology,* 1957, 90: 227–38.

Klingensmith, S. W. Child animism. *Child Development,* 1953, 24: 51–61.

Laurendeau, M., and Pinard, A. *Causal Thinking in the Child.* New York: International Universities Press, 1962.

Looft, W. R., and Charles, D. C. Modification of the life concept in children. *Developmental Psychology,* 1969, 1.

Lowrie, D. E. Additional data on animistic thinking. *Scientific Monthly,* 1954, 79: 69–70.

Munn, N. L. *The Evolution and Growth of Human Behavior*. (2nd ed.) Boston: Houghton Mifflin, 1965.

Murchison, C. (Ed.) *A Handbook of Child Psychology*. Worcester, Mass.: Clark University Press, 1931.

Nass, M. L. The effects of three variables on children's concept of physical causality. *Journal of Abnormal and Social Psychology*, 1956, 53: 191–96.

Piaget, J. *The Child's Conception of The World*. New York: Harcourt, Brace, 1929.

Piaget, J. *The Child's Conception of Physical Causality*. London: Kegan Paul, 1930.

Piaget, J. Children's philosophies. In C. Murchison (Ed.), *A Handbook of Child Psychology*. (2nd ed.) Worcester, Mass.: Clark University Press, 1933.

Piaget, J. *Play, Dreams, and Imitation in Childhood*. New York: Norton, 1951.

Piaget, J. Esquisse d' autobiographie intellectuelle. *Bulletin de Psychologie*, 1959, 13: 7–13.

Russell, R. W. Studies in animism: II. The development of animism. *Journal of Genetic Psychology*, 1940, 56: 353–66. (a)

Russell, R. W. Studies in animism: IV. An analysis of concepts allied to animism. *Journal of Genetic Psychology*, 1940, 57: 83–91. (b)

Russell, R. W. Studies in animism: V. Animism in older children. *Journal of Genetic Psychology*, 1942, 60: 329–35.

Russell, R. W., and Dennis, W. Studies in animism: I. A standardized procedure for the investigation of animism. *Journal of Genetic Psychology*, 1939, 55: 389–400.

Russell, R. W., and Dennis, W. Note concerning the procedure employed in investigating child animism. *Journal of Genetic Psychology*, 1941, 58: 423–24.

Russell, R. W. Dennis, W., and Ash, F. E. Studies in animism: III. Animism in feeble-minded subjects. *Journal of Genetic Psychology*, 1940, 57: 57–63.

Safier, G. A study in relationships between the life and death concepts in children. *Journal of Genetic Psychology*, 1964, 105: 283–94.

Simmons, A. J., and Goss, A. E. Animistic responses as a function of sentence contexts and instructions. *Journal of Genetic Psychology*, 1957, 91: 181–89.

Stevenson, H. W. (Ed.) *Child Psychology, the 62nd yearbook of the National Society for the study of Education*. Chicago: National Society for the Study of Education, 1963.

Voeks, V. Sources of apparent animism in students. *Scientific Monthly*, 1954, 79: 406–407.

Werner, H., and Carrison, D. Animistic thinking in brain-injured, mentally retarded children. *Journal of Abnormal and Social Psychology*, 1944, 39: 43–62.

REVIEW QUESTIONS

1. Properties of "life" and "living" are usually defined in junior high school science classes. Would it be worthwhile to discuss the meaning of *life* and *living* in the elementary grades? Why, or why not?

2. What is the relationship between Piaget's four stages of animistic thinking and his four stages of cognitive growth described by Tuddenham in article 13?

3. Would the question "Is the sun dead or alive?" stimulate a lively high-school session on semantics?

seventeen

Birth Order and School-Related Behavior: A Heuristic Review

RICHARD W. BRADLEY

Abstract: As evidence accrues there appears to be a redoubtable link between birth order and college matriculation. Overwhelming evidence shows that first-borns of both sexes attend college in greater numbers than their later-born peers. While explanations of this phenomenon are tenuous, substantial evidence exists indicating that early personality factors favoring firstborns are substantiated and extended while in school. Firstborns seem to more frequently (a) meet teachers' expectations and (b) show more susceptibility to social pressure than later borns. Exhibiting (c) greater information-seeking behavior and (d) being more sensitive to tension-producing situations, firstborns may be judged by others as (e) serious and (f) low in aggression. These behaviors may (g) strengthen firstborns' achievement motivation and (h) help to enhance their academic performance.

The intuitive notion that differential treatment and behavior occur as a result of ordinal position among siblings has led to more than a century of interest in birth order. Hundreds of studies have been published which make some use of birth order as a criterion variable. The physiological, psychological, and sociological correlates of birth order which have been studied range from affiliation and alcoholism to schizophrenia and school performance. Relatively few conclusions can be drawn, however, on the basis of relationships studied.

One concept which continues to be demonstrated in report after report is that birth order seems related to college matriculation. At many institutions information on birth order is included as part of general demographic data collected on entering freshmen. Over the years interested researchers and bureaus of student statistics have compiled and reported numerous descriptions of those matriculating. Studies particularly concerned with birth order show consistently that more

Source: From *Psychological Bulletin*, 1968, 70:45–51. Copyright 1968 by the American Psychological Association. Reprinted by permission of the author and the publisher.

firstborns enter college than would be expected on the basis of the proportion of firstborns in the total college-age group. Apparently birth order is operating in school and social environments in such a way as to result in more firstborns' aspiring to higher education.

In order to clarify relationships between college attendance and ordinal position, some knowledge of percentages of firstborns and later borns in the total population is needed which can then be used as the basis for comparison. The United States Bureau of Vital Statistics (1937–1966) compiles and publishes the number of births occurring in ordinal positions, from first to fifteenth, during each calendar year. Proportions of births in each ordinal position calculated from these data show first ordinal births fluctuating yearly from a high of 42.9 per cent in 1947 to a low of 25 per cent in 1933, while generally ranging between 33 per cent and 38 per cent.

Since education up to the age of 15 or 16 is compulsory, percentages of eldest children in the elementary and secondary schools should be approximately the same as percentage of firstborns in the total school-age population. To check this concept Schachter [1963] gathered birth order information on all students attending a Minneapolis public high school in a lower-middle-class neighborhood. The distribution did not differ from expectations. About 35 per cent were firstborns. These results and additional evidence presented in the same report gave no indication of disproportionate numbers of firstborns prior to college.

But in college the number of firstborns amounts to 50–65 per cent of all students. Studies of student populations at Columbia University [Schachter, 1963], Dartmouth College [Bender, 1928], Kansas State University [Danskin, 1964], University of Minnesota [Schachter, 1963], Reed College [Altus, 1966], University of California [Altus, 1966], University of Florida [Hall and Barger, 1964], University of Nebraska [Warren, 1966], and Yale [Capra and Dittes, 1962] all showed such overrepresentation of firstborns. Findings appeared to be consistent throughout the country. The Columbia and California studies also demonstrated consistency over time. Schachter [1963] presented information on a random sample of members of two-child families who entered Columbia College between 1943 and 1962. Yearly percentages of firstborns ranged from 52.5 per cent to 66 per cent. At the University of California, Santa Barbara, Altus [1966] found a similar pattern from 1959 through 1963. Sixty-three per cent of all members of two-child families were firstborns, 50.5 per cent of those from three-child families were firstborns, and 50.5 per cent of the enrollees from four-child families were firstborns. By the time students enroll in graduate and professional school, proportions of firstborns tend to be even greater [Schachter, 1963]. Thus the overall relationship between birth order and enrollment in higher education appears to be firmly established. The reason this relationship occurs has yet to be discovered.

A possible explanation concerns relative intelligence levels of firstborns and later borns. If it could be shown that firstborns are more intelligent than their siblings, this would probably account for overrepresentations of firstborns in college. Studies supporting this point of view can be found in the literature, but when viewed en masse results of research concerned with this topic are contradictory. In a review of birth order literature, Murphy, Murphy, and Newcomb [1973] provided a section on studies which indicated that firstborns are more intelligent. Another section reviewed work indicating that later borns are more intelligent, and a third indicated that there were no systematic intelligence differences between firstborns and later borns. Since 1937 results have been no more consistent.

Some evidence has appeared, however, that ordinal differentiation may occur among the very bright. The first indication of this trend appeared 40 years ago when Terman [1925] published the first volume of his study of 1,000 high-performance children. One of the criteria for selection in this study was an IQ of 140 or higher. This cutoff point provided a sample of the top 1 per cent of the total population in intelligence test performance. There is an interesting similarity between the birth order breakdown found for this sample and ordinal position distributions found among some classes of matriculating college students. Terman's study was one of the few research attempts focusing on the very bright which included birth order information. Apparently little research was done which added to this information until recently when Nichols [1964] showed a preponderance of firstborns and only children among 1,618 finalists in the National Merit Scholarship competition. Qualification as a Merit finalist typically indicates scholastic ability in the top 0.5 per cent of the United States population. From this entire group of finalists Nichols presented information about 1,226 students from two-, three-, and four-child families. Percentages of firstborns were 66, 52, and 59, respectively. Expected proportions would be about 50, 33, and 25 per cent, respectively. Later, Nichols [1966] observed similar overrepresentations in five successive large groups of finalists. According to the Nichols and Terman data, superior scholastic performance of firstborns is evident among the very top students. If this is true, it could account, in part, for the overrepresentation of firstborns among college populations. But at this stage, very high test scores may be used to account for only about 1 per cent of all college students. This is insufficient to account for the 15 per cent to 30 per cent excess of firstborns found among entering freshmen classes.

SCHOOL-RELATED BEHAVIOR

An adequate explanation of this phenomenon probably involves several complex types of related behaviors in addition to those cited above. No single body of evidence can be used to explain overrepresentations of first-borns in college, however, a review of literature in education, psychology, and sociology suggests several possibilities. These are discussed below in the context of performance and behavior in education.

Insofar as achievement in school is concerned, there is no conclusive evidence favoring firstborns. It is known that more firstborns go to college, but evidence is not available to show that they perform better. Campbell [1933] found no difference in scholarship between only children and children with siblings at the University of Oregon. Although this study was conducted for purposes other than checking scholastic performance by ordinal position, it is one of the few which even touches on this question. For high school groups, evidence is also sparse but somewhat more appropriate. Pierce [1959] looked at students who scored high on tests and divided them into those who did and those who did not achieve well. The high-achieving group contained mainly first and only children. Elder [1962] and Schachter [1963] reported that firstborns achieved higher grade point averages than later borns.

Work on achievement motivation seems to support the tentative inference that firstborns will achieve higher grade point averages than later borns. Sampson [1965] reported a significantly higher need for achievement among firstborn high school students from two-sibling families. Other research on achievement motivation does not deal directly with school situations, but perhaps the findings are relevant to achievement in school. Early life experiences should shape traits manifested in school behavior. Krebs [1958] and Winterbottom [1958] both found that a high need for achievement was associated with early training in independence and responsibility. Rosen [1961] also found this relationship and presented evidence indicating that parents affect their children's self-reliance and autonomy in problem-solving and decision-making situations. These findings support the importance of early training as well as the argument that firstborns will have higher need for achievement because parents have greater expectations for them and tend to overestimate their abilities. In school eldest children may tend to achieve (if parents place emphasis on education) because they are more sensitive to parents' wishes and demands. Sampson [1962] found the relationship between birth order and need for achievement stronger for females than males. Bossard and Boll [1955] found that in large families, parents place greater responsibility demands on firstborn girls than on firstborn boys. The oldest female child, even when a later born, seems to be the most responsible sibling. Thus, differential training for females may partially account for better elementary school performance of girls than of boys.

In the United States the majority of elementary school teachers are women. Women teachers may value certain behavior traits more than others and reward students who portray these traits accordingly. Rosen [1961] found that firstborns were reared to be more adult oriented and to command more adult attention. Such an adult orientation may help the child to perform better to the satisfaction of teachers. Dittes [1961] found firstborn male subjects not only had an adult orientation but were more vulnerable to variations in the amount of positive regard expressed by other persons; thus, they tended to be more susceptible to social pressure. By experimental manipulation Dittes varied the degree and situations in which positive regard toward others could be expressed. Later borns appeared to be less vulnerable to differences in acceptance. Additional support for this notion was found at three different age levels. Dean [1947] studied families having only two children of the same sex under seven years of age. Mothers judged their firstborns to be more dependent. In a study reported by Sears [1950], elementary school teachers also rated firstborns more dependent than later borns. Schachter [1964] found that firstborn members of college fraternities and sororities were more dependent on others and more easily influenced than are later borns. The consistency of these findings suggests that firstborns are more dependent on adults and are more oriented toward them than are later borns. If this is the case, then perhaps firstborns may be more inclined to adhere to desired classroom behavior patterns and teacher expectations.

If oldest children in families are more vulnerable to variations in expressed positive regard and are more dependent on adults, it might be expected that later borns will be oriented in different directions. Sells and Roff [1963] asked over 1,000 elementary school children to make peer nominations for most-liked and least-liked classmates. Mean scores for peer acceptance were computed and ranked on a 6-point scale. Though firstborns constituted the largest single ordinal group they ranked next to last on peer acceptance. Schachter [1964] found similar results with college students. Members of fraternities and sororities were asked to respond to two questions concerning whom they would prefer for roommates (ideal choice) and with whom they spend the most time in informal social activities (actual choice). Analysis of these data showed that later borns were considerably more popular than firstborns. Ordinal differentiations in popularity may be connected to the attitudinal structure of siblings. Hall and Barger [1963] used a multivariate analysis technique on data gathered in previous studies to factor out sibling differences. The prime factor for firstborns was seriousness. Among second borns the prime factor was gregariousness. Goodenough and Leahy [1927] also ascertained that the middle child (who could have been second or third born depending on family size) was more gregarious but described firstborns as likely to be seclusive rather than characterizing them as serious. Still other results support these differences although semantic labels differ. In a study by Dean [1947], mothers who judged their pair of siblings agreed that the older spent more time "just thinking" and had his feelings hurt more easily. Information available on second borns indicated that they were more popular among their peers and tended to seek association with age mates, whereas firstborns were not so popular and tended to be serious or seclusive. These differences would seem to account for the higher self-esteem found among later-born children. After reviewing studies in this area, Sampson [1965] concluded that there was tentative support for the notion that firstborns develop lower levels of self-esteem than later borns. These generalized personality traits may have the long-range effect of influencing school performance. Apparently firstborns more frequently exhibit behaviors which help them gain academic recognition while later borns more frequently seek social recognition.

Even though second borns are more socially oriented, Schachter [1959] brought forward evidence indicating that under stress firstborn children are more likely to want the company of other persons. Since 1959 there has been an increasing amount of research on affiliation. Warren [1966] reviewed recent affiliation studies and concluded that firstborn women seemed more sensitive to tension-producing situations than later-born women. For men, however, the effect of stress on affiliative behavior is not clear. Variations in the nature of stressful situations employed have produced contradictory results. Thus far, research investigations have been conducted in laboratory settings with artifically produced tension (usually electric shock). If artificially produced anxiety is similar to real frustration and stress felt by students there may be real connections between coping styles of firstborns and later borns in educational settings. The wish to be with others may be interpreted as the desire for information [Festinger, 1954, 1957; Heider, 1958]. Thus, it may be that firstborns exhibit more information-seeking behavior in order to better prepare themselves for stressful educational situations like tests.

Any attempt to connect affiliation and education is speculative, but control of aggression seems to have a firm educational foundation. Aggressive students may upset teachers because they can easily disrupt a classroom situation. Persons who are extremely aggressive may be asked to leave the classroom for periods of time or even be denied further access to the school. Their general presence will, at any rate, create a less happy situation for teachers. Macfarlane, Allen, and Honzik [1954] found that second-born boys in the California Growth Study showed more overt and competitive aggressive patterns than firstborn boys. In two-child families with one sibling in the first grade Koch [1956] found that teachers rated as low in aggression firstborn boys who had a younger sister. Dean [1947] reports that mothers of two children judged the younger to be more physically aggressive. Gewirtz's study [reported by Sampson, 1965], based on observation of young children in a school setting, suggested similar tendencies. Recently Sampson [1965] reviewed the positive and negative evidence concerning ordinal position and aggression. He concluded that, in general, second-born children appear more aggressive than firstborns. Therefore firstborns may be less likely to get into trouble. . . .

If the behavior patterns described above continue to hold up under critical investigation, educators should pay more attention to ordinal variables when working with students. The effect of school requirements and expectations may alter performances of firstborns and latter borns. Much of the research tentatively points to ordinal position differences, which school situations could confound, resulting in wider birth discrepancies. A better understanding of birth order effects may indicate the need to alter expectations or treatment on the part of school personnel. But at this stage, only casual inferences can be drawn from the data. Inferences drawn may be limited because some reports cited are based on small samples and have not been replicated. When replications have taken place results are often contradictory and confusing. In such cases the judicious conclusions of critical reviewers have been relied upon whenever available. Therefore, the behavioral considerations included in this review should not be considered definitive. They are intended to serve as impetuses to encourage others to consider, and possibly, investigate further. Empirical studies specifically designed to look at birth order and school-related behavior are necessary before any extension of these hypothetical relationships can be made.

DISCUSSION

This review has attempted to find some unifying patterns for studying ordinal position. Theoretical underpinnings have generally rested on specific events occurring in a child's life which are difficult to relate to later events. Adler [1928] was one of the first to offer a theoretical explanation of differential channeling as a consequence of birth order. Adler's idea that the oldest feels "dethroned" by the second child and fights to restore his place in the family has received considerable support. In conjunction with the derived attitudes of the child are the rearing practices of the parents. Lasko [1954] reported that until the 1950's almost all statements concerning parental behavior toward children were based on clinical experience. Since Lasko's report empirical evidence has accumulated which indicates the importance of early experiences on personality development, but it is difficult to relate these early experiences to later life. School experiences seem to offer one avenue for exploring continuing and relatively consistent patterns for all children (at least up to age 16). Explorations of values and attitudes developed in early childhood can then be continued as pupils progress through school.

The most redoubtable link between birth order and education is suggested by the information on college attendance. Overwhelming evidence shows that firstborns of both sexes attend college in greater numbers than later-born peers. There is no definitive explanation for this overrepresentation, but several explanations are tenable. Recent evidence [Nichols, 1964, 1966] has revived the notion that, at least among the very able, greater numbers of eldest children may rank higher on achievement tests. Yasuda [1964] reported that primogeniture is still in operation, even in the United States, but to what extent this would account for over-representations of firstborns is still unknown. The higher education-seeking behavior of firstborns may be the result of better scholastic performance, although data illustrating this are rather limited. While there has not been adequate measuring of school performance stratified by order of birth, information available on need for achievement would seem to predict that firstborns will perform at higher levels. Behavior attributes which may link birth order to education are an adult orientation, dependability, susceptibility, and seriousness of firstborns and greater popularity and gregariousness of second and later borns. Combinations of these characteristics indicate that firstborns should respond more affirmatively to school situations and succeed more frequently in winning teachers' approval. Meeting expectations is part of the educational game and firstborns appear to be more oriented toward doing what adults expect of them. Throughout elementary and secondary school, teachers may reinforce types of behaviors firstborns frequently exhibit. Such long-range reinforcement could account for higher educational aspirations of firstborns.

An amount of ambiguity is involved in linking social-psychological and educational parameters to ordinal position at birth. Relationships are unresolved or at best dimly comprehended. To gain a better understanding of the relationship involved, further research may profit by considering the following questions:

1.   Will a preponderance of firstborns and only children continue to appear among individuals in the very top percents in measured scholastic ability?

Nichols [1966] has observed overrepresentations of firstborns in successive groups of National Merit finalists. Similar findings using different samples of very able students would tend to substantiate this finding.

2.   Do firstborns actually perform better than later borns on academic criteria in high school and college?

There is already some evidence to the affirmative. Continued substantiation should help explain relationships between birth order and higher education.

3.   Are firstborns, rather than later borns, more frequently selected by their teachers for awards, special recognitions, or inclusions in unique programs?

What types of behavioral criteria are used by teachers in making these selections?

Do firstborns strive toward meeting teachers' expectations more than later borns?

Research in this area may give more definite information concerning the notion that firstborns adhere to classroom climates.

4.   Do second borns orient themselves toward nonacademic extracurricular activities and athletics in greater proportions than firstborns?

If this is true it would support the hypothesis that later borns strive toward popularity more than they strive toward school achievement.

Questions 3 and 4 may also help clarify the assumption that firstborns more frequently exhibit behaviors and engage in activities which will help them gain academic recognition while later borns more frequently seek social recognition.

5.   Do colleges with more stringent admission standards enroll higher proportions of firstborns than colleges with lower standards for admission or "open door" policies?

Altus [1966] points out that data on college matriculants suggests this. If this is true, then California Institute of Technology, Harvard University, Massachusetts Institute of Technology, and Reed College will enroll a much higher proportion of firstborns than state colleges and public junior colleges, which may indicate significantly higher aspiration levels for firstborns.

6.   Do firstborns exhibit greater information-seeking behaviors which enable them to better cope with stressful educational situations?

Prior research on affiliation gives some indications this might be a productive area for investigation. Studies using academic performances as dependent variables may help clarify the above question.

After a century of research on birth order it still appears necessary to know *what* differences occur before a theoretical model can be augmented. Once outcome variables are identified, explorations can turn to *why* differences occur.

REFERENCES

Adler, A. Characteristics of the first, second, and third child. *Children,* 1928, 3: 14.

Altus, W. D. Birth order and its sequelae. *Science,* 1966, 151: 44–49.

Bender, I. E. Ascendance-submission in relation to certain other factors in personality. *Journal of Abnormal Psychology,* 1928, 23: 137–43.

Bossard, J. H. S., and Boll, E. S. Personality roles in the large family. *Child Development,* 1955, 26: 71–78.

Campbell, A. A. A study of the personality adjustments of only and intermediate children. *Journal of Genetic Psychology,* 1933, 43: 197–206.

Capra, P. C., and Dittes, J. E. Birth order as a selective factor among volunteer subjects. *Journal of Abnormal and Social Psychology,* 1962, 64: 302.

Danskin, D. G. An introduction to KSU students. Unpublished report, Kansas State University, Student Counseling Center, September 1964. Cited by J. B. Warren, Birth order and social behavior. *Psychological Bulletin,* 1966, 65: 38–49.

Dean, D. A. The relation of ordinal positions to personality in young children. Unpublished master's thesis, State University of Iowa, 1947. Cited by R. Sears, Ordinal position in the family as a psychological variable. *American Sociological Review,* 1950, 16: 397–401.

Dittes, J. E. Birth order and vulnerability to differences in acceptance. *American Psychologist,* 1961, 16: 358.

Elder, G. H., Jr. Family structure: the effects of size of family, sex composition and ordinal position on academic motivation and achievement. In, Adolescent achievement and mobility aspirations. Chapel Hill, North Carolina: Institute for Research in Social Science, 1962. (Mimeo) Cited by E. E. Sampson, The study of ordinal position: antecedents and outcomes. In B. A. Maher (Ed.), *Progress in Experimental Personality Research.* New York: Academic Press, 1965.

Festinger, L. A theory of social comparison processes. *Human Relations,* 1954, 7: 117–40.

Festinger, L. *A Theory of Cognitive Dissonance.* Evanston, Ill.: Row, Peterson, 1957.

Goodenough, F. L., and Leahy, A. M. The effect of certain family relationships upon the development of personality. *Journal of Genetic Psychology,* 1927, 34: 45–72.

Hall, E., and Barger, B. Attitudinal structures of older and younger siblings. *American Psychologist,* 1963, 18: 356.

Hall, E., and Barger, B. Background data and expected activities of entering lower division students. Mental Health Projects Bulletin No. 7, May 1964, University of Florida. Cited by J. B. Warren, Birth order and social behavior. *Psychological Bulletin,* 1966, 65: 38–39.

Heider, F. *The Psychology of Interpersonal Relations.* New York: Wiley, 1958.

Koch, H. L. Some emotional attitudes of the young child in relation to characteristics of his siblings. *Child Development,* 1956, 26: 393–426.

Krebs, A. M. Two determinants of conformity: Age of independence training and achievement. *Journal of Abnormal and Social Psychology,* 1958, 56: 130–31.

Lasko, J. K. Parent behavior toward first and second children. *Genetic Psychology Monographs,* 1954, 49: 97–137.

Macfarlane, J. W., Allen, L., and Honzik, M. P. A developmental study of the behavior problems of normal children between twenty-one months and fourteen years. *University of California Publications in Child Development,* 1954, 2: 1–222.

Murphy, G., Murphy, L. B., and Newcomb, T. H. *Experimental Social Psychology.* New York: Harper, 1937.

Nichols, R. C. Birth order and intelligence. Unpublished research study, National Merit Scholarship Corporation, 1964. Cited by W. D. Altus, Birth order and scholastic aptitude. *Journal of Consulting Psychology,* 1965, 29: 202–205, and W. D. Altus, Birth order and its sequelae. *Science,* 1966, 151: 44–49.

Nichols, R. C. The origin and development of talent, *National Merit Scholarship Corporation Reports,* 1966, 2, No. 10. Evanston, Ill.: National Merit Scholarship Corporation. (Mimeo)

Pierce, J. V. *The Educational Motivation of Superior Students Who Do Not Achieve in High School.* Washington, D. C.: United States Department of Health, Education and Welfare, Office of Education, November 1959.

Rosen, B. C. Family structure and achievement motivation. *American Sociological Review,* 1961, 26: 574–85.

Sampson, E. E. Birth order, need achievement, and conformity. *Journal of Abnormal and Social Psychology,* 1962, 64: 115–59.

Sampson, E. E. The study of ordinal position: Antecedents and outcomes. In B. A. Maher (Ed.), *Progress in Experimental Personality Research.* New York: Academic Press, 1965.

Schachter, S. *The Psychology of Affiliation.* Stanford, Calif.: Stanford University Press, 1959.

Schachter, S. Birth order, eminence, and higher education. *American Sociological Review,* 1963, 28: 757–67.

Schachter, S. Birth order and sociometric choice. *Journal of Abnormal and Social Psychology,* 1964, 68: 453–56.

Sears, R. R. Ordinal position in the family as a psychological variable. *American Sociological Review,* 1950, 15: 397–401.

Sells, S. B., and Roff, M. Peer acceptance-rejection and birth order. *American Psychologist,* 1963, 18: 355.

Terman, L. (Ed.) *Mental and Physical Traits of a Thousand Gifted Children: Genetic Studies of Genius.* Stanford, Calif.: Stanford University Press, 1925.

Vital Statistics of the United States. Washington, D.C.: United States Office of Vital Statistics, Government Printing Office, 1937–1966.

Warren, J. B. Birth order and social behavior. *Psychological Bulletin,* 1966, 65: 38–49.

Winterbottom, M. R. The relation of need for achievement to learning experiences in independence and mastery. In J. W. Atkinson (Ed.), *Motives in Fantasy, Action, and Society.* Princeton, N.J.: Van Nostrand, 1958.

Yasuda, S. A methodological inquiry into social mobility. *American Sociological Review,* 1964, 29: 16–23.

REVIEW QUESTIONS

1. Which of the following seem to characterize firstborn children:

    a. winning more National Merit Scholarships.

    b. more likely to attend college.

    c. more dependent.

    d. more aggressive.

    e. higher achievement motivation.

    f. high levels of aspiration.

    g. more oriented toward athletics and popularity.

    h. greater needs for affiliation.

    i. probably better achievers.

2. Does birth order information have significance for a high school teacher?

Answers to question 1: a, b, c, e, f, h, i.

part iii

MOTIVATION

The primary concern of every school teacher is motivation. Traditionally, learning theory concepts of motivation were based upon such physiological needs as hunger, thirst, avoidance of pain, and the related principles of reinforcement and punishment. From Sigmund Freud had come unconscious and mysterious drives in the form of the id, the oedipal complex, as well as the life and death instincts. Other psychologists, especially Murray and Maslow, created lists, for example, of needs for play, safety, love, and realizing the potential of the self. This part, while short, is composed of four very contemporary and penetrating approaches to motivation. All four articles relate directly to stimulating that high level of interest, involvement, and attention necessary for meaningful learning.

In article 18, Day and Berlyne emphasize the distinction between motivation that is *extrinsic* to the task at hand—such as smiles, stars, and grades—and motivation *intrinsic* to the learning situation. Basing their theory upon the psychophysiological concept of arousal, the authors explain how individual differences in arousal levels lead some people to be more alert, tense, energetic, and excitable than others. Also, some individuals prefer higher levels of stimulation (arousal) than others. The authors also suggest that the curiosity-stimulating effects of novelty, complexity, ambiguity, and uncertainty may be used to activate exploration and information-seeking in the school.

Every parent has witnessed the eagerness with which young children explore and learn, for no other reason than to become wiser and more able. Frank Nardine in article 19 explains the dynamics of *competence* motivation, the idea that man possesses a natural curiosity and a desire to cope successfully with his world. The learning stimulated by such motivation is its own reward. Nardine points out that the natural development of a child's competence may be impaired by parents or teachers who are excessively directive, or who have expectations that are either too low or too high. Finally, dividing competence into the two factors of school performance and self-confidence, the author outlines instructional ideas for children who are either high or low in school ability and high or low in self-confidence.

We often speak of underachieving, overachieving, and educational achievement in general. In article 20 John Atkinson summarizes his theory of achievement motivation through the aid of equations. For example:

$$T_s = M_s \times P_s \times I_s$$

where T_s = overall strength of tendency to achieve success

M_s = motive to achieve success

P_s = probability of success

I_s = incentive value of success.

In regard to I_s, Atkinson notes that the attractiveness of success is greater the more difficult the task, which we probably already knew. However, it may not have occurred to us that the tendency to achieve is most strongly aroused by tasks of intermediate difficulty—easy tasks pose no challenge, while exceedingly difficult ventures promise little success. On the other hand, for the anxious student, motivated more by his fear of failure than by his motive to achieve, the intermediate-difficulty tasks also pose the greatest threat.

Humanist Carl Rogers in article 21 itemizes his answers to the question "How does a person learn?" Emphasizing a student's natural motivation to learn, Rogers points out that material relevant to the self can be mastered in a fraction of the time needed to learn "required" material. Also, he notes that learning will generally be reduced unless activities and information that threaten the self are removed. Rogers further suggests that self-initiated learning and learning-by-doing motivate total involvement, including both feelings and intellect, which results in highly effective and permanent learning. Finally, the author describes the climate-setting and resource role of the leader of learning, a leader who must accept and resolve his judgmental, nonfacilitative feelings.

eighteen

Intrinsic Motivation

H. I. DAY AND D. E. BERLYNE

It is the premise of this chapter that a better understanding of the forces inherent in intrinsic motivation can lead to a marked improvement in learning through greater efficiency in teaching methodology, and to greater achievement by the learners. Moreover, the cultivation of intrinsically motivated behavior in the classroom will ultimately lead to the development of adults who continue to learn and explore their environments after completing their formal course of education. Too many adults remember school as the place where learning was a painful experience and have negative feelings at the thought of reading a non-fiction book or studying any new subject formally or informally.

At one time, great emphasis was laid on intelligence in learning, and individual differences in academic success were related to differences in aptitudes and abilities. Motivational factors were alluded to usually in a discussion of classroom behavior and discipline with the assumption that the teacher's role was to control the class while goading pupils toward a high level of achievement.

Underachievers, for example, were considered to be children who failed to live up to their intellectual potential and required extra effort on the part of a teacher to drive them to achieve. *Overachievers,* much more difficult to explain, were those who performed at a level greater than appeared possible from their intelligence test scores, and were viewed as pupils who were overextending their abilities, and were sure to fall flat on their faces at any moment.

But recently it was pointed out that intelligence accounts for only about half of the variability in achievement and that the next most potent factor is probably motivation.

Motivational factors can be dichotomized into long-term motivators (extending over weeks, months, and even years) and short-term or immediate motiva-

Source: Abridgment of Chapter 11 from *Psychology and Educational Practice* by Gerald S. Lesser (Ed.). Copyright © 1971 by Scott, Foresman and Company. Reprinted by permission of the authors and the publisher.

tors. The former influence the process of education toward a particular goal. The goals, of course, are always intrinsic to the task at hand, but are displayed to the pupil either verbally or by a model, as appropriate. To extend the motivation of the pupil over a long range of years, intermediate goals are established and intermediate rewards (and punishments) are distributed. Thus high grades, prizes, and other marks of intermediate achievement are used to help motivate the pupil toward his "final" vocational goal. The use of these rewards and reinforcers is predicated on the existence of needs and drives within the pupil which seemingly can only be satisfied by the achievement of particular goals. These needs and drives, measured by interest inventories and personality batteries, are used to counsel pupils and encourage them toward definite educational and vocational ends.

Immediate motivation can be both *extrinsic or intrinsic* to the task at hand. Extrinsic motivation is usually applied by the teacher in the form of physical or social reinforcement (stars, a pleasant remark, good marks on a test, etc.). It is related to the task at hand and used to affect attention, performance, and learning of that task.

Intrinsic motivation is derived, not from the teacher, but from the interaction of the task and the pupil. It is intrinsic to the performance of the task and also affects attention, performance, and learning. While intrinsic motivation is relevant to immediate problems, its influence can pervade long-range attitudes and education both within the classroom and eventually throughout one's life.

EARLY MOTIVATIONAL THEORIES

Over the years, many attempts have been made to define motivation, describe its importance, and classify sources of motivation in human beings. While it is not the intention of this chapter to review these numerous theories, it is well to point out a few of the more prominent ones and show how they contributed to the modern concepts of curiosity and intrinsic motivation.

Motivation has not yet been defined in a universally acceptable manner. In fact, almost every theorist has begun by supplying his own definition, sometimes vaguely resembling another definition, but often in a novel manner.

Generally, motivation speaks to the "why" of behavior. It seeks to identify one or more of three kinds of factors:

1. The environmental forces which act upon the organism,
2. Internal feelings, drives or instincts, and
3. The goals of the behavior.

While some theorists stress one of these factors, others may emphasize different factors or may redefine the same factor with novel nuances and emphases.

Another possibility is to consider motivation as having both an *energizing* function and one of *directing* or patterning behavior. While some theories argue that only the energizing component is the proper domain of motivation, others include the latter factor as an area of interest toward which the study of motivation is directed.

Although early psychological theories used the concepts of motivation without treating it as a separate area of study, a few attempts were made to organize these concepts into definite theoretical formulations. For many years, motivation theory in America was dominated by the concept of *instincts* and *needs*. These concepts, traceable to the Stoics of ancient Greece and carried on through the ages by scientist-philosophers such as St. Thomas Aquinas and Descartes, were expounded clearly in modern times by McDougall and Freud, who suggested that people behave in certain ways because of internal wishes, urges, or instincts. However, the concept fell into disrepute among American psychologists because of the possibility of generating new "instincts" to account for behaviors which the familiar instincts could not explain. Furthermore, the term seemed to carry within it the connotation of innateness and immutability.

Freud received much publicity for his advocacy of the importance of unconscious motivators, especially that of the sex urge. His major contribution was his insistence that one should look within the individual for an explanation of his manifest behavior, and that motivations arise not only from conflicts between the individual and his environment but also from conflicts among forces within himself. He suggested that there are tendencies within individuals toward maintaining a certain level of tension characteristic for the organism. But to Freud, as to most theorists of this time, motivational states were seen as having mainly aversive qualities that instigate behavior to reduce that state.

Murray formulated a list of twenty-seven *psychogenic needs* which he suggested could account for all the motivations in the behavior displayed by people. An examination of this need-system structure suggests that the list is fairly comprehensive and even somewhat redundant. However, the outstanding feature of Murray's need system is the possibility of postulating additional needs whenever deemed necessary. This may seem to be a positive feature, but it may decrease the effectiveness of the whole structure if the list becomes too large and unwieldy for predictability. (One might even postulate a need to postulate needs.) Moreover, it is conducive to circularity, for the existence of a need can be inferred from the kind of behavior the postulated need is supposed to explain.

Of special interest in this chapter are Murray's needs for play, order, and understanding, for these needs suggest the existence of intrinsic driving forces in human motivation.

Maslow's need system has the advantage of categorizing all needs into six general groups and suggesting a hierarchical system in which the satisfaction of certain needs takes precedence over that of other needs higher in the hierarchy.

Maslow considered the primary needs to be physiological, and an individual is expected to act to satisfy these before safety needs, and so on up the hierarchy. At the top are the needs to know, to understand, and the need for *self-actualization*. Maslow argued that when the basic needs are gratified, only then will a person attend to the satisfaction of the higher needs and impulses. He also stressed that these higher impulses are desirable and that gratification increases the desire for more, whereas gratification of the physiological and safety needs only prevents illness.

However, examination of any pupil's classroom behavior, as well as a child's or adult's behavior in the everyday world, shows that people indulge in activities that fulfill the need to know and understand despite the fact that it may be more important, at that particular moment, to gratify one of the physiological or safety needs. Thus, we find jaywalkers blithely reading newspapers while crossing the road against traffic, a major threat to their need for safety. We find too, that, given options for a course of study, students will often elect difficult subjects which carry the threat of hard work and possible failure, but promise the excitement of learning. Children will investigate objects and events which may be threatening to life and limb because they seem interesting and provoke curiosity, and grownups will climb mountains and skydive for no apparent reason other than the satisfaction of the act itself.

DEFINITION OF INTRINSIC MOTIVATION

Motivation is of two kinds, extrinsic and intrinsic. Behavior which is extrinsically motivated can be considered that which has a goal external to the act itself. For example, if a person eats in order to alleviate his hunger, the motivation for the behavior is extrinsic to the eating. Intrinsic motivation, on the other hand, is in effect when the goal is inherent within the act itself. Eating for the pleasure of the act itself would be intrinsically motivated.

Similarly, learning a piece of information for the purpose of passing an examination and reaching a vocational goal which, in turn, would increase income, enhance security, self-esteem, and self-actualization, or even the prospect of sexual gratification, is learning which is motivated by a drive or need extrinsic to the task. Learning for the satisfaction of knowing or the reduction of uncertainty intrinsic to the situation is learning motivated by an intrinsic drive.

It is often difficult to distinguish clearly between these two kinds of motivation for, when an individual is eating or learning, probably both intrinsic and extrinsic elements collaborate in the situation. An extremely hungry individual, for example, may be willing to eat anything, even food he normally dislikes. But, as hunger is reduced, the extrinsic motivation is gradually diminished and the individual eats for the enjoyment of eating and becomes more particular about the choice of foods or the place where he eats.

Extrinsic motivators also include those which are normally aversive, such as hunger, thirst, and pain. They often act to disrupt the learning process, demanding immediate satisfaction and often being cyclic or recurrent. These motivators may sometimes influence behavior in directions that are not entirely congruent with the goals of the activity itself. Such factors include externally applied rewards, punishments, and competition.

As stated earlier, intrinsic types of motivation have been defined in a number of ways: conflict among forces within oneself, needs to know and understand, and needs for self-conceptualization. Such definitions must remain vague and untestable unless they can be made quantifiable, be manipulated and measured, and are anchored to more clearly identifiable constructs. The chapter is based on a psychological model which in turn is based on a physiological concept— the arousal system. It suggests that intrinsic motivation is directed towards the search for information with the purpose of reducing a heightened level of arousal which resulted from a situation in which adequate information to select an appropriate response was not available. Situations characterized by uncertainty, complexity, novelty, and ambiguity seem to induce a state of high tension, the alleviation of which is the goal of exploration and information search which may result in the acquisition of knowledge.

This chapter presents a provisional model, and examples of the research which is being conducted to test the model, which may be used to explain much of the behavior in a classroom and may serve to suggest ways of improving the motivating functions of a teacher.

AN AROUSAL MODEL

In the 1930's, theories based on the concept of *drive* became popular in American psychology. These conceptualizations tended to be rigidly experimental and more interested in behavior than in feelings. They were generally based on the premise that individuals tend to remain in a state of rest or *homeostasis* unless displaced from this state by one of the drives. Drives were generally limited to hunger, thirst, pain, and sexual appetite, were regarded as aversive or discomforting, and were seen to activate and direct behavior. Sources of drive could be both external or internal but invariably caused some kind of physiological or biochemical imbalance in the system. Hunger, for example, was seen as a state of reduced sugar level in the body.

The principle of homeostasis was introduced from the physiological and biochemical sciences and may have been influenced by Newtonian principles dealing with the effect of forces applied to stationary bodies, for the physiological version suggested that each organism tends to remain in a state of balance and when disturbed by external forces or by internal physiological and biochemical conditions will initiate activities to restore the balance. Superficially, this adaptation seems reasonable. When a person becomes hot, he begins to perspire and the evaporation of the water reduces surface temperature. Similarly, when the salt level in the blood is reduced, the individual becomes thirsty and seeks to restore the blood-salt level. However, closer examination of the principle reveals distinct flaws. If a drop in the blood-sugar level initiates hunger and eating, why does eating not continue until the blood-sugar level is restored (usually hours after termination of eating)? Moreover, if homeostasis is the goal of behavior, why do some people overeat, or why do people tend to eat approximately the same amount after a fast regardless of how long they had fasted?

Psychologically, there is even greater difficulty for the drive-homeostasis model to explain certain behaviors. Why, for example, do people go mountain climbing or gamble, or children learn to read even when they are not forced to? None of these behaviors are directly explained by the classical drive theories. Explanations suggesting the existence of *secondary* drives derived from the primary drives of hunger, thirst, and other basic needs were proposed, but these sometimes appeared cumbersome and overly complex. For example, it could be argued that mountain climbers are really trying to impress themselves and others with their capabilities, thus gaining them respect that might eventually lead to a better job, more money, greater security, less exposure to hunger and thirst, and greater opportunity for sexual activity.

Yet, no such explanation will explain the behavior of the well-fed, well-rested baby who refuses to remain in a state of rest and instead plays with his toes, explores his environment, crawls, stands up, and learns to walk and talk. Nor can it explain the fidgeting behavior of a bored child in a classroom who stimulates himself by shifting attention rapidly rather than succumbing to sleep, or the persistence with which people tackle difficult problems, insoluble puzzzles, or obviously risky business ventures.

Many of these questions had been ignored or avoided before 1950. Around that time two discoveries were made in the field of physiology which forced some psychologists to re-examine the bases for their conceptual models.

The first advance was made when Moruzzi and Magoun [1949; Magoun, 1950] demonstrated the existence of the *reticular activating system* (also called the arousal system or the *RAS*). They showed that stimulation sensed by the nerve fibers actually travels to the brain via two pathways: a specific sensory tract which transmits external stimulation by direct projection onto the cortex, and a second set of fibers which transmits energy through a diffuse network (reticulum) of fibers in the midbrain to the cortex of the cerebrum.

Activity in the RAS appears to affect the degree to which the directly projected stimulation will be received by the cortex, be acted upon, and eventually be translated, if necessary, into motor activity. The greater the arousal level, the more pronounced the level of activity that can be induced in the cerebral cortex. For example, during sleep, activity in the RAS is minimal and the amount of specific stimulation received by the cortex is very small. When the RAS is extremely active, the cortex may be bombarded by an overwhelming amount of stimulation.

The second physiological discovery was that nerve fibers tend to fire spontaneously. Indeed, it appears that nerve fibers, while opposed to overactivity, may also abhor inactivity. It follows then that stimulation may originate intrinsically, arising from some need of the nervous system for excitation.

While the RAS was originally described from a physiological-neurological viewpoint, psychologists such as Lindsley [1951] and Hebb [1955] revised their thinking about motivation, incorporating the new physiological evidence into a psychological model. Hebb [1955] outlined a theory of the relationship of performance to arousal as represented in Figure 1.

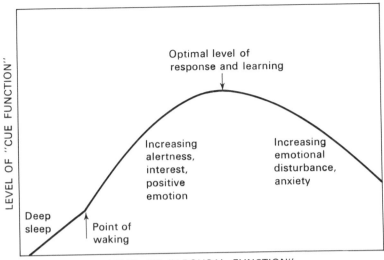

Figure 1. Performance as a function of arousal level. (Hebb, D. O. Drives and the CNS. *Psychological Review,* Vol. 63, 1955, p. 250. © 1955 by the American Psychological Association. Used by permission.)

Psychologically, arousal has been approached from a number of directions, some of which have tended to incorporate physiological thinking into their theoretical framework. Thus, *arousal* to some is synonymous with *level of activation,* while to others it is directly concerned with the degree of measurable physiological and biochemical change in the body following exposure to an event or a stimulus. Moreover, some psychologists point to the fact that arousal is not a simple reaction but may affect some parts of the body to a greater extent than other parts. However, within the model proposed here, it is unnecessary to detail all the differences. We must also recognize that there are differences among individuals in the localization of maximum arousal effect in the body, such that some people react to an arousing stimulation by tensing their muscles more than others, by perspiring more, or by manifesting greater changes in heart rate or respiration pattern. While recognizing the known physiological elaborations and possible distinctions, we will restrict our discussion to the premise that arousal can be recognized as *a general increase in tension in any part of the body* together with various biochemical, physiological, and neurological changes.

An increase in arousal may not be recognized as such even by extremely reflective and sensitive people. But it can usually be recorded on physiological recording devices of which the "lie detector" is one example. Tension or activation exists in every living person to some extent, and its level fluctuates continuously. It is important to study the arousal system not only because of the effects of extreme peaks of arousal on behavior but also because of the relation of existing levels of arousal and/or any changes in arousal level on behavior and learning.

THEORETICAL PROPOSITIONS

The exposition of this arousal model and its availability for the postulation of intrinsic motivation allows the ready explanation of many of the difficulties encountered by earlier motivation theories. But in order to apply this model to classroom learning and behavior, a number of statements must be proposed and ·discussed. Some of these have already been proposed by Hebb [1955] and Berlyne [1963, 1965] and some are derived from empirical data. It would be unreasonable to expect that these propositions can explain all behavior easily, that all empirical data are in accord with the model, or that other theories cannot be adapted to the evidence. However, the simplicity and clarity of the arousal model may induce a new perspective for the teacher in the classroom and may suggest different approaches to the solution of old problems.

1.   Each individual seeks to maintain a tonus level of arousal. This postulate is a reiteration of the homeostatic principle, somewhat similar to that expounded by drive theorists. The goal of behavior is to maintain a *tonus level* of arousal, that is, a condition of mild, steady activity in the nerve and muscle fibers. When arousal is increased (see postulate 4 for more detail) the individual initiates behavior to restore the tonus. This tonus level is at some intermediate point on the arousal continuum and not at a zero point as postulated by earlier drive theory.

2.   The tonus level varies among individuals, within each individual over time, and with extended exposure to a particular environment. People differ in the degree of tension or arousal they maintain even in a resting state. Some people always seem to have more energy available and some always seem to be more tense and excited. According to Figure 1, we should be able to relate this to efficiency of performance and describe some people as characteristically more efficient than others.

Within each person, the tonus level drifts upwards or downwards depending on the time of day, month, and year because of physiological and biochemical changes and extended exposure to specific environmental conditions. Industrial psychologists tell us that people tend to be more active, alert, and efficient in the early hours of the workday. According to arousal theory, we would therefore expect the tonus level to be close to the optimum level for peak efficiency. As morning passes, the tonus level seems gradually to drift downward toward a low at about 10:30 A.M., with a resultant decrease in alertness and efficiency. The coffee break at about this time often serves to raise the tonus level.

Teachers who spend all morning with the same class can readily recognize this syndrome: high excitement level and alertness at 9:15 A.M. (except Mondays), with a lot of noise and distractibility (which can be channeled into concentrated efficient work) and a gradual downward drift until recess time as children become weary and sloppy. Children need to revive their tonus levels at recess (while teachers need that coffee break) about 10:30 A.M.

When a person is first exposed to an environment of loud noise, he immediately reacts with a startle response, i.e., strong tension and arousal. But with prolonged exposure this tension subsides somewhat, he adapts to his environment, and his arousal level settles again. But the tonus does not return to its original level; it remains higher than before, even when the individual seems to be relaxing again. This fits our belief that city folk live at a constantly higher tension level than their country cousins, and it can readily be demonstrated in the laboratory.[1]

3.   Change in arousal level may be induced both externally and internally. Change in arousal may be induced by any change in stimulation especially when it is sudden, intense, and/or frightening. (This postulate will be further elaborated in the section *Sources of Arousal Change* and *Attention*.) Not only does an increase in level of stimulation have the potential to increase arousal but so may a decrease in level of stimulation, sensory isolation, boredom, and repetitiveness.

Furthermore, an individual may increase his arousal level with self-imposed problems and exciting thoughts. When he is asleep, this stimulation may take the form of dreams or nightmares. During dreaming, his body tenses and measures of cortical electrical activity in the brain show patterns of alertness.

Sometimes, when a person is relaxed, his body may suddenly stiffen or move spasmodically. This flash of involuntary activity may simply be the firing of motor nerve fibers through self-stimulation. Similarly, sensory fibers may fire autonomously and we may momentarily sense flashing lights or sounds which are not related to the external environment. These sudden bursts remind us that our bodies crave stimulation and abhor extended inactivity.

4.   Moderate increases in strength of stimulation are perceived as pleasant, but large changes are abhorred and induce behavior aimed at reducing arousing qualities in the stimulus. The tonus level of arousal may have an indifferent *affect* or feeling value. Slight changes in level of stimulation have moderate arousal potential and are perceived as pleasant. Thus, a little sugar in a cup of tea, a gentle swaying motion in a boat or automobile, or a TV or radio adjusted to a moderate level is pleasant, but a great deal of sugar, violent swaying, and a loud television or radio are aversive (except to those who have adjusted to these quantities and consider them to be normal).

---

[1] A person may be brought for an experiment involving GSR apparatus. This apparatus measures Galvanic skin resistance, that is, the resistance to an imperceptibly slight electrical current between two electrodes fixed to the surface of the body, one of which is attached to a sweat area of the body, usually the palm of the nondominant hand. If sudden tension is introduced, the hand becomes moist and resistance to the current drops. The individual may soon recover from the experience and the resistance to the current is restored. If, on the other hand, mild tension continues for an extended period of time, the individual will show a gradually decreasing basal level of resistance without the specific responses. People who stay awake for long periods of time, or are exposed to loud sounds for extensive periods show this change.

This theory has roots in early philosophical concepts of hedonism as expounded by Greek philosophers and later by Jeremy Bentham and John Stuart Mill in England. Its central assumption is that behavior is directed toward pleasure and away from pain. Slight variations in stimulation are considered to have positive valence and are sought. Large changes have negative valence and are avoided, or, if forced upon the individual, will cause behavior to reduce the arousing elements in the stimulation.

5.   There are individual differences in tolerance and preference for arousal potential. When confronted by a specific amount of arousal potential, some people will react with positive affect, interest, and exploration. Others may become overly tense and inefficient, and try to reject, avoid, or withdraw from the source of stimulation. Similarly, some people will seek to induce large changes into their environments while others will try to maintain the *status quo* as much as possible. This tolerance and preference for arousal potential has been labeled *curiosity* and will be explored later in the chapter.

In summary, the model suggested in this chapter is one which argues for the importance of awareness of the arousal level in any individual in order to understand and predict how he will behave and what he will choose to do. It is postulated that each person has a tonus level which, although not fixed at any point, is peculiar to him. This tonus level usually lies somewhere below the point of optimum efficiency, so that the induction of additional arousal will generally increase efficiency. But if arousal continues to rise, efficiency will begin to drop. Every individual prefers some optimal intake of arousal potential but abhors too much or too little. His behavior is aimed at maintaining a constant flow of information input.

AROUSAL AND LEARNING

A series of interesting studies demonstrated a possible relationship between arousal, performance, and learning. These studies showed that material learned under a condition of heightened arousal may not be recalled well immediately, but the learner may *reminisce* about the material and can recall it better at some later time.

As an illustration of this phenomenon, Kleinsmith and Kaplan [1963] presented a series of words to subjects one at a time for a brief interval and asked them to recall the words. Some of the words tended to be personally disconcerting to the subjects (e.g., *vomit, rape*) while others were received nonchalantly (e.g., *swim, dance*). The results . . . showed that while the arousing words were poorly recalled two minutes after learning, they were remembered much better later . . . . These studies suggest that the arousing words really must have been learned much better than the neutral words if they could be recalled so well a week later. Thus, performance in this instance was a poor indicator of learning.

There is a dictum that "only aroused persons learn." The evidence here is that people learn better those things which arouse or excite them and that they learn better when aroused to some intermediate level. Blurredness of stimulation has also been shown to increase arousal. In a recent experiment by Helzel [personal communication, 1969], students were shown a series of words for two seconds, and, without being directed to learn, were asked to recall the words either immediately after the experiment or twenty-four hours later. Some of the words were preceded by six seconds of the same word in a fairly clear condition (second carbon copy), some by six seconds in a slightly blurred condition (sixth copy), some by six seconds of an intermediately blurred condition (tenth copy), and some by six seconds of an extremely blurred condition (sixteenth copy). Subjects were asked to try to identify each blurred word during the six seconds. Thus, the words preceded by the slightly blurred conditions were actually viewed for eight seconds while the words preceded by the highly blurred condition were seen for only two seconds .... Of great interest are the findings that blurring the words to be presented enhanced both performance and learning and that blurring to the point of greatest uncertainty (i.e., the point where the greatest amount of effort at guessing the word correctly is required) is most effective.

Teaching was earlier defined to include the manipulation of motivational conditions to optimize the learning process in pupils; the judicious application of reinforcers to shape particular behaviors; the presentation of information to pupils under conditions of repetition until learning is consolidated; but, of greatest interest in this chapter, the skillful manipulation of environmental variables which will produce optimal arousal conditions in the pupils contiguous with the presentation of information to be learned.

If, then, the teacher is to be effective in stimulating pupils in order to optimize learning, it is essential that he recognize three important conditions:

1.   The tonus level of each pupil under relaxed conditions in the classroom,

2.   The student's characteristic level of intrinsic motivation, i.e., his willingness to receive additional stimulation and change in arousal, and

3.   The conditions in the classroom and in the material to be learned that can induce change in arousal.

ATTENTION

The term attention has been used in various ways with somewhat different meanings. As such it seems to denote something akin to arousal — to be alert or awake. But often the phrase used is "to pay attention to . . ." that is, to orient oneself toward a particular element in the environment excluding other elements, or to one aspect of a stimulus array. It is in this latter sense that the word attention is relevant here; not as the activation of arousal, but as the director of behavior toward a segment of the universe.

At any moment in time, our senses are exposed to an infinite array of stimuli, many more than can be perceived by our sense organs and transmitted to our brains. Our neural capacities are too limited to transmit so much stimulation and our brains inadequate to receive, record, and cope with all the input that can be transmitted. There must be a *gating mechanism* that excludes some of the stimulation from reaching the brain, even though it may have been perceived by the sense organs.

This filtering mechanism must have some criteria for allowing passage of particular stimulation and excluding others. One criterion is to transmit material which is relevant and which carries information. Not all stimulation is relevant or informative. *Information* is considered to be that which reduces uncertainty, and if no uncertainty about a particular facet of our environment exists, we stand to gain no information from it and we are not interested in attending to it.

Suppose a person enters a strange small, quiet room almost bare of furnishings. Unsure of how to react, his arousal level is elevated and he explores the room by looking, listening, smelling, and touching, in search of potentially threatening, interesting, attractive, and informative items. He sees a chair and sits in it, glancing about to continue the information-processing activity. But soon most of the uncertainty in the environment has been reduced and no more information is left to be readily extracted. He relaxes; his arousal level drops and his information search is reduced to a minimum. Should the environment change in some way, he again becomes alert and attentive, seeking the source of change for the information it may yield to him. If no change occurs in the environment, the person may continue to relax until he falls asleep or, conversely, may become bored and overly tense because of the lack of change and may begin to pace around the room in order to change his point of focus in the room with the hope of finding new perspectives which might prove informative and interesting.

Although it may take more time to process the information in an unchanging classroom, it must be assumed that a pupil will eventually extract most or all the information from the room and its usual contents. He will "know" the room and seek or create excitement elsewhere. He will attend to any change in the room, whether it is produced by the teacher, by his behavior or that of other pupils, or by sources of information introduced by the teacher.

Thus, we note that attention is a concomitant of arousal increase and is directed toward the source of change. People become unaware of familiarity in their environment and react to it neither physiologically nor with attention. Change in stimulation attracts attention and raises arousal. Extended sameness and lack of change also raises arousal, but initiates a search for stimulation, rather than attracting attention to a particular segment of the environment. Attention, therefore, may be seen as a particular type of behavior which directs us to explore the sources of arousal change in the environment.

SOURCES OF AROUSAL CHANGE

Berlyne [1963, 1965] has distinguished three groups of properties that enable stimulation to arouse us and attract our attention: *psychophysical, ecological,* and *collative* properties. The first two groups are fairly clearly defined. Psychophysical properties include characteristics of intensity, size, color, and pitch. Any sudden change in intensity of a stimulus, for example, will almost invariably attract attention and raise one's level of arousal, if only momentarily. Stimuli loaded with emotional overtones will quicken our pulses, make us catch our breath, and will attract attention. These are ecological properties, for they are associated with events of biological significance. The third set of variables has been defined to include properties which cause an interaction between the observer and the stimulus, the characteristics of which are dependent on his previous experience and expectations of the stimulus event.

Collative properties are considered by Berlyne to be of supreme influence with regard to the induction of curiosity and exploratory behavior and in advancing education in the classroom. Whereas other properties either affect individuals momentarily or are colored by emotional overtones so that they are hardly manipulable by the teacher, *collative variability* can easily be brought under the teacher's control and used to keep a classroom alert and attentive.

Collative properties depend on the collation or comparison of information from different sources. These sources may be contiguous or may involve the collation of present stimulus with past stimuli or experiences. Collative properties include *novelty, complexity, ambiguity, incongruity,* and other properties which contain a measure of unexpectedness and uncertainty. Their effectiveness depends on the observer's experiences, and his ability to distinguish elements in the universe from each other. For example, the perception of complexity in visual stimulation may develop over time, the infant being limited in his visual perception and the young child limited in his conceptualization of the subtleties in visual perception. Novelty, too, must be a function of previous experience, and should be viewed from two perspectives: that of absolute novelty—never having been perceived—and relative novelty—having been perceived at some time in the past.

It often becomes difficult to distinguish between the various properties which are subsumed under the rubric of collative variability. A stimulus such as an *elephish* (see Figure 2) may be incongruous to some, but children might be more

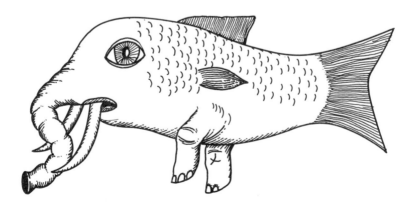

Figure 2. An incongruous stimulus, the elephish.

prone to call it a novel animal. Regardless of the label imposed on the stimulus, the reactions are the same: 1. Orientation toward the stimulus, 2. A rise in arousal level, 3. The induction of a state of curiosity, and 4. The initiation of exploration and epistemic behavior.

CURIOSITY AND SPECIFIC EXPLORATION

Berlyne [1963, 1965] has dichotomized exploration into *specific* and *diversive*. He sees the former as having the purpose of intensifying stimulation from specific portions of the stimulus field and is therefore exploration of a specific object— finding out about something. Diversive exploration, on the other hand, has the purpose of establishing contact with new sources of stimulation, i.e., looking *for* collative variability.

Day [1968a,b] has suggested that curiosity also can be dichotomized into similar groupings: specific and diversive. The former is a state induced by a condition of fairly high uncertainty arising from exposure to stimulation high in collative properties. It causes an elevation in arousal level and overt external responses of specific exploration. Similarly, Day sees diversive curiosity as a state of high arousal induced by an environment lacking in interesting stimulation, boring, repetitive, or homogenized. It too results from uncertainty, but leads to diversive exploration—the search for an interesting environment that approximates the optimal level of stimulation variability.

Collative properties act by inducing a state of *response conflict,* i.e., uncertainty about the nature of the stimulus and thus a conflict among the various response tendencies toward it. For example, the sight of an *elephish* may arouse opposing response tendencies—to react as though to an elephant and as though to a fish. If the response tendencies to both are alike (e.g., to run away) there would be little conflict (unless one runs away from an elephant faster than from a fish). If the observer had never seen or heard of a fish there would also be little conflict, for he would only be uncertain as to whether or not the novel or incongruous creature is really a type of elephant. But having experienced both elephants and fish, the viewer would surely be torn between identifying the strange objects as one or the other and choosing an appropriate response to the creature.

The degree of response conflict thus seems to depend upon the nature of previous experiences with similar stimulations. It also depends on the number of opposing response tendencies, their degree of opposition, their relative strengths and their absolute strength. This last factor is somehow related to how meaning-ful the whole situation is to the observer, for the more meaningful, the greater is the intensity of conflict.

The strength of response conflict determines the strength of the exploration which reduces the conflict. Unimportant specific curiosity, as from a comic cartoon, may induce only slight arousal and casual exploration. A meaningful situation with a high level of uncertainty (e.g., being lost in a fun house) will probably induce intense exploration.

Specific exploration can take many forms. Berlyne [1963, 1965] has categorized them into *receptor adjusting, locomotor,* and *investigatory.* The first consists of changes in orientation of parts of the body toward the source of stimulation and changes in sensitivity of sense organs. These responses include turning the head, dilating the pupils, and, fixating attention on a specific object. Locomotor exploration includes changes in the whole body, i.e., moving toward the source of stimulation. Investigatory behavior is mainly manipulative, handling a strange object, moving things aside to get to it, and similar actions. Often an exploratory response includes more than one type of behavior.

Berlyne [1965] also identified another type of behavior which has much in common with exploratory behavior. He called it *epistemic* behavior and reserved this nomenclature for behavior whose function is to equip the individual with knowledge. He attempted to distinguish between these two types of behavior, arguing that one deals mainly with the perception of objects or events while the other is directed toward reducing conflict about concepts and symbolic representations.

Berlyne divided the forms of epistemic exploration into three classes: *epistemic observation, consultation,* and *directed thinking.* He suggested that when an individual is aroused by events which create conceptual conflict, that is, conflict between incompatible symbolic response patterns (beliefs, attitudes, thoughts, and ideas) he will search for information which will reduce the conflict.

The types of conceptual conflict which can exist are really innumerable, but a listing of some of these may be of interest to educators.

1. *Doubt.* This is a conflict between tendencies to believe and to disbelieve a proposition, idea, or reality of an event. If an authority tells someone something which is hardly credible in his conceptual organization, conceptual conflict will arise and may lead to epistemic exploration.

2. *Perplexity.* This conflict occurs when an individual can think of several different but contradictory meanings for a concept and must decide on the "true" one.

3. *Contradiction.* This is a form of conflict, obtained when a teacher or person of authority makes definitive statements which are clearly opposed to an individual's attitude and belief system.

4. *Conceptual incongruity.* This is similar to perceptual incongruity (recall the example of an *elephish*) but arises from hearing or reading about the existence of events or objects which have mutually exclusive elements.

5. *Confusion.* Like ambiguity in the perceptual field, this state results from poorly received communication, due to conflicting elements. Confusion usually results from the presence of a large number of poorly defined elements rather than a conflict between two definite response tendencies.

6. *Irrelevance.* This is a conflict arising from a problem which appears insoluble and toward which the person is utterly at a loss. He can produce many alternative responses, but none of them appear to be relevant to the solution of the problem.

All of these conditions promote one or more of the forms of epistemic behavior. A pupil in a classroom, confronted with situations which induce conceptual conflict, becomes aroused and may initiate such exploratory behaviors that permit arousal and conflict to be reduced.

The category of epistemic observation, one form of epistemic behavior, is very similar to exploratory behavior, directing all one's resources to the exploration of the source of conflict for the purpose of gaining information. But rarely is this a solitary response. It usually occurs together with the other forms—consultation and directed thinking. Consultation includes many forms of search for information: asking questions, searching through books, catalogues, maps, and so on. Directed thinking, probably ubiquitous in all forms of exploratory and epistemic behavior, is thinking with a definite goal—that of choosing a successful response which will successfully solve a problem and eliminate a specific conflict.

Translating the preceding into an actual classroom situation, one would point out that a pupil is susceptible to the induction of conceptual conflict in a large number of ways, many of them manipulable by a teacher, and all of them serving to initiate exploratory and epistemic behavior. The form of exploration which the pupil chooses will probably depend to a great extent on the source of conflict, the type of conflict, and his previous success or lack of it with conflict reduction.

Teachers may have some difficulty in identifying highly curious children because much of the exploration of a curious child may be internalized. If a child asks questions, manipulates objects and orients his body in an obvious manner (e.g., waving his arm in the air) a teacher may indentify this behavior as a response to curiosity. However, if a child cogitates and sits quietly immersed in directed thinking, or consults books at home, a teacher may fail to realize that these responses are exploratory and epistemic. That child may instead be labeled as dreamy, inattentive, or dull. An active, questioning child may not be the most curious, although questioning is one method of conflict reduction. Instead he may be very anxious, or more likely one who has merely been reinforced previously at home or at school with attention for question-asking behavior.

A state of specific curiosity need not be unpleasant. An individual who is excited by, and interested in, some element in his environment may be happy while tense or cheerful while concerned. He may be faced with a problem, but he is willing to tackle and solve it.

OTHER FORMS OF MOTIVATION

Certainly it would be unreasonable not to acknowledge the role of other forms of motivation in education. Intrinsic motivation, while extremely potent, is but one of the many useful ways to enhance the learning and educational process.

Youth dreams of self-fulfillment and a world in which he can find involvement in significant matters. He seeks relevant material and ways which can help him contribute to the world's well-being as well as that of his own. A teacher must not miss the opportunity to utilize these potent motivational forces to move the pupil through periods when the stimulus material has lost some if its intrinsic appeal.

The promise of tomorrow is often neglected or avoided by teachers who find it easier to manipulate immediate satisfactions. In our present-day society we emphasize quick returns for our investments and immediate gratification. But teachers must not fear to expose their pupils to dreams and their possible outcomes—success for some and failure for others. The teacher must overcome the forces of TV, movies, and the pulp books which are usually success oriented, and wherein success is measured by material possessions. Children must be made to realize that self-fulfillment and self-actualization are far more satisfying goals.

This use of the future to shape today's behavior can be a subtle and powerful tool in a dedicated teacher's hands. But sometimes he must rely on more intermediate goals, not as distant as those achieved with maturity. . . .

One method of shaping behavior uses principles based on modeling theory. It has been shown that children learn by modeling themselves on their peers and on their elders. The models may be heroes (or antiheroes) of novels, TV and movies, or parents and teachers. If the teacher is a person who merits respect and is accepted as a model by the pupils, they will try to emulate his behavior, attitudes, and mannerisms. By seeing a teacher receive reinforcement for his behavior in the form of respect from his peers and other pupils, they will themselves be reinforced for initiative behavior. It therefore becomes important that teachers display the positive characteristics of curious people—they must seek novelty, complexity, and socially acceptable forms of excitement, and they must show interest in and persist in exploring collative variability in the environment.

When intrinsic motivation is inadequate in a particular situation and the manipulation of wishes and dreams is inappropriate, the teacher must have recourse to the direct and immediate reinforcement of the pupils' behaviors. Here the teacher may use principles derived from the study of conditioning to reinforce and shape behaviors which are considered desirable by society.

Shaping of behavior can be done in a number of ways: reinforcing desirable behaviors, ignoring unwanted behaviors, or punishing undesirable behaviors while emphasizing alternatives. The principles have been tested on animals and humans, and their applicability to the control of behavior in classrooms has been clearly demonstrated. There are many articles and books available illustrating and teaching the methodology of conditioning and behavior modification, and there is no reason to discuss it here. Only one *caveat* must be mentioned: Sometimes the modification of behavior relies on complete control and management by an agent external to the individual. There are times when control must be external—when there is reason to believe that the individual does not have the ability or maturity to manage himself well, for his own safety and self-development. This can be justified with autistic children and regressed schizophrenics, and perhaps less so with behavior problems of addiction and socially undesirable behaviors. Only in extreme cases should the external control of normal humans be delivered into the hands of external agents, even well-intentioned teachers. When this is done it must be with the full and conscious anticipation of the transfer of control back to the pupils themselves at the first opportunity.

Today there is greater emphasis on behavior-modification techniques which are based on the solicitation of cooperation of the pupil himself. The pupil may be asked to record his own behavior and to apply his own reinforcement. When this technique is well applied, the reinforcement may often become the satisfaction derived from the behavior itself.

CONCLUSION

We have presented an outline of intrinsic motivation with the hope that it may serve to develop an understanding by the teacher of the reasons for some of the activities and inactivities in the classroom. We have refrained from presenting too much of the voluminous data from which the propositions and hypotheses were derived in order to confine the chapter to a reasonable length. There are many arguable points in the chapter and many speculative ideas. But the hope is that the chapter will contribute a clear exposition of an arousal theory, and enough examples of its usefulness in the explanation of past and present behavior, to serve as a guide in understanding and predicting behavior.

Curiosity or intrinsic motivation was described as a state of tension arising from response conflict due to uncertainty or insufficient knowledge about a percept or concept that leads to further study or exploration, with the goal of obtaining additional information and so relieving the conflict and tension. We attempted to anchor the conceptualization to an arousal system in the brain, measurable by psychological, neurological, and biochemical changes.

We argued that performance, attitudes, and emotions were related to level of activity in the arousal system and to response conflict, and suggested that learning, measured by delayed performance, is also related to arousal and conflict.

A possible division of curiosity into two types, specific and diversive, was proposed. Specific curiosity was defined as a state of conflict arising from insufficient information from a particular source, external or internal to the individual, leading to increased exploration of that source. Diversive curiosity was explained as response conflict arising from monotony or insufficient stimulus change instituting a search for diverse sources of stimulation, this behavior often being termed recreation, play, or daydreaming.

Finally, throughout the chapter we attempted to make the reader aware of the motivational forces within each person, and the potency of the intrinsic motivational drive when it is judiciously stimulated through a deliberate manipulation of environmental conditions for the purpose of optimizing attention, performance, and learning.

REFERENCES

Berlyne, D. E. Motivational problems raised by exploratory and epistemic behavior. In S. Koch (Ed.), *Psychology: A Study of a Science*, Vol. 5. New York: McGraw-Hill, 1963, pp. 284–364.

Berlyne, D. E. Curiosity and education. In J. D. Krumboltz (Ed.), *Learning and the Educational Process*. Chicago: Rand McNally, 1965, pp. 67–89.

Day, H. I. Role of specific curiosity in school achievement. *Journal of Educational Psychology*, 1968, 59:37–43. (a)

Day, H. I. A curious approach to creativity. *The Canadian Psychologist*, 1968, 9:485–97. (b)

Hebb, D. O. Drives and the CNS (conceptual nervous system). *Psychological Review*, 1955, 62:243–54.

Kleinsmith, L. J., and Kaplan, S. Paired-associate learning as a function of arousal and interpolated interval. *Journal of Experimental Psychology*, 1963, 65:190–93.

Lindsley, D. B. Emotion. In S. S. Stevens (Ed.), *Handbook of Experimental Psychology*. New York: Wiley, 1951, pp. 473–516.

Magoun, H. W. Caudal and cephalic influences of brain-stem reticular formation. *Physiological Review*, 1950, 30:459–74.

Moruzzi, G., and Magoun, H. W. Brainstem reticular formation and activation of the EEG. *EEG Clinical Neurophysiology*, 1949, 1:455–73.

REVIEW QUESTIONS

1. True or false:
   a. A pat on the head would be an *extrinsic* reinforcer.
   b. Murray and Maslow formulated lists and hierarchically organized categories of needs.
   c. The RAS controls the level of arousal.
   d. The higher the *tonus level of* arousal, the sleepier you are.
   e. Individuals differ in levels of arousal (alertness, energy, excitability).
   f. Individuals also differ in their preferences for higher stimulation levels.
   g. Moderate changes in stimulation (hence arousal) are pleasant.
   h. Optimum learning occurs at an intermediate arousal level.
   i. Attention seems to include a *gating* or *filtering* mechanism which prevents some incoming information from reaching the brain.
   j. *Epistemic behavior* is information-seeking to reduce conceptual conflict.

2. As a result of reading this article, do you better understand why some children are more active than others? Do you have any ideas for stimulating *intrinsic* motivation?

Answers to question 1: a. true, b. true, c. true, d. false, e. true, f. true, g. true, h. true, i. true.

nineteen

The Development of Competence

FRANK E. NARDINE

THE CONSTRUCT OF COMPETENCE

BACKGROUND AND DERIVATION

The construct of *competence* as it generally appears in psychological literature today was proposed and refined by Robert W. White [1959, 1960, 1965]. White [1965] reports that his interest in competence grew out of his "grave discontent with psychological theories in which the person was treated as the result of the influences acting upon him, not as himself an effective agent in events" [p. 1]. In White's view, a person is *not* merely the sum of the influences of his experiences, but rather a competent and reasoning being who can take a hand in his own course of development. The term *competence* is used to describe an individual's ability to take the initiative and act upon his environment rather than standing by passively and allowing the environment to control him and determine his every act. The competent individual sees himself as master of his own destiny and captain of his own fate rather than as a pawn of capricious and uncertain fortune. The competent person has both the skills necessary to interact successfully with his world and the confidence required to brave new ventures. This view of competence coincides with the popular definition of competence as denoting being able, proficient, adept, and effective in some aspect of life.

The first criterion or dimension of competence, then, is the attainment of a specified degree of knowledge and associated level of performance, often that which Bloom [1968] refers to as *mastery*. Generally, the degree of competence is judged by the effectiveness with which an individual is able to deal with his world, or, as White [1959] terms it, an "... organism's capability to interact effectively with its environment" [p. 279].

Source: Abridgment of Chapter 12 from *Psychology and Educational Practice* by Gerald S. Lesser (Ed.). Copyright © 1971 by Scott, Foresman and Company. Reprinted by permission of the author and the publisher.

In addition to the mastery criterion of competence, there is a second dimension ideally associated with the construct, namely an individual's self-confidence or *sense* of being competent and able to *cope*. This sense of competence permits the individual to enter and explore new situations, new areas of learning, and skill development.

COMPETENCE AND THE SCHOOLS

The competent person might be described as an effective and affective agent or force. Our schools can be very influential in the development of such a person. Their role in promoting and fostering cognitive growth and development is widely accepted and indeed generally regarded as the schools' *raison d'être*. The obligation of the schools to promote a positive self-concept and sense of achievement is less intuitively obvious. Nonetheless, a feeling of efficacy and sense of achievement are necessary adjuncts of cognitive growth, without which the individual will not have the confidence and self-assurance requisite for ventures into the new areas of learning and skill dvelopment. The relationship between skills and self-confidence is a spiral one, and growth requires that both be present. Knowledge and mastery ideally lead to development of confidence in one's skills and ability, and confidence supports the efforts to master new skills, the achievement of which in turn buttresses confidence. Thus, self-confidence is a *sine qua non* of competence growth as it provides the basis for taking risks and for expanding one's skills into new areas.

The modern approach to schooling emphasizes the need for expansion or continuous learning in a technological society where the skills acquired in school may shortly thereafter become obsolete. We seek to produce students who not only have acquired a sound base in learned skills, but who also are able and motivated to expand that base and to acquire for themselves new skills when they are needed. The role of the school, then, must be to foster both cognitive growth and an appropriate sense of confidence in one's efficacy and ability to learn new skills if we are to graduate competent individuals who will initiate their own further or ongoing education.

THE GROWTH OF COMPETENCE

GENERAL COURSE OF DEVELOPMENT

White maintains that man is naturally curious. He starts learning to interact with his environment shortly after birth and continues to explore and experiment with the infinite facets of his world for the rest of his life. During the first years of his life the small child engages in a wide range of exploratory activities. Experimentation with the environment is natural and a part of normal development. Witness, for example, the typical behavior of a young child during feeding in which he investigates the utensils and explores the behavior of spilled food. Such behavior, White suggests, is directed and selective, and constitutes the child's attempts to interact with and manipulate his environment. The child's *fitness* to interact with his environment comes about through a very gradual process of accumulated and prolonged learning. Through this process of inquiry, children learn to bring their environment more into service. This process of mastering and to some extent controlling his world affords the individual great satisfaction. When, as he grows older, *efficient action* allows an individual to manipulate his environment, when he is successful in his dealings with his world, or when he is able to function effectively, the individual is apt to be pleased with himself and positive about his abilities. The feeling of confidence which he possesses may motivate or lead him to engage in further exploration of the world and further attempts to manipulate the environment in his service.

White [1965] would thus argue that learning and achievement are intrinsically satisfying and rewarding in and of themselves: The child does not require an external reward such as a gold star given by the teacher to spur him on to further efforts, pleasant as such recognition may be to him, since . . . "intrinsic satisfaction comes from expending effort and producing consequences" [p. 4]. The satisfaction generated by real accomplishment provides the basic and most powerful motivation for further efforts and learning.

IDEAL DEVELOPMENT OF COMPETENCE

Ideally, competence and self-confidence will have developed from a child's earliest days through the interaction between the child and his environment. The child affects his environment and in turn the environment affects him; this transaction is a perpetual testing ground for a child, and he discovers a more-or-less endless stream of consequences for what he does. From these experiences the child derives some facility or degree of competence in dealing with his world. The level of competence is ultimately contingent upon the degree of success the individual achieves.

The outcomes of the child's interaction with his environment lead to certain perceptions, learnings, differentiations, ways of structuring and interpreting his experience, and strategies of future attack. In other words, competence grows out of a continuous process of testing the environment and of observing the results one has produced. From this interaction, certain behavioral patterns for dealing with day-to-day events emerge. Thus, the child begins to perceive, think, and act in regularly established and often predictable ways. Throughout this process, he begins to view himself in relation to the degree of success he has had in coping with whatever has confronted him. Ideally, the child has had successful dealings with his world and has experienced gratification through his own efforts and achievements. If this is indeed the case, he will have a measured degree of competency and, under the ideal situation, a realistic level of confidence proportionate to his skill. An accurate assessment of abilities becomes the basis for future levels of aspiration, and both skills and self-confidence increase and develop as the child meets progressively more difficult challenges during his school years.

The early school years are of critical importance to the development of a child's competence. The school is responsible for the development and nurturing of the child's cognitive skills. Without real and actual achievement, the child must either regard himself as a failure or fantasize some accomplishment which is in fact an idle and empty boast. The teacher is central to the ideal development of competence, first for her skill in nurturing cognitive growth and facility, and second, but equally important, for her skill in encouraging and developing the child's confidence in the cognitive area. The importance of the confidence level cannot be underestimated, for it certainly affects and may well determine the child's future attitude toward learning.

The academic aspects of schools can thus be seen as being of vital importance to a child's growth in competence. The process of testing the environment and thereby determining one's powers and limitations also occurs in the social area. A child develops social and interpersonal abilities and social self-confidence through his interactions with other children in the classroom. Although the teacher's primary responsibility lies in developing cognitive competence, she has an opportunity to aid and abet a child's growth in social areas also, thereby encouraging balanced and healthy personality development.

CRITICAL STAGES

Certain periods or stages of development present critical challenges to the growth of competence. One of these developmental stages occurs at about the age of two years and can be very trying to a parent, tempting him to resolve the situation in a decisive manner which is not conducive to the growth of competence in the child. Most children go through a stage of experimentation and exploration of feeding, for example, in which the child insists upon doing it himself and brooks no interference or suggestion from parents. Often the child's activity seems inefficient and time consuming to the parent who in exasperation finally intervenes or takes over, wrests the spoon from the child and shovels the mashed and scattered food into his mouth. Ideally, the parent would allow the child to gain coordination and competency through manipulating his utensils and feeding himself. Similarly, the teacher may later discourage the autonomy strivings of the young child who is fumbling with words, trying to make a circuit with the batteries upside down, or otherwise engaged in awkward or inefficient behavior, by taking over and doing for the youngster what he wishes and should be allowed to do for himself. In order to encourage the growth of competence, the parent and teacher must bear with the child's efforts, respecting his desire to manipulate his world himself and offering aid only when it is wanted.

The time of school entrance is another of the critical stages in the growth of competence. Ideally, the home situation will have provided opportunities for the child to deal successfully with his environment. Thus, the child comes to school expecting further opportunities for successful functioning and eager for new explorations and learning experiences. Erikson [1950] points out that "Many a child's development is disrupted when family life may not have prepared him for school life, or when school life may fail to sustain the promises of earlier stages" [p. 227]. It is at this stage of school entrance that the child experiences, often for the first time, the full weight of the world outside his family. The ideal situation will provide an initial confrontation that allows the child opportunities to succeed, thereby strengthening his skills and confirming his status in his own eyes as a worthy and competent individual. The danger, as Erikson warns, lies in a sense of *inadequacy* and *inferiority* which the child may gain if his initial efforts in school result in consistent failure. It does not take long for the child who is not learning to read to recognize his failure and to develop feelings of inadequacy about his ability, feelings which often result in a defeat or failure syndrome. Failure becomes a self-fulfilling prophecy. The child fails, leading him to expect failure which, in turn, produces further failure. Thus, early school experiences are crucial in the determination of competence or incompetence, and the teacher is a prime determinant of the child's sense of accomplishment or defeat.

IMPEDIMENTS TO THE DEVELOPMENT OF COMPETENCE

White asserts that the most critical period of competence development is during childhood. In these formative years the growth of competence is either fostered or impeded. Failure to master a task regarded or designated as important, or even the feeling that one has failed to master the task, can lead to debilitating anxiety and a sense of oppressive frustration. The effect of a major or prolonged failure can be so dire that the child may refuse to venture again or to try new things. The following section focuses on the etiology of those children who have low competence—the children who have failed.

In the ideal development of competence, the child tests his abilities in a range of areas and, by observing the results of his efforts, acquires an accurate estimate of his capabilities. However, numerous factors can intervene in the development of competence and its associated feelings. Often the misguided efforts of adults seriously interfere with growth in competence and cause lasting damage.

EXCESSIVE EXTERNAL DIRECTIONS AND REWARDS

Parents and teachers who insist on directing or overseeing the child's every action may stifle a child's natural curiosity and cause him to become dependent on external guidance and support. If the child is rewarded only when he follows directives, he may abnegate his prerogative to think for himself and passively await suggestions or "spoon feeding." Eventually, this child probably loses even the desire to make his own judgments and finds security in executing the ideas and directives of other people. Such a child is apt to be *other-directed,* that is, oriented toward and excessively dependent upon the direction and approbation of other people.

UNREALISTICALLY LOW EXPECTATIONS

Adults who hold low expectancies for a child's performance may place barriers on the growth of competence, for some children readily accept others' estimates of their ability. . . . If the child's efforts are constantly disparaged or if adults convey to him that he is in some sense inferior, the child will internalize the negativism expressed and regard himself and his efforts as failures. Believing that he is capable only of inferior work, the child generally does not exert a real effort to learn or master, or his anxiety interferes with his learning. Consequently, he does not learn or achieve, and his failure only serves to reinforce his feelings of inferiority. Not experiencing success, he does not have the opportunity to revise his low estimate of his ability. The circular effect of failure resulting in expectation and feelings of failure resulting in further failure are well documented in psychological literature.

A few examples will suffice to illustrate the point. The relationship between one's expectations for himself and achievement is described in Lecky's [1945] case study in which a student of his, though intelligent, was an extremely poor speller. As is sometimes the case with a person weak in spelling, this child had been subjected to a strong dose of extra practice in this area, but without any appreciable success or improvement. It was difficult for his teachers to explain why this student, who showed considerable facility in his other subjects, should have such difficulty learning to spell. His success in his other school work indicated that his impairment in spelling was not due to lack of ability. Upon investigation, Lecky discovered that this pupil actually believed that he was, once and forever, a poor speller. Extra instruction aimed at overcoming his deficiency was ineffective in the face of the student's conviction that he was and would be unable to spell. Lecky [1945] reported that ". . . the resistance arises from the fact that at some time in the past the suggestion that he was a poor speller was accepted and incorporated into his definition of himself, and became an integral part of his total personality" [p. 178]. In effect, this poor speller had a definition of himself as a poor speller and expected future behavior to be in consonance with this low standard. In a very general sense, then, what a person is able or unable to learn will depend to some extent upon the nature of his past learning experience. Self-expectation, in other words, can become a self-fulfilling prophecy.

FAILURE IN MEETING EXCESSIVELY HIGH
PERFORMANCE STANDARDS

Adults often create competitive situations for children on the assumption that competition will act as a stimulus or perhaps a goad spurring the child on to greater efforts. Competition, if channeled and controlled, may result in behavior which contributes to gaining mastery by inspiring the individual to exert that little extra something that makes a superior performance possible. However, competitive situations also can result in the child's acquiring a crippling feeling of inadequacy and despair if he continually loses, especially to his peers. The competition may in reality be unfair; that is, the child may be pitted against a larger, more mature, more popular, or more intelligent peer so that his defeat is almost assured from the beginning. Usually the child will not perceive the competition as unequal or realize that he may have made a good showing, all things considered. He may mutter that "it isn't fair," but the anger, hurt, and discouragement at being a constant loser, always being chosen last, or being in the slow reading group may create attitudes and patterns of behavior that tend to enhance continued failure. Failure in competition thus may discourage a child from additional attempts at mastering the environment. Persistent failure may lead to anxiety and failure-avoidant patterns of effort in which the child simply refuses to try or else selects a task so difficult that no one will expect him to succeed and hence will not condemn him for failing.

A teacher who sets a common standard of performance for the whole class will inevitably contribute to the failure of some children to develop competence. One fact of life that faces the teacher is that children enter school with varying degrees of competencies and proceed to develop at uneven rates, with the result that divergency increases with each passing year. A teacher who grades the class on a sliding scale with A's going to the children who complete the most problems correctly or write the most imaginative or sophisticated themes and B's, C's, and D's awarded to the other children as their work compares to that of the A children, is setting up a competitive situation that will defeat some children all of the time. A child whose mind is not as agile as that of the best student, or whose personality or approach is different from that which the teacher favors or ranks as most desirable, is doomed to spend six hours a day, week after week, in a failure situation or, in the current phrase, contemplating his inferiority. Interestingly, some of the children who appear as mediocre or even as slow in one setting may show to much greater advantage placed in a different class or school. Thus, a child who is rated as a C student in an elite private school whose entrance exams have eliminated all but the brightest children may be rated as a B child or even as an A child in a school with a more normal distribution. A child who does not excel in this group might have been one of the pacesetters of the class had he just come along one year sooner or later and had lesser or different competition. The child does not change; only the context in which he appears determines whether he is to be an A, B, or C child. Yet this child placed in a context where he is rated as C will think of himself as mediocre, and his further performances will probably reflect his attitude and his battered self-concept.

What of the child who is in fact a slow or below-average learner? This child faces the continual discouragement of always finding himself at the bottom of the academic heap. He is not developing competency according to the teacher's judgment as reflected in his grades, and his feelings about his ability and his motivation to stand on his own feet flag with each additional F. The first-grade teacher, in an attempt to salvage some modicum of self-respect for the low-ability child, may have appointed him chief eraser clapper, but such a distinction hardly balances the realization of academic nonachievement and recognition of intellectual incompetency that the child sees in his marks. For this child, school is probably a maintenance situation at best and perhaps more of a treadmill on which his incompetencies and the resultant feelings of defeat increase as he marks time and stays in place.

IDENTIFICATION AND TEACHING STRATEGY

As indicated earlier, discovering the competence level of a particular child requires careful observation and analysis. The teacher will be engaged in the complicated task of interpreting human behavior, and, on the basis of his interpretation, forming a professional judgment concerning the best instructional strategy for the child. The guidelines below are intended to aid the teacher in his observation and analysis. The general descriptions are meant as an aid in the recognition and classification of different types of children, and the teaching strategies which follow the descriptions are included as suggestions of kinds of strategies appropriate for the child to facilitate his growth toward greater competence.

A CLASSIFICATION OF COMPETENCE LEVELS

Although children differ from one another in an infinite number of ways that defy categorization, they can generally be classified in four rather distinct ways, depending upon their levels of cognitive competence, i.e., their level of performance and self-confidence. The chart below represents the four general classifications of competence:

A child in group I is high in both performance and confidence (a plus-plus child); a child in group II is high in performance but low in confidence (a plus-

COGNITIVE COMPETENCE

Group	Performance	Confidence
I	+	+
II	+	—
III	—	+
IV	—	—

(Plus [+] signifies high; minus [—] signifies low.)

minus child); a child in Group III is low in performance but high in confidence (a minus-plus child); and a child in Group IV is low in both performance and confidence (a minus-minus child).

This model is not intended to group all children once and forever into one of these four cells, nor is it meant to imply that children who have been grouped together in any category are alike in every respect. . . . Also, it is highly probable that a child will fall into one group in a particular curriculum area and into another group in a different area, as in the example previously given of the boy lacking in performance ability and confidence in the area of spelling only. The purpose of the model is to provide teachers with a useful tool by which to effect an initial recognition of children's competency levels.

Group I (plus-plus); high performance—high confidence. This type of child shows a willingness to take risks. This willingness seems to stem from his proven or demonstrated abilities and his feeling that he can manipulate or control his environment. He feels free to explore his hunches and his original, sometimes "way-out" ideas. He welcomes new experiences and challenges and is continually reaching outward and inward in search for new meaning. This child is able to analyze his failures in an objective way without a feeling of personal threat. His investigation in this respect is a search for causality, a "What went wrong here?" approach. Unless he feels extremely frustrated by the school environment or is trapped by a personality clash with a particular teacher, this child exercises considerable intellectual independence relative to his age group. His expectations for success are high and he persists in a given task, usually achieving the standard he has set for himself. This child profits greatly when given a relatively free rein in his learning experiences.

The plus-plus child will have relatively few academic weaknesses. His most likely weakness is impatience with the routine drill and practice required to master certain basic skills such as number facts, spelling, or handwriting. Thus, he may exhibit deficits or lacks in certain low-level learning which may hinder his progress in later high-level learning and produce an erratic or uneven academic profile.

Instructional strategy. Since this child is well on his way toward mastering skills, tools, and other school objectives, he personifies overall cognitive facility and high confidence about his learning prowess. An important dimension of his competency is his capacity to learn new competencies when they are desired or needed. In the classroom, the territory and the ground rules for learning can be established by the teacher, by the child, or by both jointly. When the teacher specifies or delineates the learning task in a manner which is arbitrary or restrictive, the plus-plus child is apt to react in one of three ways depending upon the particulars of the situation:

1.   The child may reject the task or goals entirely, and either balk at participating or dash off something which will be the bare minimum letter of the assignment but will not involve any thinking or effort.

2.   He may modify the task in some creative way, embellishing it with his own original twist or interpreting it in the light of his own interests and learning desires.

3. He may expand the original assignment far beyond the teacher's specification, the project growing with his developing interest.

When this child accepts an assignment, he assimilates it and makes it his own, with the result that his work is highly individual and bears his own personal touch.

The child is, in essence, engaging in the highly sophisticated process of setting his own standards, and the teacher acts as a facilitator of learning, promoting and freeing inquiry. Even with the highly competent child, the teacher's help will be needed in defining areas or problems, focusing on the pertinent data, and providing feedback to the student's hypotheses and findings. Suchman [1961] suggests that the teacher should serve as a model of an inquirer as well as a resource and guidance figure; the plus-plus child probably offers the teacher the greatest opportunity to assume this subtle and sophisticated role of guide and model. The teacher must accord this child sufficient latitude to generate ideas and chart his own progress along the route. The teacher can assist the child along the way when he is stuck by making suggestions that will enable the child to think through an issue or overcome an obstacle. He has to resist telling the child and allow the suggestions he makes to be rejected. The trick is for both the teacher and the child to understand one another's territorial rights. The teacher neither gives nor does the child accept *unnecessary* aid. The teacher has to be prepared to accept some deviation from the agreed-upon task, for the child has an inquiring mind and inquiry must run its own course.

The teacher *has to supervise* the plus-plus child, but at a safe distance so as not to interfere when his aid is not needed. The teacher should strive to cultivate a free and relaxed classroom atmosphere that encourages the child to come for help when he feels the need. The clear expectation on the part of the teacher is for the child to do his very best work. The plus-plus child has internalized this expectation to an extensive degree. Interestingly enough, the most effective quality control the teacher can exert if he suspects substandard work is contained in the question, "Is this your very best work?" The highly competent, highly confident child will answer this question fairly accurately. Usually a negative reply on the part of the child is motivation enough for him to strive for a higher quality of performance. Perhaps this appeal to pride in performance is the best way to persuade this type of child to put forth the effort necessary to master the basic skills, the acquisition of which so often bores him. In essence, this is a *subtle* kind of encouragement of self-evaluation and self-competition. If one word has to describe the teacher's role in regard to the plus-plus child, it is the word *subtle*. The teacher ceases to teach but begins to educate in the true sense of the word by leading forth and leading out. The teacher has to challenge the highly competent, highly confident child without competing with him. The criterion of ultimate success for the teacher is that he is no longer needed as teacher, but serves as a guide or facilitator, posing alternative goals and strategies for the plus-plus child to consider.

Few classrooms today contain more than a handful of plus-plus children. For the majority of children, competency growth has been in some way restricted or damaged. The kind of teaching strategy appropriate for the plus-plus child is not appropriate for the rest of the children, at least not at first. Thus, while the child whose performance and confidence levels are high may profit from an instructional process where the teacher serves as guide and remains largely in the background, the instructional process will need some modification for children whose competency growth is damaged or otherwise incomplete. Here again the exact teaching strategy depends upon the learning and motivational characteristics of the child under consideration. For some children the teacher must first seek to build the level of confidence the child has in himself; for others the teacher has to decide how best to increase the child's level of performance in order that he may feel justifiable pride and satisfaction. Still others will need help from the teacher in developing both greater confidence and higher performance levels.

The three groups of children described below encompass the vast majority of pupils found in today's classrooms. The teaching strategies are illustrative of practices that teachers can use to increase growth in competence for these children.

Group II (plus-minus); high performance—low confidence. This type of child, though capable of doing a good job, seeks constant assurance from others. Again and again he approaches the teacher or his peers with such questions as "Am I doing this right?" or "Is this what we're supposed to do?" This type of child seeks approval, of himself and his work, and does not derive intrinsic satisfaction from accomplishment of the task itself. Although the child's work is often above average, his feeling of inadequacy may impel him to seek reassurance and approval in even such personally expressive areas as art and music. Small errors and misunderstandings are magnified, and often the child engages in self-recrimination. Generally, he has little faith in his own abilities and is, therefore, highly susceptible to the influence and opinion of others. His emotional dependence is related to his intellectual dependence. A child with these characteristics is not adept at setting realistic standards for himself but will work hard to meet those set for him. Usually he finds freedom to choose his own course of action threatening.

Instructional strategy. The competent but nonconfident child presents a particular challenge to the teacher on two counts. First, this plus-minus child plainly has definite areas of performance ability. Nevertheless, he frequently seems to bid for support and verification from others concerning his performance on a given task. Second, the low confidence that the child has in himself often inhibits the growth of existing competencies as well as the development of new skills. The child may well seek to preserve a maintenance situation because enhancement situations where new levels of performance come about are threatening since they involve greater risk. Thus, the teacher's job is, first, to arrange situations that trigger the process whereby the child will gain realistic satisfaction from that which he already does well and, second, to break ground toward achieving additional competencies. Often the teacher has accepted the plus-minus child's adequate performance at the expense of a broader view of the performance-attitude relationship because the child's incapacities appear slight. However, long-term intellectual dependence and external reliance are apt to increase if the teacher does not intervene.

The teacher has to plan his interaction with this type of child so that he refrains from reinforcing dependency but still provides an environment of encouragement. The task is made easier by the existing competencies of the child because they serve as a foundation for promoting growth of confidence. With these competencies in mind, the teacher can design lessons which demand that the child set goals for himself. Part of the assigned task can be setting sights or fixing goals. Thus the structuring of the problem or the decision, e.g., "What constitutes a good report," is in itself the end goal. The process of setting standards places responsibility squarely upon the child.

The child can be encouraged to express his own opinions about his work. If he is unduly critical, the teacher can ask him what he is most pleased or satisfied with in the paper and what exactly he is dissatisfied with. In this way, the teacher can wean the child from wholesale "This is no good" condemnations of his efforts to a more realistic evaluation based upon a discussion of *specific* strengths and weaknesses. Another way of getting the child to reflect upon his own accomplishment without direct teacher presence is to comment extensively in writing on papers that the child hands in. The comments have to be judiciously written so as to earmark portions exemplifying demonstrated competence. The generative power of the written comments in terms of confidence building is great because the child can keep these as records or signposts. Instead of allowing the child to seek out the teacher continually for assurance throughout the day, time can be set aside after school for an informal school conference in which the progress of the child can be assessed. Plans and strategies can be developed which will enable the child to get through a short period of time without leaning on the teacher unnecessarily. The teacher can actively encourage greater periods of independent activity by the child. For example, when asked for comments or suggestions the teacher may reply that he prefers to wait until the child has completely finished the assigned task before commenting. Actually, it may seem more expedient to give the child immediate answers or solutions, but in the long run the child may learn much more if he is encouraged to work and make decisions with a minimum of help. Some assignments readily lend themselves to built-in evaluation where the child can judge his progress for himself, thereby promoting greater intellectual independence. Another technique which often can facilitate performance and confidence growth is the placing of the plus-minus child in a group with plus-plus children. The teacher can arrange interactions that contain a high probability that imitation or modeling will occur.

Once the teacher recognizes the plus-minus child's excessive reliance on others for setting goals and executing assignments, a corrective course of action almost prescribes itself. However, this initial recognition often does not occur readily because with the support of others the child seems to be functioning quite adequately. The teacher has to be particularly alert that the plus-minus child does not escape notice. The fact that he seems always to be striving for improvement may mislead the teacher into giving the kind of help which, although it does increase the child's competencies, at the same time increases his reliance upon outside support and approval.

Group III (minus-plus); low performance—high confidence. This type of child does not demonstrate competence. His evaluation of himself is unconnected with his particular school performance. His sense of control over his environment does not seem to be related to his actual school achievement. Often he excuses his mistakes by blaming outside factors or circumstances beyond his control. The minus-plus child is apt to demonstrate overestimation of his abilities by constantly volunteering for tasks beyond his persistence span or his capabilities. This type of child can be characterized as unsystematic in accomplishing assignments and impatient. He finds it difficult to accept evaluation of his performance by others. Often he may set unrealistic goals for himself and when they don't seem to be materializing, shift his goals or explain away his lack of progress. In short, this kind of child "talks a good game." His opinion of himself, however, is not lowered by a poor performance, and he appears to believe his excuses and rationalizations. This mismatch seems, as was previously discussed, to stem from parental attitudes toward the child and a parental tendency to regard everything that he does as right or exceptional.

In identifying this type of child, the teacher must exercise caution and be alert to the possibility that the minus-plus child may actually be a minus-minus child in disguise, with his expressions of confidence merely a bravado designed to conceal his deep-seated feelings of incompetency. If the case is such, the teacher's treatment would follow the lines that will be suggested for the minus-minus child.

Instructional strategy. This child, who is low in level of performance but high in confidence, presents the teacher with the most difficult challenge. Since this minus-plus child's confidence ratings often originate with his parents, the corrective measures which the teacher attempts may be interpreted as a personal attack on the parents. Thus, the best approach is to gain the confidence of the parents initially and to obtain their cooperation in effecting a strategy for the child. If the parents are receptive, changes are more apt to have a chance to occur. Unfortunately, parents will not always cooperate, and the teacher and the minus-plus child may find themselves pitted against one another, owing to their wide differences in evaluation of the child's performance. A personality clash often results. Obviously such a situation is unhealthy and should be avoided.

Difficult as it may sometimes be, the teacher has to refrain from tearing down the inflated and unsupported notions that the child has about himself. Instead, he must aid the child in developing abilities to perform specific and concrete tasks which will yield genuine achievements evident to both the child and others. The teacher will have to exert great patience in dealing with the minus-plus child because his accumulated experience of always having a high value placed upon his performance by his parents is not easily overcome. The child may find it extremely difficult to accept weaknesses, not to mention admitting or talking about them to others. Chances are when the teacher undertakes an analysis of the child's academic progress, he will probably be surprised at the deficits he finds. Often, because of the child's confident air and ability to persuade or divert the teacher, it has been assumed that certain skills have been mastered. At this point the teacher must insist that these missing skills be acquired, and he must plan instruction based upon his analysis of the child's learning capabilities. In one respect, the minus-plus child has an advantage over the other groups. Because he is so imperceptive of his incompetence, this type of child is sometimes incredibly optimistic and positive about his ability to progress. A teacher can capitalize upon his motivation and initial enthusiasm to get the child working hard at a level appropriate to his actual abilities. Later the teacher can point out the child's actual successes and realistic possibilities in response to his overzealous claims or espousal of overly ambitious projects. In this way, the teacher does not cause the child to lose face by denying or correcting his exaggerated claims, but rather he modifies the child's claims so that real success is possible for him.

It is difficult to indicate specific strategies to deal with the child fitting into this group because so much is predicated upon the particular personality and abilities involved. But as a general rule of thumb, the teacher has to create situations that prevent the child from losing face. It may be a temptation to attack the overconfidence of the child. However, open or public criticism of his inabilities or work habits will destroy any future basis for effective teacher intervention. A preferable approach is private communication between the teacher and the child, and even private instructional lessons within the classroom. Not only are these techniques informative in terms of assessing the child's learning difficulties and progress, but they allow the teacher to point out how effort is related to results. If the child does not engage in the task, then increased levels of performance cannot accrue. A good way to trigger the process is to place the child in a position of some responsibility where he is expected to produce tangible results. He might be chairman of a committee so that the other children expect him to take an active lead in the group's productivity and to get something done. Often other children's expectations can be more motivating than those of the teacher. The teacher might also link effort and result by constructing a visual record of the child's work progress which tracks his daily achievement. Such a record can serve as an impetus to work harder, and as the child puts more effort into the task at hand better results should occur. The teacher is then able to point out and compliment the child's specific acts or learnings. The minus-plus child's praiseworthy performance based on real achievement and paired with teacher acknowledgment is the beginning of competence training. As the child begins to acquire substantial competency in performing tasks well he will legitimize the confidence he has in himself. This kind of child is accustomed to monopolizing the limelight, and the teacher may need to structure opportunities for him to receive his due share of recognition, perhaps through such areas as the expressive arts rather than in academic areas in which his performance does not warrant such recognition. Some provision for praise must be made to bridge the period during which the child is acquiring academic skills and before he can demonstrate achievement. In summary, the teacher's prime responsibility is to see that the child's school tasks are geared correctly to his actual levels of performance so that legitimate successes are possible for him and situations which encourage distortion of achievement are minimized.

Group IV (minus-minus); low performance—low confidence. This type of child is one who experiences the least amount of success in today's classrooms. He is all too visible to both teachers and his peers, and he readily acquires a reputation as a slow learner in school subjects. This reputation, whether justified or not, is not easily shaken and often influences the child's own self-appraisal. The low-performance, low-confidence child reacts typically in one of two ways. On the one hand if he does not simply give up trying to succeed in his school tasks, he certainly does not invest much time or energy in accomplishing assignments, because he has learned that the investment fails to pay dividends. On the other hand, this type of child may be acutely sensitive to his inability to succeed, and this realization serves to make him even more dysfunctional in the school setting. In either case, a child fitting the Group IV description is easily threatened or intimidated. Thus, he views new experiences with anxiety and is reluctant to try them. There is little reason for him to display initiative, and low performance or even school failure is accepted as inevitable. The minus-minus child is apt to be quiet in the classroom hoping he won't be noticed. Sometimes in desperation when he is pressured to complete some bit of schoolwork he may copy or take the successful ideas of others, a process which detracts from the building of badly needed performance skills and self-confidence. Ultimately, the minus-minus child just gives up and rejects the whole school scene if for no other reason than self-preservation.

Instructional strategy. Through accumulated school experience the minus-minus child has learned that he is incompetent in school tasks. The child is submerged by a feeling of being involved in situations completely over his head and constantly senses that he is being threatened and defeated. It is this sense of defeat that the teacher must combat.

In part, this feeling can be attributed to the institutional routine that characterizes many classrooms. Inadvertently the instructor may be aiming educational happenings to the great middle class, and the too-rapid pacing of instruction passes over the low-performance, low-confidence child without any actual educational residue. The child, in effect, serves his time, but competencies are difficult to achieve. With full realization of the child's inability to grasp and master new skills and materials quickly, the teacher and curriculum specialist must devise alternate modes or levels of performance for him. Practices of endless repetition along with fierce determination on the part of the teacher to stick with a particular lesson until it sinks in should be abandoned because the learning process of the minus-minus child can be characterized as gradual and cyclical. That is, he needs longer exposure time to master a set of operations interspersed with new and different sets of operations. Prolonged, uninterrupted exposure should be replaced by calculated intervals which permit the child to focus and refocus. Each time around, the child assimilates more of the set of operations and gradually achieves increasing degrees of competency. The circling back takes into consideration the child's inability to obtain and retain the learnings during the first exposure. The focus begins to be placed correctly on the child's developing ability to perform instead of his existing inabilities.

An important component of developing genuine competence is completion of what one sets out to do. The surest way to begin to feel incompetent is never to experience *closure* or completion. By helping the child to write a realistic work-production contract the teacher can try to ensure specific accomplishment as well as to reduce the feeling of being overwhelmed. While the child is in the process of executing the contract, he needs considerably more help than children in the other three groups. The minus-minus child is least independent and has to be carefully observed to discern those precise moments when he is "stuck." The importance of this should not be underestimated because the child low in both performance and confidence is unable to discriminate whether his difficulties are attributable to himself or to the task or material. He merely assumes that he is at fault and his image of himself as incompetent is unjustifiably strengthened. One reason for this is the difficulty which this type of child has in seeing patterns and relationships. Therefore, the teacher should use all possible means at his disposal —analogies, charts, diagrams, and stories—to help the child to see how particular tasks fit into a larger framework.

The degree of genuine competence or mastery that the minus-minus child achieves over his school environment may be relatively less than that of the other children in the class, but the important experience for this child is the quality of success and not its quantity. The teacher has the resources at his command to ensure that the child's self-confidence is not destroyed because of his rate of learning. If steps are taken to ensure that some initial, though small, mastery over schoolwork and assignments occurs, greater degrees of competency will follow in due course. Since this kind of child, through the protective coloring of silence, is often the "invisible" child in the classroom, the teacher may be able to affect his self-image positively by making a special effort to know him personally and to let him know that he is liked and respected as a person, despite his low level of performance in school tasks.

CONCLUSION

The process of educating children, in the fullest sense of the word, is difficult and hazardous. The teacher must make decisions concerning the child and his education, the consequences of which may not be known for weeks, months, or even years. In terms of the teaching-learning process in the classroom, the crux of the matter is what Erikson [1950] calls *the process of mutual regulation*. An understanding of the construct of competence can aid the educator in promoting the process of shifting from teacher regulation to child regulation. That is, as the child develops and proceeds through the grades, the teacher must expect and promote increasingly higher levels of performance and must encourage greater degrees of confidence. A child's increasing competence is linked with more complex activities and more complicated behaviors. Thus, a changing relationship emerges between the child's developing capacities and teacher behavior and demands. The teacher's role and responsibilities must shift to accommodate the child's changing role and responsibilities. The shift occurs through a series of crucial, even decisive teacher-pupil encounters that play an integral part in the child's ultimate growth. The child gains mastery or control over his environment to the degree that the shift occurs. Thus, to an ever increasing extent the child must be given and assume the responsibility for his own learning. Only when the child is performing competently, and knows it through the realization of successful school experiences, can the teacher have any certainty that he is aiding the child to become functionally adequate in the world outside the classroom.

The process of competence training and growth is delicate and complex. The task of setting adequate performance levels and healthy expectations for individual children is very difficult, and to do so the teacher must come to know each child well enough to encourage him and demand that he do as well as he can, without imposing unrealistic expectations. The line between wasting a child's potential through underexpectancy and destroying self-confidence through overexpectancy is a fine distinction indeed, one which can be drawn only by a teacher highly sensitive to the performance and confidence levels of the children in his classroom. Paradoxically, the criterion of ultimate success for the teacher is a child who is competent to direct his own learning with minimal guidance and help from the teacher.

REFERENCES

Bloom, B. S. *Learning for Mastery: Evaluation Comment.* Los Angeles: Center for the Study of Evaluation of Instruction Programs, University of California, 1968, 1, No. 2.

Erikson, E. H. *Childhood and Society.* New York: Norton, 1950.

Lecky, P. *Self-consistency: Theory of Personality.* Hamden, Conn.: Shoe String Press, 1945.

Suchman, J. R. Inquiry training: building skills for autonomous discovery. *Merrill-Palmer Quarterly,* 1961, 7:147–70.

White, R. W. Motivation reconsidered: the concept of competence. *Psychological Review,* 1959, 66:297–333.

White, R. W. Competence and the psycho-sexual stages of development. *Nebraska Symposium on Motivation.* Lincoln: University of Nebraska Press, 1960, pp. 97–141.

White, R. W. Competence as a basic concept in the growth of personality. Paper prepared for the Social Science Research Council's Conference on the Socialization and Evaluation of Competence, San Juan, Puerto Rico, 1965.

REVIEW QUESTIONS

1.   Do you have college friends who seem to fit the four competence categories outlined by the author? Where do you belong?

2.   In what ways would teaching the plus-plus child be different from teaching the minus-minus person?

twenty

The Mainsprings of
Achievement-Oriented Activity

JOHN W. ATKINSON

The psychology of motivation must provide a useful way of thinking about the several factors that combine to produce interest in the various activities which constitute the curriculum in education. We have passed the day when there is any consensus that motivation, conceived merely as drive, must be present and reduced for learning to occur. But no one disputes that a student must be sufficiently motivated to attend school, at least, if he is to get an education, and sufficiently interested in what is going on in the classroom to pay attention once in a while if educational curricula are to have any of their intended effects on him.

The sources of interest in schoolwork and in those activities outside of classrooms which educational institutions try to encourage may vary substantially from one person to the next. For one, attention to the task at hand may be a matter of compliance with the wishes of an authority; for another, a way of gaining the warm approval of nurturant teachers and parents; for another, the expression of curiosity; for another, an avenue for expressing an interest in meeting the challenge of intellectual tasks and performing as well [as] or better than others; for another, the first practical step toward some long-term goal; for another, the competitive challenge may produce debilitating anxiety. The combination of all of these constitutes what we habitually refer to as motivation for learning in school. It is still an open empirical question whether one kind of interest in schoolwork enhances learning more than another and whether learning is influenced in any substantial way by the strength or degree of interest. These questions, as important as they are, have yet to be systematically explored.

Source: Abridgment of "The Mainsprings of Achievement-Oriented Activity" by John W. Atkinson from *Learning and the Educational Process* by J. D. Krumboltz (Ed.). Copyright © 1965 by Rand McNally and Company, Chicago. Reprinted by permission of the author and the publisher.

... Today there could be an integrated rather than a sporadic attack on many interrelated problems of motivation in education. Some useful techniques of study are available to replace the conventional wisdom, and so, also, are the enthusiastic and competent researchers. Perhaps the attack has already begun. Most needed to give it impetus and direction are a common understanding of the problem of motivation and a conceptual scheme which will provide a more enlightening initial guide than traditional psychological concepts of motivation generated in the study of lower animals. Those who are primarily concerned with the learning process frequently assume that the *kind* of motivation sustaining problem solving and practice is irrelevant as long as there is *some* motivation. I believe that this assumption is one of those shared oversimplifications derived from our common scientific heritage—the inadequate and nonfertile theory of drive.

The progress made in several programs of experimental study of human motivation since 1950 deserves the special attention of researchers in the field of education. One such program is Berlyne's work on curiosity. ... The others are the work on effects of anxiety on performance, which originated at Iowa [Spence, 1958; Taylor, 1956] and at Yale [Sarason et al., 1960], and the analysis of achievement motivation centered at Michigan and Harvard [Atkinson, 1958; Atkinson, 1964; Atkinson and Feather, 1966; McClelland et al., 1953; McClelland, 1961]. These programs of research on anxiety and achievement motivation ... have produced fruitful tools for research—the self-report tests of anxiety and the method for content analysis of imaginative behavior to assess the strength of achievement motive and other important social motives. And each has produced a fund of experimental findings describing how these components of motivation affect human learning and performance.

My immediate aim is to draw attention to a conceptual scheme which has evolved in the fifteen-year program of research on achievement motivation, particularly as it applies to analysis of the problems of aspiration and persistence in problem-solving behavior. These are central aspects of the problem of motivation in education. I hope to encourage some of you to begin to think a certain way about these issues—not because I believe this theoretical scheme or model represents the truth in any final sense, but because I believe it provides a very adequate memory aid and initial guide. It summarizes most, if not all, of what we know about the dynamics of achievement-oriented behavior, and it suggests new and nonobvious hypotheses about motivation which constitute potential tests of the scheme itself. ...

THE TENDENCY TO ACHIEVE SUCCESS

First, it is assumed that the strength of the tendency to achieve success *(Ts)*, which is expressed in the interest of an individual in some task and his performance, is a multiplicative function of three variables: motive to achieve success (M_S), conceived as a relatively general and relatively stable disposition of personality; and two other variables which represent the effect of the immediate environment—the strength of expectancy (or subjective probability) that performance of a task will be followed by success (P_S), and the relative attractiveness of success at that particular activity, which we call the incentive value of success (I_S). In other words, $T_S = M_S \times P_S \times I_S$.

... Following the early proposal of Lewin, Escalona, and Festinger, it is assumed that the incentive value or attractiveness of success is greater the more difficult the task. This idea is now stated as a relationship between the incentive value of success (I_S) and the strength of expectancy or subjective probability of success (P_S): viz., $I_S = 1 - P_S$. ... Consider, for example, what happens in a ring-toss game when each subject in one group is asked to stand at various distances from the peg and indicate how many times out of ten he thinks he can hit the target from that distance and each subject of another group is asked to recommend a monetary prize for hitting the target from various distances. Figure 1 shows that the average estimate of P_S decreases with distance, and the average

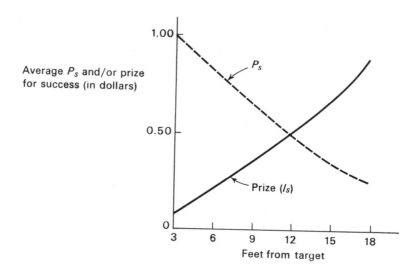

Figure 1. Estimated probability of success (P_s) and prize recommended for success (I_s) by 20 college students in ring-toss game [after Litwin, 1958].

monetary prize proposed, which we assume to be symbolic of an individual's estimate of his reaction to success at that distance, increases with distance. The result is similar when immediately after success at tasks which differ in difficulty, subjects are asked to rate the degree of their pleasure in success [Brown, 1963].

... The tendency to achieve is more strongly aroused by tasks having intermediate probability of success than either very easy or very difficult tasks. ...

THE TENDENCY TO AVOID FAILURE

For some years, our studies focused only on the behavioral consequences of differences in achievement motive until the unsolved problems and accumulated evidence in them, as well as in the independent programs of work employing the Manifest Anxiety Scale and the Test Anxiety Questionnaire, made it patently clear to us that whenever performance is evaluated in relation to some standard of excellence, what constitutes the challenge to achieve for one individual poses the threat of failure for another. The tendency to avoid failure associated with anxiety is as fundamentally important a factor in achievement-oriented action as the tendency to achieve success. We treat this tendency, which is conceived as an inhibitory tendency that functions to oppose and dampen the tendency to undertake achievement-oriented activities, as the source of the conscious experience of anxiety. The tendency to avoid failure is also considered a multiplicative function of a motive, an expectancy, and an incentive. We speak of the motive to avoid failure (M_{AF}) and refer to a disposition which is separate and distinct from the achievement motive. It might be thought of as a capacity for reacting with humiliation and shame when one fails. This is considered the source of individual differences in the anticipatory emotional reaction called anxiety or fear of failure. The tendency to avoid failure (T_{AF}) is aroused and expressed when there is an expectancy that some act will lead to failure (P_F), and it is also influenced by the incentive value of failure at that particular activity (I_F). That is, $T_{AF} = M_{AF} \times P_F \times I_F$. The incentive value of failure is negative, signifying that it functions like shock for a rat. It is a noxious event to be avoided. It is assumed that the negative incentive value of failure, i.e., the repulsiveness of failure, is greater the easier the task. No one feels very bad when he fails at a very difficult task, but to fail when a task appears easy is a source of great embarrassment.

... As with the achievement motive, we expect the effect of differences in disposition to anxiety to be more apparent in tasks of intermediate difficulty than in very easy or very difficult tasks. ...

THE RESULTANT ACHIEVEMENT-ORIENTED TENDENCY

We study achievement-oriented behavior today assuming that all individuals have acquired a motive to achieve (M_S) and a motive to avoid failure (M_{AF}). That is to say, all persons have some capacity for interest in achievement and some capacity for anxiety about failure. Both are expressed in any situation when it is apparent to the individual that his performance will be evaluated in reference to some standard. One of these motives produces a tendency to undertake the activity; the other produces a tendency to avoid undertaking the activity. There is what we traditionally call an approach-avoidance conflict. It is suggested by the conceptual scheme that we might better begin to think of this as a conflict between an *excitatory* tendency and an *inhibitory* tendency. It is assumed that the two opposed tendencies combine additively and yield a resultant achievement-oriented tendency which is either approach (excitatory) or avoidant (inhibitory) in character and of a certain strength depending upon the relative strength of motive to achieve success and motive to avoid failure in the individual. That is, the resultant tendency equals $T_S - T_{AF}$. . . .

MOTIVATIONAL EFFECTS OF ABILITY GROUPING

. . . In the traditional heterogeneous class, where all levels of ability are represented, the chance of being a standout performer relative to peers must seem almost impossible for the student of low ability and is virtually assured for the student of very high ability. According to theory, when P_S is either very low or very high neither interest in achievement nor anxiety about failure will be aroused. Hence only the students of average ability are likely to be very motivated to achieve or anxious in the traditional heterogeneous class.

What happens when students of comparable ability are brought together in the same class? According to theory, the student of high ability now faces a more competitive situation. His P_S should drop from near certainty towards .50, an intermediate risk. Just the opposite should happen for the student of very low ability. Now, for the first time he is surrounded by peers of equal ability and so he has the opportunity for success relative to the others. His P_S is increased towards .50. In other words, homogenization in terms of ability should make the learning situation one of intermediate achievement risk for more students than the traditional heterogeneous class. Is this good? The theory asserts that ability grouping should enhance interest and performance when the achievement motive is strong and the motive to avoid failure is weak. But it should heighten the tendency to avoid failure when that motive is dominant in the person. The same treatment should, in other words, have *diametrically opposite motivational effects* depending upon the personality of the students. . . .

THE LAW OF EFFECT—A MISLEADING GUIDE

Equally important is another general implication of the conceptual scheme which deserves some explicit comment. It is the argument that the Law of Effect is fundamentally inadequate as a guide to understanding in the domain of achievement-oriented activity. Success does not invariably produce a strengthening of the tendency to undertake the same activity on another occasion. Sometimes success weakens the subsequent tendency to engage in the same activity. The individual strongly motivated to achieve normally raises his level of aspiration following success: his behavior changes.

Gordon Allport [1943] noted this inadequacy of the Law of Effect more than twenty years ago, and now, at last, we have a reasonably clear explanation of why the traditional generalization does not hold. The law does not hold because in the domain of achievement-oriented activity an increase in the expectancy of success, which is the effect on the person of success, produces a change in the incentive value of success. Sometimes the effect of this change is an increase in the strength of the tendency to undertake the same activity. Sometimes it is just the reverse. It depends upon the personality of the subject—whether the motive to achieve or the motive to avoid failure is dominant in him—and it depends upon the initial strength of the expectancy of success at the task. The matter is complicated, certainly more complicated than the Law of Effect would ever lead us to imagine.

REFERENCES

Allport, G. The ego in contemporary psychology. *Psychological Review* 1943, 50: 451–78.

Atkinson, J. W. (Ed.) *Motives in Fantasy, Action, and Society.* Princeton, N. J.: Van Nostrand, 1958.

Atkinson, J. W. *An Introduction to Motivation.* Princeton, N.J.: Van Nostrand, 1964.

Atkinson, J. W., and Feather, N. T. (Eds.) *A Theory of Achievement Motivation,* New York: Wiley, 1966.

Brown, M. Factors determining expectancy of success and reactions to success and failure. Unpublished manuscript, University of Michigan, 1963.

Litwin, G. H. Motives and expectancies as determinants of preference for degrees of risk. Unpublished honors dissertation, University of Michigan, 1958.

McClelland, D. C. *The Achieving Society.* Princeton, N. J.: Van Nostrand, 1961.

McClelland, D. C., Atkinson, J. W., Clark, R. A., and Lowell, E. L. *The Achievement Motive.* New York: Appleton-Century-Crofts, 1953.

Sarason, S. B., Davidson, K. S., Lighthall, F. F., and Ruebush, B. K. *Anxiety in Elementary School Children.* New York: Wiley, 1960.

Spence, K. A theory of emotionally based drive (D) and its relation to performance in simple learning situations. *American Psychologist* 1958, 13: 131–41.

Taylor, Janet A. Drive theory and manifest anxiety. *Psychological Bulletin* 1956, 53: 303–20.

REVIEW QUESTIONS

1. Can you explain: $T_{AF} = M_{AF} \times P_F \times I_F$?

2. a. Can you explain why ability grouping—according to the theory—should have positive motivational effects upon students high in achievement motivation, but negative effects upon students motivated to avoid failure?

   b. Do you understand why these opposite effects are *independent* of whether the student is high or low in ability?

twenty-one

"Regarding Learning and its Facilitation" from *Freedom to Learn*

CARL ROGERS

How does a person learn? How can important learnings be facilitated? What basic theoretical assumptions are involved? In this chapter I have tried to answer these questions in a "bare-bones" fashion, simply stating the core of my views on these questions.

It is customary to begin a presentation with theoretical and general principles, and then to indicate the way in which these principles might be carried out in practice. I have followed the opposite course in this book. I have endeavored to present a wealth of practical experience and descriptions of methods, all of which have been used to set students free for self-initiated, self-reliant learning. Now I would like to make a succinct general statement of some of the principles (or hypotheses) which can reasonably be abstracted, it seems to me, from these and other similar experiences. I will be drawing on my own experience, on the work of many other facilitators of learning who have sent me accounts of their work and its outcomes, and upon relevant research. . . .

LEARNING

Here are a number of the principles which can, I believe, be abstracted from current experience and research related to this newer approach:

1. *Human beings have a natural potentiality for learning.* They are curious about their world, until and unless this curiosity is blunted by their experience in our educational system. They are ambivalently eager to develop and learn. The reason for the ambivalence is that any significant

Source: Chapter 7 from *Freedom to Learn*, published by Charles E. Merrill Publishing Co., Columbus, Ohio, 1969. Reprinted by permission of the author and the publisher.

learning involves a certain amount of pain, either pain connected with the learning itself or distress connected with giving up certain previous learnings. The first type of ambivalence is illustrated by the small child who is learning to walk. He stumbles, he falls, he hurts himself. It is a painful process. Yet, the satisfactions of developing his potential far outweigh the bumps and bruises. The second type of ambivalence is evident when a student who has been absolutely tops in every way in his small town high school enrolls in a superior college or university where he finds that he is simply one of many bright students. This is a painful learning to assimilate, yet in most instances he does assimilate it and goes forward.

This potentiality and desire for learning, for discovery, for enlargement of knowledge and experience, can be released under suitable conditions. It is a tendency which can be trusted, and the whole approach to education which we have been describing builds upon and around the student's natural desire to learn.

2. *Significant learning takes place when the subject matter is perceived by the student as having relevance for his own purposes.* A somewhat more formal way of stating this is that a person learns significantly only those things which he perceives as being involved in the maintenance of or the enhancement of his own self. Think for a moment of two students taking a course in statistics. One is working on a research project for which he definitely needs the material of the course in order to complete his research and move forward in his professional career. The second student is taking the course because it is required. Its only relationship to his own purposes or the enhancement of himself is simply that it is necessary for him to complete the course in order to stay in the university. There can hardly be any question as to the differences in learning which ensue. The first student acquires a functional learning of the material; the second learns how to "get by."

Another element related to this principle has to do with the speed of learning. When an individual has a goal he wishes to achieve and he sees the material available to him as relevant to achieving that goal, learning takes place with great rapidity. We need only to recall what a brief length of time it takes for an adolescent to learn to drive a car. There is evidence that the time for learning various subjects would be cut to a fraction of the time currently allotted if the material were perceived by the learner as related to his own purposes. Probably one third to one fifth of the present time allotment would be sufficient.

3. *Learning which involves a change in self organization—in the perception of oneself—is threatening and tends to be resisted.* Why has there been so much furor, sometimes even lawsuits, concerning an adolescent boy who comes to school with long hair? Surely the length of his hair makes little objective difference. The reason seems to be that if I, as a teacher or administrator, accept the value which he places on non-conformity then it threatens the value which I have placed on conforming to social demands.

If I permit this contradiction to exist I may find myself changing, because I will be forced to a reappraisal of some of my values. The same thing applies to the former interest in "beatniks" and the current interest in "hippies." If their rejection of almost all middle class values is permitted to stand, then an individual's acceptance of middle class values as a part of himself is deeply threatened, since to most people it seems that to the degree *others* are right, *they* are wrong.

Sometimes these painful and threatening learnings have to do with contradictions within oneself. An example might be the person who believes "every citizen in this country has equal right to any opportunity which exists." He also discovers that he has the conviction, "I am unwilling for a Negro to live in my neighborhood." Any learning which arises from this dilemma is painful and threatening since the two beliefs cannot openly co-exist, and any learning which emerges from the contradiction involves a definite change in the structure of self.

4. *Those learnings which are threatening to the self are more easily perceived and assimilated when external threats are at a minimum.* The boy who is retarded in reading already feels threatened and inadequate because of this deficiency. When he is forced to attempt to read aloud in front of the group, when he is ridiculed for his efforts, when his grades are a vivid reflection of his failure, it is no surprise that he may go through several years of school with no perceptible increase in his reading ability. On the other hand, a supportive, understanding environment and a lack of grades, or an encouragement of self evaluation, remove the external threats and permit him to make progress because he is no longer paralyzed by fear. This is also one of the great advantages of the teaching machine, when properly used. Here the poor reader can begin at his own level of achievement and practically every minute step he makes is marked by reward and a feeling of success.

It is fascinating to me how completely we have tended to disregard the evidence which clearly supports this principle. Nearly forty years ago Herbert Williams, then a teacher, was put in charge of a classroom in which all of the most serious delinquents in a large school system were brought together. They were the "worst boys" in a city of 300,000. He could not hope to carry on much individualized instruction, and the boys were at all levels of school achievement. As might be expected, they were retarded intellectually (average I. Q. 82) as well as in their school achievement. He had very little special equipment. Besides the usual desks and blackboards, there was a large table in the room on which he placed picture books, readers, story books, and textbooks in various subjects, appropriate to all levels of reading achievement. There were also art materials available. There were but two rules. A boy must keep busy doing something, and no boy was permitted to annoy or disturb others. Each child was told, without criticism, of his results on an achievement test. Encouragement and suggestions were given only after an activity had been self initiated. Thus, if a boy had worked along artistic lines he might be given assistance in getting into a special art class. If activities in mathematics or mechanics had engaged his interest, arrangements might be made for him to attend courses in these subjects. The group remained together for four months. During this period the measured educational achievement (on the Stanford Achievement Test) of those who had been in the group for the major part of this period increased fifteen months on the average, and this improvement was evident in reading, arithmetic, and other subjects. The increase was more than four times the normal expectation for a group with this degree of retardation, and this in spite of the fact that reading and other educational disabilities abounded. This incredible improvement came about through informal, self-directed, activity. It is my belief that studies such as this have been disregarded primarily because they provide a threat to the teacher. Here is evidence that the most unpromising students learn rapidly when they are simply given opportunities to learn and when no attempt is made to teach them. This must seem to many teachers that they might be deprived of their jobs and hence the information is simply not assimilated.

One reason for the success of this highly unorthodox and inexpensive venture must have been the attitude of Mr. Williams himself. He surmises that his interest in each child's home conditions, neighborhood, health, and in each boy individually may have stimulated the youngsters. He states that he wanted to get acquainted with each boy, and spent his time in this sort of activity rather than in teaching. That he had a strong and sympathetic interest in, and belief in, juvenile delinquents is shown by the fact that he went on to become superintendent of a highly progressive institution for delinquents.

5. *When threat to the self is low, experience can be perceived in differentiated fashion and learning can proceed.* In a sense this is only an extension of, or an explanation of, the preceding principle. The poor reader is a good illustration of what is involved in this principle. When he is called upon to recite in class the internal panic takes over and the words on the page become less intelligible symbols than they were when he was sitting at his seat before he was called upon. When he is in an environment in which he is assured of personal security and when he becomes convinced that there is no threat to his ego, he is once more free to perceive the symbols on the page in a differentiated fashion, to recognize the differing elements in similar words, to perceive partial meanings and try to put them together—in other words, to move forward in the process of learning. Any sort of learning involves an increasing differentiation of the field of experience and the assimilation of the meanings of these differentiations. Such differentiations, it seems to me, are most effectively made under two sharply differing kinds of conditions. They may occur when the threat to the *organism* is intense, but such threats are quite different than threats to the *self* as perceived. The combat soldier, for example, learns very quickly to distinguish

the shriek of a shell going high overhead from the whine of one which is coming in his direction. He learns to discriminate very readily a normal footpath from one whose surface has been disturbed, since the latter may be a land mine. He is, in these instances, responding to threat of a very serious nature, but this is threat to his organism and not a threat to the self he perceives himself to be. In fact the more quickly he can learn these discriminations the more his self is enhanced. In the ordinary educational situation, however, such realistic life and death threats are rare and when these exist pupils respond well to them. Children learn traffic rules, for example, quite readily and comfortably. But humiliation, ridicule, devaluation, scorn and contempt—these are threats to the person himself, to the perception he has of himself and as such interfere strongly with learning. On the other hand, as described above, when threat to the self is minimized, the individual makes use of opportunities to learn in order to enhance himself.

6. *Much significant learning is acquired through doing.* Placing the student in direct experiential confrontation with practical problems, social problems, ethical and philosophical problems, personal issues, and research problems, is one of the most effective modes of promoting learning. Illustrations range from the class group which becomes involved in a dramatic production, selecting the play and the cast, designing and making the scenery and costumes, coaching the actors, and selling tickets, to much more sophisticated confrontations. I have always been impressed with the fact that brief intensive courses for individuals on the firing line facing immediate problems—teachers, doctors, farmers, counselors—are especially effective because the individuals are trying to cope with problems which they are currently experiencing.

7. *Learning is facilitated when the student participates responsibly in the learning process.* When he chooses his own directions, helps to discover his own learning resources, formulates his own problems, decides his own course of action, lives with the consequences of each of these choices, then significant learning is maximized. There is evidence from industry as well as from the field of education that such participative learning is far more effective than passive learning.

8. *Self-initiated learning which involves the whole person of the learner —feelings as well as intellect—is the most lasting and pervasive.* We have discovered this in psychotherapy, where it is the totally involved learning of oneself which is most effective. This is not learning which takes place "only from the neck up." It is a "gut level" type of learning which is profound and pervasive. It can also occur in the tentative discovery of a new self-generated idea or in the learning of a difficult skill, or in the act of artistic creation—a painting, a poem, a sculpture. It is the whole person who "lets himself go" in these creative learnings. An important element in these situations is that the learner *knows* it is his own learning and thus can hold to it or relinquish it in the face of a more profound learning with-

out having to turn to some authority for corroboration of his judgment.

9. *Independence, creativity, and self-reliance are all facilitated when self-criticism and self-evaluation are basic and evaluation by others is of secondary importance.* The best research organizations, in industry as well as in the academic world, have learned that creativity blossoms in an atmosphere of freedom. External evaluation is largely fruitless if the goal is creative work. The wise parent has learned this same lesson. If a child is to grow up to be independent and self reliant he must be given opportunities at an early age not only to make his own judgments and his own mistakes but to evaluate the consequences of these judgments and choices. The parent may provide information and models of behavior, but it is the growing child and adolescent who must evaluate his own behaviors, come to his own conclusions, and decide on the standards which are appropriate for him. The child or adolescent who is dependent both at school and at home upon the evaluations of others is likely to remain permanently dependent and immature or explosively rebellious against all external evaluations and judgments.

10. *The most socially useful learning in the modern world is the learning of the process of learning, a continuing openness to experience and incorporation into oneself of the process of change . . . .* A static kind of learning of information may have been quite adequate in previous times. If our present culture survives it will be because we have been able to develop individuals for whom *change* is the central fact of life and who have been able to live comfortably with this central fact. It means that they will not be concerned, as so many are today, that their past learning is inadequate to enable them to cope with current situations. They will instead have the comfortable expectation that it will be continuously necessary to incorporate new and challenging learnings about ever-changing situations.

FACILITATION

So much has been presented in preceding chapters about various methods of facilitating learning and various qualities of the facilitator that only the briefest summary of some of the guidelines which can be abstracted will be presented here.

1. *The facilitator has much to do with setting the initial mood or climate of the group or class experience.* If his own basic philosophy is one of trust in the group and in the individuals who compose the group, then this point of view will be communicated in many subtle ways.

2. *The facilitator helps to elicit and clarify the purposes of the individuals in the class as well as the more general purposes of the group.* If he is not fearful of accepting contradictory purposes and conflicting aims, if he is able to permit the individuals a sense of freedom in stating what they would like to do, then he is helping to create a climate for learning. There

is no need for him to try to manufacture one unified purpose in the group if such a unified purpose is not there. He can permit a diversity of purposes to exist, contradictory and complementary, in relationship to each other.

3. *He relies upon the desire of each student to implement those purposes which have meaning for him, as the motivational force behind significant learning.* Even if the desire of the student is to be guided and led by someone else, the facilitator can accept such a need and motive and can either serve as a guide when this is desired or can provide some other means, such as a set course of study, for the student whose major desire is to be dependent. And for the majority of students he can help to utilize the individual's own drives and purposes as the moving force behind his learning.

4. *He endeavors to organize and make easily available the widest possible range of resources for learning.* He endeavors to make available writings, materials, psychological aids, persons, equipment, trips, audiovisual aids—every conceivable resource which his students may wish to use for their own enhancement and for the fulfillment of their own purposes.

5. *He regards himself as a flexible resource to be utilized by the group.* He does not downgrade himself as a resource. He makes himself available as a counselor, lecturer, and advisor, a person with experience in the field. He wishes to be used by individual students, and by the group, in the ways which seem most meaningful to them insofar as he can be comfortable in operating in the ways they wish.

6. *In responding to expressions in the classroom group, he accepts both the intellectual content and the emotionalized attitudes, endeavoring to give each aspect the approximate degree of emphasis which it has for the individual or the group.* Insofar as he can be genuine in doing so, he accepts rationalizations and intellectualizing, as well as deep and real personal feelings.

7. *As the acceptant classroom climate becomes established, the facilitator is able increasingly to become a participant learner, a member of the group, expressing his views as those of one individual only.*

8. *He takes the initiative in sharing himself with the group—his feelings as well as his thoughts—in ways which do not demand nor impose but represent simply a personal sharing which students may take or leave.* Thus, he is free to express his own feelings in giving feedback to students, in his reaction to them an individuals, and in sharing his own satisfactions or disappointments. In such expressions it is his "owned" attitudes which are shared, not judgments or evaluations of others.

9. *Throughout the classroom experience, he remains alert to the expressions indicative of deep or strong feelings.* These may be feelings of conflict, pain, and the like, which exist primarily within the individual. Here he endeavors to understand these from the person's point of view and to communicate his empathic understanding. On the other hand, the feelings may be those of anger, scorn, affection, rivalry, and the like—

interpersonal attitudes among members of the group. Again he is as alert to these as to the ideas being expressed and by his acceptance of such tensions or bonds he helps to bring them into the open for constructive understanding and use by the group.

10. *In his functioning as a facilitator of learning, the leader endeavors to recognize and accept his own limitations.* He realizes that he can only grant freedom to his students to the extent that he is comfortable in giving such freedom. He can only be understanding to the extent that he actually desires to enter the inner world of his students. He can only share himself to the extent that he is reasonably confortable in taking that risk. He can only participate as a member of the group when he actually feels that he and his students have an equality as learners. He can only exhibit trust of the student's desire to learn insofar as he feels that trust. There will be many times when his attitudes are not facilitative of learning. He will find himself being suspicious of his students. He will find it impossible to accept attitudes which differ strongly from his own. He will be unable to understand some of the student feelings which are markedly different from his own. He may find himself angry and resentful of student attitudes toward him and angry at student behaviors. He may find himself feeling strongly judgmental and evaluative. When he is experiencing attitudes which are non-facilitative, he will endeavor to get close to them, to be clearly aware of them, and to state them just as they are within himself. Once he has expressed these angers, these judgments, these mistrusts, these doubts of others and doubts of himself, as something coming from within himself, not as objective facts in outward reality, he will find the air cleared for a significant interchange between himself and his students. Such an interchange can go a long way toward resolving the very attitudes which he has been experiencing, and thus make it possible for him to be more of a facilitator of learning.

CONCLUSION

It is hoped that this article may provide a view of the skeleton of hypotheses and principles which underlie the practices and methods of the individuals and groups whose experience has been described in earlier chapters.

REVIEW QUESTIONS

1. True or false:
   a. Students have a natural desire for learning and discovery.
   b. If the material is relevant to the self, it could be learned in one third or one fifth of the present time allotment.

c. Information that is threatening to the self may be rejected.

d. Threat of ridicule stimulates efficient learning.

e. Learning by direct experience with practical problems is no better than reading about such problems.

f. Being open to experience allows us to adapt to change.

g. The effective facilitator of learning primarily sets the climate, clarifies purposes, provides materials, then takes a resource-person role.

h. The leader must admit and resolve his nonfacilitative (e.g., judgmental, resentful) attitudes.

2. Would the philosophy represented in this article result in chaotic or ideal classrooms?

Answers to question 1: a. true, b. true, c. true, d. false, e. false, f. true, g. true, h. true.

part iv

NEW LOOKS IN EDUCATION: CRITICAL AND CONSTRUCTIVE

This part might be thought of as having two related major themes: "We are in trouble" and "I think there is a way out." No writer shows a hint of complacency. From John Holt's angry blast at many "sacred cows" of education to Joseph Featherstone's description of the British primary schools, they all imply that things must get better. Some contribute by stating the problems; others focus upon experiences and strategies that show promise.

More specifically, John Holt's short article summarizes many of the criticisms he has leveled in his books. He argues that educational priorities must change drastically. Children are victims of distorted goals and counterproductive practices. Not only must schools be run by different persons, but also the concept of the school itself must change. Previously untapped community resources and individuals can help; so can revamped financing and learner-directed teaching.

Herbert Kohl considers his book *The Open Classroom* as "... a handbook for teachers who want to work an open environment." The excerpts comprising article 23 give examples of Kohl's own initial illustrations and eventual success in attempting to create a nonauthoritarian classroom atmosphere. Against the gloomy picture of schools dominated by order and delusion, Kohl gives hope that the situation can be purposefully changed.

A. S. Neill has developed a school that is a legend in his own lifetime. Some of Summerhill's success derives from its private status, the supportive parents, and its uncompromised philosophy. A major factor is the person of Neill. In article 24, Thomas Warren examines features of Summerhill and asks the question, "What can be borrowed from this free English school that will have a good chance of working in other situations?"

On this side of the Atlantic, Jonathan Kozol is a leader among persons who have worked in free schools. As explained in article 25, he wants them to survive and not fall prey to uninformed, biased criticism. But he is also concerned with several problems within the free-school movement. Especially, he claims, many teachers are reluctant to demonstrate their expertise and show their values and convictions, preferring instead to appear as "... ethical and pedagogical neuters."

Robert Rosenthal and Lenore Jacobson's names have become closely linked to "expectancies" and "self-fulfilling prophecies." In article 26 these writers stress that the way a person is treated influences how he will behave. Their research on what happens because of what people think will happen is recognized as an important contribution to educational research and practice. Certainly, the implications are enormous, and it is no wonder that Rosenthal and Jacobson have caught the attention of those who are disturbed about impersonal dehumanizing education.

Janet Elashoff and Richard Snow summarize in article 27 why they do not especially like the publicity and enthusiasm generated by Rosenthal and Jacobson's work. They caution against unquestioning endorsement before fully-reported data are available. They admonish also the "overdramatized generalities" of the Rosenthal and Jacobson book *Pygmalion in the Classroom* as well as the carelessness of overzealous and ill-informed journalists.

Article 28 by Neil Postman and Charles Weingartner is concerned with goals. Their main question asks, "What's worth knowing?" The answer: important questions. They state that a basis for a new curriculum can be built upon carefully constructed student and teacher probing. In order for worthwhile questions to emerge, however, certain criteria must be noted.

David Ausubel also is a questioner. In article 29 he questions whether certain, ostensibly student-centered, real-life learning situations are rigorous and meaningful. Do they give sufficient attention to abstractions? Are verbal concepts unreasonably deemphasized? Can discovery learning be oversold?

Herbert Klausmeier in article 30 describes a comprehensive program emphasizing individualized education for elementary school students and new roles for their staff members. The multi-unit school and individually guided education have grown out of work at the Wisconsin Research and Development Center for Cognitive Learning. MUS-IGE was designed to coordinate improvements in organization and instruction. Feedback from schools where the program is in operation has led to refinements and to the elimination of many practical problems. The plan, which began in a handful of Wisconsin schools in the mid-1960's, involves in 1973–74 about two thousand schools in thirty-six states.

William Glasser also evolved a plan that has gained popularity and support in recent years. Based upon the premise that all children must be responsible for what they do and be accepted by themselves and others, he tells how teachers and students can avoid failure. Classroom meetings, described in article 31, form the heart of a school without failure.

"Good noise" is coming from British primary schools these days, and Americans who visit them are often impressed. "Why can't something like that happen over here?" they often ask. Joseph Featherstone in article 32 explains the success and problems of the British plan. He also talks about implications for the United States. British primary schools have moved a long way and on a large scale toward achieving individualized instruction, nongraded classes, and new roles for teachers, while deemphasizing the memorization that previously characterized British education.

twenty-two

Why We Need New Schooling

JOHN HOLT

Knowledge is increasing so fast, a recent ad said, that the problem of education is to find better ways "to pack it into young heads." This popular belief is wrong, and causes much of what is so wrong with our schools. For years, it is true, learned men used their brains to store and retrieve information. Today, the child who has been taught in school to stuff his head with facts, recipes, this-is-how-you-do-it, is obsolete even before he leaves the building. Anything he can do, or be taught to do, a machine can do, *and soon will do,* better and cheaper.

What children need, even just to make a living, are qualities that can never be trained into a machine—inventiveness, flexibility, resourcefulness, curiosity, and, above all, judgment.

The chief products of schooling these days are not these qualities, not even the knowledge and skills they try to produce, but stupidity, ignorance, incompetence, self-contempt, alienation, apathy, powerlessness, resentment, and rage. We can't afford such products any longer. The purpose of education can no longer be to turn out people who know a few facts, a few skills, and who will always believe and do what they are told. We need big changes, and in a hurry. Here, in no particular order, are some things to change.

We must get rid of the notion that education is different and separate from life, something that happens only in school. Everything that happens to us educates us, for good or for bad. To answer "What makes a good education?" we must ask, "What makes a good life?"

Teachers must have, like doctors with patients, the professional freedom to work with their students as *they* think best. Only the child himself should have more to say than the teacher about what is learned, and when, and how; today, in most places, only the child has less. So, out with lesson plans, fixed schedules, so many hours a week per subject, prescribed texts, grades, normal curves, censorship, supervisors—the whole deadening, humiliating, intimidating regime under which too many teachers have to work.

Children and their parents should not have to submit, for lack of choices, to school experiences that seem degrading, painful, or harmful. School is neither jail nor the Army. People should be free to find or make for themselves the kinds of educational experiences they want their children to have. Anything in law that makes this impossible or even very difficult should be changed.

In most of history, children have been educated by the whole community, the whole society they lived in. Nothing else makes any sense. We must get as much as possible of the outside world into our schools, and get the schools and the children into the outside world, as in the Parkway project in Philadelphia, where hundreds of students use the city itself as their classroom.

Abolish compulsory attendance laws. We cannot measure growth and learning by the day or hour. A child, finding out what he wants to find out, fully alive and alert, learns more in an hour than most students learn in school in weeks or months. Schools are only one place, among many, where people can learn about and grow into the world. Let them compete with other educational resources for the time and attention of children.

Abolish all certification requirements for teachers. They don't make teachers better, often make them worse, and keep or drive out of teaching many excellent people. Let the people who run a school use as teachers anyone they think can help the children.

Teachers, or teachers and parents, should run schools, not specialists in school administration. Whoever pays the bills and sees that the floors are swept and the windows washed should be under the teachers, not over them.

Abolish the required curriculum. Children want to learn about the world and grow into it; adults want to help them. Let them get together, and the proper curriculum will grow out of what the children need and want, and what the adults have to give.

Abolish all compulsory testing and grading. If a student wants his teacher to test his knowledge or competence, so that he may know how to improve, fine. All other testing and grading is destructive and inexcusable. Students should organize to refuse to take tests for other people's purposes, and teachers should organize to refuse to give them.

Abolish the required use of so-called intelligence tests and other psychological prying. Such tests should only be given with the consent of parent and child, and the results should belong to them *exclusively*. Establish by law that *any and all* records of what a child does in a school shall go with him, as his exclusive property, when he leaves that school.

In all educational institutions supported by tax money, or enjoying tax-exempt status (with the possible exceptions suggested below), abolish all entrance exams or other selective admissions requirements. An educational institution, like a library, museum, lecture hall, park, or theater, should be open at least until full, to any and all who want to use it. A few exceptions might be made for institutions where performance skill is involved, as in the performing arts, crafts, skilled trades, or in flying, surgery, perhaps some sciences. But even here, the institutions should have to show that selection is really needed, and not just a concession to institutional vanity, or a way, as in some professions and trades today, to keep the cost of services high by limiting the number of people able to provide them.

Abolish all requirements for schools. *Parents and parents alone* should decide whether a school is right for their children; it is no one else's business. Health and safety? Let parents decide. Our cities do not enforce health and safety codes in the homes of the poor. Why should these codes be used to harass poor people's schools, or to prevent people from trying to solve their problems?

Every school charging no tuition and open to all should be considered an independent public school and entitled to tax support per pupil-day on the same basis as state-run schools in its district. Why should the state have a monopoly on public education?

As Peter Marin and others have suggested, we should radically revise all laws that deny children the right to work, travel, and live independently. The laws once passed to protect children now oppress more than they protect. We ought not to deny any child the right to take part in society as fully as he wishes and is able.

Students of any age should get academic credit, as some college students now do, for holding down a job. Better yet, schools should get out of the business of granting credentials as the proof, and only proof, of job-worthiness.

As Christopher Jencks and others have suggested, the best way to finance education might be to give every child an education allowance, for him to spend on his education as he chooses. Parents and their children might in many places develop forms of education vastly more efficient than our present schools.

Too many of our schools are too big to be human, instead, we could have, in any of our giant school buildings, a number of small schools, each independently run and using its own ideas and methods, and all sharing whatever facilities needed to be shared.

Let students, whose time is taxed by the schools, and who really know and care about them, vote in school-board elections.

Give more time, money, and space in all schools for all the arts and for developing physical fitness, strength, and skill. Sports, games, athletics are too important to be for just the varsity.

For part of people's lives, we tell them they can't get out of school, and once they're out, we tell them they can't get back in. Let people, of whatever age, go in and out of school when they see fit, using it when it seems most useful to them. Let the learner direct his own learning.

REVIEW QUESTIONS

1. Do you agree with this attack? Is it possible to make a list of "What's right with schools"? Try it.

2. Think about the implications of having a "student ombudsman," that is, a person whose job is to investigate complaints about the teachers, requirements, tests, and so on. What might be gained? What might be considered to increase its chances of success?

twenty-three

The Open Classroom

HERBERT R. KOHL

When I began teaching I felt isolated in a hostile environment. The structure of authority in my school was clear: the principal was at the top and the students were at the bottom. Somewhere in the middle was the teacher, whose role it was to impose orders from textbooks or supervisors upon the students. The teacher's only protection was that if students failed to obey instructions they could legitimately be punished or, if they were defiant, suspended or kicked out of school. There was no way for students to question the teachers' decisions or for teachers to question the decisions of their supervisors or authors of textbooks and teachers' manuals.

My school happened to be in a black ghetto in New York City, and I thought for a while that it was a pathological case. In the last few years I have spoken with many teachers throughout the country and visited many schools—urban, suburban, black, white, integrated, segregated, elementary, secondary. There is the same obsession with power and discipline everywhere; for most American children there is essentially one public school system in the United States, and it is authoritarian and oppressive. Students everywhere are deprived of the right to make choices concerning their own destinies. My experiences in a Harlem elementary school were not special, and I think the discoveries I made about myself and my students apply to most schools.

The authoritarian environment of the school I taught at encouraged a collusive atmosphere in which everyone except the students pretended that the school was functioning smoothly and effectively and that the teachers were "doing a good job." It was not proper to talk about troubles or admit failures.

There was no one for me to talk with, to share my despair and confusion. I was having troubles with the curriculum, with my students, with bureaucratic details, with other teachers, and, most of all, with myself. I was bewildered and angered by what was expected of me, and overwhelmed by my contact with students. I was supposed to teach the fifth-grade curriculum, no matter who my students were or what they cared about. I was also supposed to take attendance; sign circulars; contribute to a fund for purchasing birthday presents for colleagues who refused to acknowledge my existence; take my turn at yard duty, hall duty, and lunchroom duty. The demands were as frequent as they were senseless. Yet they were insignificant when compared with the pressure to fulfill the function considered most essential to a teacher's success—controlling the children.

The entire staff of the school was obsessed by "control," and beneath the rhetoric of faculty meetings was the clear implication that students were a reckless, unpredictable, immoral, and dangerous enemy.

I found myself following the usual methods. The textbooks bored me, yet I went along and tried to impose them upon my students. The clerical work seemed to me absurd, yet with my students I tried to make it seem important. They weren't impressed, and because I didn't have the heart to harass them, they mocked and harassed me. My students hated school and let me know it by running about the room, screaming, falling out of their seats. There were a few times when something developed in the classroom that led the students to become absorbed in learning. Yet for the most part I was having trouble, and I wanted to talk to someone about it. In the authoritarian atmosphere of the school no one wanted to hear about my troubles—if the system didn't work in my case, I probably wasn't suited to the job.

After a few months of teaching, however, I met another teacher in my school who spoke honestly about teaching. His class was a wonder to me—the atmosphere was open, there was a casual and friendly exchange between him and his pupils. This absence of hostility was accompanied by the intense involvement of the students in things they seemed to care about. What he had achieved seemed unattainable for me, given the state of my class. I couldn't believe that he had ever confronted problems with students or had ever been uncertain about his role in the classroom. But we talked about my problems and he told me of his own difficulties during his early years as a teacher. Knowing that he had similar problems made me somewhat more hopeful. He helped me to locate the source of my difficulties in myself and in the pathology of the classroom instead of in the students. He also showed me the need to find alternatives to textbooks and to the domination of the teacher.

That first six months I just managed to survive. The next year was much better and I learned how to make the classroom more interesting for my pupils. I also learned how to give up my power as a teacher (not delegate it but abrogate it) and how to help my pupils as well as become someone they could talk with. I learned to listen to them, to be led by their interests and needs. In turn I became involved in creating things in the classroom—in doing research on myths and numbers, in learning from the experience of the students. My students and I resembled a community much more than a class, and I enjoyed being with them. We worked together in an open environment which often spilled out of the school building into the streets, the neighborhood, and the city itself.

Yet these things didn't happen magically or quickly. I needed a great deal of help, and very little was available. I did learn to function in a non-authoritarian way within an authoritarian institution, though I had little impact on the school, and ultimately quit. Still I gradually found ways of teaching that were not based on compulsion but on participation; not on grades or tests or curriculum, but on pursuing what interested the children.

Other teachers are going through the same process of yielding some of their authority and freeing themselves to teach without using compulsion. Many have been fired for trying to teach in non-authoritarian ways; others have been trying to change and finding themselves confused or impatient. It is difficult to yield power and develop a sense of community with young people (or even with one's peers, for that matter).

This book is a handbook for teachers who want to work in an open environment. It is difficult to say exactly what an open classroom is. One almost has to have been in one and feel what it is. However there are certain things that it is not. It is important not to equate an open classroom with a "permissive" environment. In an open classroom the teacher must be as much himself as the pupils are themselves. This means that if the teacher is angry he ought to express his anger, and if he is annoyed at someone's behavior he ought to express that, too. In an authoritarian classroom annoying behavior is legislated out of existence. In a "permissive" classroom the teacher pretends it isn't annoying. He also permits students to behave only in certain ways, thereby retaining the authority over their behavior he pretends to be giving up. In an open situation the teacher tries to express what he feels and to deal with each situation as a communal problem.

This book is based upon the experience of teachers: their problems, failures, and frustrations, as well as their successes. It is about the battles with self and system that teachers encounter in the schools. But it is not a handbook that gives teachers a step-by-step account of how to change their classrooms and themselves. Each teacher must obviously go through the process of change in ways consistent with his own personality. This handbook does, however, try to anticipate problems, to present possibilities and make suggestions. It presents some strategies for change, for dealing with the administration and other teachers, for creating different kinds of textbooks, lesson plans, etc. It can and I hope will be used by different people in different ways.

This book is primarily addressed to public school teachers. However, much is I think relevant to other teachers in community schools, in private schools, and at colleges and universities. Power is a problem for all of us. The development of open, democratic modes of existence is essentially the problem of abandoning the authoritarian use of power and of providing workable alternatives. That is a problem that must be faced by all individuals and institutions that presume to teach.

Teachers' expectations have a tendency to become self-fulfilling. "Bad" classes tend to act badly, and "gifted" classes tend to respond to the special consideration that they expect to be given to them if they perform in a "superior" way.

All of this is inimical to an open classroom, where the role of the teacher is not to control his pupils but rather to enable them to make choices and pursue what interests them. In an open classroom a pupil functions according to his sense of himself rather than what he is expected to be. It is not that the teacher should expect the same of all his pupils. On the contrary, the teacher must learn to perceive differences, but these should emerge from what actually happens in the classroom during the school year, and not from preconceptions.

I remember an incident where the effect of a teacher's expectations in one of my classes was pernicious. I have always been unable to avoid having favorites in my classes. I like defiant, independent, and humorous people, and my preferences naturally come out in my teaching. One year, several students were puzzled by my choice of favorites. The class had been together for three years and each year teachers chose the same four children as their favorite students. However, I had chosen different students and it upset most of the class, especially the ones who had been favorites in the past. All the students were black. It took me several months to realize that the former favorites were all the lightest-skinned pupils in the class—in other words, the whitest were (by their white teachers) expected to be the nicest and most intelligent.

A teacher in an open classroom needs to cultivate a state of *suspended expectations*. It is not easy. It is easy to believe that a dull class is dull, or a bright class is bright. The words "emotionally disturbed" conjure up frightening images. And it is sometimes a relief to discover that there are good pupils in the class that is waiting for you. Not reading the record cards or ignoring the standing of the class is an act of self-denial; it involves casting aside a crutch when one still believes one can't walk without it. Yet if one wants to develop an open classroom within the context of a school which is essentially totalitarian, such acts of will are necessary.

What does it mean to suspend expectations when one is told that the class one will be teaching is slow, or bright, or ordinary? At the least it means not preparing to teach in any special way or deciding beforehand on the complexity of the materials to be used during a school year. It means that planning does not consist of finding the class's achievement level according to the record cards and tailoring the material to those levels, but rather preparing diverse materials and subjects and discovering from the students as the year unfolds what is relevant to them and what isn't.

Particularly it means not reading I.Q. scores or achievement scores, not discovering who may be a source of trouble and who a solace or even a joy. It means giving your pupils a fresh chance to develop in new ways in your classroom, freed from the roles they may have adopted during their previous school careers. It means allowing children to become who they care to become, and freeing the teacher from the standards by which new pupils had been measured in the past.

There are no simple ways to give up deeply rooted expectations. There are some suggestions, however:

—talk to students outside class

—watch them play and watch them live with other young people

—play with them—joking games and serious games
—talk to them about yourself, what you care about
—listen

In these situations the kids may surprise you and reveal rather than conceal, as is usual in the classroom, their feelings, playfulness, and intelligence.

REVIEW QUESTIONS

1.   What would your own list of priorities be if you were starting in a challenging teaching position such as the one Kohl held?

2.   What is the minimum length of time a person must be in a school in order to make a valid critique of it? What factors other than time are involved?

twenty-four

Summerhill Is an Island

THOMAS F. WARREN

Summerhill has been called many things: an inspiring religion, a model of what a school should be, a womb, a personality cult, "twaddle," undisciplined, antischolastic, worse than a brothel, and a nonschool. Some love it and some, quite obviously, hate it. The main purpose of this article is to take a brief look at Summerhill and try to relate how its successes might be transferred a little. I'm not suggesting a "Summerhill West"[1] in any sense, nor am I recommending many little Neillian-inspired free schools or a Montessori-type missionary movement. Instead, I'm hoping that some ideas can be borrowed from Summerhill and used in any educational setting.

Summerhill is a small, private boarding school for children from under five years old to late adolescence. It is located near the North Sea in Leiston, Suffolk County, England. Summerhill's headmaster, A. S. Neill, has been with the school since he opened it in 1921. He is still alive and active at this writing. Neill has written about his experiences, and the books have sold well. Few people are neutral regarding A. S. Neill and Summerhill. Supporters generally note the child-centered learning, and a free, loving atmosphere. Critics are concerned about the nonacademic curriculum and lack of direction from adults. In some respects Summerhill is like the Stroget in Copenhagen where tourists from more inhibited countries can gaze at explicit sensual sights that are only partially realized in their nations' media or in their own fantasies. Summerhill gives vicarious excitement to many educators because they know something is happening that can't be realized in their own schools without turning things upside down.

Freedom dominates at Summerhill, but one who is familiar with the school

[1] "... Summerhill cannot be reproduced. It is doubtful that even the original Summerhill will be able to survive its founder. ... Neill's successor, of course, will not be a martinet or scoundrel, although he may seem so to the children, but he will at best be a disciple. Disciples rarely save any enterprise or idea." [Hechinger, 1970, p. 37]

would never confuse this freedom with license. Rules, made by the students, are periodically reviewed and revised. Each person—students (regardless of age), faculty, and headmaster—has one vote in school meetings. Probably the most controversial aspect of the freedom is that children are not required to go to lessons. Most do quite regularly, but one pupil was enrolled at Summerhill for thirteen years without attending classes. The Ministry of Education for England mentioned this in their 1949 report to illustrate that Summerhill's freedom is genuine "... and is not withdrawn as soon as its results become awkward." [Neill, 1960, p. 77] But that does not mean children make all the decisions. Safety and health issues, for example, are not subject to voting.

Summerhill is Neill's school to a far greater extent than most schools are the domain of a single person. He knows his sphere of influence outside the school (modest, he says) and his freedom within. Neill is intensely optimistic about children, claiming that he has never seen a lazy child. He suggests that the problem of laziness would be solved if adults made every attempt to recognize what is important to the child and use that as a starting point. Then they are allies in the child's education and even the adult learns more than when he is in a didactic role. Like William Glasser, Neill knows that a positive, self-perceived role must be a top priority, far more important than an adult-defined goal or role. Only if a child sees himself as a loved, competent, and responsible person can a school or family consider itself successful.

Neill's success as a headmaster can be attributed to his understanding of children and their development as well as to his commitment to freedom and individualism. In both areas he is a man of many specific likes and dislikes. Among the latter are: time-table feeding, repressed sex, doctors untrained in child-rearing, spotless suits, authority, irrational fear, guilt, inferiority, books, bad consciences, unreachable standards of morality, neuroses, rewards and punishments, preaching, license, and sarcasm. On the other hand he supports: self-regulation, rights and dignity for children, candor, tools, responsibility, subjectivity, toys that interest children, manners, empathy, humor, clarity in explaining, and self-acceptance.

Neill is very willing to make himself the butt of jokes or the fall guy of a story in order to learn more about his students. Once he told a tale of his own death. "Each face brightened as I told of the funeral," he relates. "The group was especially cheery that afternoon." [Neill, 1960, p. 301–302] Neill interprets such joy as an indication of adult-hating coming to the surface.

Children are egotistic. Neill knows it and does not get upset when his students show it. Using a different vocabulary, he is saying much the same thing as did Piaget and Lawrence Kohlberg; namely, that children go through stages in their moral development, and it is futile to push them far beyond where they naturally are. Intermediate steps must be lived through before internally consistent, altruistic behavior dominates. Do not pressure them, Neill would warn.

Sex and toilet-related topics are constantly on the minds of older children who come to Summerhill after starting out somewhere else. Neill believes in letting them talk about and play about with their obsessions until they get tired of them. He tells of one eleven year old girl fascinated by toilets. He changed her lessons to include them, and she was happy for a few days. But after ten days Neill made a comment about toilets, and the girl said, "Don't want to hear about them. I'm fed up with talking about toilets." [Neill, 1960, p. 172]

Few educators anywhere have Neill's persistence and depth of understanding plus access to the constantly-renewing resource that is his school. Summerhill's greatest asset is the personal force of A. S. Neill. Ashley Montagu [1970, p. 58] put it this way:

> Very simply, before anyone can undertake the education of anyone else, be it infant or child or adolescent or adult, he must first be an educated person himself—that is he must understand what, at his particular stage of development, the individual in need requires. There are some persons who seem to possess this knowledge almost intuitively. A. S. Neill is undoubtedly one of those persons. Intuition constitutes a combination of sensitivity and quick intelligence; and here, once more, is a trait terribly neglected in the education of children.

It is futile to try to imitate Summerhill because the main ingredient, Neill, would be missing. But ideas basic to Summerhill can be transferred and can succeed in other settings. The fact is that an elusive commodity, such as uncompromised freedom for children, can deliberately be made real. The mere knowledge that such a possibility exists can breed optimism, which is so important to a persistent effort at duplicating the feat elsewhere. The headmaster at Summerhill did it his way; part of this freedom and respect for children may be reproduced *your way*. Remember that real freedom to teach (or to guide or facilitate) comes from breaking away from a model, however ideal, in order to adapt the model's ideas to your own. In other words, let us consider imitating Neill and borrowing ideas from him and from Summerhill, but at the same time let us realize that the amount of imitation is a very personal issue depending on many factors.

In a sense Summerhill is an island: unique, isolated, alone. Its success is tied to many variables that are impossible to duplicate. Realizing this, we should not even try to copy it identically, but get down to the more important and feasible task of carefully borrowing ideas.

While on the subject, one might ask if Summerhill itself could profit from outside ideas. Novelty can be worshipped to such an extreme that creative elaboration on existing themes is minimized. A still richer, more diversified experience could derive from a planned emphasis on borrowing good ideas from various sources. Other observers of Summerhill agree. Montagu [1970, p, 54] says:

> I believe Neill errs in overlooking or underemphasizing the importance of giving the child roots in the background of his culture and humanity. It would seem to me that this would be desirable in providing the child with the sort or referents from which he can wing his way to fulfillment and independence.

Ames [1970, p. 66] puts it in stronger words:

> He seems to have an almost pathological need to remove all customary bounds
> of discipline from the child, as well as an almost desperate need to identify him-
> self with the rebelling child against parental or any other adult authority, includ-
> ing his own.

Hechinger [1970, p. 41] adds:

> Summerhill claims to be noncoercive; but the model and the life style of those
> who teach do, in fact coerce, however gently. The priorities of Summerhill are so
> non-intellectual as to place the book, the literary masterpiece, the evolution of
> thought at a disadvantage.

Certainly, the self-directed learning advocated by Neill has its positive side,
and Summerhill is indeed a sanctuary of freedom for children. However, a sel-
dom-mentioned corollary to student freedom also exists. Just as children should
be given leeway in what they choose to study, teachers, especially beginners,
should also be given a chance to build upon their strengths and interests. The
particular *modus operandi* of a new teacher makes a crucial difference in whether
or not his influence is positive. To be able to select goals and activities from all
those possible and to teach what one feels comfortable with and challenged by
are ingredients for a good start.

Summerhill has also been a model to emulate in its age-grouping policies.
Chronological age, as the sole criterion of togetherness, disappears. Fortunately,
other educationists are beginning to recognize the benefit of such a mix of ages.
For example, many English infant schools stress 'family" or "vertical" grouping,
and ungraded schools are gaining acceptance in the United States.

So, how can we best learn from Summerhill? Certainly not by trying to copy it
point by point. Rather, a beginning may emerge from what happens there that is
similar to other successful situations where children are learning. And then, by
daring to try some of these things on our own, something good could develop.

What happens at such a school? What can we borrow? For starters, kids can
make mistakes. So can adults. Not much preaching goes on. Good music, literature, art, and drama are defined primarily in terms of whether a child likes the
particular work or not. Work and play are difficult to distinguish. Age differences
are not very important. Everyone seems to do at least something pretty well. More
heads nod vertically than horizontally when creative new ideas appear. Academic
and nonacademic subjects are related to each other. Questions are more important than answers. There are a lot of right answers but right ones are not always
better than wrong ones. Things are not timed very much. Students listen to other
students as well as to the teacher. In a school that works, teachers may not seem
to know as much as other teachers when you first meet them, but after knowing
them for a while, you realize their depth of understanding. Outside of class,
teachers actually talk about the good things students do more than the bad things.

Teachers listen to students. No one gets very excited about little things. Students help plan ahead as well as reflect on the past. Children are taken seriously and listened to. Their hopes are supported. Most important of all, adults are on their side.

REFERENCES

Ames, L. B. In H. Hart (Ed.), *Summerhill: For and Against*. New York: Hart, 1970, pp. 64–82.

Hechinger, F. M. In H. Hart (Ed.), *Summerhill: For and Against*. New York: Hart, 1970, pp. 34–46.

Montagu, A. In H. Hart (Ed.), *Summerhill: For and Against*. New York: Hart, 1970, pp. 48–63.

Neill, A. S. *Summerhill: A Radical Approach to Child Rearing*. New York: Hart, 1960.

REVIEW QUESTIONS

1. To what extent is Summerhill not a free school?

2. After you read Kozol's article "Free Schools: A Time for Candor" (article 25), how do you reflect upon Summerhill?

3. Compare Summerhill with the British schools described by Featherstone (article 32). (Food for thought: Warren once walked into the office of a British primary school headmaster with a copy of an A. S. Neill book under his arm. The headmaster's attack on Neill was instant and from the heart.)

twenty-five

Free Schools: A Time for Candor

JONATHAN KOZOL

For the past six years free schools have almost been pets of the media. Too little of this coverage, however, has focused on the deep and often overwhelming problems that confront some of these schools: the terrible anguish about power and the paralyzing inhibition about the functions of the teacher.

The difficulties begin with a number of foolish, inaccurate, and dangerous clichés borrowed without much criticism or restraint from fashionable books by fashionable authors who do not know very much about either life within the cities or responsibilities that confront a free school for poor children in a time of torment and in a situation of great urgency and fear. It is almost axiomatic that the free schools that survive are those that start under the stimulus of a neighborhood in pain and that remain within the power of that neighborhood. Those that fail are, time and again, those that are begun on somebody's intellectual high or someone's infatuation with a couple of phrases from the latest book and then collapse after six months or a year of misery among the cuisenaire rods.

It is time for us to come right out and make some straightforward statements on the misleading and deceptive character of certain slogans that are now unthinkingly received as gospel. It is just not true that the best teacher is the one who most successfully pretends that he knows nothing. Nor is it true that the best answer to the blustering windbag of the old-time public school is the free-school teacher who attempts to turn himself into a human inductive fan.

Free schools that exist under the siege conditions of New York, Boston, or one of the other Northern cities should not be ashamed to offer classroom experience in which the teacher does not hesitate to take a clear position as a knowledgeable adult. Neither should these free schools be intimidated in the face of those who come in from their college courses with old and tattered copies of *How Children Fail* and *Summerhill*. Many of these people, fans of John Holt or A. S. Neill though they may be, are surprisingly dogmatic in their imposition of modish slogans on the real world they enter. Many, moreover, have only the most vague and shadowy notion of what the free school represents.

Free schools at the present moment cover the full range of beliefs from the Third World Institute of all black kids and all black teachers, operated by a group of revolutionary leaders wearing military jackets, boots, and black berets, to a segregated Summerhill out in the woods of western Massachusetts offering "freedom" of a rather different kind and charging something like $2,000 or $3,000 yearly for it. The free schools that I care most about stand somewhere in between, though surely closer to the first than to the second. The trouble, however, is that the intellectual imprecision of the school-reform movement as a whole, and the very special imprecision of the free schools in particular, allow *both* kinds of free schools to advertise themselves with the same slogans and to describe themselves with the same phrases.

The challenge, then, is to define ourselves with absolutely implacable precision—and to do so even in the face of economic danger, even in the certain knowledge of the loss of possible allies. "This is what we are like, and this is the kind of place that we are going to create. This is the kind of thing we mean by freedom, and this is the sort of thing we have in mind by words like 'teach' and 'learn.' This is the sort of thing we mean by competence, effectiveness, survival. If you like it, join us. If you don't, go someplace else and start a school of your own."

Such precision and directness are often the rarest commodities within free schools. Too many of us are frightened of the accusation of being headstrong, tough, authoritarian, and, resultingly, we have tried too hard to be all things to all potential friends. It is especially difficult to resist the offered assistance when we are most acutely conscious of the loneliness and isolation of an oppressive social structure.

The issue comes into focus in the choice of teachers and in the substance of curriculum. In an effort to avoid the standard brand of classroom tyranny that is identified so often with the domineering figure of the professional in the public system, innovative free-school teachers often make the grave mistake of reducing themselves to ethical and pedagogical neuters. The teacher too often takes the role of one who has *no* power.

The myth of this familiar pretense is that the teacher, by concealing his own views, can avoid making his influence felt in the classroom. This is not the case. No teacher, no matter what he does or does not say, can ever manage *not* to advertise his biases to the children.

A teacher "teaches" not only or even primarily by what he *says*. At least in part, he teaches by what he *is*, by what he *does*, by what he seems to *wish to be*. André Gide said, "Style is character." In the free school, life-style is at the heart of education. The teacher who talks of "redistribution of the wealth" yet dresses in expensive clothes among the poor and spends the Christmas holidays in San Juan gets across a certain message, with or without words, about his stake in some of the nice things privilege can offer. A black woman with a conspicuous

Afro and a certain definite quality of suppressed intensity in her manner and voice gets across a whole world of feelings and biases concerning race and rage and revolution. A white woman who dresses in old sandals, blue work shirt, Mexican skirt, whose long hair is frequently uncombed, who wears love beads or a molded-steel medallion on her breast, who calls things "neat," "right on," "downers," and "together" presents a living advertisement for a whole body of implied ideas, political tendencies, and ideological directions.

In certain respects, the things a teacher does not even *wish* to say may well provide a deeper and more abiding lesson than the content of the textbooks or the conscious message of the posters on the wall. When war is raging and when millions of people in our land are going through a private and communal hell, no teacher—no matter what he does or does not do—can fail to influence his pupils. The secret curriculum is in the teacher's own lived values and convictions, in the lineaments of his face, and in the biography of passion (or self-exile) that is written in his eyes. The young teacher who appears to children to be vague or indirect in the face of human pain, infant death, or malnutrition may not teach children anything at all about pain, death, and hunger, but he will be teaching a great deal about the capability of an acceptable adult to abdicate the consequences of his own perception and, as it were, to vacate his own soul. By denying his convictions during class discussion, he does not teach objectivity. He gives, at the very least, a precedent for nonconviction.

It is particularly disabling when a strong and serious free school begun by parents of poor children in an urban situation finds itself bombarded by young teachers who adhere without restraint or self-examination to these values. Not only does such behavior advertise gutlessness and weakness to the children, it also represents a good deal of deception and direct bamboozlement. The willingness of the highly skilled white teacher to blur and disguise his own effectiveness and to behave as if he were less competent and effective than he really is provides the basis for a false democracy between himself and the young poor children he works with. The children, in all honesty, *can't do nothing.* The young man from Princeton only *acts* as if he can't. The consequence of this is a spurious level of egalitarian experience from which one party is always able to escape, but from which the other has no realistic exit.

I believe, for these reasons, in the kind of free school in which adults do not try to seem less vigorous or effective than they are. I believe in a school in which real power, leverage, and at least a certain degree of undisguised adult direction are not viewed with automatic condescension or disdain. I believe in a school in which the teacher does not strive to simulate the status or condition of either an accidental "resource-person," wandering mystic, or movable reading lab, but comes right out, in full view of the children, with all of the richness, humor, desperation, rage, self-contradiction, strength, and pathos that he would reveal to other grownups. Nevertheless, some of the free schools that describe and advertise their high-priced, all-white, innovative education in the pages of *New Schools Exchange* seem literally to build the core of their life-style around the simulation of essential impotence, with competence admitted only in those areas of basic handiwork and back-to-nature skills where no serious competition from the outside world exists. "Wow!" I hear some of these free-school people say. "We made an Iroquois canoe out of a log!" Nobody, however, *needs* an Iroquois canoe. Even the Iroquois do not. The Iroquois can buy aluminum canoes if they should really need them. They don't, however. What they need are doctors, lawyers, teachers, organizers, labor leaders. The obvious simulation-character of the construction of an Iroquois canoe by a group of well-set North American children and adults in 1972 is only one vivid example of the total exercise of false removal from the scene of struggle that now typifies the counterculture. There may be some pedagogic value or therapeutic function in this form of simulation for the heartsick or disoriented son or grandson of a rich man. It does not, however, correspond to my idea of struggle and survival in the streets and cities I know.

In the face of many intelligent and respected statements on the subject of "spontaneous" and "ecstatic" education, the simple truth is that you do not learn calculus, biochemistry, physics, Latin grammar, mathematical logic, Constitutional law, brain surgery, or hydraulic engineering in the same organic fashion that you learn to walk and breathe and make love. Months and years of long, involved, and—let us be quite honest—sometimes nonutopian labor in the acquisition of a single unit of complex and intricate knowledge go into the expertise that makes for power in this nation. The poor and black cannot survive the technological nightmare of the next ten years if they do not have this expertise.

There is no more terrifying evidence of the gulf of race and class that now separates oppressor and oppressed within this nation than that so many of those people who are rich and strong should toil with all their heart to simulate the hesitation, stammer, and awkward indirection of impotence, while blacks in Roxbury, in Harlem, and in East St. Louis must labor with all their soul to win one-tenth of the *real effectiveness* that those white people conspire to deny. If there is a need for some men and women to continue in that manner of existence and that frame of mind, and if it is a need that cannot be transcended, then let there be two very different kinds of free schools and two very different kinds of human transformation and human struggle. But, at least within the urban free schools that we build and labor to sustain, let us be willing to say who we are and what we think and where we stand, and let us also say what things *we do not want*.

Those who fear power in themselves fear it still more in those whom they select to lead them. Several free schools that I know firsthand have gone through nightmarish periods in which they all but pick apart the man or woman they have chosen to be their headmaster or headmistress. The process is dangerous and debilitating not only because it does so much direct damage in terms of simple pain and hurt to many decent and courageous men and women but also because it wastes our time in minor skirmishes and diverts us from the serious struggle for the well-being and real survival of our children.

More importantly, however, fear of power places a premium on mediocrity, nonvital leadership, insipid character, and unremarkable life-style. An organization, of whatever kind, that identifies real excellence, effectiveness, or compelling life-style with the terrifying risk of despotism and authoritarian manipulation will, little by little, drive away all interesting, brilliant, and exhilarating people and will establish in their stead norms of communal mediocrity. The label reserved for those who do not learn to respect these norms is "ego-tripper." Without question, there is a need for realistic caution, but not every straightforward, unequivocal statement of position can be construed as an instance of ego-tripping. The perfect way to avoid an ego trip, of course, is to create a community of utterly alienated, dull, and boring people. There is no risk of ego-tripping if there is no ego. But there isn't any life or strength or truth or passion either.

Free schools, if they wish to stay alive and vital, must learn to separate the fear of domination from the fear of excellence. If a free school were ever able to discover or train a leader with the power and vision of a Jesse Jackson or, in a different sense, a George Dennison or a Truman Nelson, I hope it would have brains enough not to attempt to dull his edge or obscure his brilliant provocations with communal indecision. "Participation" and "the will of the full group," inherently eloquent and important aspects of a democratic and exciting free school, can easily turn into the code words for a stylized paralysis of operation and for a new tyranny of will and function.

It may well be that certain free schools, within a rural, safe, and insulated situation, will find it possible to function and survive without formal structure, leadership, or power apparatus. It is their choice if they should wish to do it in that way; but those who look for leaders, place them in power, and invest them with the trust and confidence of numbers ought then to stand beside them and help to make them stronger and less frightened in the face of the dangers they confront. Angry parents who never before had power in their hands and young white people who have forever hated anyone who wielded it, can together paralyze the operations of a free school and can gradually destroy the finest qualities in anyone that they select to lead them.

Statements of this kind run counter to a large part of the jargon that the media tend to associate with the free schools. Jargon, however, does not often correspond to the realities of struggle and survival. In every free school that has lasted longer than two years there is—*there always is*—some deep down and abiding power center. Free schools do not hang photographs of unremarkable individuals. They put up photographs of Malcolm X, of César Chavez, of Martin Luther King, of Tolstoy, of José Martí. What is true in history and on the poster-photograph is also true in our own numbers: Some women and some men *are* more powerful and more interesting than others. Behind every free school that survives are the special dedication, passion, and vocation of one woman, one man, or one small and trusted group of men and women. It is by now almost a rule of thumb that the less the free-school bylaws speak of "power" the more one person or one group turns out to hold it. It may be only by a look, a shrug, or a sense of peace within the quiet center of the pedagogic storm. Is A. S. Neill the "ego-tripper" or the "power center" or the "ethical fire" in the heart of his own school? Ask anyone who has ever been to Summerhill.

Still another dangerous tendency included in the syndrome of pretended impotence and threatening the survival of urban free schools is what Bernice Miller speaks of as an inclination toward The Insufficient—or what I think of sometimes as The Cult of Incompletion. It is the kind of hang-loose state of mind that views with scorn the need for strong, consistent, and uninterrupted processes of work and aspiration and, instead, makes a virtue of the interrupted venture, the unsuccessful campaign. I have in mind an almost classic picture of a group of rural free-school people I know, sitting on the lawn of someone's country farm or "radical estate" in an almost too comfortable mood of "resting on our elbows at a place of satisfying retrospect on our own failure" or at a kind of "interesting plateau of our half-success."

I think that it is time for us to face head on this problem of our own inherent fear of strength and effectiveness. We must be prepared to strive with all our hearts to be strong teachers, efficacious adults, unintimidated leaders, and straightforward and strong-minded provocators in the lives of children. We must work with all our hearts to overcome the verbal style of debilitation and subjunctive supposition—the interposition, for example, of the preposition or conjunction of arm's length invalidation ("like") before all statements of intense commitment or denunciation. I know some free-school leaders and writers who now begin to justify and defend the will-to-failure by making a virtue of the capability to start and stop things in response to sudden impulse. It is a curious revolution that builds its ideology and its morale upon the cheerful prospect of surrender. Men who walk the city streets with minds uncluttered by their own internal need for self-defeat, aware of the pain around them, could not make barbarous recommendations of this kind.

The free-school press and writers speak more often of Bill Ayers's free school in Ann Arbor, Michigan, which did not work out, than they do of Edward Carpenter's remarkable and long-sustained success at Harlem Prep. I have a good deal of respect and admiration for Bill Ayers. Still, it cannot be ignored that, insofar as the free schools are concerned, Bill Ayers's experience is perhaps the prototype of the eloquent exercise in self-defeat. I believe we ought to honor people like Bill Ayers in the same way many of us revere the name of Che Guevara. There is also Fidel, however, who was not afraid to sit in the victor's chair, and there are also strong and stable people like Ed Carpenter. It would not hurt to have upon the walls or in the stairways of our little schools photographs not only of those who do not fear to die for their beliefs but also of those who do not fear to win. I think that the children of the black and poor ought to be able to know and believe, right from the first, that the struggle for liberation does not need to end with sickness in the mountains or with steel helmets in Chicago or with a T-group in Manhattan. It can also end with personal strength, political passion, psychological leverage, and the deepest kind of moral and pragmatic power.

I do not intend to mock young people, or myself, or my own friends, who really try and honestly do fail; but I am thinking also of the anguish in success and in "too much effectiveness" of those who look upon effectiveness itself as bearing the copyright of evil men. There is no need for us to choose between a contaminated sense of competence and a benign sense of ineptitude. The opposite of the cold and avaricious doctor earning his $250,000 yearly in the kingdom of lighted pools and begonia hedges in Lexington, Massachusetts, does not need to be the spaced-out flautist in the shepherds's jacket on a mountain in Colorado or the mystical builder of the Pakistani mud hut in New Hampshire; it can also be the radical, bold, and inexhaustible young doctor working his heart out in the storefront clinics of Chicago. The opposite of the sleek corporation lawyer spooning up the cool lime sherbet from a silver dish in the air-conditioned confines of the Harvard Club in Boston does not need to be the barefoot kid in blue jeans in New Hampshire; it can also be the strong and passionate young woman who nails down her law degree while working nights to tutor kids within the nightmare of the Pruitt-Igoe projects in St. Louis—and then comes back to be their representative before the law. The preference for the unsuccessful, for the interrupted enterprise, for hesitation and low-key aspiration is not surprising or inexplicable in a hard and driving nation such as our own.

One final point: Free schools often prove to be almost irresistibly attractive to some of the most unhappy and essentially aggresive people on the face of the wide earth. In many instances, the very same people who have been "evicted" from someone else's free school precisely for the pain and hurt they cause will shop around until they come to us. There is, as many people in the free schools find, a rather familiar kind of man or woman who does not, in fact, care a great deal about children but who enjoys a power struggle. There is a kind of "energy of devastation" in such people that can be helpful when it is directed at external obstacles but that can be incredibly destructive when it turns in on our own small numbers.

I have seen one of the kindest black people I know pause, and look gently, almost with sadness, into the eyes of someone of this sort and say quietly: "Well, you don't seem to be somebody that I want to work with. There has been too much unhappiness among us since you came. You do not seem to think we are sufficiently enlightened. You do not seem to think that we have read the right books. You may be right. We have not read many books in the past year. We have been too busy trying to build up our school and trying to keep off people who bring sadness and unhappiness into our ranks. We think that you are just that kind of person. We would rather have the courage of our errors than the kind of devastation forced upon us by your intellectual wisdom."

I do not like to end with a passage of this kind. It shows too much of the bitterness and the deep pain that have been part of the free schools I know. I am trying, however, to be as realistic and as candid as I can. There is a time when we must sit down and compose rhapsodic stories to raise money for the free schools; there is another time when we have to be as honest as we can. In 1972 the free schools have come into their own hour. It is the time for candor.

REVIEW QUESTIONS

1. What are some criticisms that an outsider might level at free schools? How might Kozol or another defender of free schools respond?

2. How might the label "free school" lead to unrealistic expectations?

twenty-six

Teachers' Expectations as Self-Fulfilling Prophecies

ROBERT ROSENTHAL AND LENORE JACOBSON

There is increasing concern over what can be done to reduce the disparities of education, of intellectual motivation and of intellectual competence that exist between the social classes and the colors of our school children. With this increasing concern, attention has focused more and more on the role of the classroom teacher, and the possible effects of her values, her attitudes, and, especially, her beliefs and expectations. Many educational theorists have expressed the opinion that the teacher's expectation of her pupils' performance may serve as an educational self-fulfilling prophecy. The teacher gets less because she expects less.

The concept of the self-fulfilling prophecy is an old idea which has found application in clinical psychology, social psychology, sociology, economics, and in everyday life. Most of the evidence for the operation of self-fulfilling prophecies has been correlational. Interpersonal prophecies have been found to agree with the behavior that was prophesied. From this, however, it cannot be said that the prophecy was the cause of its own fulfillment. The accurate prophecy may have been based on a knowledge of the prior behavior of the person whose behavior was prophesied, so that the prophecy was in a sense "contaminated" by reality. If a physician predicts a patient's improvement, we cannot say whether the doctor is only giving a sophisticated prognosis or whether the patient's improvement is based in part on the optimism engendered by the physician's prediction. If school children who perform poorly are those expected by their teachers to perform poorly, we cannot say whether the teacher's expectation was the "cause" of the pupils' poor performance, or whether the teacher's expectation was simply an accurate prognosis of performance based on her knowledge of past performance. To help answer the question raised, experiments are required in which the ex-

Source: From a paper presented at the meeting of the American Psychological Association, Washington, D. C., September 1967. Reprinted by permission of the authors.

pectation is experimentally varied and is uncontaminated by the past behavior of the person whose performance is predicted.

Such experiments have been conducted and they have shown, that in behavioral research, the experimenter's hypothesis may serve as self-fulfilling prophecy [Rosenthal, 1966]. Of special relevance to our topic are those experiments involving allegedly bright and allegedly dull animal subjects. Half the experimenters were led to believe that their rat subjects had been specially bred for excellence of learning ability. The remaining experimenters were led to believe that their rat subjects were genetically inferior. Actually, of course, the animals were assigned to their experimenters at random.

Regardless of whether the rat's task was to learn a maze or the appropriate responses in a Skinner box, the results were the same. Rats who were believed by their experimenters to be brighter showed learning which was significantly superior to the learning by rats whose experimenters believed them to be dull. Our best guess, supported by the experimenters' self-reports, is that allegedly well-endowed animals were handled more and handled more gently than the allegedly inferior animals. Such handling differences, along with differences in rapidity of reinforcement in the Skinner box situation, are probably sufficient to account for the differences in learning ability shown by allegedly bright and allegedly dull rats.

If rats showed superior performance when their trainer expected it, then it seemed reasonable to think that children might show superior performance when their teacher expected it. That was the reason for conducting the Oak School Experiment [Rosenthal and Jacobson, 1966].

THE "OAK SCHOOL" EXPERIMENT

To all of the children in the Oak School, on the West Coast, the "Harvard Test of Inflected Acquisition" was administered in the Spring of 1964. This test was purported to predict academic "blooming" or intellectual growth. The reason for administering the test in the particular school was ostensibly to perform a final check on the validity of the test, a validity which was presented as already well-established. Actually, the "Harvard Test of Inflected Acquisition" was a standardized relatively nonverbal test of intelligence, Flanagan's Tests of General Ability.

Within each of the six grades of the elementary school, there were three classrooms, one each for children performing at above-average, average, and below-average levels of scholastic achievement. In each of the 18 classrooms of the school, about 20 per cent of the children were designated as academic "spurters." The names of these children were reported to their new teachers in the Fall of 1964 as those who, during the academic year ahead, would show unusual intellectual gains. The "fact" of their intellectual potential was established from their scores on the test for "intellectual blooming."

Teachers were cautioned not to discuss the test findings with either their pupils or the children's parents. Actually, the names of the 20 per cent of the children assigned to the "blooming" condition had been selected by means of a table of random numbers. The difference, then, between these children, earmarked for intellectual growth, and the undesignated control group children was in the mind of the teacher.

Four months after the teachers had been given the names of the "special" children, all the children once again took the same form of the nonverbal test of intelligence. Four months after this retest the children took the same test once again. This final retest was at the end of the school year, some eight months after the teachers had been given the expectation for intellectual growth of the special children. These retests were not, of course, explained as "retests" to the teachers but rather as further efforts to predict intellectual growth.

The intelligence test employed, while relatively nonverbal in the sense of requiring no speaking, reading, or writing, was not entirely nonverbal. Actually there were two subtests, one requiring a greater comprehension of English—a kind of picture vocabulary test. The other subtest required less ability to understand any spoken language but more ability to reason abstractly. For shorthand purposes we refer to the former as a "verbal" subtest and to the latter as a "reasoning" subtest. The pretest correlation between these subtests was $+.42$.

For the school as a whole, the children of the experimental groups did not show a significantly greater gain in verbal IQ (2 points) than did the control group children. However, in total IQ (4 points) and especially in reasoning IQ (7 points) the experimental group children gained more than did the control group children ($p = .02$). In 15 of the 17 classrooms in which the reasoning IQ posttest was administered children of the experimental group gained more than did the control group children ($p=.001$). Even after the four month retest this trend was already in evidence though the effects were smaller ($p<.10$).

When we examine the results separately for the six grades we find that it was only in the first and second grades that children gained significantly more in IQ when their teacher expected it of them. In the first grade, children who were expected to gain more IQ gained over 15 points more than did the control group children ($p< .002$). In the second grade, children who were expected to gain more IQ gained nearly 10 points more than did the control group children ($p<.02$). In the first and second grades combined, 19 per cent of the control group children gained 20 or more IQ points. Two-and-a-half times that many, or 47 per cent, of the experimental group children gained 20 or more IQ points.

When educational theorists have discussed the possible effects of teachers' expectations, they have usually referred to the children at lower levels of scholastic achievement. It was interesting, therefore, to find that in the present study, children of the highest level of achievement showed as great a benefit as did the children of the lowest level of achievement of having their teachers expect intellectual gains.

At the end of the school year of this study, all teachers were asked to describe the classroom behavior of their pupils. Those children from whom intellectual growth was expected were described as having a significantly better chance of becoming successful in the future, as significantly more interesting, curious, and happy. There was a tendency, too, for these children to be seen as more appealing, adjusted, and affectionate and as lower in the need for social approval. In short, the children from whom intellectual growth was expected became more intellectually alive and autonomous or at least were so perceived by their teachers. These findings were particularly striking among the first grade children; those were the children who had benefited most in IQ gain as a result of their teachers' favorable expectancies.

We have already seen that the children of the experimental group gained more intellectually so that the possibility existed that it was the fact of such gaining that accounted for the more favorable ratings of these children's behavior and aptitude. But a great many of the control group children also gained in IQ during the course of the year. Perhaps those who gained more intellectually among these undesignated children would also be rated more favorably by their teachers. Such was not the case. The more the control group children gained in IQ the more they were regarded as *less* well adjusted ($r = -.13$, $p<.05$), as *less* interesting ($r = -.14$ $p<.05$) and as *less* affectionate ($r = -.13$, $p<.05$). From these results it would seem that when children who are expected to grow intellectually do so, they are considerably benefited in other ways as well. When children who are not especially expected to develop intellectually do so, they seem either to show accompanying undesirable behavior or at least are perceived by their teachers as showing such undesirable behavior. If a child is to show intellectual gain it seems to be better for his real or perceived intellectual vitality and for his real or perceived mental health if his teacher has been expecting him to grow intellectually. It appears that there may be hazards to unpredicted intellectual growth.

A closer analysis of these data, broken down by whether the children were in the high, medium, or low ability tracks or groups, showed that these hazards of unpredicted intellectual growth were due primarily to the children of the low ability group. When these slow track children were in the control group so that no intellectual gains were expected of them, they were rated more unfavorably by their teachers if they did show gains in IQ. The greater their IQ gains, the more unfavorably were they rated, both as to mental health and as to intellectual vitality. Even when the slow track children were in the experimental group, so that IQ gains were expected of them, they were not rated as favorably relative to their control group peers as were the children of the high or medium track, despite the fact that they gained as much in IQ relative to the control group children as did the experimental group children of the high group. It may be difficult for a slow track child, even one whose IQ is rising to be seen by his teacher as a well-adjusted child, and as a potentially successful child, intellectually.

THE QUESTION OF MEDIATION

How did the teachers' expectations come to serve as determinants of gains in intellectual performance? The most plausible hypothesis seemed to be that children for whom unusual intellectual growth had been predicted would be more attended to by their teachers. If teachers were more attentive to the children earmarked for growth, we might expect that teachers were robbing Peter to see Paul grow. With a finite amount of time to spend with each child, if a teacher gave more time to the children of the experimental group, she would have less time to spend with the children of the control group. If the teacher's spending more time with a child led to greater gains, we could test the "robbing Peter" hypothesis by comparing the gains made by children of the experimental group with gains made by children of the control group in each class. The robbing Peter hypothesis predicts a negative correlation. The greater the gains made by the children of the experimental group (with the implication of more time spent on them) the less should be the gains made by the children of the control group (with the implication of less time spent on them). In fact, however, the correlation was positive, large and statistically significant (rho $= +.57$, $p = .02$, two tail). The greater the gain made by the children of whom gain was expected, the greater the gain made in the same classroom by those children from whom no special gain was expected.

Additional evidence that teachers did not take time from control group children to spend with the experimental group children comes from the teacher's inability to recall which of the children in her class were designated as potential bloomers and from her estimates of time spent with each pupil. These estimates showed a tendency, which was not significant statistically, for teachers to spend *less* time with pupils from whom intellectual gains were expected.

That the children of the experimental group were not favored with a greater investment of time seems less surprising in view of the pattern of their greater intellectual gains. If, for example, teachers had talked to them more, we might have expected greater gains in verbal IQ but, the greater gains were found not in verbal but in reasoning IQ. It may be, of course, that the teachers were inaccurate in their estimates of time spent with each of their pupils. Possibly direct observation of the teacher-pupil interactions would have given different results, but that method was not possible in the present study. Even direct observation by judges who could agree with one another might not have revealed a difference in the amounts of teacher time invested in each of the two groups of children. It seems plausible to think that it was not a difference in amount of time spent with the children of the two groups which led to the differences in their rates of intellectual development. It may have been more a matter of the type of interaction which took place between the teachers and their pupils.

By what she said, by how she said it, by her facial expressions, postures, and perhaps, by her touch, the teacher may have communicated to the children of the experimental group that she expected improved intellectual performance. Such communications, together with possible changes in teaching techniques, may have helped the child learn by changing his self-concept, his expectations of his own behavior, his motivation, as well as his cognitive skills. It is self evident that further research is needed to narrow down the range of possible mechanisms whereby a teacher's expectations become translated into a pupil's intellectual growth. It would be valuable, for example, to have sound films of teachers interacting with their pupils. We might then look for differences in the way teachers interact with those children from whom they expect more intellectual growth compared to those from whom they expect less. On the basis of films of psychological experimenters interacting with subjects from whom different responses are expected, we know that even in such highly standardized situations, unintentional communications can be subtle and complex [Rosenthal, 1967]. How much more subtle and complex may be the communications between children and their teachers, teachers who are not constrained by the demands of the experimental laboratory.

SOME IMPLICATIONS

The results of the experiment just now described provide further evidence that one person's expectation of another's behavior may serve as a self-fulfilling prophecy. When teachers expected that certain children would show greater intellectual development, those children did show greater intellectual development.

It may be that as teacher training institutions acquaint teachers-to-be with the possibility that their expectations of their pupils' performance may serve as self-fulfilling prophecies, these teacher trainees may be given a new expectancy—that children can learn more than they had believed possible.

The methodological implications of the evidence presented in this paper are best introduced by citing the results of a well-known "total-push" educational program, which, after three years, led to a 10-point IQ gain by 38 per cent of the children and a 20-point IQ gain by 12 per cent of the children. Such gains, while dramatic, were smaller than the gains found among the first and second grade children of our control group and very much smaller than the gains found among the children of our experimental group.

It is not possible to be sure about the matter, but it may be that the large gains shown by the children of our control group were attributable to a Hawthorne effect. The fact that university researchers, supported by federal funds, were interested in the school in which the research was conducted, may have led to a general improvement of morale and teacher technique on the part of all the teachers. In any case, the possibility of a Hawthorne effect cannot be ruled out either in the present experiment or in other studies of educational practices. Any educational practice which is assessed for effectiveness must be able to show some excess of gain over what Hawthorne effects alone would yield.

When the efficacy of an educational practice is investigated, we want to know its efficacy relative to the Hawthorne effect of "something new and important" but the present paper suggests that another baseline must be introduced. We still want to know, too, whether the efficacy of an educational practice is greater than that of the easily and inexpensively manipulatable expectation of the teacher. Most educational practices are more expensive in time and money than giving teachers names of children "who will show unusual intellectual development."

When educational innovations are introduced into ongoing educational systems, it seems very likely that the administrators whose permission is required, and the teachers whose cooperation is required, will expect the innovation to be effective. If they did not, they would be unlikely to give the required permission and cooperation. The experimental innovation, then, will likely be confounded with favorable expectations regarding their efficacy.

When educational innovations are introduced into newly created educational systems with specially selected and specially trained teachers and administrators, the problems are similar. Those teachers, and those administrators, who elect to go, and are selected to go, into newly created educational systems, are likely to have expectations favorable to the efficacy of the new program. In this situation as that in which changes are introduced into pre-existing systems, teachers' and administrators' expectations are likely to be confounded with the educational innovations. All this argues for the systematic employment of expectancy control groups, a type of control described elsewhere in detail [Rosenthal, 1966]. Without the use of expectancy control groups, it is impossible to tell whether the results of experiments in educational practice are due to the practices themselves or to the correlated expectations of the teachers who are to try out the educational reforms.

But to come to an end, we shall want a summary. Perhaps the most suitable summary of the hypothesis discussed in this paper and tested by the described experiment has already been written. The writer is George Bernard Shaw, the play is *Pygmalion* and the speaker is Eliza Doolittle:

> You see, really and truly, ... the difference between a lady and a flower girl is not how she behaves, but how she's treated. I shall always be a flower girl to Professor Higgins, because he ... treats me as a flower girl, ... but I know I can be a lady to you, because you always treat me as a lady, and always will.

REFERENCES

Rosenthal, R. *Experimenter Effects in Behavior Research*. New York: Appleton-Century-Crofts, 1966.

Rosenthal, R. Covert communication in the psychological experiment. *Psychological Bulletin*, 1967, *67*: 356–67.

Rosenthal, R., and Jacobson, Lenore. Teachers' expectancies: Determinants of pupils' IQ gains. *Psychological Reports*, 1966, *19*: 115–18.

REVIEW QUESTIONS

1.   How do you suppose a *student's* expectations influence his success in school and later life?

2.   Could ability grouping (or "tracking") influence a student's self-expectations?

twenty-seven

From *Pygmalion Reconsidered*

JANET D. ELASHOFF AND RICHARD E. SNOW

Before discussing methodological aspects of the RJ study, we consider it appropriate to examine the RJ book [Rosenthal and Jacobson, 1968] as a report of original research. A researcher's responsibility does not end when the experiment has been conducted and analyses concluded; he must report to the public his methods and findings. This is not a trivial final step but a crucial part of the research process. If the reader is misled about the results, it no longer matters how much care went into the performance of the experiment. A careful reading of the report should provide the reader with sufficient information to allow replication of the study, to allow replication of the data analyses if provided with the data, and to allow him to draw his own conclusions about the results. Stated conclusions, tables, and charts should be carefully presented so that the uninformed reader will not be misled. All studies have weaknesses in design, execution, measurement, or analysis. These should be carefully discussed in the report because they affect the interpretation of results.

Careful reporting is especially important when the report receives considerable attention from methodologically unsophisticated readers, as in the case of *Pygmalion*. The phenomenon of teacher expectancy might be of central importance in the improvement of education, particularly if the scholastic development of disadvantaged children were strongly dependent on such effects. The problem then is of considerable social moment and the results of the RJ work have been widely distributed with noticeable impact in the news media. The following represents a sample of popular reaction:

> Can the child's performance in school be considered the result as much of what his teachers' attitudes are toward him as of his native intelligence or his attitude as a pupil? ... *Pygmalion in the Classroom* is full of charts and graphs and statistics and percentages and carefully weighed statements, but there are conclu-

Source: From *Pygmalion Reconsidered*, published by Charles A. Jones Publishing Company, Worthington, Ohio. Copyright © 1971 by Charles A. Jones Publishing Company. Reprinted by permission of the first author and the publisher.

sions that have great significance for this nation. . . . Among the children of the first and second grades, those tagged "bloomers" made astonishing gains. . . . TOGA's putative, prophecy was fulfilled so conclusively that even hard-line social scientists were startled. [Coles, *The New Yorker*, April 9, 1969]

Here may lie the explanation of the effects of socio-economic status on schooling. Teachers of a higher socio-economic status expect pupils of a lower socio-economic status to fail. [Hutchins, *San Francisco Chronicle*, August 11, 1968]

Jose, a Mexican American boy . . . moved in a year from being classed as mentally retarded to above average. Another Mexican American child, Maria, moved . . . from "slow learner" to "gifted child," . . . . The implications of these results will upset many school people, yet these are hard facts. [Kohl, *The New York Review of Books*, September 12, 1968]

The findings raise some fundamental questions about teacher training. They also cast doubt on the wisdom of assigning children to classes according to presumed ability, which may only mire the lowest groups into self-confining ruts. [*Time*, September 20, 1968]

Other comments appeared in the *Saturday Review* [October 19, 1968], and a special issue of *The Urban Review* [September 1968] was devoted solely to the topic of expectancy and contained a selection from *Pygmalion*. Rosenthal was even invited to discuss the results on NBC's "Today" show, thus reaching millions of viewers with the idea. The study was also cited in at least one city's decision to ban the use of IQ tests in primary grades:

The Board of Education's unanimous action was founded largely on recent findings which show that in many cases the classroom performance of children is based on the expectations of teachers.

In one study conducted by Robert Rosenthal of Harvard University, the test results given to teachers were rigged, but the children performed just as teachers had been led to expect based on the IQ scores. [McCurdy, *Los Angeles Times*, Janurary 31, 1969]

Because the book received wide attention and will likely stimulate more public discussion and policy decisions as well as much further research, it is imperative that its results be thoroughly evaluated and understood. Unfortunately, a complete understanding of the data and results are not obtainable from the published accounts alone.

Pygmalion in the Classroom can be severely criticized as a research report. We summarize our criticisms briefly here and then return to each in more detail. The RJ report is misleading. The text and tables are inconsistent, conclusions are overdramatized, and variables are given prejudicial labels. The three concluding chapters represent only superficial, and frequently inaccurate, attempts to deal with the study's flaws. Descriptions of design, basic data, and analysis are incomplete. The sampling plan is not spelled out in detail. Frequency distributions are lacking for either raw or IQ scores. Comparisons between text and appendix tables are hampered by the use of different subgroupings of the data and the absence of intermediate analysis-of-variance tables. Many tables and graphs show only differences between difference scores, i.e., gain for the experimental group minus gain for the control group. There are technical inaccuracies: charts and graphs are frequently drawn in a misleading way and the p-value or significance level is incorrectly defined and used. Statistical discussions are frequently oversimplified or completely incorrect. . . .

[Regarding] RJ's experimental design and sampling procedures, the major difficulties discussed are the lack of clarity about the details of assignment to treatment groups, subject losses during the experiment, and the lack of balance in the design. These difficulties are especially important in the RJ study since the experimental group showed higher pretest scores on the average.

[Also, we must] examine the IQ scores actually obtained by children in Oak School, and questions of norming, reliability, and validity for these measurements. Histograms of the score distributions in each grade are shown. The number of IQ scores below 60 and above 160, especially for verbal and reasoning subscores, raises doubts about the validity of the experiment as a whole and the results of certain statistical techniques in particular.

In short, our criticisms can be stated in the more general words of D. Huff [1954]:

> The fault is in the filtering-down process from the researcher through the sensational or ill-informed writer to the reader who fails to miss the figures that have disappeared in the process.

INTERPRETATIONS AND CONCLUSIONS

Conclusions are frequently overstated and do not always agree from place to place in the book. Text and tables are not always in agreement. Again, our concern is well stated by Huff [1954, p. 131]:

> When assaying a statistic, watch out for a switch somewhere between the raw figure and the conclusion. One thing is all too often reported as another.

RJ use labels for their dependent variables that presume interpretations before effects are found, a practice especially to be condemned in publications aimed at the general public. "Intellectual growth" is used in referring to the simple difference between a child's pretest IQ score and his IQ score on a posttest. It is questionable whether simple gain from first to a later testing (with some adjustments for age) using the same test represents anything so global as intellectual growth.

The difference in gains shown by the experimental group over the control group is described as an "expectancy advantage." This term presupposes that the difference is always positive. In fact it is not. What particular "advantage" or "benefit" accrues to the child showing a large gain score is not made clear.

Words like "special" and "magic" are also frequently used to refer to experimental children, when less provocative terms would serve as well.

Looking at RJ's main results for Total IQ, as reported in their Table 7-1 (see our Table 1), the first- and second-grade experimental groups show a large, significant expectancy advantage, the fourth-graders show a small, nonsignificant

TABLE 1. Mean Gain in Total IQ After One Year by Experimental and Control-Group Children in Each of Six Grades (Reprinted from RJ, their table 7–1, p. 75)

		Control		Experimental		Expectancy Advantage	
Grade	N	Gain	N	Gain	IQ Points	One-tail p
1	48	+12.0	7	+27.4	15.4	.002
2	47	+ 7.0	12	+16.5	9.5	.02
3	40	+ 5.0	14	+ 5.0	0.0	
4	49	+ 2.2	12	+ 5.6	3.4	
5	26	+17.5	9	+17.4	−0.1	
6	45	+10.7	11	+10.0	−0.7	
Total	255	+ 8.42	65	+12.22	3.80	.02

advantage, the third- and fifth-graders show no difference and the sixth-graders show a small, nonsignificant disadvantage. So RJ's table reports an "expectancy advantage" for the first- and second-graders (and possibly the fourth-graders) and reports no "expectancy advantage" for the other grades. The significant "expectancy advantage" reported by RJ is thus based only on the 19 first- and second-graders in the experimental group. But RJ conclude:

We find increasing expectancy advantage as we go from the sixth to the first grade.... [p. 74]

Here is how RJ describe the results elsewhere in the text:

When the entire school benefitted as in Total IQ and Reasoning IQ, all three tracks benefitted. [p. 78]

When teachers expected that children would show greater intellectual development, these children did show greater intellectual development. [p. 82]

The evidence presented in the last two chapters suggests rather strongly that children who are expected by their teachers to gain intellectually in fact do show greater intellectual gains after one year than do children of whom such gains are not expected. [p. 121]

After the first year of the experiment a significant expectancy advantage was found, and it was especially great among children of the first and second grades. [p. 176]

There is thus a clear tendency to overgeneralize the findings. When the authors are explaining away the results of *contradictory* experiments, however, the conclusions sound quite different:

> The ending that only the younger children profited after one year from their teachers' favorable expectations helps us to understand better the [negative] results of two other experimenters. . . . [p. 84]

> The results of our own study suggest that after one year, fifth-graders may not show the effects of teacher expectations though first- and second-graders do. [p. 84]

Another important inconsistency is between the form of analysis and the stated conclusions. All analyses were done in terms of means, yet conclusions are stated in terms of individuals; for example ". . . when the entire school benefitted . . . ." or ". . . these children did show greater intellectual development." That is, the analyses performed by RJ could only show that average gains by experimental children were larger than average gains by control children, but RJ's statements imply that each individual experimental child gained and that these gains were all larger than those shown by any control group child.

There is a strong presumption throughout the book that teacher expectations have an effect. Contrary evidence is explained away. RJ cite other studies which in general did not support the conclusions drawn in this book. The discussion of these adverse findings de-emphasizes the possibility that teacher expectations have little effect on IQ scores and becomes almost absurd with references to all possible alternative hypotheses—"there is such an effect, but . . . ." [RJ, p. 57]

One of RJ's closing chapters takes steps toward answering specific methodological criticisms. Unfortunately, much of this discussion is superficial and some is incorrect . . . . RJ's chapter also offers speculation on possible processes of intentional and unintentional influence between the teachers and students, but fails to face the full implications of the fact that after the study the teachers could not remember the names on the original lists of "bloomers" and reported having scarcely glanced at the list.

RJ's last chapter provides a capsule summary and some general implications. It is here that the inadequacy of statistical summaries of these data should be clearly specified. But it is not. The reader expecting careful conclusions is given overdramatized generalities instead.

REFERENCES

Huff, D. *How to Lie with Statistics*. New York: Norton, 1954.

Rosenthal, R., and Jacobson, L. *Pygmalion in the Classroom: Teacher Expectation and Pupils' Intellectual Development*. New York: Holt, 1968.

REVIEW QUESTIONS

1. Put yourself in Rosenthal and Jacobson's place. How might they respond to this article?

2. Reflect on your own school experience with expectations. How crucial a variable has it been to you?

twenty-eight

"What's Worth Knowing?" from
Teaching as a Subversive Activity

NEIL POSTMAN AND CHARLES WEINGARTNER

Suppose all of the syllabi and curricula and textbooks in the schools disappeared. Suppose all of the standardized tests—city-wide, state-wide, and national—were lost. In other words, suppose that the most common material impeding innovation in the schools simply did not exist. Then suppose that you decided to turn this "catastrophe" into an opportunity to increase the relevance of the schools. What would you do?

We have a possibility for you to consider: suppose that you decide to have the entire "curriculum" consist of questions. These questions would have to be worth seeking answers to not only from your point of view, but, more importantly, from the point of view of the students. In order to get still closer to reality, add the requirement that the questions must help the students to develop and internalize concepts that will help them to survive in the rapidly changing world of the present and future.

Obviously, we are asking you to suppose you were an educator living in the second half of the twentieth century. What questions would you have on your list?

Take a pencil and list your questions on the next page, which we have left blank for you. Please do not be concerned about defacing our book, unless, of course, one of your questions is going to be "What were some of the ways of earning a living in Ancient Egypt?" In that case, use your *own* paper.

Now, if one of your questions was something like "Why should you answer someone else's questions?," then you undoubtedly realize that we will submit our own sample list with some misgivings. As we have said, the ecology of the inquiry environment requires that the *students* play a central, but not necessarily

Source: Abridgment of Chapter 5 from *Teaching as a Subversive Activity* by Neil Postman and Charles Weingartner. Copyright © 1969 by Neil Postman and Charles Weingartner. Reprinted by permission of the authors, and the publishers Delacorte Press, New York, and Pitman Publishing, London.

CURRICULUM QUESTIONS

exclusive, role in framing questions that they deem important. Even the most sensitive teacher cannot always project himself into the perspective of his students, and he dare not assume that *his* perception of reality is necessarily shared by them. With this limitation in mind, we can justify the list we will submit on several grounds. First, many of these questions *have* literally been asked by children and adolescents when they were permitted to respond freely to the challenge of "What's Worth Knowing?" Second, some of these questions are based on our careful *listening* to students, even though they were not at the time asking questions. Very often children make declarative statements about things when they really mean only to elicit an informative response. In some cases, they do this because they have learned from adults that it is "better" to pretend that you know than to admit that you don't. (An old aphorism describing this process goes: Children enter school as question marks and leave as periods.) In other cases, they do this because they do not know *how* to ask certain kinds of questions. In any event, a simple translation of their declarative utterances will sometimes produce a great variety of deeply felt questions.

Our final justification rests with our own imagination. We have framed—as we asked you to do—some questions which, in our judgment, are responsive to the actual and immediate as against the fancied and future needs of learners in the world as it *is* (not as it *was*). In this, we have not surveyed thousands of students, but have consulted with many, mostly in junior and senior high school. We have tried variations of these questions with children in primary grades. By and large, the response was enthusiastic—and serious. There seemed to be little doubt that, from the point of view of the students, these questions made much more sense than the ones they usually have to memorize the right answers to in school. At this point it might be worth noting that our list of questions is intended to "educate" students. Contrary to conventional school practice, what that means is that we want to elicit from students the meanings that they have already stored up so that they may subject those meanings to a testing and verifying, reordering and reclassifying, modifying and extending process. In this process, the student is not a passive "recipient"; he becomes an active *producer* of knowledge. The word "educate" is closely related to the word "educe." In the oldest pedagogic sense of the term, this meant drawing out of a person something potential or latent. We can, after all, learn only in relation to what we already know. Again, contrary to common misconceptions, this means that, if we don't know very much, our capability for learning is not very great. This idea—virtually by itself—requires a major revision in most of the metaphors that shape school policies and procedures.

Reflect on these questions—and others that these can generate. Please do not merely react to them.

> What do you worry about most?
> What are the causes of your worries?
> Can any of your worries be eliminated? How?
> Which of them might you deal with first? How do you decide?

Are there other people with the same problems? How do you know? How can you find out?

If you had an important idea that you wanted to let everyone (in the world) know about, how might you go about letting them know?

What bothers you most about adults? Why?

How do you want to be similar to or different from adults you know when you become an adult?

What, if anything, seems to you to be worth dying for?

How did you come to believe this?

What seems worth living for?

How did you come to believe this?

At the present moment, what would you most like to be—or be able to do? Why? What would you have to know in order to be able to do it? What would you have to do in order to get to know it?

How can you tell "good guys" from "bad guys"?

How can "good" be distinguished from "evil"?

What kind of a person would you most like to be? How might you get to be this kind of person?

At the present moment, what would you most like to be doing? Five years from now? Ten years from now? Why? What might you have to do to realize these hopes? What might you have to give up in order to do some or all of these things?

When you hear or read or observe something, how do you know what it means?

Where does meaning "come from"?

What does "meaning" mean?

How can you tell what something "is" or whether it is?

Where do words come from?

Where do symbols come from?

Why do symbols change?

Where does knowledge come from?

What do you think are some of man's most important ideas? Where did they come from? Why? How? Now what?

What's a "good idea"?

How do you know when a good or live idea becomes a bad or dead idea?

Which of man's ideas would we be better off forgetting? How do you decide?

What is "progress"?

What is "change"?

What are the most obvious causes of change? What are the least apparent? What conditions are necessary in order for change to occur?

What kinds of changes are going on right now? Which are important? How are they similar to or different from other changes that have occurred?

What are the relationships between new ideas and change?

Where do *new* ideas come from? How come? So what?

If you wanted to stop one of the changes going on now (pick one), how would you go about it? What consequences would you have to consider?

Of the important changes going on in our society, which should be encouraged and which resisted? Why? How?

What are the most important changes that have occurred in the past ten years? twenty years? fifty years? In the last year? In the last six months? Last month? What will be the most important changes next month? Next year? Next decade? How can you tell? So what?

What would you change if you could? How might you go about it? Of those changes which are going to occur, which would you stop if you could? Why? How? So what?

Who do you think has the most important things to say today? To whom? How? Why?

What are the dumbest and most dangerous ideas that are "popular" today? Why do you think so? Where did these ideas come from?

What are the conditions necessary for life to survive? Plants? Animals? Humans?

Which of these conditions are necessary for all life?

Which ones for plants? Which ones for animals? Which ones for humans?

What are the greatest threats to all forms of life? To plants? To animals? To humans?

What are some of the "strategies" living things use to survive? Which unique to plants? Which unique to animals? Which unique to humans?

What kinds of human survival strategies are (1) similar to those of animals and plants; (2) different from animals and plants?

What does man's language permit him to develop as survival strategies that animals cannot develop?

How might man's survival activities be different from what they are if he did not have language?

What other "languages" does man have besides those consisting of words?

What functions do these "languages" serve? Why and how do they originate? Can you invent a new one? How might you start?

What would happen, what difference would it make, what would man *not* be able to do if he had no number (mathematical) languages?

How many symbol systems does man have? How come? So what?

What are some good symbols? Some bad?

What good symbols could we use that we do not have?

What bad symbols do we have that we'd be better off without?

What's worth knowing? How do you decide? What are some ways to go about getting to know what's worth knowing?

It is necessary for us to say at once that these questions are not intended to represent a catechism for the new education. These are samples and illustrations of the kinds of questions we think worth answering. Our set of questions is best regarded as a metaphor of our sense of relevance. If you took the trouble to list your own questions, it is quite possible that you prefer many of them to ours. Good enough. The new education is a process and will not suffer from the applied imaginations of all who wish to be a part of it. But in evaluating your own questions, as well as ours, bear in mind that there are certain *standards* that must be used. These standards may also be stated in the form of questions.

Will your questions increase the learner's *will* as well as his capacity to learn?

Will they help to give him a sense of joy in learning?

Will they help to provide the learner with confidence in his ability to learn?

In order to get answers, will the learner be required to make inquiries? (Ask further questions, clarify terms, make observations, classify data, etc.?)

Does each question allow for alternative answers (which implies alternative modes of inquiry)?

Will the process of answering the questions tend to stress the uniqueness of the learner?

Would the questions produce different answers if asked at different stages of the learner's development?

Will the answers help the learner to sense and understand the universals in the human condition and so enhance his ability to draw closer to other people?

If the answers to these questions about your list of questions are all "yes," then you are to be congratulated for insisting upon extremely high standards in education. If that seems an unusual compliment, it is only because we have all become accustomed to a conception and a hierarchy of standards that, in our opinion, is simultaneously upside-down and irrelevant. We usually think of a curriculum as having high standards if "it" covers ground, requires much and difficult reading, demands many papers, and if the students for whom it is intended do not easily get "good" grades. Advocates of "high standards" characteristically and unwittingly invoke other revealing metaphors. One of the most frequently used of these is "basic fundamentals." The most strident advocates of "high, and ever yet higher, standards" insist that these be "applied" particularly to "basic fundamentals." Indulging our propensity to inquire into the language of education, we find that the essential portion of the word "fundamental" is the word "fundament." It strikes us as poetically appropriate that "fundament" also means the buttocks, and specifically the anus. We will resist the temptation to explore the unconscious motives of "fundamentalists." But we cannot resist saying that *their* "high standards" represent the *lowest possible standards imaginable* in any conception of a new education. In fact, so low, that the up-down metaphor is not very useful in describing it.

What one needs to ask of a standard is not, "Is it high or low?," but, "Is it appropriate to your goals?" If your goals are to make people more alike, to prepare them to be docile functionaries in some bureaucracy, and to prevent them from being vigorous, self-directed learners, then the standards of most schools are neither high nor low. They are simply apt. If the goals are those of a new education, one needs standards based on the actual activities of competent, confident learners when they are genuinely engaged in learning. One must be centrally concerned with the hearts and minds of learners—in contrast to those merely concerned with the "fundament." No competent learner ever says to himself, "In trying to solve this problem, I will read two books (not less than thirty pages from each). Then, I will make a report of not less than twenty pages, with a minimum of fifteen footnotes. . . ." The only place one finds such "standards" is in a school syllabus. *They do not exist in natural, human learning situations, since they have nothing to do with the conditions of learning—with what the learner needs to be and to do in order to learn about learning, or indeed about anything.* Any talk about high standards from teachers or school administrators is nonsense unless they are talking about *standards of learning* (as distinct from standards for grading, which is what is usually meant). What this means is that there is a need for a new—and "higher"—conception of "fundamentals." Everyone, at present, is in favor of having students learn the fundamentals. For most people, "the three R's," or some variation of them, represent what is fundamental to a learner. However, if one *observes* a learner and asks himself, "What is it that this organism needs without which he cannot thrive?," it is impossible to come up with the answer, "The three R's." The "new fundamentals" derive from the emotional and intellectual realities of the human condition, and so "new" answers (well beyond the three-R's type) are possible in response to the question. In *In Defense of Youth,* Earl Kelley lists five such possible answers:

1. The need for other people.
2. The need for good communication with other people.
3. The need for a loving relationship with other people.
4. The need for a workable concept of self.
5. The need for freedom.

One does not need to accept all of these in order to accept Kelley's *perspective* on what is fundamental. Obviously, we would want to add to his list "the need to know how to learn," as well as some others which are suggested by our list of "standards" questions. The point is that any curriculum that does not provide for needs as viewed from this perspective—"What does the organism require in order to thrive?"—is not, by our definition, concerned with "fundamentals."

. . . It is certainly true that "historians" ask different kinds of questions from "biologists," and "biologists" from "linguists." But such men are finding, increasingly, that what they thought was someone else's "field" turns out to be theirs as well. We now have mathematical biologists, biophysicists, anthropological psychologists, and so on. They are discovering that the traditional ways of structuring ("seeing") what is out there are both inadequate and arbitrary. As Alan Watts says, the universe is wiggly. Our attempts to take snapshots of the wiggles must not lead us to think that the photograph *is* the wiggle. Besides, someone else may take another photograph and capture an altogether different aspect of the wiggle. And that is exactly what happens when children are allowed to function as question askers and answer seekers. They frequently perceive relationships that others have not noticed before. Let them start with a question in "biology"—for example, "What are the conditions for sustaining life in plants?"—and they will soon start asking questions about "physics," "anthropology," "chemistry," etc. This will happen over and over again unless the teacher insists that they "stick to the subject." But who is to say what the subject is or is not? Besides, the students don't particularly care what *name* is given to the subject. They are engaged in finding things out, in "structuring" what they think they see. And when you are doing that, you have to look where you think there's something to be found. If there's no "official category" for what you're looking at—or for—well, that may even be an advantage. Leeuwenhoek invented the microscope, and the Wright brothers invented the airplane, not knowing that they "couldn't." At least, authorities of their times "knew" and could "prove" that they couldn't. The career of Charles Kettering, one of America's most prolific inventors, is a chronicle of his "doing things that couldn't be done" mostly because he was not suffering from "hardening of the categories." Alfred North Whitehead made the point that taxonomy is the death of science. And, we would add, the memorization of taxonomies is the death of education.

And so in our questions curriculum, "subjects" frequently lose their "clear" and arbitrarily limiting dimensions. We will need to start talking more about the "structure of the learner and his learning" and less about the "structure of the subject."

There are two other characteristics of our questions curriculum that should be mentioned here. The first has to do with that recently discovered (invented?) category of human beings called "disadvantaged children." Generally speaking, these children are reputed to be "slower" learners than other types of children. If this is true, it simply means that they do not function so well as others *in the existing school environment.* It cannot be inferred from this that "disadvantaged children" would be a "problem" if the ecology of the school environment were entirely different. If we may paraphrase Heisenberg: "We have to remember that what we observe children doing in schools is not what they *are,* but children exposed to us by our methods of teaching." We are, in fact, confident that the disadvantaged child is much more likely to find the conditions which will satisfy him as a learner in the kind of environment we have been trying to describe than in any other. In a way, this statement is a tautology since the environment we are describing is devoted to making the learner "satisfied." It is based on what we know about learners, and not on what we know about what we want them to learn.

Finally, note that the questions we listed are capable of being pursued by children at every grade level. Their answers, as well as their *way* of answering, will vary depending on their experience: where they've been, what they believe, and what their purposes are. This curriculum does not call for a single set of answers. Therefore, it does not require a single set of *answerers.* There is an old joke about a school administrator who was dismayed when he and his staff had taken great trouble to prepare a new and wonderful curriculum, only to discover that the "wrong" kids showed up. That's the trouble with the old education and its functionaries: it virtually insures an endless and increasing number of "wrong" students.

It remains for us to say here that the function of the "What's-Worth-Knowing Questions Curriculum" is to put two ideas into clear focus. The first is that the art and science of asking questions is the source of all knowledge. *Any curriculum of a new education would, therefore, have to be centered around question asking.* This means that, even if a school system is unwilling to scrap its present curriculum structure (i.e., "history," "English," "science," etc.), it will need to transform its instructional program so that the major content of what is to be learned by the students results from inquiries structured by the questions that are raised. This implies that students will spend a great deal of their time finding answers to their questions. Question asking and answer finding go hand in hand. And answer finding requires that students go to books, to laboratories, to newspapers, to TV sets, to the streets, to wherever they must go to find their answers.

The second idea is that question asking, if it is not to be a sterile and ritualized activity, has to deal with problems that are perceived as useful and realistic by the learners. We do not mean to suggest that a child's perception of what is relevant is an unalterable given; indeed, the thrust of the "curriculum" we have been describing is to extend the child's perception of what is relevant and what is not.

Simply said: There is no learning without a learner. And there is no meaning without a meaning maker. In order to survive in a world of rapid change there is nothing more worth knowing, for any of us, than the continuing process of how to make viable meanings.

REVIEW QUESTIONS

1. Fill up the authors' blank page with questions, if you have not done so already.

2. Look again at the questions listed by Postman and Weingartner. Would most of all of these form the basis of a truly relevant curriculum? Why or why not?

twenty-nine

Is Drill Necessary?
The Mythology of Incidental Learning

DAVID P. AUSUBEL

One of the strongest legacies of the progressive education movement and of Thorndikian educational psychology that still remains on the pedagogic scene is a confused and contradictory attitude toward structured practice or drill. On the one hand, we minimize the value of drill in educational theory, regarding it as rote, mechanical, passive, and old-fashioned, as psychologically unnecessary for the learning process, and as actually harmful for active, meaningful learning. On the other hand, as teachers, parents, coaches, and students, we still implicitly accept the old maxim that "practice makes perfect." The upshot of this conflict in our beliefs is that we still place considerable reliance on drill in actual classroom practice, but do so half-heartedly, apologetically, and in ways that detract from its effectiveness.

The progressivists, of course, did not entirely deny the value of practice. As a matter of fact, both their espousal of activity programs and their battle cry of "learning by doing" carried an implied endorsement of the importance of appropriate practice. But by appropriate practice they meant direct (concrete, manipulative), nondeliberate, and autonomous learning encounters with different examples of the same concept or principle in uncontrived, "real-life" situations. Their mistake lay in assuming that all structured practice (drill) is necessarily rote; that unstructured, unguided, and unintentional (incidental) practice is maximally effective for school learning tasks; and that "doing" necessarily leads to learning simply because it involves direct experience and occurs repeatedly in natural, problem-solving situations.

Actually, for practice to result in meaningful mastery of material, the only really essential conditions are that the learning task be potentially meaningful; that the learner exhibit a meaningful learning set and possess the necessary back-

Source: From *The Bulletin of the National Association of Secondary School Principals*, 1963, 47 (287): 44–50. Reprinted by permission of the author and the publisher.

ground concepts; and that the number, distribution, sequence, and organization of practice trials conform to empirically established principles of efficient learning and retention. Not only is the uncontrived or unstructured quality of practice an unessential condition of meaningful, effective learning, but it also often leads to no meaningful mastery whatsoever.

The fetish of naturalism and incidental learning embodied in the activity program movement emphasizes these five points:

1. Unstructured and uncontrived learning situations;
2. Direct kinds of experience, in a concrete, manipulative sense;
3. Unintentional or nondeliberate learning effort;
4. Learning by autonomous, unguided discovery; and
5. Exposure to diversified rather than repetitive experience.

LEARNING IN NATURAL SETTINGS

How desirable is it that factual information and intellectual skills be acquired in the real-life, functional contexts in which they are customarily encountered, rather than through the medium of artificially contrived drills and exercises? It is true, of course, (providing that all other factors are equal) that learning is enhanced when the conditions of practice closely resemble the conditions under which the skill or knowledge in question will eventually be used. Wholly natural settings, however, rarely provide the practice conditions that are either necessary or optimal for efficient learning. Generally it is only during the latter stages of learning, *after* component aspects of the learning task have already been identified and mastered in structured practice sessions that naturalistic "dress rehearsals" become feasible.

This is so, in the first place, because unstructured learning settings typically fail to furnish examples that come along frequently, repetitively, and close enough together to make possible the learning of concepts and principles. Under these circumstances there is also inadequate opportunity for differential practice of particularly difficult components. Contrary to Thorndike's generally accepted but unwarranted inferences from his well-known experiments on the "law of frequency," the weight of the research evidence clearly indicates that repetition *per se* is typically necessary both for the learning and retention of associations and meanings. Second, unstructured practice does not receive the benefit of either skilled pedagogic selection, presentation, and organization of material or of careful sequencing, pacing, and gradation of difficulty.

DIRECT EXPERIENCE

Many features of the activity program were based on the quite defensible premise that the elementary school child perceives the world in relatively specific and concrete terms, and requires considerable first-hand experience with diverse concrete instances of a given set of relationships before he can acquire genuinely meaningful concepts and propositions. Thus, an attempt was made to teach factual information and intellectual skills through the medium of direct, manipulative experience in natural settings rather than through verbal exposition and drill.

In older pupils, however, once a sufficient number of basic concepts is consolidated, new concepts are primarily abstracted from verbal rather than concrete experience, and new propositions are comprehended without any direct reference to or manipulation of concrete props. Hence, in secondary school, it may be desirable to reverse both the sequence and relative balance between abstract concepts and supportive data. There is good reason for believing that much of the time presently spent in cookbook laboratory exercises in the sciences could be more advantageously employed in formulating precise definitions, making explicit verbal distinctions btween concepts, generalizing from hypothetical situations, etc.

John Dewey correctly recognized that meaningful understanding of abstract concepts and principles in childhood must be built on a foundation of direct, empirical experience, and for this reason advocated the use of activity methods in the elementary school. But he also appreciated that once a firmly grounded first-story of abstract understandings was established, it was possible to organize secondary and higher education along more abstract and verbal lines. Unfortunately, however, some of Dewey's disciples blindly generalized over the entire life span the conditions that limit abstract verbal learning during childhood.

NONDELIBERATE LEARNING

Although individuals can acquire much miscellaneous information and some skills incidentally, deliberate effort is required for the efficient learning of most types of academic material. Countless experiments show that deliberate learning in response to explicit instructions is both more effective and more precise than is unintentional or implicitly instructed learning.

Especially for long-term meaningful learning of subject matter, doing *per se* is not sufficient in the absence of the felt needs and interests that give rise to deliberate intent. Inability to see any need for a subject is the reason students mention most frequently for losing interest in high-school studies. Doing, without being interested in what one is doing, results in relatively little permanent learning. Only that material can be meaningfully incorporated into an individual's structure of knowledge, on a long-term basis, which is relevant to areas of concern in his psychological field.

Learners who have little need to know and understand, quite naturally expend little learning effort and manifest an insufficiently meaningful learning set. They fail to develop precise meanings, to reconcile new material with existing concepts, and to reformulate new propositions in their own words. Finally, they do not devote enough time and effort to practice and review. Material is therefore never sufficiently consolidated to form an adequate foundation for sequential learning. Hence it is unrealistic to expect that school subjects can be effectively learned and retained until pupils develop a felt need to acquire knowledge as an *end in itself*—since much school learning can never be rationalized as necessary for meeting the demands of daily living.

AUTONOMOUS, UNGUIDED DISCOVERY

The unquestioning faith which advocates of incidental learning have in autonomous, unguided discovery is justified neither by logic nor by research evidence. In the first place, laboratory and problem-solving exercises are not inherently or necessarily meaningful. They may lead to little or no meaningful learning if a student's learning set is simply to memorize rotely type problems or techniques of manipulating reagents and symbols, and if he has inadequate background in or appreciation of the substantive and methodological principles underlying specific problem-solving or laboratory procedures.

Second, what is typically called "the discovery method" is really a contrived type of discovery that is a far cry from the truly autonomous discovery activities of the research scholar or scientist. Pure discovery techniques could lead only to utter chaos and waste of time in the classroom, inasmuch as immature students generally lack sufficient subject-matter sophistication both to formulate workable problems and to devise appropriate and relevant research methods. Before students can "discover" concepts reasonably efficiently, problems must be structured for them in such a way as to make ultimate discovery almost inevitable.

Third, many short-term studies have demonstrated that guided discovery is more efficacious for learning, retention, and transfer than is either completely autonomous discovery or the provision of complete guidance. Guidance under these circumstances sensitizes the learner to the salient aspects of the problem, orients him to the goal, and promotes economy of learning by preventing misdirected effort. However these findings do not necessarily indicate that guided discovery is more effective for teaching subject-matter content than is simple didactic exposition. For one thing, the solving by a naive subject of a few novel problems in a laboratory setting is hardly comparable to the learning of a large body of sequentially organized material by a learner with varying degrees of subject-matter sophistication. For another, even contrived discovery techniques are incomparably more time-consuming than expository teaching.

Lastly, guidance in the form of prompting has been shown to be very helpful during the early stages of learning. At this point in the learning process, the learner has not mastered sufficient material to receive much practice benefit from unaided recitation. Furthermore, the provision of prompts can prevent the learning of errors and thus obviate the necessity for costly unlearning.

DIVERSIFIED EXPERIENCE

Proponents of activity programs tend to favor task heterogeneity in practice. That is, they seek, in part, to escape the opprobrium associated with drill by stressing diversity both in the types of learning tasks and in the examples of each type that are presented to the learner. This approach undoubtedly has merit in that, other factors being equal, the defining attributes of a new concept are learned most readily when the concept is encountered in many different contexts. Such experience obviously enhances the generality of abstract knowledge and transferable skills. It also minimizes the possibility of boredom and of a rote and rigid approach to learning.

However, if diversity of learning task content is provided at the expense of attaining mastery of the particular component tasks which comprise it, its over-all effect on learning is detrimental. Positive transfer from one learning task to another reqires that particular examples of a given type of tasks as well as particular types of tasks first be considered (i.e., mastered, overlearned) before new task content is introduced.

Many cases of disability in such academic skills as arithmetic, reading, spelling, and grammar can undoubtedly be attributed to overemphasis on the importance of diversified experience in unstructured learning situations. Failure to provide sufficient repetitive practice (drill) in antecedent learning tasks does not allow for the adequate mastery of these tasks that is essential if sequentially related tasks are to be successfully handled in the acquisition of concepts, generalizations, and intellectual skills.

REVIEW QUESTIONS

1. How do the factors of student age and academic subject matter differences affect Ausubel's thesis?

2. Ausubel often talks about meaningfulness. Doesn't any meaningful learning have to include aspects of both reception and discovery?

thirty

The Multi-Unit Elementary School and Individually Guided Education

HERBERT J. KLAUSMEIER

For the first time in the history of American education, a practical alternative to age-graded, self-contained elementary schooling has emerged. It is the multi-unit school, established to implement an individually guided education (IGE) system at the elementary school level. The system is a product of the Wisconsin Research and Development Center for Cognitive Learning, where the staff, with cooperating educational agencies, began to develop IGE in 1965.

Essentially, the system is a planned transformation of the free, tax-supported education for all children which has been evolving since colonial times. The IGE system has been refined to produce higher education achievements by means of these components:

1. An organizational pattern for instruction, building-level administration, and central-office-level administration. Together, these elements constitute what we call the multi-unit school—elementary (MUS-E).

2. A model of instructional programming for the individual, with related guidance procedures. This model is designed to provide for differences among students in their rates and styles of learning, levels of motivation, and other characteristics. Based on educational objectives of the school, it is used to develop curriculum materials and implement IGE (see Figure 1).

3. A model for developing measurement tools and evaluation procedures. The model includes pre-assessment of children's readiness, assessment of progress and final achievement with criterion-referenced tests, feedback to the teacher and the child, and evaluation of the IGE design and its components.

4. Curriculum materials, related statements of instructional objectives,

Source: From *Phi Delta Kappan*, November 1971, pp. 181–84. Reprinted by permission of the author and the publisher.

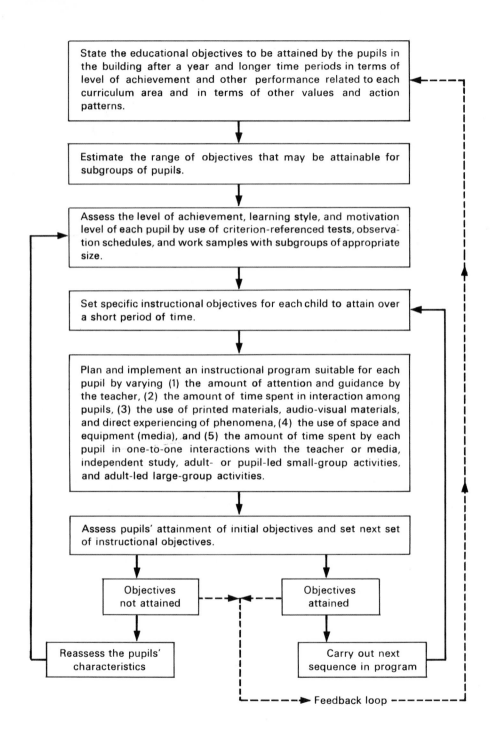

Figure 1. Instructional programming model in individually guided education.

and criterion-referenced tests and observation schedules. The R and D Center in 1971–72 is developing materials and instructional procedures in reading, pre-reading, mathematics, environmental education, and motivation.

5. A program for home-school communication that reinforces the school efforts by generating the interest and encouragement of parents and other adults whose attitudes influence pupil motivation and learning.

6. Facilitative environments in school buildings, school system central offices, state education agencies, and teacher education institutions that encourage IGE practices.

7. Continuing research and development by center and school personnel to generate knowledge and to produce improved curriculum materials and instructional procedures.

ORGANIZATIONAL ARRANGEMENTS

The MUS-E was designed to produce an environment in which the other six components of IGE can be introduced and refined. It may be thought of as an invention of organizational arrangements that have emerged since 1965 from a synthesis of theory and practice. It incorporates instructional programming for individual students, horizontal and vertical organization for instruction, role differentiation, shared decision making by groups, open communication, and administrative and instructional accountability. These terms themselves imply fundamental changes in the nature of elementary education to satisfy many unmet needs of children, teachers, and other school personnel.

Figure 2 shows the prototype organization of a MUS-E of 600 students. Variations from the prototype are made in terms of such factors as the number of students enrolled in the building, the availability of noncertified personnel, and the size of the school district. The organizational hierarchy consists of interrelated groups at three distinct levels of operation: the instructional and research (I and R) unit at the classroom level, the instructional improvement committee (IIC) at the building level, and the systemwide policy committee (SPC) or a similar administrative arrangement at the system level. Each element, though being responsible and taking the initiative for certain decisions, must secure information from and be responsive to one or both of the other elements. Personnel who serve at each of two levels, as noted in Figure 2, provide the communication link.

The I and R Unit. The nongraded I and R unit replaces the age-graded, self-contained classroom. Research is included in the title to reflect the fact that the staff must continuously do practical research in order to devise and evaluate an instructional program appropriate for each child. The main function of each unit is to plan, carry out, and evaluate, as a hierarchical team, instructional programs for the children of the unit. Each unit engages in a continuous

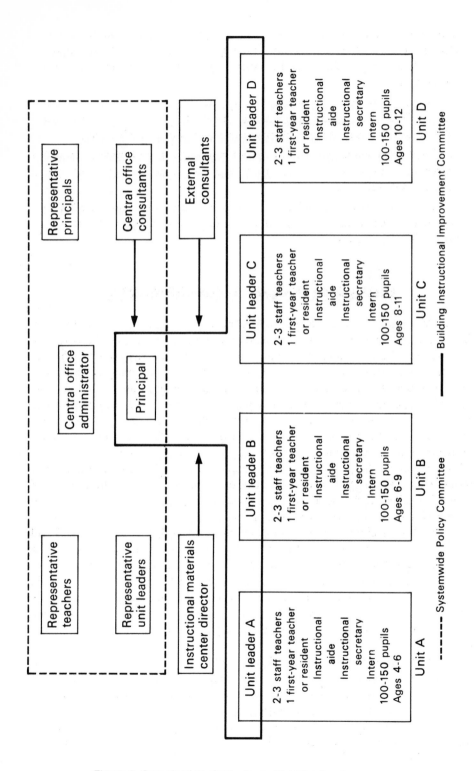

Figure 2. Organization chart of a multi-unit school.

on-the-job staff development program. Some units plan and conduct research and development cooperatively with other agencies, and some are involved in pre-service education.

The IIC. At the second level of organization is the IIC, a new organization that became possible in 1967 when the first six elementary school buildings in Wisconsin were organized completely into units. The four main functions for which the IIC takes primary initiative are stating the educational objectives and outlining the educational program for the entire school building; interpreting and implementing systemwide and statewide policies that affect this educational program; coordinating the activities of the various I and R units to achieve continuity in all curriculum areas; and arranging for the use of facilities, time, material, etc., that the units do not manage independently. The IIC thus deals primarily with planning and coordinating functions related to instruction.

The SPC. Substantial changes are required to move from the self-contained classroom organization to that of the I and R unit and the IIC. The SPC, at the third organizational level, was created to facilitate this transition. As shown in Figure 2, the prototypic committee, chaired by the superintendent or his designee, includes consultants and other central office staff and representative principals, unit leaders, and teachers. Four decision-making and facilitative responsibilities for which the SPC takes primary initiative are identifying the functions to be performed in each MUS-E of the district, recruiting personnel for each MUS-E and arranging for their in-service education, providing instructional materials, and disseminating relevant information within the district and community. A central office arrangement other than an SPC may be responsible for these functions; considerable flexibility is required, since local school districts differ greatly in size.

Unlike some differentiated staffing programs that call for a proliferation of new roles and titles for personnel, the MUS-E establishes only one new position, that of unit leader or lead teacher. Other roles that changed somewhat are those of the building principal, staff teacher, first-year teacher or resident, teacher intern, instructional aide, and instructional secretary. The MUS-E pattern does not preclude the identification and establishment of other new, specialized roles such as those connected with instructional media or neighborhood relations.

EVALUATION RESULTS, 1966–70

In-service and on-campus staff development programs for IGE/MUS-E personnel are still being refined, as are the other components. Despite this limitation, a massive amount of evaluative information has been collected and reported each year since 1966.

FEASIBILITY

To be a feasible alternative to age-graded elementary education, the MUS-E concept must be sound, practical in terms of costs and benefits, and adaptable to conditions in a variety of local school settings. One indication of such feasibility is that the number of MUS-Es has greatly increased each successive school year, starting with 1967–68 and extending through 1970–71. In 1967–68 there were nine MUS-Es in Wisconsin; in 1970–71 there were 99. In 1968–69 the first three MUS-Es were started in Ohio and Pennsylvania; in 1970–71 there were 164 MUS-Es in seven states. This year there will be about 400 new schools.

The National Evaluation Committee of the R and D Center has expressed its strong support of the multi-unit school, noting that these features are "provided by this unusual combination of educational and organizational concepts":

1. Attention is focused on the individual learner as a person with unique characteristics, concerns, and motivations.

2. Teachers and other educational personnel are helped to employ systematic problem-solving processes in the identification and satisfaction of the educational needs of individuals—both in the student body and on the staff.

3. The basic organizational units are small enough to allow every person to be known and treated as an individual and large enough to permit role differentiation and complementarity of contributions.

4. Provisions for staff training and continuing development are an essential part of the approach.

5. There is a good reconciliation of the values of autonomy and accountability, small-group responsibility, and intergroup coordination.

ATTAINING ORGANIZATIONAL OBJECTIVES

Performance objectives are stated for each component of IGE, including the organizational arrangements. As part of a longitudinal study, data were collected in a MUS-E and a control school in each of three Wisconsin school districts. The results show comparative attainment of organizational objectives in well-established control schools and in first-year MUS-Es. It was found that:

1. MUS-E teachers spent more time planning for instruction and diagnosing individual children's needs.

2. MUS-E teachers specialized more, some working primarily with individual pupils, others working mainly with small groups or class-sized groups, a few working with larger groups.

3. The unit leaders in the MUS-E schools facilitated interaction among the staff and served as the connecting links between the teachers and the principal.

4. In the three self-contained schools, decisions affecting each classroom were the prerogative mainly of each individual classroom teacher and of the principal, who provided advice or set the limits within which the teacher had discretion, whereas MUS-E decisions about instruction were generally made by the unit leaders and teachers in a group setting.

5. Finally, job satisfaction and teacher morale were higher among the staff teachers of MUS-Es.

STUDENT ATTAINMENT OF OBJECTIVES

The Wisconsin Design for Reading Skill Development (WDRSD), under development by the R and D Center, includes a word attack program with subskills presumed to lead to independence in attacking phonetically regular words. Pre- and post-testing of MUS-E children who had worked with WDRSD for a year yielded encouraging results. Successive administration of criterion-referenced tests of reading subskills and of the Doren Diagnostic Reading Test showed that the children, many of whom qualified for Title I support, acquired the subskills at a rate indicating that most of them would be able to read phonetically regular words with independence by the end of the fourth year (third grade) of school or earlier. A higher percent of children mastered more of the subskills after working with WDRSD. The mean scores of the children on the Doren Diagnostic Reading Test were higher after one year of experience with WDRSD.

These results indicate the desirable combined effects of the MUS-E organization and a concerted attack on curriculum improvement along the individual instructional programming model.

COST AND IMPLEMENTATION

As of 1970–71, most MUS-Es in Wisconsin were on the same pupil-teacher ratio as the other schools of the same school district and the average cost of instruction per pupil was about the same. Although unit leaders were receiving salaries that ranged from four to ten per cent above staff teachers (the center recommends twenty per cent), and aides and full-time teaching interns were being employed, the pattern in Wisconsin was to operate a MUS-E at little or no increase in cost.

On the basis of its experimental programs, however, the R and D Center can recommend these guidelines to school districts and state educational agencies that plan to implement individually guided education in multi-unit schools:

—Allocate at least $10 per pupil during the first two years for any combination of one instructional aide per 150 children, additional instructional materials, and higher pay for the lead teacher. Title I or Title III funds should be available for this.

—Remodel the "eggcrate" type school building so that there will be one well-supplied instructional resource center to accommodate at least ninety intermediate-age children and another center to accommodate at least sixty primary-age children. Local funds should be available for the remodeling and Title I, II, or III funds for the materials and equipment.

—Participate in a staff development program starting with a one-day workshop for chief school officers, a three-day workshop for the prospective building principal and unit leaders of the various MUS-Es, a one-week workshop for the entire staff of each MUS-E prior to the opening of the MUS-E in the fall (this may be spread out during a semester), four half-day workshops for the entire staff of each building during the first year, and a one-week institute for central office consultants in the curriculum area which will be given most attention during the first year. Here the local school should pay time and travel expenses of its personnel and the state educational agency should provide its staff to lead all the workshops except the one which occurs prior to the opening of the school. This is staffed by the local school district. In Wisconsin the Department of Public Instruction and local school districts have been implementing this program since 1968.

This year the R and D Center has undertaken to stimulate the nationwide establishment of multi-unit schools. With support from the Bureau of Education Professions Development and the National Center for Educational Communication, it has begun a four-phase sequence of awareness, installation, maintenance, and refinement.

After a printed brochure was sent to a nationwide sample of elementary school principals, a series of one-day information conferences was held for the interested principals at five sites throughout the country.

Then the R and D Center contracted with the state educational agencies of Colorado, Connecticut, Illinois, Indiana, Minnesota, New Jersey, Ohio, South Carolina, and Wisconsin, each agency agreeing to help start twenty to fifty new multi-unit schools. By this procedure a projected 250–300 new multi-unit schools were slated to open.

The R and D Center staff conducted a one-week institute to assist the cooperating agencies and teacher education institutions to carry out their staff development programs for multi-unit school personnel. Installation teams were organized by the center to help the nine state coordinators conduct staff development workshops of the kind described earlier for Wisconsin. In addition to the preceding, the R and D Center is also working with a few school districts of other states.

I/D/E/A/, an affiliate of the Kettering Foundation, began a parallel implementation effort in 1970 and is helping over 100 schools change to the multi-unit pattern in the first semester of this year.

Multi-unit schools have started and survived reasonably well with a minimum amount of assistance. However, in spite of participating in the staff development programs described earlier, not all staff members of multi-unit schools acquire all of the primary concepts and skills. To remedy this situation, several universities last summer offered one-week institutes for principals, unit leaders, and staff teachers in reading who had prior experience in multi-unit schools.

The refinement-institutionalization phase includes residential programs for lead teachers, building principals, and reading staff teachers at the University of Wisconsin, Wisconsin State University—Eau Claire, and Marquette, with related practical experiences in multi-unit schools. The plan is for these teacher education institutions to develop and describe model programs that may subsequently be adapted by other teacher education institutions helping to prepare the educated personnel needed.

In summary, the IGE system offers a practical alternative to age-graded, self-contained elementary schooling. At the same time, a second-level career position in elementary teaching, namely that of the lead teacher, is being established. Principals of multi-unit schools are assuming much initiative for instructional improvement. A staff development program has been organized to promote a self-renewing capability in the staff of each building, so that less assistance from external sources is needed. Instructional programming for the individual student is producing higher student achievement and other desired objectives. Teachers and other school personnel are experiencing higher job satisfaction and are looking with greater enthusiasm toward a lifetime career in elementary education.

REVIEW QUESTIONS

1.   MUS-IGE is an elementary program. What might happen to secondary programs in a school district that goes MUS-IGE?

2.   How compatible is MUS-IGE with Glasser's ideas (article 31)?

thirty-one

"Classroom Meetings" from
Schools Without Failure

WILLIAM GLASSER

In this . . . article I shall give a detailed description of . . . classroom meetings, meetings in which the teacher leads a whole class in a nonjudgmental discussion about what is important and relevant to them. There are three types of classroom meetings: the *social-problem-solving* meeting, concerned with the students' social behavior in school; the *open-ended* meeting, concerned with intellectually important subjects; and the *educational-diagnostic* meeting, concerned with how well the students understand the concepts of the curriculum. These meetings should be a part of the regular school curriculum. In my experience, they are warmly supported by teachers who agree with the educational philosophy of this article.

SOCIAL-PROBLEM-SOLVING MEETINGS

The many social problems of school itself, some of which lead to discipline of the students, are best attacked through the use of each class as a problem-solving group with each teacher as the group leader. Teachers in their faculty meetings will do essentially the same thing that each class does in the classroom meeting: *attempt to solve the individual and group educational problems of the class and the school.* When children enter kindergarten, they should discover that each class is a working, problem-solving unit and that each student has both individual and group responsibilities. Responsibility for learning and for behaving so that learning is fostered is shared among the entire class. By discussing group and individual problems, the students and teacher can usually solve their problems within the classroom. If children learn to participate in a problem-solving group when they enter school and continue to do so with a variety of teachers throughout the six years of elementary school, they learn that the world is not a mysterious and sometimes hostile and frightening place where they have little control over what happens to them. They learn rather that, although the world may be difficult and that it may at times appear hostile and mysterious, they can use their brains individually and as a group *to solve the problems of living in their school world.* Over and above the value of learning to solve their problems through class meetings, students also gain in scholastic achievement. This gain is described by Dr. Edmund Gordon, Professor of Psychology and Education at Yeshiva University, in his detailed review of the Coleman Report [1960]:*

> In addition to the *school* characteristics which were shown to be related to pupil achievement, Coleman found a *pupil* characteristic which appears to have a stronger relationship to achievement than all the school factors combined. *The extent to which a pupil feels he has control over his own destiny is strongly related to achievement.* This feeling of potency is less prevalent among Negro students, but where it is present *"their achievement is higher than that of white pupils who lack that conviction"* (emphasis added).

School children have many social problems, some of which may call for discipline, some not. Under ordinary conditions, because there is no systematic effort to teach them social problem solving, school children find that problems that arise in getting along with each other in school are difficult to solve. Given little help, children tend to evade problems, to lie their way out of situations, to depend upon others to solve their problems, or just to give up. None of these courses of action is good preparation for life. The social-problem-meeting can help children learn better ways.

Working with an eighth-grade class of an elementary school, I recently held a social-problem-solving meeting that can serve as an example. Although I do conduct social-problem-solving meetings, they are more difficult for an outsider such as I to hold than for the classroom teacher; students usually feel that someone who doesn't know them well has no business probing into their problems. In terms of Reality Therapy, before one can successfully change behavior, one must be involved. It is difficult for a class and a total stranger to become sufficiently involved with each other to make the meeting successful enough to serve as a demonstration. In contrast, the other kinds of meetings, open-ended and educational-diagnostic, are very easily led by someone the class does not know because these meetings do not present nearly the threat of the social-problem-solving meeting.

A serious problem with the eighth-grade class in the spring of 1967 was truancy. On some of the warmer days, as many as six or eight out of a class of thirty-five would be absent from school. The same children were not absent every day, although some missed school more than others and some always came to class. I was asked to focus on truancy during the meeting. Although no one expected that one meeting would solve such a serious problem, my goals were to get the class to think both about their own motives in cutting school and about some ideas that might help the whole class toward better attendance. The meeting started with my asking the class if everyone were present that day. There was considerable discussion, timid at first but shortly more frank, revealing that about eight students were absent and that those present knew that most of the absentees were not ill that beautiful spring day. When I asked whether some of the students present also frequently skipped class, many admitted that they did. The students sensed that I was nonpunitive and that I was inquiring because I was concerned about their not coming to school.

We discussed at some length what they gained by cutting school and what problems it was causing. We also discussed the school's methods of handling truancy and their parents' reactions to these methods. The students maintained that school was dull and that they saw little sense in what they were learning. They gave the impression that their lives were so full of interesting things to do outside of school that they didn't feel they could attend regularly. They rationalized their position by saying that this year was the last time they would have a chance to cut because next year, when they entered high school, they would have to toe the mark. Questioning their rationale, I said that I doubted that they would attend high school any more regularly. I added that I did not believe that the things they complained about in the eighth grade would be much different in high school. As we continued to talk, most of the students admitted that the reference to high school was rationalization; from their experience with sisters, brothers, and friends, truancy was just as common in high school as in the eighth grade.

At this point we had accomplished what in Reality Therapy would be called exposing the problem for open, honest discussion. My warm and personal attitude helped the class to open up. Talking only about the present problem, we got it out on the table for everyone to examine. Getting this far probably would have been sufficient for the first of a series of meetings aimed at a real solution to the truancy problem. Because the meeting was a demonstration, however, I wanted to go further, and I started pressing the class for a solution. I asked them if they would talk to the absent students to try to get them to stop cutting and to attend school regularly. I knew that unless the students made a value judgment that going to school is worthwhile, they would not attend regularly. It was clear that the statements they made about the value of school were merely lip service. Unless their attitude toward school could be changed, I or anyone else faced an impossible task in trying to get them to come regularly. . . . The relevance of the school work must be taught, and where too much irrelevant material is in the curriculum, it must be replaced by material more meaningful to the children.

I attempted, nevertheless, to get from the students present a commitment to attend school the next day. Their wariness toward me and toward anyone who suggested change was apparent in their refusal to make this commitment. The refusal was also a perfect example of the difficulty we have in getting students to participate in irrelevant education. They gave every reason they could think of why they might not be in school the following day. To end the meeting and to help the students understand the importance of making a commitment, I introduced a technique that sometimes works even when a value judgment has not been made: I asked the class to sign a statement promising to come to school the next day. About one-third of the twenty-nine students were willing to sign the statement. The others were very leery about it, giving all kinds of excuses such as that they might be sick or they might be run over on the way to school. They did not want to do anything as binding as signing a piece of paper saying they would attend school. To the nonsigners I said, "If you won't sign a paper stating you will come to school tomorrow, will you sign a paper stating that you won't sign a paper? In other words, will you put your lack of commitment in writing?" After much heated discussion, about one-third more said they would sign the second paper. Although signing this paper did not commit them to come to school, it might still help them to understand the commitment process. One-third of the students remained who refused to sign either paper. I asked them if they would sign a paper stating that they would sign nothing, but they were too smart for me and still refused to sign. I said, "Under these circumstances, will you allow your names to be listed on a piece of paper as students who refuse to commit themselves in any way regarding truancy?" I would put their names on the paper; they would not have participated in the commitment process in any way. To this they agreed, and we obtained the three lists at the end of the meeting.

One meeting with little involvement, no real value judgment, and weak commitment produced, as I expected, no improvement in attendance. There was, however, much discussion not only among these students but also in the entire seventh and eighth grades concerning the class meeting. I had set the stage for a series of meetings to attack the problem of truancy. If this first meeting could have been followed with regular meetings several times a week, the students could have discussed the importance of attending school and been led toward value judgments, plans, and commitments. In class meetings teachers must listen to the reasons given for poor school attendance. When reasons with some validity are given, we must consider changing our teaching to make the school worthwhile to the students where it is not. In addition, we must teach the value of school.

Social-problem-solving meetings such as the one just described are valuable to students and to the school. I suggest that all students in elementary schools wishing to implement the meetings meet regularly during the week for a reasonable time to discuss the problems of the whole class and of individual students within the class. Both students and teachers should consider the class meetings as important as reading, history, or math. The social-problem-solving meetings should be conducted according to the following guidelines that have proved effective both in the public schools and at the Ventura School for Girls, where I first used this technique. Although better guidelines may be developed as the meetings progress, the following should give a good start.

All problems relative to the class as a group and to any individual in the class are eligible for discussion. A problem can be brought up by an individual student about himself or someone else, or by the teacher as she sees a problem occur. In a school with a unified faculty involved with each other and with all school problems, subjects for discussion can be introduced in any class by any student or any teacher, either directly by a note to the group or indirectly by an administrator with knowledge of the problem. In addition to school problems, problems that a child has at home are also eligible for discussion if the child or his parents wish to bring them up.

To adults reading this book, my suggestions may seem strong. As adults, we usually either struggle with our own problems in privacy with little help from friends and family, or we sweep our problems under the rug and try to act as if they don't exist. Thus it may sound as if I am demanding too much of small children. Having held meetings for several years, I have found that children do not think that discussing their problems openly is as difficult as we adults do. The children are concerned because they are learning to deny the existence of their problems. They would much rather try to solve them, and school can give them a chance to do so. Before they come to school, children discover that it is reasonable to try to solve problems. We must be careful, therefore, not to do as we do too often at present: extend our adult anxieties and inadequacies to children and thereby teach them to be evasive as they grow to maturity. In my experience, a class of six-year-olds will freely discuss difficult problems, even one such as stealing (ordinarily a very emotional subject for older children and adults), and try to work out a solution. A solution may require more than just trying directly to get the child to stop stealing, although this of course is the ultimate goal. A solution may include the discovery in the meeting that a child steals because he is lonely, hungry, or jealous, and the working out of ways to correct these causes. Teachers learn during meetings that small children can stand only small temptations. Teachers who do not adequately safeguard lunch money, for instance, are subjecting children to temptation that they may not have the strength to withstand. If children can find a reasonable solution at age six and can concomitantly learn the value of honesty, it is likely that they will never steal again. If someone does steal in a school where discussions are a continuing part of the school program, the stage is set for solving the problem later. The students know that the purpose of all discussion is to solve problems, not to find fault or to punish. Experience in solving social problems in a non-fault-finding, nonpunitive atmosphere gives children confidence in themselves as thinking, worthwhile people.

We have stated that the social-problem-solving meeting is open for any subject that might be important to any child, teacher, or parent related to that class or school. *The discussion itself should always be directed toward solving the problem; the solution should never include punishment or fault finding.* The children and the teacher are oriented from the first meetings in the first grade that the purpose of the meeting is not to find whose fault a problem is or to punish people who have problems and are doing wrong; rather the purpose is to help those who have problems to find better ways to behave. The orientation of the meetings is always positive, always toward a solution. When meetings are conducted in this way, the children learn to think in terms of a solution—the only constructive way to handle any problem—instead of the typical adult way soon learned by school children—fault finding and punishment.

It is important . . . in class meetings for the teacher, but not the class, to be nonjudgmental. The class makes judgments and from these judgments works toward positive solutions. The teacher may reflect the class attitude, but she should give opinions sparingly and make sure the class understands that her opinions are not law. Each child learns that he is important to every other child, that what he says is heard by everyone, and that his ideas count. When children experience the satisfaction of thinking and listening to others, they are not afraid to have ideas, to enter into a discussion, and to solve their own problems and the problems of their class by using their brains.

Once an atmosphere of thinking, discussing, and problem solving is established, and it can be established rather quickly, situations that ordinarily would cause serious disturbances in class and that might cause a child to be sent to the principal's office can be handled effectively within the class. Children learn that their peers care about them. They learn to solve the problems of their world. Then it is easy to accept the teacher who says, "We have a problem; these two boys are fighting. At our next class-meeting time we are going to discuss the fight, but now would you boys be willing to stop fighting and wait for the meeting?" This simple request has proved to be effective. The boys stop fighting and wait because they know there is a reasonable alternative to their misbehavior—a solution from the meeting. When they believe that even if they stop fighting they will be punished or expelled from the class, they often continue to fight because the alternatives offered aren't any better than fighting. Classroom meetings can serve to siphon off steam in the class by providing a better alternative. Often the problem is dissipated before the meeting, and the children agree it would be a waste of time to discuss it. The availability of the meeting allowed the children to use the normal ways children have to solve problems.

Meetings should always be conducted with the teacher and all the students seated in a tight circle. This seating arrangement is necessary if good meetings are to occur.

Classroom meetings should be short (ten to thirty minutes) for children in the lower grades and should increase in length (thirty to forty-five minutes) as the children grow older. The duration of a meeting is less important than its regular occurrence and the pertinence of the problems discussed.

Children who must be excluded from the class because their behavior is not tolerable to the teacher or the students will have a better avenue for reentry into the class through the use of class meetings than they have at the present time. Under ordinary school procedures, a principal dealing with a problem child who has been sent out of class finds himself meting out some sort of punishment. He usually swats the child, lectures him, calls in his parents, excludes him from school, or assigns detention time after school or during school. These procedures tend to work less well each time they are applied to any individual child. When the classroom meetings are a part of the school program, the principal has an important added wedge in working with the child. He asks the child sent to his office what he was doing and helps the child understand that *what he did* caused him to be excluded. The principal conducts the discussion with a goal of sending the child back to a class meeting in which the same points will be pursued. The principal counsels the individual child in a way that emphasizes what the child did. In an atmosphere of problem solving instead of punishment, the child usually will discuss his part in whatever happened. The principal then asks the child whether he has any plan to go back to class. Working with the principal, the child is asked to make a plan to get back into his class. If he does not want to go back, he is told that the class will nevertheless try *to help him* the best they can without him. He is asked to work out a plan in some detail, which usually does not take much time. For example, the boy may have been fighting with another boy so much that the teacher finally sends him out of the class. In a school where he is not threatened with punishment, he will admit to the principal that he was fighting and, after a while, admit the part he played in the fight. The principal then asks him to think about how he could stop fighting. Usually he says he would do better away from the other boy. This discussion sometimes takes a little time; maybe the other boy has to come in so that they can agree together on a plan to stay apart for a while. Both boys take the plan back to the class and the class may agree to help by not egging them on. In future meetings the class can work on the underlying problem, which may be jealousy, and the teacher can work on the boys' failure in school, which usually is a part of behavior problems.

The principal works with the child in a nonpunitive, problem-solving way. Using the class meeting, the child has a built-in entrée to return to class. As the procedure becomes operational and the children see that it works, they are happy to use it because it makes their lives easier. The whole disciplinary structure of a school should revolve around the class meeting. Individual discussions with children concerning their problems should be directed toward individual, and then group-accepted, solutions.

As time goes on, fewer and fewer disciplinary problems arise, so that class meetings about behavior disturbances become infrequent. Children learn through problem solving in the group how to avoid trouble in school and sometimes at home, although it is the rare home where children are encouraged to solve problems by discussion and planning. If they learn to do so in school, however, the knowledge will prove of value all their lives. Although social-problem-solving meetings often deal with behavior problems, many other subjects can be discussed: friendship, loneliness, vocational choice, and part-time work are examples.

. . . It can be shown that classroom meetings, initiated to solve disciplinary problems, can be used effectively to gain and to sustain educational relevance. To understand how this is done, we need to describe two additional kinds of classroom meetings, neither of which directly relates to behavior problems.

OPEN-ENDED MEETINGS

Probably the cornerstone of relevant education is the open-ended classroom meeting. It is the type of meeting that should be used most often, even where behavior problems are common. When behavior and other social problems are minimal, social-problem-solving meetings will be used infrequently. The open-ended meeting, however, is always applicable; the more it is used, the more relevance can be added to education. In the open-ended meetings the children are asked to discuss any thought-provoking question related to their lives, questions that may also be related to the curriculum of the classroom. The difference between an open-ended meeting and ordinary class discussion is that in the former the teacher is specifically not looking for factual answers. She is trying to stimulate children to think and to relate what they know to the subject being discussed.

For example, in meetings with second-grade classes, I have introduced the subject of blindness. In answer to my question, "What is interesting to you?" one class said they would like to talk about eyes and ears. Although the five senses are not a specific part of the second-grade curriculum, from this introduction an open-ended meeting was held that provided a way for the students to gain greater motivation to read and to take more interest in the world around them. In the central-city school where I first held this discussion, the second graders usually did not show much intellectual curiosity. What they didn't know about the world didn't seem to interest them; at least, it appeared that way. Yet, when an unknown was introduced in a way that made sense to them, they became excited and showed as much curiosity and as much good thinking as children who come from more stimulating environments. I asked the children what they did with their eyes, and they all said, "See"—a good, simple, factual answer. In a discussion with small children, it is best to let them begin at a simple level where they have confidence in their ability to give a good answer.

Going to a more complex question, I asked, "What do you see with your eyes?" They mentioned many things, including "the words in our books." Again they were succeeding in answering a question; they enjoyed it and were becoming involved. At the same time, I was able to direct them toward books and reading in a way new to them. Children are just as stimulated by new approaches as we are, and they are just as bored with sameness as we are. One value of the open-ended meeting is to give new ways a chance to be used. I then asked them about people who can't see, and they said, "They are blind." A short discussion on what blindness means followed. Despite an apparent understanding of blindness, most of the children believed that blind people could really see if they tried hard. We worked at length before everyone understood that blind people could not see at all. The children closed their eyes tight and kept them closed. Slowly, through this participation and discussion, it began to dawn on the class that if you are blind, you cannot see.

By now the children were all involved, but so far they hadn't done much thinking or problem solving. It was important at this time to introduce a problem related to their school work that they could solve if they worked hard. I asked,

"Could a blind man read?" The reaction I received from the second graders was laughter, puzzlement, and incredulity. To think that a blind man could read, after they had just confirmed that a blind man couldn't see, was absurd. I asked them to keep thinking to see if someone could figure out some way that a blind man could read. Of course, I implied that there was an answer. I wouldn't ask second graders a question that had no answer, although in this case the answer was not easy. I insisted that they keep trying to solve the problem; their first reaction when the going got tough was to give up. In school the children had rarely used their brains to solve problems. Accustomed to simple, memorized answers, they gave up when these answers didn't work.

The discussion so far had piqued the children's interest and awakened their faith in their brains. They kept trying, but they were in trouble. The leader must judge when to give them help; he must not do so too soon. I decided to help them at this time by asking if someone would like to take part in a little experiment. We had an immediate raising of hands; they were all eager to help, partly because they sensed that the experiment was a way to keep the discussion going. I selected a boy who, I detected, was not one of the better students or better behaved members of the class. He was waving his hand, eager to volunteer. Calling him over, I told him to shut his eyes very tight and hold out his hands. I asked him if he were peeking; he said, "No." Putting a quarter in one of his hands and a dollar bill in the other, I asked him if he could tell me what I had put in his hands. The entire class was now glued to the experiment. Some of the brighter students immediately began to glimpse the idea. The boy was able to tell me what was in his hands. I asked him how he knew. Although he wasn't very verbal, he finally said that anyone could tell a dollar bill from a quarter. When I took the dollar bill away and put a nickel in his hand instead, he was still able to distinguish the nickel from the quarter. I then asked him to sit down. Again I asked the class, "How could a blind man read?" Thoughtful students now began to express the idea that if a blind man could feel the letters on a page, he might be able to read. I said, "How could he feel the letters on a page? The page is smooth." And I ran my fingers over a page. One bright child said, "If you took a pin and poked it through the page, you could feel where the pin poked through." From that, most of the class—and they were very excited—was able to get the idea: you could feel the letters on a page!

I still wasn't satisfied, however. I said, "Suppose you *could* feel the letters on the page; I still don't think you could tell one from another." They said they could. I said they couldn't. Suggesting another experiment to try to prove whether or not they could recognize a word by tracing the letters without seeing them, I asked whether they could write their names on the blackboard with their eyes closed. During this discussion I had noticed a little girl sitting next to me trying desperately to follow what was going on. Now she raised her hand vigorously. Every other hand in the class was also raised, but I called on her. Very slowly, somewhat inaccurately although still recognizably, she wrote her name on the board. While she was at the board the teacher, with some alarm, passed me a note saying that the girl was mentally retarded and cautioning me to be prepared for her to fail. Retarded or not, she was fully involved in the experiment. She had managed to scratch something on the board that both she and the class could recognize as her name. Because they were bursting to try, I let some of the other students go to the board to write their names. Most of them did it very well. Through this effort they were able to see the possibility that if they could write their names with their eyes closed, a blind person might feel words in a book. And the smile and eagerness of the "mentally retarded" girl proved that she was as much involved in the discussion as anyone else in the class. Later the class asked what books for the blind look like. They wanted the teacher to bring some in, which she promised to do.

In the discussion after the meeting with the class teacher and several other teachers who were observing, I noted that the meeting could be used as a way to stimulate children to learn to read. The teacher could point out, or have the children point out to her, the advantage of having eyes; reading, difficult as it is for many of these children, is much easier for them than for the blind. The children were deeply involved in the meeting, enjoyed it, and used their brains to think about and solve what seemed at first an insoluble problem. They experienced success as a group and success as individuals. Meetings such as this one in the second grade can be used as motivators in many subjects of the curriculum. In addition, a class that is involved, thinking, and successful will have few disciplinary problems.

In the lower grades, the open-ended meeting may have to be related to the curriculum by the teacher; in the higher grades the class can make the connection. Having a thoughtful, relevant discussion on any subject, however, is more valuable than forcing a connection to the curriculum. In fact, if enough thoughtful discussions are held on subjects not in the curriculum, we should study the curriculum to see where it should be changed.

EDUCATIONAL-DIAGNOSTIC MEETINGS

A third type of class meeting, the educational-diagnostic, is always directly related to what the class is studying. These meetings can be used by the teacher to get a quick evaluation of whether or not teaching procedures in the class are effective. For example, in an eighth-grade class in another school district, I was disappointed to find that the students, despite studying the Constitution for a semester and a half, seemed to know very little about it. Although they had studied its clauses and many of them could recite certain sections from memory, the students had a nonthinking view of the Constitution. Even before the meeting, based on my experience with other classes, I doubted that the students understood the meaning of the Constitution to them as individuals or to the community. To test my opinion, I was given a bright class for the meeting. The questions I asked might be considered unfair by some educators, but we did get a discussion going, and the audience learned that the students had some extremely unconstitutional ideas about the Constitution. Because I had previously com-

plained to the superintendent of schools that the students seemed to have difficulty in handling concepts, I had invited him to join me that day; the meeting
I was proposing might pinpoint the difficulty.

My first question to the class was, "What is the Constitution?" The class
seemed to be taken aback by this question, but I repeated it several times, adding,
"I just want to know if anyone here can tell me what the Constitution is."
Looking for some sort of definition or description to start the meeting, I saw
immediately that the students were in trouble. It had never occurred to them
that anyone would ever ask them what the Constitution is; assuming that everyone, including themselves, knew, they hadn't bothered to think the idea through.
The best answer I could get was that the Constitution is something written in
books to be studied. I asked them, "Does the Constitution exist? Is there a
Constitution on a piece of paper nailed to a wall somewhere that people can
see?" The class doubted that it existed in the form I had described. Finally I had
to tell them that the Constitution did exist and that people could go to Washington, D.C., and see it. (I usually don't give answers, but I was filled with frustration at this point.)

From this small factual start, I went on to see whether the students understood
the ideas of the Constitution. Following their assurance that they had studied
it in detail, I asked them to name some of its important features. When they
mentioned the Bill of Rights, I said, "Do these rights pertain to you?" It took
some time before they understood what I meant and more time to agree that
in fact the Bill of Rights did pertain to the students sitting there. Some of them
thought the Bill of Rights did pertain to them, while others thought that it was
just for adults.

The key question, however, which brought on a discussion confirming my
doubts about the students' understanding of the Constitution, was, "What happens if you do something on your own property that is against the law? For
example, may you drive a car on your own property even though you don't
have a driver's license and are too young to drive? May you drink a can of beer
in your home if your father offers it to you, even though you are legally too
young to drink?" I don't know the correct legal answers in these two examples,
but that was not the point of the questioning. There was heated discussion.
Many of the students suggested that you have no right to break the law on your
own property and that you should be punished if you do. I then raised the
question of how you could be caught. "Do the police have the right to spy on
your home and then come in and arrest you if they think you are drinking beer
with your father?" The class said they thought the police did have the right
and should do so. I then asked them how the police would know whether a child
was having a glass of beer with his father. Although they said that this would
be hard to discover, they did have some constructive ideas. One of them was
that the police should have a television set focused in everybody's home and, as
soon as the police saw anyone doing anything wrong, they should come and get
him! Many in the class agreed with this idea and no one disagreed strongly. At
that point we dropped the discussion.

It was clear that the discussion was provoking individual thinking about the

Constitution. My affirmation of the existence of the Constitution in Washington was the only time during the discussion that I corrected the class or offered them a right answer. In the educational-diagnostic meeting, the leader should not incorporate value judgments into the discussion. The students should feel free to voice their opinions and conclusions in any way they see fit. The teacher learns points of weakness that require additional teaching by her and additional study and discussion by the class. In memory education, where discussions probing understanding rarely occur, students may get answers right on tests and still have no working, living knowledge of something as important as the Constitution and how it pertains to them. Unless the teacher takes a completely nonjudgmental attitude, however, she will never discover these distortions. Cueing to her judgments, students see no reason to discuss their own ideas and opinions.

It is hard for a teacher to conduct an educational-diagnostic meeting because of her involvement with the subject and consequent possible inability to recognize the points that the class may have missed. To see more clearly what a class knows, therefore, teachers might sometimes exchange classes to run these meetings. The blind spots could thereby be eliminated. The educational-diagnostic class meeting should never be used to grade or evaluate the students. It should be used only to find out what students know and what they don't know.

I have described the three kinds of class meetings that I have used during the past several years in my work in the schools. These meetings have proved interesting to students and teachers alike. The technique is not easy for teachers to learn because the required class leadership is not ordinarily taught. Few teachers will conduct meetings without some guidelines, some chance to observe a group, and much approval and encouragement from their superiors. Successful meetings occur only through practice, through evaluating what happens, and through following the guidelines given earlier in the chapter. Unless the meetings are nonjudgmental and open-ended, they will fail.

Enough teachers are conducting class meetings now so that some feedback is available. Many teachers are starting to use some of the techniques involved, especially the circle and the open-ended question, in regular teaching. Going from the open-ended question to some factual material, they encourage students to use judgment and to give opinions. As I write this book, however, most teachers in the schools in which I work have not incorporated classroom meetings into an integral part of their class program. Unfortunately, it is usually isolated from regular teaching. Most teachers conduct meetings one, two, or three times weekly; some report successful, continuing meetings every day. Although some teachers, despite their principal's permission to conduct meetings, still feel guilty about "wasting time" or "playing games," the success of the meetings is slowly winning them over. Students have responded very favorably in every class. Reminding the teacher when a meeting is due, they become involved quickly in the meetings. Because the students don't know that it is hard to have a good meeting, they soon have good meetings, especially in the lower grades. They are eager to participate in discussions relevant to their lives.

When one asks students whether their school work is in any way related to their lives outside of school, most of them reply incredulously, "Of course not." By the tenth grade, students are firmly convinced that school is a totally different experience from life. One learns to live and, completely separately, one learns at school. The three types of class meetings described herein can provide a stable bridge across the gap between school and life.

Although I suggest that class meetings be held at a regular time at least once a day in elementary school and perhaps two or three times a week in high school, there is no reason that teachers cannot use the technique for arithmetic, history, science, and other subjects. Whole-class teaching reduces isolation and failure. We use large, cooperative groups in most of the extracurricular subjects. The team, for example, is the basis of competitive athletics. But in the class curriculum, where it could be equally effective, it is little used. By treating the whole class as a unit, the same spirit of cooperation can arise as arises on athletic teams. By eliminating failure, by accepting each child's thinking (at least during the time of the meeting), and by utilizing his mistakes as a basis for future teaching, we have a way of approaching the child that supports him. The present system of accentuating his mistakes tears the child down and makes him unable or unwilling to think.

Another advantage of class meetings is the confidence that a child gains when he states his opinion before a group. In life there are many opportunities to speak for oneself. The more we teach children to speak clearly and thoughtfully, the better we prepare them for life. When a child can speak satisfactorily for himself, he gains a confidence that is hard to shake.

REVIEW QUESTIONS

1.   Try "reverse brainstorming" with Glasser's idea of classroom meetings. In other words, think of as many things as you can that might go wrong with them. Then see if these difficulties can be remedied. (If they can, the meetings should seem more credible to you.)

2.   Glasser has often said that many of his schools-without-failure strategies are being used in different ways and forms by successful teachers who never have heard of his writings. Can you think of some other ways that the main goals of classroom meetings might be realized without doing exactly as Glasser says?

thirty-two

The Primary School Revolution in Britain

JOSEPH FEATHERSTONE

I. Schools for Children: What's Happening in British Classrooms

My wife and I have just spent a month in England visiting classes in primary schools, talking to children and teachers. Friends told us about good things happening in British classrooms, but we were scarcely prepared for what we found; in recent decades there has been a profound and sweeping revolution in English primary education, involving new ways of thinking about how young children learn, classroom organization, the curriculum and the role of the teacher. We saw schools in some good local educational authorities: Bristol, Nottingham, Leicestershire, Oxfordshire, and a few serving immigrant areas in cities like London.

In the first part of what follows, I'm going to be as specific as I can about how classes work in a good English school, how the room is laid out, what sort of things are in it, how the teacher and the children spend the day and, in some detail, how a child learns to read, as an example of the kind of learning that goes on. I know that teachers in this country, particularly good ones, are rightly suspicious of most talk on education, because so little of what they hear ever relates to actual classroom practice. I hope I can be specific enough. The relevance of these classrooms to us is another, more difficult question which I'll leave for later. I don't have any easy answers.

Primary schools divide into "infant" and "junior" schools. Much of this report will focus on the infant schools, which take children from the age of five to seven, and in some authorities eight. (As in Israel, children begin compulsory schooling at the early age of five in England.) It is in the infant schools that people learn to read and write and to work with numbers. Junior schools take

Source: Abridgment of three chapters from *Schools Where Children Learn* by Joseph Featherstone. Copyright © 1971 by Joseph Featherstone. Reprinted by permission of Liveright Publishing, New York.

children from seven or eight to 11, when they go on to secondary school. Infant and junior schools sometimes occupy the same building, and some authorities— Oxfordshire, for example—have a policy of putting them together in one unit, like an American elementary school.

It is important to understand that what goes on in the good infant schools is much the same. The approach is similar, though the quality of teaching and children's work varies greatly.

Westfield Infant School is a one-story structure, like any of a thousand American buildings, on a working-class housing estate in Leicestershire. If you arrive early, you find a number of children already inside, reading, writing, painting, playing music, tending to pets. Teachers sift in slowly, and begin working with students. Apart from a religious assembly (required by English law) it's hard to say just when school actually begins, because there is very little organized activity for a whole class to do together. The puzzled visitor sees some small group work in mathematics ("maths") or reading, but mostly children are on their own, moving about and talking quite freely. The teacher sometimes sits at her desk, and the children flock to her for consultations, but more often she moves about the room, advising on projects, listening to children read, asking questions, giving words, talking, sometimes prodding.

The hallways, which are about the size of those in our schools, are filled with busy children, displays of paintings and graphs, a play grocery store where children use play money and learn to count, easels, tables for collections of shells and plants, workbenches on which to pound and hammer nails and boards, big wooden boxes full of building blocks.

Classrooms open out onto the playground, which is also much in use. A contingent of children is kneeling on the grass, clocking the speed of a tortoise, which they want to graph against the speeds of other pets and people. Nearby are five-year-olds, finishing an intricate, tall tower of blocks, triumphantly counting as they add the last one, "23, 24." A solitary boy is mixing powders for paint; on a large piece of paper attached to an easel, with very big strokes, he makes an ominous, stylized building that seems largely to consist of black shutters framing deep red windows. "It's the hospital where my brother is," he explains, and pulls the visitor over to the class-library corner, where a picture book discusses hospitals. He can't read it yet (he's five), but says he is trying. And he is; he can make out a number of words, some pretty hard, on different pages, and it is clear that he has been *studying* the book, because he wants badly to know about hospitals. At another end of the hall there is a quieter library nook for the whole school. Here two small boys are reading aloud; the better reader is, with indifferent grace, correcting the grateful slower boy as he stumbles over words.

The rooms are fairly noisy—more noisy than many American teachers or principals would allow—because children can talk freely. Sometimes the teacher has to ask for quiet. With as many as forty in some classes, rooms are crowded and accidents happen. Paint spills, a tub overflows, there are recriminations. Usually the children mop up and work resumes.

The visitor is dazed by the amount and variety and fluency of the free writing produced: stories, free-verse poems, with intricate images, precise accounts of experiments in "maths" and, finally, looking over a tiny little girl's shoulder, he finds: "Today we had visitors from America. . . ."

After a time, you overcome your confusion at the sheer variety of it all, and you begin making more definite observations. The physical layout of the classrooms is markedly different from ours. American teachers are coming to appreciate the importance of a flexible room, but even in good elementary schools this usually means having movable, rather than fixed, desks. In these classes there are no individual desks, and no assigned places. Around the room (which is about the size of one of ours) there are different tables for different kinds of activities: art, water and sand play, number work. (The number tables have all kinds of number lines—strips of paper with numbers marked on them in sequence on which children learn to count and reason mathematically—beads, buttons and odd things to count; weights and balances; dry and liquid measures; and a rich variety of apparatus for learning basic mathematical concepts, some of it homemade, some ready-made. The best of the commercial materials were familiar: Cuisenaire rods, the Dienes multi-base material, Stern rods and attribute or logical blocks. This sort of thing is stressed much more than formal arithmetic.)

WENDY AND PUPPETS

Every class has a library alcove, which is separated off by a room divider that also serves as a display shelf for books. Some library corners have a patch of carpet and an old easy chair. Every room has a "Wendy House," a play corner with dolls and furniture for playing house. Often there is a dress-up corner, too, with different kinds of cast-off adult clothes. The small children love the Wendy houses and dress-up corners, but you see older ones using them as well. Some classes have puppet theatres for putting on improvised plays with homemade puppets—although many make do with the legs of one table turned upside down on top of another for a makeshift stage. Often, small children perform dance dramas involving a lot of motion and a minimum of words.

Gradually it becomes clear how the day proceeds in one of these rooms. In many infant and some junior schools the choice of the day's routine is left completely up to the teacher, and the teacher, in turn, leaves options open to the children. Classes for young children, the visitor learns, are reaching a point in many schools where there is no real difference between one subject in the curriculum and another, or even between work and play. A school day run on these lines is called, variously, the "free day," the "integrated curriculum," or the "integrated day." The term scarcely matters.

In a school that operates with a free day, the teacher usually starts in the morning by listing the different activities available. A lot of rich material is needed, according to the teachers, but the best stuff is often homemade; and, in any case, it isn't necessary to have thirty or forty sets of everything, because most activities are for a limited number of people. "Six children can play in the

Wendy House," says a sign in one classroom. The ground rules are that they must clean up when they finish and they mustn't bother others.

A child might spend the day on his first choice, or he might not. Many teachers confess they get nervous if everybody doesn't do some reading and writing every day; others are committed in principle to letting children choose freely. In practice, a lot of teachers give work when they think it's needed. In this, as in any other way of doing things, teachers tailor their styles to their own temperament and the kind of children they have. But the extent to which children really have a choice and really work purposefully is astonishing.

How they learn reading offers a clear example of the kind of individual learning and teaching going on in these classrooms, even in quite large ones. (The mathematics work shows this even better, but I'll talk of math in another context.) Reading is not particularly emphasized, and my purpose in singling it out is purely illustrative, though the contrast between English classes and most American ones, where reading is a formidable matter, is vivid and depressing.

At first it is hard to say just how they do learn reading, since there are no separate subjects. A part of the answer slowly becomes clear, and it surprises American visitors used to thinking of the teacher as the generating force of education: children learn from each other. They hang around the library corners long before they can read, handling the books, looking at pictures, trying to find words they do know, listening and watching as the teacher hears other children's reading. It is common to see nonreaders studying people as they read, and then imitating them, monkey doing what monkey sees. Nobody makes fun of their grave parodies, and for good reasons.

A very small number of schools in two or three authorities have adopted what they call "family," or "vertical," grouping, which further promotes the idea of children teaching children. In these schools, each class is a cross-section of the whole school's population, all ages mixed together. This seems particularly successful in the early school years, when newcomers are easily absorbed, and older children help teach the young ones to clean up and take first steps in reading. Family grouping needs smaller classes, teachers say, because it requires close supervision to make sure small children don't get overshadowed and big ones are still challenged. Teachers using it swear by the flexibility it provides.

BOOKS IN PROFUSION

Teachers use a range of reading schemes, sight reading, phonics, and so forth, whatever seems to work with a child. (Only about five percent of English schools use the Initial Teaching Alphabet, an improved alphabet, not a method of reading, that has proved successful with poor readers and adults both in England and in this country; heads of good schools we visited thought that ITA was unnecessary with a truly flexible reading program, but that in a rigid scheme, it gave the slow reader another chance, and thus a break.) Increasingly in the good infant schools, there are no textbooks and no class readers. There are just books, in profusion. Instead of spending their scanty book money on 40 sets of every-thing, wise schools have purchased different set of reading series, as well as a great many single books, at all levels of difficulty. Teachers arrange their classroom libraries so they can direct students of different abilities to appropriate books, but in most classes a child can tackle anything he wants. As a check, cautious teachers ask them to go on their own through a graded reading series—which one doesn't matter.

However a child picks up reading, it will involve learning to write at the same time, and some write before they can read; there is an attempt to break down the mental barrier between the spoken, the written and the printed word. When a child starts school, he gets a large, unlined notebook; this is his book for free writing, and he can put what he wants in it. On his own, he can draw a picture in it with crayon or pencil, discuss the picture with the teacher, and dictate a caption to her, which she then writes down for him: "This is my Dad." He copies the caption, writing just underneath. In this way he learns to memorize the look and sound of his dictated words and phrases, until he reaches a point where, with help, he can write sentences. Often his notebook serves as his own first reading book.

He also gets a smaller notebook, his private dictionary, in which he enters words as he learns them. "I got a new word," a five-year old brags to the visitor. Children are always running to the teacher for words, as they find they have more and more to write. Good teachers don't give in without a struggle; the children have to guess the first letter and sound the word out before they get it. Thus they pick up phonetic skills informally, although some teachers do use sight cards at the outset with their children. Gradually as a child amasses a reading and writing vocabulary, he reaches a fluent stage and you see six-year-olds writing stories, free-verse poems, accounts of things done in class, for an audience that includes other children as well as the teacher.

As a rule, teachers don't pay much attention to accuracy or neatness until a child is well on in his writing. They introduce grammar and spelling after a time, but not as separate subjects or ends in themselves: they are simply ways to say what you want better and more efficiently. Under these methods, where the children choose the content of their writing, there seems in fact to be more atten-tion paid to content than externals, such as punctuation, spelling and grammar. In the good schools, these are presented as what they are, living ways to get a meaning across, to be understood. Even some unimaginative teachers, who quib-ble with children about other work, can respect the content of the free writing books and take it seriously. This emphasis on self-chosen content has produced a flowering of young children's literature in schools working with many kinds of teachers and children. There is growing recognition that different people flourish on different kinds of writing; storytellers and poets are not necessarily the same as those who can do elegant and graceful writing about mathematics.

I've focused on reading, although of course children spend their time doing other things, and the teachers in the schools we saw would be annoyed at the manner in which I've singled out one academic subject. The very best often argued that art was the key. Miss Nash, the head of Sea Mills School in Bristol, said firmly that if the art is good, all else follows. All else does follow, richly, at Sea Mills, where the infants sat us down and performed a concert of skillful poetry and songs they made up on musical instruments.

But my purpose was to show not reading, but the changed role of the classroom teacher. Formal classroom teaching—the instructor standing up front, talking to the group, or even the first-grade room divided up into reading groups which the teacher listens to separately as she tries desperately to keep order—has disappeared from many infant and a number of junior schools. It has disappeared because it is inflexible, because it imposes a single pattern of learning on a whole group of children—thus forcing the schools to "track," or to group classes by ability—because it ignores the extent to which children teach each other, and because in many workaday schools other methods are working better. Ordinary teachers, trained formally, take to the new role when they can see with their own eyes that the result is not chaos.

INFORMALITY IS HARD WORK

These methods mean more work for the teacher, not less. In informal conditions, it is essential for the teacher to keep detailed and accurate accounts of what a child is learning, even though at any given moment she might not know what he's up to. Children help by keeping their own records: in some schools, they have private shelves where they store writing books, accounts of experiments and work in "maths," lists of the books they've read, and dates when they checked in with the teacher to read aloud. If American parents could ever see some of the detailed histories kept of each child's separate path, including his art work, they would feel, quite rightly, that a report card is a swindle.

When the class seldom meets as a unit, when children work independently, discipline is less of a problem. It does not disappear as a problem, but it becomes less paramount. The purposeful self-discipline of these children is, we were told, just as surprising to middle-aged Englishmen as it is to Americans. It is a recent development, and by no means the product of luck: much hard work and thought go into the arrangement of these classrooms and their rich materials. When they work at it, teachers find they can make time during the day for children who need it. "I can give all my attention to a child for five minutes, and that's worth more to him than being part of a sea of faces all day," said a teacher in an East London school overlooking the docks. Other teachers say they can watch children as they work and ask them questions; there is a better chance of finding out what children really understand.

What we saw is no statistical sample. The practices of the good schools we visited in different kinds of communities are not universal; but there are reasons for thinking that they are no longer strikingly exceptional. The schools we saw are, for the most part, staffed by ordinary teachers; they are not isolated experiments, run by cranks and geniuses. A government advisory body—the Plowden

Committee—published a massive, and to American eyes, a radical report early this year, in which it indicated that about a third of England's 23,000 primary schools have been deeply influenced by the new ideas and methods, that another third are stirring under their impact, and that the remaining third are still teaching along the formal lines of British schools in the thirties, and of American schools now.

The change is most widespread and impressive in the infant schools, and becomes more scattered on the junior level. Junior schools in some authorities are playing stunning variations on the free themes developed by the infant schools; but, in general, change in the junior schools is slower, more diffident and faces more problems.

Many formal schools—English and American—are probably doing a more effective job, in conventional terms, than many of these schools. It doesn't do to dogmatize. For example, by and large, in terms of measurable achievement on conventional tests, children in traditional, formal classes in England do slightly better than children from the freer classes. (The survey is submitted by the Plowden Report.) The difference is greatest in mechanical arithmetic, and least in reading. These are facts, but there are reasons for discounting them, apart from evidence that the differences disappear in later school years. Formal schools teach children to take conventional tests; that is their function, and it would be surprising if all their efforts didn't produce some results. In view of the lack of test training in the freer schools, the students' results seem to me surprisingly high. It is perfectly clear that the mathematics taught in the informal schools—mathematical relationships in which process of thought counts for more than arithmetical skill—and the English—free writing, rather than grammar and so on—put their students at a disadvantage on achievement tests, whose authors would probably be the first to admit this. England and America badly need new kinds of tests. My own very strong impression is that in areas easy to define and probably not hard to test—ability to write, for example, or understanding of the math they were doing—the children in the good schools I saw, including slum schools, were far ahead of students in good schools in this country.

The external motions teachers go through in the schools matter less than what the teachers are and what they think. An organizational change—the free day, for example, or simply rearranging classroom space—is unlikely to make much difference unless teachers really believe that in a rich environment young children can learn a great deal by themselves and that most often their own choices reflect their needs. But when you see schools where teachers do believe in them, it is easy to share the Plowden Report's enthusiasm for informal, individual learning in the early years of school. (The Plowden Committee is in a sense the official voice of the primary school revolution.) The infant schools are a historical accident—nobody years ago gave much thought to why children should begin school at five—but British teachers are now realizing their advantages. With kindergarten and the first few years fused together, children have an extended time in which to learn to read and write and work with numbers. This is especially effective if the pattern of learning is largely individual; if the teacher is important, but she doesn't stand in the way or try to take over the whole job. Many of the difficulties that plague formal first-grade classes disappear; children aren't kept back from learning, nor are they branded as problems if they take their time.

II. How Children Learn

The British Plowden Committee's Report, *Children and Their Primary Schools,* is a complicated document in social history, and to draw one single lesson from it would be a mistake. Some of its surveys are of universal interest—one careful study suggests convincingly what common sense has often suggested before, that parents' attitudes play a larger role in a child's life than anything the school does on its own. Some chapters will be items of political controversy: its excellent proposals for nursery schools and aid to poor areas, for example, have little immediate hope of being pushed through by a government whose finances are in a melancholy state. Some are of purely British interest—the earnest and troubled discussion of compulsory religious education, for example. But an American may be pardoned if one aspect of the report fixes his attention: the extent to which this official document is a radical, if stately hymn of praise to the kinds of classrooms described in my first report. . . .

There is no doubt that this remarkable report celebrates a fairly recent change. Until not long ago, heads of many schools could point to a chart in their office showing what each class was doing every minute of the week, and the number of minutes spent on each subject. (English, for example, being divided up into periods for spelling, grammar, exercises, composition, recitation, reading, handwriting, and so on.) It is obvious, as the Plowden Report tartly points out, "that this arrangement was not suited to what was known of the nature of children, of the classification of subject matter, or the art of teaching."

How did change come about? In the first place, a tradition has developed over the last 50 years that gives heads of British schools great freedom in matters of scheduling and curriculum, and teachers a fair amount of say about what goes on in the classroom. By itself this freedom did not produce much change, it is important to note. But it was clearly a prerequisite for reform. Also British schools traditionally feel relatively free from public and parental opinion. This independence seems less of a necessary prerequisite to reform, since parents seem to approve the new methods when they understand them; but it is true that people in British schools are not running as scared as their American counterparts, who often see public opinion not as a source of policy, but as a shadowy, yet massive veto.

Another element in the reform was a different emphasis in the work of the HMI's (government inspectors). As long as the inspectors acted as educational policemen, making the schools toe the mark, their effect over the years was to dampen innovation. But as their role took on more and more of an advisory character, they became important agents for disseminating new ideas. There is a clear moral here: external rules enforced from without not only have little positive effect on schools, but they tend to make their practices rigidify through fear. Where government and local inspectors have ceased inspecting and taken up advising, the results have been excellent. Some of the lively authorities, such as Leicestershire, set up distinct advisory offices, with no administrative responsibilities except to spread ideas and train teachers in new methods.

The shadow of IQ and achievement tests lay heavy in British schools until recently, and the reform has been linked to a partial lifting of the shadow. The pressure has eased most in a few authorities that have successfully abolished the "eleven-plus" examination which used to separate English children at the age of 11 into goats and sheep; a small number of goats went to a "grammar school" that prepared them for a university, while the large number of sheep went to a "secondary modern school" that frequently prepared them for nothing. Some are very good indeed, but all too many are merely custodial institutions, like American slum high schools, with the difference that they speak to students in the very English accents of Mr. Dombey: "I am far from being friendly to what is called by persons of leveling sentiments, general education. But it is necessary that the inferior classes should continue to be taught to know their position and to conduct themselves properly. So far, I approve of schools." Grammar schools, on the other hand, have traditionally been obsessed with the highly competitive tests for university placement, and therefore, like many crack American high schools, their patterns of instruction are very brittle. ("This is a rat race and I am a rat," as a friend of mine who went to Philadelphia's Central High School put it.) Most British educators are ready now to admit that the eleven-plus was fearfully wasteful of talent, and that a test at that age is not a sound prediction of a child's future—except that it becomes a self-fulfilling prophecy, with children defined as stupid coming to act stupid.

MORAL FOR REFORMERS

... It is worth emphasizing that the authorities which are establishing alternatives to a system dominated by IQ and achievement tests are also those where reform has moved farthest, even into the junior schools. The moral for reformers on both sides of the Atlantic is, again, obvious.

Math offers an excellent illustration of the fusion of classroom practice with new ideas on child development that is characteristic of the primary school revolution, and I want to go into this important matter in some detail.

Developmental psychology—the study of the growth of intellect and the order in which various abilities flower—has a great influence on the British schools, but the influence is of a special sort. The same theorists, Baldwin, Isaacs, Bruner, and especially the Swiss psychologist, Jean Piaget, are read in America (along with the dominant American behaviorist school), but to less practical effect. As a rule, theorists have less impact on schools than most people suppose—schools, like girls, are seldom ruined by books—and when they do, it is usually because their theories seem to confirm successful or popular practices. This is generally the case in Britain today, except that the work of the developmental psychologists, and Piaget in particular, has proved so fruitful and suggestive in the area of mathematics that their assumptions are beginning to pervade classrooms and shape the direction of educational innovation.

Some of the most important assumptions are that a great majority of primary school children can't be told things, that they learn basic mathematical concepts much more slowly than adults realize, and that the patterns of abstract thought used in mathematics must be built up from layer after layer of direct experience—seeing, hearing, feeling, smelling. According to Piaget, each of us needs to forge, through direct experience, a mental scheme of the world, with a hierarchy of meanings; a learner has to organize material and his own behavior, adapting and being adapted in the process. He learns by his own activity. In a lifetime's work with young children, including his own, Piaget has advanced the idea that children learn to think in stages, and that in the early stages they learn mainly from the testimony of their senses, and not so much through words. At first, small children think intuitively and even magically; at another stage they can deal practically with concrete experiences; and still later they proceed to a point where they can think abstractly and make use of mathematical abstractions. In a series of classic experiments, Piaget has offered persuasive evidence that ideas which seem obvious to an adult are by no means obvious to a small child. Certain mathematical principles are difficult to grasp, except through repeated experience. Take the principle of invariance of number, for example: if you rearrange five pebbles there are still five. It seems hard for children to grasp that. Or reversibility: if you reverse a process—take two beads from eight then return them—you arrive at the same state of affairs from which you began. Or the principle of conservation: if you put a given amount of water in a flat saucer and pour the contents of the saucer into a tall glass, many children will say that the amount of liquid has changed, and it takes both time and experience to get them to see that the amount is really the same. All this has practical consequences for teaching mathematics: it is of little use to a boy if he can do sums in a workbook but still fails to understand reversal or the conservation of number.

CONSERVATION AND CONVERSATION

. . . Children are encouraged to talk in the good British primary schools, because, among other reasons, it seems that they make better intellectual progress when they can speak freely about what they're doing and when the teacher is ready from time to time with questions and appropriate terms.

Piaget himself has spelled out a fairly exact sequence of development, from intuitive thinking to being able to reason concretely to the use of abstractions, and he has assigned these stages to definite chronological ages. Many teachers have questioned any scheme that pretends to be able to predict what a six- or a seven-year-old can learn, just as some critics have argued that Piaget pays too little attention to the social context of learning—the child's feelings, the expectations of the teacher, and more important, those of the parents. And yet there is a growing respect for Piaget's general outline of the stages of a child's development, based on experience in teaching mathematics. Whether or not his theories are ultimately accepted as true, it is clear that he and other developmental theorists have pushed British schools in directions that are pedagogically sound, toward an understanding that abstract concepts and words are hard for children, that children learn best from their own activity, and that they need time in which to grow.

Hence the belief of the good infant schools that what adults call play is a principal means of learning in childhood, a belief that seems more plausible when you consider how much children learn without formal instruction in the years before they come to school. Hence the sand and water tables, the rich variety of number apparatus, the clay, the wood, the geometric shapes to play with, the weights and balances, the Wendy Houses, and the dress-up clothes (to explore adult roles, as well as the materials that make up the world) ; hence, too, the conviction that a classroom should offer myriads of rich activities to choose from, that allowing children to repeat activities is often good, and that language and experience should link together in conversations among children and with the teacher.

The Schools Council's admirable *Mathematics in the Primary Schools* has a handy checklist of the areas of mathematical knowledge of an ordinary seven-year-old by the time he leaves a good infant school. The list is accurate, and I'm going to restate some of the main categories and describe some of the classroom activities related to each. Remember that in many schools there is no timetable and no division of the curriculum into separate subjects, so "math" will be going on in the classroom at the same time as painting or reading or writing—much writing, in fact, consists of accounts of things done in math.

An ordinary seven-year-old knows:

1. Sorting and classifying things into sets (a set is any defined group of objects) ; comparing the sizes of two sets, the number of objects in each; the use of terms for expressing inequalities, more than, smaller than and so on. As soon as they come to school, children begin sorting out all manner of things around the classroom, from buttons to pieces of material to building blocks. Sorting out merchandise in the play store is one way to learn about sets, as is laying the dinner table in the Wendy House, making sure to get the right number of forks and knives. On their own, small children sort endlessly, like monks at their beads, "four of these, and five of these."

2. Counting; conservation of number; the composition of numbers up to 20—how a number like 7 can be made up of smaller numbers added together (4 plus 3) ; knowing the numbers up to 20 well enough to see that 14 and 6 are 20 without having to count on fingers. Just as children in these classes learn to write by writing, not by filling words in workbooks,

they learn counting by counting. They roam around the classroom making inventories of other children, windows, shoes, chairs, always writing the number down. As in reading, they get unfamiliar numbers from each other or the teacher. "Twenty-seven is on the calendar," a boy advises a perplexed little girl who has just finished a count of some milk bottles. They weigh things on scales and balances endlessly: "How many bolts balance nine beans?" Here again the play shop is useful.

3.   Knowing the number line—all the numbers in order up to 100; understanding place value in number notation—the fact that each of the 4's in 444 has a value that depends on its place. Many classes have actual number lines, homemade strips of paper a few inches wide and 100 inches long, with the numbers written one per inch in sequence from one to 100, and with the 10's marked prominently with colored magic marker. Along with the big one come number strips of different sizes from one to 10 inches in length; these are used with the big number line to find answers to various problems—addition, subtraction, multiplication. Just by playing with the number line, children can begin to see patterns: if you add 10 to 7 and then keep going, you begin to sense regularities, 17, 27, 37, and so on.

4.   Measurement; rulers and other instruments of measurement, including units of money; conservation of measures, liquid and dry (a quart is a quart, whatever the shape of its container); knowledge of the relationship between one unit and another—inches to feet, for example. They invent their own units—their hands, their feet. Children measure the classroom, the playground and everything within. They measure each other, making graphs of heights. They play games guessing the measurement of something and then finding out who guessed best and writing an account to explain why.

5.   Simple fractions: the children learn these by dividing up all kinds of real things into halves, quarters, and three-quarters.

6.   Aspects of addition, multiplication, and division as these arise from real situations in the classroom. The idea is to have all the first steps performed on real materials, not as abstract exercises. Before a child tackles two times seven, he handles two sets of seven things, and seven sets of two things, using different kinds of objects.

7.   Shape and size, including some simple proportions—such as four times as heavy as, twice as tall as, nearly as old as. Children play with shapes, making and copying patterns. Cardboard boxes are cut out, flattened and then rebuilt, the children slowly acquiring a sense of what a cube is; here work with shapes touches on solid geometry. At one school in Bristol, children noticed that the wooden floor of the assembly hall consisted of squares about a foot on a side, and on a teacher's suggestion, with the help of some 50-foot lengths of rope, they worked out a game. Following the squares on the floor, pairs of children made polygons with their rope; some were simply large rectangles, most were intricate, with many

sides. Then each child would find the area of his polygon by counting (hopping from square to square) the number of squares inside the perimeter.

When an American visitor reflects on all these varied activities he is impressed not so much by the amount learned—though that is certainly staggering—as by its fundamental nature. What the children know, they know for sure; they have time in which to establish an understanding of extremely basic things that are seldom even taught in American classrooms. First-grade teachers in this country are sometimes astonished when they discover how many of the children successfully solving workbook sums have no appreciation of, say, the conservation of number; the same is true of children taught to memorize multiplication tables without ever having had a chance to understand what multiplication means, and what number relationships are involved.

A CREATIVE INFLUENCE

The approach is mathematical—stressing learning to think—rather than arithmetical, stressing mechanical computation. Rote learning and memorizing have been abandoned by good British primary schools, partly because they are dull, but more because they are poor ways to learn. It is assumed as a matter of course that children will proceed each at a different pace, doing different things. The idea of readiness is seldom used as a justification for holding a child back—a sure sign that Piaget's influence has been creative, rather than restrictive, since his theories could be used that way. The result of these practices—in perfectly measurable or in less tangible terms—are striking. By giving children an opportunity to explore and experiment—play if you will—and by putting teachers in a position where they can watch children and talk to them about what puzzles or intrigues them, good British primary schools are producing classes where mathematics is a pleasure, and where, each year, there are fewer and fewer mathematical illiterates.

Mathematics not only illustrates the fusion of development psychology with actual classroom practice, it is also becoming in itself an important catalyst for schools making the change from formal to informal methods of learning. This is in some part owing to the efforts of the Nuffield Foundation and the Schools Council, whose excellent curriculum materials for primary schools are not textbooks or set courses, but rather practical handbooks of suggestions for teachers, a large amount of whose space is given over to actual samples and pictures of children's work. (The Nuffield math books are dedicated to Piaget.) In sharp contrast to America, where many of the good curriculum projects are the work of university people, the British have taken enormous pains to enlist ordinary primary school teachers in the process of creating and spreading new ideas and materials. This is an important aspect of the great change, and offers a partial explanation for its success.

These are some of the various elements that have gone into the revolution in the British primary schools. Many are distinctly British, and not for export; but there are some lessons for American schools in this great transformation. My next and final report will attempt to sift them out.

III. Teaching Children to Think

. . . These methods, I've indicated, are successful in fairly measurable, as well as other, terms. They are not guaranteed to make bad teachers, or people who dislike children, into good teachers. But they are more suited than formal methods to the nature of small children and to the kinds of subjects that should be taught in primary school; and they encourage many ordinary teachers, who find that they are happier using them and less likely to spend all their time worrying about keeping order. Such methods assume that children can respond to courteous treatment by adults, and that to a great extent they can be trained to take the initiative in learning, if choices are real, and if a rich variety of material is offered them. As the Plowden Report concedes, these assumptions are not true for all children (some will probably always benefit more from formal teaching) or for every child all of the time. But the Plowden Report is itself testimony to a growing conviction in Britain that they can be a workable basis for an entire nation's schools.

Are they a workable basis for American schools? The task of creating American schools along these lines will be formidable, to say the very least. This is not the place to rehearse the institutional and cultural obstacles to change in American education, but I do want to anticipate some of the most serious questions that many people will raise about the kinds of schools I've described. In reform, as in anything else, there must be priorities, and in this case the first stark priority is simply to see clearly.

One thing that troubles some Americans about these schools is discipline. They may acknowledge that good British schools are doing better work than good American schools, but they are reluctant to admit that the results stem from, among other things, giving children freedom to choose from among selected activities in the classroom, and to move around the room, talking to each other. If they are teachers, they may react to such a proposition with contempt, because they know how hard it is to maintain discipline in many American classrooms. Where the class is taught as a unit, and every child is supposed to pay attention as the teacher talks, discipline can be a serious matter; it is even more of a problem when the class splits into groups for reading out loud, as any first-grade teacher knows. Quick children get restless; slow children dread the ordeal, and act accordingly. Any teacher who can keep good order under the circumstances, has a certain amount of talent, however wasted. Tony Kallet, a perceptive American now working as an adviser in Leicestershire, has written of the difficulties in maintaining control of the class in the good, but very formal American school in which he apprenticed. Some children managed quite well, he recalls, but others, especially the "problem children," found the discipline too much, too little was permitted them, and "their problems were in part, being created, rather than mitigated by control." After working with English classes, he felt very different about the problem, but for all the time he was in an American classroom, "it did truly seem that every single control imposed was necessary if anything was to be accomplished," a view that many American teachers will understand.

Some American teachers who have seen the spectacle of children in British classes working diligently on their own have raised another question: they have wondered whether British children are fundamentally different from American children. Certainly British grown-ups are different from Americans, and there may well be important differences in national character. Yet middle-aged English visitors to the informal schools often react with the same disbelief as Americans: they find it hard to credit British children with so much initiative and so much responsibility. Also, formal schools in Britain suffer from discipline problems, so it is hard to know how to speculate intelligently on the question. American teachers working on their own—and how lonely they seem—have often succeeded with methods similar to those of the good British primary schools: a forthcoming book by Herbert Kohl (see article 23) describes a sixth-grade class in Harlem run along fairly free lines—he includes some extraordinarily powerful samples of the children's free writing. A British teacher from one of the good local authorities recently came over to a large American city to teach a demonstration class of 8- to 11-year-olds in a slum school. Before he went, he was assured—by Americans—he would find American children as different from British as day is from night. Yet, he reported, the children reacted exactly as English children to a classroom thoughtfully laid out to permit choices. At first, the American children couldn't believe he meant what he said. After a timid start, they began rushing around the room, trying to sample everything fast, as though time were going to run out on them. Then they "settled remarkably quickly to study in more depth and to explore their environment with interest and enthusiasm." The teacher noticed that for the first two weeks no one did any written English or math, and when he asked them why, they said they hated those subjects. Eventually he got more and more of the class interested in free writing, but he never could get them interested in mathematics.

REASSURING THE PARENTS

Another, more serious, argument against this kind of education is that it won't prepare children for life. The answer the Plowden Report makes to this seems to me remarkably sensible: the best preparation for life is surely to live fully as a child. Sometimes this fear takes the reasonable form of a parent's question: will these informal methods handicap a child if he moves on to a school run on formal lines? This problem is now fairly common in England as children move from good infant schools to old-fashioned junior schools, or from primary school to rigid secondary school. I went to a parents' meeting at one superb infant school; the parents, who clearly were completely won over by the methods of the school, were nonetheless apprehensive of what could become of their children in a new situation. The head of the infant school said—which was true— that the children did in fact do very well in the very formal junior school. There was only one repeated complaint about them: they were not good at sitting still for long periods of time.

BRANDED AS STUPID

In England, as in America, there are many reasons why a practical alternative to tracking would be desirable. Tracking in a primary school brands children as stupid at an early age, with profound and unhappy effects on them.

"I'll never forget the look on the faces of the boys in the lower stream," an East London junior school head told me. His school has successfully abolished the practice, but he is unable to forget the look completely: "I still see it when my boys in the lower streams of secondary modern school come back to visit." Tracking has a profound effect on teachers, too: it tempts them to think that a single pattern of instruction can apply to a whole class, and it increases the odds that they will deal with their children in terms of abstract categories, IQ or whatever. In England, as here, the upper tracks of a school tend to be middle class, which makes the school an instrument for reinforcing social inequality. In America, of course, tracking is commonly a means of maintaining segregation within a supposedly integrated school.

After watching British classes, another argument against tracking occurs to you: it ignores the extent to which children learn from each other, slow children learning from the quick, and the bright ones, in turn, learning from the role of teacher they adopt with the slow. This is most evident in the small number of schools that have adopted family, or vertical, grouping: where there is not only no grouping by ability, but no grouping by age, and every class contains a mixed bag of older and younger children. Yet while all this is true, it makes little sense to condemn tracking unless you can show teachers alternatives to formal classroom teaching. This is where the pedagogical bite of the primary school revolution is so impressive: when a British school today stops tracking, it is not simply returning to the past, it is shifting to a different definition of the roles of teacher and student, and setting up a new kind of classroom in which students are trained to do work independently. With the blessing of the Plowden Report, fewer and fewer infant schools track and it is increasingly common for junior schools to abandon tracking in the first two years, and in some cases in the third. How far this trend will carry depends on the impact the primary school revolution makes on the secondary schools. A survey in the Plowden Report shows that English teachers, who used to be overwhelmingly in favor of streaming as a general policy for primary schools, are coming to approve of unstreaming. The reason, clearly, is that they are beginning to see workable alternatives.

Tracking is regarded as a necessary evil in this country, as are IQ and standardized achievement tests, formal class teaching, specified curriculum materials, set hours for set subjects, fixed ages for entering school and being promoted and so on. Teachers and administrators often realize that children's intellectual and emotional growth varies just as widely as their physical growth, yet they seldom feel able to act on their understanding, to treat each child differently. The good British schools raise serious doubts as to whether these evils are in fact necessary. In this country, as in England, there is a growing, and on the whole healthy skepticism about education: people are questioning the standard methods of the schools, and they are becoming realistic about the limited extent to which any school can be expected to pick up the marbles for the rest of society. (One interpretation of last year's Coleman Report would be that it calls into question our standard techniques of education, in slums as well as suburbs.) No British teacher would claim that his methods could solve our deepest historical and social problems. But, as far as education can make a difference, the work of the British schools in many different kinds of communities, suggests working models of individual learning to those who believe, as I do, that what American education needs is definitely not more of the same.

REVIEW QUESTIONS

1. What aspects of the British primary school "revolution" can take place in virtually any class, anywhere?

2. Are the earlier grades really the most appropriate ones for educational innovation?

part v

THE CULTURALLY DIFFERENT LEARNER

In recent years, we are beginning to attend seriously to the education of our poor and our culturally different children. In article 33, however, Jonathan Kozol, one of America's more articulate critics of discrimination, passionately spells out that we are hardly doing enough. We have given black people little reason to trust or like white-controlled schools, and we have allowed the use of textbooks containing racially offensive material. The author catches the readers' serious attention with insults and criticisms for everyone. Even our young liberals are attacked for giving their energies to the Peace Corp or SDS, instead of to black inner-city children. What are you doing, he asks, and which side are you on?

In article 34 Dean Luvern Cunningham paints a chaotic picture of his visiting principalship in a ghetto junior high school. Characterizing the school as a live volcano, Dean Cunningham describes dirty and hot study conditions, teachers being shot and slugged, outmoded and irrelevant curricula, high absenteeism (except during federally-sponsored lunch periods), and fights, chair-throwing, and crap-shooting in the cafeteria. Small wonder teachers feared lunchroom duty. The author concludes that the best authorities on ghetto education are not in the colleges, but are on the firing line in the schools. And having served his apprenticeship, our author proposes some semi-radical changes: Allow the principal to close the school if necessary, adopt a problem-solving orientation among staff and students, use summers for planning, segregate boys and girls, and abandon compulsory attendance.

The apparently ambiguous Coleman Report has been cited to support virtually any argument pertaining to the value of desegregation or readiness and remediation programs. In careful reanalysis, Christopher Jencks in article 35 concludes that, as hypothesized by Coleman, black and white students do attend different schools and that black students learn less as measured by standardized achievement tests. Contrary to predictions, the vast majority of white schools do not spend more money per pupil than black schools (except in the obvious comparison of ghetto schools with schools in nearby affluent suburbs). Also, the level of school expenditures did not relate to student achievement. Examining some criticisms of the Coleman Report, such as biased sampling, Jencks decided that the main conclusions are correct. As for implications of the report for educational reform, the author asserts that typical improvements—more materials, better teachers—will do little. Rather, intellectual development would best be promoted by changing the whole cultural and social system. Finally,

Jencks perceptively observed that since self-discipline, honesty, punctuality, and self-respect contribute more to job success than knowledge of history or physics, schools should attend more to developing these personal characteristics.

Herbert Kohl's *36 Children* has been a best-selling portrait of teaching in a New York slum school. In the excerpts of *36 Children* comprising article 36, Kohl lets each child describe life in his neighborhood. Telling it, quite naturally, "like it is."

Article 37, from *Up the Down Staircase* by Bel Kaufman, is a sensitive description of a teacher's first day in a rough school. Between put-ons by students and arbitrary school policies, Miss Barrett has an unforgettable day.

Defining mental health as living with a minimum of disorder, functioning with personal satisfaction, and maintaining an adequate self-concept, Stanley Charnofsky in article 38 indicates that the powerlessness of the uneducated poor relates directly to severe feelings of inadequacy. One prescription is the identification with and commitment to a person's subculture, thus increasing his control over his destiny, his sense of personal power, and therefore his psychological health.

The remaining three articles in Part V are aimed at clarifying some of the unique language and cultural patterns of American blacks which make life difficult in white schools. In article 39 linguist William Labov describes the "Black English Vernacular" of Harlem adolescents, a language that had led wayward educational psychologists to believe that black children suffer a verbal and conceptual deficiency. In a formal interview described by Labov, one black boy said almost nothing. In a second session, with potato chips and a friend present, and using comfortable obscenities, the same boy proved highly verbal and logical—emphasizing the critical effects of the social situation upon verbal fluency. The author further notes that the middle-class writing of high school and college students is usually unclear and pretentious verbiage. Labov demonstrates that the Black English Vernacular in some instances may not only be clearer and more precise, but more logical as well. Finally, Labov rightly observes that the misguided deficit position is tragically damaging to the welfare and self-respect of black children.

Joan Baratz in article 40 agrees with William Labov that psychologists and educators are completely off base in concluding that black children are verbal cripples. Black English, or Negro nonstandard English as Baratz prefers, is demonstrated to be as well ordered and highly structured as any other language. The author lists grammatically consistent sentence structures and word usages which the white reader should find fascinating. Black readers may see these rules as their first formal exposure to a linguistic analysis of Black English.

If you are not convinced that black culture is so different from the culture of white middle-class America, try the "Chitling" test by Adrian Dove, presented in article 41. We should mention, incidentally, that there are about twelve distinct black subgroups in America, and this test would not be valid for all of them. Many black people, however, would be quite comfortable with this black-oriented intelligence test.

thirty-three

A Talk to Teachers

JONATHAN KOZOL

We meet, I'm afraid, at a tragically appropriate moment. The nation is divided between a false facade of superficial mourning for a dead man (Martin Luther King) it seldom genuinely honored and a more authentic and gut-level terror that we are soon going to be obliged to pay a terrible price for the racism and brutality his murder symbolizes.

The over-riding fear, the constant question, is whether or not we are about to have a summer of unending urban riots. To my own mind the most saddening fact of all is that, in the long run, in terms of the ultimate issues, it is not going to much matter. More people may die and another thousand buildings may perhaps be burned or battered but the same problems will be with us even after the wreckage has been cleared away and, riots or not, destruction blatant and overt or destruction only gradual and ordinary, the same bitter problems of a divided society and of a nation torn by bigotry will still be with us in September.

I think that in America we love to believe in apocalyptic interventions. It would be comforting almost to think that a rebellion, no matter how devastating, no matter how expensive, would at least have the ultimate result of settling our problems. It is—unhappily—not so.

Broken glass and streams of blood will be good covers for news magazines in the middle of the summer—but they will not even begin to solve our problems. Probably they will not even destroy us.

They will *scare* us for a while and force our newspapers to write long editorials. And then we will go back to our ordinary American lives again and to our old, more quiet ways of dying.

It is for this reason, I believe, that now is as good a time as any to take an unforgiving second look at some of the ways in which we have defined the basic problems. I would like to focus on the schools. I would like to focus on the teachers. And I would like to get beyond some of the unproductive things that have been said already.

Source: From the *English Record*, October 1968, 19:2–14. Reprinted by permission of the New York State English Council.

The problem within the ghetto, stated in the very simplest possible terms, comes down to a very few plain and painful facts: Black kids, black parents and black leaders do not—by and large—either like or trust their schools or the kinds of white people who work in them. A great many black people, given even half a chance, would dearly love to burn the whole mess down and—unhappily, in a good many cases—would not be very much the losers if they succeeded.

I say this not facetiously but because I believe that many Negro people have been fortunate enough to recognize fairly early in their lives that the schools were not their friends, that the schools were not going to stand beside them in a struggle, that the teachers were not likely to stick out their necks on crucial issues.

I am going to try to be as frank as possible in attempting to anticipate the reactions to this statement among many of the people in this audience. Many of you, I can imagine, will protest at this kind of disloyal assertion on my part and will want to stand up and tell me that I am being insolent and speaking out of turn, needlessly defiant and unjustly disrespectful to my fellow-teachers: Don't I know—these people will want to ask—how many of the dedicated teachers of the inner city schools have given their lives to the education of young children?

To this, I am afraid that there is only one real answer. It does not matter, in the long run, what I *think*—what matters in the long run is what the black communities BELIEVE. And what they *do* believe at the present time, throughout the nation, is that professional teaching hierarchies, principals, superintendents—are servants and acolytes of a hostile, unfriendly and ultimately unmerciful white structure which has trodden them down and kept their souls and lives in prison for over three hundred years and which still today oppresses their children, murders their leaders and disdains their own humanity.

If this is the case—if this is what the black communities believe—then the challenge for us is *not* to withdraw into a militant and stiff defensive posture in which we ward off criticism with our pious platitudes of "professional experience" and "long years of dedication" but to ask ourselves instead just exactly why it is that all our "professionalism" and all our inheritance of reiterated "dedication" seem to have had the ultimate effect of compelling most black people to despise us?

The deepest, most direct and most immediate personal experience that a black child in America is ever likely to have of white society is that which he will have within a public classroom—in the person of the school teacher. That experience, as we well know, is anything but happy. Bitterness and cyicism are the primary inheritance that most black children in America take from the classroom.

"Hate whitey!" cries the 14-year-old Negro student standing on the corner.

"Hate whitey!" repeats the 16-year-old drop-out as he sees a white policeman cruising through the ghetto.

But who is this whitey?? What white people do they *know?* What white man or white woman have they ever faced directly, known with intimacy, had a chance to assess and study and evaluate and learn how to trust or distrust—hate or admire?

Well, you know the answer as readily as I do: sometimes it's a slum-lord, a grocer, a money-lender, police officer or social worker—but in almost *all* cases it is a white school principal or a white school teacher. And it is from us, whether we know it or not, whether we like it or not, whether we can admit it or not, that black kids sooner or later get the message that white men and white women are people who—for one reason or another—they cannot take for real. Some teachers keep on repeating the same question, as though they haven't an idea in the world of a possible answer: Why don't they trust us? What on earth could we be doing wrong?

I don't think we really have to look far to find the answer. Teachers go out on strike for all sorts of good and palpable and powerful reasons: they strike for pay, they strike for better working conditions, they strike for extra benefits, occasionally they even strike for issues which have something to do, specifically, with the immediate demands of education: but *when, the black community asks us, did we ever strike to bring about racial integration? When—they want to know— did we ever strike to get racist Scott Foresman readers taken out of any grade- school classrooms? When—they ask—did the junior high school teachers of the ghetto ever strike to have the dishonest and openly bigoted and destructive Allyn and Bacon social studies textbooks taken out of their shelves and classrooms?*

You called us *culturally deprived*—the black parents tell us—you told us that we were the ones who lacked stability and values. All the while you, as the teacher, remained the keeper of the classroom and the guardian of its books and values. You were the ones who could examine those tests and prepare the lessons, ready the lesson-plans, state your approach, your purpose, your methods, and your evaluations. Yet all the while you failed for some reason to make the one most important and most obvious and necessary evaluation of them all: Are these books, are these values, are these areas of evasion and dishonesty consistent with democratic principles and with all that you (the teacher) are supposed to have known about the "professionalism" and "moral dignity" of education?

Allyn and Bacon, publishers: *Our America*—a textbook for fourth-grade children on our nation's history:

> "Our slaves have good homes and plenty to eat." . . . Most Southern people treated their slaves kindly. . . . "When they are sick, we take good care of them." No one can truly say, "The North was right" or "The Southern cause was the better." For in Our America all of us have the right to our beliefs.

You were there—you were in the classroom—you were the one who had the education and the professional judgment and, supposedly, the moral character: *What did you do—what did you say?* (the Negro mother asks us) *If you ever protested, you must have done it in a whisper: we never heard you. . . .*

American Book Company, publishers: *Our Neighbors Near and Far:*

> The streets of this Oasis city of Biskra (in North Africa) are interesting. There are many different people upon them. Some who are white like ourselves have come here from Europe. Others are Negroes with black skins, from other parts of

Africa. And many are bronze-faced Arabs who have come in from the desert to trade in the stores. . . .

These people are fine looking. Their black eyes are bright and intelligent. Their features are much like our own, and although their skin is brown, they belong to the white race, as we do. It is the scorching desert sun that has tanned the skin of the Arabs to such a dark brown color.

Yumbu and Minko are a black boy and a black girl who live in this jungle village. Their skins are of so dark a brown color that they look almost black. Their noses are large and flat. Their lips are thick. Their eyes are black and shining, and their hair is so curly that is seems like wool. They are Negroes and they belong to the black race.

Two Swiss children live in a farmhouse on the edge of town. . . . These children are handsome. Their eyes are blue. Their hair is golden yellow. Their white skins are clear, and their cheeks are as red as ripe, red apples.

You were there—you were in the classroom—what did you say? What did you do? We were the uneducated—(the Negro mother, the Negro father tells us)—we were your maids and ironing-ladies, garbagemen and janitors. We were the ones who were illiterate, we were the ones who were culturally deprived. Daniel Moynihan has told the whole world what was wrong with *us*—but who has yet been able to explain to the world what in God's earth could have been wrong with *you?*

Allyn and Bacon, publishers: *Our World Today,* another geography textbook, this one for junior high school:

The people of South Africa have one of the most democratic governments now in existence in any country.

Africa needs more capitalists. . . . White managers are needed . . . to show the Negroes how to work and to manage the plantations . . .

The white men who have entered Africa are teaching the natives how to live.

You were there—you were the guardian of our children—what did you do?

And this (these things) the Negro child remembers—and the child who read that book five years ago, of course—is the full-grown black teenager of today, and he wants to know what you were doing or saying on these matters: He wants to know why you were silent, when you were the one who was the adult, the grown-up—the professional in that public classroom. You kept the cupboard. You prepared the meal. And what you fed the child—without remorse—was poison. Whether you taught math or physics, Russian, Chinese, English, French or cooking—you were there. You were an adult and you said nothing. There is no way in which you can escape responsibility.

The Negro mother and the Negro father speak to you, quietly: You went on strike (they say—you went out on strike for your "professional rights and dignities" but you never once went out on strike for your rights *or* our rights as respectable human beings.

"Why is it they don't trust us?" ask the sweet and bewildered white schoolladies to each other.

Because we're frauds and it took the Negroes a long time to figure it out: but now they know it.

A couple of years back a highly respected board of inquiry sponsored by the Massachusetts State Board of Education issued a report documenting the fact of racial segregation in the Boston Schools. The report was signed by outstanding figures in all areas: the Catholic Archbishop, leaders of the Jewish and Protestant communities, the presidents of Boston University, M.I.T., Brandeis, and Northeastern. . . .

In response to this report, a young Boston teacher, assigned to a third-grade class within the ghetto, initiated a brief letter simply asserting in an unbelligerent manner that she, and other school teachers, were aware of the presence of racial segregation in their classroom, were aware of the deficiencies of their school buildings, and shared the sense of impatience and of discontent evinced both by the State Report and by the Black Community. She—like others—had heard the children singing when they were walking on the picket lines and she knew very well the words of one of the songs they sang:

"Which side are you on?" the song was asking, "Which side are you on?" It came out of the labor union struggles of the 1930s and was taken over by the white and Negro people in the Freedom Movement.

So here was this young white girl in the school system trying, with a good heart, to give an answer and she appealed to her fellow-teachers in the system to do the same.

Ladies and gentlemen—there were at least 4,000 professional employees of the Boston Public Schools at that time. *Not 20 people would stand beside that one young teacher by affixing their signatures at the bottom of her letter.*

"Which side are you on?" the black parents were demanding.

And 3,980 professional employees of the Boston School System gave their answer. Then . . . in their faculty rooms, over their sandwiches and over their cups of coffee, the dedicated white ladies sat and stared at each other in sweet bewilderment—asking the time-honored question: "Why is it they don't trust us?"

Because they have done nothing to *deserve* being trusted: because they were not *trustworthy.*

The distance and the withdrawal on the part of a school faculty from its immediate community is, I think, well-known to many of us. Those among us who are acquainted with the classic faculty-room dialogue within a ghetto grade-school or a junior-high know well, I think, how older teachers coach the younger ones about the ways in which to deal and talk with Negro people: *Be careful,* is the message: *Don't be unguarded or informal. Don't let yourself be known to the black community in any way that might be vulnerable, that might reveal your feelings.*

The first advice that I received from my school supervisor was not to make use of the informal and casual word OKAY.

"I noticed you used the word OKAY three times this morning, Mr. Kozol"— said my superior. "OKAY is a slang word, Mr. Kozol. In the Boston schools we say ALL RIGHT, we do not say OKAY."

It seemed not worth the pain, not worth the trouble to reason with the man—to try to tell him that OKAY could be a very good and powerful word, that ALL RIGHT says nothing, that OKAY says everything, that President Kennedy used to say the word OKAY to his brothers, that good reporters say OKAY to their editors, football captains to their managers, pilots to the airport. I wanted to tell him that OKAY was a good word, an American word, an OKAY word—a word with life in it, and energy. But I didn't even argue with him. I just looked at him and nodded—and denied myself and said quietly, "All right."

There was the time, too, when I took a child over to visit in Cambridge. We visited the museums, went to call on an old classmate, had lunch with my girl friend, and went back to my own place and set up an electric train lay-out in the kitchen. The principal of my school heard of this visit in short order and later wrote of it in her report on me. She indicated in her report that unattractive conclusions might well be drawn of a man who takes a young child to visit in his home. Said the principal in her report, "I told Mr. Kozol of the possibilities. . . ."

I think, also, of the tragedy of a PTA meeting in my building at which I arrived a little late—late enough to stand a moment in the doorway and look out at the extraordinary scene in front of me. Parents on one side—teachers way over on the other. In the middle—a huge safe space of unoccupied and untouched chairs.

I looked and watched and wondered:

How did this happen?

Was it conceivably a random accident?

Was it just a fluke of timing?

Obviously—with all mercy, all reservation, all wish to be wise and kindly and compassionate and back-bending—one could not CONCEIVABLY write off the professional STUPIDITY, VULGARITY and sheer ROTTENNESS of the school principal and faculty in allowing this kind of situation to develop.

Was it not, I had to ask myself, part and parcel of the same stupidity that prevented white teachers from dropping in on Negro families, from driving kids home, from fooling around in a comfortable and easy-going way out in the schoolyard? Was it not the same tragedy, the same ignorance, the same brutality which allowed a school faculty to drive through the ghetto every morning with eyes looking neither to left nor to right, nor, in some cases, one felt, even down the middle? Teachers on one side—parents on the other. In the center, an area of graphic sterilization. No germs might travel, no blackness, no ugliness, no race-contagion, could journey the distance from the seated mothers of a black community and the prissy teachers, their legs and souls up-tight together in their safe and sexless little corner on the aisle.

I would like to be able to deserve to be called generous by my fellow-teachers and I recognize all too well that, in ringing such a note of outright indignation, I bring upon myself once again, as I have done before, the concerted rage of a profession of embattled people, teachers in panic, principals in frenzy, aroused to vengence at the implications of their personal cowardice, deceitfulness and pathos.

Yet it is true. It is there before us every day. And the very rare exceptions only stand out to prove the rule.

Avoidance of intimacy—avoidance of blackness—avoidance of humanity. At times, the tragedy involved in such a stance withdrew into the background and all that remained was a kind of wild absurdity.

Absurdity seemed uppermost in a confrontation that developed once between our principal and one of the other Fourth-Grade teachers. The teacher in question, a woman, happened to be Negro and happened to live in Roxbury and happened, as a matter of fact, to live in the precise neighborhood in which the school was situated. The principal had advised us to observe unusual caution in regard to any casual or day-to-day involvements with the black community. She did not, of course, use those words, but it was apparent to us all that this was her real meaning. So this teacher, the Negro woman I have just mentioned, went up and asked the principal what she expected of her.

"What if I'm in the supermarket," she asked, " and I meet the mother or father of one of my pupils there? What do you think I'm going to say?"

The principal was taken aback, obviously baffled by the situation. It did not accord properly with a reasonable understanding of such matters that a person ought to be living within the same community in which she was a teacher. Our principal, however, was good at regaining her composure—she never lost it for long, nor lacked of authoritative resources for regaining it. And so in this case too she soon regained her self-possession, looked directly into the eyes of this young teacher, and said to her simply:

"Well then, in such a case all I can do is to advise you not to forget your professional dignity."

It is hard to know exactly how she meant this, or how indeed one is to lose dignity in the purchasing of groceries except by confirming to the mothers and fathers of a community that you, like them, possess an alimentary canal, need food, spend money, buy things cheaply. It is hard to know—but I don't even want to ask. What I would like to do instead is to ask what we can do for our part to change these things and to break down these walls of inhumanity.

I think, to start with, we have got to ask ourselves straightforwardly where most of these teachers and administrators *come* from—and in what ways they have been prepared for teaching. This, of course, is the real question and I am afraid—no matter what we say—the majority of us already know the answer.

They come from schools of education.

They come from teachers' colleges.

They do *not*, by and large, come from the liberal faculties of our major universities, but from those faculties which are geared to teacher-training.

I think it is time to place some of the blame where it belongs and to cease trying to placate those who are most likely to take offense at words of frankness.

Some schools of education (a few) are relatively competent and provide a rich and humane education. (For the sake of politeness, let us assume that the education faculty from which any of my listeners may have graduated was one of the exceptions.) By and large, this is simply not the case. Education schools, in their great numbers, are institutions which perpetuate precisely the kinds of uneasy and defensive behavior which I have been describing. At times they offer, I suppose, certain courses which may be truly helpful in a very few and highly selective areas of learning. Much of what they teach, however, is *not* necessary at all, has little relevance to the human or intellectual or moral demands to be placed upon a classroom teacher, and leaves her worse off than she was before she started.

In every other field we are willing to acknowledge the failure of a process of preparation when the products of that preparation prove unequal to the responsibilities for which they had thought that they had been prepared. *Only in education, it appears, do we attribute the blame for failure not to the training institution, not to the Education School nor even to the teacher—but to the consumer, the victim, the public, the Negro family and the Negro child.* Teachers, filled full with all the newest codification—with all the most recent and most sophisticated formulas of condescension concerning the supposedly undermotivated, lethargic and culturally disadvantaged Negro child—go out into the ghetto, memorize the words of their sociologists and suddenly find themselves bewildered and helpless, overwhelmed by the realities which are imposed upon them. Sometime—seeing the bewilderment with which so many education school graduates respond—I wonder if they would not have been better off in the beginning if they had had their courses, their training, their preparation right on the spot, right in the ghetto all along? What did they gain from all their courses in the philosophy of education, in methods and materials, in sociological examination of so-called "culturally deprived" but a wearisome and inappropriate and somehow dehumanizing sense of condescension—and an inflated and artificial image of their own individual importance as "professionals"?

Teachers tell us very frequently of the hostilities they encounter, the disappointments they face, the distrust their presence repeatedly engenders in their Negro pupils.

There was no such distrust of teachers in the Freedom Schools of Alabama and Mississippi.

There is no such distrust of teachers in the tutorial classes run by the various militant Negro community organizations in this country.

There is no such distrust in the classrooms of those experimental grade-schools begun and operated by the black communities.

Nor, I think we remember, has there ever been distrust of that sort within the Headstart Classes, Upward Bound Programs, or other independent educational projects of the War On Poverty.

Yet none of these programs that I have named are dominated by those whom we designate "professionals." It is, indeed, one is almost tempted to believe, the adamant *non*-professionalism—the amateur exuberance and uninhibited sense of personal commitment—which makes such programs possible and successful.

Why can we not bring some of the same energy and exuberance into the public classrooms? Is there no way to bring into these classrooms right away the kinds of people who will be able to earn the confidence of a black community because they will in fact share its aspirations? There are thousands of young, bright, brave and revolutionary pupils in the liberal colleges of this country and I know from my experience—from recent weeks and hours of long discussion among the parents and leaders of the black communities—that they are still needed and still *wanted* within the schools that serve the inner cities.

For all the recent militance, for all the rhetoric of separation, for all the talk about black schools with all-black children and black teachers, the authentic leaders of the black community will still tell us frankly that they cannot go it alone without white teachers. For a long while to come, the situation is going to remain the same—and the only question is whether we are going to give those children the worst or the best—the dreariest or the most exciting—the narrowest or the freest—that we have to offer.

The liberal and radical kids are there in our colleges right now. We send them to the Peace Corps, we give them to SNCC and SDS or else we let them out on loan to Senator McCarthy but—poor economists that we are—we do not allow them to give their lives to the black children of the inner cities. Not, that is, unless they have previously agreed to have their brain picked dry and their outlook rendered sterile within the thankless surgery of one of our schools of education.

It is a reasonable question, I suppose, whether such kids would stick it out forever in a public classroom. Would they remain in teaching? Would they last for ten years? Would they last for forty? Would they be "dedicated" forever to their "professional" responsibility and obligation? In a curious sense, I almost hope that they would *not*—not, at any rate, in the manner in which those have been interpreted up to now.

Rather an impulsive and energetic and unpredictable amateur than a drearily predictable, dedicated and dehydrated professional—and rather a person dedicated to life, and love, and danger, and activity, and action than to the wearisome and unchangeable sterility of chalk and stick and basic reader.

Recently in Newton a parent complained to a school official at an open meeting: "There is so much teacher-turnover within this system. Many of our teachers seem to leave so soon, after only three or four years in many cases, sometimes after seven."

Said the school official: "Of this we are not in the least ashamed. We would rather have teachers we can't keep than teachers we can't get rid of."

There, I believe, in few words, is a very good and adequate answer.

I see no shame in having high teacher-turnover—if what we are turning over is something fertile and exciting. Rather have a lively, attractive and exciting girl who will quit after five years because she has the healthy urge to marry— than a girl who will never quit for that reason because she will never get an offer.

Many older people, I can well imagine, might consider the kind of proposal I have made impractical. They will tell me that young people, by and large, are selfish and ambitious to settle down, raise families, buy their ranch homes in the country, hire maids, have holidays abroad, earn lots of money. Young people, they say, may *talk* idealism but they will not act upon it. They will not make the sacrifice to stand up and serve as teachers.

When people tell me this—I always look at them for a moment—to think about their motives—and then I say that I do not know the kinds of young people they are speaking of. It was not the selfish and self-centered spoiled daughter of the selfish and the opulent rich man who ran the Freedom Schools in Mississippi and Alabama, who worked with the poor and the hungry for the Peace Corps in Argentina, Bolivia and Brazil. It was not the young man dreaming about a ranch-house and a million dollars who gave up his studies and his comfort and his security to go down South and risk his life, his respectability or his career, to walk a Negro citizen to the City Hall and give him the courage to go in and demand the right to register to vote.

Michael Schwerner was not thinking about cocktails, about sports cars or ranch-wagons when he lay down his life three years ago in Mississippi to help to make this nation free.

James Chaney was not calculating how he could make it to the top when he was buried at the bottom of the mud beneath a wall made out of stone in Mississippi, because he believed that black people still had the privilege to be free.

The young Unitarian minister, James Reeb, murdered three years ago in Selma, Alabama was not worrying about nailing down a fancy parish, sending his kids to fancy schools and buying his wife a fancy way of living when he walked out upon the streets of that racist city and received a club over his head; and fell; and died.

There is a new nation within the old one in America. It is better than the old one; it is honest and it is not selfish and it is not afraid. The oldtime teachers, the oldtime autocrats, the oldtime political school administrators do not really want to believe that this can be the case. It is too threatening. It hurts them very badly. They are involved with guilt and with the memory of cowardice and with the fear of an unspeakable retribution. They knew about the racist books within their shelves and did not speak. They saw the Negro parents across the room and did not smile. They heard the moral challenge—the plea—coming out from within the black community and they did not answer. And now they are unwilling— they are unable—to believe that we can be more decent.

It is up to us to prove that they are wrong.

400,000 Negro kids are going to be attaining the age of eighteen this season. Of those 400,000, not 10% will have received an education equal to the white standards.

It will not be due to their mothers and their fathers.

It will not be due to a defective family-structure.

It will not be due to any inherent lack of intelligence or motivation.

It will be due to ineffective and irrelevant and dishonest EDUCATION.

There is no way to get around it. The facts are there and they are devastating.

We are going to have to look those facts straight in the face and take them seriously. The sweet white lady in the classroom who wears blinders, cannot make her way through to a rebellious generation of black children. The white bigot or false liberal who teaches his lesson, locks up his room, and hops into his car to return to his nice home within the safe suburbs, cannot and should not have a serious role within a ghetto classroom. There is only one kind of person who can make it work—and that is the person who, in his class and in his life, is ready to take a militant stand beside the black community. There is no other way to do it.

Often now, when I have finished with a lecture of this sort, young people come up to me, teachers just beginning or people who believe that they would like to teach, and they question me, and they ask me, it seems—almost as if it were an amazing and undecipherable riddle: "How is it, Mr. Kozol, that you were able to go in, as you did, to an angry and revolutionary Negro area and into a tur- bulent and unhappy and properly embittered classroom, a room in which kids had had substitutes half the winter, or emotionally unstable teachers, or teachers who despised them, or—more frequently—teachers who simply didn't really ever care—and did not right on the spot receive a knife in the side or, at the very least, an eraser or an elastic or a paperclip or a spitball in the eye?"

When this question is asked, I often am aware that the questioner expects a complicated answer—a subtle and elaborate and self-complimenting explanation of how I worked out and contrived some amazing and fascinating English lessons guaranteed to hook the most apathetic and lethargic students. It just is not so. There is a far more simple-minded answer. "Listen," I say; "I walked into a ghetto classroom, an inept amateur, knowing nothing. In my lapel there was a tiny little button that the children in that classroom recognized. It was white and black—an equal sign—you remember it, I hope—it was the symbol of the Civil Rights Movement in America. The children had *eyes* and they could *see*—and they had hearts and minds and they could feel and know. And they knew what that little button stood for. On Saturdays sometimes they saw me on a picket line in front of a dilapidated building whose absentee white landlord had been negli- gent. On Fridays sometimes, a little while before supper, they would see me and my girlfriend coming up the stairs of their own home to visit with their mother and their father and sometimes stay for dinner.

If it was revolutionary you may say, with a smile, it certainly was the most natural and easy and deeply satisfying kind of a revolution that a man or a wo- man could conspire.

Then—on Monday—I was in the classroom; and the kids would say "We saw you Saturday." Or another child would say, 'He's got a pretty girlfriend.' Or another one would say, "He's got a junky old beat-up raggedy car."

But the thing is—they were not angry any longer. And I wasn't a very excel- lent or fancy teacher—I can assure you—but I was someone they'd seen out in the real world and someone they were willing to take on as a real friend.

Well, there aren't many picket-lines any longer in America, and they don't sing Freedom Songs in this country any more, but the kids out in the ghettos are still turning to us in the same way and asking us the same question that they asked before.

"Which side are you on?" is what they're saying.

And, truly, there is no way to get around that question.

It hurts sometimes. It hurts terribly, I know. But each and every one of us has got to come up with his own answer.

REVIEW QUESTIONS

1. Does Kozol's article make you feel that you might be less liberal and less dedicated than you thought you were? (If not, read the article more carefully.)

2. Is re-zoning, busing, or some other form of school integration the best solution? What problems—social or educational—would be aided? Are new problems created by, for example, busing?

thirty-four

Hey, Man, You Our Principal?
Urban Education As I Saw It

LUVERN L. CUNNINGHAM

This is a report. It is as objective as I can make it. The remarks that follow are based on a few days' experience as principal of an inner-city junior high school—a problem-saturated place.

I want it known that although what I say here is critical, it is not intended to be critical of any person or group of persons. But it is an indictment of us all—educators and laymen, critics and the criticized.

The notion of an exchange cropped up out of the woodwork. Someone had an idea that this would be a good thing to do. The big-city people agreed and we agreed and so we were off and running. We didn't have the luxury of much advanced planning time. Had we had a chance to contemplate the event in Columbus (in the peace and quiet and solitude of the ivory tower) we could have lost our courage and copped out on the whole deal. We didn't have that time, so we did appear at our respective schools at the appointed hour, Monday, May 5. On that fateful morning (like little kids going to kindergarten) we picked up our pencil boxes and marched off to the school house.

I arrived at about 7:45 A.M. I had read about the city's riots in 1966 and I knew it was near here that they had started. I was aware too that this was a junior high that had been having its share of trouble. I knew that the faculty had walked out in January in protest of school conditions. Most of the faculty stayed away for two days, saying that this school was an unfit place in which to carry on professional activity.

My first several minutes as the new helmsman were exciting, to say the least, I walked in through the front door and introduced myself to the regular principal's secretary. She was most cordial and smiled knowingly. I think she chuckled to herself, thinking that this guy is really in for an education. If those were her feelings she was quite right.

Source: From *Phi Delta Kappan*, November 1969, pp. 123–28. Reprinted by permission of the author and the publisher.

I walked into the office and was about to set my briefcase down. I looked up and there must have been twenty faces, most of them black, all around. And others were coming through the office door. Some were students, some were faculty members with students in tow, others were clerks who wanted me to make some monumental decisions about events of the day.

They weren't even in line. They were all just kind of standing around there competing for attention. And to make life more exciting a little black fellow with a flat hat and a cane about two feet long came up to me. He whipped that cane around on his arm and stuck it in my stomach and said, "Hey, man, you our principal?" I began thinking longingly of Columbus and said, "Well, no, I'm not. But I'm here for a week and I am going to be taking his place." I was back-pedaling and trying to think of some answer that would make sense to this eighth-grade student.

A number of youngsters who were crowding around were just curious; others had problems. One was a girl who had recently been released from a correctional institution and was under court order to come back to school. She was there for an appointment, but she didn't want to come back to this or any other school. She was openly hostile, asking harshly that she not be made to come back. I had no file. I didn't have any background on this young lady. I was unprepared to make a decision. So instead of displaying administrative genius, I said, "Would you sit down over there and I'll talk to you later." She sat—head down, sullen, oblivious to the confusion surrounding us. It was an hour before I got back to her problem.

There was tragedy and comedy. A teacher who was obviously disturbed about something had a very attractive sixteen-year-old girl by the hand. She came in and said, "I understand you're the new principal, Mr. Cunningham. Look at that skirt. Look at that mini-skirt. It's entirely too short. Just look at that thing. I think we ought to send her home. Aren't you going to send her home?"

She turned to the girl and said, "Is your mother home?" The girl said "No." "When will she be home?" "Well, she'll be home about 6:15 tonight."

The teacher turned to me and said, "We can't send her home." Then she marched the girl over in front of me, rolled that brief skirt up several inches and said, "Look at that, it's got a hem in it. It's got a hem in it that long. We ought to be able to take that hem out. Let's go back to the classroom." I didn't have a chance to say a word.

In the meantime other kids were still clustered around. They had their own brand of problems so I said, "Would you go and wait outside the office please and come in one at a time?" They kept coming in with their questions, some that I could answer, most that I could not.

When the first bell rang and the students had to go to their homerooms, faces disappeared, the corridors cleared a bit, and there was an atmosphere of temporary calm. I was able to sit down and try to get my bearings. It was an inauspicious beginning, to say the least.

Let me comment a bit about Lester Butler. Lester was assigned to the principal's office. His responsibility was to be available during free periods for phone calls, delivery of messages, and any other tasks that might appropriately be handled by an eager, intelligent seventh-grader. After quiet had been established in the office on that first day he gave me a quick tour of the building. He took me to the obvious places like the library, the auditorium, the gymnasium, and special classrooms, but he also pointed out the nooks and crannies, the special recesses, the hideaways of the old structure. With his special brand of radar he was able to track me down and bring messages to me during the week when I was about the building. We became unusually fine friends.

This junior high school building is old. The oldest part was built sixty-five years ago. It has had two additions. Despite its age the building has been refurbished from time to time; it was painted and the windows were in. It's not particularly unattractive from the inside, but as a structure to house education it's a nightmare of inefficiency. Traffic patterns are unbelievable. You have to go upstairs to get downstairs. You go upstairs across a kind of plateau and down the other side to reach another part of the building. The arrangements for science and home economics facilities, as well as classrooms housing other particular specialized aspects of the curriculum, do not accommodate decent traffic patterns. When the bell sounds and classes pass it is a wild place. It's wild in between times, too, for that matter.

The absentee rate is very high. Of the nearly 1,800 enrolled, between 350 and 400 were absent every day. Where they were no one really knows. There was no apparent relationship between my presence and the absentee rate; that's the way it is every day. During my first day a counselor took me in his car and just crisscrossed the neighborhood. He wanted to point out the housing, the neighborhood, the fact that the streets were crowded with humanity just milling around. It was a warm week, the first week in May. People were outside. Kids of all ages were all over. There appeared to be as many youngsters on the street as there were in the elementary school and junior and senior highs.

Ironically, everybody shows up during the lunch period. The lunches are partly financed with federal funds and the youngsters are admitted to the lunchroom by ticket. Kids who are truant get into the building (despite door guards) and into the cafeteria. They have something to eat and then melt into the community.

The building is a sea of motion—people are moving about all the time. Adults (teachers, teaching assistants, observers, student teachers, door guards, other people who get in through the doors despite the guards) and students are in the halls all the time. Some of the students have passes to go somewhere given by somebody, but most students are just there. Those who don't have passes have excuses. As a newcomer seeing all of this motion, what should I have done? Should I have gotten tough? Should I have tried to shout them back to class? Should I have threatened such and such? Or should I have turned my head and let them go on about their own purposes? I turned my head.

When I was in my office students would come in with all sorts of questions, grievances, or requests for excuses. Apparently the pattern in the building is that if you can't get a hearing for your complaint anywhere else you end up in the principal's office. I had a steady flow of customers.

The school has eighty-five teachers. There is a high absence rate each day among teachers too. They fail to show up for many reasons. The teacher absentee numbers (while I was there) would range from eleven to fourteen per day. If you have a faculty of eighty-five and fourteen teachers fail to show (and you don't get substitutes), you have to make some kind of ad hoc arrangements quickly to handle the crises. Each day three to five substitutes would appear and they would be assigned quickly to cover classes. But they were not enough. Furthermore, there was little relation between the substitutes' teaching fields and their assignments. The first priority is to put live people in classes to maintain some semblance of order.

The youngsters, as I said, were in motion. I had the feeling that I was walking on a live volcano. Classes were often noisy and rowdy. Fights and squabbles broke out frequently. Fights between girls occurred about five to one more often than fights among boys. But the fights among the girls were often over boys. The adult population was on pins and needles from the time the building opened in the morning until school was out at 3:30 in the afternoon. Everyone hoped to make it through the day without large-scale violence.

The day is organized around eight periods. Students have a number of free periods, during which time they are assigned to study halls. Some go to a large auditorium; others go to classrooms with teachers assigned to study hall duty there. Large numbers congregate in the cafeteria on the ground floor for "study." The cafeteria accommodates around three hundred youngsters. Teachers are reluctant to supervise the cafeteria study halls. When they do it is with fear and trembling. The place is noisy. Kids move around despite the efforts of several teachers to keep them seated. They shoot craps. Some play other games. There is bickering and fighting. Kids pick up chairs and fling them across the room at one another. It's dirty and hot.

The whole building is hot, because the custodians cannot shut off the heat. It is the only way to provide hot water for the lunch program. So they keep the stokers going to have hot water for the federally subsidized lunches. Everybody complains about it: the principal, the assistant principals, the teachers, the students, and the PTA.

The lunchroom study halls are unbearable. The undermanned custodial staff is unable to keep the table tops clean; a slimy film covers them. They are neither attractive for eating nor for study purposes. Because of the danger of intruders coming in off the streets, the major cafeteria emergency exit has been nailed shut. Teachers asked the principal to have the custodians do this. The custodians refused because of fire regulations. In desperation the principal himself nailed it shut. Each day he lives in fear that a fire will break out and students will be trapped. Large numbers might not get out through the narrow passageways that serve as entrances and exits. Thus a measure taken to protect the teachers could lead to another type of disaster.

We called the police only once during my stay. It was different at another junior high school where my colleague Lew Hess served as principal. At night following his first day a fire bomb was thrown through his office window. It was a dud and didn't go off. On his last day three fire bombs were thrown inside the building and they did go off. The police and fire department had to be summoned each time.

On the second day, in a classroom study hall right across from my office, a young boy was late. His name was Willy Denton. He was about a minute and a half tardy and his excuse was that he had been next door signing up for a special program of summer employment. The study hall supervisor had obviously had a hectic morning. As Willy entered the room a few words were exchanged. The supervisor grabbed Willy, put a hammerlock around his neck, kind of choked him, and wrestled him out into the corridor. The noise attracted other kids. Immediately there were about forty students as well as door guards right around the teacher and Willy. Willy got free for a moment but the supervisor caught him again, this time grabbing him by the shoulders. He shook him against the lockers and that was like whomping a big bass drum. The sound reverberated around that part of the building and more people came. The supervisor got a fresh hammerlock on Willy, dragged him over to my office, threw him in and across to the other side, and said, "Take charge."

I suppose that I turned whiter in that sea of black, but I took charge. I closed the door and asked Willy to sit down. All of a sudden another teacher opened the door about six inches and shouted, "Willy's got a good head on his shoulders," slammed the door, and left.

It was about 12 noon. The period had just started. There were nearly thirty-five minutes until Willy was to go to another class. So Willy and I just talked. I didn't think that lining him up for swats would make much difference. He was livid. If he had been white he would have been purple. He was furious, and so we just sat and talked.

We talked about what he liked and what he disliked. I asked him if he had worked last summer, since he was going to be employed this coming summer. He said that he had. I asked where and he said, "I worked in a church." And he added, "You know I teach Sunday School." I asked how old his class members were and he said, "Well they're about the same age as I am." "How many do you have?" "About fifteen, and sometimes I teach on Saturdays too." "Do you like to teach?" He said, "Well, it's okay. But boy those first Sundays my stomach just kind of turned around and I didn't know what I was doing. But it's better now. Like last Sunday, did you hear about that plane that was shot down in Korea? You know, we just talked about that. I sat down and we talked about that."

It was clear that Willy loved what he was doing in Sunday School. He liked math too and he planned to go to high school. But he was so angry at that study hall supervisor. He trembled for several minutes; he just couldn't get control. We talked through the balance of the hour till the bell rang. I sent him on to his next class sans swats.

The PTA leaders came in to meet with me on Wednesday. They shared their definitions of the school's problems. I held a faculty meeting on Thursday. And I was amazed at the similarity between faculty and parent sentiments on the issues facing the school.

The teachers, by and large, are a very dedicated lot. Many of them are young; some of them are coming out of MAT programs. Despite their youth they, like the rest of the faculty, are tired, disheartened, even despondent. But they don't want to fail.

One of the teachers was shot ten days before I arrived on the scene. He missed his lunch break and went across the street to get a coke and a bag of potato chips. Coming back he was held up on the street and shot with a pellet gun. He came back into the building, walked into the principal's office, with his hand pressed against his side. Blood was spewing between his fingers and he said, "I'm shot, I'm shot, I'm shot." The principal called an ambulance and got him to the hospital. But he was back teaching while I was there, with the pellet still in him. He hadn't had time to have it taken out. He was going to the hospital that weekend to have the bullet removed.

I tried to visit classes and meet teachers. As I became known around the building, it was rather like walking down the hall and being attacked by aardvarks. Teachers would come out, grab me by the arm, pull me back into the teachers' lounge or their classrooms, and say, "Let me tell it like it is here." Every one of them had deep feelings for the school and for the kids, but an inability to define the specific changes that would make a difference. Their intense desire to solve the school's problems mixed with overwhelming despair is one of the powerful impressions that remains with me as a consequence of those days.

In many ways it is an overmotivated but underprepared staff. As one young fellow who came in March said, "This is an overpeopled and understaffed school. We've got lots of special people running around under federal grants doing their particular thing. But they don't fit into any kind of mosaic that has meaning for solving the problems of the school."

Many teachers have the too-little-and-too-late kind of feeling. No one is apologetic about it. There is no sense of humiliation about being assigned to the school. But most of them want to get out because they feel that it is an absolutely hopeless situation, that they can't afford to spend whatever psychic energy they have in fighting a losing battle. Even though they are emotionally committed to the place they still want to leave. So the turnover rate is high. Some youngsters had had several different teachers in some of their classes since the beginning of the year.

After the early chaos of my first morning I was able to visit a class being taught by a Peace Corps returnee. She was a young woman with an MAT degree. She had two adults with her in the room assisting with the youngsters. And it was pandemonium. She was trying to teach social studies. She was obviously searching desperately to locate something that might motivate or have some interest for fifteen seventh-graders. Her Peace Corps assignment had been in Africa, so she was showing slides of how people construct thatched cottages there. It was something she knew about first-hand—she had been on the scene. But the kids tuned her out. They were making funny remarks and fighting.

One of the other adults in that room was a young man, a practice teacher who had arrived that morning. He had already been slugged twice by students before my 11 A.M. visit. I talked with him later in the week trying to find out whether he was going to give up or stick around. I had to admire his tenacity. He was going to stay; he wasn't going to be licked by that set of events.

During the lunch hour a group of seventh-grade teachers who were cooperating in a transitional program (transitional from the sixth grade into junior high) were meeting for a planning session. I was invited to sit in. The young Peace Corps returnee came in with a tear-stained face. She just couldn't manage her situation. She didn't know what to do. She had to go back and face those classes that afternoon and the next day and the next. She had been advised by the principal and by others to turn in her chips and move to another school. But she just wouldn't do it. She had been fighting it since September, facing failure all year long, but she just would not give up. Others like her were having similar experiences.

The curriculum at this junior high is archaic, outmoded, irrelevant, and unimportant in the minds of the kids who are there. The faculty has agreed for the most part that this is true. But no one is able to design a pattern of change which will remedy or act upon all of the deficiencies that are so prominent in the program of studies. Because of the way the building is constructed (room sizes, locations, and the like) they are locked into an eight-period day. There just are not enough classrooms to handle a six-period organization. Furthermore, there is ambiguity about who is responsible for curriculum reform. Everyone wants change but no one knows how to achieve it.

They were administering the Stanford Achievement Test the week I was there. Large numbers of kids couldn't read it. Many couldn't even read the name of the test. Some of them would mark all of the alternative responses; some wouldn't mark any; some would just casually draw pictures on the test; some would stare; others would raise their hands and ask for help from those who were monitoring the testing.

A few teachers raised the question with me, "Why test?" It is a good question. Or why use that kind of testing for youngsters in a junior high school like this one? Apparently standardized testing is a system-wide requirement which may have had historical significance and is continued merely because no one has has considered not doing it.

As I have said, most of the teachers' energy goes into control. I found few classrooms where I could say with any confidence that there was excitement relative to learning. The only place where I saw interest and motivation and product was in home economics, which enrolls both boys and girls. In other areas interest and motivation appeared to be near zero. It seems to me that the traditional school "subjects" have to be very carefully analyzed in terms of some relevancy criterion.

We toss that word around a great deal—relevance. It's in everybody's language. It has reached cliché status more rapidly than most similar words in our professional jargon. Nevertheless, there is some meaning there.

When I ask myself what would be relevant to the young people at this school I reach an impasse very quickly. It is hard to know what is relevant. Certainly it ties to motivation. If we were insightful enough to know what the prominent motivations are among such young people, then maybe we could organize a program of studies in keeping with interest areas. The program might look quite unlike the traditional subject-centered arrangement in these schools.

I mentioned earlier the "leakage" of the building, both inside out and outside in. The staff walkout in January, 1969, took place because the school was an unsafe place in which to teach. The Board of Education responded by putting door guards on the doors. The measure was to protect teachers and students from a range of intruder types. It was also to control students coming in and going out during the day. The guards have helped a bit in keeping invaders out of the building, but this move hasn't solved the pupil "leakage" problem. An outsider (or an insider for that matter) will cause a disturbance at one of the doors. Door guards come quickly from their posts to help out, leaving their own stations unattended. Other kids will then open the unprotected doors and run out or run in, whichever suits their fancy.

Administrators and teachers resort to corporal punishment. The chief vehicle for control is the swat system. The teachers worked out a scheme to improve control following the January walkout. Teachers volunteer to help with discipline in the "gym balcony," a little area overlooking the gymnasium. During free periods kids who have misbehaved, for whatever reason, are brought there. They queue up, outside, both boys and girls, waiting to be swatted. Teachers take their turns up there in the gym balcony. Similar disciplinary lineups occur outside of the office doors of the three assistant principals, who have paddles or razor straps hanging from their belts. If they need to use them in the corridors they do.

Disciplinary cases are brought first to their door. If they or the principal are too busy, in juvenile court or at home with a case of nerves or whatever it might be, then the students go to the gym balcony to get their swats. Afterward they go back to class or study hall or library or get out of the building.

I didn't administer corporal punishment. I don't know whether I was psychologically capable of it. I don't think I could have forced myself. Teachers on a few occasions brought students to my office. One teacher just threw them in, saying "Take charge" and leaving.

There doesn't seem to be any intrinsic motivation, any way of appealing to the interests of pupils to stay and learn. So everyone (adults and students) adjusts to the corporal punishment routine. No one likes it; no one wants it. Teachers hate it; the principals hate it. But they have no other alternative. They have not been able to discover any better control measure.

And now about death. There is an astonishing callousness about death among the students here. One of them had been killed a few days earlier. He was shot in a car wash down the street. I have mentioned the shooting of the teacher; fortunately that did not end in death. There were other shoot-outs in the neighborhood ending in fatalities. Lester Butler, on my last day, sought an excuse to attend a funeral. I asked for particulars. He said, "It's for my friend's father. He was killed a week ago. He was shot right outside the school. I want to attend the funeral. I'll come right back after it's over." I wrote the excuse.

Lester described the event without emotion, with placidness, with matter-of-factness. Death is a part of life here. Life is filled with its own brand of violence. Its violence is routine. It is not necessarily racial. It is grounded in hate which feeds upon itself. It is cancerous and spreads and spreads and spreads.

The cancer of hate is latent within the student body. You sense its power. You sense its presence and the prospect for its release at any moment. You do not know when it will burst forth and cascade around you. It is everywhere; it is nowhere. Lester sensed that the school was a powder keg. He would even try to describe it to me in his own way.

In many ways life at this junior high is a charade. People go about the business of routine schooling. Teachers laugh and smile. They walk through the corridors ignoring the rowdiness. They try at times, halfheartedly, to establish a bit of order. The administrative staff takes the problem more seriously; they shout and cajole and urge and plead. The counselors do their thing. They talk with students. They describe worlds of glitter and gold. The students squirm and stare and ignore. The counselors' cubicles, tucked away here and there, are temporary refuges from the storm.

I was impressed with the door guards. They try. They understand the charade. Many of them have played the game for a lifetime. They represent well the male image. They are for the most part young, strong, handsome. They are on the side of the angels. That is, they try to support the purposes of the school. They work closely with teachers and administrative officials. They do their job. It involves keeping hoodlums off the street out of the building, avoiding physical encounters but not turning away from them. There is no training for their positions. They must exercise amazing discretion every minute of the day. Most of them have little formal education. But they have established a bond with the professional staff that is harmonious and marked by mutual respect. Each day I issued up a silent prayer of thanks that they were there.

What to do about this school? And other similar junior highs in other places? An archaic building, a largely uncaring community, an irrelevant program of studies, a student population that is out of hand, an underprepared, overpressured staff, a sympathetic but essentially frustrated central administration, a city that wishes such schools would go away. A proposal from the staff and administrators was to burn the school down. Destroy it. Get the symbol out of the neighborhood. This was more than a half-serious proposal.

Short of that, what can be done? This question haunted me during my stay. What could be done? Only a few feeble proposals occurred to me.

I would argue for complete building-level autonomy. The principal and faculty should run the show without concern for other places. They should be allowed to organize the program of studies without adherence to district-wide curriculum guides and the like. The principal should be free to select his own faculty without reference to certification. He should look for talented people anywhere and everywhere. They could be found across the street or across the nation. The principal should build his own budget and make internal allocations in terms of the faculty and staff's definition of need.

More radically, I would ask that the principal be given complete control over time. That is, he should be able to open and close the school at will. If in his judgment events are getting out of hand, he should have the power—indeed be expected—to close the school down for a day, a week, or a month. During the time the building is closed, all of the adults in the school, in cooperation with students and community leaders, should focus on the problems that are overwhelming them. They should develop a problem-solving ethos. They should include genuine and substantial neighborhood participation. They should zero in on questions one by one, work them through and seek solutions. The state, the city, and the central school administration should support but not interfere. What is required in schools like these is a set of solutions. There is no justification for keeping the building open simply to observe the state code.

The staff should be kept on during the summer. Give them an air-conditioned retreat; allow them to plan for the year ahead. Work on the program of studies, work on motivation, work on community linkage, work on patterns of staffing, work on everything.

It occurred to me that it might be wise for the boys and girls to be separated— have boys' schools and girls' schools. There are some research data to support this recommendation. I remembered a study in Illinois that I directed a few years ago. There we tried to discover the impact of segregated learning on achievement. We examined a small district where youngsters were feeding into one junior high school out of white schools, black schools, and integrated schools. We were interested in such factors as pupil alienation, attitudes toward schooling, and achievement in the traditional subject fields. We discovered some significant differences, but the overwhelming difference was how boys responded to the learning environments in contrast with how girls responded. The boys were getting the short end of the stick on most things.

Systems should depress the emphasis on attendence. I would even support abandoning compulsory education for this part of the city. Emphasize programs of interest and attractiveness; deemphasize regimentation. Much of the faculty's energy goes into keeping kids in school. And once in school, keeping them in class. Why fight it? Jettison the pressure toward control. Enroll students on the basis of interest only. Such policies violate the rich American tradition of education for everyone, but why carry on the charade? Why?

Again I want it understood that I came away from this school with profound admiration and respect for the regular principal, the three assistant principals, the several counselors, the many teachers, and the many special staff members, as well as the central administration. And I came away with respect for the students. The adults in the building are struggling feverishly. They are dedicated. They are in their own way in love with the school. But they are shell-shocked, exhausted, and desperate. They need help but they are not sure what kind of help. And I am not sure. I have advanced a few notions but they need careful scrutiny and considerable elaboration.

It is clear that we have no experts in this sort of urban education anywhere. The most expert may be those professionals who are there every day engaging in the fray. But they are reaching out, and it is for this reason that some kind of liaison with universities and other sources of ideas is critical. Refined, umbilical relationships need to be developed. We are just scratching the surface at Ohio State. No one has *the* answer. Anyone who thinks he has is a fool. At best there are only partial answers—pieces of a larger mosaic that could at some point in the future fit together in a more productive fashion than today's mosaic.

There are many schools in America like the one I have described. We don't want to admit it but there are. And all of us who bear professional credentials must carry that cross.

Such educational institutions are an indictment of presidents and senators; of justices and teachers; of governors and legislators. It is ludicrous the way we behave. Our pathetic politicians wailing and wringing their hands, spouting platitudes and diatribes. They advance shallow excuses. They say that bold acts will not find favor with unnamed constituencies. And we educators stand impotent, frightened, disheveled in the face of such tragedy.

REVIEW QUESTIONS

1. In the article by Jonathan Kozol and again in this one, a serious recommendation for improving the school was to burn the whole thing down. Which problems itemized by Cunningham would this strategy solve?

2. Without a ten-million-dollar replacement, what could be done to improve Cunningham's junior high school?

thirty-five

A Reappraisal of the Most Controversial Educational Document Our Time: The Coleman Report

CHRISTOPHER JENCKS

Three years have passed since James Coleman and his colleagues issued their now famous report on "Equality of Educational Opportunity." Virtually unnoticed at the time of its publication, this 737-page monograph has since become the best-known and most controversial piece of educational research of our time.

Like a veritable Bible, the "Coleman Report" is cited today on almost every side of every major educational controversy, usually by people who have not read it and almost always by people who have not understood what the authors meant when they wrote it. It has been used to support arguments for increasing integration in the schools—and to buttress the position of those who would accept segregated schools with community control. It has been cited as evidence that what black children need is good teachers—and as proof that such increases in per pupil expenditure will not close the educational gap between black and white.

The report has also inspired a growing body of scholarly exegesis, interpretation and criticism, so that anyone who wants to know what the report "really" proves must now plow through not only the baffling charts and tables of the original document but dozens of subsequent critiques and reanalyses, most of which are available only in mimeographed form to the cognoscenti. The time has clearly come for a reappraisal.

The Coleman Report was a political football from its very inception. Like much American social science, it was initiated in order to avoid confronting a difficult political problem. In the summer of 1964 Congress had decided to pass a civil-rights law which was expected to end *de jure* school segregation in the South by cutting off Federal funds from segregated systems. The question inevitably arose:

Source: From *The New York Times Magazine*, August 10, 1969, pp. 12–13, 34–38, 42. © 1969 by the New York Times Company. Reprinted by permission of the author and the publisher.

what about *de facto* segregation in the North? The expedient answer was that the Commissioner of Education should investigate the problem and report back in two years.

After nearly a year of bureaucratic squabbling and indecision in the U. S. Office of Education, Commissioner Frank Keppel decided to conduct an "Equality of Educational Opportunity" survey. The survey, theoretically covering nearly a million pupils in 6,000 different schools across the nation, was carried out in the fall of 1965. Prime responsibility for planning and analyzing it fell on James Coleman, a distinguished sociologist from Johns Hopkins University with a long record of interest in both education and survey research.

Coleman expected the survey to demonstrate three rather conventional propositions:

1. *Nonwhite pupils. North and South, usually attend different schools from white pupils.*

2. *Nonwhite schools usually have less adequate facilities, inferior curriculums and worse teachers, as well as less affluent and academically adept student bodies.*

3. *Because they attend those inferior schools, nonwhite pupils learn less than white pupils.*

The survey confirmed the first proposition. Black and white pupils are seldom in the same schools, even in the North. Not only that, but the black pupils do learn much less than the white pupils, at least judging by standardized tests of verbal and nonverbal skill, reading comprehension, arithmetic skill and general information. The typical black first grader scores below about eighty-five per cent of white first graders. This relative disparity persists throughout elementary and secondary school, and thus the absolute difference between black and white children grows wider as they grow older. A six-year-old who scores below eighty-five per cent of his classmates is about one year behind, while a sixteen-year-old is more than two years behind.

The survey did *not* support the second proposition, that black schools spend significantly less money per pupil than white ones, have substantially larger classes, get worse trained and less experienced teachers, operate in more antiquated and crowded facilities, rely on less adequate textbooks and equipment and *so* forth. On the contrary, the survey uncovered only one major measurable difference in these items between black and white schools: the black schools had more black teachers. This means that the black children's teachers also come from poorer homes and do worse on tests of academic ability. Black schools in the urban North also tended to have somewhat older buildings and smaller play areas. In other respects, however, black and white schools proved surprisingly similar. Later analyses, while largely confined to Northern urban elementary schools, have shown that schools which serve rich and poor children also have quite similar facilities, curriculums and teachers.

How could the conventional wisdom have been so wrong? The apparent answer is that claims of discrimination have usually been based on the obvious contrast between Northern ghetto schools and white schools in a few affluent nearby suburbs or in the city itself. In most (but not all) cities, the black schools get short-changed. What all such comparisons evidently ignore, however, is the fact that most white Americans live in smaller (and poorer) cities and towns, where the school facilities, curriculum and teachers evidently leave almost as much to be desired as they do in the big-city ghettos, where most blacks live.

More important, even, was the report's conclusion on the third proposition, the expected cause-and-effect relationship between inadequate school resources and low student achievement. In fact, neither black nor white children of a given family background did significantly better in schools with high expenditures, large libraries, accelerated curriculums and so forth. Coleman and his colleagues believed that pupils did slightly better in schools with experienced and articulate teachers, but even this difference was surprisingly small—and the evidence supporting their belief has subsequently proved to be rather shaky.

The report suggests—though it does not state in so many words—that black children clearly get less satisfactory schooling than white children in only one major respect. If a child happens to have a black skin, the odds are very strong that he or she will end up with classmates from impoverished homes and a plethora of learning and behavior problems. A child who attends such a school may be short-changed even if it has first-rate facilities and teachers. Most black sixth-graders, for example, attend schools in which the majority of their classmates are reading at the fourth- or fifth-grade level. This means that even if a black child has the ability to read at sixth-grade level, he will probably not be pushed to do so. The instruction in his classroom will be aimed not at him but at the laggard majority. Furthermore, there is reason to believe that children learn more from one another than from their teachers. If black children attend schools where this "informal curriculum" is based on a vocabulary half as large and on concepts far less abstract than in a white school, their chance of developing academic skills is reduced.

Coleman and his colleagues were extremely anxious to determine whether individual achievement was dependent on a school's social composition. After analyzing their data, they concluded that it was, but that a child was influenced by his classmates' social class background and aspirations rather than by their race. This implied that a poor black child would *not* benefit from attending school with poor white children, but that he *would* benefit from attending with middle-class children, black or white. Coleman and his colleagues also tentatively concluded that black children were more sensitive to peer influences than white children. This implied that a black child would benefit substantially from integration, while a white child would suffer very little. The apparent effects of integration were always small, however, relative to over-all differences in achievement between races, socio-economic groups and individuals.

If differences between schools do not account for most of the observed differences in achievement, what does? By far the most important factor measured in the survey was the ethnic and socio-economic background of the individual child. In addition, there is a strong association between children's achievement levels and their attitudes. Among black children in particular, there is a marked relationship between their achievement and their personal sense of control over their own destinies. Yet even when family background and attitudes are taken into account, more than half the variations in individual achievement remain completely unexplained. Whether this reflects unmeasured genetic differences in aptitude or unmeasured differences in environmental influence is a matter for speculation. One thing it did not seem to represent, however, was unmeasured effects of differences between school environments. The survey showed that the differences between the best and the worst pupils in the same school are invariably far larger than the difference between the best and the worst schools. Indeed, eliminating all school-to-school differences would only reduce the total variation in achievement by about twenty per cent. This does not definitely prove that schools have no role in generating inequality, since there could theoretically be systematic discrimination against certain kinds of pupils within most schools. Still, it is hard to believe that within-school differences play a large role in inequality when between-school differences play such a small role. Coleman and his colleagues therefore concluded that the major reasons for unequal academic achievement must lie outside the school.

This brief summary of the Coleman Report's major findings hardly does justice to the voluminous text, but it does suggest why the report became a major focus of political debate. The report was published at a time when America was vacillating between two different strategies for helping the disadvantaged. Some people advocated racial and socio-economic integration of the schools—and of the larger society. Others argued that integration was unattainable, undesirable or both; the only realistic strategy was to accept segregation and make black schools as good as white ones. The Coleman Report implied—though it did not say explicitly—that *neither* strategy would help achievement much. But insofar as anything was likely to work, the report seemed to indicate that integration was a better bet than what had come to be called "compensatory" education. Yet at the same time the finding that parental interest and pupil attitudes were strongly associated with achievement seemed to give oblique support to those who believed that parental participation and/or control over all-black schools might make a critical difference to student achievement.

The report's conclusions were inevitably subjected to stringent and sometimes extravagant criticism. The report had been prepared in great haste to meet the Congressional deadline, and the authors had had no time to examine many obvious objections to their tentative conclusions. Skeptics have been able to offer a variety of speculative reasons why the report's conclusions might be wrong, and those who have political reasons for wanting to discredit or ignore the report have naturally found such speculations very persuasive. For the past two years I have been part of a group of Harvard social scientists trying to determine whether any of the hypothetical objections to the report's conclusions are actually correct. My judgment is that the report's broad conclusions were sound, even though many of its specific methods and findings were wrong.

One common criticism of the survey has been that more than ten per cent of the school districts in the original sample refused to cooperate, including such major cities as Chicago and Los Angeles. Some districts evidently feared that the Federal Government would use the survey to prove they were discriminating against minority groups. Other districts—especially those being sued for *de facto* segregation—feared that minority groups would get hold of the survey results and use them in court or in the press. Some districts also feared that simply asking questions about sensitive racial issues might stir up trouble in the schools. In addition, many schools in nominally cooperative districts failed to return data because it was too much bother or perhaps—a more serious matter—because they had something to hide. As a result, complete returns were received from only about sixty per cent of the schools in the original sample.

There were clearly some small differences between participating and nonparticipating schools, and selective participation may well have led to a slight underestimate of the qualitative differences between black and white schools. But there is no reason to suppose that nonparticipation led to an underestimate of the relationship between school quality and student achievement. It hardly seems likely, for example, that the dynamics of education in Chicago and Los Angeles, which refused to participate, differ significantly from Detroit and San Francisco, which agreed to do so. On the contrary, the dynamics of education are probably much the same in one big city as in another. The problem of nonparticipation is therefore probably a nonproblem.

A second criticism of the survey has been that the information provided by the superintendents, principals, teachers and pupils in the sample schools may not have been accurate. This criticism arose largely because of doubt that black children's teachers and facilities could really be the equal of those given white children. Since the Office of Education made no site visits to check up on the accuracy of replies given by principals and teachers, no definite answer to this charge is possible. Data supplied by state departments of education suggest, however, that the principals' replies about facilities were probably fairly accurate. Direct interviewing of parents in two communities likewise showed that most (though not all) of the pupils' responses were reasonably accurate. And the replies of principals, teachers and students to similar questions show a fairly high level of internal consistency for most "objective" items. On the other hand, questions which involved subjective judgment of any kind did *not* elicit internally consistent answers. The results of such subjective "attitude" questions must therefore be treated with great caution.

A third criticism of the report has been that the authors should not have concentrated on the determinants of verbal ability to the exclusion of reading, mathematics and general information. Those who believe that black people are peculiarly "nonverbal" have even argued that the decision to stress verbal ability was fundamentally racist. Unfortunately, black children did as badly on the tests of other abilities as on the verbal tests. Furthermore, while some individual children did well on one test and badly on another, schools as a whole either did well on them all or badly on them all. A Northern urban elementary school's mean verbal score, for example, correlated almost perfectly with its mean reading and math scores. Under these circumstances it hardly matters which test we use to measure over-all school achievement.

A fourth line of attack on the report has been more technical. The authors of the report employed a number of dubious statistical techniques and made a variety of mechanical errors in handling and labeling their data. But they also recognized that such errors were likely, given the extreme haste with which they worked, and they were generous in helping others reanalyze the data more meticulously. These analyses have shown that while the report's broadest conclusions were correct, many important details were wrong. In particular, and contrary to what some critics have argued, the net effect of the report's various errors was to *under*-estimate the importance of family background and *over*-estimate the importance of school in determining achievement.

A fifth criticism of the report has been that the authors made unwarranted causal inferences from their one-shot survey, which by its very nature could reveal only patterns of association rather than prove causation. Two examples illustrate the problem.

The report uncovered a strong association between teacher verbal ability and student achievement in secondary schools. Though they listed a number of qualifications, the authors concluded that able high school teachers probably boosted student achievement. Yet the report's data could equally well lead to the conclusion that school systems were assigning able students to schools with able teachers, or that they were assigning able teachers to schools with able pupils. Since we know from experience that both practices are widespread at the secondary level, it seems rash to assume that there need be any direct causal link between teacher ability and student achievement to explain the observed association between the two.

Fortunately, these problems are far less serious at the elementary level. Students are allocated to elementary schools largely on the basis of residence, race and social status, all of which were measured in the survey. With luck and ingenuity the effects of such allocation can be discounted and the effects of various school characteristics can then be estimated. Since there is little evidence that student transfers at the elementary school level are based on ability (as distinct from family background), the mean achievement of first-graders entering a given elementary school can also be used to estimate the mean initial ability of sixth-graders in the same school. With these precautions, causal inferences are considerably safer than at the secondary level; and when these precautions are taken, it turns out that facilities, curriculum and teacher characteristics are even less important than Coleman and his colleagues supposed. A student's peers may, however, have a modest effect on his achievement.

Another instance of ambiguous causation was the association between attitudes and achievement. The survey showed, for example, that students who did well on achievement tests were more likely to say that their parents expected them to go to college. The authors concluded that parental expectations probably had an important influence on children's achievement. Yet it would be equally reasonable to conclude that children's achievement had an important influence on their parent's expectations. Most parents know that if their child cannot read competently he is unlikely to attend college, and the child is likely to be aware of this attitude and report it when asked. This same difficulty arises with all the report's inferences about the effects of attitudes on achievement.

What, then is the present consensus about the policy implications of Coleman's survey? The answer is that no consensus exists, even among experts. My own judgments are as follows:

1. The resources—both fiscal and human—devoted to black and white children's schooling are not dramatically different, except perhaps in certain parts of the South. Nor do we devote substantially greater resources to educating middle-class children than to educating lower-class children.

2. Variations in schools' fiscal and human resources have very little effect on student achievement—probably even less than the Coleman Report originally implied.

3. The report's assertion that peers have a consistent effect on achievement may or may not be correct. My guess, based on available data, is that peers *do* have an effect, but that it is relatively small.

None of this denies that unusually dedicated and talented individuals can create schools in which initially disadvantaged children learn a remarkable amount. But it does deny that the achievement levels of large numbers of disadvantaged children can be appreciably enhanced by spending more money, hiring better teachers, buying new textbooks or making any of the other changes that reformers normally advocate.

If improved student achievement is our goal, the Coleman Report's implication is obvious: we must alter the whole social system rather than just tinker with the schools. There is plenty of evidence that major changes in a child's social and cultural environment will affect his intellectual development, often dramatically. Bruno Bettelheim and others have chronicled the impact of the Israeli kibbutz on hitherto deprived North African and Yemenite Jews. Here in America we know that children raised on Long Island do far better, even in first grade, than those raised in Appalachia. Similarly, children raised in Jewish homes do better than those raised in Christian homes, even in the same city. And the World War II draftees who grew up in the America of 1917–1941 did far better on standard tests than the World War I draftees who grew up in the America of 1900–1917. Intellectual skills are, therefore, not just a function of genetic differences. But neither are they a function of school differences. If the Coleman survey convinces us of that basic truth, it will have served its purpose.

Does this mean that we should simply let inferior schools rot? I think not. Good schools *can* make a difference—if we know what kind of a difference we want them to make.

Underlying the comments of most people who discuss the Coleman Report is the assumption that academic achievement is the most important objective of schooling, and that if school reform does not affect achievement, it is worthless.

Yet despite much popular rhetoric, there is little evidence that academic competence is critically important to adults in most walks of life. If you ask employers why they won't hire dropouts, for example, or why they promote certain kinds of people and not others, they seldom complain that dropouts can't read. Instead, they complain that dropouts don't get to work on time, can't be counted on to do a careful job, don't get along with others in the plant or office, can't be trusted to keep their hands out of the till and so on. Nor do the available survey data suggest that the adult success of people from disadvantaged backgrounds depends primarily on their intellectual skills. If you compare black men who do well on the Armed Forces Qualifications Test to those who do badly, for example, you find that a black man who scores as high as the average white still earns only about two-thirds what the average white earns. Not only that, he hardly earns more than the average black. Even for whites, the mental abilities measured by the A.F.Q.T. account for less than a tenth of the variation in earnings.

With these observations in mind, go visit a slum school and ask yourself what the school is actually doing. You will usually find that it seems to share the employers' priorities. It devotes very little time to academic skills. Instead, the teachers spend their days in a vain effort to teach the children to behave in what they (and probably most employers) regard as the proper way. The teachers' ideas about proper behavior are silly in some respects. Nonetheless, they are probably right in feeling that what their children need first and foremost is not academic skill but such "middle-class" virtues as self-discipline and self-respect. It is the school's failure to develop these personal characteristics, not its failure to teach history or physics or verbal skill, that lies behind the present upheavals in the schools. And it is this failure to which reformers should be addressing themselves.

From this perspective the best index of a school's success or failure may not be reading scores but the number of rocks thrown through its windows in an average month. The Coleman survey does not speak to this question.

REVIEW QUESTIONS

1. True or false:
    a. Overall, black schools spend less money per pupil than white schools.
    b. Schools for black and white children have similar facilities, curricula, and teachers.
    c. A normal sixth-grade black child may be slowed down because teaching is geared to his slower-reading classmates.
    d. The social-class background and the aspirations of classmates are more important than race or school expenditures in determining achievement.
    e. Differences between pupils in a given school are larger than the average differences between schools.

   f. The author did not feel that the refusal to cooperate of school districts in Los Angeles, Chicago, and other big cities was a significant problem.

   g. The broad conclusions of the Coleman Report are basically correct.

   h. Academic skills are more important for job success than personal characteristics.

2.   Jencks suggests the best solution is to alter the whole social system. How would this influence the individual black child? Is the social system changing in the right direction?

Answers to question 1: a. false, b. true, c. true, d. true, e. true, f. true, g. true, h. false.

thirty-six

"What My Block Is Like" from *36 Children*

HERBERT KOHL

I would arrive at the school at eight. Several of the children would be waiting and we would walk the five flights up to the room. One of the boys would take my briefcase, another the keys. Once in the room the children went their own ways. Maurice and Michael went to the phonograph, Alvin to his latest project with Robert Jackson. The girls would play jacks or wash the boards. Grace explored the books on my desk. Every once in a while one of the children would come up to my desk and ask a question or tell me something. The room warmed up to the children, got ready for the day. At first the questions were simple, irrelevant.

"Mr. Kohl, what's today's date?"

"Where is Charles this morning?"

Then there was some testing.

"Mr. Kohl, when are you going to be absent?"

"Will you come back here next year?"

By the end of October a few children were coming to my desk in the morning and saying things that nothing in my life prepared me to understand or respond to.

"Mr. Kohl, the junkies had a fight last night. They cut this girl up bad."

"Mr. Kohl, I couldn't sleep last night, they was shouting and screaming until four o'clock."

"I don't go down to the streets to play, it's not safe."

"Mr. Kohl, those cops are no good. They beat up on this kid for nothing last night."

I listened, hurt, bruised by the harshness of the children's world. There was no response, no indignation or anger of mine, commensurate to what the children felt. Besides, it was relief they wanted, pronouncement of the truth, acceptance of it in a classroom which had become important to them. I could do nothing about the facts, therefore my words were useless. But through listening, the facts remained open and therefore placed school in the context of the children's real world.

At eight o'clock on October 22, Alvin pushed Ralph up to my desk. Ralph handed me "The Rob-Killing of Liebowitz," and retreated.

> Last night on 17 St. Liebowitz collected the rent. They told him not to come himself but he came for many years. The junkies got him last night. He wouldn't give them the money so they shot him and took it. They was cops and people runny all over roofs and the streets.
>
> There were people from the news and an ambulance took Liebowitz.

I read Ralph's article to the class and asked them if it were true. There was an awkward silence, then Neomia said with bitterness:

"If you don't believe it you can look in the *Daily News*."

"Mr. Kohl, you don't know what it's like around here."

The others agreed, but when I pressed the class to tell me, silence returned. The more I tried to get the class to talk the dumber the children acted, until they finally denied that there was any truth in Robert's article whatever. The topic was too charged for public discussion; it somehow had to be made private, between each individual child and myself. After all, not everybody saw the same things, and worse perhaps, if things were so bad it would be natural for some of the children to be afraid. So I asked the class to write, as homework in the privacy of their apartments, and tell me what their block was like, what they felt about it. The papers were not to be marked or shown to anybody else in the class. If anybody objected, he didn't have to do the assignment. This was probably the first time in their school lives that the children wrote to communicate, and the first sense they had of the possibilities of their own writing.

The next evening I read the responses.

Neomia   WHAT A BLOCK!

My block is the most terrible block I've ever seen. There are at least 25 or 30 narcartic people in my block. The cops come around there and tries to act bad but I bet inside of them they are as scared as can be. They even had in the papers that this block is the worst block, not in Manhattan but in New York City. In the summer they don't do nothing except shooting, stabbing and fighting. They hang all over the stoops and when you say excuse me to them they hear you but they just don't feel like moving. Some times they make me so mad that I feel like slaping them and stuffing and bag of garbage down their throats. Theres only one policeman who can handle these people and we all call him "Sunny." When he come around in his cop car the people run around the corners, and he wont let anyone sit on the stoops. If you don't believe this story come around some time and you'll find out.

Marie

My block is the worse block you ever saw people getting killed or stabbed men and women in building's taking dope. And when the police come around the block the block be so clean that nobody will get hurt. There's especially one police you even beat woman you can't even stand on your own stoop he'll chase you off. And sometimes the patrol wagon comes around and pick up al the dope addicts and one day they picked up this man and when his wife saw him and when she went to tell the police that that's her husband they just left so she went to the police station and they let him go. You can never trust anyone around my block you even get robbed when the children in my building ask me to come down stairs I say no because you don't know what would happen. Only sometimes I come down stairs not all the time.

Sonia THE STORY ABOUT MY BLOCK

My block is dirty and it smell terrible
The children picks fights. And it hardly have room to play. Its not a very long thing to write about, but if you were living there you won't want to stay there no longer. it have doopedics and gabbage pan is spill on the side walk and food is on the ground not everyday but sometimes children make fire in the backyard. on the stoop is dirty. I go out to play that the End about My block.

Phyllis MY BLOCK

My block has a lot of kids who thing that the can beat everybody (like a lot of blocks) They pick on children that they know they can beat. There trouble makers and blabbers mouths.

Charisse MY BLOCK

I live 62 E 120st My neighborhood is not so bad. Everyone has children in the block. Many of the children are Spanish. Some of them run around nude and dirty. Some of the house are so dirty you would be sacre to come in the door. Sometime the drunks come out and fight. Some of the house are nice and clean. The block is not to dirty its the people inside of it. At night it's very quite. But if you come in my building at about 10:00 you would be surprised to see some naked children running around like animals. The mothers don't even seem to care about them. Many of the children ages run from 1 to 4 years of age. Many of the people in the block drink so much they don't have time for the children. The children have no place to play they have the park but the parents don't care enough to take them. Now you have a idea of what my block is like.

Ralph MY NEIGHBORHOOD

I live on 117 street, between Madison and 5th avenue. All the bums live around here. But the truth is they don't live here they just hang around the street. All the kids call it "Junky's Paradise." Because there is no cops to stop them. I wish that the cops would come around and put all the bums out of the block and put them in jail all their life. I would really like it very much if they would improve my neighborhood. I don't even go outside to play because of them. I just play at the center or someplace else.

Gail MY BLOCK

My block is sometimes noisy and sometimes quiet when its noisy children and grownups are out side listening to the boys playing the steel drums or there's a boy who got hit by a car or something. When the block is quiet, there is a storm, raining or snowing and people don't come out side. Farther down the block near Park Avenue, some of the houses are not kept clean.

There's a lot right next to a building and there's a lot of trash, you can see rats running back and forth. The Sanitation Department cleans it every week, but it just gets dirty again because people throw garbage out the windows. From Madison Ave. to about the middle of the block the houses are kept clean. The back yards are keep swept and the stoops are clean. I like my building and block.

Carol

Around my block all you can see is drug addits. The other day the Cops came and took over 15 men in the cops wagon and they came out the next day but one man shim they kept him beated him from 7 in the morning until 1:30 in the afternoon because they thought he had something to do with the Rob Killing of Lebrowize.

Ronnie

I think my block is not as lively as it use to be cause all the jive time people are moving out. I think my block is nice compare to 117 St were people be getting kill.

Charles

My block is a dirty crumby block.

Thomas S.

Ounce their was a gang fight around my block and the police came and a man got shot. And their was detives around my block and junkies shot at a copes and a lady curse out the copes and they broke in a lady house. Around 119 street a cop was bricked and kill and junkies took dop and needles.

Kathleen   ABOUT MY BLOCK

Around my block theirs no trees on the side walks like the Park on the outside but of course theres not going to be any trees on the side walks but there are some trees on the side walks mabe in brooklyn or long island. New Jersey and Queens but I know there are some in long island I know that because thats like a little country in some parts of it. And around my block I have nice friends and nice neighbors of my mother, people are nice around my block I go to Church with my friends and we all go together and learn more and more about God and I like it very much Because when I grow up to be a lady (if I live to see and if gods willing) and know all about God and understand the facts I want to be a nice mannered lady and go to church as long as I live to see.

The day after we talked about them. I had asked for the truth, and it presented its ugly head in the classroom, yet I didn't know what to do about it. That was all

I could say to the children—that I was moved, angry, yet as powerless to change things as they were. I remembered How We Became Modern America, the books I couldn't use, and felt dumb, expressionless—how else can one put up with such lies of progress, prosperity, and cheerful cooperation when we do face problems. The next day the children wrote of how they would change things if they could.

Thomas S.   IF I COULD CHANGE MY BLOCK

If I could change my block, I would first get read of all of the wine heads and clean up the gobash and then try to improve the buildings and paint the apartments. That's what I would do.

Neomia

If I could change my block I would stand on Madison Ave and throw nothing But Teargas in it. I would have all the people I liked to get out of the block and then I would become very tall and have big hands and with my big hands I would take all of the narcartic people and pick them up with my hand and throw them in the nearest river and Oceans. I would go to some of those old smart alic cops and throw them in the Oceans and Rivers too. I would let the people I like move into the projects so they could tell their friends that they live in a decent block. If I could do this you would never see 117 st again.

Kathleen   MY BLOCK

If I could change my block I would have new house but in it I would have all the bums take out of it. There would be garden where I live. There would be some white people live there we would have all colors not just Negro. There would be 7 room apt. There be low rent for the poor family. The poor family would have the same thing as the average or rich family have. There would be club for the boys and girls. There would be place where the Old could come. Where the young can share there problem

Brenda T.

If I could change my block I would put all the bums on an Island where they can work there. I would give them lots of food. But I wouldn't let no whiskey be brought to them. After a year I would ship them to new York and make them clean up junk in these back yard and make them maybe make a baseball diamond and put swings basketball courts etc. When I get thought they'll never want whiskey or dope cause If I catch them I'll make a them work day and night with little food. Lunch would be at 5:00 super 10:00 bed 1:00 (If caught 2 times) breakfast 8:30. Get up at 3:00

Marie   HOW I WOULD CHANGE MY BLOCK

If I could change my block I would take out all of the junkies and I would take out all of the old buildings and put in new ones and give hot water every day and make a play street out of my block.

That's what I would do if I could

Thomas C.

Well I would like to change my block into a play street, first I'd take all the junkies out the block and take the parking cars out the block and make whaw that everyman put their cars in a garage at nights. Because too many children get hit by cars and make all the buildings neat and clean with stream and hot and cold water.

Anastasia

The very first thing that I would like to do to change my block if I could, put up a no litering sign to keep away stange people who hang aroung the steps. Nexs I would have less garbage containers on the sidewalks, especially those that are uncovered because they are unsightly and unhealthy, and last bus at least. I would make a carfew at least 5 p.m. for ander age children to be upt the corners, sidewalks, and if they are not, hold their parents severly responsible for any harm that befails them.

Charles

If I could do anything to chang my block tear down the buildings on both sides. And have a school on one side and a center on the other. Inside the center there would be a swimming pool inside and also a gym. And outside a softball field and also four baskball courts.

Sonia

if I could of change my block I would make it cleaner no gabbage pans open and falling down and not so many fights and don't let it have dead animals in the street.

thirty-seven

"Hi Teach!" from
Up the Down Staircase

BEL KAUFMAN

Hi, teach!
Looka *her!* She's a teacher?
Who she?
Is this 304? Are you Mr. Barringer?
No. I'm Miss Barrett.
I'm supposed to have Mr. Barringer.
I'm Miss Barrett.
You the teacher? You so young.
Hey she's cute! Hey, teach, can I be in your class?
Please don't block the doorway. Please come in.
Good afternoon, Miss Barnet.
Miss Barrett. My name is on the blackboard. Good morning.
O, no! A *dame* for homeroom?
You want I should slug him, teach?
Is this homeroom period?
Yes. Sit down, please.
I don't belong here.
We gonna have you all term? Are you a regular or a sub?
There's not enough chairs!
Take any seat at all.
Hey, where do we sit?
Is this 309?
Someone swiped the pass. Can I have a pass?
What's your name?
My name is on the board.
I can't read your writing.

Source: From the book *Up the Down Staircase* by Bel Kaufman. © 1964 by Bel Kaufman.
Published by Prentice-Hall, Inc., Englewood Cliffs, New Jersey, and McIntosh and Otis, Inc.

I gotta go to the nurse. I'm dying.

Don't believe him, teach. He ain't dying!

Can I sharpen my pencil in the office?

Why don't you leave the teacher alone, you bums?

Can we sit on the radiator? That's what we did last term.

Hi, teach! You the homeroom?

Pipe down, you morons! Don't you see the teacher's trying to say something?

Please sit down. I'd like to——

Hey, the bell just rung!

How come Mrs. Singer's not here? She was in this room last term.

When do we go home?

The first day of school, he wants to go home already!

That bell is your signal to come to order. Will you please——

Can I have a pass to a drink of water?

You want me to alphabetize for you?

What room is this?

This is room 304. My name is on the board: Miss Barrett. I'll have you for homeroom all term, and I hope to meet some of you in my English classes. Now, someone once said that first impressions——

English! No wonder!

Who needs it?

You give homework?

First impressions, they say, are lasting. What do we base our first——Yes? Do you belong in this class?

No. Mr. McHabe wants Ferone right away.

Who?

McHabe.

Whom does he want?

Joe Ferone.

Is Joe Ferone here?

Him? That's a laugh!

He'll show up when he feels like it.

Put down that window-pole, please. We all know that first impressions——Yes?

Is this 304?

Yes. You're late.

I'm not late. I'm absent.

You are?

I was absent all last term.

Well—sit down.

I can't. I'm dropping out. You're supposed to sign my Book Clearance from last term.

Do you owe any books?

I'm not on the Blacklist! That's a yellow slip. This here is a green!

Hey, isn't the pass back yet?

Quit your shoving!

He started it, teach!

I'd like you to come to order, please. I'm afraid we won't have time for the discussion on first impressions I had planned. I'm passing out——

Hey, she's passing out!

Give her air!

——Delaney cards. You are to fill them out at once while I take attendance from the Roll Book. Standees—line up in back of the room; you may lean on the wall to write. Print, in ink, your last name first, your parent's name, your date of birth, your address, my name—it's on the board—and the same upside down. I'll make out a seating plan in the Delaney Book. Any questions?

In ink or pencil?

I got no ink—can I use pencil? Who's got a pencil to loan me?

I don't remember when I was born.

Don't mind him—he's a comic.

Print or write?

When do we go to lunch?

I can't write upside down!

Ha-Ha. He kills me laughing!

What do you need my address for? My father can't come.

Someone robbed my ball-point!

I can't do it—I lost my glasses.

Are these going to be our regular seats—the *radiator?*

I don't know my address—we're moving.

Where are you moving?

I don't know where.

Where do you live?

I don't live no place.

Any place. You, young man, why are you late?

I'm not even here. I'm in Mr. Loomis. My uncle's in this class. He forgot his lunch. Hi, Tony—catch!

Please don't throw—Yes, what is it?

This Mrs. Singer's room?

Yes. No. Not anymore.

Anyone find a sneaker from last term?

Hey, teach, can we use a pencil?

You want these filled out *now?*

There's chewing gum on my seat!

First name last or last name first?

I *gotta* have a pass to the Men's Room. I know my rights; this is a democracy, ain't it?

Isn't—What's the trouble now?

There's glass all over my desk from the window.

Please don't do that. Don't touch that broken window. It should be reported to the custodian. Does anyone——

I'll go!

Me! Let *me* go! That's Mr. Grayson—I know where he is in the basement!
All right. Tell him it's urgent. And who are you?
I'm sorry I'm late. I was in Detention.
The what?
The Late Room. Where they make you sit to make up your lateness when you come late.
All right, sit down. I mean, stand up—over there, against the wall.
For parent's name, can I use my aunt?
Put down your mother's name.
I got no mother.
Well—do the best you can. Yes, young lady?
The office sent me. Read this to your class and sign here.
May I have your attention, please. Please, class!
There's been a change in today's assembly schedule. Listen carefully:

PLEASE IGNORE PREVIOUS INSTRUCTIONS IN CIRCULAR #3, PARAGRAPHS 5 AND 6, AND FOLLOW THE FOLLOWING:
THIS MORNING THERE WILL BE A LONG HOMEROOM PERIOD EXTENDING INTO THE FIRST HALF OF THE SECOND PERIOD. ALL X2 SECTIONS ARE TO REPORT TO ASSEMBLY THE SECOND HALF OF THE SECOND PERIOD. FIRST PERIOD CLASSES WILL BEGIN THE FOURTH PERIOD, SECOND PERIOD CLASSES WILL BEGIN THE FIFTH PERIOD, THIRD PERIOD CLASSES WILL BEGIN THE SIXTH PERIOD, AND SO ON, SUBJECT CLASSES BEING SHORTENED TO 23 MINUTES IN LENGTH, EXCEPT LUNCH, WHICH WILL BE NORMAL.

I can't hear you—what did you say?
They're drilling on the street!
Close the window.
I can't—I'll suffocate!
This is a long homeroom?
What's today's date?
It's September, stupid!
Your attention, please. I'm not finished.

SINCE IT IS DIFFICULT TO PROVIDE ADEQUATE SEATING SPACE FOR ALL STUDENTS UNDER EXISTING FACILITIES, THE OVER-FLOW IS TO STAND IN THE AISLES UNTIL THE SALUTE TO THE FLAG AND THE STAR-SPANGLED BANNER ARE COMPLETED, AFTER WHICH THE OVERFLOW MAY NOT REMAIN STANDING IN THE AISLES UNLESS SO DIRECTED FROM THE PLATFORM. THIS IS A FIRE LAW. DR. CLARKE WILL EXTEND A WARM WELCOME TO ALL NEW STUDENTS; HIS TOPIC WILL BE "OUR CULTURAL HERITAGE." ANY STUDENT FOUND TALKING OR EATING LUNCH IN ASSSEM-BLY IS TO BE REPORTED AT ONCE TO MR. McHABE.

Water! I gotta have water! My throat is parching!
He thinks he's funny!

May I have your attention?
No!

TOMORROW ALL Y2 SECTIONS WILL FOLLOW TODAY'S PROGRAM
FOR X2 SECTIONS WHILE ALL X2 SECTIONS WILL FOLLOW TO-
DAY'S PROGRAM FOR Y2 SECTIONS.

Where do we go?
What period is this?
The two boys in the back—stop throwing that board eraser. Please come to order;
there's more:
Is this assembly day?

BE SURE TO USE THE ROWS ASSIGNED TO YOU: THERE IS TO BE
NO SUBSTITUTION.

Excuse me, I'm from Guidance. Miss Friedenberg wants Joe Ferone right
away.
He isn't here. Will you pass your Delaney cards down, please, while I——
I didn't start yet! I'm waiting for the pen.
How do you spell your name?
Hey, he threw the board eraser out the window!
Will you please——
Here's my admit. He says I was loitering.
Who?
McHabe.
Mr. McHabe.
Either way.
Now class, please finish your Delaney cards while I call the roll.
I didn't finish!
I never got no Delaney!
Any. Yes?
Mr. Manheim next door wants to borrow your board eraser.
I'm afraid it's gone. Please, class———
You give extra credit for alphabetizing?
We go to assembly today?
You want me to go down for the stuff from your letter-box, Miss Barnet?
All right. Now we'll just have to——
I can't write—I got a bum hand.
You gonna be our teacher?
Please come to order while I take attendance. And correct me if I mispronounce
your name; I know how annoying that can be. I hope to get to know all of you
soon. Abrams, Harry?
Here.
Quiet, please, so I can hear you. Allen, Frank?
Absent.

Absent?

He ain't here.

Isn't. Amdur, Janet?

Here.

Mr. Grayson says there's no one down there.

How can he say that when he's there?

That's what he says. Any answer?

No. Amdur, Janet?

I was here already.

Arbuzzi, Vincent? Yes, what do I have to sign now?

Nothing. I came back from the bathroom.

Can I have the pass?

Me, I'm next!

I said it first!

Blake, Alice?

I'm present, Miss Barrett.

Blanca, Carmelita?

Carole. I changed my name.

Blanca, Carole

Here.

Borden——Yes?

Miss Finch wants you to make this out right away.

I'm in the middle of taking attendance. Borden——

She needs it right away.

Excuse me, class.

IN THE TWO COLUMNS LABELED MALE AND FEMALE, INDICATE
THE NUMBER OF STUDENTS IN YOUR HOMEROOM SECTION
BORN BETWEEN THE FOLLOWING DATES—

Please don't tilt that chair____Boy in the back__I'm talking to you____Oh!

So I fell. Big deal. Stop laughing, you bums, or I'll knock your brains out!

Are you hurt?

Naw, just my head.

You've got to make out an accident report, Miss Barrett, three copies, and
send him to the nurse.

Aw, she ain't even allowed to give out aspirins.

Only tea.

Get your feet offa me!

You call this a *chair?*

He can sue the whole Board of Education!

Perhaps you'd better go to the nurse. And ask her for the accident report blanks.

Yes, what can I do for you?

Miss Friedenberg wants last term's Service Credit cards.

I wasn't here last term. And what do you want?

Miss Finch is waiting for the attendance reports and absentee cards.
I'm in the middle of——Yes?
The office wants to know are the transportation cards ready?
The what cards?
Bus and subway.
No. Yes?
You're supposed to read this to the class. It's from the liberry.
Library. May I have your attention, please?

THE SCHOOL LIBRARY IS YOUR LIBRARY. ALL STUDENTS ARE ENCOURAGED TO USE IT AT ALL TIMES.

STUDENTS ON THE LIBRARY BLACKLIST ARE NOT TO RECEIVE THEIR PROGRAM CARDS UNTIL THEY HAVE PAID FOR LOST OR MUTILATED BOOKS.

THE LIBRARY WILL BE CLOSED TO STUDENTS UNTIL FURTHER NOTICE TO ENABLE TEACHERS TO USE IT AS A WORKROOM FOR THEIR PRC ENTRIES.

Yes, who sent you here?
You did. Here's the stuff from your letter-box.
Where do I dump it?
Is that all for me?
Excuse me, the nurse says she's all out of accident reports, but she wants the missing dentals.
The missing what?
Dental notes.
I see. And what is it you want?
New change in assembly program. Your class goes to different rows. X2 schedule rows.
I see. And you?
Mr. McHabe says do you need any posters for your room decoration?
Tell Mr. McHabe what I really need is——Yes?
The office wants the list of locker numbers for each student.
I haven't even——Yes?
This is urgent. You're supposed to read and sign.

TO ALL TEACHERS: A BLUE PONTIAC PARKED IN FRONT OF SCHOOL HAS BEEN OVERTURNED BY SOME STUDENTS. IF THE FOLLOWING LICENSE IS YOURS—

Tell Mr. McHabe I don't drive. Now, class——
Hurray! Saved by the bell!
Just a minute—the bell seems to be fifteen minutes early. It may be a mistake.
We have so much to——Please remain in your——
That's the bell! You heard it!

All the other teachers are letting them out!
But we must finish the——
When the bell rings, we're supposed to *go!*
Where do we go, assembly?
Please sit down. I'd like to____We haven't____Well. It looks as if you and I are the only ones left. Your name is____?
Alice Blake, Miss Barrett. I just wanted you to know how much I enjoyed your lesson.
Thank you, but it wasn't really a——*Yes, young lady?*
I'm from the office. She says to announce this to your class right away.

PLEASE DISREGARD THE BELLS. STUDENTS ARE TO REMAIN IN THEIR HOMEROOMS UNTIL THE WARNING BELL RINGS.

I'm afraid they've all gone.
I've got to go too, Miss Barrett. I wish I had *you* for English, but my program says Mr. Barringer.
I'm sure he's a fine teacher, Alice, and that you'll do well with him.
You Barrett?
What's that, young man?
Late pass.
That's no way to hand it to me. Throwing it like that on my desk——
My aim is bad.
There's no need for insolence. Please take that toothpick out of your mouth when you talk to me. And take your hands out of your pockets.
Which first?
What's your name?
You gonna report me?
What's your name?
You gonna give me a zero?
I'm afraid I've had just about——*What's your name?*
Joe.
Joe what?
Ferone. You gonna send a letter home? Take away my lollipop? Lecture me? Spank me?
All I asked——
Yeah. All you asked.
I don't allow anyone to talk to me like that.
So you're lucky—you're a teacher!

thirty-eight

Psychological Health of the Poor

STANLEY CHARNOFSKY

Minstrel Man*

Because my mouth
Is wide with laughter
And my throat
Is deep with song,
You do not think
I suffer after
I have held my pain
So long?

Because my mouth
Is wide with laughter
You do not hear
My inner cry?
Because my feet
Are gay with dancing
You do not know
I die?

Classic studies of behavior patterns of people who live in poverty emphasize the incidence of measurable neuroses or psychoses compared to the middle-class or upper-class populations. Statistical studies [Hollingshead and Redlick, 1958] have implied greater psychoses among people in Class V (lower class) and greater neuroses among people in Classes I and II (upper classes). Other researchers [Miller and Mishler, 1964] have challenged such findings by computing the data

Source: From *Educating the Powerless* by Stanley Charnofsky. © 1971 by Wadsworth Publishing Company, Inc., Belmont, California 94002. Reprinted by permission of the author and the publisher.

*From *The Dream Keeper and Other Poems* by Langston Hughes. Copyright 1932 by Alfred A. Knopf, Inc., renewed 1960 by Langston Hughes. Reprinted by permission of the publisher.

from different angles and with different statistical devices. In short, there is not complete agreement about psychological health or its lack among people of poverty. One finds himself examining carefully the numerous definitions of "health." Rather than employing the standard definitions of mental illness or mental health, we shall consider the situation from a very practical, nonmedical viewpoint. We shall define mental (psychological) health to be: living with a minimum of personal and social disorder, functioning with some personal satisfaction, and containing a self-concept that is adequate and dynamic.

But phrased thusly, and without further clarification, it is also easy to see how people of poverty could be considered, in many instances, as generally rather less than psychologically healthy. The hypothesis could be presented that the psychological health of any subgroup, measured within, and compared to, a given culture, can be made to appear poor because of, *ipso facto,* the definitions of good and poor health: Those are healthy who are in harmony with the social order and those are not who are in disharmony.

This, however, can also be simplistic if not carefully analyzed. Our above definition of good health emphasizes the individual's personal (phenomenological) conceptualizing of himself as a human being of worth and value. While this certainly cannot be done independent of a social order, it can be done *despite* the values of a given social order. A person of poverty, then, feeling himself rejected by the larger culture could *still* be psychologically healthy by identifying his "self" and his behavior with other reference groups or subcultures. The angry and militant black nationalist groups, by these definitions, serve a valuable function in providing one segment of the society with a meaningful identification.

We are saying that the poverty-stricken individual, despite alienation from the culture at large, can be in a state of satisfactory equilibrium with himself through some felt relationship to a subsegment of the culture. But we must also ask how long the person can tolerate the rejection by the larger culture, and when and in what form he begins to manifest signs of alienation, disorder, and unhappiness within himself, and a subsequent failure to function in a progressive, fulfilling way. We also ask how many people of poverty do *indeed* have any kind of reference group with which they can identify and which can give them meaningful social involvement. This will not be discussed in a statistical sense, nor with psychiatric labels. Rather, we shall explore the functional equality of people in poverty as they are forced to react to and interact with the prejudices, controls, power, bureaucracies, politics, economics, and general whimsy of the American scene.

THE FEELING OF ADEQUACY

Most people who live in poverty just don't think very much of themselves. There are many confusing, complicated reasons for this, a significant one being the message they are constantly getting from the culture at large. It was noted earlier that mass communication offers opportunities for instant comparisons.

People of poverty can see at a glance the accumulation of goods the larger culture enjoys; but even more significant, they can see and hear and feel the thematic pertinence of most of the shows and stories and games that television and theaters present. The irrelevance of much of this material to the lives of most of the ghetto viewers is instantly apparent. The pervasive domestic situation comedies, for example, are saying: "Here are the tricky and superficial problems that an affluent family spends its time confronting." And they are also saying: "*You* do not spend your time at these problems because you cannot gain the position that permits you to engage in such leisure-time tomfoolery."

But even more profound is the message that the bureaucratic structure pumps out with unending regularity; a message which is, indeed, becoming so complex that to be able to cope adequately, the standard requirement, even for middle-class citizens, has become a college degree. The bureaucracies confound, frustrate, humiliate, and degrade the poor. The poor are managed, manipulated, and chastised for not knowing, and criticized for not being industrious. They avoid the bureaucracy and are accused of law breaking. They confront it and are exploited. The result is a totally helpless feeling—a feeling of inadequacy.

I made a rather significant personal discovery a short while back, while working as a counseling psychologist in a college counseling center. In the course of a year, of some sixty student-clients who came for academic-personal counseling, virtually everyone seemed to have a "hang-up" on some sexual problem, either guilt feelings for too much sexual activity, or panic because of fear of the opposite sex. The evidence seemed to show that Freud was indeed correct: Sex is the basic human motivation.

But upon deeper reflection and a more critical case-analysis approach, it soon became clear that in *every* case, the young man or woman did not think very much of himself. He did not like himself very much, he could not cope well, he did not feel very adequate. This saturated all areas of his life, including the sexual, which at that age (18–25) is certainly at a high-energy point. I found that to approach these clients' problems as basically sexual did little to raise their level of personal confidence and ability to function dynamically. Approaching the problems as more general feelings of inadequacy opened the clients to a self-investigation that seemed, empirically, to direct them to fuller personal lives.

The hypothesis that emerges herein parallels much that is being said about the poor and the powerless. The feeling of inadequacy seems to saturate their lives and to restrict their functioning at high levels of personal achievement and satisfaction.

But *inadequate* is really another way of saying *powerless*. If we reason carefully it may be seen that when a person is feeling better about himself, he is feeling some control over a given area of his human activity. The more areas he feels adequate in, the more control he has over his performance—the more he has power.

Of course, with our college students, the opportunity to gain feelings of adequacy and to have power over their activities was interpersonal in nature and was available so long as the contaminating personal relationships could be confronted.

With powerless people of poverty, the avenue to adequacy is less personally available; the relationship is more cultural-personal and less interpersonal. . . . Through its oppression and complexity, the culture imposes upon its poor a feeling of inadequacy, and the way to better functioning is impeded by the refusal of those who have power to relinquish it.

The psychological health of the poor, then, can be considered in relationship to their opportunity for meaningful control over their own lives. And if the larger culture denies them this, the poor must seek alternatives. One of these is to ignore the larger culture and commit themselves to their own, internally defined, internally rewarding subculture. A corollary is to reject and condemn that culture which has denied them access and personal enhancement: And so the "revolution of the urban poor."

But are the poor uniformly in poor psychological health? They can find adequacy and, therefore, some sense of power, by identification with and subsequent reward from groups and causes germane to the urban poverty condition. This can give the committed poor psychological health. But those poor who have no reference group, who have no basis for self-identification, who suffer from "anomie," who feel inadequate and powerless to confront the daily struggle, are indeed suffering from poor psychological health. (It must be reemphasized here that the imputation of personal, genetic, hereditary, congenital, or ethnic inadequacy is totally rejected; our thesis holds that the urban slum dweller is psychologically inadequate in direct relationship to the environmental control he is experiencing.) The implications for educating the poor in our public schools that stem from this notion are enormous.

POVERTY AND POWER

One excellent comparison between the generally accepted "truths" about the poor and an alternate thesis of personal power or its lack has been made by Haggstrom [1964], who has gathered a quantity of data from publications relating to poverty written by social scientists over a fifteen-year span. In general, these publications stress widely varying hypotheses in describing behavior patterns of the poor. A primary hypothesis has been that money is the key to successful participation in the American scene. That is, the major problem of the poor is their poverty. This supposes that because the psychological characteristics of poor people represent certain inadequacies in behavior and attitude, such characteristics are the *result of* being poor. The cause and effect thesis, according to Haggstrom, has not been successfully demonstrated. In fact, he cites several instances where economic poverty exists (certain religious groups, leaders of the poor, college students from poverty homes) and psychological inadequacy does not. The latter tend to be quite committed to personal fulfillment, to various causes which they have pursued and embraced, and to have some form of future-time allegiance.

Other observations have cited:

1. Lack of future orientation of the poor;

2. Hostility toward those who have made it;

3. Suspicion and resentment of outside influence;

4. A consequent trusting to "chance," "luck," or "fate";

5. An apathetic approach to problems;

6. A futility about where everything is going and what everything means; and

7. Childlike dependency on those who are gifted or capable or affluent or powerful.

While these findings cannot be refuted, a critical point must be made—that none of the above is more than an observation about what exists. None of the above is explanatory, but rather largely descriptive. None of it gets at the heart of the matter.

Haggstrom explores these phenomena by citing the syndrome of psychological dependency and its concommitant loss of self-esteem. His notion of psychological dependency would appear to neatly parallel our earlier hypothesis about feelings of inadequacy. The dependent person has lost the capacity to make decisions and to rely upon his own abilities. Completing the circle, he then diminishes in his belief that he has any control over his own destiny, and he feels lost and helpless, inadequate, powerless. This description of the existential situation of the poor, when read with an understanding of the thesis of inadequacy or of powerlessness, becomes much more comprehensible.

The debilitating aspect of the dependency of the urban poor, in contrast with the dependency of other segments of our society (workers dependent upon their management, or children upon their parents), is their lack of opportunity to influence personally and actively a change in their situation. If the poor had access to the means for change or saw some slight opportunity for choice in their condition, the psychological impact of their situation would be lessened.

THE DO-IT-YOURSELF THESIS

But what might alter this helplessness of spirit that characterizes poor people? Middle-class Anglo citizens are becoming increasingly aware of their own historical neglect of the poor in their cities; but are they yet aware that it behooves *them* to see the situation drastically altered? The militant blacks in our ghettoes have been crying out to the world that the awakening has come, that self-awareness is now upon the black poor, and that this country will survive if the power structure does not bend to the demands of reality. What then, can white middle-class America do? In short, how is it possible to raise the personal expectations of those who feel inadequate and to enhance their lives so that they feel emotionally and psychologically capable?

In society at large, the poor must personally and collectively take social action to influence their own condition. They must also be unquestionably aware that *they* are the source of such action. The poor must see themselves as able to influence their own lives and environments. Thus, psychologically, they will begin to develop a sense of their own personal power and adequacy. Also, such action must have the effect of being able to move existing social institutions. It must have the ring of success—failure in self-initiated activities is likely to be as damaging in the beginning as failure in middle-class activities has always been.

And so we say that the poor must do it for themselves. Not without help, certainly, and not without many false starts and mistakes. But the ultimate thrust cannot be applied from the outside. Good health is generated from the energy released during meaningful thought and action. But middle-class, white, established powerful America cannot sit on its hands and demand that the poor help themselves "as we did when we were working our way up." One cannot demand that people pull themselves up by their own bootstraps if the people have never had boots. The poor must be involved, activated, motivated—and the nonpoor must be economically and emotionally receptive, willing to give away segments of their power, tolerant of diversely paced and managed activities mingling with and affecting their own, eager to cut tape and bend rules to help others as well as themselves.

I recently witnessed a black college student verbally castigate an important college administrator because the administrator had deferred a significant question (concerning recruitment of black college students) for "committee action." The student literally used the language of the streets in exhorting the administrator to "break the rules to bring more black kids in here, because you sure break 'em fast enough when it's somethin' *you* want!" It is true that we all could think of incidents where we have "exercised our power" to get tickets to a play or ball game, or to get a more favorable number at registration, or whatever. We call it pulling strings; divorced of metaphor, it is simply expressing our control or power over our environment.

The black student was soundly criticized by other administrators and faculty for his "disgusting exhibition" and his "humiliating display." One young college administrator noted that the student was "psychotic, disturbed, paranoid," in the lack of control he displayed over his emotions. I profoundly disagree.

We have argued that personal power to control one's environment brings a sense of identity and a more sound psychological encounter with living. If this is true, then the person who has escaped the lethargy of dependency, who has attached himself to a cause or an ideal, and who takes dynamic action to forward his cause, is illustrating emerging psychological stability. That this student was actively pursuing, with shrewd volatility, a personally identified critical goal, was evidence of his growing emotional health. That he used a language and a style of presentation that proved offensive to the power structure was evidence of their absorption with the delivery and not with the message. This is not to say that "dirty" language must become the vogue, but we must not let the style cloud the message.

Ironically, the campus administration responded to the confrontation by implementing (within a forty-eight-hour period) several programs of tutoring and curriculum revision that would remarkably and positively affect incoming minority students. Red tape was left strewn all over the campus. . . .

PARTICIPANTS, NOT RECIPIENTS

It is fitting that we should close this section by citing the writings of Charles V. Hamilton, who with Stokely Carmichael wrote *Black Power: The Politics of Liberation in America* [Carmichael and Hamilton, 1967]. It was Carmichael who first frightened powerful, middle-class America with his demands for black power. Subsequently, in the light of emerging strategies and increasing positions of importance for black people (and also, for Mexican-Americans, Puerto Ricans, and others), the rationale behind Carmichael's demands has become more comprehensible, less shocking to the general society.

Hamilton [1968], in an article in the *New York Times Magazine,* has written that the aim of black power is to "reduce black dependence upon whites." He also writes that black power seeks to ". . . work to establish legitimate new institutions that make participants, not recipients, out of a people traditionally excluded from the fundamentally racist processes of this country." Gauged within the framework of our hypothesis, such writing appears indeed wise.

How many of our people of poverty do identify with a cause, do feel personal strength, and meaningful social involvement? Our guess is, not many. Certainly not enough. But the tide is moving. *Power* becomes a rallying cry, and power is the key to dynamic living.

And so, we come to our schools. What kind of education can offer sound psychological health through meaningful involvement and a relevant curriculum?

REFERENCES

Carmichael, S., and Hamilton, C. V. *Black Power: The Politics of Liberation in America.* New York: Random House, 1967.

Haggstrom, W. C. The power of the poor. In F. Riessmen, J. Cohen, and A. Pearl (Eds.), *Mental Health of the Poor.* New York: Free Press, 1964, pp. 205–23.

Hamilton, C. V. An advocate of Black Power defines it. *New York Times Magazine,* April 14, 1968.

Hollingshead, A. B., and Redlick, F. C. *Social Class and Mental Illness.* New York: Wiley, 1958.

Miller, S. M., and Mishler, E. G. Social class, mental illness and American psychiatry: An expository review. In F. Reissman, J. Cohen, and A. Pearl (Eds.), *Mental Health of the Poor*. New York: Free Press, 1964, p. 16–36.

REVIEW QUESTIONS

1. According to the concepts in this article, what does black power have to do with psychological health?

2. Think about it: Which would you rather be?
    a. poor
    b. unable to control your destiny
    c. psychologically unstable
    d. uneducated
    e. none of the above

thirty-nine

Academic Ignorance and
Black Intelligence

WILLIAM LABOV

*The controversy over why children in the inner-city schools show such low
educational achievement has been examined in several recent issues of* The
Atlantic. *In the September 1971* Atlantic, *R. J. Herrnstein summarized the position of psychologists and others who believe that heredity is substantially more
important than environment in determining intelligence, as measured by IQ tests.
In its issue of December 1971,* The Atlantic *published a number of letters (the
correspondents included sociologists, anthropologists, economists, educators, and
a few psychologists) taking issue with Professor Herrnstein's article. Many of
those who wrote maintained that environmental factors, rather than any genetic
deficit, explain the poor performance of lower-class inner-city children.*

*A third position held by linguists and many anthropologists locates the problem
not in the children, but in the relations between them and the school system. This
position holds that inner-city children do not necessarily have inferior mothers,
language, or experience, but that the language, family style, and ways of living
of inner-city children are significantly different from the standard culture of the
classroom, and that this difference is not always properly understood by teachers
and psychologists. Linguists believe that we must begin to adapt our school system
to the language and learning styles of the majority in the inner-city schools. They
argue that everyone has the right to learn the standard languages and culture in
reading and writing (and speaking, if they are so inclined); but this is the end
result, not the beginning of the educational process. They do not believe that the
standard language is the only medium in which teaching and learning can take
place, or that the first step in education is to convert all first-graders to replicas
of white middle-class suburban children.*

*This article grew out of my attempt to state the linguistics position on these
issues at a Georgetown Round Table in 1968. While psychologists are obviously
divided, linguists find (somewhat to their own surprise) that they all agree. My*

Source: From the *Atlantic Monthly*, June 1972, pp. 59–67. Copyright © 1972 by the Atlantic
Monthly Company, Boston, Mass. Reprinted by permission of the author and the publisher.

own statement here is based on research carried out in South Central Harlem from 1965 to 1968 by a team of two white and two black investigators, supported by the Office of Education. Our aim was to describe the differences between the standard English of the classroom and the vernacular language used by members of the street culture. We carried out long-term participant-observation with a number of black adolescent peer groups: the Jets, the Cobras, the Thunderbirds, the Aces, the Oscar Brothers. Their dialect will be referred to below as the Black English Vernacular (BEV). *It is a remarkably consistent grammar, essentially the same as that found in other cities: Detroit, Chicago, Philadelphia, Washington, San Francisco, Los Angeles, New Orleans. It is important to note that this Black English Vernacular is only a small part of what might be called "Black English." Black Americans do not, of course, speak a single dialect, but a wide range of language forms that cover the continuum between this vernacular and the most formal literary English.*   —W. L.

In the past decade, a great deal of federally sponsored research has been devoted to the educational problems of children in ghetto schools. To account for the poor performance of children in these schools, educational psychologists have tried to discover what kind of disadvantage or defect the children are suffering from. The viewpoint which has been widely accepted and used as the basis for large-scale intervention programs is that the children show a cultural *deficit* as a result of an impoverished environment in their early years. A great deal of attention has been given to language. In this area, the deficit theory appears as the notion of "verbal deprivation": black children from the ghetto area are said to receive little verbal stimulation, to hear very little well-formed language, and as a result are impoverished in their means of verbal expression. It is said that they cannot speak complete sentences, do not know the names of common objects, cannot form concepts or convey logical thoughts.

Unfortunately, these notions are based upon the work of educational psychologists who know very little about language and even less about black children. The concept of verbal deprivation has no basis in social reality; in fact, black children in the urban ghettos receive a great deal of verbal stimulation, hear more well-formed sentences than middle-class children, and participate fully in a highly verbal culture; they have the same basic vocabulary, possess the same capacity for conceptual learning, and use the same logic as anyone else who learns to speak and understand English. The myth of verbal deprivation is particularly dangerous because it diverts the attention from real defects of our educational system to imaginary defects of the child; and as we shall see, it leads its sponsors inevitably to the hypothesis of the genetic inferiority of black children, which the verbal-deprivation theory was designed to avoid.

The deficit theory attempts to account for a number of facts that are known to all of us: that black children in the central urban ghettos do badly on all school subjects, including arithmetic and reading. In reading, they average more than two years behind the national norm. Furthermore, this lag is cumulative, so that they do worse comparatively in the fifth grade than in the first grade. The information available suggests that this bad performance is correlated most closely with socioeconomic status. Segregated ethnic groups, however, seem to do worse than others: in particular, Indian, Mexican-American, and black children.

We are obviously dealing with the effects of the caste system of American society—essentially a "color-marking" system. Everyone recognizes this. The question is, By what mechanism does the color bar prevent children from learning to read? One answer is the notion of "cultural deprivation" put forward by Martin Deutsch and others: the black children are said to lack the favorable factors in their home environment which enable middle-class children to do well in school. These factors involve the development, through verbal interaction with adults, of various cognitive skills, including the ability to reason abstractly, to speak fluently, and to focus upon long-range goals. In their publications, the psychologists Deutsch, Irwin Katz, and Arthur Jensen also recognize broader social factors. However, the deficit theory does not focus upon the interaction of the black child with white society so much as on his failure to interact with his mother at home. In the literature we find very little direct observation of verbal interaction in the black home; most typically, the investigators ask the child if he has dinner with his parents, and if he engages in dinner-talk conversation with them. He is also asked whether his family takes him on trips to museums and other cultural activities. This slender thread of evidence is used to explain and interpret the large body of tests carried out in the laboratory and in the school.

The most extreme view which proceeds from this orientation—and one that is now being widely accepted—is that lower-class black children have no language at all. Some educational psychologists first draw from the writings of the British social psychologist Basil Bernstein the idea that "much of lower-class language consists of a kind of incidental 'emotional accompaniment' to action here and now." Bernstein's views are filtered through their strong bias against all forms of working-class behavior, so that Arthur Jensen, for example, sees middle-class language as superior in every respect—as "more abstract, and necessarily somewhat more flexible, detailed and subtle." One can proceed through a range of such views until one comes to the practical program of Carl Bereiter, Siegfried Engelmann, and their associates. Bereiter's program for an academically oriented preschool is based upon the premise that black children must have a language which they can learn, and their empirical findings that these children come to school without such a language. In his work with four-year-old black children from Urbana, Illinois, Bereiter reports that their communication was by gestures, "single words," and "a series of badly connected words or phrases," such as *They mine* and *Me got juice*. He reports that black children could not ask questions, that "without exaggerating ... these four-year-olds could make no statements of any kind." Furthermore, when these children were asked, "Where is the book?" they did not know enough to look at the table where the book was lying in order to answer. Thus Bereiter concludes that the children's speech forms are nothing more than a series of emotional cries, and he decides to treat them "as if the children had no language at all." He identifies their speech with his interpretation of Bernstein's restricted code: "The language of culturally deprived children ... is not merely an underdeveloped version of standard English, but is a basically non-logical mode of expressive behavior." The basic program of his preschool is to teach them a new language devised by Engelmann, which consists of a limited series of questions and answers such as *Where is the squirrel? / The squirrel is in the tree.* The children will not be punished if they use their vernacular speech on the playground, but they will not be allowed to use it in the schoolroom. If they should answer the question "Where is the squirrel?" with the illogical vernacular form "In the tree," they will be reprehended by various means and made to say, "The squirrel is in the tree."

Linguists and psycholinguists who have worked with black children are likely to dismiss this view of their language as utter nonsense. Yet there is no reason to reject Bereiter's observations as spurious: they were certainly not made up. On the contrary, they give us a very clear view of the behavior of student and teacher which can be duplicated in any classroom. Our own research is done outside the schools, in situations where adults are not the dominant force, but on many occasions we have been asked to help analyze the results of research into verbal deprivation in such test situations.

Here, for example, is a complete interview with a black boy, one of hundreds carried out in a New York City school. The boy enters a room where there is a large, friendly white interviewer, who puts on the table in front of him a block or a fire engine, and says, "Tell me everything you can about this!" (The interviewer's further remarks are in parentheses.)

[*12 seconds of silence*]
(What would you say it looks like?)
[*8 seconds of silence*]
A spaceship.
(Hmmmmm.)

[*13 seconds of silence*]
Like a je-et.

[*12 seconds of silence*]
Like a plane.

[*20 seconds of silence*]
(What color is it?)
Orange. [*2 seconds*]. An'whi-ite. [*2 seconds*]. An' green.
[*6 seconds of silence*]
(An' what could you use it for?)
[*8 seconds of silence*]
A je-et.

[*6 seconds of silence*]
(If you had two of them, what would you do with them?)
[*6 seconds of silence*]
Give one to somebody.
(Hmmm. Who do you think would like to have it?)
[*10 seconds of silence*]
Cla-rence.
(Mm. Where do you think we could get another one of these?)
At the store.
(Oh-ka-ay!)

We have here the same kind of defensive, monosyllabic behavior which is reported in Bereiter's work. What is the situation that produces it? The child is in an asymmetrical situation where anything he says can, literally, be held against him. He has learned a number of devices to *avoid* saying anything in this situation, and he works very hard to achieve this end.

If one takes this interview as a measure of the verbal capacity of the child, it must be as his capacity to defend himself in a hostile and threatening situation. But unfortunately, thousands of such interviews are used as evidence of the child's total verbal capacity, or more simply his verbality: it is argued that this lack of "verbality" *explains* his poor performance in school.

The verbal behavior which is shown by the child in the test situation quoted above is not the result of ineptness of the interviewer. It is rather the result of regular sociolinguistic factors operating upon adult and child in this asymmetrical situation. In our work in urban ghetto areas, we have often encountered such behavior. For over a year Clarence Robins had worked with the Thunderbirds, a group of boys ten to twelve years old who were the dominant pre-adolescent group in a low-income project in Harlem. We then decided to interview a few younger brothers of the Thunderbirds, eight to nine years old. But our old approach didn't work. Here is an extract from the interview between Clarence and eight-year-old Leon L.:

CR: What if you saw somebody kickin' somebody else on the ground, or was using a stick, what would you do if you saw that?

LEON: Mmmm.

CR: If it was supposed to be a fair fight—

LEON: I don' know.

CR: You don' know? Would you do anything? . . . huh? I can't hear you.

LEON: No.

CR: Did you ever see somebody get beat up real bad?

LEON: . . . Nope? ? ?

CR: Well—uh—did you ever get into a fight with a guy?

LEON: Nope.

CR: That was bigger than you?

LEON: Nope.

CR: You never been in a fight?

LEON: Nope.

CR: Nobody ever pick on you?

LEON: Nope.

CR: Nobody ever hit you?

LEON: Nope.

CR: How come?

LEON: Ah 'on' know.

CR: Didn't you ever hit somebody?

LEON: Nope.

CR: [*incredulous*] You never hit nobody?

LEON: Mhm.

CR: Aww, ba-a-a-be, you ain't gonna tell me that.

This nonverbal behavior occurs in a relatively *favorable* context for adult-child interaction, since the adult is a black man raised in Harlem, who knows this particular neighborhood and these boys very well. He is a skilled interviewer who has obtained a very high level of verbal response with techniques developed for a different age level, and has an extraordinary advantage over most teachers or experimenters in these respects. But even his skills and personality are ineffective in breaking down the social constraints that prevail here.

When we reviewed the record of this interview with Leon, we decided to use it as a test of our own knowledge of the sociolinguistic factors which control speech. We made the following changes in the social situation; in the next interview with Leon, Clarence:

1. Brought along a supply of potato chips, changing the "interview" into something more in the nature of a party.

2. Brought along Leon's best friend, eight-year-old Gregory.

3. Reduced the height imbalance. When Clarence got down on the floor of Leon's room, he dropped from 6 feet, 2 inches to 3 feet, 6 inches.

4. Introduced taboo words and taboo topics, and proved to Leon's surprise that one can say anything into our microphone without any fear of retaliation. It did not hit or bite back. The result of these changes is a striking difference in the volume and style of speech.

[The tape is punctuated throughout by the sound of potato chips.]
CR: Is there anybody who says, "Your momma drink pee"?
LEON: *[rapidly and breathlessly]* Yee-ah!
GREG: Yup.
LEON: And your father eat doo-doo for breakfas'!
CR: Ohhh! *[laughs]*
LEON: And they say your father—your father eat doo-doo for dinner!
GREG: When they sound on me, I say "C.B.M."
CR: What that mean?
LEON: Congo booger-snatch! *[laughs]*
GREG: Congo booger-snatcher! *[laughs]*
GREG: And sometimes I'll curse with "B.B."
CR: What that?
GREG: Oh, that's a "M.B.B." Black boy. *[Leon crunching on potato chips]*
GREG: 'Merican Black Boy.
CR: Oh.
GREG: Anyway, 'Mericans is same like white people, right?
LEON: And they talk about Allah.
CR: Oh, yeah?
GREG: Yeah.
CR: What they say about Allah?
LEON: Allah—Allah is God.
GREG: Allah—
CR: And what else?
LEON: I don' know the res'.

GREG: Allah i—Allah is God. Allah is the only God, Allah—
LEON: Allah is the *son* of God.
GREG: But can he make magic?
LEON: Nope.
GREG: I know who can make magic?
CR: Who can?
LEON: The God, the real one.
CR: Who can make magic?
GREG: The son of po'—(CR: Hm?) I'm sayin' the po'k chop God! He only a po'k chop God! [*Leon chuckles*]

The "nonverbal" Leon is now competing actively for the floor; Gregory and Leon talk to each other as much as they do to the interviewer. The monosyllabic speaker who had nothing to say about anything and could not remember what he did yesterday has disappeared. Instead, we have two boys who have so much to say that they keep interrupting each other, who seem to have no difficulty in using the English language to express themselves.

One can now transfer this demonstration of the sociolinguistic control of speech to other test situations, including IQ and reading tests in school. It should be immediately apparent that none of the standard tests will come anywhere near measuring Leon's verbal capacity. On these tests he will show up as very much the monosyllabic, inept, ignorant, bumbling child of our first interview. The teacher has far less ability than Clarence Robins to elicit speech from this child; Clarence knows the community, the things that Leon has been doing, and the things that Leon would like to talk about. But the power relationships in a one-to-one confrontation between adult and child are too asymmetrical. This does not mean that some black children will not talk a great deal when alone with an adult, or that an adult cannot get close to any child. It means that the social situation is the most powerful determinant of verbal behavior and that an adult must enter into the right social relation with a child if he wants to find out what a child can do. This is just what many teachers cannot do.

The view of the black speech community which we obtain from our work in the ghetto areas is precisely the opposite from that reported by Deutsch, Engelmann, and Bereiter. We see a child bathed in verbal stimulation from morning to night. We see many speech events which depend upon the competitive exhibitions of verbal skills: singing, sounding, toasts, rifting, louding—a whole range of activities in which the individual gains status through his use of language. We see the younger child trying to acquire these skills from older children—hanging around on the outskirts of the older peer groups, and imitating this behavior. We see, however, no connection between verbal skill at the speech events characteristic of the street culture and success in the schoolroom; which says something about classrooms rather than about a child's language.

There are undoubtedly many verbal skills, which children from ghetto areas must learn in order to do well in school, and some of these are indeed characteristic of middle-class verbal behavior. Precision in spelling, practice in handling abstract symbols, the ability to state explicitly the meaning of words, and a richer knowledge of the Latinate vocabulary may all be useful acquisitions. But is it true that *all* of the middle-class verbal habits are functional and desirable in school? Before we impose middle-class verbal style upon children from other cultural groups, we should find out how much of it is useful for the main work of analyzing and generalizing, and how much is merely stylistic—or even dysfunctional. In high school and college, middle-class children spontaneously complicate their syntax to the point that instructors despair of getting them to make their language simpler and clearer.

Our work in the speech community makes it painfully obvious that in many ways working-class speakers are more effective narrators, reasoners, and debaters than many middle-class speakers, who temporize, qualify, and lose their argument in a mass of irrelevant detail. Many academic writers try to rid themselves of the part of middle-class style that is empty pretension, and keep the part necessary for precision. But the average middle-class speaker that we encounter makes no such effort; he is enmeshed in verbiage, the victim of sociolinguistic factors beyond his control.

I will not attempt to support this argument here with systematic quantitative evidence, although it is possible to develop measures which show how far middle-class speakers can wander from the point. I would like to contrast two speakers dealing with roughly the same topic: matter of belief. The first is Larry H., a fifteen-year-old core member of another group, the Jets. Larry is being interviewed here by John Lewis, our participant-observer among adolescents in South Central Harlem.

JL:	What happens to you after you die? Do you know?
LARRY H:	Yeah, I know. (What?) After they put you in the ground, your body turns into—ah—bones, an' *shit.*
JL:	What happens to your spirit?
LARRY:	Your spirit—soon as you die, your spirit leaves you. (And where does the spirit go?) Well, it all depends. (On what?) You know, like some people say if you're good and 'shit, your spirit goin' t'heaven . . . 'n' if you bad, your spirit goin' to hell. Well, *bullshit!* Your spirit goin' to hell anyway, good or bad.
JL:	Why?
LARRY:	Why? I'll tell you why. 'Cause, you see, doesn' nobody really know that it's a God, y'know, 'cause, I mean I have seen black gods, pink gods, white gods, all color gods, and don't nobody know it's really a God. An' when they be sayin' if you good, you goin' t'heaven, tha's *bullshit,* 'cause you ain't goin' to no heaven, 'cause it ain't no heaven for you to go to.

Larry is a gifted speaker of the Black English Vernacular (BEV) as opposed to standard English (SE). His grammar shows a high concentration of such characteristic BEV forms as negative inversion [*don't nobody know*], negative concord [*you ain't going to no heaven*], invariant *be* [when they be sayin'], *dummy it* for SE *there* [*it ain't no heaven*], optional copula deletion [*if you're good . . . if you bad*], and full forms of auxiliaries [*I have seen*]. The only SE influence in this passage is the one case of *doesn't* instead of the invariant *don't* of BEV. Larry also provides a paradigmatic example of the rhetorical style of BEV: he can sum up a complex argument in a few words, and the full force of his opinions comes through without qualification or reservation. He is eminently quotable, and his interviews give us a great many concise statements of the BEV point of view. One can almost say that Larry speaks the BEV culture.

It is the logical form of this passage which is of particular interest here. Larry presents a complex set of interdependent propositions which can be explicated by setting out the SE equivalents in linear order. The basic argument is to deny the twin propositions:

(A) If you are good,   (B) then your spirit
                                will go to heaven.

(not A) If you are bad.   (C) then your spirit will go
                                to hell.

Larry denies (B), and allows that if (A) or (not A) is true, (C) will follow. His argument may be outlined:

1. Everyone has a different idea of what God is like.
2. Therefore nobody really knows that God exists.
3. If there is a heaven, it was made by God.
4. If God doesn't exist, he couldn't have made heaven.
5. Therefore heaven does not exist.
6. You can't go somewhere that doesn't exist.

(not B) Therefore you can't go to heaven.
(C) Therefore you are going to hell.

This hypothetical argument is not carried on at a high level of seriousness. It is a game played with ideas as counters, in which opponents use a wide variety of verbal devices to win. There is no personal commitment to any of these propositions, and no reluctance to strengthen one's argument by bending the rules of logic as in the (2, 4) sequence. But if the opponent invokes the rules of logic, they hold. In John Lewis' interviews, he often makes this move, and the force of his argument is always acknowledged and countered within the rules of logic.

JL: Well, if there's no heaven, how could there be a hell?
LARRY: I mean—ye-eah. Well, let me tell you, it ain't no hell, 'cause this is hell right here, y'know! (This is hell?) Yeah, this is hell right here!

Larry's answer is quick, ingenious, and decisive. The application of the (3–4–5) argument to hell is denied, since hell is here, and therefore conclusion (not B) stands. These are not ready-made or preconceived opinions, but new propositions devised to win the logical argument in the game being played. The reader will note the speed and precision of Larry's mental operations. He does not wander, or insert meaningless verbiage. It is often said that the nonstandard vernacular is not suited for dealing with abstract or hypothetical questions, but in fact, speakers of the BE Vernacular take great delight in exercising their wit and logic on the most improbable and problematical matters. Despite the fact that Larry H. does not believe in God, and has just denied all knowledge of him, John Lewis advances the following hypothetical question:

JL: ... But, just say that there is a God, what color is he? White or black?

LARRY: Well, if it is a God ... I wouldn't know what color, I couldn' say— couldn' nobody say what—

JL: But now, jus' suppose there was a God—

LARRY: Unless'n they say ...

JL: No, I was jus' sayin' jus' suppose there is a God, would he be white or black?

LARRY: ... He'd be white, man.

JL: Why?

LARRY: Why? I'll tell you why. 'Cause the average whitey out here got everything, you dig? And the nigger ain't got *shit*, y'know? Y'unnerstan'? So—um—for—in order for *that* to happen, you know it ain't no black God that's doin' that *bullshit*.

No one can hear Larry's answer to this question without being convinced of being in the presence of a skilled speaker with great "verbal presence of mind," who can use the English language expertly for many purposes.

Let us now turn to the second speaker, an upper-middle-class, college-educated black man being interviewed by Clarence Robins in our survey of adults in South Central Harlem.

CR: Do you know of anything that someone can do, to have someone who has passed on visit him in a dream?

CHAS. M.: Well, I even heard my parents say that there is such a thing as something in dreams, some things like that, and sometimes dreams do come true. I have personally never had a dream come true. I've never dreamt that somebody was dying and they actually died (Mhm), or that I was going to have ten dollars the next day and somehow I got ten dollars in my pocket. (Mhm.) I don't particularly believe in that, I don't think it's true. I do feel, though, that there is such a thing as—ah—witchcraft. I do feel that in certain cultures there is such a thing as witchcraft, or some sort of *science* of witchcraft; I don't think that it's just a matter of believing hard enough that there is such a thing as witchcraft. I do believe that there is such a thing that a person can put himself in a state of *mind* (Mhm), or that—er—something could be given them to intoxicate them in a certain—to a certain frame of mind—that—that could actually be considered witchcraft.

Charles M. is obviously a "good speaker" who strikes the listener as well-educated, intelligent, and sincere. He is a likable and attractive person—the kind of person that middle-class listeners rate very high on a scale of "job suitability" and equally high as a potential friend. His language is more moderate and tempered than Larry's; he makes every effort to qualify his opinions, and seems anxious to avoid any misstatements or overstatements. From these qualities emerges the primary characteristic of this passage—its *verbosity*. Words multiply, some modifying and qualifying, others repeating or padding the main argument. The first half of his extract is a response to the initial question on dreams, basically:

1. Some people say that dreams sometimes come true.
2. I have never had a dream come true.
3. Therefore I don't believe 1.

This much of Charles M.'s response is well directed to the point of the question. He then volunteers a statement of his beliefs about witchcraft which shows the difficulty of middle-class speakers who (a) want to express a belief in something but (b) want to show themselves as judicious, rational, and free from superstitions. The basic proposition can be stated simply in five words:

But I believe in witchcraft.

However, the idea is enlarged to exactly one hundred words, and it is difficult to see what else is being said. The vacuity of this passage becomes more evident if we remove repetitions, fashionable words, and stylistic decorations:

But I believe in witchcraft.
I don't think witchcraft is just a belief.
A person can put himself or be put in a state of mind that is witchcraft.

Without the extra verbiage and the OK words like *science, culture* and *intoxicate,* Charles M. appears as something less than a first-rate thinker. The initial impression of him as a good speaker is simply our long-conditioned reaction to middle-class verbosity: we know that people who use these stylistic devices are educated people, and we are inclined to credit them with saying something intelligent.

Let us now examine Bereiter's own data on the verbal behavior of the black children he dealt with. The expressions *They mine* and *Me got juice* are cited as examples of a language which lacks the means for expressing logical relations —in this case characterized as "a series of badly connected words." In the case of *They mine,* it is apparent that Bereiter confuses the notions of logic and explicitness. We know that there are many languages of the world which do not have a present copula, and which conjoin subject and predicate complement without a verb. Russian, Hungarian, and Arabic may be foreign, but they are not by the same token illogical. In the case of Black English we are not dealing with even this superficial grammatical difference, but rather with a low-level rule which carries contraction one step further to delete single consonants representing the verbs *is, have,* or *will.* We have yet to find any children who do not sometimes use the full forms of *is* or *will,* even though they may frequently delete it.

The deletion of the *is* or *are* in Black English is not the result of erratic or illogical behavior: it follows the same regular rules as standard English contraction. Wherever standard English can contract, black children use either the contracted form or (more commonly) the deleted zero form. Thus *They mine* corresponds to standard English *They're mine,* not to the full form *They are mine.* On the other hand, no such deletion is possible in positions where standard English cannot contract: just as one cannot say *That's what they're* in standard English. *That's what they* is equally impossible in the vernacular we are considering. The appropriate use of the deletion rule, like the contraction rule, requires a deep and intimate knowledge of English grammar and phonology. Such knowledge is not available for conscious inspection by native speakers: the rules we have worked out for standard contraction have never appeared in any grammar, and are certainly not a part of the conscious knowledge of any standard English speakers. Nevertheless, the adult or child who uses these rules must have formed at some level of psychological organization clear concepts of "tense marker," "verb phrase," "rule ordering," "sentence embedding," "pronoun," and many other grammatical categories which are essential parts of any logical system.

Bereiter's reaction to the sentence *Me got juice* is even more puzzling. If Bereiter believes that *Me got juice* is not a logical expression, it can only be that he interprets the use of the objective pronoun *me* as representing a difference in logical relationship to the verb; that the child is in fact saying that "the juice got him" rather than "he got the juice"! If on the other hand the child means "I got juice," then this sentence form shows only that he has not learned the formal rules for the use of the subjective form *I* and oblique form *me.*

Bereiter shows even more profound ignorance of the rules of discourse and of syntax when he rejects "In the tree" as an illogical or badly formed answer to "Where is the squirrel?" Such elliptical answers are of course used by everyone, and they show the appropriate deletion of subject and main verb, leaving the locative which is questioned by *wh* + *there.* The reply *In the tree* demonstrates that the listener has been attentive to and apprehended the syntax of the speaker. Whatever formal structure we wish to write for expressions such as *Yes* or *Home* or *In the tree,* it is obvious that they cannot be interpreted without knowing the structure of the question which preceded them, and that they presuppose an understanding of the syntax of the question. Thus if you ask me, "Where is the squirrel?" it is necessary for me to understand the sentence from an underlying form which would otherwise have produced *The squirrel is there.* If the child had answered *The tree,* or *Squirrel the tree,* or *The in tree,* we would then assume that he did not understand the syntax of the full form, *The squirrel is in the tree.* Given the data that Bereiter presents, we cannot conclude that the child has no grammar, but only that the investigator does not understand the rules of grammar. It does not necessarily do any harm to use the full form *The squirrel is in the tree,* if one wants to make fully explicit the rules of grammar which the child has internalized. Much of logical analysis consists of making explicit just that kind of internalized rule. But it is hard to believe that any good can come from a program which begins with so many misconceptions about the input data. Bereiter and Engelmann believe that in teaching the child to say *The squirrel is in the tree* or *This is a box* and *This is not a box,* they are teaching him an entirely new language, whereas in fact they are only teaching him to produce slightly different forms of the language he already has.

If there is a failure of logic involved here, it is surely in the approach of the verbal-deprivation theorists, rather than in the mental abilities of the children concerned. We can isolate six distinct steps in the reasoning which has led to programs such as those of Deutsch, Bereiter, and Engelmann:

1. The lower-class child's verbal response to a formal and threatening situation is used to demonstrate his lack of verbal capacity, or verbal deficit.

2. This verbal deficit is declared to be a major cause of the lower-class child's poor performance in school.

3. Since middle-class children do better in school, middle-class speech habits are said to be necessary for learning.

4. Class and ethnic differences in grammatical form are equated with differences in the capacity for logical analysis.

5. Teaching the child to mimic certain formal speech patterns used by middle-class teachers is seen as teaching him to think logically.

6. Children who learn these formal speech patterns are then said to be thinking logically, and it is predicated that they will do much better in reading and arithmetic in the years to follow.

This article has proved that numbers 1. and 2. at least are wrong. However, it is not too naïve to ask, What is wrong with being wrong? We have already conceded that black children need help in analyzing language into its surface components, and in being more explicit. But there are, in fact, serious and damaging consequences of the verbal-deprivation theory. These may be considered under two headings:

a. the theoretical bias and

b. the consequences of failure.

It is widely recognized that the teacher's attitude toward the child is an important factor in the latter's success or failure. The work of Robert Rosenthal on "self-fulfilling prophecies" shows that the progress of children in the early grades can be dramatically affected by a single random labeling of certain children as "intellectual bloomers." When the everyday language of black children is stigmatized as "not a language at all" and "not possessing the means for logical thought," the effect of such a labeling is repeated many times during each day of the school year. Every time that a child uses a form of BEV without the copula or with negative concord, he will be labeling himself for the teacher's benefit as "illogical," as a "nonconceptual thinker." This notion gives teachers a ready-made, theoretical basis for the prejudice they may already feel against the lower-class black child and his language. When they hear him say *I don't want none* or *They mine,* they will be hearing, through the bias provided by the verbal-deprivation theory, not an English dialect different from theirs, but the primitive mentality of the savage mind.

But what if the teacher succeeds in training the child to use the new language consistently? The verbal deprivation theory holds that this will lead to a whole chain of successes in school, and that the child will be drawn away from the vernacular culture into the middle-class world. Undoubtedly this will happen with a few isolated individuals, just as it happens in every school system today for a few children. But we are concerned not with the few but the many, and for the majority of black children the distance between them and the school is bound to widen under this approach.

The essential fallacy of the verbal-deprivation theory lies in tracing the educational failure of the child to his personal deficiencies. At present, these deficiencies are said to be caused by his home environment. It is traditional to explain a child's failure in school by his inadequacy; but when failure reaches such massive proportions, it seems necessary to look at the social and cultural obstacles to learning and the inability of the school to adjust to the social situation.

The second area in which the verbal-deprivation theory is doing serious harm to our educational system is in the consequences of this failure and the reaction to it. As Operation Head Start fails, the interpretations which we receive will be from the same educational psychologists who designed this program. The fault will be found, not in the data, the theory, or the methods used, but rather in the children who have failed to respond to the opportunities offered them. When black children fail to show the significant advance which the deprivation theory predicts, it will be further proof of the profound gulf which separates their mental processes from those of civilized, middle-class mankind.

A sense of the failure of Operation Head Start is already commonplace. Some prominent figures in the program have reacted to this situation by saying that intervention did not take place early enough. Bettye M. Caldwell notes that

> the research literature of the last decade dealing with social-class differences has made abundantly clear that all parents are not qualified to provide even the basic essentials of physical and psychological care to their children.

The deficit theory now begins to focus on the "long-standing patterns of parental deficit" which fill the literature. "There is, perhaps unfortunately," writes Caldwell, "no literacy test for motherhood." Failing such eugenic measures, she has proposed "educationally oriented day care for culturally deprived children between six months and three years of age." The children are returned home each evening to "maintain primary emotional relationships with their own families," but during the day they are removed "hopefully to prevent the deceleration in rate of development which seems to occur in many deprived children around the age of two to three years."

There are others who feel that even the best of the intervention programs, such as those of Bereiter and Engelmann, will not help the black child no matter when they are applied—that we are faced once again with the "inevitable hypothesis" of the genetic inferiority of the black people. Arthur Jensen, for example, in his *Harvard Educational Review* paper [1969], argues that the verbal-deprivation theorists with whom he has been associated—Deutsch, Whiteman, Katz, Bereiter—have been given every opportunity to prove their case and have failed. This opinion forms part of the argument leading to his overall conclusion that the "preponderance of the evidence is . . . less consistent with a strictly environmental hypothesis than with the genetic hypothesis."

Jensen argues that the middle-class white population is differentiated from the working-class white and black population in the ability for "cognitive or conceptual learning," which Jensen calls Level II intelligence as against mere "associative learning," or Level I intelligence.

Thus Jensen found that one group of middle-class children were helped by their concept-forming ability to recall twenty familiar objects that could be classified into four categories: animals, furniture, clothing, or foods. Lower-class black children did just as well as middle-class children with a miscellaneous set, but showed no improvement with objects that could be so organized.

But linguistic data strongly contradict Jensen's conclusion that these children cannot freely form concepts. In the earliest stages of language learning, children acquire "selectional restrictions" in their use of words. For example, they learn that some verbs take ANIMATE subjects, but others only INANIMATE ones: thus we say *The machine breaks* but not *John breaks; The paper tears* but not *George tears.* A speaker of English must master such subtle categories as the things which *break,* like *boards, glasses,* and *ropes;* things which *tear,* like *shirts, paper,* and *skin;* things which *snap,* like *buttons, potato chips,* and *plastic,* and other categories which *smash, crumple,* or *go bust.*

In studies of Samoan children, Keith Kernan has shown that similar rules are learned reliably long before the grammatical particles that mark tense, number, and so on. The experimentation on free recall that Jensen reports ignores such abilities, and defines intelligence as a particular way of answering a particular kind of question within a narrow cultural framework. Recent work of anthropologists in other cultures is beginning to make some headway in discovering how our tests bias the results so as to make normally intelligent people look stupid. Michael Cole and his associates gave the same kind of free recall tests to Kpelle speakers in Liberia. Those who had not been to school—children or adults—could only remember eight or ten out of the twenty and showed no "clustering" according to categories, no matter how long the trials went on. Yet one simple change in the test method produced a surprising change. The interviewer took each of the objects to be remembered and held it over a chair: one chair for each category, or just one chair for all categories. Suddenly the Kpelle subjects showed a dramatic improvement, remembered seventeen to eighteen objects, and matched American subjects in both recall and the amount of clustering by categories. We do not understand this effect, for we are only beginning to discover the subtle biases built in our test methods which prevent people from using the abilities that they display in their language and in everyday life.

Linguists are in an excellent position to demonstrate the fallacies of the verbal-deprivation theory. All linguists agree that nonstandard dialects are highly structured systems; they do not see these dialects as accumulations of errors caused by the failure of their speakers to master standard English. When linguists hear black children saying *He crazy* or *Her my friend* they do not hear a "primitive language." Nor do they believe that the speech of working-class people is merely a form of emotional expression, incapable of relating logical thought. Linguists therefore condemn with a single voice Bereiter's view that the vernacular can be disregarded.

There is no reason to believe that any nonstandard vernacular is in itself an obstacle to learning. The chief problem is ignorance of language on the part of all concerned. Our job as linguists is to remedy this ignorance: Bereiter and Engelmann want to reinforce it and justify it. Teachers are now being told to ignore the language of black children as unworthy of attention and useless for learning. They are being taught to hear every natural utterance of the child as evidence of his mental inferiority. As linguists we are unanimous in condemning this view as bad observation, bad theory, and bad practice.

That educational psychology should be strongly influenced by a theory so false to the facts of language is unfortunate; but that children should be the victims of this ignorance is intolerable. If linguists can contribute some of their valuable knowledge and energy toward exposing the fallacies of the verbal-deprivation theory, we will have done a great deal to justify the support that society has given to basic research in our field.

REFERENCES

Jensen, A. R. How much can we boost IQ and scholastic achievement? *Harvard Educational Review*, 1969, 39:1–123.

REVIEW QUESTIONS

1. What is the "verbal deprivation" position?

2. Why does the author conclude that the ideas of Bernstein, Bereiter and Engelmann, and Jensen are damaging to the welfare of black children?

3. Should Black English and black texts be used in black elementary schools?

forty

Teaching Reading in an
Urban Negro School System

JOAN C. BARATZ

In his recent report on the Washington, D. C. School System, Passow [1967] indicated that the central question that must be answered is: "What are the educationally relevant differences which the District's pupils bring into the classroom and what kinds of varied educational experiences must be provided by the schools to accommodate these differences?" One major educationally relevant difference for Washington, D. C., as for ghettos across the nation, is that of language. The Negro ghetto child is speaking a significantly different language from that of his middle-class teachers. Most of his middle-class teachers have wrongly viewed his language as pathological, disordered, "lazy speech." This failure to recognize the interference from the child's different linguistic system, and consequent negative teacher attitudes towards the child and his language, lead directly to reading difficulties and subsequent school failure. Understanding that the inner-city child speaks a language that is well-ordered, but different in many respects from standard English, is crucial to understanding how to educate him. Unfortunately, there is a tendency for the educator to think of the black child with his nonstandard speech as a "verbal cripple" whose restricted language leads to, or is caused by, cognitive deficits.

If we look briefly at the research and research assumptions concerning the language of Negro children, we can see how this erroneous notion of verbal inadequacy evolved.

When reviewing the literature, one finds three major professions concerned with describing the language and cognitive abilities of black children: educators, psychologists (mainly child development specialists), and linguists. The educators were the first to contribute a statement about the language difficulties of these children—a statement that amounted to the assertion that these children

Source: Abridgment of "Teaching Reading in an Urban Negro School System" by Joan C. Baratz. In J. Baratz and R. Shuy (Eds.), *Teaching Black Children to Read*. Washington, D. C.: Center for Applied Linguistics, 1969. Reprinted by permission of the publisher.

were virtually verbally destitute, i.e., they couldn't talk, and if they did, it was deviant speech, filled with "errors." The next group to get into the foray—the psychologists—reconfirmed initially that the children didn't talk, and then added the sophisticated wrinkle that if they did talk, their speech was such that it was a deterrent to cognitive growth. The last group to come into the picture were the linguists, who, though thoroughly impressed with the sophisticated research of the psychologist, were astonished at the naiveté of his pronouncements concerning language. The linguist began to examine the language of black children and brought us to our current conceptions of the language abilities of these children, namely, that they speak a well-ordered, highly structured, highly developed language system which in many aspects is different from standard English.

We have a fascinating situation here where three professions are assessing the same behavior—the child's oral language production and comprehension—but with varying assumptions, so that they see different things. However, it is not merely another example of the parable of the six blind men describing the elephant and asserting that an elephant equaled that portion of the elephant that the blind man happened to be touching—for in the parable all men were partially correct, and an elephant could be adequately described in the sum total of their "observations." But when we look at the assumptions of the educator, the psychologist, and the linguist, we find that there are actually some premises held by one profession, e.g., the psychologists' view that a language system *could* be underdeveloped, that another profession sees as completely untenable, e.g., linguists, who consider such a view of language so absurd as to make them feel that nobody could possibly believe it and therefore to refute it would be a great waste of time. The educator worked under the assumption that there is a single correct way of speaking and that everyone who does not speak in this "grammar book" fashion is in error. (Indeed, although the psychologist may not recognize it, he tacitly adheres to this principle when he defines language development in terms of "correct" standard English usage.) This assumption is also untenable to the linguist, who is interested in the structure and function of an utterance. To him the discussion of a hierarchial system that says that a double negative, e.g., *they don' have none,* is inferior to a single negative, e.g., *they haven't any,* is meaningless. The linguist simply wishes to describe the rules of the system that allow a speaker of that system to generate a negative utterance—or any other complex structure—that is considered grammatical and is understood as intended, by the speakers of the system.

The linguist takes it as basic that all humans develop language—after all, there is no reason to assume that black African bush children develop a language and black inner-city Harlem children do not! Subsumed under this is that the language is a well-ordered system with a predictable sound pattern, grammatical structure and vocabulary (in this sense, there are no "primitive" languages). The linguist assumes that any verbal system used by a community that fulfills the above requirements in a language and that no language is structurally better than any other language, i.e., French is not better than German, Yiddish is not better than Gaelic, Oxford English is not better than standard English, etc. The second assumption of the linguist is that children learn language in the context of their environment—that is to say, a French child learns French not because his father is in the home or his mother reads him books, but because that is the language that he hears continually from whatever source and that is the language that individuals in his environment respond to. The third assumption that the linguist works with is that by the time a child is five he has developed language—he has learned the rules of his linguistic environment.

What are those rules and how have they been determined? By using ghetto informants, linguists such as Stewart [1964, 1965, 1967, 1968], Dillard [1966, 1967], Bailey [1965, 1968], Labov [1967], Loman [1967] and Shuy, Wolfram and Riley [1968] have described some of the linguistic parameters of Negro nonstandard English. Differences between standard English and Negro nonstandard occur to varying degrees in regard to the sound system, grammar and vocabulary.

Although Negro non-standard has many phonemes similar to those of standard English, the distribution of these phonemes varies from standard English. For example, /i/ and /e/ may not be distinguished before nasals, so that a "pin" in Negro nonstandard may be either an instrument for writing a letter or something one uses to fasten a baby's diaper. Sounds such as 'r' and 'l' are distributed so that 'cat' may mean that orange vegetable that one puts in salads—standard English *carrot*—as well as the four-legged fuzzy animal, or a "big black dude." The reduction of /l/ and /r/ in many positions may create such homonyms as "toe" meaning a digit on the foot, or the church bell sound—standard English *toll*. Final clusters are reduced in Negro nonstandard so that "bowl" is used to describe either a vessel for cereal or a very brave soldier—standard English *bold*.

These are but a few of the many instances where Negro non-standard sound usage differs from standard English. It is no wonder then, that Cynthia Deutsch [1964] should find in her assessment of auditory discrimination that disadvantaged black children did not "discriminate" as well as white children from middle-class linguistic environments. She administered a discrimination task that equated "correct responses" with judgments of equivalences and differences in standard English sound usage. Many of her stimuli, though different for the standard English speaker, e.g., *pin-pen*, are similar for the Negro nonstandard speaker. She attributed the difference in performance of disadvantaged children to such things as the constant blare of the television in their homes and there being so much "noise" in their environment that the children tended to "tune out". However, black children make responses based on the kind of language they consider appropriate. In the same way *cot* (for sleeping), *caught* (for ensnared) ; or *marry* (to wed), *Mary* (the girl), and *merry* (to be happy) are not distinguished in the speech of many white people (so that they would say on an auditory discrimination test that *cot* and *caught* were the same), *pin* and *pen* are the same in the language of ghetto blacks. The responses that the black child makes are on the basis of the sound usage that he has learned in his social and geographical milieu, and do not reflect some difficulty in discriminating.

The syntax of low-income Negro children also differs from standard English in many ways (unfortunately the psychologist, not knowing the rules of Negro nonstandard has interpreted these differences not as the result of well-learned rules, but as evidence of "linguistic underdevelopment"). Some examples of the differences are provided below:

1. When you have a numerical quantifier such as 2, 7, 50, etc., you don't have to add the obligatory morphemes for the plural, e.g., *50 cent; 2 foot.*

2. The use of the possessive marker is different. For example, the standard English speaker says "John's cousin"; the nonstandard Negro speaker says *John cousin.* The possessive is marked here by the contiguous relationship of *John* and *cousin.*

3. The third person singular has no obligatory morphological ending in nonstandard, so that "she works here" is expressed as *she work here* in Negro nonstandard.

4. Verb agreement differs, so that one says *she have a bike, they was going.*

5. The use of the copula is not obligatory—*I going! he a bad boy.*

6. The rules for negation are different. The double negative is used: standard English "I don't have any" becomes *I don' got none* in Negro nonstandard.

7. The use of "ain't" in expression of the past—Negro nonstandard present tense is *he don't go,* past tense is *he ain't go.*

8. The use of "be" to express habitual action—*he working right now* as contrasted with *he be working every day.*

These are just a few of the rules that the nonstandard speaker employs to produce utterances that are grammatical for other speakers in his environment.

Baratz and Povich [1967] assessed the language development of a group of five-year-old black Head Start children. They analyzed speech responses to photographs and to CAT cards, using Lee's [1966] developmental sentence types model. A comparison of their data and Menyuk's [1964] restricted and transformational types of white middle-class children was performed. Results indicated that the Negro Head Start child is not delayed in language acquisition—the majority of his utterances are on the kernel and transformational levels of Lee's developmental model. His transformational utterances are similar to those appearing above—he has learned the many complicated structures of Negro nonstandard English.

But how did the psychologist manage to come to the erroneous conclusion that the black child has an insufficient or underdeveloped linguistic system? The psychologist's basic problem was that his measures of "language development" were measures based on standard English [Bereiter, 1965; Thomas, 1962; Deutsch, 1964; Klaus and Gray, 1968]. From these he concluded that since black children do not speak standard English, they must be deficient in language development.

Despite the misconceptions of the educator and psychologist concerning language and linguistic competence, the linguists for their part have described the differences between Negro nonstandard and standard English in some detail. The following is a list of some of the syntactic differences between the two systems:

Variable	Standard English	Negro Nonstandard
Linking verb	He is going.	He _ goin'.
Possessive marker	John's cousin.	John_ cousin.
Plural marker	I have five cents.	I got five cent_ .
Subject expression	John lives in New York.	John he live in New York.
Verb form	I drank the milk.	I drunk the milk.
Past marker	Yesterday he walked home.	Yesterday he walk_ home.
Verb agreement	He runs home.	He run home.
	She has a bicycle.	She have a bicycle.
Future form	I will go home.	I'ma go home.
"If" construction	I asked if he did it.	I ask did he do it.
Negation	I don't have any.	I don't got none.
	He didn't go.	He ain't go.
Indefinite article	I want an apple.	I want a apple.
Pronoun form	We have to do it.	Us got to do it.
	His book.	He book.
Preposition	He is over at his friend's house.	He over to his friend house.
	He teaches at Francis Pool.	He teach _ Francis Pool.
Be	Statement: He is here all the time.	Statement: He be here.
Do	Contradiction: no, he isn't.	Contradiction: No, he don't.

But what of these differences? All the linguists studying Negro nonstandard English agree that these differences are systematized structured rules within the vernacular; they agree that these differences can interfere with the learning of standard English, but they do not always agree as to the precise nature of these different rules. This leads to varied disagreements as to why a particular feature exists (i.e., phoneme deletion vs. creolization), but it does not dispute the fact that the linguistic feature is present. No one would fail to agree that standard English has a grammatical structure and uniqueness, and many descriptions of that structure have been written. Yet it is probably true that no two linguists would agree in all details on how to write the grammar. This equally explains the current controversy among linguists as to how one writes the grammar of Negro nonstandard English.

This language *difference,* not deficiency, must be considered in the educational process of the black ghetto child. In 1953, the UNESCO report regarding the role of language in education stated that: "It is axiomatic that the best medium for teaching a child is his mother tongue. Psychologically, it is the system of meaningful signs that in his mind works automatically for expression and understanding. Sociologically, it is a means of identification among the members of the community to which he belongs. Educationally he learns more quickly through it than through an unfamiliar medium."

But does the black nonstandard speaker have to contend with interference from his own dialect on his performance in standard English? The following experiment clearly suggests that he does.

The subjects in this experiment were third and fifth graders from two schools in the Washington, D. C. area. One was an inner-city, impact-aid school; all the children in this school were Negroes. The other was a school in Maryland, located in an integrated low-middle-income community; all the children from that school were white.

	Negro	White	Total
Fifth grade	15	15	30
Third grade	15	15	30
	30	30	60

A sentence repetition test was constructed that contained thirty sentences, fifteen in standard English and fifteen in Negro nonstandard. The sentences were presented on tape to each subject, who was asked to repeat the sentence after hearing it once.

The kinds of "errors" the two groups made (e.g., white subjects adding the third person -s to nonstandard stimuli and Negroes deleting the third person -s on standard stimuli) represent an intrusion of one language code (the dominant system) upon the structure of the other code (the newly acquired system). If, indeed, nonstandard were not a structured system with well-ordered rules, one would expect that Negro children would not be able to repeat the nonstandard structures any better than did the white children, and one would also expect that nonstandard patterns would not emerge systematically when lower-class Negroes responded to standard sentences. Neither of these expectations was upheld. The Negro children were in fact able to repeat nonstandard structures better than were the white children, and they did produce systematic nonstandard patterns when responding to standard sentences. The converse was true for the whites; they responded significantly better to standard structures and exhibited systematic standard patterns when responding to nonstandard stimuli.

The results of this research clearly indicate that

1. There are two dialects involved in the education complex of black children (especially in schools with a white middle-class curriculum orientation);

2. Black children are generally not bi-dialectal; and

3. There is evidence of interference from their dialect when black children attempt to use standard English.

Since the disadvantaged Negro child, as the previous study suggests, like the Indian having to learn Spanish in Mexico, or the African having to learn French in Guinea, has to contend with the interference from his vernacular in learning to read, how does his task of learning to read differ from that of the middle-class "mainstream American" child? When the middle-class child starts the process of learning to read, his is primarily a problem of decoding the graphic representation of a language which he already speaks. The disadvantaged black child must not only decode the written words, he must also "translate" them into his own language. This presents him with an almost insurmountable obstacle, since the written words frequently do not go together in any pattern that is familiar or meaningful to him. He is baffled by this confrontation with

1.   A new language with its new syntax;

2.   A necessity to learn the meaning of graphic symbols; and

3.   A vague, or not so vague, depending upon the cultural and linguistic sophistication of the teacher, sense that there is something terribly wrong with his language.

Because of the mismatch between the child's system and that of the standard English textbook, because of the psychological consequences of denying the existence and legitimacy of the child's linguistic system, and in the light of the success of vernacular teaching around the world, it appears imperative that we teach the inner-city Negro child to read using his own language as the basis for the initial readers. In other words, first teach the child to read in the vernacular, and then teach him to read in standard English. Such a reading program would not only require accurate vernacular texts for the dialect speaker, but also necessitate the creation of a series of "transition readers" that would move the child, once he had mastered reading in the vernacular, from vernacular texts to standard English texts. Of course, success of such a reading program would be dependent upon the child's ultimate ability to read standard English.

The advantages of such a program would be threefold. First, success in teaching the ghetto child to read. Second, the powerful ego-supports of giving credence to the child's language system and therefore to himself, and giving him the opportunity to experience success in school. And third, with the use of transitional readers, the child would have the opportunity of being taught standard English (which cannot occur by "linguistic swapping," since his school mates are all vernacular speakers) so that he could learn where his language system and that of standard English were similar and where they were different. Such an opportunity might well lead to generalized learning and the ability to use standard English more proficiently in other school work.

REFERENCES

Bailey, B. Linguistics and nonstandard language patterns. Paper presented at the annual meeting of the National Council of Teachers of English, 1965.

Bailey, B. Some aspects of the impact of linguistics on language teaching in disadvantaged communities. *Elementary English,*1968, 45: 570–79.

Baratz, J., and Povich, E. Grammatical constructions in the language of the Negro preschool child. ASHA paper, 1967.

Bereiter, C. Academic instruction and preschool children. In R. Cobin and M. Crosby (Eds.), *Language Programs for the Disadvantaged.* Champaign, Ill.: National Council of Teachers of English, 1965.

Deutsch, C. Auditory discrimination and learning: Social factors. *Merrill Palmer Quarterly,*1964, 10: 277–96.

Dillard, J. The Urban Language Study of the Center for Applied Linguistics. *Linguistic Reporter,*1966, 8 (5): 1–2.

Dillard, J. Negro children's dialect in the inner city. *Florida FL Reporter,*1967, 5 (3).

Klaus, R., and Gray, S. The early training project for disadvantaged children: A report after five years. *Society for Child Development,* Monograph 33, 1968.

Labov, W. Some sources of reading problems for Negro speakers of nonstandard English. In A. Frazier (Ed.), *New Directions in Elementary English.* Champaign, Ill.: National Council of Teachers of English, 1967.

Lee, L. Developmental sentence types: A method for comparing normal and deviant syntactic development. *Journal of Speech and Hearing Disorders,* 1966, 31: 311–30.

Loman, B. *Conversations in a Negro American Dialect.* Washington, D. C.: Center for Applied Linguistics, 1967.

Menyuk, P. Syntactic rules used by children from preschool through first grade. *Child Development,*1964, 35: 533–64.

Passow, A. *Toward Creating a Model Urban School System: A Study of the District of Columbia Public Schools.* New York: Teachers College, Columbia University, 1967.

Shuy, R., Wolfram, W., and Riley, W. *Field Techniques in an Urban Language Study.* Washington, D.C.: Center for Applied Linguistics, 1968.

Stewart W. Foreign language teaching methods in quasi-foreign language situations. In W. Stewart (Ed.), *Non-standard Speech and the Teaching of English.* Washington, D. C.: Center for Applied Linguistics, 1964.

Stewart, W. Urban Negro speech: Sociolinguistic factors affecting English teaching. In R. Shuy (Ed.), *Social Dialects and Language Learning.* Champaign, Ill.: National Council of Teachers of English, 1965.

Stewart, W. Sociolinguistic factors in the history of American Negro dialects. *Florida FL Reporter,*1967, 5 (2).

Stewart, W. Continuity and change in American Negro dialects. *Florida FL Reporter,*1968, 6 (2).

Thomas, D. Oral language sentence structure and vocabulary of kindergarten children living in low socio-economic urban areas. *Dissertation Abstracts,* 1962, 23: 1014.

REVIEW QUESTIONS

1. Would white middle-class children encounter "language problems" in a school where the spoken language and all texts, movies, and other materials— including achievement and ability tests—were in Negro nonstandard English?

2. How do you think black children would react to primary grade readers written in Black English?

forty-one

Soul Folk "Chitling" Test
(The Dove Counterbalance Intelligence Test)

ADRIAN DOVE

You might find this test useful in evaluating your verbal aptitude. The verbal aptitude tested is not slanted toward middle-class experience, however, but to nonwhite lower-class experience. This test is to be self-administered. You may allow yourself no longer than twelve minutes in taking this test.

People from nonwhite, lower-class backgrounds are required to do well on aptitude tests keyed to white, middle-class culture, before they are allowed to perform in that culture. By the same standard, it seems only fair that people of white middle-class background should be required to do well on tests keyed to nonwhite lower-class culture before they are allowed to perform in such a milieu.

The following test was developed by Watts social worker Adrian Dove to measure intelligence as the term applies in lower-class black America. Gilbert W. Merkz, instructor in Public Health and Sociology at Yale University, administered this schedule to a small nonrandom sample of Dixwell Avenue residents (a ghetto area in New Haven) who achieved a mean score of twenty-nine correct answers to the thirty questions (97 per cent accuracy).

If you score less than twenty (67 per cent) on the test, you are virtually failing by Yale standards, and might therefore conclude that you have a low ghetto IQ. As white middle-class educators put it, you are "culturally deprived." Who knows, perhaps OEO will fund a program in remedial education for you.

As usual, the honor system applies here—you are neither to receive nor give aid in this examination. Set your watch. Now, BEGIN! ! Good luck. (When you have finished, the correct answer key and score interpretation data are to be found on pages 411 and 412.)

1. "T-Bone Walker" got famous for playing what? (a) trombone (b) piano (c) "T-flute" (d) guitar (e) "hambone"

Source: Reprinted with permission of Adrian Dove.

2. Who did "Stagger Lee" kill (in the famous blues legend)? (a) his mother (b) Frankie (c) Johnny (d) his girl friend (e) Billy

3. A "gas head" is a person who has a _____. (a) fast moving car (b) stable of "lace" (c) "process hair" (d) habit of stealing cars (e) long jail record for arson

4. If a man is called a "blood," then he is a _____. (a) fighter (b) Mexican-American (c) black (d) hungry hemophile (e) redman or Indian

5. If you throw the dice and "7" is showing on the top, what is facing down? (a) "seven" (b) "snake eyes" (c) "boxcars" (d) "little Joes" (e) "eleven"

6. Jazz pianist Ahmad Jamal took an Arabic name after becoming really famous. Previously, he had some fame with what he called his "slave name." What was his previous name? (a) Willie Lee Jackson (b) LeRoi Jones (c) Wilbur McDougal (d) Fritz Jones (e) Andy Johnson

7. In "C. C. Rider," what does the C. C. stand for? (a) Civil Service (b) church council (c) country circuit, preacher or an old time rambler (d) country club (e) "Cheatin' Charlie" (The "Boxer Gunsel")

8. Cheap "chitlings" (not the kind you purchase at a frozen food counter) will taste rubbery unless they are cooked long enough. How soon can you quit cooking them to eat and enjoy them? (a) 15 minutes (b) 8 hours (c) 24 hours (d) 1 week (on a low flame) (e) one hour

9. "Down home" (the South) today, for the average "Soul brother" who is picking cotton (in season from sunup until sundown), what is the average earning (take home) for one full day? (a) $0.75 (b) $1.65 (c) $3.50 (d) $5.00 (e) $12.00

10. If a judge finds you guilty of "holding weed" (in California), what is the most he can give you? (a) indeterminate (life) (b) a nickel (c) a dime (d) a year in county (e) $100.00

11. "Bird" or "yardbird" was the "jacket" that jazz lovers from coast to coast hung on _____. (a) Lester Young (b) Peggy Lee (c) Benny Goodman (d) Charlie Parker (e) "Birdman of Alcatraz"

12. A "hype" is a person who _____. (a) always says he feels sickly (b) has water on the brain (c) uses heroin (d) is always ripping and running (e) is always sick

13. Hattie Mae Johnson is on the county. She has four children and her husband is now in jail for nonsupport, as he was unemployed and was not able to give her any money. Her welfare check is now $286.00 per month. Last night, she went out with the biggest player in town. If she got pregnant, nine months from now, how much more will her welfare check be? (a) $30.00 (b) $2.00 (c) $35.00 (d) $150.00 (e) $100.00

14. "Hully gully" came from _____. (a) "East Oakland" (b) Fillmore (c) Watts (d) Harlem (e) Motor City

15.   What is Willie Mae's last name? (a) Schwartz (b) Matauda (c) Gomez (d) Turner (e) O'Flaherty

16.   The opposite of square is _____. (a) round (b) up (c) down (d) hip (e) lame

17.   Do the "Beatles" have soul? (a) yes (b) no (c) gee whiz or maybe

18.   A "hankerchief head" is _____. (a) a cool cat (b) a porter (c) an "Uncle Tom" (d) a hoddi (e) "preacher"

19.   What are the "Dixie Hummingbirds"? (a) a part of the KKK (b) a swamp disease (c) a modern gospel group (d) a Mississippi Negro, paramilitary strike force (e) deacons

20.   "Jet is _____. (a) an "East Oakland" motorcycle club (b) one of the gangs in *West Side Story* (c) a news and gossip magazine (d) a way of life for the very rich

FILL IN THE MISSING WORDS THAT SOUND BEST

21.   "Tell it like it _____." (a) Thinks I am (b) baby (c) try (d) is (e) y'all

22.   "You've got to get up early in the morning if you want to _____." (a) catch the worms (b) be healthy, wealthy, and wise (c) try to fool me (d) fare well (e) be the first one on the street

23.   And Jesus said, "Walk together children _____." (a) don't you get weary. There is a great camp meeting. (b) for we shall overcome (c) for the family that walks together talks together (d) by your patience you will win your soul (Luke 21:9) (e) find the things that are above, not the things that are on Earth (Col. 3:3)

24.   "Money don't get everything it's true _____." (a) but don't have none and I'm so blue (b) but what it don't get I can't use (c) so make with what you got (d) but I don't know that and neither do you

25.   "Bo-Diddley" is a _____. (a) camp for children (b) cheap wine (c) singer (d) new dance (e) majo call

26.   Which word is out of place here? (a) splib (b) blood (c) grey (d) spook (e) black

27.   How much does a "short-dog" cost? (a) $0.15 (b) $2.00 (c) $0.35 (d) $0.05 (e) $0.86 + tax

28.   True or false: A "pimp" is also a young man who lays around all day. (a) true (b) false

29.   If a pimp is up tight with a woman who gets state aid, what does he mean when he talks about "Mother's Day"? (a) second Sunday in May (b) third Sunday in June (c) first of every month (d) none of these (e) first and fifteenth of every month

30.   Many people say that "Juneteenth" (June 10) should be made a legal

holiday because this was the day when _____. (a) the slaves were freed in the USA (b) the slaves were freed in Texas (c) the slaves were freed in Jamaica (d) the slaves were freed in California (e) Martin Luther King was born (f) Booker T. Washington died

ANSWERS TO SOUL FOLK "CHITLING" TEST (honor system)

(1) d (2) e (3) c (4) c (5) a (6) d (7) c (8) c (9) d (10) c (11) d (12) c (13) c (14) c (15) d (16) d (17) b (18) c (19) c (20) c (21) d (22) c (23) a (24) b (25) c (26) c (27) c (28) a (29) c (30) b

After you have taken this exam you may try to console yourself (that is, minimize cognitive dissonance or rationalize your performance, or lack of performance) by attempting to discredit the test by questioning its validity, reliability, etc. If you fall into this category, then you have missed the *entire* point: the point being that there does exist such a phenomenon as "cultural bias" in a test and that, indeed, exams can even be constructed in such a way as to inquire into matters beyond normal middle-class experience and therefore, to discriminate against persons of such "deprived" backgrounds. If nothing more, the hope is that this little quiz illustrates that there is *not* cultural homogeneity in the U.S. and that an effort to understand the "black man's psyche" cannot possibly be successful without, first an understanding of the norms and values on which is based his perception of the world.

Interestingly studies by psychologists reveal that persons from the lower socioeconomic brackets—who must of necessity be ever concerned with the question of where the next dollar and meal will come from—tend to perform better than middle-class oriented persons on tests (purporting to be measurement of "IQ" or "problem-solving ability") which inquire more into the solving of problems of a more immediate, concrete character (such as problems dealing with food and shelter) rather than into problems that are more removed and abstract in character. A test based on the norms, values, traditions, and the individual's experiences of a specific milieu, therefore, can be said to have part validity only when given to persons with the necessary exposure and only when testing to learn at what level a person is presently equipped to function in that milieu. The problem of devising a test with universal applicability (culture notwithstanding) is a formidable, if not impossible, one.

(Scores and IQ ranges on next page.)

No. Correct	IQ range	No. Correct	IQ range
30	106 or above (you may need a more difficult test)	20	56–60
		19	51–55
		18	45–50
29	101–105	17	41–45
28	96–100	16	36–40
27	91–95		
26	86–90	15	31–35
		14	26–30
25	81–85	13	21–25
24	76–80	12	16–20
23	71–75	11	11–15
22	66–70		
21	61–65	10	6–10
		9	1–5

part vi

CLASSROOM CREATIVITY

Developing creative thinking is regularly named as a major goal of education. Unfortunately, this is one of those situations where everyone talks, but nobody does. The problem is that the misty concept of "creativity" is difficult enough to define and understand, let alone teach.

In Part VI about half of the articles are geared toward understanding creativity and the creative person; the other half offer concrete suggestions for stimulating creative thinking in the classroom. In article 42 Robert Samples relates the plight of Kari, a sensitive poetic girl who must conform to the demands and meet the needs of rigid teachers. The author points out that despite clichés about "respecting each child's individuality," teachers continue to reward logical, clear thinking but not metaphorical and intuitive kinds of thinking. The solution to Kari's predicament is, at first, a surprising one.

Gary Davis, in article 43, points out that creative people possess a particular set of attitudes and habits. For example, they are flexible and curious in their thinking, and they consciously prefer originality. He suggests that these and other attitudes, motivations, and habits may be encouraged in the classroom by: a. using creative methods and materials, b. letting students practice creating, and c. providing a psychologically safe creative atmosphere.

Complementing Davis's emphasis on the significance of attitudes in creative development, Charles Clark in article 44, with help from Thomas Warren, lists some subtle and not-so-subtle ways a creative student or an innovative teacher may be squelched. The reader will recognize many of the non-ideas in this list.

No one has contributed more to classroom creativity than E. Paul Torrance. In article 45 Torrance itemizes numerous strategies for stimulating original thinking through open-ended instruction. For example, he suggests brainstorming, combining ideas, asking "What could happen if . . ." and other provocative questions, free-associating to abstract sounds, and many others. Straining the imaginations of students and teacher alike, one exercise requires the teacher to role-play a storybook rabbit. The rabbit-teacher answers all questions about his life in the forest and cabbage patch.

In article 46 Davis, Helfert, and Shapiro contrast children's theatre, whose function is to develop on-stage actors, with creative dramatics, a curious endeavor intended to develop the senses, creativity, and especially self-confidence of all students. The authors list simple exercises for stimulating sensory awareness and body control and further describe pantomime and playmaking activities. Particularly with adults, the effects of even a brief creative dramatics session are usually exciting and profound.

It would seem difficult to teach our youngest elementary school children to write poetry, let alone create in them a desire to continue writing potery. Kenneth Koch, however, summarizes in article 47 some simple devices he engineered for eliciting quite fanciful poems from children in a New York elementary school. Such strategies as beginning each line with "I wish . . ." or "I used to be . . . , but now I am . . .," telling tall tales, and other structures elicit amazingly successful poetry.

Abraham Maslow in article 48 makes an intriguing distinction between the type of creative genius exemplified by great artists, composers, and writers—a form of creativity that may or may not include good psychological health—and the creativeness of the well-adjusted, "self-actualized" person. Self-actualizing creativeness springs from the personality and appears in the child-like freedom, spontaneity, expressiveness, and self-acceptance of the fully functioning person. For this, great talent is not needed.

Finally, in article 49, Clark Moustakas summarizes his humanistic views of, first, the creative and then the conforming person. According to Moustakas, the better-adjusted creative individual is in contact with nature and with himself, faces life honestly and openly, and expresses his individual identity. The conformist, on the other hand, loses touch with his own real feelings since his role performance is geared toward status and approval at the expense of valuing his own judgment and perceptions.

forty-two

Kari's Handicap—
The Impediment of Creativity

ROBERT E. SAMPLES

Of course. The only way it could be explained is that snow is a cloud lying down. The ocean breathes a cloud into the air and it becomes tired as it ripples up and down across the desert. When it must rest, it will lie down on a mountain. Maybe it's making love to the mountain. Oh, if it is, I wish I were a mountain. If it stops too long, it can't leave the way it came. The mountains bleed their cloud away and it becomes soiled. But what beautiful punishment ... it can escape out of the inside of an aspen tree to get back into the air ... but only a little at time. That's what it costs to be too tired. Maybe though, it could ...

"Kari!"

Damn you! It was silent, but she thought it. Aloud, she said, "Yes, Mr. Clyde?"

"Have you solved the problem yet?"

"Oh, ... no; I'll need more time."

The teacher's voice rang with bitterness, "You're the only one who needs more time. Have it here by 8 in the morning."

If you saw her running between classes with too many books in her arms and a little bit late, you would never notice that she was different. When she sat in class engrossed in the patterns the window light made on the floor, she seemed commonly inattentive. But once you got to know her, you fully realized that she was different. She flushed with a kind of awareness. Kari was handicapped. But her handicap wasn't a limp or a distorted speech pattern. Her handicap was creativity.

What is creativity? Sometimes creative connection is done in a manner unique to mankind, but most often such connections bring a spark of "newness" to the connector only. In our society those who have the "duty" of determining what is creative and what is not are the critics. They are armed with peculiar kinds of subjective authority focused upon those who attempt to create. The prejudices they bring to their decision making are erudite and usually are not in the realm of the commonplace.

Source: From *Saturday Review*, July 15, 1967, pp. 56–57. Copyright 1967 Saturday Review, Inc. Reprinted by permission of the author and the publisher.

Teachers and other adults who must work with younger people are shadowed by the awareness of the critics' role. As a result, there is often the tendency to use the societal definitions of uniqueness when viewing the creative efforts of individual children. Few realize that both effective surprise and connecting the unconnected are *firstly* individual and *secondly* societal. A child whose perception is acute enough to see the road as a "ribbon of moonlight" cannot be punished because Alfred Noyes saw it first. Yet in many instances they are.

Teachers are instruments of society, and, in an awkward way, they are the judicial branch of society's government. The term in court called the school year is served by each child. The child is sentenced to these years of examination and indoctrination by a society bent on self-perpetuation. In this environment Kari is a misfit. Her teachers have been spawned by a society that has provided them with a host of clichés that guide their perception. They go into rooms full of thirty children with the knowledge that "each child has his own personality" and "each child is an individual" and that "the individual should respect the rights of others." In their implementing of these clichés pervasive concepts of democratic behavior and underdog worship cloud the teachers' analysis of class needs. Protectivism and conformity are built into Kari's school walls.

Kari has too many classmates. But the high numbers are only one excuse for the response of the teachers. Actually, if there were only ten students in each class, Kari would still be mistreated. The school reflects the society from which Kari comes. The school's compartmental treatment of intellectualism is a microcosm of society's patterns. Words, numbers, and activities are separated by fences labeled LANGUAGE, MATH, and GYM.

Kari tries to synthesize all the elements of her world into relevance. In doing so, *she* makes the choices—an act which gives her the plague mark of individuality. She sees an algebraic solution as symbolic poetry that rhymes in the symmetry of logic. The logic doesn't matter, but the meter she perceives does. Her teacher is disgusted by her lack of effort to please him. He makes his requirements clear and is piqued by her apparently intentional effort to ignore *his* needs.

The mathematician Jules Henri Poincaré once described the way he solved a knotty group of problems in the following manner:

> *For fifteen days I strove to prove that there could not be any functions like those I have since called Fuchsian functions. I was then very ignorant; every day I seated myself at my work table, stayed an hour or two, tried a great number of combinations and reached no results. One evening, contrary to my custom, I drank black coffee and could not sleep. Ideas rose in crowds; I felt them collide until pairs interlocked, so to speak, making a stable combination. By the next morning I had established the existence of a class of Fuchsian functions.... I had only to write out the results....*

This suggests something that has been known by psychologists for a long time—more than one mode of thought guides our approach to solving problems. The substantive and internally consistent mode is the "logical, clear-thinking" one that is most admired and accepted by society. More metaphoric and intuitive kinds of thought are regarded suspiciously and only a small segment of society is permitted license to perform them. Regardless the breadth of society's approval, the capabilities for both modes exist in each of us.

In addition to these two, Lawrence Kubie cites the kind of thought whose source lies within the unconscious realm. Substantive thought is born of the conscious realm, and the intuitive is the product of the preconscious realm. Noncreative people, when solving problems and patterning their world, draw

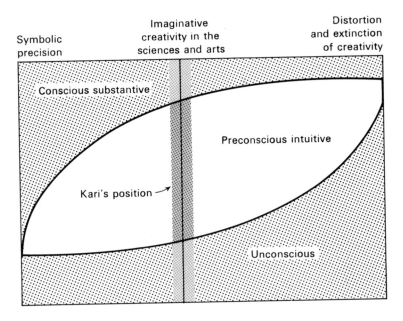

"Substantive thought is born of the conscious realm, and the intuitive is the product of the preconscious realm. The capabilities for both modes exist in each of us."

heavily upon conscious or substantive modes of thought. Creative people, on the other hand, are dependent upon their use of the preconscious or intuitive. Thoughts and behavior resulting from the interference of these two modes from the unconscious realm inhibit both logic and creativity. Thought in the unconscious realm is the kind over which the individual has no control. When this kind of thought predominates, the individual is "sick."

Schools are most dedicated to rewarding substantive thought. Thus, they are effective mirrors of society's rules, and operationally they force the position of the student toward the logical and chronological. The substantive is identified with our professional life while the intuitive dominates our personal lives. At the same time that an awareness that the leisure segment of our lives is increasing, the schools perpetrate the substantive reward patterns. What this means is that while claiming to be attendant to developing the individual to lead a better life, the schools yet serve the institutions recognized by the group. The professional and societal aspects of the role of the individual are stressed by deed and innuendo. The microsociety of the school is modeled after the industrial patterns which pervade the "real world." This means that the clichés prevail while in deed Kari and her kin are discriminated against. The teachers *say* they will serve the individual, but in action they homogenize individuals into anonymous, ineffective groups. This efficiency overwhelms effectiveness.

Kari begins to learn that society expects her, as a female, to act in an intuitive fashion. The adjectives society uses, however, are "emotional" and "irrational." She learns early that upon the male image is bestowed "logical" and "rational" expectations. The fetish of efficiency is superimposed upon the expected behavior of Kari and her classmates. The goals society has set must be reached almost ritualistically and this is what so offends this girl. She does not want to *have* to be a bright mother of two. Nor is she interested in becoming "man-like" and "rational" so that career success will be hers. Kari is just interested in being honest and free.

When the school bells ring, Kari is required to cast an experience full of the brilliant orange of paint and the smell of linseed into a new form. This new image form is called civics. Here she learns to be "civil" by memorizing other new rules structured into a language so formulated that it brings tears to her throat as she reads them. She learns that laws are written by individuals and interpreted by groups. She learns that when she respects her own rights, the chances are she infringes on another's.

Kari obviously has begun to reject elements of the role that she has inherited. She watches fads drift like culture clouds across the scene. She sees paisley print blouses give way to ragged tennis shoes. None of these elements of controlled change apply, for they are not relevant to her. She appears strange to the conformity-cloistered society around her, for it sees her respond to herself rather than to its collective voice. She creates a guilt in the cliché-makers which they transform to resentment for their own self-preservation. They decide that she is the element of abnormality and ply her toward the norm. Her resistance is interpreted as immaturity and stubbornness that must be overcome.

She and those like her are called immoral and they are often admonished by phrases like, "These kids are getting worse every day." The difference between Kari and the voices of rebellion around her is that Kari's questions will continue. Her *why* will not be relinquished when she graduates or marries or has children. Kari is not a victim of her youth. Rather, youth, is asking similar questions and bathing in uninhibited perception, is a victim of a state of mind that is too temporary. With Kari a question is a beginning, an answer, a challenge. Kari somehow resents the giving of an answer. It makes things too pat, and its precision is immediately subject to mistrust.

Kari was the one student in the class who defended the heroine in Hawthorne's *The Scarlet Letter* for having the courage to be apart from the society. At the same time Kari damned her for her dishonesty to herself. The teacher was angry because virtue wasn't winning out in the analysis. Kari said virtue was in doing what *had* to be done, rather than "obeying like a starved rat the corridors of a maze somebody else built." The teacher was so frightened by Kari's argument that he gave her a "D" for her participation.

Kari's uniqueness is only in part due to her creativity, for most children exhibit high creative potential in their youth. Kari's main mark of difference is her courage. It requires courage to ignore the matrix defined by others. She is aware of society's rule of order as surely as she is alert to the way that $F = Ma$ in physics. Her courage is expressed in the way that she behaves. She knows that the subjectivity of society's rule, "Thou shall not," is very different from science's rule, $F = Ma$. In the first case, man's subjectivity is highly influential in guiding the interpretation, while in the second, subjectivity is far less relevant.

By knowing this, Kari has learned to trust the natural far more than the societal. Her courage is displayed by her acceptance of the responsibility that is attendant with mediation. She mediates her experience and ignores the way society claims the right to influence her conclusions. Because the schools fundamentally speak in a language of mediated clichés, they do not greatly affect Kari. She once expressed her role in society by likening herself to a tree. She claimed that the tree could not want, for a tree could use only what it needed; all else was simply irrelevant.

The creative person is able to convert substance into metaphor. Instead of a natural fact, like $F = Ma,$ being a deductive end to the experience of the scientist who investigates relationship between mass and force, it is an inductive beginning. Kari weaves the substance of formalized experience into her intuition.

Her attendance to nature reflects her rejection of mediated sources of experience. Kari sees within the commonplace elements of the natural world a source of elements that are infinitely repatternable. The realm of the commonplace in the world of society is filled with already mediated devices. She is not content with the reassembling of other people's ideas or products. She instead prefers to deal with the source—nature.

In a line of poetry she once wrote, Kari claimed that "Before you can love you must know how to walk in the snow leaving no tracks." She knew the thrill of dashing chaotically through a virgin field of snow. In addition, she knew the excited fulfillment of willing abstinence. Both of these ideas were synthesized into the beautiful statement that applied to all love.

Kari is sixteen and growing up. She and her generation will soon be ours. The structured constraints of society are becoming real to these young people, and we must accept the responsibility to guarantee the nature of their course. Are they to preserve the structure or alter it? It would be foolish to claim that the structure will remain the same, so it *will* evolve. We need the Karis, all of them, but how can they be saved? The simplicity of the answer is as frightening as it is demanding: We must be more like Kari.

REVIEW QUESTIONS

1. Do you think students like Kari are recognized as talented or as classroom headaches? What happens to students like this in college?

2. What would you do for students like Kari?

forty-three

Teaching for Creativity:
Some Guiding Lights

GARY A. DAVIS

The purpose of this article is to summarize three foundational rules or guidelines for increasing creative potential. Before describing these, however, we first must consider what *being creative* is, and further, what is it we do when we *teach creativity*.

There is no doubt that the shapes and forms of human creativity are without limit. Almost daily we see creative products emerging from the fields of music, entertainment, literary and graphic arts; and from science, medicine, industry and other technologies. We might encounter a creatively planned children's room, an innovative repair of a basement leak, a list of creative Christmas gifts, or some problem solution found by imagination rather than repetition. The commonality in this diversity of creative acts is simply the abstract quality of fanciful resourcefulness itself.

It would seem then, that whatever the specific nature of the problem, a person is more likely to respond creatively if he possesses a particular constellation of attitudes and habits which lead him to consciously seek creative solutions. Indeed, creative individuals often have been characterized by their habitual preference for originality, their curiosity and flexibility, and their willingness to differ and to take risks. It is these attitudes and habits which are taught by every course or program seeking to foster creative development, from the Torrance and Myers [1970] elementary-level *Idea Books* through Osborn's [1963] and Gordon's [1961] principles for professional group problem solving. The author's research with sixth-, seventh-, and eighth-grade students has shown that, in fact, students can be taught to hunt for new problem approaches and to value original thinking. A student's awareness of the importance of creative innovation in the larger world and in his own life can be increased. The student can be taught some

Source: From *Journal of Research and Development in Education*, 1971, 4:29–34. Reprinted by permission of the publisher.

simple techniques for forcing new idea combinations such as modifying product attributes or looking for metaphorically-related solutions [Davis, 1969, 1971; Davis and Scott, 1971]. Since the goal of creativity training is to change conscious attitudes and habits in the direction of more creative thinking, the author has developed three guidelines for fostering creative growth, in accord with the goal of creativity training, which concern:

1.   Using creative teaching tactics,

2.   Letting students learn creative attitudes and habits by actually creating, and

3.   Providing a psychologically safe atmosphere for creativity.

USE OF CREATIVE TACTICS

Whether one is writing materials for stimulating creativity or teaching creative attitudes and habits directly to the class, imaginative teaching methods are a must. Traditional methods (including such new traditions as team teaching, nongraded schools, and even computer-assisted instruction) have evolved for imparting information—teaching facts and concepts about science or history, or teaching conceptual skills of mathematics or language usage. On the other hand teaching for creativity aims at strengthening flexibility and open-mindedness, teaching some conscious techniques for producing new idea combinations, and all the while reinforcing the use of innate creative abilities. A different end requires a different means.

A much more important reason for using creative teaching methods and creatively prepared materials has been found in the benefits reaped by teaching creativity by example. The teaching-creativity-by-imitation principle cannot be emphasized enough. It is one thing to tell students that creative thinking requires a nimble imagination, as when in college we teach "about creativity"; it is much more effective to demonstrate what "being creative" is like, through creative classroom activities and creatively written and illustrated materials. The actual teaching can and should demonstrate a lively imagination by the teacher, the materials developer, or preferably both.

Teaching creativity by example may be illustrated with two introductory pages from *Saturday Subway Ride* [DiPego, 1970], a professionally written workbook likely to bend the mind of anyone above adolescent age:

> Let me tell you about last Saturday.
> I took a ride on a new super subway that travels a fast circle from Kansas City to Pittsburgh to Dublin to Tokyo to Santa Monica and back.
> What's wrong?
> You say there's no such subway, and you're about to close the book and stare out the window?
> Well, maybe you're wrong. Maybe I zipped around the world on an underground thought, a daydream, a nightdream, or a 'superfastspecialfivecity' idea.

That's what this book is all about.

Ideas.

You say my subway ride is just a wild idea and pretty silly, and you'd rather pitch pennies?

Well, what about flying? People said that men flying around in machines was a wild idea and pretty silly. Then the Wright brothers took off and ZIP!

People once thought that TV was just a wild idea and probably wouldn't work—and bicycles, too, and life insurance and polio vaccine.

A wild idea is something that people find hard to accept because it's new and sounds strange and looks funny and maybe it's light green suede and smells of paprika. Anyway, it's something people haven't seen before, and that makes them afraid.

Some people only feel safe with old, comfortable, tried-out ideas. I guess those people never learned to stretch their minds.

That's what this book is all about, too—learning to stretch your mind, learning to reach out for big, new, different, and even wild ideas.

Why?

So you can solve problems and create new things and improve old things and have more fun. Ideas are good anywhere, anytime, in any climate and even underwater.

The goal of *Saturday Subway Ride* is to change attitudes and consciously orient students toward using their creative capabilities. It does this by example, as much as by exhortation and exercise.

The various creative thinking materials of Myers and Torrance also demonstrate to the student what "being creative" is like, while asking the student to flex his own inventive muscles. Only writers with imagination, hoping to increase a student's receptiveness to far-fetched idea combinations, would ask, "What could happen if cats could bark when they wanted to?" [Myers and Torrance, 1965a] or "What could a dish made of olives, peanut butter, bread crumbs, and boiled cucumbers be called?" [Myers and Torrance, 1965b].

Still another delightful strategy for altering attitudes and habits is that of Koch, who wanted to ". . . get the gradeschool kids excited about poetry" [Koch, 1970]. For example, with his *Class Collaboration Strategy* for creative poetry writing, Koch asked each child to contribute one line, beginning with "I wish" and containing a color, a comic-strip character, and a city or country (e.g., "I wish I were with Charlie Brown in a blue shirt in France"). Later, his very young students wrote entire poems structured by beginning each line with "I wish" ("I wish I had a pony with a tail like hair"); or beginning alternate lines with "I use to" and "But now" ("I used to be a rose, but now I am a leaf"). Other simple patterns asked for comparisons, clang associations, and metaphors. The result of this creative strategy? Students not only found they could write sensitive, colorful poetry, but they wanted to write more and more of it.

In sum then, teaching for creative growth requires innovative teaching methods and materials because: (1) the goal is teaching attitudes and habits conducive to creative behavior, which requires a departure from instructional methods aimed at imparting factual information, and (2) students benefit tremendously from a model—the teacher, the material, or both—showing what "being creative" is like.

LEARNING CREATIVITY BY DOING CREATIVITY

The second guideline to be emphasized is simply Dewey's time-tested principle of learning by doing. Actively "doing creativity" will stamp in creativity-conscious thinking habits in the same intuitively-sound way that learning-by-doing will improve ice skating, speaking French, or figuring a math problem.

The overall strategy of the Myers and Torrance *Idea Books* evolves around creating conditions which actively elicit creative responses in many forms and in many modes. The examples previously cited bring forth student speculation on the consequences of surprising events (cats barking) and associations to novel idea combinations ("the dish"). Other exercises elicit empathetic, metaphorical thinking almost involuntarily: "What would your shoes say to you as you get ready for a bath on the day you come in last in a race at school?" or "Write a letter from the viewpoint of your pet. And be sure it's newsy" [Myers and Torrance, 1966b]. Memories, combinatory play, sensory awareness and other facets of creative experience and expression are brought out by asking, "Do you remember when you saw (smelled, touched, tasted) something strange or surprising?" [Myers and Torrance, 1966a]. Torrance and Myers [1970] further recommend using incompleteness, for example, asking students to project into the future. The teacher (or materials writer) also may pose such thought-provoking questions as: What use can be made of Polar ice formations? or How might an *odor* be used as a communications device?

Saturday Subway Ride also tries to increase creative strength by extracting from every reader some fanciful thoughts and sensations.

Try to avoid responding creatively to these two exercises:

> Two astronauts are orbiting their spacecraft around the moon.
> Suddenly, there is a knock on the spaceship door.
> Astronaut 1.:
>
> Astronaut 2.:
>
> Answer one of these questions with a tall tale, a couple of paragraphs just for the fun of it, and just for the brain-stretching exercise:
> 1. Where were you born?
> 2. What did you do last Saturday?
> 3. What does your dad do for a hobby?

Research conducted to evaluate the effectiveness of creative thinking programs has concluded that actual participation in creative thinking is the most critical component of the overall experience. The *Purdue Creativity Program* of Feldhusen, Treffinger, and Bahlke [1970; WBAA, 1966] is a set of twenty-eight audio tapes, with three or four printed exercises to accompany every tape. Each tape consists of two components, a three- to four-minute presentation designed to teach a principle of creative thinking (e.g., being open to new ideas, putting ideas together in new ways, valuing creative problem solving) and a story depicting creative, adventurous behavior by such pioneers as Christopher Columbus, Alexander Bell, John Glenn, and Jonas Salk. A series of experimental studies evaluated the relative contributions of each of three training components, the presentations of the creativity principles, the stories, and the exercises, and all possible two-way combinations of these. Students whose experimental treatments included working through the printed exercises alone, or in combination with the presentations or the stories, typically displayed the greatest improvement in their tested creative thinking abilities.

Our own field research also has pointed to the critical role of active participation in improving creative potential. Our most successful field trial included a teacher and class who, day after day, spent a little time on principles and a lot of time on wild, far-out creative thinking [Davis, Houtman, Warren, and Roweton, 1969]. A subsequent study with inner-city students further confirmed that teachers who promote class and individual activities were more successful in increasing measured creative potential than teachers who felt they could not allow group problem-solving or discussion in fear of losing disciplinary control [Davis, Houtman, Warren, Roweton, Mari, and Belcher, 1972].

In sum, the active involvement of the student in thinking of creative ideas and problem solutions is essential in teaching for creativity. Learning by doing acquaints the student first hand with the flexible openness necessary for imaginative problem-solving.

THE CREATIVE ATMOSPHERE

Perhaps the most obvious yet most critical guideline for stimulating creative thinking lies in creating an atmosphere of receptiveness and encouragement for the free expression of ideas. Whether in classroom brainstorming or in creative art, writing, or science projects, the student must be free to create. Or he won't.

Carl Rogers [1962] used the concepts of *psychological safety* and *psychological freedom* to describe the acceptance of both the complete individual and his spontaneous, playful thinking. Osborn's [1963] fundamental principle of deferred judgment also states in flashing neon that successful brainstorming depends upon a psychologically safe, encouraging atmosphere. In fact, in professional brainstorming the chronic growler or idea-squelcher may be invited to leave an otherwise creative problem-solving session.

New ideas often are funny though, and it is quite consistent with the spirit of group problem-solving to laugh at surprising new ideas so long as this levity is not taken as criticism or punishment. Certainly, the substance of both creativity and humor is new and surprising juxtaposition of ideas; and so it is common for successful brainstorming sessions to be humorous and entertaining.

Humor also may be used deliberately, as the author and others have reported

[Davis, 1971; Davis and Houtman, 1968; DiPego, 1970], to contribute the open and safe creative atmosphere so essential for unrestrained creative functioning. For example, *Saturday Subway Ride* displays a far-fetched, humorous, playful attitude throughout—intentionally loosening up the student's conditioned reluctance to challenge strong forces of conformity and tradition. In the *Idea Books* [Myers and Torrance,1965a, 1966a, 1966b] and in *Sound and Images* [Cunnington and Torrance, 1965] Torrance also cultivates the playful associative behavior which is both the cause and the effect of a creative atmosphere.

CONCLUSIONS

In teaching for creative development, both the classroom teacher and the developer of training materials try to increase an individual's capacity for and likelihood of behaving creatively in his personal, educational, and future professional life. If the view is accepted that conscious attitudes and habits related to flexible, imaginative thinking are important and transferable components of creative behavior—common to all forms of creative endeavor—three suggestions should guide teaching for creativity. First, imaginative teaching methods and creatively devised materials must be used since a. the goal is not the traditional one of transmitting scholarly facts and concepts; and b. students may learn what "being creative" is like by using creative teaching activities and creatively prepared materials as models. Second, active participation—learning creativity by doing creativity—is critical. Attitudes and habits of creative thinking must be learned first hand. Third, the psychologically safe and encouraging creative atmosphere is an obvious yet essential part of any successful effort to train imagination. Humor is one good way to stimulate the playful, associative behavior intrinsic to free idea expression.

REFERENCES

Cunnington, B. F., and Torrance, E. P. *Sounds and Images*. Boston: Ginn & Co., 1965.

Davis, G. A. Training creativity in adolescence: a discussion of strategy. In R. E. Grinder (Ed.), *Studies in Adolescence II*. New York: Macmillan, 1969, pp. 538–45. Reprinted in Davis, G. A., and Scott, J. A. (Eds.) *Training Creative Thinking*. New York: Holt, 1971, pp. 261–69.

Davis, G. A. *Psychology of Problem Solving: Theory and Practice*. New York: Basic Books, 1973.

Davis, G. A., and Houtman, S. E. *Thinking Creatively: A Guide to Training Imagination,* Wisconsin Research and Development for Cognitive Learning, University of Wisconsin, 1968.

Davis, G. A., Houtman, S. E., Warren, T. F., and Roweton, W. E. A program for training creative thinking: I. Preliminary field test. *Technical Report No. 104,* Wisconsin Research and Development Center for Cognitive Learning, University of Wisconsin, 1969.

Davis, G. A., Houtman, S. E., Warren, T. F., Roweton, W. E., Mari, S., and Belcher, T. L. A program for training creative thinking: II Inner city evaluation. *Technical Report,* Wisconsin Research and Development Center for Cognitive Learning, University of Wisconsin, 1972.

Davis, G. A., and Scott, J. A. (Eds.) *Training Creative Thinking.* New York: Holt, Rinehart & Winston, 1971.

DiPego, G. *Saturday Subway Ride.* Wisconsin Research and Development Center for Cognitive Learning, University of Wisconsin, 1970. Published as *Imagination Express: Saturday Subway Ride.* Buffalo, N.Y.: D.O.K. Publishers, 1973.

Feldhusen, J. F., Treffinger, D. J., and Bahlke, S. J. Developing creative thinking: The Purdue creativity program. *Journal of Creative Behavior,* 1970, 4:85–90.

Gordon, W. J. J. *Synectics.* New York: Harper & Row, 1961.

Koch, K. *Wishes, Lies, and Dreams.* New York: Chelsea House, 1970.

Myers, R. E., and Torrance, E. P. *Can You Imagine?* Boston: Ginn, 1965.(a)

Myers, R. E., and Torrance, E. P. *Invitations to Speaking and Writing Creatively.* Boston: Ginn, 1965. (b)

Myers, R. E., and Torrance, E. P. *For Those Who Wonder.* Boston: Ginn, 1966. (a)

Myers, R. E., and Torrance, E. P. *Plots, Puzzles and Ploys.* Boston: Ginn, 1966. (b)

Osborn, A. F. *Applied Imagination.* (3rd Ed.) New York: Scribner's, 1963.

Rogers, C. Toward a theory of creativity. In S. J. Parnes and H. F. Harding (Eds.), *A Source Book for Creative Thinking.* New York: Scribners, 1962, pp. 63–72.

Torrance, E. P. and Myers, R. E. *Creative Learning and Teaching.* New York: Dodd, Mead, and Co., 1970.

WBAA. *Creative Thinking: The American Pioneers.* (Audio tapes and a manual for teachers.) West Lafayette, Ind.: Purdue University School of the Air, 1966.

REVIEW QUESTIONS

1. What do you think characterizes a creative classroom atmosphere? How does humor fit in?

2. Can creative thinking be stimulated in a history or a science class? How?

forty-four

How to Squelch Ideas

CHARLES H. CLARK (and THOMAS F. WARREN)

We've never done it that way before . . .
It won't work . . .
We haven't the teacher-student ratio . . .
It's not in the budget . . .
We've tried that before . . .
We're not ready for it yet . . .
All right in theory but can you put it into practice?
Too academic . . .
What will the parents think?
Somebody would have suggested it before if it were any good . . .
Too modern . . .
Too old-fashioned . . .
Let's discuss it at some other time . . .
I'll have to think about that one . . .
You don't understand our situation . . .
We're too small for that . . .
We're too big for that . . .
We have too many projects now . . .
It has been the same for twenty years, so it must be good . . .
What bubblehead thought that up?
Won't we be held accountable?
Would Rafferty like it?
Sounds like something A. S. Neill might do . . .
Not academic enough . . .

Source: Abridgment of "Killer Phrases" from *Brainstorming* by Charles H. Clark, copyright ©
1958 by Doubleday & Company, Inc. Reprinted by permission of the author and the publisher.

I just know it won't work . . .

Let's form a committee . . .

Let's sit on it for a while and watch developments . . .

But that's not our problem . . .

Downtown won't accept it . . .

They'll think we're political . . .

You'll never sell it to the teachers' union . . .

Don't move too fast . . .

Why something new now? Our salaries are still going up . . .

Let's wait and see . . .

Here we go again . . .

Let's put it in writing . . .

I don't see the connection . . .

Won't work in our neighborhood . . .

We can't do it under the regulations . . .

Nuts . . .

The Board will faint . . .

We're too new for that . . .

The sisterhood will object . . .

That's not our department . . .

That's not our job . . .

That's not our role . . .

That's trouble . . .

But things have been running so smoothly . . .

I'll bet some professor suggested that . . .

Ouch . . .

But we have to be practical . . .

Sounds good, but . . .

It's not in the plan . . .

No regulations covering it . . .

But can it be evaluated objectively?

We've never used that approach before . . .

It's not in the curriculum . . .

It'll mean more work . . .

It's not our responsibility . . .

Yes, but . . .

It will increase taxes . . .

It's too early . . .

It's too late . . .

It will offend . . .
It won't pan out . . .
Our people won't accept it . . .
You don't understand the problem . . .
No adolescent is going to tell me how to run this operation . . .
No!

REVIEW QUESTIONS

1.   Do these statements have something to do with creative attitudes, a creative atmosphere, and psychological safety?

2.   Do tradition, habit, conformity, and "don't rock the boat" attitudes influence educational innovation and improvement? Can you think of specific instances?

forty-five

Creativity and Infinity

E. PAUL TORRANCE

Creativity is an infinite phenomenon. A person can be creative in an endless number of ways. The outcomes of creative behavior are inexhaustible.

The coming of the space age and knowledge explosions in every field of human inquiry are making it increasingly necessary for people to learn to be comfortable with infinity. There was a time when we thought we knew the limits to space, to man's potential, to knowledge. A person could learn some good things in school, college, or an apprenticeship and these learnings would last him for the rest of his life. This day is no more. Men of the future will have to behave creatively.

As computers do more and more of the routine or repetitive work we become freer to behave creatively and there is no limit to what we might do and become. A person may produce a few original or creative ideas by chance but sustained creativity requires an ability to continue to get glimpses of infinity. Unfortunately, we have done little about teaching children to be comfortable with infinity. Usually, infinity astonishes, wearies, confounds, and frightens us. The ancient Greeks had a favorable attitude toward infinity and attributed it to the boundless environment of our cosmos. The Romans, however, regarded infinity unfavorably and negatively. To them, it meant "obscure, variable, unfinished, bad, irrational, flowing or formless, and indefinite."[1] Theologians have emphasized God's infinity and man's finiteness.

Quite interestingly, young children seem to grasp the concept of infinity intuitively. For example, when you show them Bruno Munari's *Zoo* [1963] with the drawing of birds captioned, "An infinity of birds," they understand. They will say, "Oh, yes, there are so many birds you can't count them." Provided open-ended experiences with opportunities to use their individuality and their creativeness, young children will get glimpses into infinity.

Like the concept of infinity, open-ended kinds of education programs and

Source: From *Journal of Research and Development in Education*, 1971, 4:35–41. Reprinted by permission of the author and the publisher.
[1] *Encyclopedia Britannica*, Vol. 12, pp. 235–8.

methods of instruction give the learner the opportunity to respond in terms of his or her experiences and abilities whatever these may be. Some teachers regard such methods and programs as dangerous. When a child responds in terms of his experiences and abilities, this takes the teacher outside his own experiences and abilities. Open-ended programs and methods of instruction cannot be pre-inspected and certified for safety. One never knows for sure where the open ends will lead.

Open-endedness does not imply a lack of structure. For effective learning, there must be some structure, some guides to behavior. One must never lose sight, however, of the self-acting nature of the human mind. This recognition is especially important in the education of creatively-gifted children. It is almost as if their creativity has plugged them into infinity. No matter how much structure is provided the highly creative child, he or she will want to know about things beyond this structure. Such children will produce ideas that go beyond the wildest predictions of the teacher or curriculum maker. This requires of the teacher the most alert and sensitive kind of guidance possible.

The author's recent work with language arts activities has offered excellent opportunities that illustrate the characteristics of educational experiences that make children comfortable with the limitlessness of infinity. Any other aspect of the curriculum can provide equally good examples.

OPEN-ENDEDNESS AND INCOMPLETENESS

One of the simplest ways of giving children glimpses into infinity is through books and stories that have open ends with limitless possibilities. An example of such a book is Fenn Lasell's *Fly Away Goose* [1965]. This beautiful story is of a little girl who is hesitating over collecting the goose's egg and letting it become a part of the omelet that night. She thinks of many of the consequences that might result if she leaves the egg and it hatches into a little gosling—both the joyful consequences as well as the sorrowful ones like having to take the mature goose to market, or the goose's being shot by hunters. At the end, the little girl concluded, "I think I'll leave it for mother goose and see if it will hatch. Who knows?" Thus, this deep-moving, emotion-arousing story is left open for the children to produce a limitless number of exciting possibilities. The child is not limited to the single, most probable response. Since no one really knows, each child is free to guess, to speculate.

The following kinds of activities are effective in creating open-endedness in all curricular areas:

1. Playing with ambiguities and uncertainties
2. Freeing children from inhibiting sets or expectations—helping them find the "tops in their cages"
3. Producing awareness of incompleteness of the information presented
4. Making divergent thinking legitimate
5. Examining fantasies for solutions to everyday problems

6. Encouraging multiple hypotheses
7. Letting one thing lead to another
8. Encouraging transformation of information

COMBINING APPARENTLY IRRELEVANT ELEMENTS

When two or more somewhat unrelated elements must be synthesized into a single response, the mental leap that occurs is likely to result in something original. This can be done as in a "make-up-your-own stories" exercise such as is found in the reader, *How It Is Nowadays* [Clymer and Ness, 1969]. In one of these, the reader is asked to make up a story about a wicked king named Bong; a beloved Princess, Rose; and an errand boy, Wug.

Exercises such as these produce an endless variety of stories which, when read to a class, can give a little glimpse into infinity. Using a design similar to *Tell a Tall Tale* [Salisbury, 1966], the idea can be extended. This intriguing book contains six stories, each with two characters, two places, and three actions. These elements can be combined in such a way as to produce 279,936 stories. It is easy to show children that if 30 of them make up six such simple stories, a total of 8,398,080 stories results immediately. Then, when all 180 of their stories (instead of 6) are combined, an astronomical number of possibilities results. If this can result so effortlessly, think what would happen if we really tried.

The following ways of encouraging the combination of apparently irrelevant elements may be applied in almost any curricular area:

1. Searching for elegant solutions (i.e., simplest solutions taking into account largest number of variables)

2. Playing with analogies as a basis for searching for solutions to problems

3. Experimenting and manipulating objects, ideas, etc.

4. Encouraging children to use knowledge in one field to solve problems in another

5. Requiring reorganization of information, objects, etc.

6. Synthesizing unorganized objects, ideas, etc. into meaningful arrangements

PRODUCING ELEMENTS AND COMBINING

Open-endedness can be increased still further by having children themselves produce the elements to be combined into a story, a drama, a picture, a dance, or some other communication.

An effective procedure found in the author's research has been termed *Magic Net* technique. This procedure can be used endlessly to produce exciting stories and dramas. To produce an atmosphere of magic, pieces of colored nylon net, music, and at times lights are used. Usually, about six actors take part. Each actor selects a piece of the colored net which turns him into whatever character he wants to play. To "warm up" the actors, they are encouraged to stand, walk, and dance as their character would. Then a member of the audience is given the magic story teller's net and asked to start a story involving the six characters. When the story teller finishes the first episode, the actors enact it. A second story teller resumes the story which is then acted by the cast wearing the magic nets. This involves a continuous problem solving process in which each subsequent story teller must get the characters out of the predicament created by the previous story teller and create another predicament. Each character must translate the action of the story into bodily movement in his own way, adding still other dimensions to the production.

The following kinds of activities are useful in implementing the strategy of producing elements and then combining them:

1. Examining a problem, piece of information, or object from several points of view and then combining the insights engendered

2. Searching for all the facts in a mystery and then solving it

3. Making a series of predictions on the basis of accumulating information

4. Learning the component skills for a complex task and then combining them in the performance of the task

5. Producing multiple analogies and then combining the insights gained from their use

BRAINSTORMING WITHIN A GIVEN STRUCTURE

The brainstorming technique [Osborn, 1963; Parnes, 1967] can be used to generate an endless variety of ideas for the open-ended stories, combinations of unrelated elements, the production of elements to be combined, or any other given structure. This would be likely to increase the imaginativeness of whatever is produced and at the same time give a quicker and deeper glimpse into infinity. The usual rules of brainstorming are applicable, such as:

1. Evaluation is suspended

2. Free-wheeling and wild ideas are welcomed

3. Quantity is wanted

4. Combination and improvement are sought

5. Discussion and argument are unwelcome

The technique can be applied to the production of cinquains, for example. We could follow one of the usual structures such as the following:

First line—one word (title)

Second line—two words describing the title

Third line—three words, expressing action

Fourth line—four words expressing feeling

Fifth line—another for the title

Let us say we wanted to make up a cinquain about the color "blue." We would brainstorm words to describe "blue" and then select the two that do the best job. Then we would brainstorm words telling what "blue" does and select the three words that tell best what "blue" does. Next we would brainstorm words to describe how "blue" feels or makes us feel and select the four most appropriate words. Finally, we would brainstorm words that synthesize all of these things and select the one that best distills the essence of "blue."

WARM-UP EXPERIENCES

Well designed and executed *warm-up* experiences can be quite useful in helping children free their imagination and plug them into infinity. The experience may be a field trip, a musical recording, a socio-drama, a poem, creative movement, or about any other experience having high arousal value.

The Cunnington and Torrance [1965] *Sounds and Images* materials provide one model for designing warm-up experiences. The *Sounds and Images* recordings provide a series of four sounds, ranging from a familiar, coherent sound effect to a strange one consisting of six rather unrelated sound elements. As each sound is played, the listener is asked to think of an image and express it in a word picture. The sounds are presented a second time and the listener is asked to let his imagination swing wider. Finally, they are presented a third time with the listener being asked to let his imagination "go the limits." These materials can be then used for stories, drawings, and the like. This can be done by having the listener select the most interesting of the storehouse images that he produced or some combination of them.

The following kinds of warm-up activities may be applied in almost any subject in the curriculum:

1. Heightening anticipation and expectation
2. Heightening concern about a problem
3. Building onto existing information or skills
4. Stimulating curiosity and wanting to know
5. Making purpose of activity clear and meaningful
6. Giving minimal clues and direction

ENVIRONMENTAL WARM-UP

Classroom environments frequently inhibit the *warm-up* necessary for creative language arts activity and make it difficult to help children catch glimpses of infinity. Some classrooms can be modified easily to create a mood or arouse affect. To facilitate the creation of such moods, Gerard Pottebaum [1970] and his associates have created what they call *The Tree House Learning Environment.* These environments give the intimacy, excitement, and delight of a tree house and consist of panels or flexible dividers that make possible an endless variety of environments within a given classroom. One set of panels might create a jungle environment free from the distractions of the frozen Arctic environment of another group. These settings make it easier for children to transcend the commonplace and obvious and make those mental leaps that result in original productions, if not in glimpses of infinity.

IDENTIFYING GAPS IN KNOWLEDGE

Infinity is incompatible with completeness, but as children learn to read and progress in school, they tend to accept what they read or see as complete. To break this up and make them more comfortable with infinity, teachers can show children that an endless number of questions remain and employ exercises to develop question-asking skills based upon pictures, objects, or stories.

For this purpose, puzzling or ambiguous pictures are desirable. An example of this is one of a dog driving an unusual-looking automobile on a busy city street in *The Dog Next Door* [Clymer and Martin, 1969]. The best stories for this purpose are those which are emotionally involving. A favorite for this purpose with preschool and primary grade children is Aileen Fisher's [1964] *Listen, Rabbit.* Throughout this beautifully written story, a little boy wants to make friends with a rabbit. He wonders what the rabbit is doing, whether it be on a moonlight night or when it is snowing. Finally, in the spring he finds the rabbit's nest with five little cottontails. After reading this very moving story, the children are asked to pretend that the teacher is the rabbit and that they can ask any question they like about the life of the rabbit in the story. To facilitate this, the author makes use of a puppet rabbit similar to the one in the story. Whether the children get glimpses into infinity is not known. In his role of the rabbit, however, the author knows that the story teller does.

PLAYING WITH IMPROBABILITIES

Another kind of experience that gives children glimpses of infinity is playing with improbabilities. This may take any of several formats. One is the "what-could-happen-if" technique Myers and Torrance [1965] used in *Can You Imagine?* Examples are:

What could happen if it always rained on Saturday?
What could happen if it were against the law to sing?

Another is the "just-suppose" technique used in tests of creative thinking

[Torrance, 1966] and in preprimary programs in recent years. Examples of these are:

> Just suppose you could make the kind of weather you want by dancing certain ways?
>
> Just suppose you could visit the prehistoric section of the museum and the animals could come alive?
>
> Just suppose you could enter into the life of a pond and become whatever you wanted to become?

These "just-supposes" can be brainstormed and enacted. For example, each child might be asked to decide what he wants to be and do in the pond. We can then enact life in the pond or enact each child's version of life in the pond. After such experiences as these, children find it easy to make up interesting stories, songs, and poems about life in the pond.

MULTI-MODAL EXPRESSION

Frequently, we involve children in an experience and they find it almost impossible to find words to express their reactions to it. They might be able to express their reactions by creative movement, sounds, or even drawings, but we insist that they express their reaction in words. They may produce something but it is likely to lack depth and may even be irrelevant to the experience. If they could first express their reactions in the mode that seems natural, they might then be able to write or talk with deep and imaginative insight about the experience. Creative movement, producing sounds, or making drawings may provide the breakthrough that challenges the ability to express insights in words.

PROVOCATIVE QUESTIONS

The *provocative question* is one that causes people to think about something in ways that they have never thought of before. Torrance and Myers [1970] and Torrance [1970] have written rather extensively about asking provocative questions. The following types of questions are usually provocative:

1. Questions that confront the pupil with ambiguities and uncertainties

2. Questions that make the familiar strange or the strange familiar

3. Questions that cause the pupil to look at the same thing from several different physical, psychological, sociological, or emotional points of view

4. Questions that require speculation and predicitions based on limited information

5.   Questions that juxtapose apparently irrelevant or unrelated elements

6.   Questions that call for the exploration of mysteries or puzzling phenomena

7.   Questions that stimulate the explanation of fantasies to facilitate the understanding of realistic problems

CONCLUSION

The author has made a first, halting attempt to identify and illustrate the kinds of educational experiences that will give children glimpses into infinity and make them more comfortable with infinity through the use of their creative powers. There are surely others or elaboration and modification of the ones suggested in this article.

REFERENCES

Clymer, T.,and Martin, P. M. *The Dog Next Door*. Boston: Ginn and Company, 1969.

Clymer, T.,and Ness, P. H. *How It Is Nowadays*. Boston: Ginn and Company, 1969.

Cunnington, B. G.,and Torrance, E. P. *Sounds and Images*. Boston: Ginn and Company, 1965.

Fisher, A. *Listen, Rabbit*. New York: Thomas Y. Crowell, 1964.

Lasell, F. H. *Fly Away Goose*. Boston: Houghton Mifflin, 1965.

Munari, B. *Zoo*. Cleveland: World Publishing Company, 1963.

Myers, R. E., and Torrance, E. P. *Can You Imagine?* Boston: Ginn and Company, 1965.

Osborn, A. F. *Creative Imagination*. (3rd Ed.) New York: Charles Scribner's Sons, 1963.

Parnes, S. J. *Creative Behavior Guidebook*. New York: Charles Scribner's Sons, 1967.

Pottebaum, G. A. *The Tree House Learning Environment*. Kettering, Ohio: The Tree House, 1970.

Salisbury, K. *Tell a Tall Tale*. New York: Western Publishing, 1966.

Torrance, E. P. *Torrance Tests of Creative Thinking: Norms-Technical Manual (Research Edition)*. Princeton, N.J.: Personnel Press, 1966.

Torrance, E. P. *Encouraging Creativity in the Classroom*. Dubuque, Iowa: Wm. C. Brown Company, 1970.

Torrance, E. P.,and Meyers, R. E. *Creative Learning and Teaching*. New York: Dodd, Mead and Company, 1970.

REVIEW QUESTIONS

1. How does Torrance relate *creativity* and *infinity?*
2. Which of his strategies and exercises would you feel comfortable with?

forty-six

Let's Be An Ice Cream Machine—
Creative Dramatics

GARY A. DAVIS, CHARLES HELFERT, AND GLORIA SHAPIRO

Around mid-year, the janitor, secretary, and principal cornered you in the cloakroom as you were about to pile the last boot of the day in the lost-and-found. With carefully picked words the principal spoke first, "Many are called, but few are chosen. YOU have the honor of teaching the first creative dramatics course at Central. This honor is yours because of your genuine ability as a geography teacher, your homeroom victory in the clothing drive and because you are the only teacher free from 3:30 to 4:30 on Monday, Wednesday, and Friday."

The secretary was next. With script in hand, she began reciting the role expectations of every new teacher. The janitor and principal reinforced her speech with a smiling round of applause.

The janitor was last to step forward. "You can use the Girl's gym. Take off your shoes and don't leave a mess! The union sez I don't hafta clean the gym twice in one day." The trio turned and paraded out.

Stunned, you sat yourself on the lost-and-found box, looked desperately at that last boot and quietly screamed, "HELP!"

WHAT IS CREATIVE DRAMATICS?

Creative dramatics is indeed a strange school subject. There are no agreed-upon goals nor any standard course content. There are almost no published workbooks, no achievement tests, and no behavioral objectives. Rows of desks and memorizing will just get in the way. While creative dramatics is not one of your standard subjects, it can do things which no amount of traditional classwork can accomplish.

Source: Reprinted from the *Journal of Creative Behavior,* 1973, 7:37–48. Copyright 1973 by Gary A. Davis. Reprinted by permission of the authors and the publisher.

In a sense, creative dramatics is the education of the whole person by experience. For example, you can tell students how important the human senses are, or you can let them feel, hear, see, smell, and taste. You can teach concepts like *trust* or *faith* with a dictionary-type description, or you can ask some students to shut their eyes and let unknown others lead them around the room or even across a busy street.

There are many ways to stimulate thinking, problem solving, and imagination [Davis, 1973], but one of the best is creative dramatics. There are *not* many well-known methods for increasing awareness and concentration, for developing control of the physical self, for sharpening the senses, for learning to discover and control emotion, for developing pride in individuality, and for strengthening self-confidence in speaking and performing. Creative dramatics helps with these too, and quite a lot.

It is important to note that creative dramatics is not "children's theatre" or "acting." However, creative dramatics experience is guaranteed to improve any amateur theatrical performance, and we highly recommend it for the classroom teacher seeking to loosen up her memorize-your-line thespians. As a rule of thumb however, "theatre" is concerned with communication between actors and an audience; "drama" deals with the unique experiences of participants [Way, 1967]. More simply, theatre develops actors, creative dramatics develops people. In fact, the demands of formal stage play might well damage the self-confidence which creative dramatics is trying to strengthen. Further, the presence of an audience only interferes with the imaginative, sensitive involvement of successful creative drama. Few children are natural actors, but everyone can be 100 per cent successful in creative drama.

THE LEADER

An *ideal* (read: nonexistent) creative dramatics leader would be highly skilled in guiding creative thinking. She also would possess a large working knowledge pertaining to physiological and psychological development, dramatic structure, and children's literature. She also would be skilled in dancing, acting, and instrumental music. But more importantly, and more realistically, the leader must have or adopt a particular personality.

First of all, it helps to love kids, and we don't mean the old turn-it-on, turn-it-off variety that shows one face at parent conferences and the real one in the teachers' lounge. Can you pay compliments when none have been earned? How would you feel about a 7:30 Saturday morning doorbell ring, which suddenly reminds you of a casual promise to show the boys where the muskrats live? Do you often bring along an extra peanut butter and banana sandwich or two for the kids with thin lunch bags?

If love is no problem, the next hurdle is *energy*. A creative dramatics leader must be able to show, not merely tell her people what to do. She not only needs to keep up with the kids, but occasionally must out-energize them. The best teachers are usually eight jumps and a bushel of ideas ahead of their students. Can you survive swinging through the jungle like a monkey, wading through a field of flypaper, crossing a burning desert in a bouncing box, swimming in a tank of Jello, being anchor man in an imaginary tug of war—and still provide the horsepower for a giant people machine?

If you have the love and energy, the last ingredient is a good sense of humor. It may seem strange that a key ingredient for anything is funniness; but for creative dramatics high quality silliness—with all its laughs, freedom, joy and spontaneity—is essential. We are speaking now of a creative atmosphere, an atmosphere of freedom of expression and acceptance of the whole child. There is no wrong; and there is minimal direction as to *how* a student should perform. Each person invents and discovers the how for himself. He does his own imaginative thing in his own unique way, and this is creative dramatics.

AGE DIFFERENCES: THE OLDER YOU ARE, THE MORE YOU NEED IT

So far, we have said little about student age differences. Creative dramatics is a valuable experience for all ages. The first author, Davis, teaches undergraduate and graduate college courses in creative thinking and problem solving. The highlight of a given course is always the creative dramatics session. As a totally new experience, these adults (some in their thirties and forties) involve their whole bodies in creative exercises and activities. They bend and twist in dozens of forms. They beep, chug, and twirl their limbs as a people machine grinding out chocolate ice cream. They stare at a fellow student, almost a total stranger, mimicking his every move. They melt to the floor as ice cubes on a stove; and there in total silence listen intently—to fast steps in the hall above, the buzz of fluorescent tubes, a noisy bird, some laughing, a diesel-engined bus. Then these proper adults pick themselves up like rag-doll puppets with strings fixed on noses and elbows. With eyes shut, they feel the face of a fellow student—for the first time in their educational lives gathering information so they can later pick him from the class.

How do adults react to such an experience? They might take the class over before the hour is out—"Let's make another machine—do whatever you want!" "Everyone balance on one leg in an awkward position and hold on to everybody else to keep from falling over!" It is a day of true creative regression that they do not soon forget; and they likely will share their experiences with their own future students.

Naturally, the teacher must gear the activities to the age of the class. The graduate students won't feel too silly tugging on an imaginary rope or holding up a sinking ceiling, but they might be embarrassed at prancing like circus ponies or role-playing the three bears. Also, if creative dramatics activities are to continue for a long period, you the leader will need a couple of books for new ideas. While we especially recommend Way [1967], several helpful volumes are listed in our bibliography.

If you do lead a session, remember that creative activities will at first be strange and unfamiliar enough. Be sure that directions are clear and that everyone understands what to do. Examples may help, so long as the examples are not copied. How to perform is the student's creative task. Also, while you will have certain activities planned, be ready to get off-course at any instant.

SOME ACTIVITIES

For organizational purposes, we have subdivided this section into three parts—movement exercises, sensory and body awareness activities, and pantomime and playmaking. In practice, movement exercises and sensory/body awareness activities will be interwoven—for example, creative listening is a great relaxer following a robot-walk through a butterscotch swamp. Also, if you include playmaking in your session, some preliminary movement and sensory exercises will loosen up mind and body.

MOVEMENT EXERCISES

1.   *Holding up the roof.* All participants strain to hold up the roof; slowly let it down (to one knee), then push it back up. Strenuous.

2.   *Circles.* Students stand in large circle. Each participant, in turn, thinks of a way to make a circle using his body. All other students make the same circle. The circles can be made with part of the body or all of the body, it can be a fixed circle (e.g., a halo) or a moving circle (e.g., a circular motion of the foot or rolling eyeballs). Names add to the fun, e.g., "This is a *halo circle,*" "This is an *eyeball circle.*"

3.   *Tug-of-war.* Pick two five-man teams for imaginary tug-of-war. Leader narrates, e.g., "This side seems to be winning; now this other side seems to be winning. Look out! The rope broke!" Students will fall in two heaps without coaching.

4.   *Mirrors.* Form two lines facing each other; each person needs a partner. Each individual in one row becomes a mirror that mimics the movement of his partner, who might be brushing his teeth, pulling faces, or putting on clown make-up.

5.   *Puppets.* Several variations. Leader can narrate as all rag-doll marionettes are lifted from floor by strings attached to nose and elbow—then dropped! Or, with children in pairs, one is the marionette and the other is the string-pulling puppeteer.

6.   *People machine.* Infinite variations. Student can create ice cream

(or donut or environmental clean-up) machine, with or without humms, buzzes, beeps, and boops. Students can spontaneously join action, or join systematically one by one. All can move, or else every other one can make a noise to match his neighbor's movement. Slow it down, speed it up. One of the best is a people machine that makes people on an imaginary assembly belt.

7. *Invisible balls.* Form subgroups of four to six students. Each student makes up an invisible ball which, one at a time, is tossed, floated, hauled, etc., around the circle. In one variation each person in a large circle describes the new form of the ball as he passes it to his neighbor ("Now it's heavy"—or hot, gooey, stinky, etc.).

8. *Ice cubes.* Everyone is an ice cube which melts; different effects if melted by sun or by stove. A variation is to be sand bags that leak.

9. *Statues.* According to "Go" and "Stop" signals, or beginning and ending of leader's drum beat, students freeze in ugliest positions imaginable. Student observers or statues themselves describe what they are. [See Way, 1967, Ch. 5, for many extensions and variations.]

10. *Biggest thing.* Participants physically expand themselves into the biggest thing they can be. Follow with *Smallest thing.* Variations include lightest, heaviest, stiffest, angriest, happiest, most frightful, most fearless, etc. Transition from one form to its opposite may be in slow motion.

11. *Circus.* Each child becomes a different circus performer or animal. Variations include the leader directing what *everyone* should be, e.g., tightrope walkers, trained elephants, lion tamers, jugglers, etc.

12. *Obstacle.* With chalk, draw "start" and "finish" lines about eight feet apart on the floor. One at a time, each student makes up imaginary obstacles which he must climb over, dodge past, wade through, overcome, etc., to get from start to finish. Observers guess the obstacle.

13. *Gym work-out.* Participants pantomime activities as if they were in an imaginary gym. They run in place, lift weights, roll a medicine ball, climb a rope, etc.

14. *Leader game.* Students form large circle. One person goes outside the room until called. Another person is selected to start some motion which the other children follow. The first person is brought back into the center of the circle and tries to guess who the leader is. The leader changes the motion when the observer is not watching.

15. *Robot walk.* Each person is a robot with a sound. Whenever one robot touches another robot, both stop, sit down, and begin again to rise, with a new sound and a new walk.

16. *Awkward hold up.* Students balance on one leg in awkward position, holding onto the arms and ankles of others to keep from falling.

17. *Balloon burst.* All students are on the floor as *one* deflated balloon.

The leader begins to blow the balloon up and the students must work together to expand and create a shape. Variations of balloon bursting: Let the air out slowly, pop with a pin, or blow the balloon so full of air that it bursts.

18. *Making letters.* Have two people at a time make any alphabet letter with their bodies. Others guess the letter. Or have larger group spell EN-VIRONMENT or word of their choice.

19. *Nature's shapes.* Children shape their bodies to become a tree, stone, leaf, growing flower, rain, sun, etc.

20. *Sticky floor.* Have students glue a portion of their bodies (e.g., elbow) to the floor. Discover movements they can make while glued.

21. *Creative locomotion.* Have children walk like a crooked man, Jolly Green Giant, Raggedy Ann, robot; run like a mouse or Miss Muffet frightened by a spider, the fattest lady in the world running for a bus; jump like a kangaroo, popcorn, or plow horse. Music, such as Sibelius' *Peer Gynt Suite* or Moussorgsky's *Pictures at an Exhibition,* is a good movement stimulus.

SENSORY AND BODY AWARENESS EXERCISES

1. *Body movement.* Children discover moving body parts by teacher asking them to move their fingers, then hands, wrists, elbows, shoulders, neck (head rolling), face (chew, make faces, bat eyelashes), back, hips, legs, ankles, feet, and toes. Variations: Ask students for more ideas (e.g., eyeballs, tongue, stomach muscles); ask students to keep *all* parts moving as more are added.

2. *Waking up the body.* Have children lie on the floor in any position with eyes closed and body parts relaxed. With slow, quiet music have the children begin waking up the various parts of their bodies one at a time until they are on their feet.

3. *Stretching.* Beginning at their heads and working down, have the children stretch the various parts of their bodies.

4. *Swinging.* Let the group discover all of the ways a body can be made to swing—head, arms, legs, waist, etc.

5. *Warm-up at different speeds.* Have children run in place in slow motion, speed up until children are moving very fast. Variations include jumping, skipping, hopping.

6. *Rag doll-tin man.* Have children perform simple warm-up exercises as limp as a rag-doll; as stiffened tin men let them discover how their movements change.

7. *Paper exploration.* Give each child a piece of 9 x 12 construction

paper. Have them balance the paper on different parts of the body (especially the foot); run with the paper on the palms of their hands.

8. *Exploring an orange.* Give everyone an orange to examine closely. How does it feel, smell, taste? What is unique about *your* orange; could you pick it out from a crowd of oranges? Take it apart and look at it, taste, touch, and smell the inside. Eat it.

9. *Blind man.* Divide participants into pairs. Member with eyes shut (or blindfolded) is led around room, under tables and chairs, and allowed to identify objects by touch, smell, or sound. Variation: go outside. Can lead to discussion of blindness and replacement senses.

10. *Observation test.* Cover some article of apparel, such as earrings or necktie, and ask what the object looks like. Variations: Ask a particular person to close his eyes and describe what the person next to him is wearing. Ask students to shut their eyes. How many windows and lights are there? What color are the walls? Are the maps down?

11. *Focusing.* Ask students to see only things that are very close; middle distance, very far. What do they see?

12. *Empathic vision.* Ask students to inspect the room through the eyes of an artist, fire inspector, lighting engineer, a termite. Look at today's weather from the point of view of a duck, a skier, a field mouse, smoke jumpers. Who else?

13. *Listening.* Have students sit (or lie) silently, listening for whatever they can hear. Encourage concentration, letting sounds evoke associated images and memories. Variations: Listen only for close sounds or far sounds. With *all* eyes shut, have students describe source of sound with hands, communicating without words.

14. *Imaginary sounds.* Ask students to suggest sounds found in particular places—a factory, zoo, railroad station, department store, gas station, police station, etc.

15. *Touching.* Have students touch many surfaces, concentrating fully on the feel. Use strange things (e.g., a piece of coral) and familiar things.

16. *Imaginary touching.* Have children imagine the feel of different objects and surfaces, e.g., warm sand between the toes, a hot sidewalk, a wet paw and a lick on the face, ice cream, a Twinkie, mud, and so on.

17. *Body contacts.* Have participants concentrate on contacts of body places with, e.g., soles of shoes, shirt collars, chair seats, contacts between fingers. Can they feel the shirt or blouse in the middle of the back? Can they feel heart beats, stomach, lungs?

18. *Texture walk.* Have group walk through imaginary substances, e.g., Jello, flypaper, deep sand, chocolate pudding, tacks, swamp, etc., with leader and members calling out new substances and surfaces.

19. *Smelling.* Indoors and outdoors, have students shut eyes and sniff.

Can they identify individual smells? Have students imagine good smells. What are they? Can everyone imagine them? Have them imagine the smell of, e.g., tulips, their mothers, a bus, a barn, a hamburger, etc.

20.   *Tasting.* Encourage students to be aware of and to concentrate upon different tastes of foods. Imaginary tastes can be suggested; perhaps some new taste experiences can be shared, with reasonable sanitary precautions.

PANTOMIME AND PLAYMAKING

Playmaking involves acting out stories and scenes without a script. In fact, you can even do without lines. When a child is asked to pantomime an action, full attention may be given to the elements that compose it. He creates the proper shape and movements of his body and even intently fixes his eyes upon objects in his imaginary environment. With encouragement, he can use his face, hands and body to display sadness, glee, love, or fear. If this same child were allowed to speak, he might very well dismiss all bodily and facial expression and let only his words convey the message. Some suggestions for pantomime exercises are as follows. Throughout, encourage students to "show me, don't tell me."

1.   *Animal pantomimes.* Have the children imitate the way a particular animal moves. In turn, each child can come into the center of the circle to pantomime his animal. The rest of the group can guess the animal, perhaps by moving into the center to feed it. For variety, two or three animals can act out a simple plot, for example:

    a.   a cat sneaking up on a mouse,

    b.   a bear looking for honey, but finding bees,

    c.   a bloodhound tracking down a possum,

    d.   a bull spotting some picnickers, or

    e.   a fox sneaking up on a chicken.

2.   *Alice's potion.* Have two bottles filled with magic potions. One makes people very small and the other makes them very tall.

3.   *Upside down.* If the world turned upside down and your group remained right-side up, what difficulties might you encounter? Pantomime activities like walking on your hands (or the sky), pouring drinks, or changing clothes.

4.   *Hats.* Create a hat shop, real or imagined, in which various kinds of workers come in to select a hat fitting their job, e.g., baseball player, policeman, fireman, Indian chief, cowboy, movie star, milkman, etc. With hat in place, each child pantomimes the behavior matching his hat.

5.   *Picnic.* The children decide what kind of person they would like to be at a picnic. It is helpful to suggest that they give their character a quality

which makes him more readily identifiable, such as a slight limp, a brisk walk, a burly strut, or a skipping or dancing motion. Of course, their faces should match the motion. When they have decided, let them walk around together until they are in character. As leader, you become the bus driver that loads up the group and takes them to the picnic. Once there, they are ready to apply their characterization to improvised situations: They can organize sports, a food table, feeding animals, dodging the local bull, swatting ants and flies, opening the pop, etc. When the players decide to leave, repack the bus and drive off.

6.   *Inside out.* Many pantomimic activities can be explored from the inside out. Children become fish in a fish tank and others look in. Zoo animals in cages are good sources for this activity. You may wish to move into empathetic abstraction by having a child's mirror describe what it's like to be looked into all day; likewise for a book's pages, a TV set, a road map.

7.   *Add-ons.* An add-on, much like a people machine, is an environment created by the group. For example, one child begins rolling a bowling ball down a lane. Another becomes the ball, a pin, the scorecard, a drinking fountain, and whatever else they can think of until the picture is complete. If available, sound effects records are helpful. Other worthwhile subjects are fishing, croquet, baseball, hanging clothes on the line, a circus, an orchestra, marine fish and animals (octopuses, starfish, crabs, lobsters), zoo animals, farm animals, etc.

8.   *Miscellaneous pantomime.* Many brief sketches may teach characterization, for example, a jolly drugstore clerk making an ice cream soda, a fussy lady trying on hats, a scared mountain climber scaling a cliff, tired pirates digging for treasure, giggly kids watching a funny movie, a grouchy cab driver fighting 5:00 P.M. traffic, a nervous sneak thief entering a candy store, an awkward cook flipping pancakes. You and your students can think of more.

Playmaking as a form of creative drama can take many forms other than pantomime activities. With one straightforward strategy, students are given a simple scene or plot, characterization—and then turned loose. In some examples from Way [1967, pp. 107–09], one group of three students could be the Three Stooges robbing a bank. They're so half-witted they do everything wrong, backwards, or both. Other groups of the same idiots can act as a surgery team performing a heart-transplant ("Gimme a knife and a blood bucket!") ; perform as a musical quartet for trombone, drum, nose harp, and garbage can; erect a tent on a windy, rocky hill; or paint and wallpaper a kitchen.

Note that by giving students a perfectly logical reason for being silly, they are helped in overcoming feelings of self-consciousness. Fear of failure is removed and confidence is built [Way, 1967].

But mini-plays need not always be silly. Way [1967, pp. 83–4] suggests that groups can be miners working against time to reinforce a mine about to cave in; slow-moving astronauts assembling something on the moon; toyshop toys (or museum displays) coming alive at the stroke of midnight; or witches cooking up a magic brew. Historical events also present possibilities: Columbus discovering America, Boston Tea Party, Pilgrims landing at Plymouth Rock, and others.

A more involved playmaking strategy runs as follows. After a few warm-up exercises, the leader tells a story. Then she and the students review the sequence of events—What happened first? Second? The group then discusses characterization, considering physical, emotional and intellectual qualities (nervous, calm, slow-witted, happy, angry, excited, scientific-minded, beautiful, quick-stepping, limping, stuck-up, etc.). The play typically is broken into scenes and worked out scene by scene. The group may first act out a scene without dialogue to explore the physical possibilities and believability of the characters and the overall effect. After the group thinks of ways to make the scene better, it is replayed with improvised dialogue. A given scene may be played many times with different students experiencing various roles. This general strategy may be adapted for use with such familiar tales as "Goldilocks" or "Peter Rabbit" for the wee tads, "Cinderella" for third graders, and "Pandora's Box" or "Electra" for the sixth grade. Generally, fairy tales, nursery rhymes, myths, folklore, historical material, and animal stories provide fine literature sources.

Direct questioning may add to the educational experience. Ask such questions as, "Why did Electra hate her mother? Could you hate your mother?" "Why are Cinderella's ugly sisters so mean?" Questions such as "How would you feel if . . .?" and "What would happen if . . .?" also will stretch the creative, empathic imagination.

SUMMARY

Creative dramatics clearly is different in purposes, activities, and results from every other school subject. Apart from the fun—which increases appreciation of school—creative dramatics activities build confidence in speaking, behaving, and being oneself in a group. They sharpen a child's observation, listening, and other sensory skills and increase body awareness and control. Creative dramatics also provides a nonthreatening atmosphere which allows stretching the creative imagination and solving unusual problems. Students learn to empathize with humans in other roles and with other interests, needs, and problems. While creative dramatics is not the same as children's theatre, the use of creative dramatics as warm-up activities will lead to more flexible, confident, and involved acting. Creative dramatics indeed is a valuable creative experience for children of all ages.

REFERENCES

Davis, G. A. *Psychology of Problem Solving: Theory and Practice.* New York: Basic Books, 1973.

Way, B. *Development Through Drama.* London, England: Longmans, 1967.

BIBLIOGRAPHY

Alington, A. F. *Drama and Education.* Oxford, England: Blackwell, 1961.

Brown, C. *Creative Drama in the Lower School.* New York: Appleton-Century-Crofts, 1929.

Burger, I. *Creative Play Acting.* Cranbury, N.J.: A. S. Barnes, 1950.

Crosscup, R. *Children and Dramatics.* New York: Scribner's, 1966.

Hutson, N. B. *Stage—A Handbook of Ideas for Creative Dramatics.* Michigan: Educational Service Inc., 1968.

Kase, C. R. *Stories for Creative Acting.* New York: French, 1961.

Lease, R., and Siks, G. B. *Creative Dramatics in Home, School, and Community.* New York: Harper and Brothers, 1952.

McCaslin, N. *Creative Dramatics in the Classroom.* New York: McKay, 1968.

Olfson, L. *You Can Act.* New York: Sterling, 1970.

Siks, G. B. *Children's Literature for Dramatization: An Anthology.* New York: Harper, 1964.

Spolin, V. *Improvisation for the Theater.* Evanston, Ill.: Northwestern University Press, 1963.

Walker, P. *Seven Steps to Creative Children's Drama.* New York: Hill and Wang, 1957.

Ward, W. *Playmaking with Children,* New York: Appleton-Century-Crofts, 1957.

REVIEW QUESTIONS

1. What is it that "creative dramatics" is supposed to do?

2. Do you have the personality required for leading a creative dramatics session or class?

forty-seven

From *Wishes, Lies, and Dreams*

KENNETH KOCH

I was curious to see what could be done for children's poetry. I knew some things about teaching adults to write, for I had taught writing classes for a number of years at Columbia and the New School. But I didn't know about children. Adult writers had read a lot, wanted to be writers, and were driven by all the usual forces writers are driven by. I knew how to talk to them, how to inspire them, how to criticize their work. What to say to an eight-year-old with no commitment to literature?

One thing that encouraged me was how playful and inventive children's talk sometimes was. They said true things in fresh and surprising ways. Another was how much they enjoyed making works of art—drawings, paintings, and collages. I was aware of the breakthrough in teaching children art some forty years ago. I had seen how my daughter and other children profited from the new ways of helping them discover and use their natural talents. That hadn't happened yet in poetry. Some children's poetry was marvelous, but most seemed uncomfortably imitative of adult poetry or else childishly cute. It seemed restricted somehow, and it obviously lacked the happy, creative energy of children's art. I wanted to find, if I could, a way for children to get as much from poetry as they did from painting. . . .

I asked the class to write a poem together, everybody contributing one line. The way I conceived of the poem, it was easy to write, had rules like a game, and included the pleasures without the anxieties of competitiveness. No one had to worry about failing to write a good poem because everyone was only writing one line; and I specifically asked the children not to put their names on their line. Everyone was to write the line on a sheet of paper and turn it in; then I would read them all as a poem. I suggested we make some rules about what should be in every line; this would help give the final poem unity, and it would help the children find something to say. I gave an example, putting a color in

Source: Abridgment from *Wishes, Lies, and Dreams* by Kenneth Koch. Copyright © Kenneth Koch. Reprinted by permission of Kenneth Koch, International Famous Agency, and Random House, Inc.

every line, then asked them for others. We ended up with the regulations that every line should contain a color, a comic-strip character, and a city or country; also the line should begin with the words "I wish."

I collected the lines, shuffled them, and read them aloud as one poem. Some lines obeyed the rules and some didn't; but enough were funny and imaginative to make the whole experience a good one—

> I wish I was Dick Tracy in a black suit in England
> I wish that I were a Supergirl with a red cape; the city of Mexico will be where
> I live.
> I wish that I were Veronica in South America. I wish that I could see the
> blue sky . . .

The children were enormously excited by writing the lines and even more by hearing them read as a poem. They were talking, waving, blushing, laughing, and bouncing up and down. "Feelings at P.S. 61," the title they chose, was not a great poem, but it made them feel like poets and it made them want to write more.

I had trouble finding my next good assignment. I had found out how to get the children started but didn't yet know how to provide them with anything substantial in the way of themes or techniques. I didn't know what they needed. I tried a few ideas that worked well with adults, such as writing in the style of other poets, but they were too difficult and in other ways inappropriate. Fortunately for me, Mrs. Wiener, the fourth-grade teacher, asked me to suggest some poetry ideas for her to give her class. (I wasn't seeing them regularly at that time—only the sixth-graders.) Remembering the success of the Collaborations, I suggested she try a poem in which every line began with "I wish." It had worked well for class poems and maybe it would work too for individual poems, without the other requirements. I asked her to tell the children that their wishes could be real or crazy, and not to use rhyme.

A few days later she brought me their poems, and I was very happy. The poems were beautiful, imaginative, lyrical, funny, touching. They brought in feelings I hadn't seen in the children's poetry before. They reminded me of my own childhood and of how much I had forgotten about it. They were all innocence, elation, and intelligence. They were unified poems: it made sense where they started and where they stopped. And they had a lovely music—

> I wish I had a pony with a tail like hair
> I wish I had a boyfriend with blue eyes and black hair
>   I would be so glad . . .

Milagros Diaz, 4*

*Here, as elsewhere in this introduction, the number following the child's name indicates the grade he or she was in when the poem was written.

Sometimes I wish I had my own kitten
Sometimes I wish I owned a puppy
Sometimes I wish we had a color T.V.
Sometimes I wish for a room of my own.
And I wish all my sisters would disappear.
And I wish we didn't have to go to school.
And I wish my little sister would find her nightgown.
And I wish even if she didn't she wouldn't wear mine.

Erin Harold, 4

It seemed I had stumbled onto a marvelous idea for children's poems. I realized its qualities as I read over their work. I don't mean to say the idea wrote the poems: the children did. The idea helped them to find that they could do it, by giving them a form that would give their poem unity and that was easy and natural for them to use: beginning every line with "I wish." With such a form, they could relax after every line and always be starting up afresh. They could also play variations on it, as Erin Harold does in her change from "Sometimes" to "And." Just as important, it gave them something to write about which really interested them: the private world of their wishes. One of the main problems children have as writers is not knowing what to write about. Once they have a subject they like, but may have temporarily forgotten about, like wishing, they find a great deal to say. The subject was good, too, because it encouraged them to be imaginative and free. There are no limits to what one can wish: to fly, to be smothered in diamonds, to burn down the school. And wishes, moreover, are a part of what poetry is always about.

I mentioned that I had told Mrs. Wiener to ask the children not to use rhyme. I said that to all my classes as soon as I had them start writing. Rhyme is wonderful, but children generally aren't able to use it skillfully enough to make good poetry. It gets in their way. The effort of finding rhymes stops the free flow of their feelings and associations, and poetry gives way to sing-song. There are formal devices which are more natural to children, more inspiring, easier to use. The one I suggested most frequently was some kind of repetition: the same word or words ("I wish") or the same kind of thing (a comparison) in every line. . . .

In presenting these poetry ideas to the children I encouraged them to take chances. I said people were aware of many resemblances which were beautiful and interesting but which they didn't talk about because they seemed too far-fetched and too silly. But I asked them specifically to look for strange comparisons—if the grass seemed to them like an Easter egg they should say so. I suggested they compare something big to something small, something in school to something out of school, something unreal to something real, something human to something not human. I wanted to rouse them out of the timidity I felt they had about being "crazy" or "silly" in front of an adult in school. There is no danger of children writing merely nonsensical poems if one does this; the truth they find in freely associating is a greater pleasure to them—

A breeze is like the sky is coming to you . . .

Iris Torres, 4

The sea is like a blue velvet coat . . .

Argentina Wilkinson, 4

The flag is as red, white, and blue as the sun's reflection . . .

Marion Mackles, 3

. . . For the Noise Poem I used another kind of classroom example. I made some noises and asked the children what they sounded like. I crumpled up a piece of paper. "It sounds like paper." "Rain on the roof." "Somebody typing." I hit the chair with a ruler and asked what word that was like. Someone said "hit." What else? "Tap." I said close your eyes and listen again and tell me which of those two words it sounds more like, hit or tap. "It sounds more like tap." I asked them to close their eyes again and listen for words it sounded like which had nothing to do with tap. "Hat, snap, trap, glad, badger." With the primary-graders* I asked, How does a bee go? "Buzz." What sounds like a bee but doesn't mean anything like buzz? "Fuzz, does, buzzard, cousin." The children were quick to get these answers and quick to be swept up into associating words and sounds—

A clink is like a drink of pink water . . .

Alan Constant, 5

A yoyo sounds like a bearing rubbing in a machine . . .

Roberto Marcilla, 6

Before they had experimented with the medium of poetry in this way, what the children wrote tended to be a little narrow and limited in its means—but not afterwards. Their writing quickly became richer and more colorful.

After the Comparison Poem and the Noise Poem, I asked my students to write a Dream Poem. I wanted them to get the feeling of including the unconscious parts of their experience in their poetry. I emphasized that dreams didn't usually make sense, so their poems needn't either. Wishes and dreams are easy to doctor up so they conform to rational adult expectations, but then all their poetry is gone.

Their Dream Poems contained a surprising number of noises, and also comparisons and wishes—

---

*At P.S. 61 some first- and second-grade classes are combined in one primary grade.

I had a dream of a speeding car going beep beep while a train went choo choo . . .

Ruben Luyando, 4

I dream I'm standing on the floor and diamonds snow on me.
I dream I know all the Bob Dylan songs my brother knows . . .

Annie Clayton, 4

. . . A poetry theme that all my classes were ready for at this point was the contrast between the present and the past. To give their poems form and to help them get ideas, I suggested that they begin every odd line with I Used To and every even line with But Now. Like Wishes and Dreams, this poem gave the children a new part of experience to write about. It gave them a chance **too** to bring in comparisons, dreams, and other things they had learned—

I used to be a baby saying Coo Coo
But now I say "Hello" . . .

Lisa Smalley, 3

I used to have a teacher of meanness
But now I have a teacher of roses . . .

Maria Ippolito, 3

Some of the content brought into their poetry by this theme surprised me. Among the primary- and third-graders metempsychosis was almost as frequent a theme as the conventionally observed past:

I used to be a fish
But now I am a nurse . . .

Andrea Dockery, 1

I used to be a rose but now I'm a leaf
I used to be a boy but now I'm a woman
I used to have a baby but now he's a dog . . .

Mercedes Mesen, 3

I used to be a design but now I'm a tree . . .

Ilona Baburka, 3

I had forgotten that whole strange childhood experience of changing physically so much all the time. It came very naturally into the children's poems once I found a way of making it easy for them to write about change—that is, by suggesting the pattern I Used To / But Now. . . .

A poetry idea which, like I Used To / But Now, brought a new part of their experience into the children's poetry, was one about the difference between how they seemed to other people and how they felt they really were. I suggested a two-line repeating form, as in the Used To Poem: I Seem To Be / But Really I Am. The sixth-graders were particularly affected by this theme, being at an age when private consciousness and social image are sometimes seriously different. For one thing, there are hidden sexual and romantic feelings which one doesn't confess—

I seem to be shy when she passes by but inside of me I have a wonderful feeling . . .
As we went for a walk in the park I felt a wet kiss hit my dry skin.

Robert Siegel, 6

Other contrasting themes I thought of but haven't yet tried are I Used To Think / But Now I See (or Know) ; I Wish / But Really; I Would Like / But I Would Not Like. . . .

The speed with which "non-writing" children can become excited about writing poetry was made very clear to me in working with Mrs. Magnani's fourth grade "N.E." class. Ron Padgett came with me the first time I visited this class, and he, Mrs. Magnani, and I each worked with about twelve students. We had decided to do a Lie Poem Collaboration. Lying, for all its bad points in daily living, is a very quick way to the world of the imagination. It is also a competitive pastime. Like the Mississippi riverboat men in *Huckleberry Finn*, the children at P.S. 61 were eager to do each other one better, to tell an even bigger, more astonishing untruth: I live on the moon; I live half the year on the moon and half on the sun; I live on all the planets: January on Jupiter, March on Mars, December on the Planet of the Apes. Different kinds of lies could also please and astonish: I am ten years older than my teacher; I like school. These fourth-graders, with just the slightest encouragement from us, began to create strange realities with great gusto. When we read the group poems back to them, they were very excited. At all three tables they demanded to write Lie Poems of their own.

. . . As poets, the primary-graders tended to be buoyant and bouncy, the third-graders wildly and crazily imaginative, the fourth-graders warmly sensuous and lyrical, the fifth-graders quietly sensuous and intellectual, and the sixth-graders ironic (sometimes even slightly bitter), secretive, and emotional.

REVIEW QUESTIONS

1. Could the author be limiting originality by using his highly structured devices for stimulating poetry?

2. Can you think of similar devices for stimulating poetry? Ideas for short stories or themes?

forty-eight

Creativity in Self-Actualizing People

ABRAHAM H. MASLOW

I first had to change my ideas about creativity as soon as I began studying people who were positively healthy, highly evolved and matured, self-actualizing. I had first to give up my stereotyped notion that health, genius, talent and productivity were synonymous. A fair proportion of my subjects, though healthy and creative in a special sense that I am going to describe, were *not* productive in the ordinary sense, nor did they have great talent or genius, nor were they poets, composers, inventors, artists or creative intellectuals. It was also obvious that some of the greatest talents of mankind were certainly not psychologically healthy people. Wagner, for example, or Van Gogh or Byron. Some were and some weren't, it was clear. I very soon had to come to the conclusion that great talent was not only more or less independent of goodness or health of character but also that we know little about it. For instance, there is some evidence that great musical talent and mathematical talent are more inherited than acquired [Scheinfeld, 1950]. It seemed clear then that health and special talent were separate variables, maybe only slightly correlated, maybe not. We may as well admit at the beginning that psychology knows very little about special talent of the genius type. I shall say nothing more about it, confining myself instead to that more widespread kind of creativeness which is the universal heritage of every human being that is born, and which seems to co-vary with psychological health.

Furthermore, I soon discovered that I had, like most other people, been thinking of creativeness in terms of products, and secondly, I had unconsciously confined creativeness to certain conventional areas only of human endeavor, unconsciously assuming that *any* painter, *any* poet, *any* composer was leading a creative life. Theorists, artists, scientists, inventors, writers could be creative. Nobody else could be. Unconsciously I had assumed that creativeness was the prerogative solely of certain professionals.

Source: From *Toward a Psychology of Being* by Abraham Maslow © 1962, 1968 by Litton Educational Publishing, Inc. Reprinted by permission of Van Nostrand Reinhold Company.

But these expectations were broken up by various of my subjects. For instance, one woman, uneducated, poor, a full-time housewife and mother, did none of these conventionally creative things and yet was a marvelous cook, mother, wife and homemaker. With little money, her home was somehow always beautiful. She was a perfect hostess. Her meals were banquets. Her taste in linens, silver, glass, crockery and furniture was impeccable. She was in all these areas original, novel, ingenious, unexpected, inventive. I just *had* to call her creative. I learned from her and others like her that a first-rate soup is more creative than a second-rate painting, and that, generally, cooking or parenthood or making a home could be creative while poetry need not be; it could be uncreative.

Another of my subjects devoted herself to what had best be called social service in the broadest sense, bandaging up wounds, helping the downtrodden, not only in a personal way, but in an organization which helps many more people than she could individually.

Another was a psychiatrist, a "pure" clinician who never wrote anything or created any theories or researches but who delighted in his everyday job of helping people to create themselves. This man approached each patient as if he were the only one in the world, without jargon, expectations or presuppositions, with innocence and naiveté and yet with great wisdom, in a Taoistic fashion. Each patient was a unique human being and therefore a completely new problem to be understood and solved in a completely novel way. His great success even with very difficult cases validated his "creative" (rather than stereotyped or orthodox) way of doing things. From another man I learned that constructing a business organization could be a creative activity. From a young athlete, I learned that a perfect tackle could be as esthetic a product as a sonnet and could be approached in the same creative spirit.

It dawned on me once that a competent cellist I had reflexly thought of as "creative" (because I associated her with creative music? with creative composers?) was actually playing well what someone else had written. She was a mouthpiece, as the average actor or "comedian" is a mouthpiece. A good cabinet maker or gardener or dressmaker *could* be more truly creative. I had to make an individual judgment in each instance, since almost any role or job could be either creative or uncreative.

In other words, I learned to apply the word "creative" (and also the word "esthetic") not only to products but also to people in a characterological way, and to activities, processes, and attitudes. And furthermore, I had come to apply the word "creative" to many products other than the standard and conventionally accepted poems, theories, novels, experiments or paintings.

The consequence was that I found it necessary to distinguish "special talent creativeness" from "self-actualizing (SA) creativeness" which sprang much more directly from the personality, and which showed itself widely in the ordinary affairs of life, for instance, in a certain kind of humor. It looked like a tendency to do *anything* creatively: e.g., housekeeping, teaching, etc. Frequently, it appeared that an essential aspect of SA creativeness was a special kind of perceptiveness that is exemplified by the child in the fable who saw that the king had no clothes on (this too contradicts the notion of creativity as products). Such people can see the fresh, the raw, the concrete, the idiographic, as well as the generic, the abstract, the rubricized, the categorized and the classified. Consequently, they live far more in the real world of nature than in the verbalized world of concepts, abstractions, expectations, beliefs and stereotypes that most people confuse with the real world [Maslow, 1954, Chapter 14]. This is well expressed in Rogers' [1961] phrase "openness to experience."

All my subjects were relatively more spontaneous and expressive than average people. They were more "natural" and less controlled and inhibited in their behavior, which seemed to flow out more easily and freely and with less blocking and self-criticism. This ability to express ideas and impulses without strangulation and without fear of ridicule turned out to be an essential aspect of SA creativeness. Rogers [1961] has used the excellent phrase, "fully functioning person," to describe this aspect of health.

Another observation was that SA creativeness was in many respects like the creativeness of *all* happy and secure children. It was spontaneous, effortless, innocent, easy, a kind of freedom from stereotypes and cliches. And again it seemed to be be made up largely of "innocent" freedom of perception, and "innocent," uninhibited spontaneity and expressiveness. Almost any child can perceive more freely, without a priori expectations about what ought to be there, what must be there, or what has alway been there. And almost any child can compose a song or a poem or a dance or a painting or a play or a game on the spur of the moment, without planning or previous intent.

It was in this childlike sense that my subjects were creative. Or to avoid misunderstanding, since my subjects were after all not children (they were all people in their fifties or sixties), let us say that they had either retained or regained at least these two main aspects of childlikeness, namely, they were non-rubricizing or "open to experience" and they were easily spontaneous and expressive. If children are naive, then my subjects had attained a "second naiveté," as Santayana called it. Their innocence of perception and expressiveness was combined with sophisticated minds.

In any case, this all sounds as if we are dealing with a fundamental characteristic, inherent in human nature, a potentiality given to all or most human beings at birth, which most often is lost or buried or inhibited as the person gets enculturated.

My subjects were different from the average person in another characteristic that makes creativity more likely. SA people are relatively unfrightened by the unknown, the mysterious, the puzzling, and often are positively attracted by it, i.e., selectively pick it out to puzzle over, to meditate on and to be absorbed with. I quote from my description [Maslow, 1954, p. 206]: "They do not neglect the unknown, or deny it, or run away from it, or try to make believe it is really known, nor do they organize, dichotomize, or rubricize it prematurely. They do not cling to the familiar, nor is their quest for the truth a catastrophic need for certainty, safely, definiteness, and order, such as we see in an exaggerated form in Goldstein's brain-injured or in the compulsive-obsessive neurotic. They can be, when the total objective situation calls for it, comfortably disorderly, sloppy, anarchic, chaotic, vague, doubtful, uncertain, indefinite, approximate, inexact, or inaccurate (all at certain moments in science, art, or life in general, quite desirable).

> Thus it comes about that doubt, tentativeness, uncertainty, with the consequent necessity for abeyance of decision, which is for most a torture, can be for some a pleasantly stimulating challenge, a high spot in life rather than a low.

One observation I made has puzzled me for many years but it begins to fall into place now. It was what I described as the resolution of dichotomies in self-actualizing people. Briefly stated, I found that I had to see differently many oppositions and polarities that all psychologists had taken for granted as straight line continua. For instance, to take the first dichotomy that I had trouble with, I couldn't decide whether my subjects were selfish or unselfish. (Observe how spontaneously we fall into an either-or, here. The more of one, the less of the other, is the implication of the style in which I put the question.) But I was forced by sheer pressure of fact to give up this Aristotelian style of logic. My subjects were very unselfish in one sense and very selfish in another sense. And the two fused together, not like incompatibles, but rather in a sensible, dynamic unity or synthesis very much like that what Fromm [1947] has described in his classical paper on healthy selfishness. My subjects had put opposites together in such a way as to make me realize that regarding selfishness and unselfishness as contradictory and mutually exclusive is itself characteristic of a lower level of personality development. So also in my subjects were many other dichotomies resolved into unities, cognition vs. conation (heart vs. head, wish vs. fact) became cognition "structured with" conation as instinct and reason came to the same conclusions. Duty became pleasure, and pleasure merged with duty. The distinction between work and play became shadowy. How could selfish hedonism be opposed to altruism, when altruism became selfishly pleasurable? These most mature of all people were also strongly childlike. These same people, the strongest egos ever described and the most definitely individual, were also precisely the ones who could be most easily ego-less, self-transcending, and problem-centered [Maslow, 1954, pp. 232–34].

But this is precisely what the great artist does. He is able to bring together clashing colors, forms that fight each other, dissonances of all kinds, into a unity. And this is also what the great theorist does when he puts puzzling and inconsistent facts together so that we can see that they really belong together. And so also for the great statesman, the great therapist, the great philosopher, the great parent, the great inventor. They are all integrators, able to bring separates and even opposites together into unity.

We speak here of the ability to integrate and of the play back and forth between integration within the person, and his ability to integrate whatever it is he is doing in the world. To the extent that creativeness is constructive, synthesizing, unifying, and integrative, to that extent does it depend in part on the inner integration of the person.

In trying to figure out why all this was so, it seemed to me that much of it could be traced back to the relative absence of fear in my subjects. They were certainly less enculturated; that is, they seemed to be less afraid of what other people would say or demand or laugh at. They had less need of other people and therefore, depending on them less, could be less afraid of them and less hostile against them. Perhaps more important, however, was their lack of fear of their own insides, of their own impulses, emotions, thoughts. They were more self-accepting than the average. This approval and acceptance of their deeper selves then made it more possible to perceive bravely the real nature of the world and also made their behavior more spontaneous (less controlled, less inhibited, less planned, less "willed" and designed). They were less afraid of their own thoughts even when they were "nutty" or silly or crazy. They were less afraid of being laughed at or of being disapproved of. They could let themselves be flooded by emotion. In contrast, average and neurotic people wall off fear, much that lies within themselves. They control, they inhibit, they repress, and they suppress. They disapprove of their deeper selves and expect that others do, too.

What I am saying in effect is that the creativity of my subjects seemed to be an epiphenomenon of their greater wholeness and integration, which is what self-acceptance implies. The civil war within the average person between the forces of the inner depths and the forces of defense and control seems to have been resolved in my subjects and they are less split. As a consequence, more of themselves is available for use, for enjoyment and for creative purposes. They waste less of their time and energy protecting themselves against themselves.

. . . What we know of peak-experiences supports and enriches these conclusions. These too are integrated and integrating experiences which are to some extent, isomorphic with integration in the perceived world. In these experiences also, we find increased openness to experience, and increased spontaneity and expressiveness. Also, since one aspect of this integration within the person is the acceptance and greater availability of our deeper selves, these deep roots of creativeness become more available for use [Kris, 1952].

PRIMARY, SECONDARY, AND INTEGRATED CREATIVENESS

Classical Freudian theory is of little use for our purposes and is even partially contradicted by our data. It is (or was) essentially an id psychology, an investigation of the instinctive impulses and their vicissitudes, and the basic Freudian dialectic is seen to be ultimately between impulses and defenses against them. But far more crucial than repressed impulses for understanding the sources of creativity (as well as play, love, enthusiasm, humor, imagination, and fantasy) are the so-called primary processes which are essentially cognitive rather than conative. As soon as we turn our attention to this aspect of human depth-psychology, we find much agreement between the psychoanalytic ego-psychology —Kris [1952], Milner [1957], Ehrenzweig [1953], the Jungian psychology [1953], and the American self-and-growth psychology [Moustakas, 1956].

The normal adjustment of the average, common sense, well-adjusted man implies a continued successful rejection of much of the depths of human nature, both conative and cognitive. To adjust well to the world of reality means a splitting of the person. It means that the person turns his back on much in himself because it is dangerous. But it is now clear that by so doing, he loses a great deal too, for these depths are also the source of all his joys, his ability to play, to love, to laugh, and, most important for us, to be creative. By protecting himself against the hell within himself, he also cuts himself off from the heaven within. In the extreme instance, we have the obsessional person, flat, tight, rigid, frozen, controlled, cautious, who can't laugh or play or love, or be silly or trusting or childish. His imagination, his intuitions, his softness, his emotionality tend to be strangulated or distorted.

The goals of psychoanalysis as a therapy are ultimately integrative. The effort is to heal this basic split by insight, so that what has been repressed becomes conscious or preconscious. But here again we can make modifications as a consequence of studying the depth sources of creativeness. Our relation to our primary processes is not in all respects the same as our relation to unacceptable wishes. The most important difference that I can see is that our primary processes are not as dangerous as the forbidden impulses. To a large extent they are not repressed or censored but rather are "forgotten," or else turned away from, suppressed (rather than repressed), as we have to adjust to a harsh reality which demands a purposeful and pragmatic striving rather than revery, poetry, play. Or, to say it in another way, in a rich society there must be far less resistance to primary thought processes. I expect that education processes, which are known to do rather little for relieving repression of "instinct," can do much to accept and integrate the primary processes into conscious and preconscious life. Education in art, poetry, dancing, can in principle do much in this direction. And so also can education in dynamic psychology; for instance, Deutsch and Murphy's [1955] "Clinical Interview," which speaks in primary process language, can be seen as a kind of poetry. Marion Milner's [1957] extraordinary book, *On Not Being Able to Paint,* perfectly makes my point.

The kind of creativeness I have been trying to sketch out is best exemplified by the improvisation, as in jazz or in childlike paintings, rather than by the work of art designated as "great."

In the first place, the great work needs great talent which, as we have seen, turned out to be irrelevant for our concern. In the second place, the great work needs not only the flash, the inspiration, the peak-experience; it also needs hard work, long training, unrelenting criticism, perfectionistic standards. In other words, succeeding upon the spontaneous is the deliberate; succeeding upon total acceptance comes criticism; succeeding upon intuition comes rigorous thought; succeeding upon daring comes caution; succeeding upon fantasy and imagination comes reality testing. Now come the questions, "Is it true?" "Will it be understood by the other?" "Is its structure sound?" "Does it stand the test of logic?" "How will it do in the world?" "Can I prove it?" Now come the comparisons, the judgments, the evaluations, the cold, calculating morning-after thoughts, the selections and the rejections.

If I may say it so, the secondary processes now take over from the primary, the Apollonian from the Dionysian, the "masculine" from the "feminine." The voluntary regression into our depths is now terminated, the necessary passivity and receptivity of inspiration or of peak-experience must now give way to activity, control, and hard work. A peak-experience happens *to* a person, but the person *makes* the great product.

Strictly speaking, I have investigated this first phase only, that which comes easily and without effort as a spontaneous expression of an integrated person, or of a transient unifying within the person. It can come only if a person's depths are available to him, only if he is not afraid of his primary thought processes.

I shall call "primary creativity" that which proceeds from and uses the primary process much more than the secondary processes. The creativity which is based mostly on the secondary thought processes I shall call "secondary creativity." This latter type includes a large proportion of production-in-the-world, the bridges, the houses, the new automobiles, even many scientific experiments and much literary work. All of these are essentially the consolidation and development of other people's ideas. It parallels the difference between the commando and the military policeman behind the lines, between the pioneer and the settler. That creativity which uses *both* types of process easily and well, in good fusion or in good succession, I shall call "integrated creativity." It is from this kind that comes the great work of art, or philosophy, or science.

CONCLUSION

The upshot of all of these developments can, I think, be summarized as an increased stress on the role of integration (or self-consistency, unity, wholeness) in the theory of creativeness. Resolving a dichotomy into a higher, more inclusive, unity amounts to healing a split in the person and making him more unified. Since the splits I have been talking about are within the person, they amount to a kind of civil war, a setting of one part of the person against another part. In any case so far as SA creativeness is concerned, it seems to come more immediately from fusion of primary and secondary processes rather than from working through repressive control of forbidden impulses and wishes. It is, of course, probable that defenses arising out of fears of these forbidden impulses also push down primary processes in a kind of total, undiscriminating, panicky war on *all* the depths. But it seems that such lack of discrimination is not in principle necessary.

To summarize, SA creativeness stresses first the personality rather than its achievements, considering these achievements to be epiphenomena emitted by the personality and therefore secondary to it. It stresses characterological qualities like boldness, courage, freedom, spontaneity, perspicuity, integration, self-acceptance, all of which make possible the kind of generalized SA creativeness, which expresses itself in the creative life, or the creative attitude, or the creative person. I have also stressed the expressive or Being quality of SA creativeness rather than its problem-solving or product-making quality. SA creativeness is "emitted," or "emits" cheerfulness without purpose or design or even consciousness. It is emitted radiated, and hits all of life, regardless of problems, just as a cheerful person like sunshine; it spreads all over the place; it makes some things grow (which are growable) and is wasted on rocks and other ungrowable things.

Finally, I am quite aware that I have been trying to break up widely accepted concepts of creativity without being able to offer in exchange a nice, clearly defined, clean-cut substitute concept. SA creativeness is hard to define because sometimes it seems to be synonymous with health itself, as Moustakas [1956] has suggested. And since self-actualization or health must ultimately be defined as the coming to pass of the fullest humanness, or as the "Being" of the person, it is as if SA creativity were almost synonymous with, or a *sine qua non* aspect of, or a defining characteristic of, essential humanness.

REFERENCES

Deutsch, F., and Murphy, W. *The Clinical Interview* (2 vols.). New York: International Universities Press, 1955.

Ehrenzweig, A. *The Psychoanalysis of Artistic Vision and Hearing*. London, England: Routledge, 1953.

Fromm, E. *Man for Himself*. New York: Rinehart, 1947.

Jung, C. G. *Psychological Reflections*. New York: Pantheon Books, 1953.

Kris, E. *Psychoanalytic Explorations in Art*. New York: International Universities Press, 1952.

Maslow, A. H. *Motivation and Personality*. New York: Harper, 1954.

Milner, M. *On Not Being Able to Paint*. New York: International Universities Press, 1957.

Moustakas, C. (Ed.) *The Self*. New York: Harper, 1956.

Rogers, C. *On Becoming a Person*. Boston: Houghton Mifflin, 1961.

Scheinfeld, A. *The New You and Heredity*. Philadelphia: Lippincott, 1950.

REVIEW QUESTIONS

1. Can you summarize the distinction between "special-talent creativeness" and "self-actualizing creativeness"? Do you have some of each?

2. Maslow notes that any job or role can be creative or uncreative. Think about how this conclusion applies to teaching.

forty-nine

From *Creativity and Conformity*

CLARK MOUSTAKAS

Many times in my life I have been faced with a dilemma that, after much internal struggle and deliberation, turned out to be illusory. I continually discovered that only one pathway was open, that there was only one way to go—a way that grew out of my own self. The problem turned out to be not one of resolving a situation that called for a choice between unsatisfactory alternatives, but rather a question of bringing into being what already existed as self-potential, that is, it required bringing into being my own identity as it related to the challenge of a crucial situation. It is this experience of expressing and actualizing one's individual identity in an integrated form in communion with one's self, with nature, and with other persons that I call creative.

To be creative means to experience life in one's own way, to perceive from one's own person, to draw upon one's own resources, capacities, roots. It means facing life directly and honestly; courageously searching for and discovering grief, joy, suffering, pain, struggle, conflict, and finally inner solitude.

In the creative experience, every moment is unique, and contains the potentiality for original expression. There are two basic requirements: that the person be direct, honest, consistent in his own feelings and his own convictions; and that he feel a genuine devotion to life, a feeling of belonging and knowing. Creativity is an abstraction that attains a meaningful, concrete form in a particular and unique relation. The branches of a tree stretch out expansive and free, maintaining a basic identity, an essential uniqueness in color, form, and pattern. They stand out in contrast to the fixed nature of the trunk. Yet one cannot see a tree without recognizing its essential harmony, its wholeness, and its unity. Each facet attains its identity and remains a living creation within a genuine whole, within an organic communion.

Not all relatedness emerges from a sense of harmony and communion. It

Source: Abridgment of Chapter 3 from *Creativity and Conformity* by Clark Moustakas. © 1967 by Litton Educational Publishing, Inc. Reprinted by permission of the author and the publisher, Van Nostrand Reinhold Company.

sometimes begins with an issue, or conflict, or sense of deviation, or separateness. This was my experience last winter on a cold blustering day. It was a severe winter which exceeded records for frigid temperatures, ice formations, and accumulations of snow. The cold, noisy, violence of a raging wind kept me indoors. After almost two days of internment, I began to feel dull and almost completely insensible to the children's play and other events going on around me. Everything seemed colorless and toneless.

I felt trapped by the violent storm outside. The wind came swaggering through the walls and lashed against the windows, reverberating the panes, and echoing throughout the house. Screaming, fluttering sounds came through the weather stripping of the doors. Yet these auditory vibrations barely entered my center of awareness. I had been taught that the safest place in a blizzard was the warm comfort of home. And this had been my retreat for almost two days, not out of choice, but from tradition and fear. I was annoyed that a wild and fitful wind had forced me into an asylum and that I had conformed in the ordinary and intelligent way.

But something was wrong. The household scenes were gloomy. I saw only the coverings and felt the lethargy and boredom of a static life. The more I thought about my situation, the more restless I became. A growing inner feeling surged within me and I decided to face the wind. I had never been in a blizzard before by choice, but in that moment I decided to enter the turbulent outside. Immediately I experienced an exhilarating and exciting feeling. I stood before the bitter, cold, turbulent flow of wind, a wind that was inciting retreat and withdrawal in every direction. Momentarily I was stung and pushed back. I hesitated, uncertain whether I could move forward. It was a tremendous challenge. Holding my ground, I stood in the way of the wind. We met head-on. I knew for the first time the full meaning of a severe wind. I felt it in every pore of my body but realized I would not retreat. I stood firm and gradually, slowly I began to move forward in spite of the violent, shattering gusts which emerged repeatedly to block my path. Tears fell down my face. It was a painful experience but at the same time wonderfully refreshing and joyous. It was cold, yet I was warmed by a tremendous surge of emotion. I felt radiant and alive as I continued my journey. As the wind met me and moved me, I became aware of the whole atmosphere— like a powerful dynamo; crackling, crunching, clanging noises everywhere; a rushing, swaying, churning turbulence; a world charged with electric fury. For the first time in my life I truly understood the meaning of a blizzard.

All about me were shining elements and sharp, penetrating sounds which I could see, and hear, and feel without effort. It was an awesome feeling, witnessing the wild turbulence. Everything was charged with life and beauty. The meeting with the wind revived me and restored me to my own resourcefulness. I felt an expansive and limitless energy.

I returned home. Everything took on a shining light and a spark of beauty. I played ecstatically with my children, with a burst of enthusiasm and excitement. I seemed to be inexhaustible. I made repairs, painted, helped with the evening meal, assisted with the children's baths and bedtime, and spent a joyous evening reading and conversing with my wife. Out of the tumultuous experience, I found new joy in life, new energy, uniqueness and beauty. I had conquered my lethargy and discovered a lively affinity in everything I touched. Everything which had been dull and commonplace took on a living splendor. I realized how out of the wild, confused, turbulent experience, came a sense of inner exaltation, peace, symmetry, and a recognition of the vital manifestations of life; how out of the initial conflict came a sense of individual aliveness and a feeling of harmony and relatedness to a raging wind.

What I am pointing to is something altogether unconditioned and transcendent of all effort, motive, or determination. It is an ultimate, universal, concrete reality that is individual yet related, harmonious yet discordant, congruent yet dissimilar. The creative cannot be scaled down to the level of facts or observable data. It rides on the horizons and fills the heavens. It is incomparable and can never be subsumed under categories of definition, communication, and logic.

I have selected a number of examples to illustrate the meaning of creativity and the creative experience. . . . Seventh-grade student, Don Camph conveyed his understanding of creativity as follows:

> Creativity is the ability to create experience—to make joy and sorrow, to rejoice and to mourn. It is not just building skyscrapers, and having a brilliant intellect, and creating masterpieces but it is being able to set men's hearts afire when they are in despair, being able to cheer them when they are sad, and most of all being able to create friends.

From the same grade, Ron Miller wrote:

> Some things may not be beautiful or great,
> But if it is your own work,
> Your original self,
> It is creative.

I believe it is the real feelings, within a vital experience, in an intimate relation to nature or other selves, that constitute the creative encounter. When a person's involvement in a situation is based on appearances, expectations, or the standards of others; when he acts in a conventional manner, or according to prescribed roles and functions, when he is concerned with status and approval; his growth as a creative self is impaired. When the individual is conforming, following, imitating, being like others, he moves increasingly in the direction of self-alienation. Such a person fears issues and controversies. He fears standing out or being different. He does not think through his experience to find value or meaning, does not permit himself to follow his own perceptions to some natural conclusion. He avoids directly facing disputes and becomes anxious in situations which require self-awareness and self-discovery. He becomes increasingly similar until his every act erases his real identity and beclouds his uniqueness. Maslow [1958] points out that the only way such a person can achieve safety, order, lack of threat, lack of anxiety, is through orderliness, predictability, control, and mastery. If the conformist can proceed into the future on the basis of "well-tried" rules, habits, and modes of adjustment which have worked in the past (and which he insists on using in the future), he feels safe. But he experiences deep anxiety when he faces a new situation, when he cannot predetermine his behavior, when he does not know the acceptable form.

Gradually the conforming person loses touch with himself, with his own real feelings. He becomes unable to experience in a genuine way, and suffers inwardly from a dread of nothingness until finally despair nails him to himself. The torment will remain because he cannot get rid of himself. To be a self is the greatest concession made to man, but at the same time it is eternity's demand upon him [Kierkegaard, 1951].

In conformity, life has no meaning for there is no true basis for existence. Cut off from his own real wishes and capacities, the individual experiences no fulfillment and no sense of authentic relatedness. He strives to achieve safety and status. He strives to overcome his natural desires and to gain a victory over his natural surroundings. His goals are acquisition and control. Separated from nature and others yet appearing to be in harmony with them, he takes his cues from the designated authority figures. A young woman in psychotherapy has recognized this pattern [Will and Cohen, 1953].

> So you have to put everything out . . . as a question, you know. Because he's the one who knows and we're the ones who don't know. You can't (pause) you're sort of stepping onto his territory if you start giving out with pronouncements of facts. You see, what you're doing is you're competing, you're being disrespectful. You're moving into his position which—you just *don't do* that. . . . And I know that very well, but how I know it or why I know it—you see, I don't know it as intellectual concept—I just *know* it. My father didn't allow anybody but himself to be the lawgiver and statement maker. . . . And a lot of those things I know, I don't know in words, I just know.

The conformist has been forced into denying the self, not as the result of existential or valid social limits, but rather as a result of the frequent experiences of being confined, restricted, and limited. A distinction must be made here between natural limits and imposed limitations. *Limits* provide the structure through which individual identity emerges and grows. They enable the organism to use its capacities within its own defined structure and are meaningful as the inherent requirements of a situation. *Limitations* are induced and imposed from without and are external and extraneous. They are blocks and deterrents to growth and hinder creative emergence.

The conforming person does not use his own resources, his own experiences, but takes his direction from experts, authority figures, and traditional guides. Somewhere along the way he has given up his actual identity and submerged himself into acceptable group modes. He has been rejected by others as a unique, independent self and he has come to reject himself. He is cut off from vital self-resources which would enable him to grow in accordance with his talents and to find his place in the world. He has lost touch with himself.

This was the tragedy of an adult in psychotherapy, expressed beautifully in the following passages [Horney, 1949]:

From ten thousand miles away I saw it as blinding light: the importance, the necessity of a Self! One's own single self. My original life—*what had happened to it?* Chaos was here—all around and in me—that I understood in all my fragments. But was that all one could ever know? What about the perfect planets, this earth, people, objects? Didn't they exist and move? Couldn't they be known? Yes . . . but there has to be a knower, a *subject,* as well! (Meaning is a bridge between *two* things.) Beginnings, direction, movement had to be *from* a single point; and ours is where we stand, alone, our being *sui generis.*

Suddenly vistas spread out and out to the sky, and all came together at my feet. Was it possible that I had touched the key to the universe—the key which every man carries so nonchalantly in his pocket? Instantly I knew in my bones, and by grief itself, that I had discovered the very core and essence of neurosis—my neurosis and perhaps every neurosis. The secret of wretchedness WAS SELF-LESSNESS! Deep and hidden, the fact and the fear of not having a self. Not being a self. Not-being. And at the end—actual chaos.

How is it possible to lose a self? The treachery, unknown and unthinkable, begins with our secret psychic death in childhood—if and when we are not loved and are cut off from our spontaneous wishes. (Think: What is left?) But wait—it is not just this simple murder of psyche. That might be written off, the tiny victim might even "outgrow" it—but it is a perfect double crime in which he himself also gradually and unwittingly takes part. He has not been accepted for himself, *as he is.*

Oh, they "love" him, but they want him or force him or expect him to be different! Therefore he must be *unacceptable.* He himself learns to believe it and at last even takes it for granted. He has truly given himself up. No matter now whether he obeys them, whether he clings, rebels or withdraws—his behavior, his performance is all that matters. His center of gravity is in "them," not in himself—yet if he so much as noticed that he'd think it natural enough. And the whole thing is entirely plausible; all invisible, automatic, and anonymous!

This is the perfect paradox. Everything looks normal; no crime was intended; there is no corpse, no guilt. All we can see is the sun rising and setting as usual. But what has heppened? He has been rejected, not only by them, but by himself. (He is actually without a self.) What has he lost? Just the one true and vital part of himself: His own yes-feeling, which is his very capacity for growth, his root system. But alas, he is not dead. "Life" goes on, and so must he. From the moment he gives himself up, and to the extent that he does so, all unknowingly he sets about to create and maintain a pseudo-self. But this is an expediency—a "self" without wishes. This one shall be loved (or feared) where he is despised, strong where he is weak; it shall go through the motions (Oh, but they are caricatures!) not for fun or joy but for survival; not simply because it wants to move but because it has to obey. This necessity is not life—not his life—it is a defense mechanism against death. It is also the machine of death. From now on he will be torn apart by compulsive (unconscious) *needs* or ground by (unconscious) conflicts into paralysis, every motion and every instant cancelling out his being, his integrity; and all the while he is disguised as a normal person and expected to behave like one!

The individual is taught to perceive in a certain way, not his way but the way adults view things; the adult with authority, of course, perceives correctly. This begins at an early age and gradually, through repetitive conditioning and reward or fear of punishment and rejection, the individual begins to act in standard ways without being aware of conforming.

I now quote from two seventh-grade children who wrote their views on conformity.

Today there is too much effort on children conforming and being more like other people. But these people children are supposed to be like, now get this, they spend more money every year on cosmetics and alcohol than on education. And in this past year they consumed between 10 and 16 million tranquilizers. Do I want to follow slogans like, "Be like others" and "Join the group." Again, I say, "No!" I want to be an individual and think and act for myself. Why, even in a gang, we can be individuals and still be good members. We don't have to just go along with everybody else's ideas.

We, the nonconformists, are sometimes thought of as abnormal by some people, but just think of that slow learning boy who was nicknamed "old father hare" and was called unsociable. Who was this? Only Albert Einstein. This was a boy who thought for himself. Our first duty to society is to be somebody, that is to say, to be ourselves.

As a teacher or adult, you must think over the following questions, "When you see that the child has a difference do you think of it for his growth, or do you look at it to see how his neighbors might react?" "Do you want him to be successful or to follow his own talents even if he is lonely and poverty stricken? Is your child doing things against his own judgment, just because others do it or is he free to follow his own mind and ideas? You can tell if you are forcing a child to conform.

There are many times when I was made to conform when I needed to be encouraged to be myself. Last year my teacher made me conform to her many times. I was bored in class because you couldn't do anything as an individual. My parents made me conform to their ideas just for the sake of it when I knew I should have been myself. Right now I think I would be very different if I hadn't been forced into things. I would be able to make independent judgments using my own intelligence. So let's not conform. Let's not be like other people so that each of us—great and good—can think and act for ourselves.

Another child viewed conformity in this way:

In this day and age, I think people are trying to stress conformity too much. These people think that in our schools everyone should develop the same habits and skills, be given the same amount of learning, all on the same subject. This kind of conformity can keep people from using their creativeness and ability to the fullest extent.

Conformity can cause other troubles. It gives you misconceptions of people. You judge a person by his group while the person might be entirely different from the group. I do not believe in doing what the guy before you did. I think everyone can think and create for himself. Our schools and churches and homes are stressing conformity today. If we could gather up enough courage to be ourselves instead of copying our neighbors, the world would be a lot happier place to live.

The conventional person does not develop his capacities, does not have an opportunity to realize what he can do. Cut off from his own desires, from his own being, he is not free to make choices based on a growing philosophy, on a developing meaning of life, and on existential value. He may appear to be a person with great sureness, with precise and emphatic ways of living, a confident person who takes possession of life. But, these are only attributes coordinated to the conventional views of success.

In the following poem [Bynner, 1944, p. 49] Laotzu distinguishes the conventional man from the creative person:

Losing the way of life, men rely first on their fitness;
Losing fitness, they turn to kindness;
Losing kindness, they turn to justness;
Losing justness, they turn to convention.
Conventions are fealty and honesty gone to waste,
They are the entrance of disorder.
False teachers of life use flowery words
And start nonsense.
The man of stamina stays with the root
Below the tapering,
Stays with the fruit
Beyond the flowering:
He has his no and he has his yes.

I believe that much of the human misery in the world today, the serious emotional problems and conflicts, result from man's efforts to fit into conventional modes, from striving for goals of success, status, and power which provide no intrinsic value or satisfaction, and contribute to a meaningless existence. Failure to grow as a self results from a failure to maintain a unique identity in significant or crucial situations and an inability to meet others directly and honestly and with expressions of living love. Following traditional patterns and external guides, basing one's life on competitive striving and the rewards of the market place, modeling oneself after people in authority or with high status, the individual no longer knows who he is. He does not mean what he says and does not do what he believes and feels. Responding with surface or approved thoughts, he learns to use devious and indirect ways, and to base his behavior on the standards and expectations of others. He moves toward falsehood, fakery, pretense. His values and convictions do not emerge from real experience but derive from a feeling of danger and anxiety, from a fear of not keeping pace, a fear of being minimized, and a desire to be protected from rejection and attack. Cut off from his own self, he is unable to have honest experiences with others and communion with nature. His life is predicated on appearances, deceptions, and controlling behavior. Without any deep and growing roots, he moves in accordance with external signals. He does not know his place in the world, his position, where he is or who he is. He has lost touch with his own nature, his own spontaneity. He is unable to be a direct, genuine, loving human being.

To the degree that the individual strives to attain a similarity or congruity, to the degree that he acts in order to be popular, to be victorious, or to be approved of, and to the degree that he models himself after another person, he fails to emerge as a self, fails to develop his unique identity, fails to grow as a creative being consistent with his own desires and capacities and consistent with a life of genuine relatedness to others.

I have had the experience of living in a false world. One day I was deeply depressed by the severe criticisms a colleague had received—a person who was living his life in an honest and truthful sense, attempting to express his unique interests in his work. I felt especially saddened when I realized how he had suffered, when all he wanted to do was maintain a personal and creative identity, a genuine existence and relatedness. I felt especially sensitive to pretense and surface behavior, as though nothing were real. A numbness settled in, right at the center of my thought and feeling. That night even the children were unable to shake my grief and sadness. In their own spontaneous, unknowing ways, they tugged and pulled at me to draw me into life but for me there remained only suffering in the world.

After the children had gone to bed, I decided to go for a walk. The night was dark, filled with black clouds. Large white flakes of snow fell on and around me. The night was silent and serene. Suddenly, without understanding in any way, I experienced a transcendental beauty in the white darkness. It was difficult to walk on the glazed surface but as I walked I felt drawn to the black, inky streaks embedded in the ice. Dark, wavy lines, partly covered by snow, spread out in grotesque forms. I knelt down, touching the black, irregular patterns. Immediately I felt a chill but at the same time the ice began melting as my fingers touched it.

My inward heaviness lifted, and I was restored to a new capacity for exertion and endurance. I realized how, out of broken roots and fibers, in a genuine encounter with natural resources, it is possible to discover a new level of individual identity and to develop new strength and conviction. I realized how the self can be shattered in surface and false meetings when surrounded by intensive pressures to conform, and how in communion with nature the self can reach a new dimension of optimism and a new recognition of the creative way of life. Possibilities for unique and unusual meetings exist everywhere. We need only reach out in natural covering to come face to face with creation.

REFERENCES

Bynner, W. *The Way of Life According to Laotzu.* An American Version. New York: John Day, 1944.

Horney, K. Finding the real self. *American Journal of Psychoanalysis,* 1949, 9: 3–7.

Kierkegaard, Soren. *A Kierkegaard Anthology.* Edited by R. Bretall. Princeton, N.J.: Princeton University Press, 1951.

Maslow, A. H. Emotional blocks to creativity. *Journal of Individual Psychology,* 1958, 14: 51–56.

Will, O., and Cohen, R. H. A report of a recorded interview in the course of psychotherapy. *Psychiatry,* 1953, 16: 263–82.

REVIEW QUESTIONS

1.   How would you characterize yourself in regard to the "creative" and "conforming" personalities outlined by Moustakas?

2.   What are some implications of Moustakas' point of view for teaching?

part vii

THE PROBLEM OF TESTING

Every teacher is faced with the interrelated problems of measuring student progress, evaluating teaching methods, assigning grades, and, especially with high school and college students, motivating systematic study. We say these problems are interrelated because testing is one solution that, for better or worse, can solve all four. Robert Ebel in article 50 admits that while neither teachers nor students particularly like testing, evaluation is essential for effective education. Apart from the four functions listed above, Ebel further points out that testing helps individualize instruction, helps the teacher clarify course objectives and, in fact, can be a valuable learning experience in itself. Finally, the author lists a number of "do's" and don't's" for constructing better tests.

Anne Anastasi is a leading scholar in test construction. In article 51 Anastasi points out several problems underlying the current antitest revolt. The idea that testing is an invasion of privacy, confidentiality of test results, validity of individual test items, discrimination against imaginative students and minority-group students, misconceptions about the "fixity" of IQ scores, and other problems are acknowledged and responded to. The author further notes that psychologists themselves are responsible for many misconceptions about testing, and that test developers are oversophisticated in the minutiae of test construction and under-sophisticated in psychological knowledge. Listing some improvements that could be made from within the testing field, Anastasi suggests that more emphasis be placed upon *change* (as, for example, in evaluating readiness for instruction), rather than upon fixed classifications. Also, she rightly indicates that it is a serious error to consider a person's mental abilities separate from his personality characteristics (particularly motivation) and his environment, both of which also determine intellectual development.

We end our book with some direct words on testing by critic John Holt. Holt claims that testing is not used, as it profitably might be, to allow a student to evaluate his own performance or to improve our teaching methods. Rather, tests are used, first, to threaten students into working and, second, to provide a basis for assigning grades. Holt also observes that at least college students study to pass tests, rather than learning for vocational preparation or enjoyment. Finally, and again hitting the nail discomfortingly squarely, Holt notes that tests penalize students who work slowly and thoroughly and students with high test anxiety.

fifty

The Need for Better Classroom Tests

ROBERT L. EBEL

Most of the tests of educational achievement used in school and college class-rooms are prepared, administered, scored, and interpreted by classroom teachers and professors. Each student takes many such tests during the course of his formal education. They exert a direct and powerful influence on how he studies and what he learns. Hence it is not unreasonable to believe that the educational significance of locally produced classroom tests may far outweigh that of the occasional standardized tests or program tests the students take.

The term "classroom test" in this article means any written test prepared by a school or college teacher for use in his own classroom. Essay tests and tests composed of mathematical problems, as well as various types of objective tests, are included in the meaning of the term as used here. Our concern will be with important, full-period tests given either at the end of a unit of work or just before grades are issued rather than with short quizzes and other informal "tests."

THE IMPORTANCE OF CLASSROOM TESTS

The view that classroom tests are important and that they could be, and ought to be, much better than they often are is shared by most school teachers and college professors. Occasionally one hears the suggestion that education could go on perfectly well, perhaps much better than it has in the past, if tests and testing were abolished. On other occasions one hears grudging acceptance of tests as a "necessary evil" in education. But the view of the great majority of teachers at all levels is that periodic assessment of educational progress is essential to effective education and that good tests afford very useful assistance to teachers in making those assessments.

Source: Abridgment of Chapter 1 from *Measuring Educational Achievement* by Robert Ebel. © 1965, pp. 1–15, 20–21. Reprinted by permission of the author and Prentice-Hall, Inc., Englewood Cliffs, New Jersey.

One would have difficulty in finding among those who are inclined to discount the value of tests a teacher or professor who is not concerned about quality in education—about the achievements of his students, about the adequacy of their previous preparation, about his own success as a teacher, and about the effectiveness of the whole enterprise of education. But quality is a matter of degree. Unless some means exist for measuring it, for distinguishing between higher and lower quality, between better and poorer achievement, concern for quality will not mean very much. If tests are abandoned, it must be on the ground that better means are available for measuring educational achievement.

It is easy to understand why tests are sometimes characterized as a "necessary evil" in education. Almost all students, but especially students of average or inferior ability, approach a test with apprehension. Those who do less well than they had expected can easily find some basis for regarding the examination as unfair. Cheating on examinations is reported often enough to cast some shadows of disrepute over the whole enterprise.

Instructors, too, sometimes dislike to assume the role of examiners. Most of them prefer to be helpful rather than critical. There is something inconsiderate about probing the minds of other human beings and passing judgment on their shortcomings. There is even something presumptuous in assuming the right to set the standards by which others will be judged. And if the instructor has learned that he is not an infallible examiner, if he has experienced the critical retaliation of students who have been unfairly judged, his wishful dreams of education freed from the torments of examining and evaluation are also easy to understand. No doubt he sometimes feels like the Sergeant of Police in "The Pirates of Penzance," who sings, "Taking one consideration with another, a policeman's lot is not a happy one."

Unfortunately, there is no effective substitute for tests or examinations in most classrooms. Even in a generally critical leaflet on some aspects of contemporary testing in the public schools [Joint Committee of the American Association of School Administrators, 1962], the authors say,

> To teach without testing is unthinkable. Appraisal of outcomes is an essential feedback of teaching. The evaluation process enables those involved to get their bearings, to know in which direction they are going.

Anxiety, unfairness, dishonesty, humiliation, and presumptuousness can be and should be minimized, but the process of examining and evaluating cannot be dispensed with if education is to proceed effectively.

Those who would abolish tests, or who regard them as an evil which must be tolerated, usually do not mean to imply that good education is possible without any assessment of student achievement whatsoever. What they sometimes do suggest is that a good teacher, working with a class of reasonable size, has no need for tests in order to make sufficiently accurate judgments of student achievement. They may also suggest that the tests they have seen, or perhaps that they have even used themselves, leave so much to be desired that a teacher is better off without the kind of "help" such tests are likely to give. In some cases they may indeed be right in this judgment. Very bad tests have been made and used. No doubt some such tests have actually been worse than no tests at all.

But again, the majority of teachers and professors are keenly aware of the limited and unsatisfactory bases they ordinarily have for judging the relative achievement of various students and of the fallibility of their subjective judgments when based on the irregular, uncontrolled observations they can make in their classroom or office. They welcome the help that tests can give in providing a more extensive and objective basis for judgment. For testing is not really an alternative to teacher observation of student behavior. It is simply a specialized technique for extending, refining, efficiently recording, and summarizing those observations.

CAN TESTS PROVIDE VALID MEASURES OF ACHIEVEMENT?

Precise measurement requires careful control or standardization of the conditions surrounding it. Obviously this control makes the behavior being measured artificial to some degree. Artificiality is a price that usually must be paid to achieve precision. It is a price that scientists and engineers, as well as psychologists and teachers, have usually found worth paying. For tests intended to measure typical behavior such as personality, attitude, or interest, the price may sometimes be too high. That is, the behavior in the artificial test situation may be so poorly related to typical behavior in a natural situation that precise measurement of something hardly worth measuring is so much wasted effort. But for tests of educational aptitude or achievement, the gain in precision resulting from the controlled conditions that formal testing can afford usually far outweighs the slight loss in the relevance of artificial to natural behavior.

Perhaps an illustration from the field of physical ability testing may be helpful here. Judges, watching a group of children at play (the natural situation), could make rough estimates of the relative abilities of the students to run fast, jump high, or throw some object far. But the precision of the estimates obtained in such an uncontrolled, unstandardized situation would probably be quite low. The different judges would not be likely to agree with each other, or even with themselves on different occasions, in the estimates they would report. If precise estimates are desired, the judges, the children, and everyone else concerned would probably prefer to see them made under the standardized and controlled, if somewhat artificial, conditions of a regular track meet. No one would worry much about the possibility that the ones who performed best in the track and field events might seem to do similar things somewhat less well under "natural" conditions on the playground.

Because all pupils in a class usually take the same test of achievement under the same conditions, some critics have concluded that uniform written tests, particularly objective tests, disregard individual differences and even tend to suppress individuality. The fact that some classroom tests are graded by machines has served to strengthen this misconception. Mass testing and machine grading suggest a standardized uniformity in education that seems inconsistent with concern for the individual and his unique needs and potentials.

But while the tests and the process of testing are as nearly alike for all the students in a class as we can make them, the scores of the students on the tests are not alike. Those who score high reflect superior ability and achievement. Those who score low reveal deficiencies. Tests tend to reveal differences among students, not to suppress or conceal them. In fact, uniformity in the conditions of testing is a prerequisite to unequivocal indication of individual differences. If the tests are not identical for all students, not all of the differences in their scores can be attributed to differences among them in ability or achievement.

The kind of information about individual differences that uniform tests reveal so clearly is essential to effective individualization of instruction. The unique needs of individual students can be identified and met. The unique capabilities of individual students can be identified and developed. Thus can standardized measurement serve individualized education.

The emphasis in this article on the value of written tests in extending a teacher's observations of student behavior and making these observations more dependable and precise is not intended to suggest that tests should be the sole means used in judging a student's educational achievement. Written tests are efficient, versatile devices for measuring many aspects of student achievement, but they cannot do the whole job. Some educational objectives may be concerned mainly with the development of physical skills or social behaviors. Direct observation is likely to provide a much better basis for assessing such skills and behaviors than would a written test. Nor should a teacher or professor ignore his own direct observations, in the classroom or elsewhere, of a student's level of understanding or ability to use knowledge, despite the fact that written tests are especially effective in measuring educational outcomes of that kind. The broader the basis of observations on which evaluation rests, the better, provided only that each observation carries no more weight in determining the final result than its appropriateness and accuracy warrant.

THE FUNCTIONS OF CLASSROOM TESTS

The major function of a classroom test is to measure student achievement and thus to contribute to the evaluation of his educational progress and attainments. This is a matter of considerable importance. To say, as some critics of testing have said, that what a student knows and can do is more important than his score on a test or his grade in a course implies, quite incorrectly in most cases, that the two are independent or unrelated. To say that testing solely to measure achievement has no educational value also implies, and again quite incorrectly in most cases, that test scores are unrelated to educational efforts, that they do not reward and reinforce effective study, penalize unproductive efforts, or tend to discourage lack of effort.

Tests can, and often do, help teachers and professors to give more valid, reliable grades. Because these grades are intended to summarize concisely a comprehensive evaluation of the student's achievement, because they are reported to the student and his parents to indicate the effectiveness of his efforts, because they are entered in the school record and may help to determine honors and opportunities for further education or future employment, it is important that teachers and professors take seriously their responsibilities for assigning accurate, meaningful grades. Students are urged, quite properly, not to study *merely* to earn high grades. But, in terms of the student's present self-perceptions and his future opportunities, there is nothing "mere" about the grades he receives.

A second major function of classroom tests is to motivate and direct student learning. The experience of almost all students and teachers supports the view that students do tend to study harder when they expect an examination than when they do not and that they emphasize in studying those things on which they expect to be tested. If the students know in advance they will be tested, if they know the kinds of knowledge and ability the test will require, and if the test does a good job of measuring the achievement of essential course objectives, then its motivating and guiding influence will be most wholesome.

Anticipated tests are sometimes regarded as extrinsic motivators of learning efforts, less desirable or effective than intrinsic motivators would be. Learning should be its own reward, providing its own intrinsic motivation for study, it is said. Fortunately, no choice need be made between extrinsic and intrinsic motivation. Both contribute to learning. Withdrawal of either would be likely to lessen the learning of most students. For a fortunate few, intrinsic motivation may be strong enough to stimulate all the efforts to learn that the student ought to put forth. For the great majority, however, the added, extrinsic motivation provided by tests and other influential factors is indispensable.

Classroom tests have other useful educational functions. The process of constructing them, if the job is approached carefully, should cause an instructor to think carefully about the goals of instruction in a course. It should lead him to define those goals operationally in terms of the kind of tasks a student must be able to handle to demonstrate achievement of the goals. On the student's part the process of taking a classroom test, and of discussing the scoring of it afterward, can be a richly rewarding learning experience. As Stroud [1946, p. 476] has said,

> It is probably not extravagant to say that the contribution made to a student's store of knowledge by the taking of an examination is as great, minute for minute, as any other enterprise he engages in.

Hence, testing and teaching need not be considered as mutually exclusive alternatives, as competitors for the valuable classroom hours. They are intimately related parts of the total educational process.

Awareness of the important direct contributions of test taking to student learning can lead to unwarranted disparagement of tests as measuring instruments. It is sometimes said, for example, that tests should be used to promote learning *rather than* to measure achievement, as if these two uses were somehow in conflict and mutually exclusive. Or the suggestion may be made that pupils who have taken a test will learn more if the test is not graded.

While there are situations in which test materials can be used solely as learning exercises, disregarding any evidence they could provide about levels of achievement, it would be unfortunate to leave the impression that most tests should be treated in this way. For the indirect contributions of a test to the promotion of learning can be far greater in scope and in effect than the direct contributions. What a student studies, and how he studies, in the weeks before the test can have far more to do with what he learns than his mental exercise during the hour or so while he is taking the test.

Richardson and Stalnaker [1935], two leaders in the development of modern educational achievement testing, have insisted that,

> An achievement examination need not have direct pedagogical value in itself....
> The purpose of achievement examining is essentially measurement for certifying academic credit.... An achievement examination is good or valid if it simply does a good job of measuring what it purports to measure.

An educational test that does not promote learning is somehow of questionable utility. But the promotion of learning is a complex enterprise, requiring a variety of tools. Tests can be, and usually are, highly important tools for the promotion of learning. If their usefulness were judged solely in terms of what the student learns while taking the test, the greater part of their importance would be overlooked. In the case of tests, the indirect influence in promoting learning is far more potent than the direct.

It probably goes without saying that the educational value of a test depends on its quality and on the skill of the teacher in using it. Good tests, properly used, can make valuable contributions to a student's education. Poor tests, or tests misused, will contribute less and might even do educational harm.

WHO SHOULD PREPARE CLASSROOM TESTS?

Most classroom tests must be prepared by the teacher or professor who is teaching the class. While there are many standardized tests of achievement available for broad areas of subject matter, there are few that are specifically appropriate to the content and objectives of a particular unit of study, a unit that may constitute only a fraction of the whole course of study of a single subject. Some textbook publishers furnish tests to accompany their texts. These can be helpful, but too often the items included have not been carefully prepared or reviewed critically by other experts in educational measurement or in the subject field itself.

Some public education authorities, like those in New York State, prepare tests for use in state-wide programs of achievement testing. Some universities, like Michigan State, maintain evaluation services that are responsible for preparing achievement tests for their basic courses. Since these tests are usually prepared by experts in test construction, working closely with expert teachers of the subjects involved, they usually do excellent jobs of measuring educational achievement. But the substantial costs involved in the development of external tests, and the problems of matching the content of the test to the material emphasized in the classroom, make it seem unlikely that they will replace any substantial fraction of teacher-made tests in the foreseeable future.

The necessity that involves most teachers in test construction brings with it some educational advantages. As has been said, the process of test construction can help the teacher clarify and define the educational objectives of a course. Classroom tests prepared by the teacher are likely to fit the content and objectives of a particular course better than would a test prepared by anyone else. Finally, when testing and teaching are in the hands of the same person, they are likely to be more effectively integrated in the total educational process than if the testing were separated from the teaching.

The necessary and desirable direct responsibility that professors and teachers have for the tests of educational achievement used in their classes does not require that every test must be a completely new and original creation of the instructor involved. There could be, and should be, much more frequent and extensive exchange of test outlines and test items among teachers of similar courses than is usually the case. . . .

Individual teachers of similar courses can, and probably should, arrange for cooperative exchange of test items and test plans. Not only will such cooperation tend to reduce the labor of test construction, it will also make the tests less parochial in the educational understandings and values they reflect and, hence, more generally valid measures of educational achievement.

At the very least, a teacher who uses objective tests can establish and maintain a cumulative file of his own items. The best of these can be and should be reused frequently. If the items have been analyzed for discrimination and difficulty . . . , and if the analysis data is recorded with the item, the value of such a file as an aid in future test development will be greatly increased. . . .

SOME REQUIREMENTS FOR EFFECTIVE TESTING

If all teachers and prospective teachers were skilled in the arts of test development and use, there would be little need for professional training in test construction. But on their own testimony, on that of their sometimes suffering students, and on that of visiting experts called in to advise them on their testing problems, teachers do reveal shortcomings in their use of tests.

A good test constructor must know comprehensively and understand thoroughly the field of knowledge to be covered by the test so that he will be able to ask significant, novel questions, express them properly and plainly, and provide acceptable, correct answers to them. He must be accurately aware of the level and range of understanding and ability in the group to be tested so that he can choose problems of appropriate intrinsic difficulty and present them so that they will have appropriate functional difficulty. He must understand the thought processes of the students and the misconceptions which the less capable ones are likely to have so that he can make wrong answers attractive to those of low achievement.

He must be skilled in written expression so that he can communicate clearly and concisely the information and instructions which make up the test and the test items. He must be a master of the techniques of item writing, well acquainted with the most useful forms of test items with their unique virtues and limitations, and with the most common pitfalls to be avoided in using them. Finally, he must be sufficiently conscious of the importance of good measures of educational achievement and sufficiently confident of his ability to prepare tests that will provide such measures to be willing to spend the time and make the effort necessary to do a competent, workmanlike job.

The traits just enumerated fall generally into one or the other of two categories: those which contribute to good teaching as well as good testing and those which contribute uniquely to good testing. More of the shortcomings observed in classroom tests are probably attributable to deficiencies in traits of the first category than in those of the second. . . . Nothing that can be said about the techniques of test construction and use will enable an incompetent teacher to make a good test. What a book on classroom testing may do is to help good teachers make better tests than they would otherwise. . . .

COMMON MISTAKES OF TEACHERS IN TESTING

What are some of the mistakes that even expert teachers and eminent professors make in measuring educational achievement? What are some of their unsound practices in classroom testing?

First, they tend to rely too much on their own subjective judgments, on fortuitous observations, on unverified inferences, in evaluating educational achievements. The wide difference among different judges in their evaluations of the same evidence of student achievement—that is, the unreliability of those judgments—has been demonstrated over and over again, yet many teachers have never checked on the reliability of any of their tests and may not even have planned those tests purposely to make them as reliable as possible.

Second, some teachers feel obliged to use absolute standards in judging educational achievement, which can almost always be judged more fairly and consistently in relative terms. If most of the students in a class get A's on one test and most of the same students fail another, some teachers prefer to blame the students rather than the test. They believe, contrary to much evidence, that a teacher can set a reasonable passing score on a test simply by looking at the test and without looking at any student answers to it. They believe that "grading on the curve" permits the students to get the (relative and presumably fallible) standards, instead of permitting the teacher (whose standards are presumed to be absolute and infallible) to set them.

Third, both teachers and professors tend to put off test preparation to the last minute and then to do it on a catch-as-catch-can basis. A last-minute test is likely to be a poor test. Further, such a test cannot possibly have the constructive influence in motivating and directing student learning that a good test of educational achievement ought to have and that a test planned and described to students early in the course would have.

Fourth, many teachers use tests which are too inefficient and too short to sample adequately the whole area of understanding and abilities that the course has attempted to develop. Essay tests have many virtues, but efficiency, adequacy of sampling and reliability of scoring are not among them.

Fifth, teachers often overemphasize trivial or ephemeral details in their tests, to the neglect of the understanding of basic principles and the ability to make practical applications. To illustrate, it is probably far more important to understand the forces which brought Henry VIII into conflict with the Pope than to know the name of his second wife. Yet some teachers are more inclined to ask about the specific, incidental details than about the important general principles.

Sixth, the test questions that teachers and professors write, both essay and objective, often suffer from lowered effectiveness due to unintentional ambiguity in the wording of the question or to the inclusion of irrelevant clues to the correct response. Too few teachers avoid these hazards by having their tests reviewed by some competent colleague before the tests are used.

Seventh, the inevitable fact that test scores are affected by the particular questions or tasks included in them tends to be ignored, and the magnitude of the resulting errors (called *sampling errors*) tend to be underestimated by those who make and use classroom tests. Many of them believe that a test score will be perfectly accurate and reliable if no error has been made in scoring the individual items or in adding these to get a total score. Differences as small as one score unit are often taken to indicate significant differences in attainment.

Finally, many teachers and professors do not use the relatively simple techniques of statistical analysis to check on the effectiveness of their tests. A mean score can show whether or not the test was appropriate for the group tested in its general level of difficulty. A standard deviation can show how well or how poorly the test differentiated among students having different levels of attainment. A reliability coefficient can show how much or how little the scores on this test are likely to differ from those the same students would get on an independent, equivalent test.

An analysis of the responses of good and poor students to individual test items can show whether the items discriminate well or poorly and, if poorly, can suggest why and what needs to be done to improve the item. The calculation of these statistics is quite simple. There is no better way for a teacher or professor to continue to improve his skill in testing, and the quality of the tests he uses, than to analyze systematically the results from his tests and to compare the findings of these analyses with ideals standards of test quality. . . .

Articles and books and courses on testing can help instructors to make better classroom tests and to use them more effectively without devoting much more time to the processes. But real improvement is likely to cost a real increase in time and effort on the part of the classroom teacher. How far he is willing to go along this line will be determined by the value he places on accurate evaluations of achievement and on the satisfaction he gets from doing a good job with this aspect of his responsibility as a teacher. Some competent, conscientious teachers may be willing to go a considerable distance.

SUMMARY

The main conclusions to be drawn from the discussions presented in this article can be summarized in the following twelve propositions.

1.   Good achievement in education is fostered by the use of good tests of educational achievement.

2.   Most teachers recognize the essential role of measurement in education.

3.   Achievement tests are given under specially devised and carefully controlled conditions to improve the precision of measurement without impairing seriously its validity.

4.   Written tests provide an important basis, but not the only basis teachers should use in evaluating student achievement.

5.   The primary function of a classroom test is to measure student achievement.

6.   Classroom tests can help to motivate and direct student achievement, and can provide learning excercises.

7.   The development of a good classroom test requires the instructor to define the course objectives in specific, operational terms.

8.   Most classroom tests are and ought to be prepared by the course instructors.

9.   Competence in teaching is a necessary, but not a sufficient condition, for expert test construction.

10.   Construction of a good objective test requires special knowledge of testing techniques and special skill in the use of language.

11.   Some common weaknesses of teacher-made tests are attributable to:

    a.   reliance on subjective judgments,

    b.   reliance on absolute standards of judgment,

    c.   hasty test preparation,

    d.   use of short, inefficient tests,

    e.   testing trivia,

    f.   careless wording of questions,

    g.   neglect of sampling errors, and

    h.   failure to analyze the quality of the test.

12.   To improve their testing teachers will have to work harder, longer, more cooperatively, and with more frequent reference to manuals on test improvement.

REFERENCES

Joint Committee of the American Association of School Administrators. *Testing, Testing, Testing.* Washington, D. C.: American Association of School Administrators, 1962.

Richardson, M. W., and Stalnaker, J. M. Comments on achievement examinations. *Journal of Educational Research* 1935, 28: 425–32.

Stroud, J. B. *Psychology in Education.* New York: David McKay, 1946.

REVIEW QUESTIONS

1.   True or false:

    a.   According to the author, there is no effective substitute for examinations.

    b.   Tests reveal information about individual differences necessary for individualizing instruction.

    c.   Examinations motivate studying.

    d.   The author recommends teacher-made tests over published standardized tests.

    e.   A good test constructor must thoroughly understand the field of knowledge and must be able to write well.

    f.   Essay tests are known for efficiency, adequacy of information sampling, and scoring reliability.

    g.   Test items may be analyzed by comparing the responses of good versus poor students on each item.

Answers to question 1: a. true, b. true, c. true, d. true, e. true, f. false, g. true.

2.   Considering (a) above, can you think of "effective substitutes" that might serve some of the same functions as testing?

fifty-one

Psychology, Psychologists, and Psychological Testing[1]

ANNE ANASTASI

It is the main thesis of this article that psychological testing is becoming dissociated from the mainstream of contemporary psychology. Those psychologists specializing in psychometrics have been devoting more and more of their efforts to refining the techniques of test construction, while losing sight of the behavior they set out to measure. Psychological testing today places too much emphasis on testing and too little on psychology. As a result, outdated interpretations of test performance may remain insulated from the impact of subsequent behavior research. It is my contention that the isolation of psychometrics from other relevant areas of psychology is one of the conditions that have lead to the prevalent public hostility toward testing.

THE ANTITEST REVOLT

Without question the antitest revolt has many causes and calls for a diversity of remedies. No one solution could adequately meet its multiplicity of problems. These problems have been repeatedly and thoroughly discussed from several angles. For the present purpose, therefore, a brief overview of the principal objections will suffice.

The one that has undoubtedly received the greatest amount of attention, including Congressional investigations, is the objection that psychological tests may represent an invasion of privacy. Although this problem has generally been considered in reference to personality tests, it can logically apply to any type of test. When elderly illiterates are approached for testing, even with a nonverbal test,

Source: Abridged from *American Psychologist,* 1967, 22: 297–306. Copyright 1967 by the American Psychological Association. Reprinted by permission of the author and the publisher.
[1]Address of the President, Division of Evaluation and Measurement, American Psychological Association, September 5, 1966.

it is amazing how many have mislaid or broken their glasses that very morning. This mild little subterfuge is their protection against the risk of being asked to read and the resulting embarrassment of admitting illiteracy. Nor is the problem limited to tests. Any observation of an individual's behavior or any conversation with him may, of course, provide information about him that he would prefer to conceal and that he may reveal unwittingly.

For this problem—as for all other problems pertaining to testing—there is no simple or universal solution. Rather, the solution must be worked out in individual cases in terms of two major considerations. The first is the purpose for which the testing is conducted—whether for individual counseling, institutional decisions regarding selection and classification, or research. In the use of tests for research, preserving the subjects' anonymity substantially reduces but does not eliminate the problem. The second consideration is the relevance of the information sought to the specific testing purpose. For example, the demonstrated validity of a particular type of information as a predictor of performance on the job in question would be an important factor in justifying its ascertainment. The interpretation given to scores on a particular test is also relevant. An individual is less likely to consider his privacy to have been invaded by a test assessing his readiness for a specific course of study than by a test allegedly measuring his "innate intelligence."

A second and somewhat related problem is that of confidentiality. Basically, this problem concerns the communication of test information. It is a two-pronged problem, however, because the implications of transmitting test information to the individual himself and to other persons are recognizably different. With regard to the transmittal of information to other persons—such as parents, teachers, supervisors, or prospective employers—professional ethics requires that this be done only when the individual is told at the outset what use is to be made of his test results. Any subsequent change in the use of such results could then be introduced only with the individual's consent.

There is another difficulty, however, in the communication of test results, which is common to both prongs of the problem. Whether the information is transmitted to the examinee himself or to others, the likelihood of misinterpretation is a serious concern. The questions of how much information is communicated, in what form, and under what circumstances are of basic importance [Berdie, 1960, 1965; Brown, 1961; Goslin, 1963, in press]. Certainly there is no justification for reporting answers to specific questions on a personality inventory, as some laymen apparently fear will be done [see, e.g., Testing and Public Policy, 1965, p. 978]. Nevertheless, even total scores, duly referred to appropriate norms and accompanied by a suitable margin of error, can be misleading when perceived in terms of prevalent misconceptions about the nature of certain tests.

There has been considerable concern about the impact that a knowledge of test scores might have upon the individual and his associates; and the need for more research to gauge such impact has been recognized [Berdie, 1965; Goslin, 1963, Ch. 8]. Some suggestive evidence is already available, indicating that teachers' knowledge of children's intelligence test scores significantly affects the children's subsequent intellectual development [Rosenthal and Jacobson, 1968]. The mechanism of this "self-fulfilling prophecy," as it affects the individual's self-concept and the behavior of his associates toward him, is of course well known. With regard to test scores, however, detrimental effects are most likely to result from misconceptions about tests. Suppose, for example, that an IQ is regarded as a broad indicator of the individual's total intelligence, which is fixed and unchanging and of genetic origin. Under these circumstances, releasing the IQs of individuals to teachers, parents, the individuals themselves or anyone else is likely to have a deleterious effect on the subsequent development of many children.

A third major category of test criticism has centered on test content. It is a common reaction among laymen, for example, to ask what a specific test item is supposed to show. What does it *mean* if you cross the street to avoid meeting someone you know? If the psychologist falls into the trap of trying to answer the question on the layman's own terms, he will soon find himself in the untenable position of claiming high validity and reliability for a single item. Moreover, he may try to defend the item in terms of its factual or veridical content, which can be challenged on many grounds. In this sort of evaluation, the critics not only ignore the objective processes of item selection and test validation, but they also overgeneralize from a relatively small number of selected items.

In the same vein, some critics make much of the fact that multiple-choice items are sometimes misunderstood and that they may occasionally penalize the brilliant and erudite student who perceives unusual implications in the answers [see Dunnette, 1964; Educational Testing Service, 1963]. Granted that this is possible, the obvious conclusion is that the tests are not perfect. A realistic evaluation, however, requires that such tests be compared with alternative assessment procedures. How do the tests compare with grades, essay examinations, interviewing procedures, application forms, ratings, and other predictors whose utilization is practicable in specific situations? An even more appropriate question pertains to how much the introduction of a test improves predictions made with other available assessment procedures.

Attention should be called, however, to a few sophisticated critiques of certain item forms, which provide constructive and imaginative suggestions for improvements in test development [e.g., Feifel, 1949; LaFave, 1966; Sigel, 1963]. This approach includes thorough logical analyses of the limitations of such existing item forms as analogies, similarities, classification, and vocabulary, together with some ingenious proposals for the analysis of errors, qualitative grading of responses, and the development of items to identify styles of categorization. In contrast to the superficial critiques of the popular writers, these analyses merit serious consideration.

A fourth type of criticism blames the tests for any objectionable features of the criteria they are designed to predict. Thus it has been argued that objective tests of scholastic aptitude tend to select unimaginative college students, or that personality tests tend to select executives who are conformists and lack individuality. Insofar as these criticisms may be true, they are an indictment not of the tests but of the criteria against which selection tests must be validated. If we were to ignore the criteria and choose less valid tests, the persons thus selected would merely fail more often in college, on the job, and in other situations for which they were selected. Predictors cannot be used as instruments of criterion reform. Improvements must begin at the criterion level.

It should be noted, however, that criteria do change over time. The nature and personnel requirements of jobs change in industry, government, and the armed services. Educational objectives and curricula change. It is therefore imperative to conduct periodic job analyses or task analyses in these various contexts. Such analyses may themselves suggest that some of the tests in use as predictors may be outdated in a particular context. Periodic revalidation of instruments against current criteria provides a more definitive safeguard against the retention of instruments that may have become irrelevant.

A fifth type of criticism asserts that psychological tests are unfair to culturally disadvantaged groups [Anastasi, 1961; Deutsch, Fishman, Kogan, North and Whiteman, 1964]. To criticize tests because they reveal cultural influences is to miss the essential nature of tests. Every psychological test measures a sample of behavior. Insofar as culture affects behavior, its influence will and should be reflected in the test. Moreover, if we were to rule out cultural differentials from a test, we might thereby lower its validity against the criterion we are trying to predict. The same cultural differentials that impair an individual's test performance are likely to handicap him in school work, job performance, or whatever other subsequent achievement we are trying to predict.

Tests are designed to show what an individual can do at a given point in time. They cannot tell us *why* he performs as he does. To answer that question we need to investigate his background, motivations and other pertinent circumstances. No test score can be properly interpreted in a vacuum—whether obtained by a culturally disadvantaged person or by anyone else.

If we want to use test scores to predict outcome in some future situations, such as an applicant's performance in college, we need tests with high predictive validity against the specific criterion. This requirement is commonly overlooked in the development and application of so-called culture-free tests. In the effort to include in such tests only activities and information common to many cultures, we may end up with content having little relevance to any criterion we wish to predict [Anastasi, 1950]. A better solution is to choose test content in terms of its criterion relevance and then investigate the effect of moderator variables. Validity coefficients, regression weights, and cutoff scores may vary as a function of certain background conditions of the subjects [Hewer, 1965]. For example, the same scholastic aptitude score may be predictive of college failure when obtained by an upper-middle-class student, but predictive of moderate success when obtained by a lower-class student. In addition, we need to consider the interaction of initial test score and available differential treatments [Cronbach, 1957]. Given a certain score obtained by Individual A with a particular cultural background what will be his predicted college achievement following a specified remedial training program?

The inclusion of both moderator variables and differential treatments in the prediction process requires far more empirical data than are now available. Efforts should certainly be made to gather such data. In the meantime, an awareness of the operation of these variables will at least introduce some needed cautions in the interpretation of test scores. Finally, it is apparent that the use of objective selection procedures, such as appropriate tests, should serve to reduce the operation of bias and discrimination against individuals for irrelevant reasons.

A sixth objection to tests is that they foster a rigid, inflexible, and permanent classification of individuals. The objection has been directed particularly against "intelligence tests," and has aroused the greatest concern when such tests are applied to culturally disadvantaged children. It is largely because implications of permanent status have become attached to the IQ that the use of group intelligence tests has been discontinued in New York City public schools [Gilbert, 1966; Loretan, 1966]. That it proved necessary to discard the tests in order to eliminate the misconceptions about the fixity of the IQ is a revealing commentary on the tenacity of the misconceptions. Insofar as these misconceptions do prevail, of course, information about a child's IQ would undoubtedly initiate the self-fulfilling prophecy cited earlier. It can be seen that this objection to tests has much in common with questions already discussed in connection with confidentiality and with the testing of culturally disadvantaged groups.

Underlying the popular notion of the fixity of the IQ is the assumption that intelligence tests are designed to measure some mysterious entity known as "innate capacity." In the light of this assumption, the tests are then criticized for their susceptibility to environmental differences. The critics fail to see that it is these very differences in environment that are largely responsible for individual differences in qualifications or readiness for job performance, job training, and educational programs. If these differences in present developed abilities are ignored or obscured by any assessment procedure, the individual will be assigned to a job in which he will fail or be exposed to an educational program from which he will not profit. Under these conditions, he will simply fall farther and farther behind in those abilities in which he is now deficient. A recognition of his present deficiencies, on the other hand, permits the application of suitable and effective training procedures.

A seventh and final type of objection has again been directed chiefly against intelligence tests. It has been argued that, because of their limited coverage of intellectual functions, intelligence tests tend to perpetuate a narrow conception of ability. It is certainly true that the limited sample of cognitive functions included in standard intelligence tests is inconsistent with the global connotations of the test names. This is but one more reason for discarding the label "intelligence test," as some psychologists have been advocating for several decades. To be sure, all test labels are likely to imply more generality than the test possesses. A clerical aptitude test does not cover all the traits required of an office clerk, nor does a mechanical aptitude test cover all aspects of mechanical tasks. A test title that tried to provide a precise operational definition of its content would be unwieldy and impracticable. Hence the layman's tendency to judge a test by its label is always likely to mislead him. Nevertheless, the difficulty is augmented by the use of such a term as "intelligence." Not only is "intelligence" an unusually broad concept, but it has also acquired an impressive array of erroneous connotations.

DISSOCIATION OF PSYCHOLOGICAL TESTING FROM PSYCHOLOGICAL SCIENCE

It is apparent that all seven classes of objections to psychological testing arise at least in part from popular misinformation about current testing practices, about the nature of available tests, and about the meaning of tests scores. Nevertheless, psychologists themselves are to some extent responsible for such misinformation. Nor is inadequate communication with laymen and members of other professions the only reason for such prevalent misinformation. It is my contention that psychologists have contributed directly to the misinformation by actively perpetuating certain misconceptions about tests. . . .

It is noteworthy that the term "test theory" generally refers to the mechanics of test construction, such as the nature of the score scale and the procedures for assessing reliability and validity. The term does not customarily refer to psychological theory about the behavior under consideration. Psychometricians appear to shed much of their psychological knowledge as they concentrate upon the minutiae of elegant statistical techniques. Moreover, when other types of psychologists use standardized tests in their work, they too show a tendency to slip down several notches in psychological sophistication.

A common enough example is encountered when an experimenter sets out to assemble two groups of children to serve as experimental and control subjects. He first decides to equate the groups in such obvious variables as age, sex, parental education, and parental occupational level. As he looks around for other handy variables to hold constant, he thinks, "Ah, of course, the children themselves ought to be equated in IQ." Very likely there are some IQs conveniently available in the children's cumulative school records. They may not all be derived from the same test, but they will provide a good enough approximation for the experimenter's purpose. After all, he wants only a rough estimate of each child's IQ.

What does the experimenter really want to equate the children in? Does his experimental variable utilize verbal material, so that vocabulary should be held constant? Is facility in numerical computation relevant to the experiment? Or perhaps perceptual speed and accuracy or spatial visualization are appropriate. Is overall scholastic aptitude his chief concern? Would a reading achievement test serve his purposes better? What does he believe he is ruling out when he equates the groups in IQ? Perhaps the IQ merely provides a sufficiently obscure label to conceal the fuzziness of his thinking.

We shall probably always have misconceptions with us. But to hold fast to old misconceptions after they have been recognized as such seems to be needlessly conservative. Yet psychometricians themselves have contributed to the perpetuation of the IQ label, with its vast appendage of misleading connotations. Even when the original ratio IQ proved too crude and was generally supplanted by standard scores, the IQ label was retained. The standard score simply became a deviation IQ. Psychologists have even begun to adopt the popular term "IQ test." The IQ is accepted as a property of the organism, and the "IQ test" measures it, of course. . . .

All the illustrations cited so far concern intelligence tests. It is about intelligence tests that misconceptions are most prevalent. It is also in reference to intelligence tests that popular objections to testing are most closely bound with substantive matters in which psychologists themselves are involved. But let us take a brief look at personality testing in this light. Because personality testing is a more recent development than intelligence testing, misconceptions are less deeply rooted in this area. Personality testing today is characterized not so much by entrenched misconceptions as by confusion and inconsistencies. For example, there is the inconsistency—I might almost say conflict—between what clinical psychology students learn about personality tests in their psychometrically oriented testing courses and what they often learn to do with the same tests in practicum training. The same discrepancies can be found between the reviews of many personality tests in the *Mental Measurements Yearbooks* and the uses to which the tests are put in professional practice.

The examples mentioned serve to illustrate a growing dissociation between psychological testing and other psychological specialties. One reason for this dissociation is the increasing specialization of psychology itself. The psychometrician is subject to the same isolation that characterizes other specialists. He may become so deeply engrossed in the technical refinements of his specialty that he loses touch with relevant developments in other psychological specialties. Yet these developments may basically alter the meaning of the very tests he is busy elaborating and refining.

A second reason is to be found in the built-in inertia of tests. Because it takes several years to develop a test, gather adequate norms, and obtain a reasonable minimum of validity data, there is an inevitable lag between the original conception of the test and its availability for professional use. Moreover, the effectiveness of a test is likely to increase markedly as more and more data accumulate from long-term longitudinal studies and other research conducted with the test. Consequently, some of our best tests are fairly old tests. Even when they are revised, the original conception of the tests is embedded in the psychology of an earlier period. These long-lived tests are among our most valuable measurement tools. But the test user needs to be aware of intervening changes in the science of behavior and to update his interpretation of test scores.

A third reason for the widening gap between testing and psychological science is an undue willingness on the part of psychologists to accede to the layman's requests. Psychologists feel a strong social obligation to put their findings and techniques to work. In their eagerness to apply their science, they sometimes capitulate to unrealistic and unsound popular demands. The public wants shortcuts and magic. Some test constructors and users have tried to give them just that. It is an important function of the applied psychologist to help laymen re-formulate problems in ways that permit a sound solution. It is not their role to provide ready-made solutions for insoluble problems. It might be salutary if testing gave less heed to the pull of practical needs and more to the thrust of behavioral science.

When tests are used by members of other professions, such as educators, soci-ologists, or psychiatrists, the gap between testing and psychological science is likely to be even wider. In addition to the reasons already mentioned, there is a further lag in communicating substantive advances to persons in other fields. It is a curious fact that members of these related fields tend to find out about new tests sooner than they find out about developments pertaining to interpretive background.

PSYCHOLOGY AND THE INTERPRETATION OF TEST SCORES

One way to meet the outside pressures that threaten to undermine psychologi-cal testing is to make improvements from within. Improvements are needed, not so much in the construction of tests, as in the interpretation of scores and the ori-entation of test users. Existing tests need not be summarily replaced with new kinds of tests; they sample important behavior and provide an accumulation of normative and validation data that should not be lightly dismissed. It would re-quire many years to gather a comparable amount of information about newly de-veloped instruments.

How, then, can the utilization of available psychological tests be improved in the light of modern psychological knowledge? Let us consider a few examples. First, in the assessment of individual differences, attention should be focused on *change*. Tests do not provide a technique for the rigid and static classification of individuals; on the contrary, they are instruments for facilitating change in de-sired directions. Not only do they permit the measurement of change as it occurs under different experimental conditions, but they also provide essential informa-tion about the individual's initial status, prior to the introduction of any inter-vention procedures. Any program for effecting behavioral change, whether it be school instruction, job training, or psychotherapy, requires a knowledge of the individual's present condition. Readiness for a particular stage or course of aca-demic instruction, for instance, implies the presence of prerequisite intellectual skills and knowledge. How well the individual has acquired these intellectual prerequisites is what the various ability tests tell us—whether they be called intelligence tests, multiple-aptitude batteries, special aptitude tests, or achieve-ment tests. At different stages and in different testing contexts, one of these types of ability tests may be more appropriate than another; there is a place for all of them in the total testing enterprise. But we should not lose sight of the fact—so often stated and so often forgotten—that all these tests measure current developed abilities and that their scores should be interpreted accordingly. . . .

At the theoretical level, there have been some ingenious attempts to link intelligence with learning, motivation, and other psychological functions. Of particular interest are the discussions of how factors may develop through the establishment of learning sets and transfer of training [Carroll, 1962; Ferguson, 1954, 1956; Hunt, 1961; Whiteman, 1964]. The breadth of the transfer effect would determine whether the resulting factor is a broad one, like verbal comprehension, or a narrow one, like a particular motor skill. Traditional "intelligence tests" cover intellectual skills that transfer very widely to tasks in our culture. This may be one of the reasons why they can predict performance in so many contexts. Another reason may be that any given criterion task can be performed by different persons through the use of different work methods which require different patterns of ability. The characteristic heterogeneity of function which contributes to a global intelligence test score may thus fit criterion situations in which a deficiency in one ability can be compensated for by superiority in another alternative ability.

From a different point of view, intelligence has been linked with motivation through the strength of certain "experience-producing drives" [Hayes 1962]. Recognizing that intelligence is acquired by learning, this theory maintains that the individual's motivational makeup influences the kind and amount of learning that occurs. Although the theory proposes that the experience-producing drives constitute the hereditary component of intelligence, the basic relationship still holds if the drives themselves are determined or modified by environmental conditions. Regardless of the origin of the experience-producing drives, the individual's emotional and motivational status at any one time in his development influences the extent and direction of his subsequent intellectual development. It might be added that longitudinal studies of intelligence test performance have provided some empirical support for this proposition [Sontag, Baker, and Nelson, 1958; Haan, 1963]. It would thus seem that adding a measure of a child's motivational status to tests of developed abilities at any one age should improve the prediction of his subsequent intellectual development.

Personality testing itself provides a second area in which to illustrate the role of psychology in the interpretation of test scores. The hypothesis just discussed suggests one important point to bear in mind, namely, that the separation between abilities and personality traits is artificial and the two domains need to be rejoined in interpreting an individual's test scores. It is now widely recognized that an individual's performance on an aptitude test, in school, on the job, or in any other context is significantly influenced by his achievement drive, his self-concept, his persistence and goal orientation, his value system, his freedom from handicapping emotional problems, and every other aspect of his so-called personality. Even more important, however, is the cumulative effect of these personality characteristics upon the direction and extent of his intellectual development [see, e.g., Combs, 1952]. Conversely, the success the individual attains in the development and use of cognitive functions is bound to affect his self-concept, emotional adjustment, interpersonal relations, and other "personality traits." To evaluate either ability or personality traits without reference to the other, because of limited testing or compartmentalized thinking, is likely to prove misleading. . . .

As a third and final illustration we may consider the *assessment of environment*. The individual does not behave in a vacuum. He responds in a particular environmental context, which in part determines the nature of his responses. It has been suggested that the prediction of criterion behavior from test scores or from earlier criterion performance could be improved by taking situational factors into account [MacKinney, 1967]. Given an individual with a certain level of developed abilities and certain personality characteristics at Time A, how will he react in a specified criterion situation at Time B?

Even more important for prediction purposes is information about the environment to which the individual will be exposed in the interval between Time A and Time B. There is some suggestive evidence that correlations approaching unity can be obtained in predicting intelligence test performance or academic achievement when environmental variables are included along with initial test scores as predictors [Bloom, 1964, Ch. 6].

Despite the general recognition of the importance of environmental variables, little progress has been made in the measurement of such variables. The available scales for evaluating home environment, for example, are crude and the choice of items is usually quite subjective. Moreover, environments cannot be ordered along a single continuum from "favorable" to "unfavorable." An environment that is quite favorable for the development, let us say, of independence and self-reliance may differ in significant details from an environment that is favorable for the development of social conformity or abstract thinking. In this connection, a promising beginning has been made in the empirical development of home environment scales against criteria of intelligence test performance and academic achievement [Wolf, 1965].

SUMMARY

In conclusion, it was the thesis of this paper that psychological testing should be brought into closer contact with other areas of psychology. Increasing specialization has led to a concentration upon the techniques of test construction without sufficient consideration of the implications of psychological research for the interpretation of test scores. Some of the relevant developments within psychology have been illustrated under the headings of behavioral change, the nature of intelligence, personality testing, and the measurement of environment. Strengthening psychological testing from within, by incorporating appropriate findings from other areas of psychology, is proposed as one way to meet the popular criticisms of the current antitest revolt.

REFERENCES

Anastasi, A. Some implications of cultural factors for test construction. *Proceedings of the 1949 Invitational Conference on Testing Problems, Educational Testing Service,* 1950, 13–17.

Anastasi, A. Psychological tests: Uses and abuses. *Teachers College Record,* 1961, 62: 389–93.

Berdie, R. F. Policies regarding the release of information about clients. *Journal of Counseling Psychology,*1960, 7: 149–50.

Berdie, R. F. The ad hoc Committee on Social Impact of Psychological Assessment. *American Psychologist,*1965, 20: 143–46.

Bloom, B. S. *Stability and Change in Human Characteristics.* New York: Wiley, 1964.

Brown, D. W. Interpreting the college student to prospective employers, government agencies, and graduate schools. *Personnel and Guidance Journal,*1961, 39: 576–82.

Burt, C. The differentiation of intellectual ability. *British Journal of Educational Psychology,*1954, 24: 76–90.

Carroll, J. B. Factors of verbal achievement. *Proceedings of the 1961 Invitational Conference on Testing Problems, Educational Testing Service,* 1962, 11–18.

Combs, A. W. Intelligence from a perceptual point of view. *Journal of Abnormal and Social Psychology,*1952, 47: 662–73.

Cronbach, L. J. The two disciplines of scientific psychology. *American Psychologist,*1957, 12: 671–84.

Deutsch, M., Fishman, J. A., Kogan, L., North, R., and Whiteman, M. Guidelines for testing minority group children. *Journal of Social Issues,*1964, 22: 127–45.

Dunnette, M. D. Critics of psychological tests: Basic assumptions: How good? *Psychology in the Schools,*1964, 1: 63–69.

Educational Testing Service. *Multiple-Choice Questions: A Close Look.* Princeton, N.J.: ETS, 1963.

Feifel, H. Qualitative differences in the vocabulary responses of normals and abnormals. *Genetic Psychology Monographs,*1949, 39: 151–204.

Ferguson, G. A. On learning and human ability. *Canadian Journal of Psychology,*1954, 8: 95–112.

Ferguson, G. A. On transfer and the abilities of man. *Canadian Journal of Psychology,*1956, 10: 121–31.

Gilbert, H. B. On the IQ ban. *Teachers College Record,*1966, 67: 282–85.

Goslin, D. A. *The Search for Ability: Standardized Testing in Social Perspective.* New York: Russell Sage Foundation, 1963.

Goslin, D. A. The social consequences of predictive testing in education. In H. M. Clements and J. B. McDonald (Eds.), *Moral Dilemmas in Schooling.* Columbus, Ohio: Charles Merrill, in press.

Haan, N. Proposed model of ego functioning: Coping and defense mechanisms in relationship to IQ change. *Psychological Monographs*,1963, 77(8, Whole No. 571).

Hayes, K. J. Genes, drives, and intellect. *Psychological Reports*, 1962, 10: 299–342.

Hewer, V. H. Are tests fair to college students from homes with low socioeconomic status? *Personnel and Guidance Journal*,1965, 43: 764–69.

Humphreys, L. G. The organization of human abilities. *American Psychologist*, 1962, 17: 475–83.

Hunt, J. McV. *Intelligence and Experience*. New York: Ronald Press, 1961.

La Fave, L. Essay vs. multiple-choice: Which test is preferable? *Psychology in the Schools*,1966, 3: 65–69.

Loretan, J. O. Alternatives to intelligence testing. *Proceedings of the 1965 Invitational Conference on Testing Problems, Educational Testing Service*, 1966, 19–30.

MacKinney, A. C. The assessment of performance change: An inductive example. *Journal of Organizational Behavior and Human Performance*, 1967, 2:56–72.

McNemar, Q. Lost: Our itelligence? Why? *American Psychologist*, 1964, 19: 871–82.

Rosenthal, R., and Jacobson, L. Self-fulfilling prophecies in the classroom: Teachers' expectations as unintended determinants of pupils' intellectual competence. In M. Deutsch, A. R. Jensen, and I. Katz (Eds.), *Race, Social Class, and Psychological Development*. New York: Holt, Rinehart and Winston, 1968.

Sigel, I. E. How intelligence tests limit understanding of intelligence. *Merrill-Palmer Quarterly*,1963, 9: 39–56.

Smart, R. C. The changing composition of "intelligence": A replication of a factor analysis. *Journal of Genetic Psychology*,1965, 107: 111–16.

Sontag, L. W., Baker, C. T., and Nelson, V. L. Mental growth and personality development. *Monographs of the Society for Research in Child Development*, 1958, 23, No. 2.

Testing and public policy. (Special issue) *American Psychologist*, 1965, 20: 857–992.

Whiteman, M. Intelligence and learning. *Merrill-Palmer Quarterly*,1964, 10: 297–309.

Wolf, R. The measurement of environments. *Proceedings of the 1964 Invitational Conference on Testing Problems, Educational Testing Service* 1965, 93–106.

REVIEW QUESTIONS

1.   True or false:
   a. Testing is sometimes considered an invasion of privacy.
   b. One proposed solution to the confidentiality problem was to explain at the outset what use is to be made of the test scores.
   c. It is misleading to judge the validity of an entire test by examining one or two individual items.
   d. Multiple-choice tests may discriminate against bright students.
   e. According to the author, cultural factors that depress test scores also depress performance in the achievement area the test is predicting.
   f. The author argues that IQ is a fixed, innate ability.
   g. Psychologists themselves are responsible for many misconceptions about testing.
   h. Highly skilled psychometricians are equally sophisticated in psychological knowledge.
   i. Some test constructors have tried to meet public requests for magic short-cut tests.
   j. Assessing readiness is a good use of testing.
   k. Motivation and personality do not influence intelligence.

2.   In question 1 does the statement in (e) mean that tests discriminate against minority-group members or not?

Answers to question 1: a. true, b. true, c. true, d. true, e. true, f. false, g. true, h. false, i. true, j. true, k. false.

fifty-two

The Tyranny of Testing

JOHN HOLT

Let me not mince words. Almost all educators feel that testing is a necessary part of education. I wholly disagree—I do not think that testing is necessary, or useful, or even excusable. At best, testing does more harm than good; at worst, it hinders, distorts, and corrupts the learning process. Testers say that testing techniques are being continually improved and can eventually be perfected. Maybe so—but no imaginable improvement in testing would overcome my objections to it. Our chief concern should not be to improve testing, but to find ways to eliminate it.

In some circumstances, of·course, tests are necessary. If a man wants to play the violin in a symphony orchestra, it makes sense to ask him to show that he meets the orchestra's standards. If he wants to work with people who speak no English, he ought to prove that he can speak their language. If he wants a license to design and build buildings, he should show that he knows enough to keep his structures from falling down. If he wants to be a surgeon, he should prove to competent judges—on the operating table, not a piece of paper—that he can operate on people without killing them.

Very similar to these are the tests people give themselves to check their own progress. The typist types exercises to increase her rate per minute. The musician plays scales and studies, and plays difficult passages against a metronome. The tennis player serves dozens of balls, trying to place them accurately in this or that corner. The heart surgeon operates on frogs, training his fingers to work with small vessels in cramped spaces. The skater does school figures, the quarterback passes to his ends, and the pitcher throws again and again to his catcher. The pilot makes approach after approach. The student, if he is wise, puts important information on file cards—one of the most flexible, most effective, and cheapest of all teaching machines—and runs through the pack, taking the questions in many different orders. In short, all serious practice can be seen as a way in which the learner tests his own skill and knowledge.

Source: From *The Underachieving School* by John Holt, pp. 51–56, 63. Copyright 1969 by Pitman Publishing Corp. Reprinted by permission of the publisher.

But virtually *none* of the testing done in schools is of this kind.

Students are not, as a rule, tested to prove they can perform activities they have chosen for themselves, without endangering other people or ruining a collective enterprise. Testing in schools is done for very different reasons, and, by and large, we are not very honest about these reasons. To the public—and to ourselves—we teachers say that we test children to find out what they have learned, so that we can better know how to help them to learn more. This is about ninety-five per cent untrue. There are two main reasons why we test children: the first is to threaten them into doing what we want done, and the second is to give us a basis for handing out the rewards and penalties on which the educational system—like all coercive systems—must operate. The threat of a test makes students do their assignment; the outcome of the test enables us to reward those who seem to do it best. The economy of the school, like that of most societies, operates on greed and fear. Tests arouse the fear and satisfy the greed.

This system may be necessary, or at least unavoidable. We may just possibly be right—though I doubt it—to feel that it is our duty to decide what children should be made to learn. And we may just possibly be right—though again I don't think so—in thinking that the best way to make children learn what we have decided they should learn is to reward or penalize them in proportion to their success or failure at learning it. But, in any case, this is nearly always what tests in schools are for and we are deeply dishonest if we pretend that they are for anything else.

Many teachers, and even students, say and sincerely believe that even if tests do threaten students into working, they can be an accurate measure of the quality of their work. To me it seems clear that the greater the threat posed by a test, the less it can measure, far less encourage, learning. There are many reasons for this. One of the most obvious, and most important, is that whenever a student knows he is being judged by the results of tests, he turns his attention from the material to the tester. What is paramount is not the course or its meaning to the student, but whatever is in the tester's mind. Learning becomes less a search than a battle of wits. The tester, whoever he is, is no longer a guide and helper, but an enemy.

Browsing through a bookstore one day several years ago, I came upon an exhaustive sociological study of medical school students. I began to read parts of it, perhaps to find out whether medical students were hindered by the same fears and self-protective and evasive strategies that so hampered my fifth graders. I soon found that they were. The authors had interviewed a great many students, at different stages in their medical education. Over and over again, these young men said that they had entered medical school passionately eager to learn medicine, only to find themselves continually being checked up on, examined, and tested and to learn that their future careers depended almost entirely on how well they did on these tests. Soon, preparing for exams came to replace learning medicine as the fundamental business of medical school. Before long, they came to judge and label their professors, not by skill or knowledge, but according to their 'fairness,' a fair professor being one whose tests were predictable and could thus be studied for.

The feeling that a test is a trap and the tester an adversary I have often felt myself—and even in situations in which the tester has had no power over me. One of my present students likes to cut test-yourself quizzes out of newspapers and magazines, and once in a while he bustles up to me in the halls at school, waving a piece of paper and challenging, 'Let's see how smart you are!' or 'Let's see how good a driver you are!' or something like that. Instantly I feel under attack. Someone is trying to make a fool of me. If the student actually asks me some of the questions on the quiz, and I rarely let him get that far, I find myself thinking, 'What's the catch? What's this guy after? How does his mind work?' I am in a duel as intense and personal as a game of chess.

If a test is a duel with an enemy who is out to do you in, any and all means of outwitting him are legitimate. This attitude is at the root of most of the cheating that has become so prevalent lately, above all among successful students in 'good' schools. The line is not easy to draw between reading a teacher's mind, or making him think you know what you don't know, and outright cheating. In any case, it is not a distinction that many students under pressure are very worried about—or many teachers either. If a teacher is being judged by his students' performances on a standardized test, he joins forces with the children to outwit the common enemy by whatever means he can. A great many teachers and schools are utterly unscrupulous about this. I have taught fifth graders who, though their achievement test scores from previous years showed that they had adequate skill in arithmetic, were unable to add or subtract. How, then had these achievement test scores been obtained? By diligent cramming on the part of the teachers. I have at times on occasion been told to do some of this cramming myself. 'Never mind what you think the children understand or can use or remember. Just see to it that they get decent marks on those achievement tests.' Yet isn't this a kind of cheating?

Must a test be a trap? When it determines who gets the carrot and who gets the stick, it cannot help but be. Churchill once said, in words more eloquent than these, that his teachers at Harrow were not interested in finding out what he knew, but only in discovering what he didn't know. This is generally true, not because teachers are old meanies, but because the system—the need to continually separate sheep from goats—demands it. Consider the problem of the test-giver. A student who knows anything at all about a subject knows enough to write about it for hours. I, for example, have not studied American history since the eighth grade and quickly forgot most of what I learned then. What little I know or think I know about it, I have picked up from a lot of miscellaneous reading, hardly any of it in what could be called history books. Yet if I were asked to write out all I know and understand about American history, it would take many pages—perhaps a book, perhaps several. How, then, can anyone test my knowledge, let alone the knowledge of a student of history, in an hour or three hours? He can't. If a teacher gives his students a test that allows them to show how much they know, they will all run out of time long before they have run out of things to say, and he will have no way to mark them except to give them all the same mark, which his bosses will not like. To make distinctions between students, which in most schools is a teacher's duty—*everyone* can't go to Harvard—he must ask questions that some students, at least, will not be able to answer. In short, like Churchill's teachers, he must seek out ignorance so that he can 'objectively' decide who gets the rewards and who gets the penalties.

I have still more objections to tests. They almost always penalize the student who works slowly. Tests tend to favour the clever guesser, the player of percentages, and to put at a disadvantage the student who likes to be thorough and sure. They severely penalize the anxious students who worry about tests; because of their fears, many students are wholly unable to show on tests just how much they do know, and every failed test makes them more fearful of the next. And tests are misleading, indeed worthless, with those students—in our cities, I suspect, there are many—who make no effort to do well on them, pursuing the strategy of deliberate failure, perhaps to save face, perhaps to hurt their parents, perhaps to fight back at a system they despise.

It may be when tests seem to work best that they do the most harm. I have had frequent discussions with my present students—able, successful, on their way to prestige colleges—about testing and grading. It is surprising how fiercely many of them defend a system that they often complain about and rebel against. They say, angrily or anxiously, 'But if we're not tested and graded, how can we tell whether we're learning anything, whether we're doing well or poorly?' It makes me sad. I think of the two- and three-year-olds I have known, continually comparing their own talk to the talk of people around them. I think of the five- and six-year-olds I have known, teaching themselves to read, figuring out each new word on a page, continually checking what they are doing against what they have done, what they don't know against what they know. Then I think of my fifth graders, handing me arithmetic papers and asking anxiously, 'Is it right?,' and looking at me as if I were crazy when I said, 'What do you think?' What difference did it make what they thought? Rightness has nothing to do with reality, or consistency, or common sense; Right is what the teacher says is Right, and the only way to find out if something is Right is to ask a teacher. Perhaps the greatest of all the wrongs we do children in school is to deprive them of the chance to judge the worth of their own work and thus destroy in them the power to make such judgments, or even the belief that they can.

There is no reason, except to relieve our own anxieties and insecurity, that we should constantly know what children are learning, or even why they are learning. What true education requires of us instead is faith and courage—faith that children want to make sense out of life and will work hard at it, courage to let them do it without continually poking, prying, prodding, and meddling.

Is this so difficult?

REVIEW QUESTIONS

1.   In view of the needs for testing outlined by Ebel (which are true) and in view of the evils of testing outlined by Holt (which are also true), where does this leave a concerned teacher such as you?

2.   Are problems (and functions) of testing, grading, and motivation different in elementary school, high school, and college? How so?

index

Summerhill (Neill), 252
Summerhill (school). *See* United King-
   doms schools
superstition, 31–32, 34, 392–93
Suppes, Pat, 62–64, 65, 67
symbolic logic, 119, 125
Systems Development Corp., 72–73

teacher certification, 10, 240, 241
Teaching Information Processing System
   (TIPS), 74–75
teaching machines. *See* individualized instruction, programmed
Teaching Machines (Skinner), 46–53
television, 19, 51–52, 65, 377
Terman, L., 172
testing, 55, 275, 315, 475
   criticism of, 240, 477–87, 488–93, 501–
      505
   importance of, 477–79
   interpretation of, 495–97
   in programmed instruction, 70–71, 77,
      78
   teacher mistakes in, 484–86
   validity of, 479–82
tests
   achievement, 133, 245, 317, 327, 503
   Armed Forces Qualification Test, 359
   "Chitling" test. *See* Dove Test
   criterion-referenced, 287–88
   Doren Diagnostic Reading Test, 293
   Dove Counterbalance Intelligence Test,
      408–12
   Flanagan's Tests of General Ability,
      260–62
   Harvard Test of Inflected Acquisition.
      See Flanagan Tests
   intelligence, 240, 489–90, 492
   IQ, 3, 94, 245, 268–71, 317, 383, 389
   nonverbal, 260–62
   preparation of, 482–84
   psychological, 124, 488–500
   reading, 72–73, 389
   Simon-Binet, 117
   situational, 108
   standard, 358
   Stanford Achievement Test, 230, 347
   Stanford-Binet Intelligence Test, 87–88
36 Children (Kohl), 328, 361–66
Thorndike, E. L., 14, 18, 52, 103, 106,
   282, 283
Time, 268
Tolman, E., 132

tonus level, 190–92, 193
Torrance, E. P., 413, 421, 423, 424, 426,
   431–39
traditionalism, 2, 5–13, 39, 278
transfer, 3, 28–30, 34, 56, 111–12
   and discovery, 109–10
   misconceptions of, 103–105
   operations in, 105–108
   teaching for, 108–10
   as teaching goal, 101–105
truancy, 297–98, 343
Tuddenham, Read, 113, 115–26

underground school phobia, 3, 30, 99
United Kingdom schools, 29, 144, 192
   primary, 238, 309–25
   Summerhill, 237, 247–51, 256
Up the Down Staircase (Kaufman), 328,
   367–74
Upward Bound programs, 336
Urban Review, The, 268
U. S. Office of Education, 353, 356, 384

verbal ability, 46, 48–50, 238, 356–57,
   383–98, 400
vertical grouping, 312
Voeks, V., 165, 166
Vygotsky, L., 132

Walden Two (Skinner), 42, 43
Warren, J. B., 174–75
Warren, Thomas, 237, 247–51, 413,
   428–30
Watson, Goodwin, 1, 14–25
Way, B., 443, 448–49
Weingartner, Charles, 238, 273–81
Wertheimer, Max, 130
White, Mary Alice, 130
White, R. W., 132, 202, 204
Why We Need Teaching Machines (Skin-
   ner), 46–53
Wilhelms, F. T., 78
Will, O., 468
Winterbottom, M. R., 173
Wisconsin Research and Development
   Center for Cognitive Learning, 238,
   287–95
Wohlwill, J. F., 118
Wolff, P. H., 118
Woodworth, R. S., 106

Yasuda, S. A., 176

Zoo (Munari), 431

1   2   3   4   5   6   7   8   9   10